T0181606

Communications
in Computer and Information Science   1935

Rationale

The CCIS series is devoted to the publication of proceedings of computer science conferences. Its aim is to efficiently disseminate original research results in informatics in printed and electronic form. While the focus is on publication of peer-reviewed full papers presenting mature work, inclusion of reviewed short papers reporting on work in progress is welcome, too. Besides globally relevant meetings with internationally representative program committees guaranteeing a strict peer-reviewing and paper selection process, conferences run by societies or of high regional or national relevance are also considered for publication.

Topics

The topical scope of CCIS spans the entire spectrum of informatics ranging from foundational topics in the theory of computing to information and communications science and technology and a broad variety of interdisciplinary application fields.

Information for Volume Editors and Authors

Publication in CCIS is free of charge. No royalties are paid, however, we offer registered conference participants temporary free access to the online version of the conference proceedings on SpringerLink (http://link.springer.com) by means of an http referrer from the conference website and/or a number of complimentary printed copies, as specified in the official acceptance email of the event.

CCIS proceedings can be published in time for distribution at conferences or as post-proceedings, and delivered in the form of printed books and/or electronically as USBs and/or e-content licenses for accessing proceedings at SpringerLink. Furthermore, CCIS proceedings are included in the CCIS electronic book series hosted in the SpringerLink digital library at http://link.springer.com/bookseries/7899. Conferences publishing in CCIS are allowed to use Online Conference Service (OCS) for managing the whole proceedings lifecycle (from submission and reviewing to preparing for publication) free of charge.

Publication process

The language of publication is exclusively English. Authors publishing in CCIS have to sign the Springer CCIS copyright transfer form, however, they are free to use their material published in CCIS for substantially changed, more elaborate subsequent publications elsewhere. For the preparation of the camera-ready papers/files, authors have to strictly adhere to the Springer CCIS Authors' Instructions and are strongly encouraged to use the CCIS LaTeX style files or templates.

Abstracting/Indexing

CCIS is abstracted/indexed in DBLP, Google Scholar, EI-Compendex, Mathematical Reviews, SCImago, Scopus. CCIS volumes are also submitted for the inclusion in ISI Proceedings.

How to start

To start the evaluation of your proposal for inclusion in the CCIS series, please send an e-mail to ccis@springer.com.

Teresa Guarda · Filipe Portela ·
Jose Maria Diaz-Nafria

Editors

Advanced Research in Technologies, Information, Innovation and Sustainability

Third International Conference, ARTIIS 2023
Madrid, Spain, October 18–20, 2023
Proceedings, Part I

 Springer

Editors
Teresa Guarda (iD)
Universidad Estatal Peninsula de Santa Elena
Campus Matriz
La Libertad, Ecuador

Filipe Portela (iD)
Algoritmi Research Centre
University of Minho
Guimarães, Portugal

Jose Maria Diaz-Nafria (iD)
Universidad a Distancia de Madrid
Madrid, Spain

ISSN 1865-0929   ISSN 1865-0937 (electronic)
Communications in Computer and Information Science
ISBN 978-3-031-48857-3   ISBN 978-3-031-48858-0 (eBook)
https://doi.org/10.1007/978-3-031-48858-0

This Springer imprint is published by the registered company Springer Nature Switzerland AG
The registered company address is: Gewerbestrasse 11, 6330 Cham, Switzerland

Paper in this product is recyclable.

Preface

The need for a greener and more digital world leads academia, governments, industry and citizens to look for emerging, sustainable, intelligent solutions and trends.

These new solutions and ideas must promote communication and ubiquitous computing between society agents, i.e., citizens, industry, organizations, net-worked machines and physical objects, and provide a promising vision of the future integrating the real world of knowledge agents and things with the virtual world of information. The emerging approaches in study or development can address several dimensions with a technological focus like Information, Innovation and Sustainability and topics: Computing Solutions, Data Intelligence, Ethics, Security, Privacy and Sustainability.

These topics are closely related to the field of Information Systems (IS) because all of them involve the use and management of technology and data to achieve specific purposes or goals. Computing Solutions are a crucial aspect of information systems as they provide the technical infrastructure and tools for organizations to manage and process data. Data Intelligence is also a key area of information systems as it involves the collection, analysis and interpretation of data to support decision-making and problem-solving. Sustainability is becoming an increasingly important aspect of information systems as organizations are recognizing the impact of technology on the environment and are looking for ways to reduce their carbon footprint. Ethics, Security and Privacy are also essential aspects of information systems as they involve the responsible and secure use of technology and data to protect individuals and organizations from potential harm.

The change observed in society modifies the landscape of human activity, particularly regarding knowledge acquisition and production, offering new possibilities and challenges that need to be explored, assessed and disseminated.

To expose and disseminate this, ARTIIS arose in 2021. ARTIIS is an international forum for researchers and practitioners to present and discuss the most recent innovations, trends, results, experiences and concerns from several perspectives of Technologies, Information, Innovation and Sustainability. This book is split into three volumes and contains a selection of 113 papers accepted for presentation and discussion at the International Conference on Advanced Research in Technologies, Information, Innovation and Sustainability (ARTIIS 2023) and its workshops. The third edition of ARTIIS, realized in 2023, received 297 contributions from 44 countries worldwide. The acceptance rate was 38.04%, 98 regular papers and 15 short papers.

The papers accepted to ARTIIS 2023 are published in the Communications in Computer and Information Science series (Springer CCIS). It is indexed in DBLP, Google Scholar, EI-Compendex, SCImago and Scopus. CCIS volumes are also submitted for inclusion in ISI Proceedings.

The conference proceedings are published in 3 CCIS volumes. The first 2 volumes (CCIS volumes 1935, 1936) consist of the peer-reviewed papers from the main conference track. In addition, 1 volume (CCIS 1937) contains the peer-reviewed papers of the 10 Special Sessions.

The first volume of the book contains all the papers on two topics: Computing Solutions and Data Intelligence:

– Computing Solutions addresses the development of applications and platforms involving computing and concerning some area of knowledge or society. It includes topics like Networks, Pervasive Computing, Gamification and Software Engineering.
– Data Intelligence focuses on data (e.g., text, images) acquisition and processing using smart techniques or tools. It includes topics like Computing Intelligence, Artificial Intelligence, Data Science and Computer Vision.

The second volume contains all the papers about Sustainability, and Ethics, Security and Privacy:

– Ethics, Security and Privacy shows a more strict and secure area of Information Systems where the end-user is the main concern. Vulnerabilities, Data Privacy and Cybersecurity are the main subjects of this topic.
– Sustainability explores a new type of computing: more green, connected, efficient and sustainable. Topics like Immersive Tech, Smart Cities and Sustainable Infrastructures are part of this topic.

The third volume contains the papers from the ten Special Sessions:

– Applications of Computational Mathematics to Simulation and Data Analysis (ACMaSDA 2023)
– Challenges and the Impact of Communication and Information Technologies on Education (CICITE 2023)
– Workshop on Gamification Application and Technologies (GAT 2023)
– Bridging Knowledge in a Fragmented World (glossaLAB 2023)
– Intelligent Systems for Health and Medical Care (ISHMC 2023)
– Intelligent Systems in Forensic Engineering (ISIFE 2023)
– International Symposium on Technological Innovations for Industry and Society (ISTIIS 2023)
– International Workshop on Electronic and Telecommunications (IWET 2023)
– Innovation in Educational Technology (JIUTE 2023)
– Smart Tourism and Information Systems (SMARTTIS 2023)

ARTIIS 2023 had the support of Universidad a Distancia de Madrid, Madrid, Spain; Universidad Estatal Península de Santa Elena, Ecuador; and the Algoritmi Research Center of Minho University, Portugal. It was realized in a hybrid format: face-to-face and virtual at Universidad a Distancia de Madrid – UDIMA, P.º del Gral. Martínez Campos, 5, 28010 Madrid, Spain – between the 18th and 20th of October 2023. Besides the main conference, ARTIIS 2023 also hosted ten special sessions.

The Program Committee was composed of a multidisciplinary group of more than 457 experts from 60 countries, with the responsibility for evaluating, in a double-blind review process, the submissions received for each of the main themes proposed for the conference and special sessions.

We acknowledge those who contributed to this book: authors, organizing chairs, steering committee, program committee, special sessions chairs, and editors. We sincerely appreciate their involvement and support, which were crucial for the success of the International Conference on Advanced Research in Technologies, Information, Innovation and Sustainability (ARTIIS 2023). We also wish to thank our publisher, Springer, for agreeing to publish the proceedings.

The success of this third edition gives us a lot of confidence to continue the work. So, we hope to see you in the fourth edition in 2024, which will be in Chile.

We cordially invite you to visit the ARTIIS website https://artiis.org.

September 2023

Teresa Guarda
Filipe Portela
Jose Maria Diaz-Nafria

Organization

General Chairs

Teresa Guarda	Universidad Estatal Península de Santa Elena, Ecuador/Universidad a Distancia de Madrid, Spain
Filipe Portela	Algoritmi Research Centre, UM, Portugal/Minho University, Portugal

Program Committee Chairs

Teresa Guarda	Universidad Estatal Península de Santa Elena, Ecuador
Filipe Portela	Minho University, Portugal
José María Díaz-Nafría	Universidad a Distancia de Madrid, Spain

Organizing Chairs

Isaac Seoane Pujol	Universidad a Distancia de Madrid, Spain
Jorge Morato Lara	Universidad Carlos III de Madrid, Spain
José María Díaz-Nafría	Universidad a Distancia de Madrid, Spain
Maria Fernanda Augusto	BITrum Research Group, Spain
Silvia Prieto Preboste	Universidad a Distancia de Madrid, Spain

Steering Committee

Andrei Tchernykh	CICESE Research Center, Mexico
Beatriz De La Iglesia	University of East Anglia, UK
Bruno Sousa	University of Coimbra, Portugal
Enrique Carrera	Universidad de las Fuerzas Armadas ESPE, Ecuador
Modestos Stavrakis	University of the Aegean, Greece
Ricardo Vardasca	ISLA Santarem, Portugal
Wolfgang Hofkirchner	Technische Universität Wien, Austria

Special Sessions Chairs

Abrar Ullah	Heriot-Watt University, Dubai
Teresa Guarda	Universidad Estatal Península de Santa Elena, Ecuador

ARTIIS Program Committee

A. Manuela Gonçalves	University of Minho, Portugal
Abbas Aljuboori	Al Zahra College for Women, Oman
Alberto Simões	Instituto Politécnico do Cávado e do Ave, Portugal
Alejandro Rodriguez	Universidad Politécnica de Madrid, Spain
Aleksandra Djordjevic	University of Belgrade, Serbia
Alfredo Cuzzocrea	University of Calabria, Italy
Alfredo Milani	University of Perugia, Italy
Ana Azevedo	Polytechnic Institute of Porto, Portugal
Ana Cláudia Campos	University of Algarve, Portugal
Ana Paula Teixeira	Universidade de Trás-os-Montes e Alto Douro, Portugal
Ana Pereira	Polytechnic Institute of Bragança, Portugal
Ana Ramires	Universidade Europeia, Portugal
Anacleto Correia	CINAV/Escola Naval, Portugal
Andreas Fricke	University of Potsdam, Germany
Andrei Tchernykh	CICESE Research Center, Mexico
Angel Dacal-Nieto	CTAG Centro Tecnológico de Automoción de Galicia, Spain
Anisha Kumari	National Institute of Technology Rourkela, India
Antonio Dourado	University of Coimbra, Portugal
António Fernandes	Instituto Politécnico de Bragança, Portugal
Antonio Jesús Muñoz-Montoro	Universidad de Málaga, Spain
Antonio Silva Sprock	Universidad Central de Venezuela, Venezuela
António Trigo	Instituto Politécnico de Coimbra, ISCAC, Portugal
Arnulfo Alanis Garza	Instituto Tecnológico de Tijuana, Mexico
Asma Patel	Staffordshire University, UK
Attila Körei	University of Miskolc, Hungary
Babar Shah	Zayed University, United Arab Emirates
Barna Iantovics	University of Medicine, Pharmacy, Science, and Technology of Târgu Mureş, Romania
Beatriz De La Iglesia	University of East Anglia, UK
Benedetto Barabino	Università degli Studi di Brescia, Italy

Bertil P. Marques	Instituto Superior de Engenharia do Porto, Portugal
Biswajeeban Mishra	University of Szeged, Hungary
Bruno Sousa	University of Coimbra, Portugal
Camille Salinesi	Université de Paris1 Panthéon-Sorbonne, France
Carina Pimentel	University of Aveiro, Portugal
Carina Silva	Escola Superior de Tecnologia da Saúde de Lisboa, Portugal
Carla Cavallo	University of Naples Federico II, Italy
Carlos Balsa	Instituto Politécnico de Bragança, Portugal
Carlos Costa	Universidade de Lisboa, Portugal
Carlos Fajardo	Fundación Universitaria Konrad Lorenz, Colombia
Carlos H. F. Alves	Federal Center of Technological Education, Brazil
Carlos Lopezosa	Universitat Pompeu Fabra Barcelona, Spain
Carlos R. Cunha	Instituto Politécnico de Bragança, Portugal
Carmen Guida	Università degli Studi di Napoli Federico II, Italy
Cecilia Avila	Fundación Universitaria Konrad Lorenz, Colombia
Cecilia Castro	Universidade do Minho, Portugal
Celia Ramos	University of the Algarve, Portugal
Chien-Sing Lee	Sunway University, Malaysia
Christian Grévisse	University of Luxembourg, Luxembourg
Christoph Schütz	Johannes Kepler University Linz, Austria
Christos Anagnostopoulos	University of Glasgow, UK
Clara Bento Vaz	Instituto Politécnico de Bragança, Portugal
Clarice Maraschin	Universidade Federal do Rio Grande do Sul, Brazil
Claudia Seabra	University of Coimbra, Portugal
Corrado Rindone	Università degli studi Mediterranea di Reggio Calabria, Italy
Daniele Granata	Università della Campania "Luigi Vanvitelli", Italy
Dasa Munkova	Constantine the Philosopher University in Nitra, Slovakia
Dimos Pantazis	Technological Education Institution of Athens, Greece
Elena Cantatore	Politecnico di Bari, Italy
Elena Cocuzza	University of Catania, Italy
Elisabetta Ronchieri	INFN CNAF, Italy
Elisete Mourão	Universidade de Trás-os-Montes e Alto Douro, Portugal
Emmanuel Okewu	University of Lagos, Nigeria

Enrique Carrera	Universidad de las Fuerzas Armadas, Ecuador
Erica Isa Mosca	Politecnico di Milano, Italy
Ester Scotto di Perta	University of Naples Federico II, Italy
Estrella Diaz	Castilla-La Mancha University, Spain
Eugen Rusu	Dunarea de Jos University of Galati, Romania
Fabio Alberto Schreiber	Politecnico di Milano, Italy
Fabio Rocha	Universidade Tiradentes, Brazil
Fabio Silveira	Federal University of São Paulo, Brazil
Fakhri Alam Khan	King Fahd University of Petroleum & Minerals, Saudi Arabia
Federica Gaglione	Università degli Studi del Sannio, Italy
Felipe S. Semaan	Fluminense Federal University, Brazil
Felix Härer	University of Fribourg, Switzerland
Fernanda A. Ferreira	Polytechnic Institute of Porto, Portugal
Fezile Ozdamli	Near East University, Turkey
Filipe Mota Pinto	Polytechnic Institute of Leiria, Portugal
Filipe Portela	University of Minho, Portugal
Flavia Marzano	Link Campus University, Italy
Flora Ferreira	University of Minho, Portugal
Florin Pop	University Politehnica of Bucharest, Romania
Francesco Mercaldo	University of Sannio, Italy
Francesco Palmieri	University of Salerno, Italy
Francesco Santini	Università di Perugia, Italy
Francisco Alvarez	Universidad Autónoma de Aguascalientes, Mexico
Frederico Branco	Universidade de Trás-os-Montes e Alto Douro, Portugal
Frederico Lopes	Universidade Federal do Rio Grande do Norte, Brazil
Gabriel Hornink	Federal University of Alfenas, Brazil
Geert Poels	Ghent University, Belgium
George Stalidis	Alexander Technological Educational Institute of Thessaloniki, Greece
Georgios Georgiadis	Aristotle University of Thessaloniki, Greece
Gerardo Carpentieri	University of Naples Federico II, Italy
Gianni D'Angelo	University of Salerno, Italy
Giovanni Paragliola	ICAR-CNR, Italy
Guillermo Rodriguez	ISISTAN-UNICEN, Argentina
Gustavo Gatica	Universidad Andrés Bello, Chile
Héctor Bedón	Universidad a Distancia de Madrid, Spain
Helia Guerra	University of Azores, Portugal
Henrique Vicente	Universidade de Évora, Portugal

Hugo Peixoto	University of Minho, Portugal
Humberto Rocha	Universidade de Coimbra, Portugal
Ilaria Matteucci	IIT-CNR, Italy
Inna Skarga-Bandurova	Oxford Brookes University, UK
Ioan Ciumasu	Université de Versailles Saint-Quentin, France
Ioannis Politis	Aristotle University of Thessaloniki, Greece
Ioannis Vrellis	University of Ioannina, Greece
Iqbal H. Sarker	Edith Cowan University, Australia
Isabel Lopes	Instituto Politécnico de Bragança, Portugal
J. Luis Luviano-Ortiz	University of Guanajuato, Mexico
Jakub Swacha	University of Szczecin, Poland
Joanna Kolodziej	NASK Warsaw and Cracow University of Technology, Poland
Jordi Vallverdú	Universitat Autònoma de Barcelona, Spain
Jorge Buele	Universidad Tecnológica Indoamerica, Ecuador
Jorge Herrera-Tapia	Universidad Laica Eloy Alfaro de Manabí, Ecuador
Jorge Luis Bacca Acosta	University of Girona, Spain
Jorge Oliveira e Sá	University of Minho, Portugal
José Carlos Paiva	University of Porto, Portugal
Jose Guillermo Guarnizo Marin	Santo Tomás University, Colombia
José Machado	University of Minho, Portugal
José María Díaz-Nafría	Madrid Open University, Spain
José Méndez Reboredo	University of Vigo, Spain
José Rufino	Polytechnic Institute of Bragança, Portugal
Juan-Ignacio Latorre-Biel	Public University of Navarre, Spain
Kalinka Kaloyanova	University of Sofia, Bulgaria
Kanchana Rajaram	SSN College of Engineering, India
Karine Ferreira	Instituto Nacional de Pesquisas Espaciais, Brazil
Kazuaki Tanaka	Kyushu Institute of Technology, Japan
Laura Verde	Università della Campania Luigi Vanvitelli, Italy
Lelio Campanile	Università degli Studi della Campania Luigi Vanvitelli, Italy
Leonardo Soto-Sumuano	Universidad de Guadalajara, Mexico
Leticia Vaca-Cardenas	Universidad Técnica de Manabí, Ecuador
L'ubomír Benko	Constantine the Philosopher University in Nitra, Slovakia
Luigi Piero Di Bonito	University of Campania Luigi Vanvitelli, Italy
Luis Gomes	Universidade dos Açores, Portugal
Luís Matos	Universidade do Minho, Portugal
Luiza de Macedo Mourelle	State University of Rio de Janeiro, Brazil
M. Filomena Teodoro	Portuguese Naval Academy, Portugal

Manuela Cañizares Espada	Universidad a Distancia de Madrid, Spain
Manuele Kirsch-Pinheiro	Université Paris 1 Panthéon-Sorbonne, France
Marcelo Fajardo-Pruna	Escuela Superior Politécnica del Litoral, Ecuador
Marcelo Leon	Universidad Tecnológica Empresarial de Guayaquil, Ecuador
Marcin Woźniak	Silesian University of Technology, Poland
Marco Gribaudo	Politecnico di Milano, Italy
Marco Zucca	University of Cagliari, Italy
Marco Cabezas González	Universidad de Salamanca, Spain
Margherita Lasorella	Polytechnic University of Bari, Italy
Maria Isabel Ribeiro	Instituto Politécnico Bragança, Portugal
Maria João Fernandes Polidoro	Politécnico do Porto, Portugal
Maria João Rodrigues	Universidade do Porto, Portugal
Maria José Abreu	Universidade do Minho, Portugal
Maria Macchiaroli	University of Salerno, Italy
Maria Sousa	CIEO Centre for Spatial and Organizational Dynamics, Portugal
Maria Stella de Biase	Università degli Studi della Campania Luigi Vanvitelli, Italy
Mariapia Raimondo	Università degli Studi della Campania Luigi Vanvitelli, Italy
Marílio Cardoso	Instituto Superior de Engenharia do Porto, Portugal
Marilisa Botte	University of Naples Federico II, Italy
Marina Alexandra Andrade	ISCTE Instituto Universitário de Lisboa, Portugal
Mario Pérez-Montoro	University of Barcelona, Spain
Mario Pinto	Politécnico do Porto, Portugal
Maritza Placencia	Universidad Nacional Mayor de San Marco, Peru
Martinha Piteira	Instituto Politécnico de Setúbal, Portugal
Mauro Iacono	Università degli Studi della Campania Luigi Vanvitelli, Italy
Michal Baczynski	University of Silesia in Katowice, Poland
Michal Munk	Constantine the Philosopher University in Nitra, Slovakia
Michel Soares	Universidade Federal de Sergipe, Brazil
Michele Mastroianni	University of Salerno, Italy
Milliam Maxime	Zekeng Ndadji University of Dschang, Cameroon
Mirka Mobilia	University of Salerno, Italy
Modestos Stavrakis	University of the Aegean, Greece
Mohamad Molaei Qelichi	University of Tehran, Iran
Mohammadsadegh Mohagheghi	Vali-e-Asr University of Rafsanjan, Iran
Mónica Pinto	Universidad de Málaga, Spain
Muhammad Younas	Oxford Brookes University, UK

Naveed Abbas — Islamia College, Peshawar, Malaysia

Naveenbalaji Gowthaman — University of KwaZulu-Natal, South Africa

Neelam Gohar — Shaheed Benazir Bhutto Women University, Pakistan

Nguyen D. Thanh — Banking University of Ho Chi Minh City, Vietnam

Nikolaos Matsatsinis — Technical University of Crete, Greece

Nishu Gupta — Norwegian University of Science and Technology in Gjøvik, Norway

Nuno C. Marques — Universidade Nova de Lisboa, Portugal

Nuno Pombo — University of Beira Interior, Portugal

Olivier Parisot — Luxembourg Institute of Science and Technology, Luxembourg

Omar Castellanos — Universidad Estatal Península de Santa Elena, Ecuador

Omid Fatahi Valilai — Constructor University, Germany

Oscar Dias — University of Minho, Portugal

Pankaj Mishra — G. B. Pant University of Agriculture and Technology, India

Paola Britos — Universidad Nacional de Río Negro - Sede Andina/Atlántica, Argentina

Paolino Di Felice — University of L'Aquila, Italy

Patricia Cano-Olivos — Universidad Popular Autónoma del Estado de Puebla, Mexico

Paula Amaral — Universidade Nova de Lisboa, Portugal

Paula Odete Fernandes — Instituto Politécnico de Bragança, Portugal

Paulo Piloto — Polytechnic Institute of Bragança, Portugal

Paulo Vasconcelos — University of Porto, Portugal

Pedro Gago — Polytechnic Institute of Leiria, Portugal

Piedade Carvalho — Instituto Superior de Engenharia do Porto, Portugal

Rafal Scherer — Częstochowa University of Technology, Poland

Raphael Gomes — Instituto Federal de Goiás, Brazil

Ricardo Cajo — Escuela Superior Politécnica del Litoral, Ecuador

Ricardo Correia — Instituto Politécnico de Bragança, Portugal

Ricardo Queirós — Politécnico do Porto, Portugal

Ricardo Vardasca — ISLA Santarem, Portugal

Robertas Damasevicius — Silesian University of Technology, Poland

Roberto Andrade — Escuela Politécnica Nacional, Ecuador

Roberto Nardone — University of Naples "Parthenope", Italy

Roman Chertovskih — University of Porto, Portugal

Ronan Guivarch — Université de Toulouse, France

Rosa Reis — Instituto Superior de Engenharia do Porto, Portugal

Rytis Maskeliunas, Kaunas	University of Technology, Lithuania
S. B. Kulkarni	SDMCET, India
Said Broumi	Hassan II University Mohammedia-Casablanca, Morocco
Samson Oruma	Østfold University College, Norway
Sanjay Misra	Østfold University, Norway
Sanket Mishra	BITS Pilani Hyderabad Campus, India
Sara Paiva	Instituto Politécnico de Viana do Castelo, Portugal
Sergio Cappucci	ENEA, Italy
Sergio Ilarri	University of Zaragoza, Spain
Shelly Sachdeva	National Institute of Technology Delhi, India
Sherali Zeadally	University of Kentucky, USA
Shuhei Kimura	Tottori University, Japan
Silvia Araújo	University of Minho, Portugal
Silvia Rossetti	Università degli Studi di Parma, Italy
Simone Belli	Universidad Complutense de Madrid, Spain
Simone Corrado	Università degli Studi della Basilicata, Italy
Smriti Agrawal	Chaitanya Bharathi Institute of Technology, India
Socrates Basbas	Aristotle University of Thessaloniki, Greece
Sofia Almeida	Universidade Europeia, Portugal
Sonia Casillas Martín	Universidad de Salamanca, Spain
Spyros Panagiotakis	Hellenic Mediterranean University, Greece
Stefania Regalbuto	Ca' Foscari University of Venice, Italy
Stefano Falcinelli	University of Perugia, Italy
Stephan Scheele	Fraunhofer IIS, Germany
Sumit Babu	Harcourt Butler Technical University, India
Syeda Sumbul Hossain	Daffodil International University, Bangladesh
Sylwia Krzysztofik	Lodz University of Technology, Poland
Tapiwa Gundu	Sol Plaatje University, South Africa
Telmo Pinto	University of Minho, Portugal
Tengku Adil Tengku Izhar	Universiti Teknologi MARA, Malaysia
Teresa Guarda	Universidad Estatal Península de Santa Elena, Ecuador
Tetiana Biloborodova	Volodymyr Dahl East Ukraine National University, Ukraine
Tiziana Campisi	Kore University of Enna, Italy
Ugo Fiore	Federico II University, Italy
Ulises Ruiz	Instituto Nacional de Astrofisica Óptica y Electrónica, Mexico
Vanda Lourenco	NOVA University of Lisbon, Portugal
Vasileios Gkioulos	Norwegian University of Science and Technology, Norway

Vicente Ferreira De Lucena Jr.   Federal University of Amazonas, Brazil
Victor Alves   University of Minho, Portugal
Victor Darriba   Universidade de Vigo, Spain
Virginie Felizardo   Universidade da Beira Interior, Portugal
Vitor Monteiro   University of Minho, Portugal
Vladimir Tcheverda   Institute of Petroleum Geology and Geophysics,
                                 Russia

Special Session Organizers

Applications of Computational Mathematics to Simulation and Data Analysis (ACMaSDA 2023)

Carlos Balsa   CEDRI-IPB, Portugal
Victoria Espinar   CITMaga - USC, Spain
Ronan Guivarch   IRIT-UFTMiP, France
Sílvio Gama   Universidade do Porto, Portugal

Challenges and the Impact of Communication and Information Technologies on Education (CICITE 2023)

Teresa Guarda   Universidad Estatal Península de Santa Elena,
                                 Ecuador
Maria Fernanda Augusto   BITrum Research Group, Spain

3rd Workshop on Gamification Application and Technologies (GAT 2023)

Ricardo Queirós   ESMAD, Portugal
Mário Pinto   ESMAD, Portugal
Filipe Portela   University of Minho, Portugal

Bridging Knowledge in a Fragmented World (glossaLAB 2023)

José María Díaz-Nafría   Universidad a Distancia de Madrid, Spain
Jorge Morato Lara   Universidad a Distancia de Madrid, Spain
Sonia Sánchez-Cuadrado   Universidad a Distancia de Madrid, Spain
Manuela Cañizares   Universidad a Distancia de Madrid, Spain
Héctor Bedón   Universidad a Distancia de Madrid, Spain
Isaac Seoane-Pujol   Universidad a Distancia de Madrid, Spain

Intelligent Systems for Health and Medical Care (ISHMC 2023)

Arnulfo Alanis	National Technological Institute of Mexico, Mexico
Bogart Yail Marquez	National Technological Institute of Mexico, Mexico
Rosario Baltazar	National Technological Institute of Mexico, Mexico

Intelligent Systems in Forensic Engineering (ISIFE 2023)

Alessia Amelio	University "G. d'Annunzio" Chieti-Pescara, Italy
Samuele Biondi	University "G. d'Annunzio" Chieti-Pescara, Italy
Regina Finocchiaro	University "G. d'Annunzio" Chieti-Pescara, Italy
Luciano Caroprese	University "G. d'Annunzio" Chieti-Pescara, Italy
Samantha Di Loreto	University "G. d'Annunzio" Chieti-Pescara, Italy
Sergio Montelpare	University "G. d'Annunzio" Chieti-Pescara, Italy

International Symposium on Technological Innovations for Industry and Society (ISTIIS 2023)

Filipe Portela	University of Minho, Portugal and IOTECH, Portugal
Rita Miranda	IOTECH, Portugal

International Workshop on Electronic and Telecommunications (IWET 2023)

Luis Chuquimarca	Universidad Estatal Península de Santa Elena, Ecuador
Carlos Peñafiel	Universidad Nacional del Chimborazo, Ecuador
Leticia Vaca	Universidad Técnica Manabí, Ecuador
Ricardo Cajo	Escuela Superior Politécnica del Litoral, Ecuador

Innovation in Educational Technology (JIUTE 2023)

Alba García Barrera	Universidad a Distancia de Madrid, Spain
Francisco David de la Peña Esteban	Universidad a Distancia de Madrid, Spain
Lucas Castro Martínez	Universidad a Distancia de Madrid, Spain
Verónica Nistal Anta	Universidad a Distancia de Madrid, Spain

Smart Tourism and Information Systems (SMARTTIS 2023)

Isabel Lopes	Instituto Politécnico de Bragança, Portugal
Isabel Ribeiro	Instituto Politécnico de Bragança, Portugal
Carlos Rompante Cunha	Instituto Politécnico de Bragança, Portugal

Special Sessions Program Committee

Adriano Mancini	Universitá Politecnica delle Marche, Italy
Ahmad Ali	Shenzhen University, China
Alba Garcia Barrera	Universidad a Distancia de Madrid, Spain
Ana Azevedo	CEOS.PP, ISCAP, Polytechnic of Porto, Portugal
Ana Dopico	Universidade de Vigo, Spain
Andres Muñoz	Universidad de Cádiz, Spain
Angel Recalde	Escuela Superior Politécnica del Litoral, Ecuador
Angel Torres Toukoumidis	Universidad Politécnica Salesiana, Ecuador
António Fernandes	Instituto Politécnico de Bragança, Portugal
Antonio Jesús Muñoz-Montoro	Universidad de Málaga, Spain
Antonio Mauricio Silva Sprock	Universidad Central de Venezuela, Venezuela
Antonio Moreira	Polytechnic Institute of Cávado and Ave, Portugal
Asma Patel	Aston University, UK
Barna Iantovics	UMFST, Romania
Benito Mendoza Trujillo	Universidada Nacional de Chimborazo, Ecuador
Bertil P. Marques	Polytechnic Institute of Porto, Portugal
Bogart Yail Marquez	Instituto Tecnológico Tijauna, Mexico
Bráulio Alturas	Instituto Universitário de Lisboa, Portugal
Carlos Balsa	Instituto Politécnico de Bragança, Portugal
Carlos Gordon	Universidad Técnica de Ambato, Ecuador
Carlos H. F. Alves	Federal Center of Technological Education, Brazil
Carlos Peñafiel	Universidad Nacional del Chimborazo, Ecuador
Carlos R. Cunha	Instituto Politécnico de Bragança, Portugal
Celia Ramos	University of the Algarve, Portugal
Chiara Braghin	Università degli Studi di Milano, Italy
Cristian Javier Rocha Jácome	Universidad de Sevilla, Spain
Daniel Santillán	UNACH, Ecuador
Datzania Villao	Universidad Estatal Península de Santa Elena, Ecuador
David Lizcano Casas	Madrid Open University, Spain
David Moreno	ESPOCH, Ecuador
Diego Paredes	UTN, Ecuador
Douglas Plaza	ESPOL, Ecuador

Eleni Christopoulou — Ionian University, Greece
Enrique-Javier Díez-Gutiérrez — Universidad de León, Spain
Estevan Gomez — Universidad de las Fuerzas Armadas, Ecuador
Fabrizio Messina — University of Catania, Italy
Fausto Calderón Pineda — Universidad Estatal Península de Santa Elena, Ecuador
Fernando Rodríguez Varela — Universidad Rey Juan Carlos, Spain
Filipe Pinto — Polytechnic Institute of Leiria, Portugal
Filipe Portela — University of Minho, Portugal
Francesco Cauteruccio — Polytechnic University of Marche, Italy
Franklin Eduardo Samaniego Riera — Universidad Nacional de Chimborazo, Ecuador
Frederico Branco — Universidade de Trás-Os-Montes e Alto Douro, Portugal
Frederico Lopes — UFRN, Brazil
Gerhard Chroust — Johannes Kepler University Linz, Austria
Giada Gasparini — University of Bologna, Italy
Giuseppe Festa — University of Salerno, Italy
Gunta Grinberga-Zalite — University of Life Sciences and Technologies, Latvia
Hector Bedon — Universidad a Distancia de Madrid, Spain
Hugo Moreno Aviles — Escuela Superior Politécnica de Chimborazo, Ecuador
Hugo Peixoto — University of Minho, Portugal
Ijaz Ahmad — Università Telematica "Leonardo Da Vinci", Italy
Ingars Eriņš — Riga Technical University, Latvia
Inna Skarga-Bandurova — Oxford Brookes University, UK
Ioan Ciumasu — UVSQ, France
Ioannis Vrellis — University of Ioannina, Greece
Isaac Seoane Pujol — Madrid Open University, Spain
Isabel Lopes — Instituto Politécnico de Bragança, Portugal
Isabel Pedrosa — Instituto Politécnico de Coimbra, Portugal
Jaciel Gustavo Kunz — FURG, Brazil
Jeniffer García Mendoza — Grupo Ananke, Ecuador
Jessica S. Ortiz — Universidad de las Fuerzas Armada, Ecuador
Jezreel Mejía Miranda — CIMAT, Mexico
Jhonattan Javier Barriga Andrade — IT Systems Security, Ecuador
João Cordeiro — University of Beira Interior, Portugal
Jorge Bernardino — Polytechnic Institute of Coimbra, Portugal
Jorge L. Hernandez-Ambato — Escuela Superior Politécnica de Chimborazo, Ecuador
Jorge Morato — Universidad Carlos III, Spain

Jorge Oliveira e Sá   University of Minho, Portugal

Jorge Oliveira   NOVA School of Science and Technology, Portugal

José Israel Hernández Vázquez   Instituto Tecnológico de León, Mexico

José María Díaz-Nafría   Madrid Open University, Spain

José Matos   University of Porto, Portugal

José Omar Hernández Vázquez   Instituto Tecnológico de León, Mexico

José Rufino   Polytechnic Institute of Bragança, Portugal

Jose Xavier Tomalá   Universidad Estatal Península de Santa Elena, Ecuador

Juan Pablo Ciafardini   UNLP, Argentina

Juan Rodriguez-Fernandez   Universidad de León, Spain

Juan V. Capella   Universitat Politècnica de València, Spain

Karolina Baras   University of Madeira, Portugal

Lasma Licite-Kurbe   Latvia University of Life Sciences and Technologies, Latvia

Leonardo Chancay-García   Universidad Técnica de Manabí, Ecuador

Leonardo Renteria   UNACH, Ecuador

Leticia Vaca-Cardenas   Universidad Técnica de Manabí, Ecuador

Lidice Haz   Universidad Estatal Península de Santa Elena, Ecuador

Linda Groma   Latvia University of Life Sciences and Technologies, Latvia

Lorena Molina Valdiviezo   Universidad Nacional de Chimborazo, Ecuador

Luis Alfonso Gaxiola   Universidad Autónoma de Baja California, Mexico

Luis Amaya   Universidad Estatal Península de Santa Elena, Ecuador

Luis Enrique Chuquimarca Jimenez   Universidad Estatal Península de Santa Elena, Ecuador

Luís Matos   Universidade do Minho, Portugal

Luis Mazon   BITrum Research Group, Ecuador

Manuel Montaño   Universidad Estatal Península de Santa Elena, Ecuador

Manuela Cañizares Espada   UDIMA, Spain

Manuele Kirsch Pinheiro   Paris 1 Panthéon-Sorbonne University, France

Marcela Palacios   Instituto Tecnológico Superior de Purísima del Rincón, Mexico

Marcelo Zambrano   Universidad Técnica del Norte, Ecuador

Marcia Marisol Bayas Sampedro   Universidad Estatal Península de Santa Elena, Ecuador

Marcos Cevallos   UCAB, Ecuador

Maria Covelo   UA, Portugal

María del Carmen Messina Scolaro	Universidad de la República, Uruguay
Maria Isabel Ribeiro	Instituto Politécnico Bragança, Portugal
Maria João Rodrigues	Universidade do Porto, Portugal
María Verdeja Muñiz	Universidad de Oviedo, Spain
Mario Pérez-Montoro	Universitat de Barcelona, Spain
Mario Pinto	ESMAD.IPP, Portugal
Mehran Pourvahab	University of Beira Interior, Portugal
Miguel Efraín Sangurima Pacheco	Universidad Nacional de Chimborazo, Ecuador
Mirna Muñoz Mata	Centro de Investigación en Matemáticas - Unidad Zacatecas, Mexico
Modestos Stavrakis	University of the Aegean, Greece
Nelia Gonzalez	Universidad Espíritu Santo, Ecuador
Nuno Pombo	University of Beira Interior, Portugal
Omar Castellanos	Universidad Estatal Península de Santa Elena, Ecuador
Panos Fitsilis	University of Thessaly, Greece
Paul Diaz	Universidad de las Fuerzas Armadas, Ecuador
Paula Odete Fernandes	Instituto Politécnico de Bragança, Portugal
Paulo Vasconcelos	University of Porto, Portugal
Pedro Aguado	Universidad de León, Spain
Pedro Gago	Polytechnic Institute of Leiria, Portugal
Pedro Oliveira	Instituto Politécnico de Bragança, Portugal
Piedade Carvalho	Instituto Superior de Engenharia do Porto, Portugal
Radmila Jankovic	Mathematical Institute of Serbian Academy of Sciences and Arts, Serbia
Rafael Angarita	Isep, Inria, France
Rainer E. Zimmermann	UAS for Technology and Economics Berlin (HTW), Germany
Regina Finocchiaro	"Gabriele d'Annunzio" Università di Chieti-Pescara, Italy
René Faruk Garzozi-Pincay	Universidad Estatal Península de Santa Elena, Ecuador
Ricardo Cajo	Escuela Superior Politécnica del Litoral, Ecuador
Ricardo Correia	Instituto Politécnico de Bragança, Portugal
Ricardo Godinho Bilro	ISCTE-Instituto Universitário de Lisboa, Portugal
Ricardo Queirós	Polytechnic Institute of Porto & CRACS - INESC TEC, Portugal
Roberth Abel Alcivar Cevallos	Universidad Técnica de Manabí, Ecuador
Roger Idrovo	Universidad de Navarra, Spain
Roman Chertovskih	University of Porto, Portugal
Ronan Guivarch	IRIT - Université de Toulouse, France

Rosa María Martínez	University of Almería, Spain
Rosa Reis	ISEP, Portugal
Rosario Baltazar Flores	Instituto Tecnológico de León, Mexico
Sang Guun Yoo	Escuela Politécnica Nacional, Ecuador
Sebastião Pais	University of Beira Interior, Portugal
Senka Borovac Zekan	University of Split, Croatia
Sergio Magdaleno	Instituto Tecnológico de Tijuana, Mexico
Silvia Prieto Preboste	Universidad a Distancia de Madrid, Spain
Sílvio Gama	Universidade do Porto, Portugal
Simone Belli	Universidad Complutense de Madrid, Spain
Siu Ming Yiu	University of Hong Kong, China
Surendrabikram Thapa	Virginia Tech, USA
Susana Burnes R.	Universidad Autónoma de Zacatecas, Mexico
Teresa Guarda	Universidad Estatal Península de Santa Elena, Ecuador
Tiago C. Pereira	University of Minho, Portugal
Ulises Ruiz	INAOE, Mexico
Verónica Crespo	Universidade da Coruña, Spain
Victor Huilcapi	Universidad Politécnica Salesiana, Ecuador
Victoria Otero-Espinar	University of Santiago de Compostela, Spain
Virginie Felizardo	Universidade da Beira Interior, Portugal
Wendoly Julieta Guadalupe Romero Rodriguez	Instituto Tecnológico Superior de Guanajuato, Mexico
Wolfgang Hofkirchner	Institute for a Global Sustainable Information Society, Austria

Sponsors

Universidad Estatal Península de Santa Elena, Ecuador
Universidade do Minho, Portugal
Universidad a Distancia de Madrid, Spain
Algoritmi Research Centre, Portugal
BITrum Research Group, Spain
The Institute for a Global Sustainable Information Society GSIS, Austria

Contents – Part I

Computing Solutions

Systematic Review of Technological Methods of Evaluation of Executive
Functions 3
   Carlos Ramos-Galarza, Patricia García-Cruz,
   and Mónica Bolaños-Pasquel

Software Quality in the IOT in Health Sector and Commerce Sector 14
   Karina Ojo-Gonzalez, Belen Bonilla-Morales,
   and Miguel Vargas-Lombardo

Implementation of a System for Measuring the Physical Performance
of Football Players Based on Analytic Hierarchy Process Method (AHP) 26
   Jose Luis Jinez-Tapia, Luis Gonzalo Santillan-Valdiviezo,
   Carlos Ramiro Peñafiel-Ojeda Ramiro, Jaime Puetate-Paredes,
   and Paulina Valle-Oñate

A *Mathematica* Function to Get a List of Random Inequalities and Their
Respective Solution Sets 38
   Judith K. Jiménez-Vilcherrez, Robert Ipanaqué-Chero,
   Ricardo Velezmoro-León, and Marcela F. Velásquez-Fernández

Mobile App for the Payment of Electronic Tickets Using NFC Technology
in the Public Transport System in Lima Metropolitana 50
   Fabricio Dávila, Guillermo Gonzales, and Juan-Pablo Mansilla

Integration Proposal for Thermal Imaging Modality into Health
Information Systems 65
   Ricardo Vardasca, Marco Tereso, Antonio Pratas, Braulio Alturas,
   Domingos Martinho, and Fernando Bento

A Fleet Allocation with Analytic Network Process and Time Dependent
Variables 76
   Hector Borcoski, Alexis Olmedo-Navarro, Luis Amigo, Javiera Jofré,
   Gustavo Gatica, and Jairo Coronado-Hernandez

alBERTUM: A Portuguese Search Engine for Scientific and Academic
Language 88
   Sílvia Araújo, Micaela Aguiar, and José Monteiro

A Novel Optimization Algorithm for Smart Video Surveillance System
and Change Object Detection 103
  Fahad Siddiqui and Shafaq Siddiqi

Enhancing the Museum Experience: A Gamified Approach of an Interactive
Installation in the Industrial Museum of Hermoupolis 118
  Athina Bosta and Modestos Stavrakis

Need for Quality Auditing for Screening Computational Methods
in Clinical Data Analysis, Including Revise PRISMA Protocols
for Cross-Disciplinary Literature Reviews 133
  Julia Sidorova and Juan Jose Lozano

Gamification in Recommendation Systems a Systematic Analysis 143
  Agyeman Murad Taqi, Munther Qadous, Mutaz Salah, and Fezile Ozdamli

Object Projection from IR^3 to IR^4 in Bachelor's Degree with GeoGebra 154
  Judith K. Jiménez-Vilcherrez, Robert Ipanaqué-Chero,
  Ricardo Velezmoro-León, Marcela F. Velásquez-Fernández,
  Rolando E. Ipanaqué-Silva, and César Silva-More

Efficacy of Blended Learning in the Teaching of Basic Surgical Skills
in Medical Students at a Public University in Peru Between 2018 and 2022 169
  Maritza D. Placencia-Medina, María A. Valcárcel-Saldaña,
  Christian Nole-Álvarez, Isabel Mendoza-Correa,
  María E. Muñoz Zambrano, Javier Silva-Valencia,
  Julián Villarreal-Valerio, Carlos H. Contreras-Pizarro,
  and Anel J. Roca-Béjar

Technological Solution to Optimize Outpatient Waiting Time for Medical
Care Between Multiple Private Healthcare Institutions – A Preliminary
Research 182
  Cesar Castro-Velásquez, Wendy Barrera-Barrera,
  Daniel Burga-Durango, and Jimmy Armas-Aguirre

Learning for the Empowerment of High School Girl Students 193
  Manuel Delzo-Zurita, Diego Pickman-Montoya, Daniel Burga,
  and David Mauricio

Intelligent System Comparing Clustering Algorithms to Recommend
Sales Strategies 209
  Gianella Arévalo-Huaman, Jose Vallejos-Huaman,
  and Daniel Burga-Durango

Digitizing Musical Skills in Elementary School with the Use of Instagram   220
  Almudena Álvarez-Castro Lamolda and Jorge Rafael González-Teodoro

Control of Type 1 and 2 Diabetes in Middle-Aged Individuals at Private
Clinics in Metropolitan Lima: A Technological Solution Based
on Wearables and IoT   230
  Diego Zapata, Sofia Bravo, and Juan-Pablo Mansilla

Easy-Programming: Towards a Web Collaborating Algorithmic
and Programming Aid for Early Apprentices   243
  Ricardo Vardasca, Duarte Silva, Joao Fonseca, Marco Tereso,
  Fernando Bento, and Domingos Martinho

Scheme of the Software Engineering Elements that Are Part
of the Development of eHealth-Oriented Models and Frameworks   255
  Sandra Gutierrez-Rios, Clifton Clunie, and Miguel Vargas-Lombardo

Reliable Reputation-Based Event Detection in V2V Networks   267
  Vincenzo Agate, Alessandra De Paola, Giuseppe Lo Re,
  and Antonio Virga

New Open Access Interactive Multifunctional Database Management
System for Research of Biological Terminology: Technical Solutions   282
  Karina Šķirmante, Gints Jasmonts, Roberts Ervīns Ziediņš, Silga Sviķe,
  and Arturs Stalažs

An Optimization Model for the Placement of Mobile Stroke Units   297
  Saeid Amouzad Mahdiraji, Muhammad Adil Abid, Johan Holmgren,
  Radu-Casian Mihailescu, Fabian Lorig, and Jesper Petersson

Data Intelligence

Leveraging Large Language Models for Literature Review Tasks - A Case
Study Using ChatGPT   313
  Robert Zimmermann, Marina Staab, Mehran Nasseri,
  and Patrick Brandtner

Environmental Impact of Food Products: A Data Analysis Approach
Using HJ-Biplot and Clustering   324
  Johanna Vinueza-Cajas, Stadyn Román-Niemes, Isidro R. Amaro,
  and Saba Infante

WS-YOLO: An Agronomical and Computer Vision-Based Framework
to Detect Drought Stress in Lettuce Seedlings Using IR Imaging
and YOLOv8 339
    Sebastian Wolter-Salas, Paulo Canessa, Reinaldo Campos-Vargas,
    Maria Cecilia Opazo, Romina V. Sepulveda, and Daniel Aguayo

Deep Learning Model for the Recognition of Its Environment
of an Intelligent System 352
    Jesús Ocaña, Guillermo Miñan, Luis Chauca, Víctor Ancajima,
    and Luis Leiva

Steels Classification Based on Micrographic Morphological and Texture
Features Using Decision Tree Algorithm 364
    Yamina Boutiche and Naima Ouali

Amazlem: The First Amazigh Lemmatizer 375
    Rkia Bani, Samir Amri, Lahbib Zenkouar, and Zouahir Guennoun

The Method of Contextual Selection of the Functions of Cultural Heritage
Objects Based on the Urban Environment Network Model 386
    Drozhzhin Andrei, Lavrov Igor, Loktev Egor, and Mityagin Sergey

Urban Lawns State Identification Method Based on Computer Vision 400
    Roman Bezaev, Sergey Mityagin, Aleksey Sokol, Daniil Zhembrovskii,
    Alexander Kryukovskiy, and Irina Melnichuk

A Behavior-Based Fuzzy Control System for Mobile Robot Navigation:
Design and Assessment 412
    Juan Pablo Vásconez, Mailyn Calderón-Díaz, Inesmar C. Briceño,
    Jenny M. Pantoja, and Patricio J. Cruz

Optimising a Formulated Cost Model to Minimise Labour Cost
of Computer Networking Infrastructure: A Systematic Review 427
    Richard Nana Nketsiah, Richard C. Millham, Israel Edem Agbehadji,
    Emmanuel Freeman, and Ayogeboh Epizitone

Comparison of Solution Methods the Maximal Covering Location
Problem of Public Spaces for Teenagers in the Urban Environment 443
    Maksim Natykin, Sergey Mityagin, Semen Budennyy,
    and Nikita Zakharenko

Digital Transformation Assessment Model Based on Indicators
for Operational and Organizational Readiness and Business Value 457
    Daniela Borissova, Naiden Naidenov, and Radoslav Yoshinov

Domain-Specific Sentiment Analysis of Tweets Using Machine Learning
Methods 468
   Tshephisho Joseph Sefara and Mapitsi Roseline Rangata

Trends in Computer Networking Congestion Control: A Bibliometric
Analysis 483
   Richard Nana Nketsiah, Israel Edem Agbehadji, Richard C. Millham,
   Samuel A. Iwarere, and Emmanuel Freeman

Use of Anomaly Detection and Object Detection as Basic Support
in the Recognition of Outlier Data in Images 498
   Shendry Balmore Rosero Vásquez

A Machine Learning Approach for the Simultaneous Prediction
of Dynamic Modulus and Phase Angle of Asphalt Concrete Mixtures 507
   Fabio Rondinella, Fabiola Daneluz, Bernhard Hofko, and Nicola Baldo

Blockchain and Robotic Process Automation Working Together 521
   Teresa Guarda, Samuel Bustos, Manuela Cañizares Espada,
   and Daniel Gracia Garallar

Data Science Methodologies – A Benchmarking Study 531
   Luciana Machado and Filipe Portela

Characteristics of Word-of-Mouth (WOM) by the Interaction Between
Feedback Willingness and Incentivized WOM Willingness 547
   Takumi Kato and Toshikuni Sato

Author Index 561

Contents – Part II

Sustainability

Exploring the Relationship Between Innovation, Entry Modes
and Destination Countries 3
   Mónica Azevedo, Carla Azevedo Lobo, Carla Santos Pereira,
   and Natércia Durão

Flexibility and Productivity in IoT Programming: A Case Study with Mruby ... 17
   Kazuaki Tanaka, Sota Ogura, R. Krishnamoorthy, Ko-ichiro Sugiyama,
   and Miyu Kawahara

Agile Model for the Gradual and Short-Term Deployment of an Enterprise
Architecture in the Financial Sector 28
   Kevin Avalos-Varillas, Rafael Rivas-Carillo, and Daniel Burga-Durango

Digital Master Plan as a Tool for Generating Territory Development
Requirements 45
   Tatiana Churiakova, Vasilii Starikov, Vladislava Sudakova,
   Aleksandr Morozov, and Sergey Mityagin

Cooperation and Technological Capacity Development Among
Companies: Evidence from Ecuador 58
   Gustavo Hermosa-Vega, Astrid Aguilar-Vega,
   Marianela Reina-Cherrez, and Myriam Moreno-Achig

Technological Solution in Real Time Based on IoT Devices to Optimize
Soccer Team Training 72
   Hiro Macuri, Rodrigo Castro, and Juan-Pablo Mansilla

Methods of Allocation of Urban Centers 87
   Aleksandr Katynsus, Ekaterina Shapovalenko, Anna Pavlova,
   Inna Arseneva, and Sergey Mityagin

Characterization and Comparison of Maximum Isometric Strength
and Vertical Jump Among Novice Runners, Long Distance Runners,
and Ultramarathoners 102
   Mailyn Calderón Díaz, Ricardo Ulloa-Jiménez, Nicole Castro Laroze,
   Juan Pablo Vásconez, Jairo R. Coronado-Hernández,
   Mónica Acuña Rodríguez, and Samir F. Umaña Ibáñez

Energy Efficient Fill-Level Monitoring for Recycling Glass Containers 113
  Nikola Marković, Ali Raza, Thomas Wolf, Pascal Romahn,
  Arndt-Hendrik Zinn, and Dorothea Kolossa

Impact of Biometric Sensors on Physical Activity 128
  Teresa Guarda, Datzania Villao, and Maria Fernanda Augusto

A Domain Specific Language Proposal for Internet of Things Oriented
to Smart Agro 140
  Alexander Guerrero, Daniel Samaniego, Darwin Alulema,
  Mayerly Saenz, and Verónica Alulema

Survey Based Analysis on Processed Food and Organic Consumption
Pattern in India 149
  Kushi Jain, Jose Swaminathan, and Dewar Rico-Bautista

Technology and the Generation Gap: How E-Expertise Present in Youths
Positively Affects Online Purchases 159
  José Magano, Manuel Au-Yong-Oliveira,
  and José Pedro Teixeira Fernandes

Internet of Things in Business & Management: Current Trends,
Opportunities and Future Scope 175
  Swati Sharma

Ethics, Security, and Privacy

Literature Review of SMS Phishing Attacks: Lessons, Addresses,
and Future Challenges 191
  Diana Barrera, Valery Naranjo, Walter Fuertes, and Mayra Macas

One-Time Passwords: A Literary Review of Different Protocols and Their
Applications 205
  Luis E. Almeida, Brayan A. Fernández, Daliana Zambrano,
  Anthony I. Almachi, Hilton B. Pillajo, and Sang Guun Yoo

Social Engineering Shoulder Surfing Attacks (SSAs): A Literature
Review. Lessons, Challenges, and Future Directions 220
  Bryan Zurita, Santiago Bosque, Walter Fuertes, and Mayra Macas

Adaptive Key Management-Based Privacy Preservation Protocol
for Healthcare Data 234
  Pankaj Khatiwada, Nishu Gupta, Bian Yang, and Mohammad Derawi

Reflector Saturation in Amplified Reflection Denial of Service Attack
Abusing CLDAP and Memcache Protocols 248
  João José Costa Gondim and Robson de Oliveira Albuquerque

Maturity Model of Response Protocols to Ransomware Scenarios
in the Mining Sector 264
  Brignith Gomez, Saul Vargas, and Juan-Pablo Mansilla

Ethical and Legal Challenges of Holographic Communication Technologies ... 275
  Natalia Giogiou, Niki Chatzipanagiotou, and Jude Alvin

Evolution, Collaborations, and Impacts of Big Data Research in Ecuador:
Bibliometric Analysis 290
  Fátima Avilés-Castillo, Manuel Ayala-Chauvin, and Jorge Buele

Data-Driven Intelligence Can Revolutionize Today's Cybersecurity World:
A Position Paper 302
  Iqbal H. Sarker, Helge Janicke, Leandros Maglaras, and Seyit Camtepe

The Relation Between Mayer's Multimedia Theory and Berthoz's
Simplexity Paradigm for Inclusive Education 317
  Alessio Di Paolo

A Serious Game About Apps, Data-Sharing and Deceptive Design 332
  Ingvar Tjostheim

Ethical Implications of Transparency and Explainability of Artificial
Intelligence for Managing Value-Added Tax (VAT) in Corporations 344
  Zornitsa Yordanova

A Systematic Literature Review: Towards Developing a Data Privacy
Framework for Higher Education Institutions in South Africa 354
  Krithica Latchman, Hanifa Abdullah, and Adéle da Veiga

Model for a Real Estate Property Title Management System Using
Blockchain 370
  Antony Alcalá-Otero, Leonardo Enriquez-Chusho,
  and Daniel Burga-Durango

Machine Ethics and the Architecture of Virtue 384
  Beatriz A. Ribeiro and Maria Braz da Silva

DrugChecker: Blockchain-Based Counterfeit Drug Detection System 402
  Amira Zaimia and Jalel Eddine Hajlaoui

Perception of Psychological Recommendations Generated by Neural
Networks by Student Youth (Using ChatGPT as an Example) 414
   Anna Uglova, Irina Bogdanovskaya, and Boris Nizomutdinov

A Study of Online Privacy Policies of South African Retail Websites 426
   Jean Maraba and Adéle Da Veiga

Author Index 441

Contents – Part III

Applications of Computational Mathematics to Simulation and Data Analysis (ACMaSDA 2023)

A Discussion on Variants of an Anisotropic Model Applied to Depth Completion 3
Vanel Lazcano and Felipe Calderero

Chaos Analysis and Machine Learning for Forecasting Climate Change in Some Countries of Latin America 17
Guido Tapia-Riera, Saba Infante, Isidro R. Amaro, and Francisco Hidrobo

Climate Time Series Prediction by Convex Polygons and the Kalman Filter 31
Soto Jose, Infante Saba, and Hernandez Aracelis

Parametric Study of a Stochastic SEIR Model for a COVID-19 Post-Pandemic Scenario 43
Carlos Balsa, Everaldo de Padua, Luan Pinto, and José Rufino

A Simple Mathematical Model to Steering Oceanic Debris to a Targeted Region 58
Carlos Balsa, M. Victoria Otero-Espinar, and Sílvio Gama

Challenges and the Impact of Communication and Information Technologies on Education (CICITE 2023)

Software Solution to Automatize Evaluation and Accreditation Process in Higher Education 73
Hristina Kostadinova, George Totkov, and Stoyan Atanasov

Using Educational Robotics to Explore and Teach Trochoidal Curves 87
Attila Körei and Szilvia Szilágyi

Impact of Mobile Technology on Learning and Library Policies 102
Irena Peteva, Stoyan Denchev, and Elisaveta Tsvetkova

Use of Simulators as a Digital Resource for Knowledge Transference 116
Teresa Guarda and José María Díaz-Nafría

Workshop on Gamification Application and Technologies (GAT 2023)

The Foggy Frontier: Exploring the Fog and Edge Computing for Online
Games 131
    João Paulo Sousa, Rogério Tavares, and Jesús M. Torres

GERF - Gamified Educational Virtual Escape Room Framework
for Innovative Micro-Learning and Adaptive Learning Experiences 140
    Ricardo Queirós

Bridging Knowledge in a Fragmented World (glossaLAB 2023)

Factors Affecting the Reliability of Information: The Case of ChatGPT 151
    Jorge Morato, Jose María Diaz-Nafria, and Sonia Sanchez-Cuadrado

QuinuaSmartApp: A Real-Time Agriculture Precision IoT Cloud Platform
to Crops Monitoring 165
    Héctor Bedón, Miguel Chicchon, Billy Grados, Daniel Paz,
    and Jose Maria Díaz-Nafría

Digital Platforms, Digitization of Community Businesses in the Province
of Santa Elena - Ecuador 180
    L. A. Núñez, R. A. Castro, and J. R. Rodrigues

Intelligent Systems for Health and Medical Care (ISHMC 2023)

Analysis of Marketing Campaigns Results Through Unsupervised
Learning with Apriori Association Modeling 197
    Ramón Loaiza Chávez and Bogart Yail Márquez Lobato

Mobile Application to Identify Non-perishable Products Using Machine
Learning Techniques 210
    Javier Sotelo, Arnulfo Alanis, and Bogart Yail

Efficient Spike Detection with Singular Spectrum Analysis Filter 223
    Ousmane Khouma, Mamadou L. Ndiaye, and Idy Diop

MangoFruitDDS: A Standard Mango Fruit Diseases Dataset Made in Africa ... 237
    Demba Faye, Idy Diop, Nalla Mbaye, Doudou Dione,
    and Marius Mintu Diedhiou

Management System for Pregnancy Evolution Tracking 251
    Jonathan Sánchez Luna, Arnulfo Alanis, Efrain Patiño, and Bogart Yail

Intelligent Emotion Prediction System for Help in Telemedicine Therapies
of Children with ASD 265
    Denisse Herrera, Arnulfo Alanis, Rosario Baltazar, and Daniel Velazquez

Intelligent Systems in Forensic Engineering (ISIFE 2023)

Social Media Intelligence as a Tool for Conducting Intelligence Activities 281
    Antonio Teti

Geometrical Acoustics in Cultural Heritage Conservation and Promotion:
Digitalization of the Acoustic Characteristics 292
    *Sergio Montelpare, Mariano Pierantozzi, Samantha Di Loreto,
    Alessandro Ricciutelli, and Marta ferrara*

The Language of the Forensic Structural Engineering 304
    Regina Finocchiaro, Samuele Biondi, and Franco Bontempi

**International Symposium on Technological Innovations for Industry
and Society (ISTIIS 2023)**

Coffee Silverskin: Unveiling a Versatile Agri-Food By-Product for Ethical
Textile Coatings 317
    *Agata Nolasco, Francesco Esposito, Teresa Cirillo, Augusta Silva,
    and Carla Silva*

Towards a Modular IOT Simulation System for Industry 328
    Tiago Coelho, Ricardo Rodrigues, Rita Miranda, and Filipe Portela

3D Printing Using Natural Fibers – An Emerging Technology
in Sustainable Manufacturing: A Review 343
    *Cristina Oliveira, Denise Carvalho, Isabel Moura, Bernardo Ribeiro,
    and Flávio Ferreira*

aWaRe: Aiming for Water and Waste Reduction, Reuse and Recycling 357
    *Margarida Fernandes, Augusta Silva, Carla Silva, Pedro Silva,
    Ricardo Silva, Mário Silva, Filipe Rodrigues, Beatriz França,
    Helena Vilaça, Rosa Silva, José Morgado, and Pedro Magalhães*

STVgoDigital: A Digital Product Passport Solution 368
    *Miguel Sá, Catarina Guise, Filipa Costa, Paula Rodrigues,
    João Oliveira, Ana Barros, Ricardo Silva, Toni Alves, Manuel Santos,
    António Miguel Rosado da Cruz, Marcelo Alves, and Carla Joana Silva*

Automatic EPS Calculation Guided Genetic Algorithm and Incremental
PCA Based DBSCAN of Extracted Acoustic Features for Anomalous
Sound Detection 377
Xiao Tan and Siu Ming Yiu

**International Workshop on Electronic and Telecommunications
(IWET 2023)**

Comparative Analysis Between LTE RSRP Measurements and Propagation
Models in Open Area Over 2800 m.a.s.l in Riobamba-Ecuador 391
Anthony Gualli, Lessly Borja, Anderson Yanqui, and Alexis Leon

Method Hand-Driven Used for Features Extraction in OCT B-Scan Images
Processed 406
*Fabricio Tipantocta, Oscar Gómez, Javier Cajas, German Castellanos,
and Carlos Rivera*

Empowering Low-Power Wide-Area Networks: Unlocking the Potential
of Sigfox in Local Transmission 417
*Manuel Montaño Blacio, Vladimir García Santos,
Daniel Jaramillo Chamba, Washington Torres Guin,
and Luis Chuquimarca Jiménez*

Innovation in Educational Technology (JIUTE 2023)

Towards New Acoustic Narratives on University Campuses: Potential
as Non-formal Educational Tools 433
*Alberto Quintana-Gallardo, Fernando A. Mendiguchia,
and Ignacio Guillén-Guillamón*

Language as a Moderating Factor in Cyber-Safety Awareness Among
School Learners in South Africa: Systematic Literature Review (SLR) 444
Amukelani Lisa Nkuna and Elmarie Kritzinger

Data Analysis for Performance Improvement of University Students Using
IoT 457
Manuel Ayala-Chauvin, Patricio Lara-Álvarez, and Ricardo Castro

Smart Tourism and Information Systems (SMARTTIS 2023)

The Impact of Smart Tourism on Tourist Experiences 471
*Camila Lourenço Lima, Paula Odete Fernandes, Jorge Oliveira,
and Isabel Maria Lopes*

Impact of Technology Revolution on Economic Development Over
the Past Decade 485
    Maria I. B. Ribeiro, Márcia C. R. Rogão, Isabel M. Lopes,
    and António J. G. Fernandes

From Information and Communication Technology to the Smart Tourism
Experience: Value Co-creation 502
    Pedro Vaz Serra, Cláudia Seabra, and Ana Caldeira

Author Index 517

Computing Solutions

Systematic Review of Technological Methods of Evaluation of Executive Functions

Carlos Ramos-Galarza[1]([✉]) [iD], Patricia García-Cruz[2] [iD], and Mónica Bolaños-Pasquel[1] [iD]

[1] Centro de Investigación en Mecatrónica y Sistemas Interactivos - MIST, Facultad de Psicología, Universidad Tecnológica Indoamérica, Quito, Ecuador
carlosramos@uti.edu.ec

[2] Facultad de Psicología, Pontificia Universidad Católica del Ecuador, Quito, Ecuador

Abstract. Executive functions are a set of high-level skills that allow humans to consciously regulate their cognition and behavior. The main executive functions are inhibitory control, planning, working memory, cognitive flexibility, emotional regulation, among others. The use of technological resources is key to evaluate executive functions, since, in today's society; technological resources are part of the daily life of the human being and must be present in the evaluation processes of these mental abilities. In this context, this article presents a systematic review study that has sought to identify the main technological developments that are used in the evaluation of executive functions. For this study, articles published in the Scopus database were analyzed, finding 350 studies and after the inclusion and exclusion process, we worked with eight studies that developed technological devices to evaluate executive functions. The developed devices have the benefit of assessing executive functions such as inhibition, working memory, decision making, among others. Finally, it is important to mention that technological development in neuropsychological evaluation is still in its beginnings and it is necessary to work on this line of research to have more devices to achieve this goal.

Keywords: Executive functions · cognition · technology · neuropsychological evaluation

1 Introduction

Executive functions are a group of higher-order mental abilities that allow humans to consciously control their behavior and cognition [1]. These mental abilities have been described as inhibitory control, working memory, cognitive flexibility, emotional regulation, monitoring, behavioral supervision, verification, planning, initiative, organization of materials, among others [2].

The frontal lobe of the human brain has been related as the neuronal substrate that allows the work of the executive functions and when this structure is immature or affected, the human being presents a disorganization in his behavior in the different spheres in which he operates [3]. For this reason, it is of vital importance to study these mental abilities and the role in the life of the people [4].

T. Guarda et al. (Eds.): ARTIIS 2023, CCIS 1935, pp. 3–13, 2024.
https://doi.org/10.1007/978-3-031-48858-0_1

In the field of research on executive functions, it has been reported that these mental abilities play a very important role in aspects such as academic performance, success in social relationships, organization of daily activities, participation in sports, achievement of objectives, control of emotions, fidelity and other areas. For this reason, executive functions are a topic of current interest and should be investigated from various areas, as in the case of this article, from technological context [1].

There are three techniques for assessing executive functions. First, techniques developed specifically to measure these skills, e.g. with the Stroop test, Hanoi tower, Wisconsin charts, digit retention, etc. [5]. These types of tests are classically applied in neuropsychological evaluation processes of people with brain damage or some cognitive problem [6].

A second method of evaluation of executive functions are non-specific tests, which are all the psychological evaluation instruments that have been developed to evaluate other mental or behavioral functions, however, in neuropsychology they are widely used to have a clinical criterion of how work executive functions [7].

The third type of evaluation of executive functions is deferred behavioral observation, which is based on the evaluation of these mental abilities through the report of a third person (parent, teacher, psychologist, etc.) or by a self-report of the own person involved in the evaluation process [8]. In this type of evaluation, the use of questionnaires and scales on behavior in daily life is characteristic, where executive functions play an important role [9].

This article focuses on the context of neuropsychological evaluation of executive functions, since we are interested in identifying the technological developments that have been made to evaluate them. In the next part of this article, we present a systematic review study where we have delved into the different technological devices created in the neuropsychological evaluation of executive functions.

2   Method

The present study was carried out using the systematic review methodology of several academic articles. This work was carried out through two procedures: (a) first, inclusion and exclusion criteria were determined for the selection of relevant data for this study; (b) second, a protocol was carried out to analyze the information from the selected articles to achieve the objective of identifying the technological devices developed to evaluate executive functions.

For the systematic review of the research found, it was necessary to comply with five stages (See Fig. 1):

A. Identification stage: a search of academic articles was carried out in the Scopus metabase and main journals in the context of psychology. The temporal range were works published between 2015 and 2023, using keywords in English and Spanish "executive functions, technology, assessment, psychology, frontal lobe". Regarding language, the selected articles were in English or Spanish. Two searches were carried out using the respective keywords and filters in each metabase.
B. Duplicate stage: duplicate articles were removed.

C. Eligibility stage: inclusion and exclusion criteria were determined to obtain relevant data that contribute to the objective of the study.

D. Selection stage: the articles were downloaded to be read completely and through the application of the inclusion and exclusion criteria. The articles related to the investigation were selected.

E. Bias stage: An expert in systematic review processes in executive functions supervised the entire process; in addition, constant reviews were carried out to identify adequate compliance with the inclusion and exclusion criteria in the analysis of the articles worked on in the investigation.

2.1 Inclusion and Exclusion Criteria

Inclusion: The article develops or analyzes a technological device to evaluate executive functions. It is an article with the participation of human beings and measurements of the developed device.

Exclusion: The article analyzes a paper and pencil or traditional procedure, without technological elements, to evaluate executive functions. The article develops a rehabilitation investigation and not an evaluation.

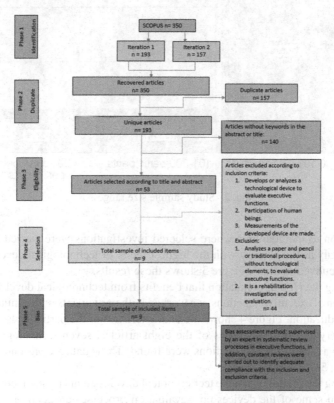

Fig. 1. Systematic review followed in this research.

Figure 1 shows the flowchart that guided this research with the phases: 1 Identification, 2 Duplicate, 3 Eligibility, 4 Selection and 5 Bias. After the analysis process of the articles, eight papers were included which are processed in the following results section.

3 Results

After carrying out the analysis, eight studies [10–18] were identified with which the results were processed. Regarding the average number of participants found in the studies, an average sample size of $M = 242.38$ $(SD = 533.79)$ was found. In most investigations were found a frequency between 0 and 100 participants. This data can be seen in Fig. 2.

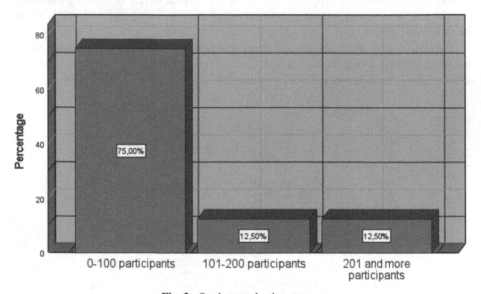

Fig. 2. Study sample size ranges.

In relation to the countries where selected investigations were carried out, it was found that Italy as the country with the highest index of technological development to evaluate executive functions. Figure 3 shows these results.

Regarding the type of population that benefits from technological developments for the evaluation of executive functions, we worked with participants with a minimum level of primary education. Figure 4 shows the characteristics of the participants.

After carrying out the analysis of the eight articles, seven technological devices developed to assess executive functions were found. These data are presented in the bar graph of Fig. 5.

Regarding the limitations of the technological developments found, it could be mentioned that in some of the devices post-evaluation processes are required, in addition to being expensive in some cases, which limits the type of population that could be evaluated.

Countries

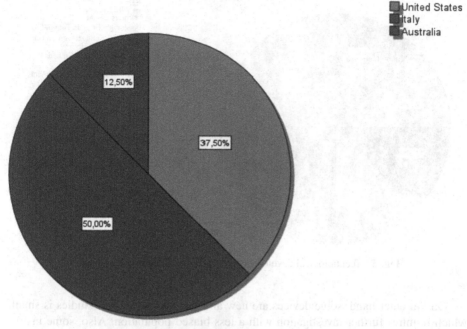

Fig. 3. Countries that have generated technology to assess executive functions.

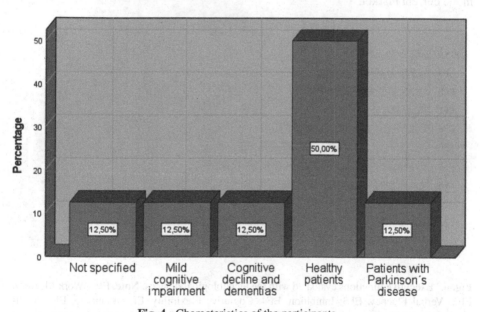

Fig. 4. Characteristics of the participants.

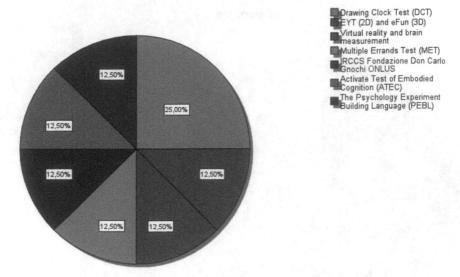

Fig. 5. Technological developments to evaluate executive functions.

On the other hand, some devices are new and the sample of their studies is small, which requires further investigation with a less biased population. Also, some instruments that use virtual reality, the resolution quality is lower compared to others available in the current market.

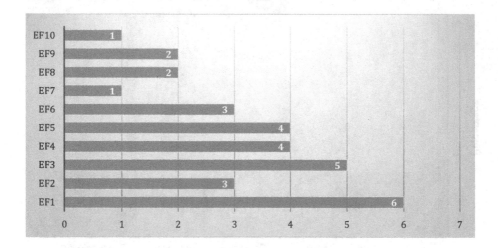

Fig. 6. Executive functions evaluated with the technological devices. **Note.** EF1: Work Memory. EF2: Verbal Fluency. EF3: Inhibition. EF4: Cognitive Flexibility. EF5: Planning. EF6: Troubleshooting. EF7: Decision Making. EF8: Attentional control. EF9: Speed of Thought. EF10: Self-regulation.

In relation to the executive functions that are evaluated in the different technological devices, it was found that working memory and inhibition are the ones that are most valued. Figure 6. Shows the executive functions evaluated.

4 Conclusions

In this article we have reported a systematic review investigation that aimed to identify technological devices developed to neuropsychologically assess executive functions. As a result of this review, eight articles were found that have developed technological devices to assess executive functions: Drawing clock test (DCT), EYT (2D) and eFun (3D), Virtual reality and brain measurement, Multiple Errands Test (MET), IRCCS Fondazione Don Carlo Gnochi ONLUS, Activate Test of Embodied Cognitivo (ATEC) and, The Psychological Experiment Building Language (PEBL).

The main aspect of the technological developments found is the evolution that is carried out in the process of neuropsychological evaluation of executive functions, since the only way to evaluate these cognitive abilities was the use of tasks that included the use of pencil and paper, or in the best of cases, some physical object. Which can be an artificial environment for today's society that bases all its activities on technology.

Advancing in this type of evaluation is a great contribution, since today's society bases the vast majority of its activities on the use of technological devices and this reality cannot be alien to the neuropsychological evaluation process. In this way, it is achieved that people who receive the evaluation of executive functions do so with devices that are more natural to their current life and not only with obsolete techniques [18].

Regarding aspects that must be improved in the analyzed applications, the fact that the clinician must have specific training for their use is highlighted. Another aspect that should be mentioned lies in the need to have regulatory data to use the devices in the general population. It is also important to motivate a change of attitude in the mental health sciences, where more space is generated for technological development to carry out the work of evaluation or rehabilitation of patients with acquired brain damage, because many times, the proposed activities generate little interest for the patient because they are not updated.

And finally, the importance of carrying out subsequent studies where technological developments are put to the test and their convergent validity with classical neuropsychological tests is assessed. In a future study we intend to carry out a systematic review of the technological devices used in neuropsychological rehabilitation.

Appendix

Table of selected articles

(*continued*)

(*continued*)

Tittle	Sample	Country	Educational level	Type of population	Technological development	Limitations of the technological device	Executive functions included in the research
Dissociating Statistically Determined Normal Cognitive Abilities and Mild Cognitive Impairment Subtypes with DCTclock	123	United States	Not specified	Patients with mild cognitive defect.	DCTclock: is a test that was digitized to evaluate cognitive functions in patients with dementia.	Requires certain subsequent computer processing for use.	Working memory, verbal fluency, inhibition.
DCTclock: Clinically-Interpretable and Automated Artificial Intelligence Analysis of Drawing Behavior for Capturing Cognition	1560	United States	Not specified	Patients with cognitive impairment and dementia.	DCTclock: is a test that was digitized to evaluate cognitive functions in patients with dementia.	There are no adaptations for different population groups.	Working memory, verbal fluency, inhibition.
A Novel Approach to Measure Executive Functions in Students: An Evaluation of Two Child-Friendly Apps	81	Australia	Primary education	Elementary, first and second grade students	EYT (2D) and eFun (3D), two applications that measure executive functions, through short and easy -to-understand tasks for young people.	It is for a specific type of population.	Working memory, cognitive flexibility, inhibition.
A virtual reality tool for the assessment of the executive functions	Not specified	Italy	Not specified	Not specified	An application that integrates the electroencephalogram and a visual tracker that can evaluate to give more information about executive functions.	It takes a long time to apply, it is very expensive, it is difficult to organize and it is poorly controlled in the application conditions and with patients with	Planning, problem solving, cognitive flexibility.

(*continued*)

(continued)

						motor deficiencies.
A neuro vr-based version of the multiple errands test for the assessment of executive functions: A possible approach	23	Italy	Not specified	Patients from 50 to 70 years old suffering from Parkinson's and cardiovascular accident	Multiple Errands Test (MET), evaluates executive functions through a virtual shopping (VR).	There may be unpredictable changes outside the control of the evaluator that disturb the patient at the time of evaluation	Planning, problem solving, cognitive flexibility.
A Psychometric Tool for Evaluating Executive Functions in Parkinson's Disease	27	Italy	Primary education	Patients between 18 and 90 years old and with no cognitive impairment	IRCCS Fondazione Don Carlo Gnochi ONLUS, cuenta de tres fases importantes: (1) tareas pre-evaluación, (2) Salida 360° y (3) tareas post-evaluación.	The screen used for the 360° device is of lower quality than those available on the current market, which reduces the quality of the (VR). In addition, there is a possible misdiagnosis of Parkinson's.	Decision making, attentional control, working memory, planning and speed of thought.
The Activate Test of Embodied Cognition (ATEC): Reliability, concurrent validity and discriminant validity in a community sample of children using cognitively demanding physical tasks related to executive functioning	55	United States	Primary education	Children of a community from 5 to 11 years of age	Activate Test of Embodied Cognition (ATEC), measures executive functions through technology that captures movements.	The ATEC measurement scale is new and requires a study with a less biased population.	Working memory, coordination, inhibition, self-regulation, cognitive processing speed.
Difference Between Young and Old Adults' Performance	70	Italy	Not specified	People from 35 to 60 years of age, from rural and urban	The Psychology Experiment Building Language (PEBL) Test Battery, is a recent computerized	It is unknown whether the computerized setting	Working memory, verbal fluency, selective

(continued)

(*continued*)

on the Psychology Experiment Building Language (PEBL) Test Battery: What Is the Role of Familiarity With Technology in Cognitive Performance?	areas of Italy without neurologic or psychiatric diseases	software that assesses cognitive functioning	could affect later cognitive performance	attention, inhibition, planning, problem solving, cognitive flexibility.

References

1. Ramos-Galarza, C., et al.: Fundamental concepts in the neuropsychological theory Conceptos fundamentales en la teoría neuropsicológica]. Revista Ecuatoriana de Neurología **26**(1), 53–60 (2017)
2. Ramos-Galarza, C., Jadán-Guerrero, J., Gómez-García, A.: Relationship between academic performance and the self-report of the executive performance of ecuadorian teenagers. Avances en Psicología Latinoam. **36**(2), 405–417 (2018)
3. Ramos-Galarza, C., Acosta-Rodas, P., Bolaños-Pasquel, M., Lepe-Martínez, N.: The role of executive functions in academic performance and behaviour of university students. J. Appl. Res. High. Educ. **12**(3), 444–445 (2020)
4. Beserra-Lagos, D., Lepe-Martínez, N., Ramos-Galarza, C.: The executive functions of the frontal lobe and its association with the academic performance of students in higher education. Rev. Ecuatoriana de Neurol. **27**(3), 51–56 (2018)
5. Ramos-Galarza, C., Benavides-Endara, P., Bolaños-Pasquel, M., Fonseca-Bautista, S., Ramos, D.: Scale of clinical observation to valuate the third functional unit of the Luria theory: EOCL-1. Rev. Ecuatoriana de Neurol. **28**(2), 83–91 (2019)
6. Silva-Barragán, M., Ramos-Galarza, C.: Etiology of brain damage: a neuropsychological contribution in its theoretical construction (First part). Rev. Ecuatoriana de Neurol. **30**(1), 154–165 (2021)
7. Ramos-Galarza, C., Cruz-Cárdenas, J., Bolaños-Pasquel, M., Acosta-Rodas, P.: Factorial structure of the EOCL-1 scale to asess executive functions. Front. Psychol. **12**(585145), 1–14 (2021)
8. Ramos-Galarza, C., Bolaños-Pasquel, M., García-Gómez, A., Martínez Siiarez, P., Jadán-Guerrero, J.: Efeco scale for assessing executive functions in self-report format. Rev. Iberoamericana de Diagnostico y Evaluacion Psicologica **51**(1), 83–93 (2019)
9. Ramos-Galarza, C., et al.: Evaluación de las Habilidades de la Corteza Prefrontal: La Escala Efeco II-VC y II VR. Rev. Ecuatoriana de Neurol. **27**(3), 36–43 (2018)
10. Matusz, E., et al.: Dissociating statistically determined normal cognitive abilities and mild cognitive impairment subtypes with DCTclock. J. Int. Neuropsychological Soc. **29**(2), 148-158 (2023)
11. Souillard-Mandar, W., Penney, D., Schaible, B., Pascual-Leone, A., Au, R., Davis, R.: DCTclock: clinically-interpretable and automated artificial intelligence analysis of drawing behavior for capturing cognition. Front. Digital Health **3**(15), 750661 (2021)

12. Berg, V., Rogers, S.L., McMahon, M., Garrett, M., Manley, D.: A novel approach to measure executive functions in students: an evaluation of two child-friendly apps. Front. Psychol. **11**(1), 1702 (2020)
13. Borgnis, F., Baglio, F., Riva, G., Cipresso, P.: A virtual reality tool for the assessment of the executive functions. Ann. Rev. Cybertherapy Telemed. **1**(1), 247–250 (2020)
14. Raspelli, S., et al.: A neuro vr-based version of the multiple errands test for the assessment of executive functions: a possible approach. J. Cyber Therapy Rehabil. **2**(4), 299–314 (2009)
15. Borgnis, F., et al.: A psychometric tool for evaluating executive functions in parkinson's disease. J. Clin. Med. **11**(5), 1153 (2022)
16. Bell, M., Weinstein, A., Pittman, B., Gorman y, R., Abujelala, M.: The activate test of embodied cognition (ATEC): reliability, concurrent validity and discriminant validity in a community sample of children using cognitively demanding physical tasks related to executive functioning. Child Neuropsychlogy **7**, 973–983, 27 (2021)
17. Scarpina, F., D´agata y, F., Mauro, A.: Difference between young and old adults' performance on the psychology experiment building language (PEBL) test battery: what is the role of familiarity with technology in cognitive performance?. Assessment **28**(6), 1–15 (2020)
18. Ramos-Galarza, C.: Adaptation of victoria stroop test in ecuadorians students. Revista Iberoamericana de Diagnostico y Evaluacion Psicologica **2**(44), 57–64 (2017)

Software Quality in the IOT in Health Sector and Commerce Sector

Karina Ojo-Gonzalez[1]([⊠]) [iD], Belen Bonilla-Morales[1] [iD],
and Miguel Vargas-Lombardo[2,3] [iD]

[1] FISC, Universidad Tecnológica de Panamá, Ciudad de Panamá, Panamá
karina.ojo@utp.ac.pa
[2] GISES, Universidad Tecnológica de Panamá, Ciudad de Panamá, Panamá
[3] Tecnología E Innovación, SNI-SENACYT Sistema Nacional de Investigación-Secretaria
Nacional de Ciencia, Clayton, Ciudad del Saber Edif.205, 0816-02852 Panama City, Panama

Abstract. The analysis of quality attributes is a vital phase that determines the functionalities and properties a software system must have from its conception and development, an aspect from which current systems do not escape. Let's add the paradigm of the Internet of Things (IoT) to the current systems, and as a result, the requirements, and capabilities of the components to be automated in the most common systems and services increase exponentially. This leads to the linking of services in the computational cloud and other contexts and domains of scientific and business interests. In this research work, a literature review supported by the ISO/IEC 25010 standard is carried out to identify the quality attributes for two application domains: Health sector and Commerce sector; the associated and attended aspects for each domain is pointed out according to the quality characteristics of the software product. This research is the basis for identifying other application domains in sectors yet to be studied, in which IOT technologies and software engineering are immersed and are necessary for the development of new experiences in the context of requirements, planning, complex processes, project development and service for software development with higher quality.

Keywords: Quality attribute · Commerce sector · Health sector · Internet of things · ISO/IEC 25010

1 Introduction

The technological development in which we live today is evidenced by the range of electronic devices on the market that allows access to various services from the palm of our hands, as in the case of smartphones. All these devices, regardless of their purpose, require software to manage their operation. The field of software engineering has had to evolve to adapt to the new needs and technologies present at the time of starting a software development project [53], not only at the level of the methodologies but also to the point of requiring modifications in the existing architectural patterns, due to the new requirements that must be satisfied for the correct operation of the systems. An example of these new trends is the Internet of Things (IoT) paradigm. The IoT [1, 6, 11] in general,

T. Guarda et al. (Eds.): ARTIIS 2023, CCIS 1935, pp. 14–25, 2024.
https://doi.org/10.1007/978-3-031-48858-0_2

consists of a network of sensors and devices that collect the data from their environment to make decisions and subsequently execute actions that improve the environment. One of its main characteristics is the interaction between the network devices without human intervention. This is one of the reasons that has led to the adapting of the traditional approach to software development and taking the specific and characteristic requirements for these systems into consideration. Therefore, through a literature review, this paper identifies the quality attributes that receive greater attention when designing an IoT system according to its application domain, taking the ISO/IEC 25010 standard [24] used for the evaluation of the properties of the IoT software products as a reference [29]. The paper is structured as follows: Section 2 presents the generalities of IoT systems, Sect. 3 discusses the methodology used for the literature review, and the execution of the review, Sect. 4 breaks down the results of the review, discusses the findings, and finally, Sect. 5 the conclusion.

2 Background

The term IoT refers to a structure composed of physical devices or "things" whose communication and interaction are controlled by a software infrastructure [1] and whose objective is to collect data from their environment, allowing subsequent analytical processing of these data with a view of generating relevant information for deciding the actions to be carried out in that environment [13, 36, 46]. This process requires a level of autonomy and intelligence on the part of the system. IoT systems are subject to the domain in which they are implemented, which is the reason why in [27], a method is proposed for performing the analysis of the system requirements. This method establishes that the first thing to be done is formally defining the purpose of the system, then comes a detailed study of the elements of the environment in which the system will be placed and the devices best suited to collect the data under the conditions of that environment, and established last is the reason that supports what expresses in [31], reference to the use of microcontrollers to improve the performance of IoT systems.

The survey of the quality attributes persists as a crucial activity for the construction of any system. Therefore, in many cases, it is necessary to modify or establish new guidelines that allow the proper analysis of the same, as detailed by [53, 59] where a set of sub-processes is proposed for the definition of the quality attributes in IoT systems; however, studies such as [1, 47] show a tendency to give greater importance to the software quality attributes. Some authors affirm the need to contemplate the aspects referring to quality attributes when designing the architectures intended to support IoT systems [57]. However, they indicate that it is a complex task as shows because it is common for conflicts to occur between the requirements, which refers to [71]. In other words, just achieving the totality of one quality attribute may have a negative impact on another requirement that is also of interest in the final product. Based on the above, the domain (purpose and environment) in which the IoT system is implemented is identified as a determining factor for the quality attributes to be considered during the design and construction of the system. Currently, IoT systems can be found in different domains such as Health sector and Commerce sector [1, 18, 44, 51]. To identify the characteristic quality attributes of the IoT systems for a given application domain, the following section details the methodology used to perform the literature review that supports this study.

3 Results of the Review

This section presents the results of the review. The methodology selected for conducting the systematic literature review is the one proposed by Barbara Kitchenham (SLR) for research related to the field of software engineering. In this section, the points concerning the preparation of the research are developed. The key questions that will serve as a guide for the collection of the information to be analyzed later are defined, based on the information presented in the background section. The following are the questions of this research:

RQ1- What are the quality attributes in an IoT system? This question aims to identify the quality attributes and the reasons why they are indispensable for a given application domain.

RQ2- What aspects of the IoT system are associated with these quality attributes in each domain? This question aims to identify possible differences in the perspective of the same quality characteristic from each of the studied domains.

3.1 Relevant Publications by Year

The graph shows an increase in the number of studies related to the identification of the non-functional requirements in IoT systems from 2018 onwards, see Fig. 1.

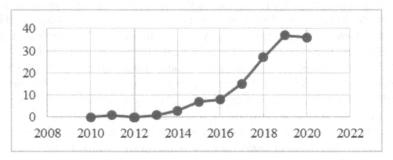

Fig. 1. Shows the distribution of the publications in the period 2010–2022.

3.2 Quality Attributes by Application Domain

The lists the quality attributes any IoT system should contemplate at the time of its design. Interoperability refers to the ability of interaction and communication between physical devices through the infrastructure in a vendor-independent manner; scalability is related to the number of devices or entities handled by the system without reducing its performance [61]; security is mostly oriented to the protection of the data collected by sensors or physical devices; sensitivity refers to the environment and the system's capacity to collect the data generated by changing conditions in the context it has been implemented in.

3.3 Prioritization of the Quality Attributes in IoT Systems

The standard used for the identification of the quality attributes is ISO 25010 [24], due to its wide international acceptance, in addition to being considered the most complete. It includes the characteristics of the systems in the production stage, omitting the attribute of functional adequacy since all the systems presented in the studies extracted during the literature review are assumed to fully comply with the purpose they were designed for. The following points show a table containing the attributes referred to or mentioned in the reviewed documents for each domain. These attributes—performance efficiency, compatibility, usability, reliability, security, maintainability, and portability—are identified as QA1, QA2, QA3, QA4, QA5, QA6, and QA7, respectively. See Table 1.

3.3.1 Health Sector

The health sector is characterized by the massive production of data as a result of daily activities such as patient monitoring, identity management, keeping medical records, and medical emergency processing [26]. These activities have no room for delays in information management and require robust and reliable automated processes.

IoT systems in the health sector not only provide many benefits that go beyond patient care and monitoring but also contribute to cost reduction and enable connections between various service providers. According to [40], the IoT systems in this application domain are usually classified into three levels: the first level is intended for real-time data collection, so it must always be kept active; the second level involves network communication protocols between devices and computing resources; the third level involves data processing and storage servers. The nature of the IoT systems in the health sector is critical, so failures could lead to the loss of human lives. Table 1, summarizes the perceived quality attributes for this domain.

Table 1. Quality attributes for an IoT system in the Health Sector

Ref	QA1	QA2	QA3	QA4	QA5	QA6	QA7
[25]	✔	✔		✔	✔	✔	
[7]				✔	✔		
[37]	✔	✔		✔	✔	✔	
[63]	✔				✔	✔	✔
[5]	✔	✔	✔	✔	✔	✔	✔
[60]	✔			✔		✔	✔
[38]	✔	✔			✔	✔	
[64]			✔				
[33]				✔	✔		
[40]	✔			✔			✔
[62]	✔	✔		✔	✔		
[34]	✔		✔			✔	
[54]			✔	✔	✔		

(*continued*)

Table 1. (*continued*)

Ref	QA1	QA2	QA3	QA4	QA5	QA6	QA7
[70]					✔		
[3]	✔	✔			✔		
[32]					✔		
[26]	✔		✔	✔	✔	✔	
[10]	✔	✔		✔	✔		
[65]	✔						✔
[17]	✔	✔	✔	✔	✔	✔	✔
[2]	✔				✔		·
[8]	✔	✔		✔	✔		✔
[46]		✔	✔		✔		
[35]	✔	✔		✔	✔		✔
[48]	✔	✔			✔	✔	✔
[15]			✔				
[58]	✔		✔		✔		
[4]	✔		✔	✔	✔		
[50]	✔	✔	✔	✔	✔		
[22]	✔	✔					
TOTAL	22	14	11	16	23	10	9

For this domain, Fig. 2 shows that compared to the two previous domains, all attributes in this domain are mentioned in at least 30% of the documents. The three main attributes coincide with those of the health sector due to this domain also having a critical nature; these attributes are safety (76.67%), performance efficiency (73.33%), and reliability (53.33%).

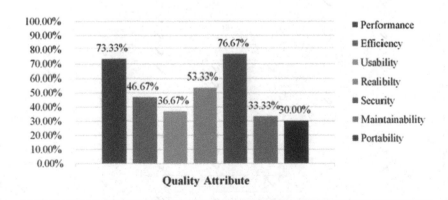

Fig. 2. Frequency of the mention of the quality attributes in the Health sector domain.

3.3.2 Commercial Sector

IoT systems for commercial activities aim to collect and analyze data to reach consumers through different channels while primarily ensuring user satisfaction and experience [55, 69]. Yet, this domain has not been able to openly obtain the benefits of IoT due to the lack of standardization and regulation policies for its use by different governments [28]. Table 2 shows the attributes mentioned in the documents collected in relation to this domain.

Table 2. Quality attributes for an IoT system in the Commercial Sector domain

Ref	QA1	QA2	QA3	QA4	QA5	QA6	QA7
[43]						✔	✔
[23]			✔				
[21]	✔	✔			✔		
[69]				✔			
[55]			✔		✔		
[42]			✔				
[67]			✔		✔		✔
[12]			✔			✔	✔
[56]	✔						
[19]	✔	✔	✔				
[16]			✔				
[28]	✔	✔	✔		✔	✔	
[49]	✔	✔		✔	✔		
[68]		✔				✔	✔
[41]	✔			✔	✔		
TOTAL	6	5	8	3	6	4	4

Although few documents were found in relation to the quality attributes for this domain, there is a notable difference from those seen previously. In this domain, usability (53.33%) tops the list of the attributes, followed by performance efficiency and security (40%), with compatibility in third place (33.33%). Frequency of the mention of the quality attributes in the commercial sector domain. See Fig. 3.

4 Discussion of Findings

This study identified the lack of a guide or plan to determine the properties of the quality attributes that must be tested in IoT systems [58] according to the domain in which they are being implemented. Besides the drawbacks detected with the existing tools, which include their focus on functional aspects, the complexity of adoption and reusability

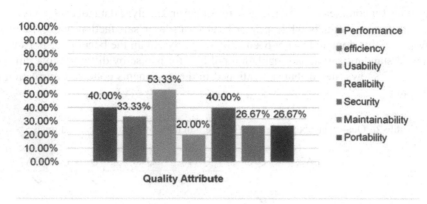

Fig. 3. Presence of quality attributes – Commercial Sector

[14, 18, 45] among other factors that influence the acceptance by the community of architects and software developers, it is proposed to first develop an updated state-of-the-art system to recognize the scenarios and contexts in which the quality attributes are present and then propose a conceptual model. We must recognize that according to [52], conceptual models can be classified as follows:

Textual: A document describing the content of each conceptual component and generating visual images of the structure of these components using narrative text. It details the objective, the output or the product of the model, its scope, and the flow of the interactions between the components.

Pictorial: In this type of model, diagrams are used to represent the flow within the model, using geometric figures and symbols connected by links that can be lines or arrows. This group includes activity cycle diagrams, process diagrams, and event networks. Multifaceted: Being the most recommended model to ensure complete documentation, the multifaceted model consists of both textual and pictorial elements, besides tending to use a set of diagrams instead of just one. In this type of model, the UML diagrams used in software engineering stand out, which define 13 types of diagrams to represent the static aspects, behavior, and interactions of the software.

Thus, the early deployment of the software platforms with marked quality attributes will be propitiated, with these first contributions being taken as a reference for the construction of the software architectures, in development models and the testing phase of IoT systems.

5 Conclusion

In this research, a literature review was conducted in which common software attributes for IoT-based systems were identified, then the specific aspects of the interest in application domains such as Health sector and Commerce sector were defined.

In the process, ISO/IEC 25010 was used as a reference for the identification of the quality attributes, showing that the same characteristic can have different perspectives, depending on the application domain or the context for which the IoT solution is to be designed.

This study evidences the need for future work to further characterize the quality attributes found through a conceptual model and, thus, provide specific guidance for the deployment of software platforms with high-quality standards based on their attributes.

Acknowledgment. We are grateful for the support provided by the Science, Technology and Innovation National Secretariat of Panama (SENACYT), Scientific Master program TIC-UTP FISC-2019, to the National Research System (SNI-SENACYT) which one author is member.

Authors Contribution. Conceptualization KO, BBM; methodology KO, BBM, MVL; formal analysis KO, BBM,; research KO, BBM, M.V.L.; original-writing KO,BBM, M.V.; writing—review and edition KO, BBM, M.V.L; Corresponding author, BBM, M.V.L.

References

1. Ahmed, B.S., et al.: Aspects of quality in Internet of Things (IoT) solutions: a systematic mapping study. IEEE Access. **7**, 13758–13780 (2019). https://doi.org/10.1109/ACCESS.2019.289 3493
2. Ahmed, M.U., Björkman, M., Čaušević, A., Fotouhi, H., Lindén, M.: An overview on the Internet of Things for health monitoring systems. In: Mandler, B., et al. (eds.) IoT360 2015. LNICSSITE, vol. 169, pp. 429–436. Springer, Cham (2016). https://doi.org/10.1007/978-3-319-47063-4_44
3. Al-khafajiy, M., et al.: Towards fog driven IoT healthcare. In: Proceedings of the 2nd International Conference on Future Networks and Distributed Systems, pp. 1–7 ACM, New York (2018). https://doi.org/10.1145/3231053.3231062
4. Almeida, A., et al.: A critical analysis of an IoT—aware AAL system for elderly monitoring. Futur. Gener. Comput. Syst. **97**, 598–619 (2019). https://doi.org/10.1016/j.future.2019.03.019
5. Arenas, C., et al.: Requirements specification of a software-intensive system in the health domain: an experience report. Pervasive Health Pervasive Comput. Technol. Healthc. (2020)https://doi.org/10.1145/3439961.3439996
6. Asthon, K.: That Internet of Things Thing. RFID J. 4986 (2010). https://doi.org/10.1038/nature03475
7. Baba-Cheikh, Z., et al.: A preliminary study of open-source IoT development frameworks. In: Proceedings of the IEEE/ACM 42nd International Conference on Software Engineering Workshops, pp. 679–686 (2020). https://doi.org/10.1145/3387940.3392198
8. de Morais Barroca Filho, I., de Aquino Junior, G.S.: Iot-based healthcare applications: A review. In: Gervasi, O., et al. (eds.) ICCSA 2017. LNCS, vol. 10409, pp. 47–62. Springer, Cham (2017). https://doi.org/10.1007/978-3-319-62407-5_4
9. Bogner, J., et al.: Using architectural modifiability tactics to examine evolution qualities of service- and microservice-based systems: an approach based on principles and patterns. Softw.-Intensive Cyber-Phys. Syst. **34**(2–3), 141–149 (2019). https://doi.org/10.1007/s00450-019-00402-z
10. Bui, N., Zorzi, M.: Health care applications: a solution based on the Internet of Things. In: ACM International Conference Proceeding Series, p. 4 (2011). https://doi.org/10.1145/2093698.2093829

11. Bures, M., Bellekens, X., Frajtak, K., Ahmed, B.S.: A comprehensive view on quality characteristics of the IoT solutions. In: José, R., Van Laerhoven, K., Rodrigues, H. (eds.) 3rd EAI International Conference on IoT in Urban Space. Urb-IoT 2018. EAI/Springer Innovations in Communication and Computing, pp. 59-69. Springer, Cham (2020). https://doi.org/10.1007/978-3-030-28925-6_6

12. Charoenporn, P.: Smart logistic system by IOT technology. In: ACM International Conference Proceeding Series, pp. 149–153 (2018). https://doi.org/10.1145/3178158.3178186

13. Chehri, A., et al.: A framework of optimizing the deployment of IoT for precision agriculture industry. Procedia Comput. Sci. **176**, 2414–2422 (2020). https://doi.org/10.1016/j.procs.2020.09.312

14. Costa, B., et al.: Specifying functional requirements and QoS parameters for IoT Systems. In: 2017 IEEE 15th International Conference on Dependable, Autonomic and Secure Computing, 15th International Conference on Pervasive Intelligence and Computing, 3rd International Conference on Big Data Intelligence and Computing and Cyber Science and Technology Congress (DASC/PiCom/DataCom/CyberSciTech), pp. 407–414 (2018). https://doi.org/10.1109/DASC-PICom-DataCom-CyberSciTec.2017.83

15. Curumsing, M.K., et al.: Understanding the impact of emotions on software: a case study in requirements gathering and evaluation. J. Syst. Softw. **147**, 215–229 (2019). https://doi.org/10.1016/j.jss.2018.06.077

16. Deng, B., et al.: Internet of Things smart restaurant design scheme. In: Proceedings of the 3rd International Conference on Computer Science and Application Engineering, pp. 1–4 ACM, New York (2019). https://doi.org/10.1145/3331453.3361283

17. Erazo-Garzon, L., Erraez, J., Cedillo, P., Illescas-Peña, L.: Quality assessment approaches for ambient assisted living systems: a systematic review. In: Botto-Tobar, M., Zambrano Vizuete, M., Torres-Carrión, P., Montes León, S., Pizarro Vásquez, G., Durakovic, B. (eds.) ICAT 2019. CCIS, vol. 1193, pp. 421–439. Springer, Cham (2020). https://doi.org/10.1007/978-3-030-42517-3_32

18. Fahmideh, M., Zowghi, D.: An exploration of IoT platform development. Inf. Syst. **87** (2020). https://doi.org/10.1016/j.is.2019.06.005

19. Faye, S., et al.: SWAM: A novel smart waste management approach for businesses using IoT. In: TESCA 2019 - Proceedings 2019 of the 1st ACM International Workshop on Technology Enablers and Innovative Applications for Smart Cities and Communities, co-located with 6th ACM International Conference System Energy-Efficient Building Cities, vol. 1, pp. 38–45 (2019). https://doi.org/10.1145/3364544.3364824

20. Gnanasekaran, R.K., et al.: Using recurrent neural networks for classification of natural language-based non-functional requirements. In: CEUR Workshop Proceedings, vol. 2857 (2021)

21. Hartner, R., et al.: Digital shop floor management: a practical framework for implementation. In: PervasiveHealth Pervasive Computer Technology Healthcare, pp. 41–45 (2020). https://doi.org/10.1145/3384544.3384611

22. Indrakumari, R., et al.: The growing role of internet of things in healthcare wearables. Elsevier Inc. (2019). https://doi.org/10.1016/B978-0-12-819593-2.00006-6

23. Isharyani, M.E., et al.: Conceptual model of consumers purchase intention towards smart retail: a literature review. In: Pervasive Health Pervasive Computer Technology Healthcare (2020). https://doi.org/10.1145/3429789.3429812

24. ISO/IEC: ISO/IEC 25010:2011 - Systems and software engineering – Systems and software Quality Requirements and Evaluation (SQuaRE) – System and software quality models (2011)

25. Jita, H., Pieterse, V.: A framework to apply the Internet of Things for medical care in a home environment. In: Proceedings of the 2018 International Conference on Cloud Computing and Internet of Things, pp. 45–54 Association for Computing Machinery, New York (2018). https://doi.org/10.1145/3291064.3291065

26. Kassab, M., et al.: Investigating quality requirements for blockchain-based healthcare systems. Proc. - 2019 IEEE/ACM 2nd International Workshop Emerging Trends Software Engineering Blockchain, WETSEB 2019, pp. 52–55 (2019). https://doi.org/10.1109/WETSEB.2019.00014

27. Kirsch-Pinheiro, M., et al.: Requirements analysis for context-oriented systems. Procedia Comput. Sci. Ant **83**, 253–261 (2016). https://doi.org/10.1016/j.procs.2016.04.123

28. Lee, I.: The Internet of Things for enterprises: an ecosystem, architecture, and IoT service business model. Internet of Things (Netherlands). **7**, 100078 (2019). https://doi.org/10.1016/j.iot.2019.100078

29. Li, Q., et al.: Smart manufacturing standardization: architectures, reference models and standards framework. Comput. Ind. **101**, 91–106 (2018). https://doi.org/10.1016/j.compind.2018.06.005

30. Marzooni, H.H., et al.: Architecture style selection using statistics of quality attributes to reduce production costs. Int. Arab J. Inf. Technol. **18**(4), 513–522 (2021). https://doi.org/10.34028/18/4/3

31. Mendoza, J.F., et al.: Architecture for embedded software in microcontrollers for Internet of Things (IoT) in fog water collection. Procedia Comput. Sci. **109**(2016), 1092–1097 (2017). https://doi.org/10.1016/j.procs.2017.05.395

32. De Michele, R., Furini, M.: IoT healthcare: benefits, issues and challenges. In: Pervasive Health Pervasive Computer Technologies Healthcare, pp. 160–164 (2019). https://doi.org/10.1145/3342428.3342693

33. Minoli, D., et al.: IoT security (IoTSec) mechanisms for e-health and ambient assisted living applications. In: 2017 IEEE/ACM International Conference on Connected Health: Applications, Systems and Engineering Technologies (CHASE), pp. 13–18 (2017). https://doi.org/10.1109/CHASE.2017.53

34. Mohamed, W., Abdellatif, M.M.: Telemedicine: an IoT application for healthcare systems. In: Pervasive Health Pervasive Computer Technologies Healthcare, pp. 173–177 (2019). https://doi.org/10.1145/3328833.3328881

35. Barroca Filho, Id.M., de Aquino Junior, G.S.: Proposing an IoT-based healthcare platform to integrate patients, physicians and ambulance services. In: Gervasi, O., et al. (eds.) ICCSA 2017. LNCS, vol. 10409, pp. 188–202. Springer, Cham (2017). https://doi.org/10.1007/978-3-319-62407-5_13

36. Motta, R.C., et al.: On challenges in engineering IoT software systems. In: ACM International Conference Proceeding Series, pp. 42–51 (2018). https://doi.org/10.1145/3266237.3266263

37. Muccini, H., et al.: Self-adaptive IoT architectures: an emergency handling case study. In: ACM International Conference Proceeding Series (2018).https://doi.org/10.1145/3241403.3241424

38. Mukhiya, S.K. et al.: An architectural design for self-reporting e-health systems. In: 2019 IEEE/ACM 1st International Workshop on Software Engineering for Healthcare (SEH). SEH 2019. iv, pp. 1–8 (2019). https://doi.org/10.1109/SEH.2019.00008

39. Nurbojatmiko, et al.: SLR on identification & classification of non-functional requirements attributes, and its representation in functional requirements. In: ACM International Conference Proceeding Series, pp. 151–157 (2018). https://doi.org/10.1145/3297156.3297200

40. Oti, O., et al.: Iot-based healthcare system for real-time maternal stress monitoring. In: Proceedings of the 2018 IEEE/ACM International Conference on Connected Health: Applications, Systems and Engineering Technologies CHASE 2018, pp. 57–62 (2019). https://doi.org/10.1145/3278576.3278596

41. Pal, K., Yasar, A.U.H.: Internet of things and blockchain technology in apparel manufacturing supply chain data management. Procedia Comput. Sci. **170**, 450–457 (2020). https://doi.org/10.1016/j.procs.2020.03.088

42. Le Pallec, M., et al.: Physical-interface-based IoT service characterization. In: ACM International Conference Proceeding Series, pp. 63–71 (2016). https://doi.org/10.1145/2991561.2991567
43. Park, J., Chi, S.Y.: A requirement for traceability of production logs in large-scale shop floor data. In: ACM International Conference Proceeding Series, pp. 151–155 (2015). https://doi.org/10.1145/2837060.2837084
44. Pereira, P.P., et al.: Enabling cloud-connectivity for mobile internet of things applications. In: 2013 IEEE Seventh International Symposium on Service-Oriented System Engineering, pp. 518–526 (2013). https://doi.org/10.1109/SOSE.2013.33
45. Pontes, P.M., et al.: Izinto: a pattern-based IoT testing framework. In: Companion Proceeding ISSTA/ECOOP 2018 Work, pp. 125–131 (2018). https://doi.org/10.1145/3236454.3236511
46. Prieto-Gonzalez, L., Tamm, G., Stantchev, V.: Towards a software engineering approach for cloud and IoT services in healthcare. In: Gervasi, O., et al. (eds.) ICCSA 2016. LNCS, vol. 9789, pp. 439–452. Springer, Cham (2016). https://doi.org/10.1007/978-3-319-42089-9_31
47. Qu, C., et al.: Aspect-oriented requirement analysis based on formal method. J. Phys. Conf. Ser. **1952**, 4 (2021). https://doi.org/10.1088/1742-6596/1952/4/042027
48. Rahmani, A.M., et al.: Exploiting smart e-Health gateways at the edge of healthcare Internet-of-Things: a fog computing approach. Futur. Gener. Comput. Syst. **78**, 641–658 (2018). https://doi.org/10.1016/j.future.2017.02.014
49. Ramakrishnan, P., Ma, Y.: Adaptive supply chain systems – IoT based conceptual framework. In: ACM International Conference Proceeding Series, pp. 62–68 (2018). https://doi.org/10.1145/3194188.3194205
50. Ray, P.P., et al.: Sensors for internet of medical things: state-of-the-art, security and privacy issues, challenges and future directions. Comput. Commun. **160**, 111–131 (2020). https://doi.org/10.1016/j.comcom.2020.05.029
51. Razzaq, A.: A Systematic review on software architectures for IoT systems and future direction to the adoption of microservices architecture. SN Comput. Sci. **1**(6), 1–30 (2020). https://doi.org/10.1007/s42979-020-00359-w
52. Robinson, S., et al.: Conceptual modeling for discrete-event simulation. In: Conceptual Modeling for Discrete-Event Simulation, pp. 337–354 (2010). https://doi.org/10.1201/9781439810385
53. Rodrigues Da Silva, A.: Model-driven engineering: a survey supported by the unified conceptual model. Comput. Lang. Syst. Struct. **43**, 139–155 (2015). https://doi.org/10.1016/j.cl.2015.06.001
54. Saraubon, K., et al.: A smart system for elderly care using IoT and mobile technologies. In: ACM International Conference Proceeding Series, pp. 59–63 (2018). https://doi.org/10.1145/3301761.3301769
55. Saraubon, K., et al.: IoT mobile-based system for business: quick service restaurant. In: ACM International Conference Proceeding Series, pp. 54–58 (2018). https://doi.org/10.1145/3301761.3301768
56. Sharma, A., et al.: SmrtFridge: IoT-based, user interaction-driven food item & quantity sensing. In: SenSys 2019 - Proceedings of the 17th Conference on Embedded Networked Sensor Systems, pp. 245–257 (2019). https://doi.org/10.1145/3356250.3360028
57. Shi, Z., et al.: Design and implementation of the mobile internet of things based on td-scdma network. In: Proceeding of 2010 IEEE International Conference Information Theory Information Security ICITIS 2010, pp. 954–957 (2010). https://doi.org/10.1109/ICITIS.2010.5689806
58. Sicari, S., et al.: A policy enforcement framework for Internet of Things applications in the smart health. Smart Heal. **3**(4), 39–74 (2017). https://doi.org/10.1016/j.smhl.2017.06.001

59. da Silva, W.M., et al.: Smart cities software architectures. In: Proceedings of the 28th Annual ACM Symposium on Applied Computing - SAC 2013, p. 1722 ACM Press, New York (2013). https://doi.org/10.1145/2480362.2480688

60. De Sousa, A.O., et al.: Quality evaluation of self-adaptive systems: challenges and opportunities. Pervasive Health Pervasive Computer Technologies Healthcare, pp. 213–218 (2019). https://doi.org/10.1145/3350768.3352455

61. Thang Nguyen, X., et al.: Optimization of non-functional properties in Internet of Things applications. J. Netw. Comput. Appl. **89**, C, 120–129 (2017). https://doi.org/10.1016/j.jnca.2017.03.019

62. Thangaraj, M., et al.: Agent based semantic internet of things (IoT) in Smart Health care. ACM International Confernce Proceeding Series Part F1305, (2016). https://doi.org/10.1145/2925995.2926023

63. Tsiachri Renta, P., et al.: Healthcare sensor data management on the cloud. In: Proceedings of the 2017 Workshop on Adaptive Resource Management and Scheduling for Cloud Computing - ARMS-CC '17, pp. 25–30 ACM Press, New York (2017). https://doi.org/10.1145/3110355.3110359

64. Tsuchiya, L.D., et al.: A study on the needs of older adults for interactive smart home environments in Brazil. In: ACM International Conference Proceeding Series, pp. 33–40 (2018). https://doi.org/10.1145/3218585.3218592

65. Wan Abdullah, W.A.N., et al.: Energy-efficient remote healthcare monitoring using IoT: a review of trends and challenges. In: ACM International Conference Proceeding Series (2016). https://doi.org/10.1145/2896387.2896414

66. Win, T.Z., et al.: Requirement prioritization based on non-functional requirement classification using hierarchy AHP. In: IOP Conference Series: Materials Science and Engineering, vol. 769, no. 1, p. 012060 (2020).https://doi.org/10.1088/1757-899X/769/1/012060

67. Xiaobing, F.: Research on perceived risk and purchase intention of smart hotel consumption. Pervasive Health Pervasive Computer Technologies Healthcare, pp. 21–24 (2020). https://doi.org/10.1145/3421682.3421708

68. Xu, F.J., et al.: A framework for developing social networks enabling systems to enhance the transparency and visibility of cross-border food supply chains. GSTF J. Comput. **3**(4), 132–144 (2014). https://doi.org/10.7603/s40601-013-0051-8

69. Yao, L., et al.: Exploring recommendations in Internet of Things. In: SIGIR 2014 Proceedings of the 37th international ACM SIGIR Conference on Research Development in Information Retrieval, pp. 855–858 (2014). https://doi.org/10.1145/2600428.2609458

70. Yassein, M.B., et al.: IoT-based healthcare systems: a survey. In: Pervasive Health Pervasive Computer Technologies Healthcare (2019). https://doi.org/10.1145/3368691.3368721

71. Zeng, R., et al.: Performance optimization for cloud computing systems in the microservice era: state-of-the-art and research opportunities. Front. Comput. Sci. **16**, 6 (2022). https://doi.org/10.1007/s11704-020-0072-3

Implementation of a System for Measuring the Physical Performance of Football Players Based on Analytic Hierarchy Process Method (AHP)

Jose Luis Jinez-Tapia[1] , Luis Gonzalo Santillan-Valdiviezo[1]([✉]) ,
Carlos Ramiro Peñafiel-Ojeda Ramiro[2] , Jaime Puetate-Paredes[3] ,
and Paulina Valle-Oñate[4]

[1] Facultad de Ingeniería, Carrera de Telecomunicaciones, GRUPO DE
INVESTIGACION GI(CT), Informática, Industria y Construcción (TEIIC),
Riobamba, Ecuador
{jjinez,lsantillan}@unach.edu.ec

[2] Facultad de Ingeniería. Carrera de Telecomunicaciones, Grupo de Investigación en
Telecomunicaciones, Informática, Industria y Construcción (TEIIC), Universidad
Nacional de Chimborazo, Riobamba, Ecuador
carlospenafiel@unach.edu.ec

[3] Universidad Nacional de Chimborazo, Riobamba, Ecuador
jpuetate.fie@unach.edu.ec

[4] Universidad Estatal de Bolivar, Guaranda, Ecuador
pvalle@ueb.edu.ec

Abstract. This research work focuses on the implementation of a system for measuring the physical performance of professional football players, through the medication of four variables: distance, speed, impacts, heart rate, and temperature, using the Analytic Hierarchy Process (AHP) Method (Analytical Hierarchical Process), the tests and detection are carried out with four professional football players of second division STAR CLUB team from the Chimborazo province. The system collects data on several variables to be analysed to evaluate player performance. The results showed that participants 3 and 4 showed the best physical performances, while participants 4 had the highest heart rate VO_2 ratings. However, more research is needed to validate the effectiveness of the system in larger sample sizes and different contexts.

Keywords: Analytic Hierarchy Process (AHP) · system · Heart rate · speed

1 Introduction

Soccer, also known as football in some countries, is one of the most popular sports in the world with more than 270 million footballers, around the world

T. Guarda et al. (Eds.): ARTIIS 2023, CCIS 1935, pp. 26–37, 2024.
https://doi.org/10.1007/978-3-031-48858-0_3

with numerous professionals and an even larger number of non-professional practitioners [4,6]. Likewise, if we observe the rankings of the best paid sports in the world, we can identify not only golf, tennis or basketball players but also football players. In fact, we could highlight some examples such as Cristiano Ronaldo, Messi, Neymar, or David Beckham, among others, and it can be considered that these athletes have good physical and physiological performance, hence the importance of the subject. [8]

In order to analyse the physical performance of a given group of football players, there are quantitative and multi-criteria assessment methods that allow this process to be carried out in an exhaustive manner, namely the Analytical Hierarchical Process (AHP), according to Leal et al. [3] the analytical hierarchical method (AHP), developed by Saaty, is a powerful multi-criteria decision making tool that has been used in numerous applications in various fields of economics, politics, engineering, and sport. The Internet of Things (IoT) has become one of the most powerful information technologies in the 21st century. The Internet of Things extends the concept of the Internet and makes it more common. The Internet of Things allows seamless interaction between different types of devices, such as medical sensors, monitoring equipment, household appliances, etc. Current wearable and IoT technologies are used in sports to monitor both the internal and external workload of athletes. However, there is still a need to obtain more information about the internal workload of the athlete, which is crucial to adjust training and increase the athlete's performance. [7,10].

Fitness assessment and training load monitoring have become a popular topic of research in sports sciences. These areas help the coaches to better understand the status of the player, as well as the functional adaptations over time [7] The aim of this particular system is to gauge the abilities of football players. This device is based on IOT technology and the AHP method, which involves a variety of physical examinations. The system is integrated into a sports waistcoat shows

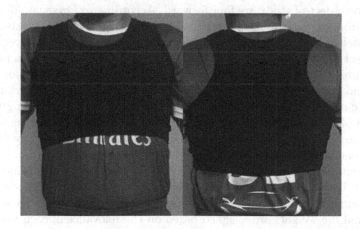

Fig. 1. Waistcoast System

as Fig. 1, which compiles and produces data. These data are then examined by a sports physician to assess the athlete's progress.

2 Methodology

This research work focusses on the implementation of a system to quantify the physical performance of football players, by adjusting four variables:

- **Heart rate (HR):** monitoring offers an objective, relatively inexpensive and convenient insight into player internal load, particularly in a team sport setting. [1]
- **Temperature:** According Calderon et.al [2] muscle activity is one of the principal heat sources of the human body. It is important to note that body temperature is one of the most commonly used indicators of health status in humans and it is infuenced by a tremendously large number of factors.
- **Distance and speed:** are measuring using gps technology. Until recently, global positioning systems (GPS) was prohibited in official competition conditions by FIFA. Despitea law change in 2015, GPS remains under-utilised due to practical reasons such as comfort and player compliance. xternal load metrics such as total distance, high-speedand sprint distance are frequently monitored in high-levelprofessional clubs across many leagues around the world-including the English Premier League, La Liga, Serie A, MajorLeague Soccer and Australian A-league [9].
- **Impacts:** It is necessary to measure the impacts because it can lead to injuries and decrease physical performance.

This work is using the AHP method (Analytical Hierarchical Process), tests, and detection are carried out with four football players from the second category STAR CLUB team from the province of Chimborazo, this club has twenty-five players, the object of study are four forward. According to Ozceylan [6] the data acquired from decision makers are pairwise comparisons of the relative importance of each of the criteria or the degree of preference of one factor over another with respect to each criterion. AHP has the advantage of permitting a hierarchical structure of the criteria, which provides users with a better focus on specific criteria and subcriteria when allocating the weights. Tests were performed on two consecutive weeks, with the first tests reflecting week 1 analyzing the current state of the participants. At week 1, the current state of the participants was analysed. In the second week, we will observe whether there is any difference or improvement compared to week 1. week, we observed if there was a difference or improvement compared to week 1. All of this will allow the athlete to be monitored, both physically and in terms of his or her health. health status. The criteria comparison matrix was created for the AHP approach, as shown in the Table 1, and the weights are assigned based on the relevance of each variable on a scale of 1 to 5.

Table 1. Criteria comparison matrix

	Distance (km)	Speed (km)	Hits Number	HR	Vo2 Max
Distance	1	1	5	3	3
Speed	1	1	5	1	1
Hits Numbre	1	1	1	1	1
Heart Frecuency	3	1	5	1	3
Vo2 Max	5	5	5	3	1

2.1 System Design

A wearable vest with a signal monitoring system consisting of heart rate measurement modules and temperature modules was designed. It will have a module for speeds, acceleration and distance for sports performance, as well as for impacts or shocks that the player experiences during training; the signal monitoring system can be shown in Fig. 2.

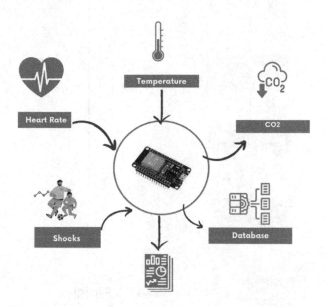

Fig. 2. Monitoring System

Heart Rate Measurement Module. The XD-58C pulse sensor installed on the Esp8266 board was used as a server and the Esp32 board as a client to perform heart rate monitoring, both are compatible with Arduino, and the signal processing is completed in Matlab and stored in the database. The block diagram of the heart rate measurement module is shown in Fig. 3.

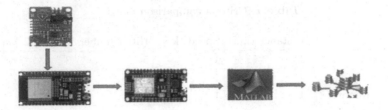

Fig. 3. Heart Rate Measurement Module

Temperature Module. For temperature monitoring, the MLX90614 sensor was used since it does not have requires contact to obtain data and communicate using the I2C protocol, in the following flowchart to the Fig. 4 you can show how the data acquisition is performed.

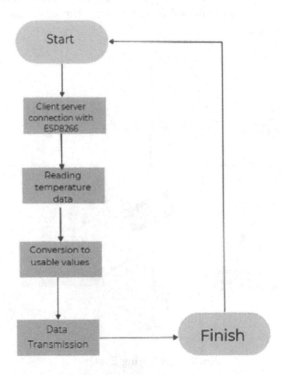

Fig. 4. Temperature Module Data Collection

Distance/Speed/Acceleration Measurement Module. The distance traveled is calculated using the Haversine Eq. 1, giving great-circle distances between two points on a sphere from their longitudes and latitudes [5].

$$d = 2r \arcsin \sqrt{\sin^2 \left(\frac{lat_2 - lat_1}{2}\right) + \cos(\phi_1)\cos(\phi_2)\sin^2\{(\frac{lon_2 - lon_1}{2})} \quad (1)$$

Where:

- Lat_2 and Lat_1: are latitudes
- Lat_2 and Lat_1: are latitudes
- r: radius of the earth: distance

From the longitude, latitude, and altitude data provided by the Neo 7m GPS module, with the data obtained the acceleration of the athlete can be calculated as shown in the Eq. 2.

$$a = \frac{v_f - v_o}{t} \quad (2)$$

Shocks Measurement Module. The player, in the course of the game, suffers several blows or collisions by his opponents in the moments of attack or recovery of the ball, these blows are necessary to count them or detect them since together with the cardiac rhythm module it will be analyzed if there is any affectation and it will be known if the player will be able to continue. and it will be known if the player will be able to continue. is created to be able to know how many hits the participants suffer during their match.

Database Design. The implementation of the database was carried out with Matlab software, which receives the data and stores them in software, which receives the data and stores them on a data sheet labelled with all the variables to be measured. Thanks to this software and to the association it has with NoSQL, it allows data interchange with relational databases.

3   Results

The study was carried out on 4 players who occupy the striker position for two weeks and who belong to the second category Star Club team of the province of Chimborazo, based on the four variables analysed. Table 2 shows the data obtained from the study of the variables analysed.

Table 2. Average data study week 1 and week 2

	Distance (km)		Avg Speed (km/h)		Hits Number		Heart Frecuency(ppm)		Vo2 Max	
	Week 1	Week 2	Week 1	Week 2	Week 1	Week 2	Week 1	Week2	Week 1	Week2
Part 1	1.45	2.773	11.52	14.94	18.33	21.83	78.00	98.00	47.89	68.04
Part 2	2.347	2.810	12.07	15.35	22.67	28.33	91.67	107.67	51.23	70.44
Part 3	3.508	4.088	16.56	16.78	35.50	37.17	114.17	122.3	77.47	77.47
Part 4	3.242	3.853	16.24	16.85	33.33	36.33	110.83	119.50	76.27	79.17

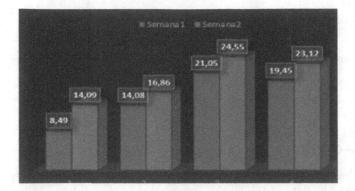

Fig. 5. Distance Comparison

Fig. 5 shows the comparison of the data from the first and second week.

The speed of each player is very important regardless of his position on the pitch. Each player has the responsibility to improve each parameter to be in optimal conditions and develop 100% of his physical capacity. In the Fig. 6 below, you can see the comparison of this parameter.

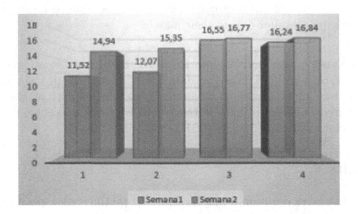

Fig. 6. Speed Comparison

The more shocks the player receives, the more actions he has, the more active the player becomes and the more he becomes the main actor in the game, he distinguishes himself and is a key player in sports. In this case, the participants with the most actions during the training are participants 3 and 4, who showed changes on the first day compared to other participants. It is the participants of the day. It can be clearly shown in Fig. 7 from the number of effects received during week 1 and week 2 in what is clearly indicated in Fig. 7.

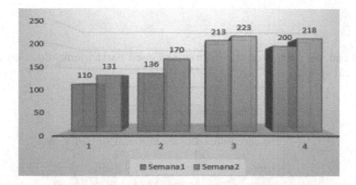

Fig. 7. Shocks Comparison

Heart rates indicate the type of work a player is doing or the condition of a player's heart rate. The player's heart rate also tells us when a player may be able to recover. Yes! It is important to keep in mind the heart rate as if the heart rate envelope is too high, the player's heart rate can be too low. Active players (with an average heart rate above the ideal pace) can be injured.

In Fig. 8 it is clear to see the improvements in the work each participant does, it is worth noting that each player can reach 100 % of his heart rate, so that his performance is improving in every step. Their performance improves and improves as they improve. Of the 4 participants, participant 3 is the one closest to his ideal heart rate, the one with the best physical condition. He is the one who is close to the heart rate of his ideal heart rate condition.

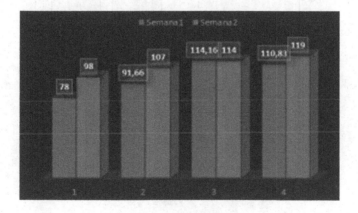

Fig. 8. Cardio Comparison

Participants' Evaluation of the AHP Method. For the AHP method, the variables to be used are:

– Distance
– Speed

To this end, we computed the intervals of each participant and their different distances and speeds, as shown in Table 3.

Table 3. Distances covered by the players

	Distance 1 (km)	Distance 2 (km)	Distance 3 (km)	Distance 4 (km)	Distance 5 (km)	Distance 6 (km)
Part. 1	1.45	2.773	11.52	14.94	18.33	21.83
Part. 2	2.347	2.810	12.07	15.35	22.67	28.33
Part. 3	3.508	4.088	16.56	16.78	35.50	37.17
Part. 4	3.242	3.853	16.24	16.85	33.33	36.33

Figure 9 shows that participants 3 and 4 perform better and have the best physical performance according to the data in Table 3, participants 3 and 4 perform the best and perform the best physically.

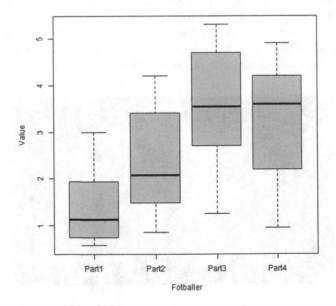

Fig. 9. Boxplot Longest distance travelled

Speed variables were also studied for evaluation as can be seen in the Table 4. The model recognizes and values those who achieve the fastest speeds during the ride and highlights the participants that are best rewarded.

Table 4. Speed Fotballer

Footballer	Sprint 1 (km/h)	Sprint 2 (km/h)	Sprint 3 (km/h)	Sprint 4 (km/h)	Sprint 5 (km/h)	Sprint 6 (km/h)
Part. 1	5.04	6.84	11.88	21.24	15.84	8.28
Part. 2	6.48	8.28	11.6	12.24	22.32	11.52
Part. 3	8.28	10.32	15.4	26.32	20.5	18.52
Part. 4	7.82	11.23	16.2	24.67	19.71	17.83

In addition to distances, participants tree and four are the ones who have reached the highest speeds 26 km/h and 24 km/h respectively, the highest speed of km/h, as can be seen in the Fig. 10, this results in excellent physical condition resulting in their own capability to overcome sports with high intensity.

The Fig. 11 below shows the rates achieved by the players.

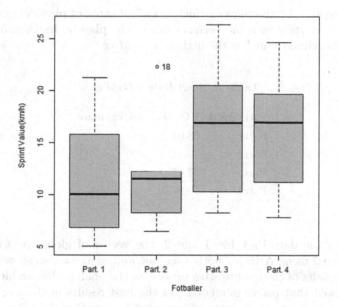

Fig. 10. Boxplot Speed Compartion

A Fig. 11 also shows that participant 3 was the fastest in measurement 4 but participant 2 was the fastest in measurement 5 because he had a slight physical recovery.

Another variable analyzed was VO_2 Max (ml/kg/min) measured in ml/kg/min, the results obtained can be seen in the Table 5, which can be seen in the table. It shows the oxygen level that the player perceives. This indicates the amount of oxygen, which is a physical performance indicator and is very important in the analysis of the players' performance. This indicates the amount of

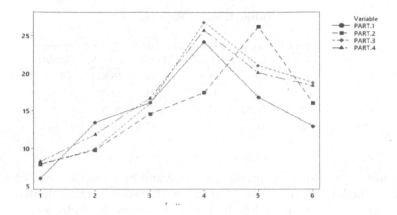

Fig. 11. Speed Compartion Four Players

oxygen perceptual by the player, which is an indicator of physical performance and is very important in a the performance of the players. In Table 5 it can be seen that participant four has the highest VO_2Max

Table 5. Heart Rate VO_2Max

Participant	VO_2Max(ml/kg/min)
Part1	68,04
Part2	70,44
Part3	77,47
Part4	79,17

Based on the data in Tables 1 and 2, the vector of global priorities, have been calculated using AHP for both week one and week two, as shown in Eqs. 3 and 4.The results of the quantitative process in the analysis-hierarchical process "AHP" showed that player number 3 get the best results in the week one and two. It is suggested to exert extra effort to meet or surpass the prior data while monitoring and concentrating on each player's heart rate since they must reach the ideal frequency. Players (4) were discovered to have put in more effort in Weeks 1 and 2, which led to the best outcomes, in the Vo_2max. The strongest athlete and the best participant both had great physical performances in Weeks 1 and 2.

$$[142.545\ 164.870\ 231.234\ 223.302] \tag{3}$$

$$[184.62\ 206.067\ 241.2058\ 238.77588925] \tag{4}$$

4 Conclusion

This study demonstrated the potential of using wearable technology and the Analytic Hierarchy Process (AHP) to measure and assess the physical performance of football players. The system collects data on various variables such as distance, speed, impact, heart rate and temperature to be analyzed to evaluate player performance. The results showed that participants 3 and 4 showed the best physical performances while participants 4 had the maximum VO2 ratings. Experts recommend working more intensely to improve player performance. The system is a potential tool used by coaches and coaches to monitor and improve the physical performance of football players. However, further research is needed to validate the effectiveness of the system in larger sample sizes and different contexts.

References

1. Burgess, D.J.: The research doesn't always apply: practical solutions to evidence-based training-load monitoring in elite team sports **12**, S2–136 (2017). https://doi.org/10.1123/ijspp.2016-0608
2. Calderón, G., et al.: Influence of artificial turf temperature on physical performance and muscle contractile properties in football players after a repeated-sprint ability test. Sci. Reports **10**, 12747 (2020). https://doi.org/10.1038/s41598-020-69720-6
3. Leal, J.E.: AHP-express: a simplified version of the analytical hierarchy process method. MethodsX **7**, 100748 (2020). https://doi.org/10.1016/j.mex.2019.11.021
4. Lu, S., Zhang, X., Wang, J., Wang, Y., Fan, M., Zhou, Y.: An IoT-based motion tracking system for next-generation foot-related sports training and talent selection. J. Healthcare Eng. **2021** (2021). https://doi.org/10.1155/2021/9958256
5. Nurul, C., Manaf, K., Rialdy, A., Khrisma, D.: Implementation of haversine formula for counting event visitor in the radius based on android application 1) (2020)
6. Ozceylan, E.: A mathematical model using AHP priorities for soccer player selection: a case study. S. Afr. J. Ind. Eng. **27**, 190–205 (2016). https://doi.org/10.7166/27-2-1265
7. Passos, J., et al.: Wearables and internet of things (IoT) technologies for fitness assessment: a systematic review. Sensors **21**, 1–18 (2021). https://doi.org/10.3390/s21165418
8. Poza, C.: Análisis del ataque posicional de balonmano playa masculino y femenino mediante coordenadas polares. RICYDE: Revista Internacional de Ciencias del Deporte **11**, 226–244 (7 2015). https://doi.org/10.5232/ricyde
9. Taberner, M., et al.: Interchangeability of position tracking technologies; can we merge the data? Sci. Med. Football **4**, 76–81 (1 2020). https://doi.org/10.1080/24733938.2019.1634279
10. Wang, S.: Sports training monitoring of energy-saving iot wearable devices based on energy harvesting. Sustain. Energy Technol. Assessments **45**, 101168 (2021). https://doi.org/10.1016/j.seta.2021.101168

A *Mathematica* Function to Get a List of Random Inequalities and Their Respective Solution Sets

Judith K. Jiménez-Vilcherrez[1] (ID), Robert Ipanaqué-Chero[2](✉) (ID),
Ricardo Velezmoro-León[2] (ID), and Marcela F. Velásquez-Fernández[2] (ID)

[1] Universidad Tecnológica del Perú, Av. Vice Cdra 1-Costado Real Plaza, Piura, Peru
C19863@utp.edu.pe
[2] Universidad Nacional de Piura, Urb. Miraflores s/n, Castilla, Piura, Peru
{ripanaquec,rvelezmorol,fvelasquezf}@unp.edu.pe

Abstract. Solving inequalities is a first step and an important achievement for undergraduate students. In fact, it is one of the first subjects studied in most of the classical courses of higher basic mathematics. This paper presents a new function, `GenerateInequalitiesList`, coded in the Wolfram programming language, which is typical of Mathematica software, to generate a random list of inequalities with their respective solutions. To encode the program, use is mainly made of the native functions RandomInteger, RandomChoice, Reduce, and Surd; as well as the paradigms of functional programming and programming based on rules and patterns (typical of symbolic programming languages). The list of inequalities obtained can be used by teachers and/or students. The former is to save time in preparing exercises and the latter to generate practice material. The problem of the high license price of Mathematica can be overcome by assembling a Raspberry Pi computer and installing the free version of Mathematica for Raspbian.

Keywords: inequalities · solution set · generate inequalities list

1 Introduction

Finding the solution set of inequalities, in $\mathbb{R}$, becomes a first step and an important achievement for most undergraduate students. Needless to say, it is one of the first topics included in the content of most of the classic courses of higher basic mathematics and that it is framed in the chapter of the real number system [17].

Currently, many software (paid or free) include functions to find the solution of various inequalities [1,6,8,27]. There are even online calculators that return step-by-step solutions to various science problems, including the [5,18] inequalities.

Several of these softwares have been included in the classroom work and satisfactory results have been obtained in student learning that exceed those obtained with traditional teaching [2–4,10,11,13,16].

T. Guarda et al. (Eds.): ARTIIS 2023, CCIS 1935, pp. 38–49, 2024.
https://doi.org/10.1007/978-3-031-48858-0_4

Using any of the aforementioned tools, the correct solutions to the proposed inequalities are obtained, but none of these tools offer the possibility of automatically generating lists of exercises with their respective solutions. Bearing in mind that, in a traditional upper basic mathematics course, the teacher has the need to assign homework to his students (perhaps he has several groups assigned to the same subject) and provide them with the answers to the exercises included in said homework, it would be quite It is beneficial for the teacher to have a tool that allows them to automatically generate a list of exercises with their respective solutions to deliver to their students in the classroom. This would save the time required to think, propose, type, and solve each of the assigned exercises.

This paper presents a new function, `GenerateInequalitiesList`, that has been coded in the Wolfram [28] programming language, the same one that is incorporated in the Mathematica software [9,27]. With this new program it is possible to generate a random list of inequalities (the number of inequalities is specified by the user) with their respective set solutions. To encode the program, use is mainly made of the native functions RandomInteger [22], RandomChoice [21], Reduce [24] and Surd [26]; as well as the functional programming paradigm and the programming paradigm based on rules and patterns [19,25] (typical of symbolic programming languages). The listability attribute of the arithmetic operators (addition, subtraction, multiplication and division) incorporated in Mathematica [20] was also used.

The problem of the high price of the Mathematica license can be overcome by assembling a Raspberry Pi [14] kit and installing the free version of this software [23] for the Raspbian operating system [15]. For more information, it is recommended to consult the book by Agus Kurniawan [12].

The structure of this article is as follows: Sect. 2 introduces certain mathematical concepts about theorems related to the solution of inequalities in $\mathbb{R}$. The code of the program is commented in Sect. 3. In Sect. 4 interesting examples are shown. Finally, Sect. 5 closes with the main conclusions of this work.

2   Mathematical Preliminaries

In this section the definitions and theorems related to inequalities in one variable and their solution in the real number system are stated.

2.1   The Real Number System

According to [29], a quatern $(\mathbb{R}, +, ., \leq)$ is the real number system if it satisfies the following three conditions:

1. $(\mathbb{R}, +, .)$ is a field.
2. $\mathbb{R}$ is a totally ordered set and the order is compatible with the operations of the field:
   if $a \leq b$ then $a + c \leq b + c$;
   if $a \leq b$ y $0 \leq c$ then $ac \leq bc$.
3. The set $\mathbb{R}$ is complete; that is, it satisfies the axiom of the supremum:
   Every non-empty, bounded set from above has a supremum.

2.2 Inequalities

1. A number $a \in \mathbb{R}$ is called positive if $0 < a$.
2. A number $a \in \mathbb{R}$ is negative if $a < 0$.
3. The "greater than" relation, denoted by $>$, is defined as:

$$a > b \Leftrightarrow b < a.$$

4. The relation "less than or equal to" ($\leq$), is defined by:

$$a \leq b \Leftrightarrow [\, a < b \vee a = b \,].$$

5. The relation "greater than or equal to" ($\geq$), is defined by:

$$a \geq b \Leftrightarrow [\, a > b \vee a = b \,].$$

6. The chain of inequalities $a < b < c$ is defined as:

$$a < b < c \Leftrightarrow [\, a < b \wedge b < c \,].$$

Theorem 1 (Sign rule). *Given $a, b \in \mathbb{R}$:*

1. $ab > 0 \Leftrightarrow a$ and b they have the same sign.
2. $ab < 0 \Leftrightarrow a$ and b they have different signs.

Theorem 2. *If $a \neq 0$, then a^{-1} has the same sign as a.*

2.3 Absolute Value

Definition 1. *The absolute value of a real number x is the non-negative number $|x|$ and it is defined by:*

$$|x| = \begin{cases} x, & si \ x > 0 \\ 0, & si \ x = 0 \\ -x, & si \ x < 0 \end{cases}$$

Theorem 3. *Let $x, a \in \mathbb{R}$, then:*

1. $|x| < a \Leftrightarrow [\, (a > 0) \wedge (-a < x < a) \,]$
2. $|x| > a \Leftrightarrow [\, (x > a) \vee (x < -a) \,]$

3   Encoding Details of the New Program

The Wolfram Language (WL) is a computer language. It is a way of communicating with a computer; in particular, to tell it what you want [28] to do. Based on this statement, it was decided to write a few lines of code (program) to generate random lists of inequalities with their respective solutions.

Next, the process followed to encode the program will be explained, taking the **quadratic inequalities** as a reference.

First of all, a quadratic inequality can be of any of the following four types:

$$ax^2 + bx + c < 0 \qquad ax^2 + bx + c \leq 0$$
$$ax^2 + bx + c > 0 \qquad ax^2 + bx + c \geq 0$$

where a is never zero.

Then, the program that generates quadratic inequalities of these forms must be implemented. A first idea to consider is to generate random numbers for the values of a, b, and c. Although it is true that a, b, and c can assume any real value (with the exception of a which cannot be zero), it is not practical (or aesthetic) to pose an inequality like the following:

$$-0.6618042060841596 - 400.793140263870324\,x - 0.6701433710320348\,x^2 < 0$$

Therefore, it was decided to use the native function RandomInteger in a range of values that go from -5 to 5.

Algorithm 1

Quadratic inequality generated according to the described convention.

```
In[1]:= RandomInteger[{-5,5}]x^2+RandomInteger[{-5,5}]x+
        RandomInteger[{-5,5}]<0
```

Out[1]= $3 + 3x + 4x^2 < 0$

If, in addition, the native Table function is used, it is possible to generate a list of quadratic inequalities.

Algorithm 2

Generating from a list of inequalities of type $ax^2 + bx + c < 0$.

```
In[2]:= Table[
        RandomInteger[{-5,5}]x^2+RandomInteger[{-5,5}]x+
        RandomInteger[{-5,5}]<0, {i,5}]
```

Out[2]= $\{3 + 4x - 4x^2 < 0, 3 - 5x < 0, -1 + 2x + 5x^2 < 0, 1 - x - 3x^2 < 0,$
$-4 - 2x - 4x^2 < 0\}$

It is clear that using this form all the quadratic inequalities obtained are of the type $ax^2 + bx + c < 0$. Also, since the contrary has not been indicated, it is possible that a acquires the value 0. One solution to these drawbacks is to use the native RandomInteger function. This way it will be sure that a will not assume the value zero.

Algorithm 3

Generating another list of quadratic inequalities of the type $ax^2 + bx + c < 0$.

In[3]:= `Table[`
   `RandomChoice[{-5,-4,-3,-2,-1,1,2,3,4,5}]x^2+`
   `RandomInteger[{-5,5}]x+RandomInteger[{-5,5}]<0, {i,5}]`

Out[3]= $\{-4-3x+5x^2 < 0, -3x+5x^2 < 0, 3-4x+4x^2 < 0, -3-x+3x^2 < 0,$
$-1+2x-4x^2 < 0\}$

Once this difficulty has been overcome, it remains to overcome the first; that is, to make the choice of the type of quadratic inequality random. For this, it must be remembered that everything in Mathematica is an expression [7]. For this reason $a < b$ can be written Less$[a, b]$; $a \leq b$ can be written as LessEqual$[a, b]$, etc.

Algorithm 4

Generating a third list of diverse quadratic inequalities.

In[4]:= `Table[`
   `RandomChoice[{Less,Greater,LessEqual,GreaterEqual}][`
   `RandomChoice[{-5,-4,-3,-2,-1,1,2,3,4,5}]x^2+`
   `RandomInteger[{-5,5}]x+RandomInteger[{-5,5}],0],`
   `{i,5}]`

Out[4]= $\{2 - 4x - 4x^2 \leq 0, -3 - x + 4x^2 \geq 0, 5 + 4x - 2x^2 \leq 0, 2x + 5x^2 < 0,$
$2 - x - x^2 > 0\}$

So far we have managed to generate a random list of quadratic inequalities, but three things are missing: list the elements, display them vertically, and include their solutions. In order to better manipulate the expressions, we will choose to use assignment variables.

Algorithm 5

Generating a third list of diverse quadratic inequalities using assignment variables.

```
In[5]:= Table[
          a=RandomChoice[{-5,-4,-3,-2,-1,1,2,3,4,5}];
          b=RandomInteger[{-5,5}];c=RandomInteger[{-5,5}];
          sym={Less,Greater,LessEqual,GreaterEqual};
          ineq=RandomChoice[sym][ax^2+bx+c,0]
          {i,5}]
```

Out[5]= $\{-2+3x-4x^2 \geq 0, -4-2x^2 > 0, -1+2x+2x^2 \geq 0, 4-4x+4x^2 > 0,$
$-3+4x-3x^2 \leq 0\}$

---

1. $-2x^2+x-4 > 0$	Sol. : False
2. $x^2-4x-1 < 0$	Sol. : $2-\sqrt{5} < x < 2+\sqrt{5}$
3. $2x^2-3x-4 \geq 0$	Sol. : $x \leq \frac{1}{4}\left(3-\sqrt{41}\right) \mid\mid x \geq \frac{1}{4}\left(3+\sqrt{41}\right)$
4. $-4x^2+x+5 \leq 0$	Sol. : $x \leq -1 \mid\mid x \geq \frac{5}{4}$
5. $4x^2-2x < 0$	Sol. : $0 < x < \frac{1}{2}$
6. $-x^2+2x+4 \leq 0$	Sol. : $x \leq 1-\sqrt{5} \mid\mid x \geq 1+\sqrt{5}$
7. $x^2+4x < 0$	Sol. : $-4 < x < 0$
8. $x^2+3x-5 \leq 0$	Sol. : $\frac{1}{2}\left(-3-\sqrt{29}\right) \leq x \leq \frac{1}{2}\left(-3+\sqrt{29}\right)$
9. $-4x^2+5x-2 \leq 0$	Sol. : True
10. $5x^2+x-1 \leq 0$	Sol. : $\frac{1}{10}\left(-1-\sqrt{21}\right) \leq x \leq \frac{1}{10}\left(-1+\sqrt{21}\right)$

Fig. 1. List of quadratic inequalities and their respective solution sets.

To format the output, WL has the native RowBox function which, in combination with the native Display function, allows to obtain an output with quite nice formats.

Algorithm 6

Presentation format for each of the quadratic inequalities.

```
In[6]:= DisplayForm[RowBox[{3,''. '',
          TraditionalForm[3x^2-2x-1<0]}]]
```

Out[6]= $3 \cdot \quad 3x^2 - 2x - 1 < 0$

Algorithm 7

Presentation format for each of the solutions of the quadratic inequalities.

```
In[7]:= DisplayForm[RowBox[{''Sol.:'',
          Reduce[3x^2-2x-1<0,x,Reals]}]]
```

Out[7]= Sol.: $-\frac{1}{3} < x < 1$

Finally, the native Grid function is used, with a change in the default values of the Spacings and Alignment options, to achieve the desired presentation.

Algorithm 8

Generating the final list of diverse quadratic inequalities.

```
In[8]:= Grid[Table[
        a=RandomChoice[{-5,-4,-3,-2,-1,1,2,3,4,5}];
        b=RandomInteger[{-5,5}];c=RandomInteger[{-5,5}];
        sym={Less,Greater,LessEqual,GreaterEqual};
        ineq=RandomChoice[sym][a x^2+b x+c,0];
        {DisplayForm[RowBox[{i,''.'',TraditionalForm[ineq]}]],
        DisplayForm[RowBox[{''Sol.:'',Reduce[ineq,x,Reals]}]]},
        {i,10}],
        Spacings->{{Automatic,5},Automatic},Alignment->{Left,Left}]

Out[8]= See figure 1
```

---

4   The Function GenerateInequalitiesList: Some Illustrative Examples

In the previous section, some details of the coding of the program developed in this work were given. However, these details correspond to a command that only allows you to generate a list of quadratic inequalities. However, this section presents examples in which lists of rational inequalities involving radicals and absolute value are generated. For this, the code of the developed program has been assigned to the new function GenerateInequalitiesList.

The new GenerateInequalitiesList function incorporates the following options (with their respective default values):

```
NumberOfExercises->10,MaxNumberOfFactors->3,RationalIneqs->False,
    Radicals->False,MaxRadicalIndex->50,AbsoluteValue->False
```

┌─── Algorithm 1 ───┐

Code of the new function `GenerateInequalitiesList`.

```
In[1]:= NSurd[n_,k_] :=
          If[EvenQ[k]&&NumericQ[n],Surd[x+n,k],Surd[n,k]]
        GenerateInequalitiesList[x_,
          OptionsPattern[{NumberOfExercises->10,
          MaxNumberOfFactors->3,
          RationalIneqs->False,Radicals->False,
          MaxRadicalIndex->50,
          AbsoluteValue->False}]]:=
        Module[{n,aa,bb,cc,dd,ee,ff,aux,noe,mnof,ri,rr,
          mri,av,h1,hh2,hh3},
          {noe,mnof,ri,rr,mri,av}=
           {OptionValue[NumberOfExercises],
            OptionValue[MaxNumberOfFactors],
            OptionValue[RationalIneqs],OptionValue[Radicals],
            OptionValue[MaxRadicalIndex],
            OptionValue[AbsoluteValue]};
          Grid[Table[
           n=RandomInteger[1,mnof];
           aa=RandomInteger[-5,5,n];
           bb=RandomInteger[-5,5,n];
           cc=RandomInteger[-5,5,n];
           h1=RandomChoice[Less,Greater,LessEqual,GreaterEqual];
           hh2=RandomChoice[Flatten[If[av,Table[Abs,k,mri],{}],
              If[rr,Table[With[k=k,NSurd[#,k]&],k,2,mri],{}],
              Table[Identity,k,mri]],n];
           If[ri,
           dd=RandomInteger[-5,5,n];
           ee=RandomInteger[-5,5,n];
           ff=RandomInteger[-5,5,n];
```

```
hh3=RandomChoice[Flatten[If[av,Table[Abs,k,mri],],
If[rr,Table[With[k=k,NSurd[#,k]&],k,2,mri],],
Table[Identity,k,mri]],n];
];
ineq=h1[Times[aux=Times@@Inner[#1[#2]&,hh2,
   aa x^2+bb x+cc,List];
   If[PolynomialExpressionQ[aux ,x],Expand[aux],aux],
   Power[If[ri,Times@@Inner[#1[#2]&,hh3,
   dd x^2+ee x+ff,List],1],-1]],0];
{DisplayForm[RowBox[{i,\[FilledVerySmallSquare],
TraditionalForm[ineq]}]],
DisplayForm[RowBox[{"Sol.:",Reduce[ineq,x,Reals]}]]},
{i,noe}],
Spacings->{{Automatic,5},Automatic},
Alignment->{Left,Left}]
]
```

With the NumberOfExercises option the user can choose the number of exercises to generate. With the MaxNumberOfFactors option the user can indicate the maximum number of factors that will appear both in the numerator and in the denominator (if any). With the RationalIneqs option the user can indicate if he wants rational inequalities to be generated. With the Radicals option the user can indicate if they want factors affected by radicals to appear. With the MaxRadicalIndex option the user can choose the maximum value of the radical indices (in case he has chosen to include factors affected by radicals). Finally, with the AbsoluteValue option, the user can choose if they want factors affected by the absolute value to appear.

┌─ Algorithm 2 ───┐
Generating   a   list   of   diverse   quadratic   inequalities   using   the   new
GenerateInequalitiesList function.

In[2]:= `GenerateInequalitiesList[x,MaxNumberOfFactors->1]`

Out[2]= See figure 2
└──┘

┌─ Algorithm 3 ───┐
Generating   a   list   of   miscellaneous   inequalities   using   the   new
GenerateInequalitiesList function.

In[3]:= `GenerateInequalitiesList[x,Radicals->True,`
        `RationalIneqs->True,NumberOfExercises->5]`

Out[3]= See figure 3
└──┘

1 ▪ $4x^2 - 4x + 1 < 0$ Sol. : False

2 ▪ $4x^2 + x \le 0$ Sol. : $-\frac{1}{4} \le x \le 0$

3 ▪ $2 - 2x \ge 0$ Sol. : $x \le 1$

4 ▪ $4x^2 + 5x - 3 < 0$ Sol. : $\frac{1}{8}\left(-5 - \sqrt{73}\right) < x < \frac{1}{8}\left(-5 + \sqrt{73}\right)$

5 ▪ $3x^2 - x - 1 < 0$ Sol. : $\frac{1}{6}\left(1 - \sqrt{13}\right) < x < \frac{1}{6}\left(1 + \sqrt{13}\right)$

6 ▪ $2x^2 - 2x - 4 \ge 0$ Sol. : $x \le -1 \,||\, x \ge 2$

7 ▪ $3 - x^2 > 0$ Sol. : $-\sqrt{3} < x < \sqrt{3}$

8 ▪ $-2x^2 - 4x + 2 \ge 0$ Sol. : $-1 - \sqrt{2} \le x \le -1 + \sqrt{2}$

9 ▪ $4x^2 + 4x - 3 \ge 0$ Sol. : $x \le -\frac{3}{2} \,||\, x \ge \frac{1}{2}$

10 ▪ $4x^2 + 3x - 5 \ge 0$ Sol. : $x \le \frac{1}{8}\left(-3 - \sqrt{89}\right) \,||\, x \ge \frac{1}{8}\left(-3 + \sqrt{89}\right)$

Fig. 2. List of quadratic inequalities, and their respective solution sets, generated with the new GenerateInequalitiesList function. Here the option MaxNumberOfFactors has been assigned the value 1.

1 ▪ $\dfrac{6x^4 - 14x^3 + 20x^2 - 22x + 10}{(2x^2 + 3x + 5)\sqrt[13]{5x - x^2}^1} < 0$ Sol. : False

2 ▪ $\dfrac{x^2 - 3x + 1}{\sqrt[4]{-4x - 3}^1} > 0$ Sol. : $x < -\frac{3}{4}$

3 ▪ $\dfrac{(-4x^2 + 3x + 2)(-2x^2 + 2x + 5)\sqrt[20]{-5x^2 - x + 5}^1}{(2x - 5)(-3x^2 - 3x - 5)(2x^2 - 4x - 1)} \le 0$

Sol. : $x \le \frac{1}{2}\left(1 - \sqrt{11}\right) \,||$

$\frac{1}{10}\left(-1 - \sqrt{101}\right) \le x \le \frac{1}{8}\left(3 - \sqrt{41}\right) \,||$

$\frac{1}{2}\left(2 - \sqrt{6}\right) < x \le \frac{1}{10}\left(-1 + \sqrt{101}\right) \,||$

$\frac{1}{8}\left(3 + \sqrt{41}\right) \le x \le \frac{1}{2}\left(1 + \sqrt{11}\right) \,||$

$\frac{1}{2}\left(2 + \sqrt{6}\right) < x < \frac{5}{2}$

4 ▪ $\dfrac{\sqrt[22]{4x^2 + x - 3}}{2x^2 - 4x - 2} \ge 0$ Sol. : $x \le -1 \,||\, x = \frac{3}{4} \,||\, x > 1 + \sqrt{2}$

5 ▪ $\dfrac{-5x^2 - x + 2}{\sqrt[5]{4x^2 + 2x + 1}} \le 0$ Sol. : $x \le \frac{1}{10}\left(-1 - \sqrt{41}\right) \,||\, x \ge \frac{1}{10}\left(-1 + \sqrt{41}\right)$

Fig. 3. List of inequalities, and their respective solutions, generated with the new GenerateInequalitiesList function. Here the options have the values indicated Radicals−>True, RationalIneqs−>True, NumberOfExercises−>5.

┌─ Algorithm 4 ─────────────────────────────────

Generating a third list of miscellaneous inequalities using the new GenerateInequalitiesList function.

In[4]:= GenerateInequalitiesList[x,Radicals->True,
          RationalIneqs->True,NumberOfExercises->5,
          AbsoluteValue->True]

Out[4]= See figure 4

$1 \cdot \dfrac{|-2x^2+2x+4|\ |4x^2+x|}{(5x^2+2x+3)\ |1-3x^2|} < 0$　　　　　　Sol. : False

$2 \cdot -\dfrac{\sqrt[39]{3}\ (2x^2-x-3)\ \sqrt[39]{x^2}\ |2x^2+2x+2|}{(-2x^2-x)\ \sqrt[25]{2x^2-2x+1}\ |-3x^2+5x-3|} \geq 0$　　　　Sol. : $x \leq -1\ |\ |\ -\dfrac{1}{2} < x < 0\ |\ |\ x \geq \dfrac{3}{2}$

$3 \cdot \dfrac{(-3x^2-2x-3)\ \sqrt[9]{-3x^2+2x-4}\ |5x^2-5x+2|}{\sqrt[14]{4x+3}\ \sqrt[9]{-5x^2-3x-1}\ |-x^2-2|} \leq 0$　　　　Sol. : $x > -\dfrac{3}{4}$

$4 \cdot \dfrac{(3x^2+1)\ |-4x^2+4x-1|}{\sqrt[39]{-2x^2+3x-3}\ |4x-4|} < 0$　　　　　Sol. : $x < \dfrac{1}{2}\ |\ |\ \dfrac{1}{2} < x < 1\ |\ |\ x > 1$

$5 \cdot \dfrac{(-2x^2-5x-5)\ |-5x^2-4x-5|}{(-3x^2-3x-3)\ \sqrt[47]{4x^2+4x}} < 0$　　　　Sol. : $-1 < x < 0$

Fig. 4. List of quadratic inequalities, and their respective solutions, generated with the new `GenerateInequalitiesList` function. Here the options have the values indicated Radicals−>True, RationalIneqs−>True, NumberOfExercises−>5, AbsoluteValue−>True.

5　Conclusions

This paper presents a new program coded in the Wolfram programming language, typical of Mathematica software, to generate a random list of inequalities together with their respective solution sets. To encode the program, the native functions RandomInteger, RandomChoice, Reduce and Surd were mainly used; as well as the paradigms of functional programming and programming based on rules and patterns. The list of inequalities obtained can be used by teachers and/or students. The former to save time in preparing exercises and the latter to generate practice material. The problem of the high price of the Mathematica license was solved by assembling a Raspberry Pi computer and installing the free version of Mathematica for Raspbian.

Acknowledgment. The authors thank the reviewers for their valuable comments and thoughtful suggestions.

References

1. Anastassiou, G.A., Mezei, R.A.: Numerical Analysis Using Sage. SUTMT, Springer, Cham (2015). https://doi.org/10.1007/978-3-319-16739-8
2. Ardiç, M., Isleyen, T.: High school mathematics teachers' levels of achieving technology integration and in-class reflections: the case of Mathematica. Univ. J. Educ. Res. 5(n12B), 1–7 (2017)
3. Ardiç, M., Isleyen, T.: Secondary School Mathematics Teachers' and Students' Views on Computer Assisted Mathematics Instruction in Turkey: Mathematica Example. Malays. Online J. Educ. Technol. 5(1), 46–64 (2017)
4. Conceição, A., et al.: Mathematica in the classroom: new tools for exploring precalculus and differential calculus. Conferência Nacional sobre Computação Simbólica no Ensino e na Investigação, CESEI2012. Lisboa (2012)
5. Course Hero Symbolab Ltd. (2023), Symbolab, https://www.symbolab.com/solver/. Accessed 03 July 2023

6. Garvan, F.: The Maple Book. Chapman and Hall/CRC (2001). https://doi.org/ 10.1201/9781420035605
7. Gray, J.: Mastering Mathematica, Second Edition. Academic Press (1997)
8. Kanagasabapathy, M.: Introduction to WxMaxima for Scientific Computations. BPB Publications (2018)
9. Maeder, R.: Programming in Mathematica, Third Edition. Addison-Wesley (1996)
10. Mohd, A., et al.: Adoption of wxmaxima software in the classroom: effect on students' motivation and learning of mathematics. Malays. J. Math. Sci. **8**(2), 311–323 (2014)
11. Karjanto, N., Husain, H.: Not another computer algebra system: highlighting wxmaxima in calculus. Mathematics **9**(12), 1317 (2021)
12. Kurniawan, A.: Raspbian OS Programming with the Raspberry Pi: IoT Projects with Wolfram, Mathematica, and Scratch. Apress (2019)
13. Makhdum, F.: Effect of using dynamic graphical utilities on students' achievements and attitudes to enhance mathematics teaching and learning at the elementary level in Pakistan: enhancingandimpeding factors. J. Positive Sch. Psychol. **7**(1), 106–116 (2023)
14. Raspberry Pi (2022), https://www.raspberrypi.com/products/raspberry-pi-4-model-b/. 02 Jan 2023
15. Raspbian (2022), https://www.raspbian.org. Accessed 02 June 2023
16. Roanes-Lozano, E., et al.: A proposal for filling the gap between the knowledge of a CAS and its application in the classroom. applications of computer algebra ACA'2007. Comput. Algebra Educ. 7–17 (2007)
17. Scribd (2016), Silabo Matematica Basica, https://es.scribd.com/document/ 312444798/Silabo-Matematica-Basica. Accessed 09 June 2023
18. Wolfram Research (2023), Wolfram Alpha, https://www.wolframalpha.com/. Accessed 03 July 2023
19. Wolfram Research (2022), Functional Programming, Wolfram Language & System Documentation Center, https://reference.wolfram.com/language/guide/ FunctionalProgramming.html. Accessed 28 Dec 2022
20. Wolfram Research (1988), Listable, Wolfram Language function, https://reference. wolfram.com/language/ref/Listable.html. Accessed 19 Dec 2022
21. Wolfram Research (2007), RandomChoice, Wolfram Language function, https:// reference.wolfram.com/language/ref/RandomChoice.html. Accessed 11 Sept 2022
22. Wolfram Research (2007), RandomInteger, Wolfram Language function, https:// reference.wolfram.com/language/ref/RandomInteger.html. Accessed 02 Aug 2022
23. Wolfram Research (2022), ¡Wolfram Language y Mathematica gratis en cada Raspberry Pi!, https://www.wolfram.com/raspberry-pi. Accessed 21 Mar 2023
24. Wolfram Research (1988), Reduce, Wolfram Language function, https://reference. wolfram.com/language/ref/Reduce.html. Accessed 13 Jan 2023
25. Wolfram Research (2022), Rules & Patterns, Wolfram Language & System Documentation Center, https://reference.wolfram.com/language/guide/ RulesAndPatterns.html. Accessed 02 July 2023
26. Wolfram Research (2012), Surd, Wolfram Language function, https://reference. wolfram.com/language/ref/Surd.html. Accessed 20 Feb 2023
27. Wolfram, S.: The Mathematica Book, Fifth Edition. Wolfram Research Inc, 2003
28. Wolfram, S.: Una Introducción Elemental a Wolfram Language. Wolfram Research Inc (2019)
29. Wikipedia (2022), Número real, https://es.wikipedia.org/wiki/N%C3%BAmero_ real. Accessed 10 Jan 2023

Mobile App for the Payment of Electronic Tickets Using NFC Technology in the Public Transport System in Lima Metropolitana

Fabricio Dávila, Guillermo Gonzales, and Juan-Pablo Mansilla[✉]

Universidad Peruana de Ciencias Aplicadas, Lima, Peru
{u201818252,u20181a750}@upc.edu.pe, juan.mansilla@upc.pe

Abstract. The current payment system for public transport on buses in Lima, Peru, is inefficient because it affects the passenger and the service provider in their economy and satisfaction, in addition to not taking advantage of mobile devices and Near-Field Communication (NFC) technology. The contactless ticket payments with NFC has been used in Sweden, Spain, Portugal, Turkey and Chile. The information on mobile payment systems for urban transport, their safety, passenger satisfaction, and payment fares was reviewed. This study proposed two hypotheses to verify that the mobile app improves the quality of service of public transport on buses. For this, the processes and architectures of the app were modeled. Once these were defined, the Android Studio platform was used to implement the native mobile app called *My LineCard* for the payment of tickets with mobile devices that have NFC technology. The validation was carried out with passengers to evaluate their experience and the usability of the app with a survey. The study concluded that this payment system is more efficient in terms of speed and security thanks to the use of the standardized fare. Finally, the best satisfaction of users for their experience with the app by having control of their payments was highlighted, as well as the ease of installing and using it on the buses.

Keywords: NFC · Contactless payment · Mobile app · Public transport · Firebase · Android Studio

1 Introduction

In the city of Lima, there are irregularities in the urban transport system at the time of payment, since collectors, on certain occasions, tend to change the rate at their discretion and convenience. According to Centeno (2018) [9], in Lima, 26.47% of all users complain about poor treatment by collectors, while 18.8% of university users are dissatisfied with the change in the price of tickets.

The manual payment system makes the payment time take between 12 and 20 s approximately, depending on the time in Lima, which causes queues to be created at "peak hours" causing chaos and annoyance to passengers [19].

© The Author(s), under exclusive license to Springer Nature Switzerland AG 2024
T. Guarda et al. (Eds.): ARTIIS 2023, CCIS 1935, pp. 50–64, 2024.
https://doi.org/10.1007/978-3-031-48858-0_5

Today, millions of people from Lima commute daily to their jobs and study centers using various means of transportation, with public transportation being the most common with 67.4% of travelers, which is equivalent to 6,742,791 people from Lima [11, 19]. The smartphone is the most used mobile device in Peru, registering approximately 41 million mobile lines [24]. According to the IPSOS researcher [26], smartphone ownership represents 83% of the population in urban areas of Peru.

NFC technology has already been used in different European countries. This technology is also used in Peru, although only with an NFC chip integrated into the cards. There are success stories such as the *Metropolitan* or the *Corredores*, which are systems implemented by the Municipality of Lima. The fact of paying through NFC is beneficial since cash is not used, it has direct and fast communication, and it is increasingly available on more devices.

The objective is to develop a mobile application that allows the digitization of ticket collection through the use of NFC technology to optimize payment time and the satisfaction of passengers and businessmen of the public transport system of Metropolitan Lima. The best alternatives were chosen for the theme of the technology used, the development environment and the type of app. Likewise, it is sought that this proposed architecture can serve as a starting point for a more economical and efficient system. The *My LineCard* app integrates the entire payment process, benefiting passengers in terms of time and user experience.

In the following sections, the points covered during the development of the project that seeks to solve these problems will be detailed: State of the art, mo tivation, hypothesis, theoretical framework, proposal, development, analysis and research, processes, architecture and standards, financial evaluation, implementation, experiment, analysis of final results, conclusions and recommendations.

2 Background

2.1 Related Works

In this section, articles about the urban transport system, its most relevant aspects, fare evasion, NFC ticket payment and security were reviewed.

The study conducted by Kholodov et al. in 2021. [18] used smart card technology as it helps users to get around more easily. Also, it is known that the use of the standard rate is a better option for users who travel to distant places compared to those who travel to near places. A tap-in validation system was implemented, which records the frequency of one trip to another and according to the zone threshold, the user's residence can be delimited. As main results, it was obtained that users who use the transport service frequently are more sensitive to change compared to those who use it sporadically. Likewise, it was revealed that the comfort of the users is greater compared to the discomfort of some, so this payment method is beneficial for this city.

In 2019, Allen et al. [4] wanted to test the hypothesis that there is a direct link between general and specific attribute satisfaction and fare avoidance behavior. Also, he wanted to demonstrate that the avoidance behavior of other users can directly affect the satisfaction of a given user. The analysis was based on a single intercept survey, designed from focus groups made to users of two modes of public transport, metro and bus in Santiago de

Chile. The main result was that evasion behavior increases according to satisfaction, that is, attitude towards other users, fare evasion behavior increases (contagion effect), and when satisfaction decreases, so does reliability.

The study carried out by Gupta et al. (2020) [16] aimed to analyze contactless smart cards that work via NFC, payment systems, techniques that are often used to protect user data, and attacks to the technologies used to make payments. It is known that NFC technology may lead to changes in the payment system and increased use in the future. But improvements are required in information security issues, since it is essential to be prepared to protect against new computer attacks and safeguard user data.

An investigation carried out by Ferreira et al. (2022) [15] demonstrated the usability of NFC technology through the development of a mobile app that provides the electronic ticketing service in urban transport for Android devices. This app allowed the passenger user to view the bus stations through which he was passing during his trip, the history of his trips made and the fares of said trips. The app was tested for more than a year, through a field test with 140 real passengers.

In 2020, the authors Brakewood et al. [7], carried out a study whose contribution was the evaluation of a mobile fee payment app in a real environment. For this, the benefits of the users who had used the app for the payment of fees were identified, since it is important for the justification of implementing or expanding mobile payment technologies. With this study it was allowed to reveal 3 benefits, the first is the reduction of time in the payment of tickets. The second benefit is the reduction of time on board the bus. And finally, the elimination of the use of cash.

2.2 Theoretical Framework

Contactless Payment System. This technology allows you to make payments and purchases without the need to place your card in the POS, simply approaching it and waiting for the reader to detect the card chip and make the payment. The contactless payment system offers the possibility of paying for a service or a product that you want to purchase through radio frequency recognition technologies, which are mostly found inside credit or debit cards, cell phones and readers [2].

Near Field Comunication (NFC). It is a short-range system for smartphones, laptops, tablets, among other devices, which allows these devices to exchange information and data through radio frequency communication when both devices are at a distance of 20 cm in theory, and 4 cm in practice [22].

Public Transportation System. It refers to the set of vehicles with different routes that seek to offer transport services to travelers. There are 2 main types of public transport, those that operate with flexible routes and those that operate with random routes. The term public transport includes various means such as minibuses, taxis, trains, among others. In certain low-demand districts there are full-route public transport companies, however, it is common for the user to select neither the route nor the speed [25].

Payment Standardization. The *Autoridad de Transporte Urbano para Lima y Callao (ATU)*, in 2020, approved the standardization of the transport payment system in Lima and Callao. With a single card, passengers can pay for their tickets on Line 1 of the metro,

Metropolitano, alternate corridors of Lima and Callao. Soon, users of urban transport in these two cities will be able to travel with a single card in complementary corridors, on Metropolitano buses or in cars on Line 1 of the Metro [5].

Android Operating System. Android is an operating system developed for mobile devices, as well as iOS, Symbian and Blackberry OS. It differs from the others in that it is based on Linux, a free, open source, cross-platform operating system kernel. This system is available so that many apps can work under this system. Android provides the necessary tools to implement apps that access cell phone functions and services, such as GPS, calls, calendar, among others, in an easy way. These native apps are developed in the Android Studio IDE, the platform par excellence for programming apps in this operating system with languages such as Java or Kotlin [1].

3   Proposed Solution

3.1   Hypothesis

1. The *My LineCard* app optimizes the time of the ticket payment process.
2. Using the *My LineCard* app, the percentage of passenger satisfaction increases.

3.2   Methodology

The research of papers and sources was conducted using the PICOC methodology divided into four categories: problem, technology, tools, and similar solutions. For the software development, the modular methodology was employed in conjunction with the Scrum methodology for testing each module and its approval through sprints. This allowed for better organization and management of the progress and prioritization of features. Once both modules were completed, they could be integrated for the passenger user and company manager. Three types of tests were conducted for app validation. First, functional tests were carried out, in which external individuals evaluated the app based on user stories to validate functionalities and provide feedback to improve certain aspects. Finally, usability and acceptance tests were performed with real users who tested the app and then were asked to complete a survey about their experience with the app.

3.3   Processes, Architecture, Standards and Standardization

Main and Secondary Processes. The payment process begins when the passenger user opens the app and has the driver as a secondary participant. If the passenger user does not have an account, proceed to register. Log in and access the main screen. Then, the passenger recharges balance. It is updated automatically. The passenger user, when he gets on the transport unit, being on the main screen, with mobile data and NFC turned on, brings his cell phone close to the card (simulated as a validator). Once the payment is accepted, he shows the screen with the message to the driver for him to give him the pass to sit down [3].

Another main process is when the company manager user registers in the app with a special validation code. Once in the home interface you can access tabs like "Statistics" where you can see the profits. Likewise, you can see and respond to the complaints and suggestions that users made.

Secondary processes are made up of browsing through the different options provided by the app such as "Payment history", "Affiliate lines", "Claims and Suggestions", among others.

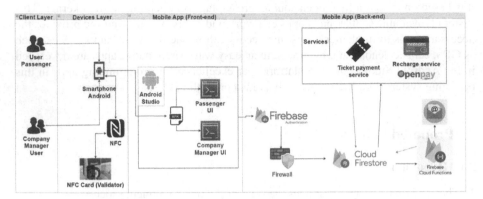

Fig. 1. Physical architecture of *My LineCard*

Physical Architecture. The physical architecture was modeled with its respective areas and hardware and software components on which the *My LineCard* app was developed (see Fig. 1).

In the physical architecture there are 4 layers: client layer, device layer, the Front-end and the Back-end of the app. First, in the client layer, the user is shown to be a passenger or a company manager. Each one of them has an Android mobile device with NFC technology that is used to bring the cell phone closer to the NFC reader that is located at the bus entrance. Once in the Front-End, the app is installed through an APK. Each type of user can interact with the interfaces that correspond to each one. For the Back-End part, the information will go through Firebase Authentication, then it will go through a Firewall to prevent the entry of third-party intruders. Later, it would arrive at the Cloud Firestore, which is where all the information is stored [3].

Payment and Money Transfer System. First, before paying, the balance is required to be greater than the cost of the ticket, so the user opens the "Recharge balance" window, the user will enter the credentials of his card so that the debit can be made and increase his balance in the app (a deal with a bank is required to have the payment gateway). In order to pay, the passenger needs to have the app open and NFC activated. The cell phone is brought closer to the validator that contains a card covered on the surface until a vibration is felt. What the cell phone reader will do is read the card ID, once it knows the identifier, it connects to the Firebase database to search for it within the "transportation" collection. When you find the document with that ID, you will know the price and other information of the unit. If it is validated that the balance is greater than the price of the ticket, it will be subtracted from the user's balance and the "Paid ticket" message will be displayed plus the day and time of the transaction so that the driver can certify its validity. This is also recorded in the user's payment history, likewise each time this action is executed, the earning field of the card increase. The payment of the recharge that was made at the beginning goes directly to the account of the founders of "My LineCard", so that later the total sum of all the earnings of each card associated with the company is delivered to the transport company.

Standards

- ISO/IEC 10118–3:2004 (Security Techniques - Dedicated Hash Functions): It provides hash functions by which the integrity of confidential user information can be ensured. From there, the fourth hash function is used, which is SHA-256 [17].
- ISO 9241–11:2018 (Usability): The definition of usability is the degree to which various interested users use a software product. It allows achieving the specific objectives set, based on effectiveness, efficiency and satisfaction in an already predetermined scenario [6]. These three UX and usability metrics are the ones used for the project.
- ISO/IEC 14443–2:2020 (Identification cards - Radio frequency signal and power interface): It establishes the operability of contactless cards used for recognition and data transmission protocols. The most widely used technology is Mifare, which complies with the higher-level protocol of 13.56 MHz. The cards that comply with the stipulated protocols are the Mifare DESFire models [14].

3.4 Fare Standardization

In order to obtain the price of the standard ticket that would be assigned to a transport company, it is necessary to calculate prices in which four factors are involved. The first is the current ticket price, the second is the interest from a banking service, the third is the app's own profit, and the fourth is the taxes. Once these factors are applied, the total price according to the company is found.

3.5 Implementation

Design. When all the concepts, tools, standards, platforms, software and hardware are already defined, mockups of the app interfaces are designed to translate them later in Android Studio. The mockups were designed in Figma and are rep-resented in Fig. 2:

Programming. The programming of the *My LineCard* app was developed in the Android Studio IDE in Java. First, the Gradle was configured so that it has the most current version of the SDK. During development, special libraries and properties were added. For example, libraries for NFC or for the Firebase database [12]. Which served to be able to use NFC functions, such as detecting when it is on or off so that there is a communication and debiting the balance as shown in Fig. 3 and Fig. 4. Second, all the possible interfaces of the passenger user and company manager were designed in the activities and fragments of Android Studio. Third, in the "java" folder, the classes were implemented where the objects were created to use the different components of the interfaces designed in the "layout" directory and assign special functions depending on the interface. Finally, it was synchronized with the Gradle to be able to build and run

Fig. 2. Interfaces for login, ticket payment and balance recharge

the project on an emulator and an APK was generated to install it [10]. Another of the important methods is *sha256* which is implemented in the registry, and which is used for encryption and security of passwords. The information was stored in the Google Firebase database, where it was organized into collections and documents (see Fig. 5).

In a Client-Server division, the client is the Android app. It is responsible for directly interacting with the user, capturing their actions, and interpreting responses from the server. Choosing a native application provides a better user experience, taking advantage of the unique features of the device, such as NFC technology for public transport payments. Firebase acts as the server. It's a Backend-as-a-Service (BaaS) service, which means it reduces the need to write server code and allows us to focus on client development. Firebase is used directly in the application. Since Firebase provides SDKs that easily integrate with platforms like Android, no additional middleware is necessary. This database has three main components in this project: First, the Cloud Firestore is used to store and retrieve data in real time. This non-relational database was chosen because of its flexibility and ability to scale horizontally. Second, Cloud Storage is used to store

```
Función ValidarNFC(contexto):
    nfcAdapter = ObtenerAdaptadorNFC(contexto)
    Si nfcAdapter es nulo:
        MostrarMensaje("Tu dispositivo no admite NFC")


Función Principal:
    ValidarNFC(contexto)
    LeerEtiquetaDesdeIntent(obtenerIntento())
    CrearTareaPendienteNFC(contexto)
    ConfigurarFiltroEtiquetaDetectada()
    MostrarMensaje("NFC habilitado")
```

Fig. 3. Pseudocode to validate the NFC on the cell phone

images efficiently and securely. Third, Firebase Authentication offers a comprehensive solution for authentication, eliminating the need to build a system from the beginning.

NFC Cards. To validate the effectiveness of the payment system we require an NFC card. First, the S50 model NFC cards and an ACR122U model NFC reader were purchased. These cards come with a default ID that refers to a transport unit. Some cards decomposed after 10 reads, so it was decided to use higher quality NFC cards (Mifare DESFire EV2 2K), which allow 500,000 read and/or write cycles, or 10 years [21].

3.6 Experimentation and Validation

An experiment was carried out to test the efficiency of the app and to verify the certainty of the hypotheses after developing and testing the app with citizens.

```
Función LeerDatosNFC(intent):
    acción = obtenerAccion(intent)
    Si acción es igual a "etiqueta detectada":
        etiqueta = obtenerExtra(intent, EXTRA_TAG)
        UID = bin2hex(etiqueta.getId())
        MostrarMensaje("Procesando pago...")
        ConsultarBDDocumentos("transportation", new OnCompleteListener() {
            Si la tarea es exitosa:
                Para cada documento en el resultado:
                    Si documento existe en BDD y tiene valor:
                        ConsultarBDDocumentoConUID("transportation", "record", UID, new OnSuccessListener() {
                            Si el documento existe:
                                Si el saldo es suficiente para el precio:
                                    ReducirSaldoUsuario(auth.getCurrentUser().getUid(), document.getDouble("price"))
                                    ActualizarGananciasEmpresa(document.getId(), UID, document.getDouble("price"))
                                    RegistrarHistorial(document, auth.getCurrentUser().getUid())
                                Sino:
                                    ReproducirSonido("soundfalse")
                                    MostrarMensaje("Saldo insuficiente. Recargue saldo")
                        Sino:
                            Si existe en "passenger":
                                Si el saldo es suficiente para el precio:
                                    ReducirSaldoUsuario(auth.getCurrentUser().getUid(), document.getDouble("price"))
                                    CrearRegistroGananciasEmpresa(document, document.getDouble("price"))
                                    RegistrarHistorial(document, auth.getCurrentUser().getUid())
                                Sino:
                                    ReproducirSonido("soundfalse")
                                    MostrarMensaje("Saldo insuficiente")
    Fin Si

Función Principal:
    LeerDatosNFC(getIntent())
```

Fig. 4. Pseudocode to make the payment with NFC

Participants. A total of 38 people were selected who performed the role of passengers who paid for their ticket through the app.

Materials. An android smartphone with NFC technology, an NFC reader and a Mifare DESFire EV2 2K NFC card that was covered by a case was required to simulate that it is a validator at the bus entrance, since the passenger in general already knows what a validator is for. Each card ID was written with the NFC reader and registered in the database (see Fig. 6).

Scenery. The experiment will be carried out the entrance of a bus, where the driver will be on one side and the NFC card (validator) will be installed in front of the passenger.

Fig. 5. My LineCard database on Firebase

Fig. 6. NFC card and reader

Tests. Before carrying out the field tests, use cases and user stories (UH) were carried out. At the HU we review in detail the functionalities of login, tab display, alternative scenarios, payment, history, bus lines, among others. While in the use cases, the entire sequentiality of a complete process was reviewed, such as the registration process, balance recharge, NFC payment, participation in the comment forum, among others. Once having verified and corrected all the functionality, we proceeded to test it in field tests.

The participants of the experiment are users not registered in the app. First, registration and login are done. Later, balance was recharged if he did not have it. Mobile data and NFC must be activated before boarding the bus. Once inside, bring your smartphone close to the NFC card and wait for the payment to be processed (see Fig. 7). The successful fare paid message is displayed to the driver and he goes to sit down (see Fig. 8). It is measured how many seconds the passenger takes to carry out this payment process. Finally, the participants answer an opinion and satisfaction survey.

Fig. 7. Passenger paying with *My LineCard* on the card (validator) [13]

Fig. 8. Showing the evidence of payment to the driver [13]

3.7 Results

After testing with users, Table 1 shows the time it took each passenger to make the payment with *My LineCard*. For which a balance of time was drawn and an average ticket payment time was obtained. Subsequently, in Table 2 the general results of *My LineCard* are compared with those of today in the fields of time, satisfaction and costs.

After obtaining the results of the experiment carried out, the respective comparisons were made with the data of the current situation and it was verified that the four hypotheses were fulfilled.

Table 1. List of passenger time and average bus fare payment with *My LineCard*

Passenger user number	Fare payment time with *My LineCard*
1	6.31 s
2	7.13 s
3	4.65 s
4	3.93 s
5	7.57 s
6	7.52 s
7	8.52 s
8	4.84 s
9	3.39 s
10	5.83 s
11	8.13 s
12	5.59 s
13	5.11 s
14	3.61 s
15	5.76 s
16	3.29 s
17	7.60 s
18	3.95 s
19	5.06 s
20	5.49 s
21	6.80 s
22	4.55 s
23	6.21 s
24	8.39 s
25	5.94 s
26	5.68 s
27	5.73 s
28	3.55 s
29	5.98 s
30	7.67 s

(*continued*)

Table 1. (*continued*)

Passenger user number	Fare payment time with *My LineCard*
31	6.06 s
32	4.84 s
33	8.20 s
34	7.16 s
35	7.57 s
36	5.80 s
37	4.03 s
38	6.78 s
Average ticket payment time	**5.90 s**

Finally, the time that would be saved by subtracting the current maximum and minimum with the time obtained (Eqs. 1 and 2).

$$\text{Max Time Saved} = 20\,\text{s}. - 5.9\,\text{s}. = 14.1\,\text{s} \tag{1}$$

$$\text{MinTimeSaved} = 12\,\text{s}. - 5.9\,\text{s}. = 6.1\,\text{s} \tag{2}$$

1. Ticket payment time (Efficiency): There was a time saving of between 6.1 to 14.1 s per person in the payment of the bus ticket. The time saving was considerable, taking into account that the payment time can be reduced by up to half. The process was optimized, since the steps of counting money, returning of change and ticket were omitted.
2. User satisfaction: Satisfaction increased by 10.4%, since the app was accepted by passengers for its fast and safe processes. This is related to what was mentioned in the previous item, about the assertion of Allen et al. (2019) [4]. This means that the user experience on public buses has improved, since mistreatment by collectors is avoided by having less interaction with passengers.

Table 2. Comparison of results with current situation

Aspects of public transport	*My LineCard*	Current payment system
Payment speed	5.9 s	12 to 20 s
Satisfaction of the passenger	6.3% Bad/Very bad - 37.5% Indifferent - 66.7% Good/Very Good	15% Bad/Very bad - 42% Indifferent - 56.3% Good/Very Good

In addition to those optimizations, there is an additional field in which there would be an improvement. Specifically, in the cost of the fee collection process. The cost of each NFC card (PEN 17.03) is very low compared to personnel costs (PEN 958 up to PEN 3,516 per month) or hardware (PEN 1,902), depending on the current fee collection system. This card is read by passengers' smartphones and can withstand thousands of read/write cycles. Users inadvertently already finance a device with NFC themselves, not because they buy it specifically for the technology, but because cell phone manufacturers are already universalizing this technology among all their devices, which is very favorable for *MyLineCard*. Therefore, this proposed vision decreases hardware and personnel costs on each bus.

4 Conclusions and Recommendations

In conclusion, the validation of *My LineCard* among experiment participants showcased the app's efficacy in facilitating electronic ticket payment through NFC technology. The app not only streamlined and secured the process but also significantly enhanced user satisfaction. A noteworthy payment time reduction of up to 14.1 s per individual was achieved, representing up to 70.5% of time saved during fare payment on transportation. This, in turn, led to a 10.4% increase in passenger satisfaction. Additionally, costs associated with the conventional ticket payment procedure were lowered. Deploying *My LineCard* on public transport units is feasible, requiring just an NFC-enabled mobile device and an NFC card (validator).

For optimal contactless payment systems, employing high-quality NFC cards capable of enduring extensive read and write cycles is advised. Using Firebase in Android Studio is recommended due to its integrated support and flexibility. Utilizing position markers for unstructured database data aids in efficient organization and retrieval. Looking forward, integrating a banking service for real debit or credit card balance top-ups could enhance future development and user convenience.

5 Financing

Universidad Peruana de Ciencias Aplicadas/UPC-EXPOST-2023- 2.

Acknowledgment. The authors thank the evaluators for their important suggestions that have allowed a significant improvement of this work. Likewise, to the Research Department of the Universidad Peruana de Ciencias Aplicadas for the support provided to carry out this research work through the UPC-EXPOST-2023–2 incentive.

References

1. ¿Qué es Android?. https://www.xatakandroid.com/sistema-operativo/que-es-android. Accessed 4 May 2022
2. ¿Qué es la tecnología 'contactless' o pago sin contacto?. https://www.bbva.com/es/tecnol ogia-contactless-pago-contacto/. Accessed 30 Jan 2023
3. Ahamad, S.S.: A novel NFC-based secure protocol for merchant transactions. IEEE Access **10**, 1905–1920 (2022). https://doi.org/10.1109/access.2021.3139065

4. Allen, J., Muñoz, J.C., de Dios, J.: On evasion behaviour in public transport: dissatisfaction or contagion? Transp. Res. Part A Policy Pract. **130**, 626–651 (2019). https://doi.org/10.1016/j.tra.2019.10.005
5. ATU aprueba estandarizar el sistema de pago de transporte en Lima y Callao. https://bit.ly/3PkyOwe. Accessed 30 Jan 2023
6. Bevan, N., Carter, J., Earthy, J., Geis, T., Harker, S.: New ISO standards for usability, usability reports and usability measures. In: Kurosu, M. (eds) Human-Computer Interaction. Theory, Design, Development and Practice, LNISA, vol. 9731, pp. 268–278. Springer, Cham (2016). https://doi.org/10.1007/978-3-319-39510-4_25
7. Brakewood, C., Ziedan, A., Hendricks, S.J., Barbeau, S.J., Joslin, A.: An evaluation of the benefits of mobile fare payment technology from the user and opera- tor perspectives. Transp. Policy **93**, 54–66 (2020). https://doi.org/10.1016/j.tranpol.2020.04.015
8. Casi cuatro millones de usuarios pagan con el móvil el metro y el autobus. https://elpais.com/economia/2020/01/11/actualidad/1578763738_098952.html. Accessed 12 Sep 2022
9. Centeno, J.: Servicio de transporte urbano en la ciudad de Lima, análisis y propuesta de mejora de la calidad, con participación de las universidades públicas y privadas. Anales científicos, **79**(1), (2018). https://doi.org/10.21704/ac.v79i1.1138
10. Cómo ejecutar apps en Android Emulator. https://developer.android.com/studio/run/emulator?hl=es-419. Accessed 27 Nov 2022
11. Cómo se moviliza la población limeña en el Transporte Público y cómo valora el servicio, http://bit.ly/3E3cfFe. Accessed 29 Oct 2022
12. Conceptos básicos de NFC. https://developer.android.com/guide/topics/connectivity/nfc/nfc?hl=es-419. Accessed 21 Nov 2022
13. Dos estudiantes crean una app que busca revolucionar el pago en el transporte público a través de la tecnología NFC. https://bit.ly/46mOHZg. Accessed 14 Jun 2023
14. Fernández, F.: Emulación de Tarjetas NFC en Android. Universidad Carlos III de Madrid, Madrid, Final Degree Project (2015)
15. Ferreira, M.C., Dias, T.G., Falcao E Cunha, J.: Anda: an innovative micro- location mobile ticketing solution based on NFC and BLE technologies. IEEE Trans. Intell. Transp. Syst. **23**(7), 6316–6325 (2022). https://doi.org/10.1109/TITS.2021.3072083
16. Gupta, B.B., Narayan, S.: A survey on contactless smart cards and payment system: technologies, policies, attacks and countermeasures. J. Glob. Inf. Manag.nf. Manag. **28**(4), 135–159 (2020). https://doi.org/10.4018/JGIM.2020100108
17. ISO/IEC: Information technology — Security techniques — Hash-functions — Part 3: Dedicated hash-functions. ISO/IEC 10118–3:2004. Geneva, Switzerland: ISO/IEC (2004)
18. Kholodov, Y., et al.: Public transport fare elasticities from smartcard data: evidence from a natural experiment. Transport Policy **105**, 35–43 (2021). https://doi.org/10.1016/j.tranpol.2021.03.001
19. Levano, J., Bernal, M.: Reducción del tiempo para abordar el corredor del sistema integrado de transporte mediante una automatización del pago del pasaje. Universidad San Ignacio de Loyola, Lima, Thesis (2021)
20. Lima supera los 10 millones de habitantes al año 2022. https://bit.ly/3XTd0sZ. Accessed 30 Jan 2023
21. MF3D(H)x2: MIFARE DESFire EV2 contactless multi-application IC. https://www.nxp.com/docs/en/data-sheet/MF3DX2_MF3DHX2_SDS.pdf. Accessed 21 Nov 2022
22. Montero, R.: Estudio de tecnología de comunicación de campo cercano, NFC. Degree Thesis, Universidad Politécnica de Madrid, Madrid (2017)
23. Olowosegun, A., Moyo, D., Gopinath, D.: Multicriteria evaluation of the quality of service of informal public transport: an empirical evidence from Ibadan, Nigeria. Case Stud. Trans. Policy **9**(4), 1518–1530 (2021). https://doi.org/10.1016/j.cstp.2021.08.002

24. Perú supera los 41 millones de líneas móviles activas al cierre del segundo trimestre del año. http://bit.ly/3O1eXj5. Accessed 5 May 2022
25. Sistema de Transporte Público. https://rno-its.piarc.org/es/conceptos-basicos-its-que-signif ica-its-servicios-y-aplicaciones-its/sistemas-de-transporte-publico. Accessed 6 May 2022
26. Usos del smartphone en la vida cotidiana 2021. https://www.ipsos.com/es-pe/usos-del-sma rtphone-en-la-vida-cotidiana-2021. Accessed 30 Jan 2023

Integration Proposal for Thermal Imaging Modality into Health Information Systems

Ricardo Vardasca[1,2](✉) (iD), Marco Tereso[1] (iD), Antonio Pratas[1] (iD), Braulio Alturas[3] (iD), Domingos Martinho[1] (iD), and Fernando Bento[1,3] (iD)

[1] ISLA Santarem, Rua Teixeira Guedes 31, 2000-029 Santarem, Portugal
ricardo.vardasca@islasantarem.pt

[2] INEGI, Universidade do Porto, Rua Dr. Roberto Frias 400, 4200-465 Porto, Portugal

[3] ISTAR, ISCTE-IUL, Av. Prof. Aníbal Bettencourt 9, 1600-189 Lisboa, Portugal

Abstract. Thermal imaging allows to map and record surface temperature in a form of images, which in medicine can document pathological states and be an important complimentary diagnostic and treatment monitoring method. It is available for six decades, but some factors contributed to its low adoption, being the main the lack of integration with the existing health information systems at the healthcare institutions. It is aim of this research to address the lack of integration with existing technological infrastructure, through documenting and proposing a procedure to integrate thermal imaging as an imaging modality in health information systems. Requirements will be outlined, supported by UML modulation for simple use cases and class diagram along with the steps to adopt the DICOM standard. Following the proposed methodology, it will be possible to integrate thermal images with the existing health information systems, contributing to better performance of the exam, increase interoperability, ensure data security and availability, and improved patient care and satisfaction.

Keywords: Health information systems · integration · thermal imaging

1 Introduction

Infrared thermal imaging allows recording and mapping temperature surface of objects remotely. It has been used in medical research since 1956 providing important physiological data related to peripheral blood flow and autonomous nervous system, being an important complimentary mean of diagnostic and treatment [1–9].

The method is a non-invasive and radiation-free imaging modality, which makes it particularly valuable in cases where repeated imaging is required or when minimizing patient exposure to radiation is essential. It is a safe and comfortable imaging technique that can be used across different patient populations, including infants, pregnant women, and individuals with contraindications for other imaging modalities [1].

It allows a comprehensive assessment of the body by capturing thermal patterns over a larger area, providing a holistic view of heat distribution and temperature variations,

T. Guarda et al. (Eds.): ARTIIS 2023, CCIS 1935, pp. 65–75, 2024.
https://doi.org/10.1007/978-3-031-48858-0_6

enabling clinicians to identify abnormalities in specific regions or even systemic conditions that may manifest as thermal changes. This whole-body assessment can assist in identifying underlying conditions and guiding appropriate treatment strategies [1, 8, 9].

This imaging modality provides objective and quantifiable data by measuring temperature variations. This objectivity reduces subjectivity and enhances diagnostic accuracy. It can be used to monitor the progress of treatment, assess response to therapy, and objectively evaluate the efficacy of interventions over time. Thermal imaging enables real-time monitoring of physiological changes and responses. It can be used to track the dynamic thermal patterns of various conditions, such as inflammation, circulation disorders, or wound healing, allowing healthcare professionals to make timely decisions and adjustments to treatment plans [1–4, 7].

It is a patient-friendly imaging modality that does not require direct contact with the body. It is non-invasive and painless, making it well-tolerated by patients. This ease of use promotes patient compliance, reduces anxiety, and improves the overall patient experience during diagnostic procedures [1–3].

Thermal imaging enables the early detection of physiological abnormalities by visualizing heat patterns and temperature variations in the body. This can assist in the early diagnosis of conditions such as inflammatory diseases, vascular disorders, and certain types of cancer. Early detection allows for timely intervention and improved treatment outcomes [1–3].

This imaging method has the potential for diverse applications across multiple medical specialties. It can be used in areas such as dermatology, rheumatology, neurology, sports medicine, vascular medicine, and oncology, among others. That versatility allows for a broad range of diagnostic and monitoring possibilities [1–4].

Overall, the importance of using a thermal imaging modality in clinical practice lies in its ability to provide early detection, non-invasive assessment, objective data, real-time monitoring, patient-friendly experience, and potential for multidisciplinary applications. By leveraging thermal imaging, healthcare professionals can enhance diagnostic accuracy, improve patient outcomes, and provide more personalized and effective care.

Despite these advantages, this imaging modality is not widely available in clinical setting and health institutions. That happens due to some factors such as: lack of training and expertise of specialists, demands on standardization and validation of specific exams, absence of reimbursement and insurance coverage and mostly lack of integration with existing technological infrastructure [10–15].

It is important to mention that due to the particularity of the infrared thermal imaging modality data acquisition and dataset requirements an existing modality implementation cannot be adapted, being this one of the major barriers to its adoption widely and at point of care.

It is aim of this research to address the lack of integration with existing technological infrastructure, through documenting and proposing a procedure to integrate thermal imaging as an imaging modality in health information systems like other medical imaging modalities.

2   Thermal Imaging Workflow

The ideal workflow of a thermal imaging modality exam involves a patient consultation, prescription of a thermal imaging examination, image acquisition, image review and analysis, report generation and report distribution and access (see Fig. 1), typically follows these steps within a health information system integrated with a Picture Archiving and Communication System (PACS), Radiology Information System (RIS), and Digital Imaging and Communications in Medicine (DICOM).

The workflow starts with a patient being consulted with a physician or healthcare professional who determines the need for a thermal imaging examination based on the patient's symptoms, medical history, and clinical assessment. If a thermal imaging examination is deemed necessary, the physician prescribes the examination and enters the order into the RIS. The RIS generates an order, which includes patient information, examination details, and any specific instructions. The RIS schedules the thermal imaging appointment based on availability and resources. The patient is notified of the scheduled appointment time and any preparation instructions.

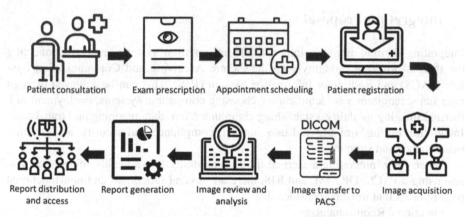

Fig. 1. Desired thermal imaging examination integrated workflow.

On the day of the examination, the patient arrives at the facility and goes through the registration process. The registration staff enters or verifies the patient's demographic information in the RIS, ensuring accurate patient identification and linking the examination to the correct patient record. The patient undergoes the thermal imaging examination. The healthcare professional operating the thermal imaging modality captures the thermal images and associates them with the patient's examination information. The modality generates DICOM-compliant thermal images and metadata.

The thermal images, along with associated metadata, are transferred from the thermal imaging modality to the PACS. This transfer can occur via DICOM network communication protocols. The PACS receives and stores the images in a secure and organized manner, associating them with the patient's unique identifier, examination details, and any other relevant information. The interpreting physician or radiologist accesses the PACS through a workstation or a dedicated image viewer. They retrieve the patient's thermal images from the PACS and review them to analyze the thermal patterns, identify abnormalities, and make a diagnosis or recommendation. After analyzing the thermal images, the interpreting physician generates a report summarizing their findings, conclusions, and recommendations. The physician uses a reporting tool integrated with the RIS to create the report, ensuring that it includes the patient's identification, examination details, relevant images, and any necessary annotations or measurements.

The finalized report is saved in the RIS, associating it with the patient's examination record. The report is typically made available in the health information system, allowing authorized healthcare professionals to access it for consultation, treatment planning, or further decision-making.

Throughout this workflow, the health information system, PACS, RIS, and DICOM facilitate seamless communication and integration of patient data, thermal images, examination orders, reports, and relevant clinical information. This integration ensures efficient and centralized management of the thermal imaging workflow within the healthcare facility, streamlining patient care and enabling accurate and timely diagnosis and treatment.

3 Integration Proposal

Integrating thermal imaging into a health information system involves connecting the thermal imaging modality with the Picture Archiving and Communication System (PACS) and Radiology Information System (RIS). This can be achieved through nine steps: requirements identification, choosing compatible systems, deployment of a thermal imaging modality, establishing communication, data mapping and translation, Integration testing, training and user support, compliance and security, and ongoing maintenance and support.

When fully integrating a thermal imaging modality into a health information system using a PACS, DICOM, and RIS, there are several functional and non-functional requirements that must be considered.

Functional Requirements:

- Patient Registration and Demographics, it should allow for accurate patient registration, including capturing and storing patient demographics such as name, age, gender, and unique identifiers.
- Order Management, it should support the creation, management, and tracking of thermal imaging examination orders, including prescription details, scheduling, and order status updates.
- DICOM Integration, it should be capable of sending and receiving DICOM-compliant data, including thermal images, from the thermal imaging modality to the PACS and RIS. It should ensure proper mapping, transmission, and storage of DICOM objects.
- Image Acquisition and Storage, it should facilitate the acquisition, transfer, and storage of thermal images in a secure and organized manner within the PACS, ensuring proper association with patient information and relevant examination metadata.
- Image Viewing and Analysis, it should provide tools for authorized healthcare professionals to access, view, and analyze the thermal images within the PACS, allowing

for proper zooming, panning, windowing, and image manipulation. It should support relevant measurement tools and overlays for image analysis.

- Reporting and Documentation, it should enable the creation, storage, and retrieval of thermal imaging examination reports, including relevant images, annotations, conclusions, recommendations, and patient identification. It should support report generation templates and customizable formats.
- Workflow and Task Management, it should support the management of the thermal imaging workflow, including task assignment, tracking, and status updates, ensuring smooth communication and collaboration among healthcare professionals involved in the process.

Non-functional Requirements:

- Security and Privacy, it should comply with relevant security standards and regulations to ensure the confidentiality, integrity, and availability of patient data and thermal images. It should include access controls, encryption, audit trails, and measures to prevent unauthorized access or data breaches.
- Performance and Scalability, it should be able to handle the data volume and processing requirements associated with thermal imaging, supporting efficient image transmission, storage, retrieval, and display. It should be scalable to accommodate future growth and increasing data demands.
- Interoperability, it should adhere to DICOM standards to ensure interoperability with other DICOM-compliant systems. It should support standard protocols for data exchange, such as DICOM and HL7, enabling seamless integration with other healthcare systems and interoperability across different facilities.
- Usability and User Experience, it should be designed with a user-friendly interface, intuitive navigation, and efficient workflows to enhance usability and user experience for healthcare professionals interacting with the system. Training and support resources should be provided to ensure proper system utilization.
- Reliability and Availability, it should have a high level of reliability, minimizing downtime and ensuring availability for accessing patient data and thermal images. It should include backup and disaster recovery mechanisms to protect against data loss or system failures.
- Compliance, it should comply with relevant regulatory requirements, such as Health Insurance Portability and Accountability Act (HIPAA) or other data protection regulations, as well as industry best practices for medical imaging systems. It should support auditing and logging functionalities for compliance monitoring.

These requirements provide a general guideline for integrating thermal imaging into a health information system using a PACS, DICOM, and RIS. Specific requirements may be required depending on the organization's needs, local regulations, and the capabilities of the chosen systems.

From the proposed requirements, UML modulation for use cases can be drawn considering the Thermal Imaging management system and the Thermal Imaging capture system (Fig. 2).

The Thermal Imaging management system, will have a physician who will prescribe a thermal imaging examination and enters the order into the RIS, access the PACS to view and analyze the thermal images, and generates a report summarizing the findings and recommendations based on the analysis of the thermal images. A registration staff can enter or verify the patient's demographic information in the RIS during the patient registration process, optionally can access the patient's information stored in the health information system (Patient Information Record System) for consultation, examination, or report generation purposes. The same actor in the RIS schedules the thermal imaging examination based on availability and resources.

At the Thermal Imaging capture system, the healthcare professional captures thermal images using the thermal imaging modality and associates them with the patient's examination details.

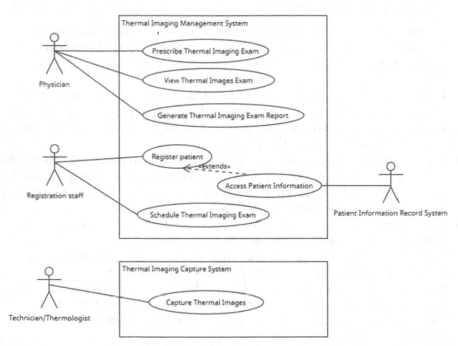

Fig. 2. The UML use cases diagram for the thermal imaging exam integration with the health information systems.

It is important to note that additional actors, use cases, and relationships based on the specific requirements and functionality of the integration may be required, this refers just to a simplest proposal of integration.

A UML class diagram for modulation of the integration of a thermal imaging modality into a health information system using a PACS, DICOM, and RIS was also defined. The "DICOMIntegration" interface represents the DICOM integration functionality (linking with the existing health information system at the facility), providing methods for sending and receiving DICOM data. The "RIS" class represents the RIS component, which handles order creation and scheduling. The "PACS" class represents the PACS component, responsible for storing and retrieving images. The "ThermalImage" class represents the thermal image entity, which encapsulates the image data, thermal values, and temperature unit. The "ExaminationOrder" class represents the examination order entity, which includes details such as the order ID, patient ID, date, and modality.

The class diagram, at Fig. 3, demonstrates the relationships and interactions between the components involved in the integration, including the DICOM integration, RIS, PACS, and the entities for thermal images and examination orders. It showcases the flow of data and functionality between these components within the health information system. Depending on the rearrangement of the integration systems requirements, new classes and associations may be required to be added.

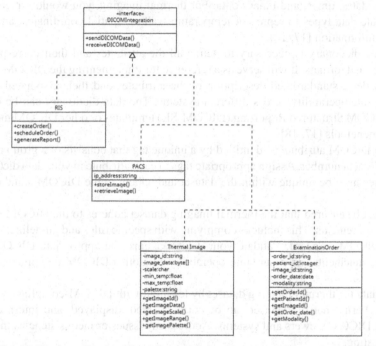

Fig. 3. The UML class diagram for the thermal imaging exam integration with the health information systems.

The DICOM standard provides a flexible framework for defining various medical imaging datasets, including thermal imaging, which has only defined the modality code. To define a medical thermal imaging dataset within the DICOM standard, apart from the data proposed by this research authors in a previous publication [16], some steps must be followed, such as: identifying relevant DICOM classes, defining necessary attributes, determining data types and formats, creating a data dictionary, assigning attribute tags, implementing DICOM conformance, testing and verifying, and documenting the whole process.

The DICOM classes and modules that are most appropriate for representing thermal imaging data need to be identified. DICOM includes a wide range of classes and modules that can be used to describe various aspects of medical images. For thermal imaging, some relevant classes and modules might include Patient, Study, Series, Equipment, Frame of Reference, Image, and Overlay Plane [17, 18].

The specific attributes are required to describe the thermal imaging data adequately. Attributes are elements that provide information about the image and its acquisition, such as patient demographics, acquisition parameters, thermal values, and image characteristics. For thermal imaging, some common attributes might include Patient Name, Patient ID, Study Date, Study Description, Body Part Examined, Thermal Scale, Thermal Map Data, and Temperature Units [17–19].

Using appropriate DICOM data types and formats to represent the thermal imaging data accurately will facilitate. DICOM supports various data types, including strings, numbers, dates, times, and binary data. For thermal imaging, you would typically use appropriate data types to represent temperature values, spatial coordinates, and other relevant information [17, 18].

A data dictionary is necessary to define all the attributes and their corresponding data types and formats. It will serve as a reference for implementing the DICOM dataset and provides a standardized description of the attributes and their associated values, ensuring interoperability across different systems. The data dictionary can be created using DICOM Structured Reporting (DICOM-SR) templates or other DICOM metadata management tools [17, 18].

Each DICOM attribute is identified by a unique tag that consists of a group number and an element number. Assign appropriate tags to each attribute in your data dictionary. Tag values must be unique within the dataset and adhere to the DICOM standard [17, 18].

It must be ensured that the thermal imaging dataset adheres to the DICOM conformance requirements. This includes complying with specific rules and guidelines defined by the DICOM standard. Validate your dataset against the appropriate DICOM conformance statements and ensure interoperability with other DICOM-compliant systems [16, 19].

Validate the thermal imaging dataset by testing it with DICOM-compliant software or tools. Verify that the dataset can be correctly read, displayed, and interpreted by different DICOM viewers and systems. Address any issues or inconsistencies that arise during testing.

The structure and content of your thermal imaging dataset, including the attribute definitions, data types, formats, and any specific implementation considerations must be documented. This documentation will be helpful for others who need to work with or integrate your dataset into their systems.

It's important to note that while the DICOM standard can accommodate thermal imaging data, there is no specific module or class dedicated solely to thermal imaging. Therefore, you may need to leverage existing DICOM modules that align closely with thermal imaging or use private tags to capture additional specific thermal imaging information not covered by the standard.

4 Discussion

There are some advantages about Integrating a thermal imaging modality system into a health information system using a PACS, DICOM, and RIS. Examples include centralized data management, enhanced workflow efficiency, improved data availability and accessibility, comprehensive patient records, data consolidation and interoperability, simplified reporting and documentation, regulatory compliance, data security, and contribute to a wider adoption of the modality improving patients care [10–15, 19].

By integrating the thermal imaging modality with the health information system, all patient data, including thermal images, examination orders, and reports, are stored centrally in a structured and organized manner. This centralization allows for easy access, retrieval, and management of patient information by authorized healthcare professionals.

Integration streamlines the workflow by automating various processes. It eliminates the need for manual data entry, reduces paperwork, and minimizes the chances of data duplication or errors. Healthcare professionals can quickly access patient records, schedule examinations, capture and store thermal images, and generate reports seamlessly, leading to improved operational efficiency.

With integration, thermal images and related patient data become readily available to authorized users within the health information system. This accessibility enables efficient collaboration, consultation, and decision-making among healthcare professionals involved in patient care. It facilitates timely access to critical information, ultimately improving patient outcomes.

Integrating thermal imaging data into the health information system enriches patient records by incorporating thermal images alongside other diagnostic images, laboratory results, and clinical documentation. This comprehensive view enables healthcare professionals to have a holistic understanding of the patient's condition, aiding in accurate diagnosis, treatment planning, and monitoring.

The integration with DICOM and other standard protocols ensures interoperability between different systems and healthcare facilities. It allows for seamless exchange of thermal images and associated data with other DICOM-compliant systems, facilitating continuity of care, referrals, and remote consultations. The consolidation of data also supports research, analysis, and population health management initiatives [17–19].

It enables efficient generation and storage of thermal imaging reports within the health information system. Physicians and radiologists can use reporting tools integrated with the RIS to create standardized reports with relevant findings, conclusions, and recommendations. This simplifies the documentation process, ensures consistency, and provides a comprehensive record of thermal imaging examinations.

Integration can help ensure compliance with regulatory requirements, such as data privacy and security regulations (e.g., HIPAA). By leveraging secure communication protocols and implementing access controls, encryption, and audit trails, the integration helps protect patient data, maintain privacy, and meet regulatory obligations.

Overall, integrating a thermal imaging modality system with a health information system using a PACS, DICOM, and RIS enhances data management, workflow efficiency, collaboration, and patient care. It promotes a more comprehensive and accessible healthcare environment, leading to improved diagnosis, treatment, and outcomes, leading to better patient care and satisfaction [15, 19].

5 Conclusion

In this research the main goal of address the lack of integration with existing technological infrastructure, through documenting and proposing a procedure to integrate thermal imaging as an imaging modality in health information systems was fulfilled. Minimal requirements, UML case studies, UML class diagram modulation and steps towards the definition of a DICOM dataset to perform a full integration.

It is important to mention that this is just a simple proposal, the implementation may differ with health institutions, since they face different scenarios and have different types of organization, which may lead to different actors, use cases, classes and relationships based on the specific requirements and functionality.

References

1. Ring, E.F.J., Ammer, K.: Infrared thermal imaging in medicine. Phys. Med. Biol. **57**(4), R1–R29 (2012). https://doi.org/10.1088/0031-9155/57/4/R1
2. Shakeel, A., Rafiq, M.H., Muhammad, G., Shakeel, A.: Medical application of infrared thermography: a review. In: Proceedings of the World Congress on Engineering, vol. 2, pp. 6–9 (2016)
3. Singh, S., Dangol, A., Yadav, A.: Medical applications of infrared thermography: a review. Biocybern. Biomed. Eng. **38**(4), 952–963 (2018). https://doi.org/10.1016/j.bbe.2018.08.007
4. Humphries, B., Finlay, D.: Infrared imaging in medical diagnostics. Infrared Phys. Technol. **71**, 28–55 (2015). https://doi.org/10.1016/j.infrared.2015.01.009
5. Bambery, K.R., Exstrom, M.A.: Thermal imaging in medical applications. In: Handbook of Imaging Materials, pp. 487–517, CRC Press (2014)
6. Gautherie, M.: Thermobiology and thermal imaging. In: Infrared Imaging, pp. 15–37, CRC Press (2014)
7. Jones, B.F.: A reappraisal of the use of infrared thermal image analysis in medicine. IEEE Trans. Med. Imaging **32**(6), 1014–1027 (2013). https://doi.org/10.1109/TMI.2013.2246565
8. Ng, E.Y., Sharma, S.: Fundamentals and applications of thermal imaging in medicine. J. Med. Eng. 875154 (2013). https://doi.org/10.1155/2013/875154
9. Sreekanth, P., Jayasree, T.: Role of infrared thermography in medicine. Int. J. Innov. Res. Sci. Eng. Technol. **2**(11), 6203–6213 (2013)
10. Adnan, M., Siddiqui, J.A., Yasin, M.: Integration of thermal imaging in healthcare applications: a review. J. Med. Syst. **43**(9), 267 (2019). https://doi.org/10.1007/s10916-019-1454-6
11. Mohareri, O., Soroushmehr, S.M.R.: Integration of thermal imaging system with PACS for predictive diagnosis of diabetic foot ulcers. J. Med. Syst. **42**(10), 196 (2018). https://doi.org/10.1007/s10916-018-1056-3
12. Mostafa, H.: Integration of Infrared Thermal Imaging with PACS in a teleradiology system. Int. J. Adv. Comput. Sci. Appl. **8**(2), 301–307 (2017). https://doi.org/10.14569/IJACSA.2017.080246
13. Siddiqui, J.A., Yasin, M.: Integration of thermal imaging in healthcare information system: a standardized approach. Int. J. E-Health Med. Commun. **7**(1), 1–15 (2016). https://doi.org/10.4018/IJEHMC.2016010101
14. Abdollahpour, I., Kharrazi, H.: Integrating thermography images with EHR systems for improving screening and diagnosis of vascular diseases: challenges and opportunities. Int. J. Telemed. Appl. 247381 (2015). https://doi.org/10.1155/2015/247381

15. Vardasca, T., Martins, H.M., Vardasca, R., Gabriel, J.: Integrating medical thermography on a RIS using DICOM standard. In: proceedings of the XII Congress of the European Association of Thermology as Appendix, vol. 1, pp. 79–81 (2012)
16. Vardasca, R., Bento, F., Tereso, M., Martinho, D.: Infrared thermal imaging: a dataset definition towards decision making and intelligence. In: Proceedings of the 16th Quantitative InfraRed Thermography conference (QIRT2022), (2022). https://doi.org/10.21611/qirt.2022.3026
17. Mildenberger, P., Eichelberg, M., Martin, E.: Introduction to the DICOM standard. Eur. Radiol. **12**, 920–927 (2002)
18. Bidgood, W.D., Horii, S.C.: Modular extension of the ACR-NEMA DICOM standard to support new diagnostic imaging modalities and services. J. Digit. Imaging **9**, 67–77 (1996)
19. Schaefer, G., Huguet, J., Zhu, S.Y., Plassmann, P., Ring, F.: Adopting the DICOM standard for medical infrared images. In: 2006 IEEE International Conference of the IEEE Engineering in Medicine and Biology Society, pp. 236–239 (2006)

A Fleet Allocation with Analytic Network Process and Time Dependent Variables

Hector Borcoski, Alexis Olmedo-Navarro[✉], Luis Amigo, Javiera Jofré, Gustavo Gatica, and Jairo Coronado-Hernandez

Faculty of Engineering, Universidad Andres Bello, Santiago, Chile
{aolmedo,luis.amigo,javiera.jofre,ggatica}@unab.cl

Abstract. A solution model to the fleet allocation problem is presented, which must attend to all customers as a methodological basis the Analytical Hierarchical Process (AHP) and the Analytical Network Process (ANP). In addition, temporal considerations of the variables coming from the traffic routes used are incorporated. As a result, a simplified proposal is generated for the assignment of values from Thomas Saaty's ratio scale to paired and reciprocal comparisons, through Assignment, Intermediate Values and Evaluation Tables. In addition, a set of alternatives from customers to dispatch schedules and from drivers to customers is proposed.

Keywords: Analytical Hierarchical AHP Process · Analytical Network Process ANP · Allocation · Transportation · Logistics

1 Introduction

Distribution logistics is faced every day with the need to decide how best to meet the delivery of products to customers with a limited number of resources. In particular, human and transportation resources, the emerging complexities of time are added. The primary goal of every organization is to maximize profits, take the largest share of the market or provide the best possible service. To implement this goal, organizations must have unique resources, i.e., human resources [13]. Even if there is a wide range of software that help to solve the best route allocation and "last mile" service, they do not consider non-quantitative or hardly measurable variables, Jansen, G. R. M., & Den Adel, D. N. [14] found that qualitative factors do influence the route choice of automobile drivers on work trips, for the authors, the two conventional variables travel time and distance are the most important; however, factors such as safety, effort (comfort) and scenery were also frequently mentioned. On the other hand, the formulations that contribute to solve the pains by incorporating qualitative variables supported by methodologies such as the Analytic Hierarchy Process (AHP) or the Analytic Network Process (ANP), do not always include time- dependent variables. Therefore, a model is proposed that includes both quantitative and qualitative variables relevant to distribution logistics planning. The contribution resides in capturing the behavior of the variables, but fundamentally it takes care of the behavior of these variables depending on the time of day when the dispatch is carried out.

© The Author(s), under exclusive license to Springer Nature Switzerland AG 2024
T. Guarda et al. (Eds.): ARTIIS 2023, CCIS 1935, pp. 76–87, 2024.
https://doi.org/10.1007/978-3-031-48858-0_7

Thus, it is possible to solve with AHP and ANP not only the sequence of dispatch fulfillment to each customer during the day, but also to assign the most appropriate driver to each dispatch. Then, the greatest benefit for the company and the best service to its customers are made compatible.

In the following section, bibliographic background is presented to understand the AHP and ANP methodologies. The third section presents the proposed methodology, the fourth section presents the results obtained and the fifth section presents some emerging conclusions.

2 Background

The AHP model is based on the proposed alternative selection model developed by Thomas Saaty in the 1980s. Thus, a new variant known as ANP is generated [7, 15]. Both methodologies are used in this work.

2.1 Analytic Hierarchy Process (AHP) Methodology

The AHP method allows optimizing decision making based on the hierarchization of a process by evaluating different criteria or decision variables. The AHP methodology [1] is a powerful and flexible multi-critier decision making tool, used in problems in which both qualitative and quantitative aspects need to be evaluated. The AHP technique helps analysts to organize the critical aspects of a problem in a hierarchical structure similar to the structure of a tree. In this way, complex decisions are reduced to a series of comparisons that allow the hierarchization of the different aspects (criteria) evaluated [2].

The four axioms of AHP defined by Saaty are:

Axiom No. 1: Referring to the condition of reciprocal judgments: If A is a matrix of paired comparisons, the intensity of preference of Ai/Aj is inverse to the preference of Aj/Ai.
Axiom No. 2: Referring to the condition of homogeneity of the elements: Elements are compared with the same order of magnitude or hierarchy.
Axiom No. 3: Referring to the condition of hierarchical structure or dependent structure: There is hierarchical dependence in the elements of two consecutive levels.
Axiom No. 4: Referring to the rank order expectations condition: Expectations must be represented in the structure in terms of criteria and alternatives [3].

The hierarchical analysis process proposes to execute the following steps:

a) Define the decision criteria in the form of hierarchical objectives. The hierarchy is structured in different levels: it starts at the top with the definition of the main objective of the hierarchy process, then the intermediate levels are defined (Criteria and Subcriteria to be evaluated) and finally, at the lowest level, the alternatives to be compared are described.
b) Evaluate (weigh) the different criteria, sub-criteria and alternatives according to their corresponding importance at each level. Qualitative and quantitative criteria can be compared using informal judgments to obtain weights and priorities. For qualitative

criteria, the AHP technique uses simple pairwise comparisons to determine weights and evaluate them. Thus, the analyst can concentrate on only two criteria at a time. In fact, the AHP technique is based on the assumption that the analyst (decision maker) can more easily choose a comparison value than an absolute value [2]. The above, leads to calculate weights or weights from comparisons or pairwise comparison. The evaluations of the comparisons, supported by the application of expert judgment, leads us to the respective eigenvectors of the matrices formed by the components of the matrix or eigenvector to finally go through the review of the consistency of the results or consistency [9]

In the Analytical Hierarchical Process (AHP) model, the hierarchical formulation is linear, leaving the goal at the top of the hierarchy, followed by the criteria, the sub-criteria, and then the alternatives at the lowest level.

2.2 Analytic Network Process (ANP) Methodology

Based on the AHP model, the Analytic Network Process (ANP) formulation was developed, which is a generalization of AHP and considers the dependence between the elements of the defined hierarchy. The ANP has as its base structure an influence network of clusters and variables or nodes contained within the clusters. Here "not only the importance of the main criterion determines the importance of the alternatives as in a hierarchy, but also the importance of the alternatives themselves determine the importance of the main criterion" [7, 15]. Meanwhile, in ANP, unlike in AHP, the scheme is presented more as a network than as a top-down hierarchy with cycles that connect its components and each component with itself, collecting the multiple relationships established between all the elements of the network, to establish the weight of these interrelationships in order to define the prioritization of the alternatives proposed. When using ANP, the weights assigned to each element of what Saaty calls the Supermatrix (there is one with and another without associated weights) of a Network or Supermatrix of a Network, which incorporates the comparisons between pairs of elements or pairwise comparison, extended to the relationships of both the clusters generated, the nodes they contain and the alternatives considered [5]. The last aspect to consider will be the incorporation of temporal aspects which allows us to generate a formulation of dynamic decisions, which can be addressed structurally by including scenarios and time periods as elements of the structure of a decision or functionally by directly involving time in the judgment element. A third possibility would be a hybrid between the first two proposals [8].

All the above leads to the calculation of the weights or weightings w_{ij}^{t} from paired comparisons, identifying the subscripts i, j to the compared elements and the superscript t to the period considered. The evaluations of the comparisons, supported by the application of expert judgment, lead to the respective eigenvectors of the matrices formed by their eigenvectors to finally go through the review of the consistency of the results (consistency). These eigenvectors then become the prioritizations of the alternatives considered [9].

3 Material and Methods

A methodological proposal is formulated in which the dispatch period is divided into "k" semi-homogeneous sub-periods in terms of the characteristics of the circulation conditions of the dispatch trucks. For each of these "k" periods, the sequence of customer priorities that could be served is determined. It uses the ANP model developed by Saaty [7, 15], with the support of the Super Decisions softwareTM. A General Objective is defined, which guides the assignment of weights in the ANP model. For each comparison table between nodes, it is also required that the matrix has an Inconsistency Index lower than 0.1 [7, 15].

Each of the "k" periods considered delivers results under the conventional BOCR (benefits, opportunities, costs and risks) criteria in these cases. An n x 4 matrix is obtained, with n the number of clients to be served and 4 four BOCR sub criteria [7, 15], the internal values of the matrix being the normalized prioritizations of each client in each period.

For the application of the ANP method, weights are defined from which Unweighted Super Matrix and Weighted Super Matrix are obtained [7, 15].

To facilitate the assignment of weights when comparing alternatives with respect to each of the nodes of the ANP structure, the model proposes the construction of Assignment Tables (AT). Then, for each node within a cluster, categorizations or states are defined, which can be quantitative or qualitative. Then, each of these categorizations or states, repeated for each BOCR sub criterion, is assigned a valuation within a closed set of integer values [9, −9].

The highest value of the adopted set is assigned to the category or state that is best oriented to achieve the General Objective of the evaluation, while the lowest value is assigned to the category or state that contributes least to the objective or is furthest away from it.

The breadth of the set of values adopted for each BOCR sub-criterion will reflect the incidence or weight of this sub-criterion within the node, in relation to its influence on the achievement of the Objective (Table 1).

Table 1. Assignment table model.

	BOCR Criteria			
Range	Benefit	Cost	Risk	Opportunities
Range 1	9	9	9	−9
Range 2	4	6	5	−7
Range 3	2	−2	2	2
Range 4	−3	−4	−5	6
Range 5	−9	−8	−8	8

For the application of the pairwise comparison between nodes and between clusters, a collective work of a group of experts must be used [7, 15], from which the values are assigned during the construction of the Assignment Tables (AT). Subsequently, based on the categories defined in the TA, the Tables of Intermediate Values (TVI) are generated, defined as the evaluation of each node contained in each cluster in relation to each of the alternatives contained in the cluster of Alternatives.

The process is repeated for each defined "k" period and within this in turn for each of the BOCR sub-criteria.

Thus, according to the example of the above TA model, if, when comparing with respect to the Node, one alternative is in Rank 1 and the other in Rank 4 in the sub-criterion Benefit, the former will take a value of 9 and the latter a value of −3.

To determine the values to be entered in the pairwise comparison tables of the Super Decisions software, the TVI values of each node are subtracted from the TVI value of the compared node, dividing the result by two, thus obtaining the Evaluation Tables (ET). Thus, for example, two nodes that are in the opposite extremes in the TVI when compared in relation to a given criterion, the value that will appear in the respective TE and will be entered into the software is given by:

$$(9 - (-9))/2 = 9 \tag{1}$$

A positive result in the TE means that the absolute value of the result must be associated to the node located in the column of the comparison matrix, a negative result means that the absolute value of the result must be associated to the node located in the row of the comparison matrix. This process is developed for each period "k", a normalized matrix of priorities of "n" × 4 is obtained for each of them, with "n" the number of alternatives and 4 the BOCR sub criteria. The structure of the matrix is described in Table 2.

Table 2. Matrix of alternatives priorities by period with BOCR sub criteria

	Period 1			
	Benefit	Cost	Risk	Opportunities
	Normalized by Cluster			
Alternative 1	0,15556	0,12973	0,10896	0,24129
Alternative 2	0,31498	0,10003	0,16985	0,26721
Alternative 3	0,19426	0,24313	0,26367	0,12349
....	0,17208	0,25722	0,26681	0,26570
Alternative n	0,16313	0,26989	0,19070	0,10231

On the other hand, the BOCR subcriteria are subjected to a pairwise comparison process, which determines the normalized weights for each of them.

The weights are used to weight each value of the "n" × 4 matrix of priorities, resulting in a vector of "n" × 1 which is finally normalized. Thus, it constitutes the final prioritization result for that given period.

Each one of these results is taken to a summary matrix of dimension "n" × "k".

Each of the values of this "n" × "k" matrix represents a valuation in each client of the best way to assign them by period and of their proximity to the fulfillment of the

General Objective, for which reason the criterion is adopted that maximizing the sum of values will provide a good approximation to the best distribution of clients by period of the day. The matrix "n" × "k" is described in Table 3.

Table 3. Matrix of alternatives priorities by period of the day

	Schedule 1	Schedule 2	....	Schedule k
Alternative 1	0,158	0,157	....	0,231
Alternative 2	0,235	0,265	....	0,241
Alternative 3	0,204	0,179	....	0,180
....	0,223	0,190	....	0,165
Alternative n	0,181	0,209	....	0,182

The maximization must be subject to three constraints, as follows:

1. Provide a transportation service to each customer (meet all customers).

$$\forall\, Customer_i \,\exists\, Period_j \tag{2}$$

2. Use all periods of the day with at least one dispatch (avoid idle dispatch resource):

$$\forall\, Period_i \,\exists\, Customer_j \tag{3}$$

3. Have a maximum number of dispatches in a period (avoid congestion at the dispatch point):

$$\exists\, t \in \aleph : \forall\, Period_j, \sum_1^n Customer \leq t \tag{4}$$

For the last maximization, the nonlinear generalized reduced gradient algorithm provided by the Excel Solver add-in is used. The result is the schedules in which the loads will be dispatched to each of the customers considered.

The second stage of the model consists of assigning the best distribution of available drivers to each office. To reach this result, the AHP model [6] is used to determine the weights that define the preferences for each driver. They are obtained by considering as the main objective of the ranking process the definition of the best driver under considerations of driving characteristics, driver experience and customer treatment [10]. It is considered to use the AHP model in this case due to its greater simplicity and given that the characteristics considered in the evaluation nodes do not present major interdependencies that suggest the convenience of using an ANP model.

For the generation of the pairwise comparison matrices, as in the case of the first stage of the model, we resort to the support of the Allocation Tables (AT) and the Intermediate Value Tables (TVI).

After having the normalized vector of weights that represents the ranking between them, we proceed to associate each driver to each customer dispatch.

To determine this association, we first construct a matrix of $n_d \times n_c$ given by the multiplication of the vector of dimension $1 \times n_c$. The latter contains the weights obtained for each customer/alternative in the schedule assigned in the prioritization stage developed with ANP, and the normalized vector of weights of the drivers with dimension $n_d \times 1$ obtained with AHP.

Thus, each customer weighting is multiplied by the respective priority weight of each driver, which then determines the maximum value for the sum of the matrix values that meets the constraints of:

1. That all drivers perform a dispatch.

$$\forall \, Customer_i \, \exists \, Period_j \tag{5}$$

2. Each client is served by a single office/driver:

$$\forall \, Period_i \, \exists \, Customer_j x \tag{6}$$

Then for the maximization of the result, we resort to the nonlinear generalized reduced gradient algorithm provided by the Excel Solver add-in.

4 Results

The model was implemented in a chemical company located in the city of Santiago de Chile, which daily supplies a group of customers with its own fleet of trucks, which has a group of drivers from the same company. The company receives daily sales requests with established dispatch dates in the respective sales notes and must tend to prioritize shipments to the most important customers. Customers are evaluated according to their economic contribution to the company by balancing the costs generated in transportation and the quality of service provided.

For the development of this case study, a fleet of 5 trucks with a capacity of less than 15 tons will be considered. The day is divided into four homogeneous periods in terms of customer requirements and circulation characteristics of the routes, previously defined for each origin-destination pair (plant-customer). Each route has a duration of 2 h, starting at 08:00 h. For each day considered, there are as many delivery trucks as customers to be served. In each hourly period the company can dispatch a maximum of two trucks, given that loading and dispatch times are a little less than 1 h. All customers must be served by only one truck and each truck supplies only one customer, due to the type of products transported.

The General Objective defined is to seek the best benefit for the company with the best service to customers. To represent the case study, the following ANP model is shown in which three clusters are defined. All nodes of the Route cluster were already defined in previous studies [10], while the nodes of the Customer cluster were defined through an evaluation team using expert criteria. The alternatives represent a group of companies to be served (Fig. 1).

Four periods are defined in which dispatches are made to customers, the first from 8:00 to 10:00; the second from 10:01 to 12:00; the third from 12:01 to 14:00 and the

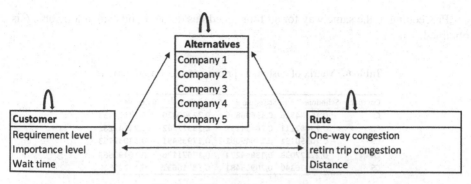

Fig. 1. ANP model for case study

Table 4. Assignment table for case study

	BOCR Criteria			
	Benefit	Cost	Risk	Opportunities
0−5 km	9	9	9	−9
5−10 km	4	6	5	−7
10−50 km		−2	2	2
50−100 km		−4	−5	6
100−n Km	−9	−8	−8	8

fourth from 14:01 to 16:00. For each period, the assignment prioritizations for each customer, as described in Table 4, must be established.

From Table 4, the intermediate values (TVI) are constructed, which allow the evaluation within the sub-criterion Benefit between the alternative of E1 and E4, then for each defined schedule the evaluations are made in each of the BOCR sub-criteria. The normalized weightings of the BOCR sub-criteria are used to weight the values of each customer in each schedule and thus, the priorities for the case study are obtained according to Table 5

Table 5. Costumer's priorities

Company	Benefit Normalized by cluster	Benefit Limiting	Cost Normalized by cluster	Cost Limiting	Risk Normalized by cluster	Risk Limiting	Opportunities Normalized by cluster	Opportunities Limiting	Normalized weights
C1	0,15556	0,02517	0,12973	0,01324	0,10896	0,00958	0,24129	0,01567	0,158
C2	0,31498	0,05096	0,10003	0,01021	0,16985	0,01494	0,26721	0,01735	0,235
C3	0,19426	0,03143	0,24313	0,02481	0,26367	0,02319	0,12349	0,00802	0,204
C4	0,17208	0,02784	0,25722	0,02625	0,26681	0,02347	0,26570	0,01725	0,223
C5	0,16313	0,02639	0,26989	0,02754	0,19070	0,01677	0,10231	0,00664	0,181
									1,000

Proceeding in the same way for all four schedules defined, the evaluation Table 6 is obtained.

Table 6. Matrix of customers priority results for all periods

Company	Schedule 1	Schedule 2	Schedule 3	Schedule 4
C1	0,15784326	0,15696896	0,22299420	0,23107433
C2	0,23482111	0,26484297	0,23527282	0,24142282
C3	0,20350191	0,17949051	0,17985491	0,18037753
C4	0,22327033	0,18964274	0,17671176	0,16490663
C5	0,18056340	0,20905481	0,18516631	0,18221869

Finally, we seek to maximize the sum of the values of the matrix that respect the defined restrictions, i.e., all customers must be served by a single truck and each truck only supplies a single customer. By applying the Solver™ add-in of Excel™, a matrix of binary values is obtained, a result that delivers the following customer dispatch assignment per schedule and the following priority values described in Table 7 (Table 8).

Table 7. Weights and priorities by schedule

Schedule 1	Schedule 2	Schedule 3	Schedule 4
0,223270326	0,26484297 0,20905481	0,17985491	0,231074329

Table 8. Customers allocation per period

Schedule 1	Schedule 2	Schedule 3	Schedule 4
C4	C2 C5	C3	C1

For the second stage of the proposed model, it is oriented to prioritize the drivers who will attend the day's dispatches through an AHP model [3]. Three clusters are defined, one for each alternative, one that includes driving characteristics and one associated with driver characteristics.

The General Objective of the stage is to assign a driver to each office to seek the greatest satisfaction of each client and the best benefit for the company (Fig. 2).

In order to assign each driver to the customer he will serve, a 5×5 matrix is generated in this case $n_d \times n_c$) formed by weighting the values of the priorities of the customers by the priorities of the drivers. Then, using the Solver™ add-in of Excel™, the sum of their products is maximized, which then becomes the objective function. This is possible given that each of these values is directly associated to the achievement of the General

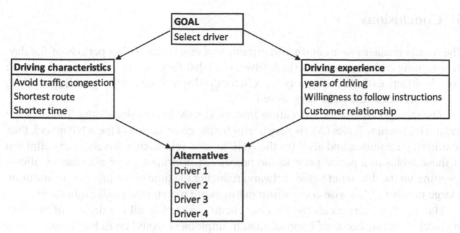

Fig. 2. AHP model for case study, driver assignment

Objective of the evaluation and that its approach to it is sized through how high its value is.

The 5 × 5 weighted value matrix is described in Table 9.

Table 9. Customers and drivers priority weights

	C4	C2	C5	C3	C1
Driver 1	0,06461	0,07664	0,06050	0,05205	0,06687
Driver 2	0,01592	0,01889	0,01491	0,01283	0,01648
Driver 3	0,05130	0,06086	0,04804	0,04133	0,05310
Driver 4	0,05275	0,06257	0,04939	0,04249	0,05459
Driver 5	0,03869	0,04589	0,03622	0,03116	0,04004

Consequently, the final allocation of customers served in each schedule of the day and with the assignment of drivers to serve each customer would be as follows at Table 10.

Table 10. Final results for client - driver - schedule assignment

		Customer	Driver
Schedule 1	08:00-10:00	C4	Driver 3
Schedule 2	10:01-12:00	C2	Driver 1
		C5	Driver 5
Schedule 3	12:01-14:00	C3	Driver 2
Schedule 4	14:01-16:00	C1	Driver 4

5 Conclusions

The model manages to establish a distribution of customers within periods of the day, by assigning each customer a certain driver, both distributions are oriented to obtain the overall objective of achieving the best profit for the dispatching company while providing the best service to the customers served.

The incorporation of the Allocation Tables (AT), the Intermediate Value Tables (TVI) and the Evaluation Tables (AT) is very useful for the construction of the ANP model, thus prioritizing customers and also, for the AHP model, prioritizing drivers. The definition of these tables in a period prior to the process of prioritization of alternatives allows speeding up the data input to the software, reducing the time of the process. In addition, a large number of pairwise comparison matrices are maintained in all evaluations.

Having characterized all the feasible clients, as well as all the drivers of the fleet in Excel™ spreadsheets, an improvement to implement would be to build macros that calculate the Evaluation Tables and a program that automatically incorporates the values determined in the Evaluation Tables into the Super Decision™ software.

References

1. Saaty, T.: How to make a decision: the analytic hierarchy process. Europ. J. Oper. Res. **48**, 9–26 (1990)
2. Taoufikallah, A.: El Método AHP, Capítulo 4. Universidad de Sevilla, Escuela Técnica Superior de Ingenieros de Sevilla (2012)
3. Saaty, R.W.: The analytic hierarchy process-what it is and how it is used. Mat/d Model. **9**(3–5), 161–176. Printed in Great Britain (1987)
4. Saaty, T.L., Vargas, L.G.: Models, Methods, Concepts and Applications of the Analytic Hierarchy Process. Kluwer, Dordrecht (2001)
5. Saaty, S.: Decision making in complex environments. In: The Analytic Network Process (ANP) for Dependence and Feedback. Creative Decisions Foundation 4922 Ellsworth Avenue Pittsburgh, PA 15213. Chap.3 (80–82) (2016)
6. Saaty, T.: The Analytic Hierarchy Process. McGraw-Hill, New York (1980)
7. Saaty, T., Vargas, L.G.: Decision Making with the Analytic Network Process: Economic, Political, Social and Technological Applications with Benefits, Opportunities, Costs and Risks. Springer; Softcover reprint of hardcover 1st ed. 2006 edition (28 December 2009) (2006)
8. Saaty, T.: Time Dependent Decision-Making; Dynamic Priorities in the AHP/ANP: Generalizing from points to Functions and from Real to Complex Variables. University of Pittsburgh, Pittsburgh, PA 15260, United States. Elsevier Ltd. (2007)
9. Saaty, T.: Decision making for leaders. The Analytic Hierarchy Process for decision in a complex world, New Edition. University of Pittsburgh, 322 Mervis Hall Pittsburgh. RWS Publications, 4922 Ellsworth Avenue, Pittsburgh, PA 15213 (2012)
10. Yang, Y., Ruan, J., Li, J., Liu, B., Kong, X.: Route choice behavior model with guidance information based on fuzzy analytic hierarchy process. Int. J. Innov. Comput. Inf. Control, **14**(1) (2018)
11. Kadoic, N., Begicevic, N., et al.: Decision making with Analytic Network Process (2017). www.semanticscholar.org
12. Saaty, T.L.: Theory and Applications of the Analytic Network Process. Pittsburgh, PA: RWS Publications, 4922 Ellsworth Avenue, Pittsburgh, PA 15213 (2005)

13. Čižiūnienė, K., Vaičiūtė, K., Batarlienė, N.: Research on competencies of human resources in transport sector: lithuanian case study. Procedia Eng. **134**, 336–343 (2016)
14. Jansen, G.R.M., Den Adel, D.N.: Car drivers route choice: an investigation into qualitative choice factors. Rapport Instituut voor Stedebouwkundig Onderzoek, (59) (1986)
15. Saaty, T.L., Vargas, L.G.: Decision Making with the Analytic Network Process, vol. 282. Berlin, Germany: Springer Science+ Business Media, LLC (2006)
16. Borcoski, E.: Propuesta etodológica para asignación de transportes utilizando proceso análítico en red (ANP) y jeráquico (AHP) con variables dependientes del tiempo. Tesis Magíster en Ingeniería Industrial, UNAB (2019)

alBERTUM: A Portuguese Search Engine for Scientific and Academic Language

Sílvia Araújo⑩, Micaela Aguiar(✉) ⑩, and José Monteiro

University of Minho, Rua da Universidade, Braga, Portugal
saraujo@elach.uminho.pt, maguiar60@gmail.com

Abstract. alBERTUM is a Portuguese search engine designed for scientific and academic language. This paper provides an overview of alBERTUM's data sources, model, architecture, and two core functions. The search engine uses a vast collection of scientific open data available in national repositories to provide bilingual terminology searches and offer a Portuguese academic writing assistant. Utilizing the deep learning model BERT, alBERTUM converts the available data and user queries into semantic vectors, enabling semantic searches for precise and contextually relevant results. The bilingual terminology search function is particularly valuable for professionals, researchers, and those working in fields that require cross-linguistic understanding, such as translation studies, linguistics, or international business. alBERTUM identifies translation equivalents in scientific documents that are not translations of each other. The academic writing assistant function seamlessly incorporates an European Portuguese academic phrase bank, which has also been developed by our team, into the search engine architecture. This integration empowers users, particularly students with limited academic vocabulary, to search for academic expressions based on their intended communicative function. The assistant not only provides contextual examples but also shows the communicative functions of these expressions, enhancing users' understanding of their usage within an academic setting.

Keywords: BERT · Open Scientific Data · Academic Writing · Information Retrieval

1 Introduction

In the fast-paced 21st century, the expansion of knowledge has outpaced the production of any tangible goods by human beings [1]. This exponential growth can be witnessed through the staggering volume of scientific articles being published annually [2], with an estimated count of 1.8 million articles in approximately 28,000 journals [3]. Price's [4] postulation in the 1960s that suggests science undergoes exponential growth, doubling in size every 10 to 15 years, is supported by recent research conducted by Bornmann, Haunschild, and Mutz [5], who found evidence indicating a growth rate of 4.10% and a doubling time of 17.3 years. In the age of Big Data and the emergence of Artificial Intelligence (AI), Price's [6] observation that "the bigger a thing is, the faster it grows" gains

T. Guarda et al. (Eds.): ARTIIS 2023, CCIS 1935, pp. 88–102, 2024.
https://doi.org/10.1007/978-3-031-48858-0_8

heightened relevance as these transformative phenomena has the potential to reshape the landscape of knowledge expansion [7]. The growth of scientific knowledge is influenced by two other crucial factors as well. Firstly, society's prevailing inclination towards specialization is also observed within scientific research [8, 9]. Secondly, there has been a substantial rise in the number of individuals with access to higher education. In fact, a recent report by UNESCO IESALC [10] highlights that over the past two decades, the percentage of people with access to higher education has soared from 19% to an impressive 38%.

From this context, three interconnected issues arise. To begin with, the research power of universities greatly outweighs their abilities (or endeavors) to adequately communicate and disseminate the knowledge they generate. Cribb & Sari [1] further highlight that approximately half of all scientific articles produced worldwide remain unread beyond their authors, editors, and reviewers, with 90% of these articles never being cited. There exists a wealth of scientific data that is being overlooked and not effectively utilized.

Secondly, the increasing specialization in various fields leads to the emergence of diverse specialized languages, as noted by Gil [11]. The concept of specialized language, also known as special language, language for special purposes, or language for specific purposes (among others), eludes a unique definition, but can be described as a language with specific features developed in response to the communicative needs of speakers, within a given area of expertise [12]. According to Gil [11], it becomes imperative to document, standardize, and inventory the new lexical units that arise from rapid scientific and technical progress. In contrast, there exists a convergence or standardization concerning the language that predominates in scientific discourse. A significant proportion of scientific texts are written in English, and there is a prevailing tendency to view it as the language universally adopted in scientific research [13]. The predominance of English in scientific investment policies, where preference is given to journals primarily published in English and indexed in Scopus and Web of Science, along with the prevalence of English in research project funding processes and scientific events [14], plays a pivotal role in consolidating its dominant position. As a means to foster multilingualism in science communication, some [15] have put forward the idea that scientific journals should provide translations of the articles they publish. It is difficult, expensive and time-consuming to translate scientific texts, and when translations do exist, they are often of poor quality.

Thirdly, in academic settings, students encounter difficulties in writing [16] due to the limited explicit teaching of academic literacy, while educational institutions struggle to adapt to changing demographics, linguistic diversity, and an increased enrollment of students in postgraduate and doctoral programs [17]. The inadequate development of academic literacy further compounds existing inequalities, as it is crucial for students to possess the necessary communication skills to fully engage and become members of the academic and scientific community [18].

The PortLinguE project endeavors to make a meaningful contribution towards tackling these issues. The PortLinguE project, funded by European funds, is an initiative led by the Digital Humanities Group of the Center for Humanistic Studies at the University of Minho. This interdisciplinary endeavor involves collaboration between ELACH and the School of Engineering, specifically the Department of Informatics and the Department of

Electronic Engineering. Through a dynamic and productive interdisciplinary dialogue, the project incorporates various fields such as Natural Language Processing, Machine Learning, Artificial Intelligence, Statistics, Corpus Linguistics, and Lexicography.

The project encompasses a set of core objectives. Firstly, it aims to foster multi-lingualism within the academic and scientific realms, with a particular emphasis on promoting Portuguese as a language of science. Secondly, it endeavors to harness the potential of open scientific data sourced from national repositories. Lastly, the project aims to develop resources for specialized languages in multilingual environments, as well as support tools for enhancing academic literacy, especially in higher education settings.

As part of this project, various resources are being actively developed to provide support for specialized languages and academic discourse. One such resource is a platform under development, enabling the visualization of hierarchical concept structures within specialized domains [19], accompanied by corresponding glossary terminology [20]. This platform will incorporate multimodal content, including videos, images, and recordings. Another noteworthy endeavor is the development of a comprehensive seven-step method for effectively navigating academic work, which will be made available online [21]. Each step will be accompanied by informative and complementary content, providing valuable guidance and assistance throughout the academic journey. However, the cornerstone of this project is the development of a dedicated search engine named alBERTUM, a search engine designed to cater to the needs of specialized languages and academic discourse. In this article, we will delve into the process of its creation, offering a detailed insight into the features and functionalities of this search engine.

In the following sections, we will take a comprehensive look at the engine's data sources, the language model powering its operations, the overarching architecture that supports its functionalities, and its two primary features: the bilingual terminology search and the Portuguese academic writing assistant. By exploring these aspects, we aim to provide an overall understanding of the engine's capabilities and its contributions to the field.

2 Data

The search engine's data is sourced from the well-established consolidated knowledge management infrastructure in Portugal, the Scientific Open Access Repository of Portugal (RCAAP) [22]. The RCAAP (Repositório Científico de Acesso Aberto de Portugal) portal, developed by FCCN (Fundação para a Computação Científica Nacional), serves as a comprehensive platform for collecting, aggregating, and indexing Open Access scientific content from various institutional repositories in Portugal. This portal grants access to an extensive collection of hundreds of thousands of scientific documents, encompassing a wide range of scholarly works such as journal articles, conference papers, theses, and dissertations. It draws from a diverse array of 360 resources, including repositories affiliated with 69 universities and institutes across the country.

The collection of such documents represents an invaluable linguistic and discursive resource. It offers not only access to a diverse range of academic genres, each with its distinct characteristics, but also provides a gateway to the specialized terminology prevalent in various domains of expertise. Therefore, this source not only aids in the exploration of language in academic contexts but also provides insights into specialized languages across different domains.

Despite the widespread availability of these documents in open access, their reliance on the PDF format presents inherent challenges for text processing and analysis. The format and structure of PDF files, while convenient for visual representation and preserving document integrity, are not inherently designed for seamless extraction and manipulation of textual content. This poses obstacles when it comes to utilizing these valuable resources for linguistic research, natural language processing, and other computational analyses. Recognizing the importance of maximizing the usability and potential of this vast resource, our search engine aims to harness and repurpose these open access scientific texts and the untapped linguistic wealth they hold.

The bilingual function utilized the British Library EThOS. The British Library EThOS serves as the national thesis service in the UK, aiming to increase the visibility and availability of doctoral research theses. It provides a centralized record of all UK doctoral theses and offers free access to as many full-text theses as possible. EThOS holds around 500,000 thesis records from over 120 institutions, with approximately 260,000 of them allowing access to the full text either through EThOS or the institution's own repository.

Wikipedia has been utilized to enhance the sources for both languages. Wikipedia is a valuable resource for specialized languages due to its comprehensive coverage and multilingual support. With a vast array of articles, it encompasses niche and specific subjects that may not be extensively covered elsewhere. The community-driven editing process ensures that specialized content is reviewed and improved by a diverse group of contributors. Additionally, the inclusion of citations and references to reliable sources enhances the credibility of the information provided.

3 Model

The BERT (Bidirectional Encoder Representations from Transformers) [23] language model serves as the driving force behind the search engine's functionality. BERT, created by Google's AI team, demonstrates extraordinary proficiency in a wide range of language processing tasks, encompassing question answering, abstract summarization, sentence prediction, and conversational response generation. Similar to how humans struggle to recall information from distant past events, earlier models like recurrent neural networks (RNNs) encountered difficulties in retaining context from previous timesteps. However, the introduction of attention mechanisms [24] revolutionized this issue by enabling simultaneous observation of all words in a sentence and learning to emphasize the relevant ones based on the specific task. Transformers [25] excel in this regard by processing sentences bidirectionally, capturing information from both directions simultaneously. This bidirectionality empowers the models to efficiently train with extensive data and generate robust pre-trained models, like BERT.

BERT's impressive capabilities are attained through its training objectives, namely masked language modeling and next sentence prediction [26]. By training on these objectives, BERT is more likely to consider context which allows it to perform semantic searches. Unlike traditional keyword-based searches, semantic searches aim to decipher the underlying intent and contextual meaning behind the words used in a person's query. BERT employs a transformative approach to convert sentences into semantic vectors, enabling effective semantic searches [27]. To transform sentences into semantic vectors, BERT follows a two-step process [28]. First, the input sentence is tokenized into subword units, which include words and subword pieces. These tokens are then fed into the BERT model, which consists of multiple layers of self-attention and feed-forward neural networks. The attention mechanisms play a crucial role in capturing the dependencies between words and their contextual significance. BERT incorporates contextualized word embeddings, meaning that the vector representation of a word is influenced by its surrounding context in the sentence. Unlike traditional word embedding models that assign a fixed vector representation to each word, BERT's contextualized embeddings adapt to the specific context in which the word appears [29]. This contextualization allows BERT to capture the nuances and variations in word meanings based on their usage within different sentences.

Semantic search plays a pivotal role in our engine, particularly in the context of the academic writing assistant function. This function is designed to cater to users who may not be proficient in academic language, yet need to effectively communicate within the academic domain. In such cases, keyword-based searches may fall short in capturing the intended meaning and context of the user's query. It takes into account the semantic relationships between words and phrases, allowing it to identify suitable expressions and structures that align with the intended communicative function.

In our engine, we incorporated pre-trained models to support its functionalities. We utilized a Portuguese language model called Bertimbau [30] (neuralmind/bert-base-portuguese-cased). This model is trained on the Brazilian Web as Corpus [31], which comprises a vast collection of Brazilian webpages containing 2.68 billion tokens from 3.53 million documents. Although this model is based on Brazilian Portuguese, it was the most suitable option available at the time of development, considering the scarcity of dedicated models for European Portuguese [32]. While there may be a slight mismatch between the model and the specific nuances of European Portuguese, we believe that Bertimbau still provides valuable insights and language patterns that are applicable to academic and specialized contexts.

The all-mpnet-base-v2 model [33] was employed for the English language task. This model facilitates the mapping of sentences and paragraphs to a dense vector space of 768 dimensions, enabling applications such as clustering or semantic search. The development of this model took place as part of the Hugging Face-organized Community Week, where NLP and CV techniques utilizing JAX/Flax were explored. Specifically, it was created for the project titled "Train the Best Sentence Embedding Model Ever with 1B Training Pairs." The primary objective of this project was to train sentence embedding models on large-scale datasets at the sentence level, utilizing self-supervised contrastive learning as the training objective. The microsoft/mpnet-base model served as the starting point and underwent fine-tuning using a dataset consisting of 1 billion sentence pairs.

4 Architecture

Figure 1 depicts the overarching architecture of our engine, which we will now delve into and will provide a comprehensive description.

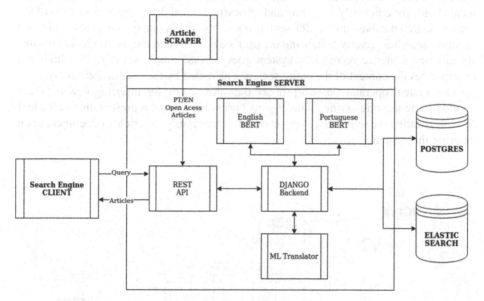

Fig. 1. An Overview of the alBERTUM's Architecture

The search engine architecture is constructed using the Django framework, a robust Python framework designed for web development. This framework offers excellent scalability and is particularly advantageous for small teams. Moreover, the extensive range of community-built packages associated with Django greatly facilitates the development process, ensuring a smoother and more efficient workflow [34]. Django serves as the backbone for connecting various components and implementing the system's logic, while the Django REST API facilitates communication between the CLIENT, SCRAPER, and the SERVER, enabling access to the different resources and functions offered. The CLIENT serves as the user-facing frontend interface, providing users with the ability to interact with the services offered by the system. It is primarily developed using REACT, a popular and widely adopted technology known for building intuitive and user-friendly interfaces.

Our system architecture utilizes a combination of Django and Docker to create and connect virtual environments, known as containers, that host different components of the system. The main container, known as the SERVER container, is responsible for hosting the majority of the system's logic. All requests and processes involving the utilization of our BERT models pass through this container. The CLIENT container serves as the gateway for users, providing access to the system's interface and redirecting user requests to the SERVER container. Another crucial component is the SCRAPER, which functions as a parallel service responsible for cycling through open access scientific articles to gather data and populate our databases. For data storage, we employ two database instances: POSTGRES [35] and ELASTIC SEARCH [36]. POSTGRES serves as a stable and reliable storage solution for storing article sentences and phrases and serves as the first stop for every document that enters our system. On the other hand, ELASTIC SEARCH is renowned for its high-speed searching capabilities, making it an ideal choice for efficiently searching and retrieving textual data. The combination of the Elastic Search database and BERT sentence vectors within our system enables fast and accurate searches, greatly enhancing the user's ability to find the most relevant results. By utilizing sentence vectors, the system goes beyond simple keyword matching and incorporates the context of the entire sentence provided by the user in their query.

Our system operates on two primary data flows: one for inserting new data and another for requesting existing data. Figure 2 provides a visual representation of the first flow, illustrating the sequential steps involved in processing an article or document upon entering the system.

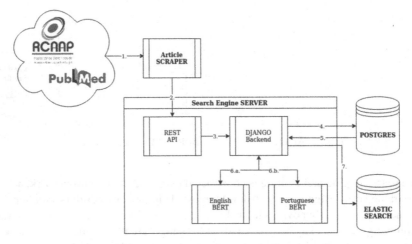

Fig. 2. Data Insertion Flow in the System

In step 1 of the data insertion flow, the SCRAPER retrieves an article from one of our trusted open access sources.

In step 2, the SCRAPER interacts with the REST API, initiating a request to insert the new document into the system.

Moving to step 3, the API directs the incoming data to the appropriate processes within the system.

In step 4, selected data from the document is stored in our POSTGRES database for future reference.

The same data is then retrieved in step 5 for further processing.

In step 6, depending on the document's language, the extracted text is passed through one of our BERT models, generating a comprehensive sentence vector that accurately captures the content and context of the document.

Finally, in step 7, the processed data is stored in our ElasticSearch database, ready to be efficiently searched and retrieved.

Figure 3 illustrates the step-by-step process followed by both users and the system to retrieve search results using our search engine.

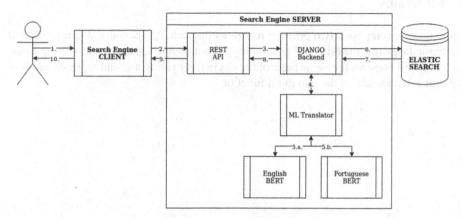

Fig. 3. Process Flow for Retrieving Search Results in the Search Engine

Here's a detailed explanation of each step:

Firstly, in step 1, users enter their search queries through our system interface, known as the CLIENT. These queries serve as the input for the search process.

Next, in step 2, the CLIENT container forwards the user's request to the SERVER using the REST API, which acts as the communication bridge between the different components of the system.

In step 3, the REST API directs the received request data to the relevant functions within the system, initiating the search process.

Based on the query language, step 4 involves our Translator recreating the query in the other language if necessary (applicable for the bilingual terminological search function). This step ensures that the search engine can handle queries in multiple languages.

In step 5, the query (the original and translated queries, for the bilingual termino-logical search function) is passed through their respective BERT models, resulting in a sentence vector.

With the sentence vectors available, step 6 involves performing a semantic search using our ElasticSearch database. This search aims to retrieve documents that align closely with the user's query, taking into account the contextual meaning of the search terms.

In steps 7, 8, and 9, the system selects the best-matching documents based on the query and specific keywords. The selected information from these documents is then forwarded back to the user, providing them with relevant search results.

Finally, in step 10, the ranked articles undergo final processing to highlight the comparable sentences requested by the user.

By following this systematic process, our search engine delivers accurate and contextually relevant search results, taking into consideration the user's query, language preferences, and the semantic meaning of their search terms.

5   Functions

Our engine encompasses two primary functions that cater to specialized languages and academic language: the bilingual terminology function and the academic writing assistant. Figure 4 presents the home page of the engine, providing a visual representation of the user interface and of the two main functions.

Fig. 4. alBERTUM's Homepage

Let's delve into each of these functions individually.

5.1   Bilingual Terminology Search

The bilingual terminological search provided by our engine is designed to assist users in finding accurate translation equivalents within the scientific domain. It currently supports two languages: Portuguese and English. This feature relies on a corpus of originally non-parallel scientific articles sourced from reputable scientific repositories. This function is particularly useful for professionals, researchers, and students working in fields that require cross-linguistic understanding, such as translation studies, linguistics, or international business.

As previously mentioned, finding aligned scientific texts and their high-quality translations can be challenging. Additionally, the increasing specialization and diversification of specialized languages presents a challenge in navigating through complex terminology manually. Our engine's semantic search capability addresses these challenges by taking context into account. By considering the context, our engine can identify comparable texts in both Portuguese and English and extract translation equivalents from them. It's important to note that the extracted equivalents are not direct translations of each other, but rather correspond to the searched term in another language. This approach ensures that the search results provide accurate and relevant translation equivalents. Furthermore, the semantic search capability of our engine proves valuable in handling the wide range of terminology encountered in scientific texts. Instead of relying solely on specific keywords, our engine looks for contextual relevance, enabling it to return more meaningful and useful results.

Figure 5 illustrates the bilingual terminology function in action.

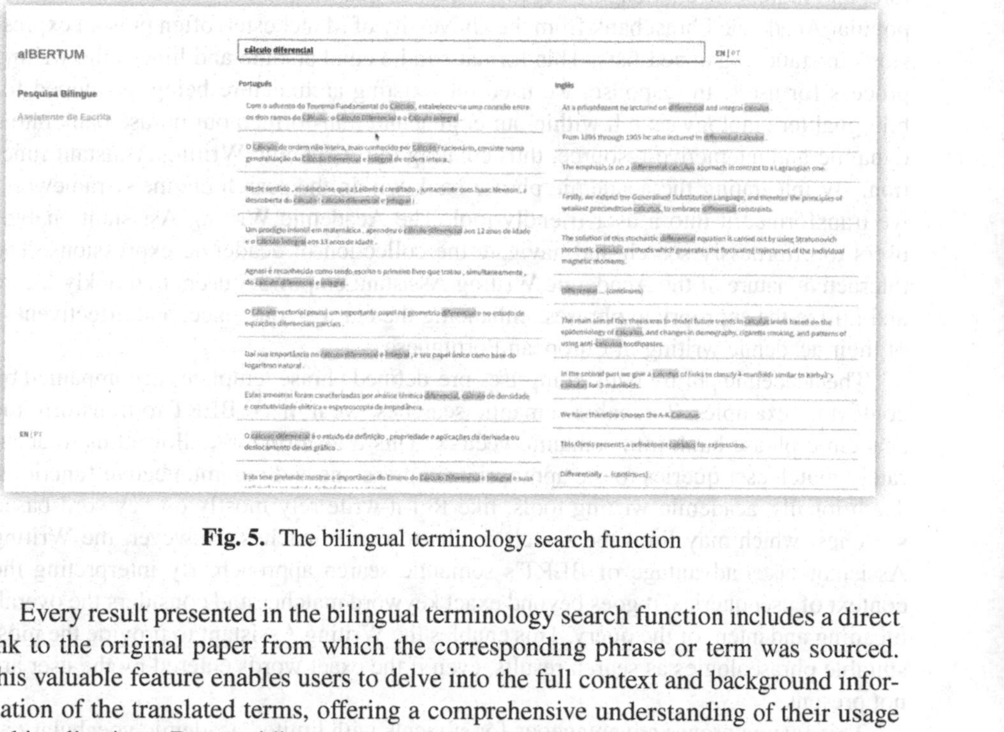

Fig. 5. The bilingual terminology search function

Every result presented in the bilingual terminology search function includes a direct link to the original paper from which the corresponding phrase or term was sourced. This valuable feature enables users to delve into the full context and background information of the translated terms, offering a comprehensive understanding of their usage and implications. By providing access to the original papers, our engine contributes to the dissemination of scientific knowledge and fosters a deeper exploration of the subject matter. Users can utilize this functionality to explore the referenced papers, gain insights from the source material, and further enhance their understanding of the terminology in its scientific context.

5.2 Academic Writing Assistant

The writing assistant function of our engine is designed to assist users in improving their academic writing. The Academic Writing Assistant is a valuable resource that emerged from the integration of two key components developed in our project: the search engine with its bilingual terminology search function and an academic phrase bank developed specifically for European Portuguese.

An academic phrase bank is a specialized resource that serves as a repository of commonly used phrases and expressions specifically designed for academic writing. It provides writers with a collection of pre-formulated language constructs that can assist in organizing thoughts, presenting arguments, and effectively conveying messages in academic contexts. To build the academic phrase bank, we built a corpus of 40 scientific articles sourced from two repositories, RepositoriUM (University of Minho) and Repositório Aberto (University of Porto). Through manual annotation, we extracted over 900 academic expressions associated with 51 distinct communicative functions. These functions encompass a wide range of writing requirements, including reporting results, indicating article structure, describing the sample, referring to consensus in the literature, and more. One challenge we recognized was that traditional phrase banks, like the popular Academic Phrasebank from the University of Manchester, often present expressions in static, organized lists. This format can be cumbersome and hinder the writing process for users. In response, we used the existing architecture being developed for bilingual terminology search within our engine and transformed our phrase bank into a dynamic and interactive resource, thus creating the Academic Writing Assistant function. By integrating the academic phrase bank within the search engine's framework, we transformed it into a user-friendly tool. The Academic Writing Assistant enables users to effortlessly search and navigate the collection of academic expressions. The interactive nature of the Academic Writing Assistant empowers users to quickly locate and utilize the appropriate phrases, enhancing the clarity, coherence, and effectiveness of their academic writing in European Portuguese.

The academic phrase bank comprises pre-defined phrase templates accompanied by contextual examples. To enable semantic searches, we utilized BERT to transform the academic phrase bank into semantic vectors. This transformation allowed us to accurately match user queries to the appropriate expressions and communicative functions. Traditionally, academic writing tools, like Ref-n-write rely mostly on keyword-based searches, which may limit the search results to exact matches. However, the Writing Assistant takes advantage of BERT's semantic search approach. By interpreting the context of user queries, it goes beyond exact keyword matches and considers the overall meaning and intent of the query. This enables the Writing Assistant to provide the most suitable phraseologies as search results, even if the exact words entered by the user are not present.

This feature proves advantageous for students with limited academic vocabulary as it grants them access to a broader array of academic language choices, thereby enhancing their writing skills. Through this tool, students can effortlessly search for academic expressions that serve their specific communicative purposes, empowering them to produce scholarly texts that are more sophisticated and coherent. Figure 6 showcases the active utilization of the Writing Assistant, presenting the search results for the expression "os resultados obtidos" ("the results obtained").

When searching for an expression, the screen is divided into two sections. On the left-hand side, expressions are shown in their generic decontextualized form, making it

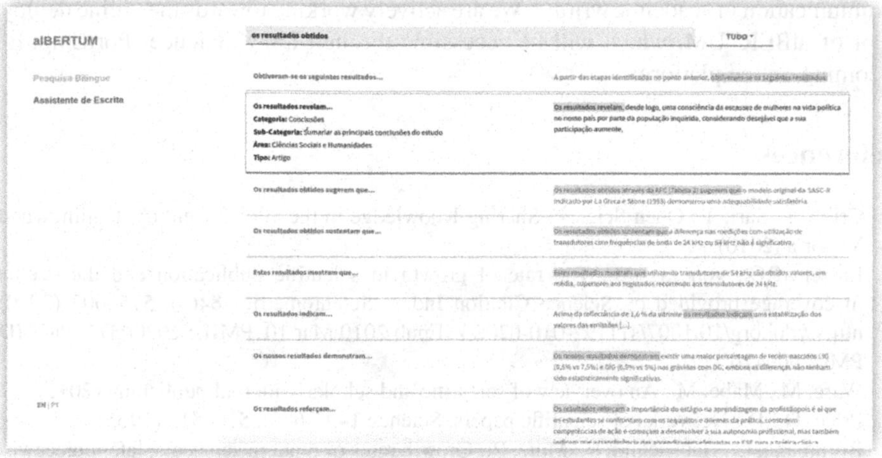

Fig. 6. The Academic Writing Assistant Function

easier for users to incorporate them into their writing without directly copying from the original source, thus avoiding plagiarism. On the right-hand side, the expressions are presented in their original context, extracted from the relevant academic text.

By selecting a search result, users can explore additional details, including the specific section of the text (such as introduction, literature review, methods, discussion, results, or conclusion) from which the expression was extracted. Furthermore, the Writing Assistant provides information on the communicative functions of the expression within the text. This valuable feature grants users a comprehensive understanding of how the expression is used in a genuine academic context, enabling them to grasp its appropriate application and contextual significance. To further refine their search, users can utilize filters that enable them to focus on specific parts of the text, such as the introduction or results section. This functionality helps users narrow down their search and find the most relevant academic expressions for their specific needs. Finally, the Writing Assistant offers additional insights, including the academic genre of the document from which the expression was sourced, as well as the subject area it belongs to. The subject areas covered include Social Sciences and Humanities, Life and Health Sciences, Natural and Environmental Sciences, and Exact Sciences and Engineering. This additional information enhances the contextual understanding of the expression and facilitates its appropriate usage within specific academic domains.

6 Conclusions

This paper aimed to showcase alBERTUM, a specialized Portuguese search engine tailored for scientific and academic language. We have provided a comprehensive overview of alBERTUM, covering its data sources, model, overall architecture, and two core functionalities: the bilingual terminology search and the academic writing assistant.We envision our system to be a valuable tool for students, researchers, and academic professionals, contributing to the dissemination of scientific knowledge and fostering effective communication in academic writing. We are actively working towards the online deployment of alBERTUM, which will be accessible through Lang2Science, PortLinguE's upcoming online platform.

References

1. Cribb, J., Sari, T.: Open Science: Sharing Knowledge in the Global Century. Collingwood, Victoria (2010)
2. Larsen, P.O., von Ins, M.: The rate of growth in scientific publication and the decline in coverage provided by Science Citation Index. Scientometrics **84**(3), 575–603 (2010). https://doi.org/10.1007/s11192-010-0202-z. Epub 2010 Mar 10. PMID: 20700371; PMCID: PMC2909426
3. Ware, M., Mabe, M.: An overview of scientific and scholarly journal publishing (2012)
4. Price, D.J.D.: Networks of scientific papers. Science **149**(3683), 510–515 (1965)
5. Bornmann, L., Haunschild, R., Mutz, R.: Growth rates of modern science: a latent piecewise growth curve approach to model publication numbers from established and new literature databases. Humanit. Soc. Sci. Commun. **8**, 224 (2021). https://doi.org/10.1057/s41599-021-00903-w
6. Price, D.J.D.S.: Little Science, Big Science... and Beyond. Columbia University Press, New York, USA (1986)
7. Zdeborová, L.: New tool in the box. Nature Phys. **13**, 420–421 (2017). https://doi.org/10.1038/nphys4053
8. Kim, J., Koh, K.: Jack of fewer trades: evolution of specialization in research. Can. J. Econ./Revue canadienne d'économique **56**, 423–452 (2023). https://doi.org/10.1111/caje.12656
9. Jain, A., Mitchell, W.: Specialization as a double-edged sword: The relationship of scientist specialization with R&D productivity and impact following collaborator change. Strateg. Manag. J. **43**(5), 986–1024 (2022). https://doi.org/10.1002/smj.3357
10. UNESCO International Institute for Higher Education in Latin America and the Caribbean: towards universal access to higher education: international trends, 86 pp. (2020). ISBN: 978-980-7175-53-1
11. Gil, I.: Algumas considerações sobre Línguas de Especialidade e seus processos lexicogénicos. Máthesis **12**, 113–130 (2003)
12. Afonso, T., Araújo, S.: Abordagem heurística das linguagens de especialidade com recurso à linguística de corpus: caso de estudo em linguagem jurídica. Polissema – Revista de Letras do ISCAP, vol. 19, pp. 9–34 (2019). https://doi.org/10.34630/polissema.vi19.3656
13. Huttner-Koros, A.: The hidden bias of science's 'universal language. The Atlantic (2015). Retrieved from https://www.theatlantic.com/science/archive/2015/08/english-universal-language-science-research/400919/
14. Assunção, C.: Internacionalização da Língua Portuguesa como língua de ciência: do passado para o futuro. In: Martins, M.L., Macedo, I. (eds.) Políticas da Língua, da Comunicação e da Cultura no Espaço Lusófono, pp. 185–197. Humus/CECS (2019)
15. Márquez, M.C., Porras, A.M.: Science communication in multiple languages is critical to its effectiveness. Front. Commun. **5** (2020). https://doi.org/10.3389/fcomm.2020.00031
16. DeFazio, J., Jones, J., Tennant, F., Hook, S.A.: Academic literacy: the importance and impact of writing across the curriculum – a case study. J. Scholarship Teach. Learn. **10**(2), 34–47 (2010)
17. Purser, E.R., Skillen, J., Deane, M., Donohue, J., Peake, K.: Developing academic literacy in context (2008)

18. Preto-Bay, A.M.: The social-cultural dimension of academic literacy development and the explicit teaching of genres as community heuristics. Read. Matrix **4**(3), 86–117 (2004)
19. Azevedo, B., Pereira, M., Araújo, S.: Being fluent in specialized languages can boost your research: designing a multilingual, multimodal and collaborative platform of resources for higher education. In: Proceedings of the 11th EAI International Conference: ArtsIT, Interactivity & Game Creation (ArtsIT 2022). November 21–22, 2022, Faro, Portugal (2022)
20. Araújo, S., Aguiar, S.: How to create digital xml-annotated glossaries in class? a multimodal approach to teaching specialized languages across all levels of education. In: Proceedings of the 15th Annual International Conference of Education, Research and Innovation (ICERI 2022). Seville, Spain, 7–9 November 2022
21. Araújo, S., Aguiar, M.: Metodiza—um recurso para a promoção de literacias em contexto académico. In: Proceedings of the 8th Congresso Nacional de Práticas Pedagógicas no Ensino Superior (CNaPPES.22). Universidade de Coimbra, 14–15 July 2022
22. Carvalho, J., Moreira, J.M., Saraiva, R.: O RCAAP e a evolução do Acesso Aberto em Portugal (2013)
23. Devlin, J., Chang, M., Lee, K., Toutanova, K.: BERT: Pre-training of Deep Bidirectional Transformers for Language Understanding. ArXiv, abs/1810.04805 (2019)
24. Vaswani, A., et al.: Attention is all you need. In: Proceedings of the 31st Conference on Neural Information Processing Systems (NeurIPS 2017). Long Beach, CA, USA
25. Wolf, T., et al.: Transformers: state-of-the-art natural language processing. In: Proceedings of the 2020 Conference on Empirical Methods in Natural Language Processing: System Demonstrations, pp. 38–45. Association for Computational Linguistics (2020)
26. Lutkevich, B.: BERT language model. TechTarget (2020). Retrieved from https://www.techta rget.com/searchenterpriseai/definition/BERT-language-model
27. Winastwan, R.: Semantic Textual Similarity with BERT. Towards Data Science (n.d.). Retrieved from https://towardsdatascience.com/semantic-textual-similarity-with-bert-fc8006 56e7a3
28. Coates, D.: Semantic Search. How It Works & Who It's For (2022). Retrieved from https:// www.algolia.com/blog/product/semantic-search-how-it-works-who-its-for/. (Consulted on August 29, 2022)
29. Mickus, T., Paperno, D., Constant, M., Van Deemter, K.: What do you mean, BERT? Assessing BERT as a Distributional Semantics Model. arXiv preprint arXiv:1911.05758 (2019)
30. Souza, F., Nogueira, R., Lotufo, R.: BERTimbau: pretrained BERT models for Brazilian Portuguese. In: Cerri, R., Prati, R.C. (eds.) BRACIS 2020. LNCS (LNAI), vol. 12319, pp. 403–417. Springer, Cham (2020). https://doi.org/10.1007/978-3-030-61377-8_28
31. Wagner Filho, J.A., Wilkens, R., Idiart, M., Villavicencio, A.: The brWaC corpus: A new open resource for Brazilian Portuguese. In: Proceedings of the Eleventh International Conference on Language Resources and Evaluation (LREC 2018), pp. 4339–4344. European Language Resources Association (ELRA) (2018). Retrieved from https://aclanthology.org/L18-1686
32. Miquelina, N., Quaresma, P., Nogueira, V.B.: Generating a european portuguese BERT based model using content from arquivo.pt archive. In: Yin, H., Camacho, D., Tino, P. (eds.) Intelligent Data Engineering and Automated Learning – IDEAL 2022: 23rd International Conference, IDEAL 2022, Manchester, UK, November 24–26, 2022, Proceedings, pp. 280–288. Springer International Publishing, Cham (2022). https://doi.org/10.1007/978-3-031-21753-1_28
33. Hugging Face. all-mpnet-base-v2 (n.d.). Retrieved from https://huggingface.co/sentence-tra nsformers/all-mpnet-base-v2
34. Vamsi, K., Lokesh, P., Reddy, K.N., Swetha, P.: Visualization of real world enterprise data using python django framework. In: IOP Conference Series: Materials Science and Engineering, vol. 1042 (2021). https://doi.org/10.1088/1757-899X/1042/1/012019

35. Stonebraker, M., Rowe, L.A.: The design of Postgres. ACM SIGMOD Rec. **15**(2), 340–355 (1986)
36. Kathare, N., Reddy, O.V., Prabhu, D.V.: A comprehensive study of Elasticsearch. Int. J. Sci. Res. **10**(6), 716–720 (2021). Retrieved from https://www.ijsr.net/archive/v10i6/SR2152923 3126.pdf

A Novel Optimization Algorithm for Smart Video Surveillance System and Change Object Detection

Fahad Siddiqui[1]([X])[ID] and Shafaq Siddiqi[2][ID]

[1] Sukkur IBA University, Sukkur, Pakistan
fahad.siddiqui@iba-suk.edu.pk
[2] Graz University of Technology, Graz, Austria
shafaq.siddiqi@tugraz.at

Abstract. Security has been a significant concern in every aspect of life. Traditional surveillance systems require a huge amount of storage capacity to save recorded videos. Moreover, as these systems are not fully automated, object detection and change detection need a lot of computational power in real-time surveillance. Finding a specific event or object in the recorded videos becomes more tedious and time-consuming. Since the last decade, researchers and developers have been working on the optimization and improvement of surveillance systems. This paper mainly focuses on surveillance system optimization by presenting an algorithm that not only optimizes objects and change detection but also requires comparatively less time in searching for a particular object from the library of recorded videos. The paper also presents a software application that offers various unique features such as searching for a specific object and on-time notification on targeted object detection.

Keywords: Object detection · surveillance system · video security · YOLOv5

1 Introduction

Nowadays, surveillance systems are getting more and more popular because the government, public and private organizations are using them to keep a check on various aspects of safety and security [4,24,29,33,38]. With the advancement in technology, the whole concept of video has changed [19] and reached a dimension of modern digital output that not only provides high-quality videos but also enhances interactive features. The impact of high-quality video resulted in high storage space as video recording in HD (720px) at the rate of 30fps normally takes up to 86 GB per day ([1,26]), and normally surveillance systems store recording for months. So, the need for storage to record and keep those high-resolution videos has increased, raising the cost of buying several storage devices.

Most of the surveillance systems today are incapable of making decisions in real-time [28] and unable to decide when to record, what to detect, and what

© The Author(s), under exclusive license to Springer Nature Switzerland AG 2024
T. Guarda et al. (Eds.): ARTIIS 2023, CCIS 1935, pp. 103–117, 2024.
https://doi.org/10.1007/978-3-031-48858-0_9

to ignore. These systems require humans to continuously monitor screens for security reasons [10]. Moreover, advancement in surveillance systems and an increased number of cameras resulted in high labor costs, useless recorded video frames, no track of change, and limitation of attention for multi-screen monitoring [32]. However, improvements in computing power, availability of large-capacity storage devices, and high-speed network infrastructure paved the way towards more robust smart video surveillance systems for security [10, 25].

Traditional surveillance systems are passive and thus keep recording continuously, increasing the cost of storage. Also, a particular object/event detection in these systems is a computationally costly and tedious job as it needs to go through the whole video track to analyze high-resolution video images [41]. However, there are few systems that perform object detection intelligently using deep learning [14, 16, 20, 37, 42] but they need high computation power for continuous processing on streaming. In contrast, machine learning-based systems could be less computationally intense but training with high accuracy is challenging in these systems as it requires huge labeled data and manual feature extraction [8].

Some systems continuously classify each captured frame before saving it into a video, increasing the number of objects in an image. It thus results in a surge of processing time [2] and requires a lot of computational resources. Moreover, the issue with these approaches is that even after classifying every image, they are unable to detect changed objects in the camera frame. This is not their incapability, but these systems are not designed to detect any change in objects which can probably miss the optimization. Additionally, due to a lack of real-time object detection, these systems do not send on-time notifications when a particular type of object is targeted. Therefore, there is a need for an efficient algorithm, which can perform real-time object detection in an optimal manner, and a system that requires comparatively less storage as well as computational power and provides intelligent object searching capability and unattended surveillance by sending an on-time notification when a particular object is detected, or a new object entered the scene.

This paper presents an algorithm that not only optimizes objects and change detection but also requires comparatively less time and effort in searching for a particular object from the library of recorded videos. The paper also presents an automated surveillance system, namely Smart Video Surveillance System (SVS System), which provides a solution for real-time surveillance.

We present the state-of-the-art in Sect. 2, and the architecture of our surveillance system and optimizations in Sect. 3 and Sect. 4 respectively. In the end, we discuss our experiments in Sect. 5.

2   Literature Review

Zhiqing Zhou et al. [43] presented optimizations in wireless video surveillance systems. The main idea was to create a modular system that reduces network complexity and optimizes overall performance. Mohammad Alsmirat et al. [3] proposed a framework that performs optimization for efficiently utilizing resources of automated surveillance systems on the edge server. For wireless bandwidth optimization, Proportional Integral Differential (PID) technique is used.

Wang and Zhao [39] and others [11,13] proposed a motion detection technique that is based on background subtraction. In this technique, a series of video images had been taken, and these images contained geometrical information of any target. Thus, relevant information is extracted for analysis and motion detection. This technique greatly improved the compression ratio.

Devi et al. [36] presented a motion detection algorithm based on background frame matching. This was a much more efficient method for motion detection. It required two frames one was a reference frame another was an input frame. Moreover, the reference frame opted to compare with the input frame and their difference in pixel values determined motion.

Nishu Singla [35] presented another technique for motion detection which used consecutive frame differencing. A reference frame was used for differencing with the current/input frame and pixel-based difference produced holes in the motion area. After that, a transformation (RGB to Gray) was applied to highlight the motion area and then another transformation (Binarizing) was applied for highlighting the motion area. The limitation of this approach was determining air effect as motion which is absolutely not acceptable for surveillance systems.

Chandana S [6] presented two more techniques for motion detection and stored video based on motion detection. The first technique was using normalized cross-correlation to find the similarity between two frames. The second technique was to calculate the sum of absolute differences between two consecutive frames.

Zhuang Miao et al. [23] presented an intelligent video surveillance system that worked on moving object detection and tracking. For object detection, three consecutive frame differencing technique was used whereas mean shift was used for tracking. Similarly, Zhengya Xu and Hong Ren Wu [21] proposed a real-time video surveillance system based on multi-camera view and moving object tracking. Moreover, other functionalities of the camera like zoom/pan/tilt for static cameras kept intact and static background modeling was used to analyze and track objects.

A. A. Shafie et al. [34] and others [7,9] presented a video surveillance system for traffic control. Basically, different vehicles were detected in real-time using blob segmentation. Every time, a new vehicle came in the range of the camera, blob segmentation drew a boundary box after classifying it.

K. Kalirajan and M. Sudha [17] proposed an object detection-based surveillance system for detecting moving objects and then performed localization for classification. For object classification, the system is used to separate background and foreground and perform classification for foreground using the Bayesian rule.

Kyungnam Kim and Larry S. Davis [18] presented another object detection methodology for real-time object detection and tracking. For object detection, background subtraction was used, and tracking was performed. Moreover, multi-camera segmentation was also implemented for parallel classification. Anima Pramanik et al. [27] presented an approach for stream processing. Frames were

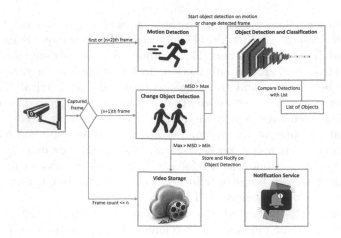

Fig. 1. Overview of SVS System.

extracted from the stream and analyzed for object detection after that they were passed for feature extraction and anomaly detection.

Hanbin Luoa et al. [22] presented a surveillance system that can detect hazards and dangerous areas in construction sites. YOLOv2 was used to detect objects and predict boundaries and proximity was calculated between people and detected objects other than humans.

Hyochang Ahn1 & Han-Jin Cho1 [2] identified that Convolutional Neural Network (CNN) based real-time object detection models are very computationally intense and face difficulty in processing every frame. Also, presented another approach with background subtraction using machine learning for real-time object detection.

Motivated by the extensive state-of-the-art, our proposed solution also builds upon the proposed technique with novel optimizations which results in less storage and runtime.

3   Design and Architecture

The Smart Video Surveillance System has Component-Based architecture and has different functionalities which are covered in distinct and independent components. The system is divided into five main components namely motion detection, change object detection, object detection and classification, video storage, and notification service.

The SVS System connects through a wired or wireless connection to the camera. Figure 1 The system captures the frame and senses motion with the motion detection component and if it finds any motion, it activates the object detection and classification component. The object detection and classification component classifies and compares the predicted output to the provided list of targeted objects. In case of the detected object matches with the targeted objects, this component will send a request to the Video Storage component to store the frames and Notification Service to trigger notification for the user. Once the recording is started, the Video Storage component will store n number of frames then pass control to change the object detection component. The change object detection will sense if there is any change in the object and based on this the control will be passed to either the Video Storage component to store n frames again or the object detection and classification component to detect new objects.

4 Methodology

In this section, we discuss the implementation details of each component with proposed optimizations and choices of parameters.

4.1 Motion Detection

Moving object detection is widely performed by taking the pixel-wise difference between the input frame and reference frame. Many improvements have been proposed to existing frame differencing and background subtraction approaches. However, these approaches have several limitations e.g., air effect, illumination effect, which may lead to unwanted results.

The proposed approach for motion detection is calculating Mean Squared Deviation (MSD). For two consecutive frames, we apply a threshold on MSD to decide a change in frames is motion or not. Moreover, to overcome the limitations of previous approaches, frames are converted into grayscale before calculating MSD which eliminates illumination and color effects (see Algorithm 1). The threshold value is set after an experimental evaluation. The reason for choosing MSD for motion detection is its fast execution and avalanche effect in minor changes. Moreover, MSD equal to zero implies similar frames, which means no motion is detected whereas increasing MSD from zero defines the intensity of dissimilarity between two consecutive frames. If this dissimilarity surpasses the threshold, it will be interpreted as motion is detected. The mathematical representation for calculating MSD is following:

$$MSD = \frac{1}{mn} \sum_{i=0}^{m-1} \sum_{j=0}^{n-1} [I_{\text{current}}(i,j) - I_{\text{previous}}(i,j)]^2$$

This algorithm first takes two grayscale frames, calculate their MSD based on the approach mentioned above, and compares the obtained MSD with a preset threshold to make any decision on motion detection.

4.2 Change Object Detection

The Change Object Detection component is one of the key components of this system. Motion Detection determines the presence of any moving object in front

---

Algorithm 1. Motion Detection in Frames

Input: *Current Frame curr, Previous frame prev*
Output: *Boolean*

1: $curr \leftarrow$ convert current frame into grayscale
2: $prev \leftarrow$ convert previous frame into grayscale
3: $m, n \leftarrow curr.shape()$ //returns current image shape
4: $MSD \leftarrow \frac{\sum (curr \quad - \quad prev)}{m \times n}$
5: **if** $MSD > Threshold$ **then**
6:     **return** True   // motion detected
7: **else**
8:     **return** False   // no motion detected
9: **end if**

---

of the camera. But, once a cycle of recording has been completed, the system will again start the new cycle from motion detection to video recording which may cause a high computational cost. To further optimize this process, Min-Max thresholding has been introduced through that the change of object will be determined and in case of the same object(s) is present in the range of the camera, the system will start recording again by eliminating the computationally expensive classification task.

Min-Max thresholding is the criteria for the Change Object Detection component to decide whether a new object has been detected in the range of the camera or the existing object(s) is still present there. In this thresholding, Min is the minimum threshold that is necessary to qualify to call any changes in the frames as 'motion'. In contrast, Max is the minimum threshold on which any change in the frames will be considered either the same object presence or a change of object(s) in the current frame.

Moreover, the Change Object Detection will apply Min-Max thresholding to determine the cause of change and decide the decision as follows:

$$MAX > MSD > MIN \quad Same\ object\ detection$$

$$MAX > MSD \quad Changed\ object\ detection$$

Change Object Detection details are given in Algorithm 2. This algorithm takes two grayscale frames and calculates its MSD similar to Algorithm 1. After obtaining MSD, it applies Min-Max thresholding to conclude if the same object is present, object has changed or there is no motion at all.

4.3   Object Detection and Classification

Smart Video Surveillance System (SVS System) uses a motion detection approach before starting real-time object classification - classifying an image with a multi-class classifier during live streaming. Once the motion detection component responds to the change in frames as motion, the next task will be to find

---

Algorithm 2. Change Object Detection in Frames

Input: *Current Frame curr, Previous frame prev*
Output: *Boolean(min, max)*

1: $curr \leftarrow$ convert current frame into grayscale
2: $prev \leftarrow$ convert previous frame into grayscale
3: $m, n \leftarrow curr.shape()$ //*returns current image shape*
4: $MSD \leftarrow \frac{\sum(curr \; - \; prev)}{m \times n}$
5: **if** $Max > MSD > Min)$ **then**
6:     **return** (True, True)   //*same object*
7: **else if** $MSD > Max)$ **then**
8:     **return** (True, False)   //*changed object*
9: **else**
10:     **return** (False, False)   //*No motion detected*
11: **end if**

---

object(s) that has caused the motion. In this regard, a multi-class classifier is needed which can process frames and return the detections efficiently.

Object detection and classification are valuable but computationally expensive in surveillance systems. There are many approaches are mentioned in the literature review for real-time object detection and a detailed comparison in terms of time and accuracy of different models including YOLO (You Only Look Once), SSD (Single Shot Detection), and R-FCN (Region-based Fully Convolutional Networks) is presented in [40]. However, they all need powerful machines with Graphical Processing Units (GPU) for surveillance systems. The proposed approach for object detection and classification is to use the You Only Look Once version 5 (YOLOv5) algorithm [15, 30] based on trade-off [12, 40] that is balanced in terms of speed and accuracy in real-time processing. Algorithm 3 presents our object detection and classification algorithm that loads the YOLOv5 model and set its type. Then it starts detection with the provided parameters.

Algorithm 3. Change Object Detection in Frames

Input: *image*
Output: *imageWithDetections*

1: *detector* $\leftarrow$ *ObjectDetection()*
2: *detector.setModelTypeAsYOLOv5()*
3: *detector.setModelPath("my_YOLO_model.h5")* //*loading weights*
4: *detections* $\leftarrow$ *detector.detectObjectsFromImage(params)*
5: **return** detections

4.4   Video Storage

While YOLOv5 is fast and accurate in real-time classification, it requires GPU to process every frame continuously. As a result, processors keep busy in classification on streaming which makes surveillance systems computational-intense.

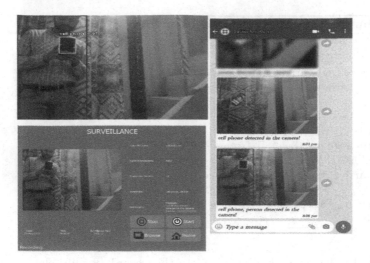

Fig. 2. Interface of SVS System.

Hence, there is a need for optimization so that surveillance systems with real-time object detection can be prevented from high computation and may also be run on computers without GPUs. The proposed approach for this optimization is to classify a single frame (if and only if motion is detected) and continuously store n number of frames if any of the specified objects are found in the classified frame. In other words, the system does not classify every frame during streaming (until there is motion and detections does not contain the specified object(s)) instead it classifies a single frame after recording n number of frames. To prevent security risks, $n-1$ frames are stored directly until the next classification is performed, if classification activates on motion detection. This approach has two limitations. First, the value of 'n' is experimental and may vary from application to application. This system is designed for home premises, but different applications may have different values of 'n'. The experiment details are shown in the experiments and threshold value section. Second, if a system detects motion continuously but none of the user's specified objects is detected in the frame, the system will start to classify every frame just like many surveillance systems.

4.5 Notification Service

SVS System has additional on-time notification services functionality which is not yet implemented in existing surveillance systems. This system allows the user to select notify option for any object and the system would generate a notification for the user if an object marked notify is detected and sends it to the user's cell phone via SMS (short message service) and send a classified image to the user's WhatsApp number. Fig 2 shows the interface and notification sample of our surveillance system.

Table 1. MSD score on different walking motions

Direction	Speed	MSD
Left to Right & Right to Left	Slow Walk	89
Left to Right & Right to Left	Normal Walk	127
Left to Right & Right to Left	Running	223
Front to Back & Back to Front	Slow Walk	66
Front to Back & Back to Front	Normal Walk	80
Front to Back & Back to Front	Running	114
Diagonally	Slow Walk	170
Diagonally	Normal Walk	287
Diagonally	Running	366

5 Experiments

This system is developed in Python 3.7 using OpenCV [5] library. The experiments are conducted on non-GPU Intel®Core™ i5-3230M CPU 2.60GHz (4CPUs) 3rd generation with 8192MB RAM and 300 GB hard disk drive.

5.1 Motion Detection Threshold

To determine the threshold for motion detection, we conducted a series of experiments. These experiments include a person's movement across the camera, throwing an object in the range of the camera, different light conditions (low, medium, high, daylight), Movement of hung clothes due to air effect and raining or water flow in front of the camera.

Experiment 1 Person Movement: In this experiment, person movement is observed. A person moved from left to right, right to left, front to back, back to front and diagonally with different speeds such as slow walking, normal walking and running. We observed that walking diagonally in front of the camera always results in higher deviation no matter the pace of walking (see Table 1).

Experiment 2 Light Effect: An observation is taken in different light conditions in front of the camera. The light conditions were low (toward darkness), medium (normal/day light on a clear sky with a temperature of 22°C) and high (very bright light a standard flashlight in a studio). Table 2 shows that MSD is very high when transitioning from high light to low and vice versa. In contrast, the MSD is very low when this transition happens in medium to low light.

Experiment 3 Throwing Objects: In this experiment, two different objects of different masses are thrown in front of the camera. The objects were an ordinary

Table 2. MSD on different light conditions

Light Condition	MSD
Low to Medium	80
Low to High	213
Medium to Low	60
Medium to High	75
High to Low	229
High to Medium	70

Table 3. MSD on different objects

Direction	Speed	MSD
Pen	Slow	30
Pen	Normal	40
Pen	Fast	60
Box	Slow	34
Box	Normal	50
Box	Fast	83

pen and a box of 10 cm * 10 cm. Table 3 show a deviation of 60 and 83 for both pen and box respectively. We repeated the experiment three times and observed higher deviation when an object of a bigger mass is thrown toward the camera.

Experiment 4 Air Effect: In the end, the air effect over the curtain and tree is evaluated in indoor and outdoor scenes. The results (Table 4) show a directly proportional relation between high air pressure and MSD. The more air pressure increases, the more MSD value increases. Similarly, the lower air pressure will result in a lower MSD value.

Table 4. MSD on different air conditions

Scene	Air Intensity	MSD
Indoor	Low	50
Indoor	High	65
Outdoor	Low	60
Outdoor	High	80

We also performed an experiment with dropping water in front of the camera and on a rainy day but did not find a significant difference in MSD on a light rainy day. On a heavy rainy day, the recorded MSD was 52. We use this information to increase the threshold value if a day is predicted as rainy. After getting the MSD for different scenarios via our experiments we took the average of these MSD values on points when a motion was detected and when a motion was not detected. Using these average values, we found the min and max values for Min-Max thresholding as **90** and **270** respectively.

Table 5. Number of stored frames between classifications.

Camera	Direction	Speed	# Frames	Time (s)
Camera 1	Left to Right	Slow	175	41.10
Camera 1	Front to back	Slow	135	30.24
Camera 1	Diagonally	Slow	140	31.20
Camera 1	Left to Right	Medium	110	25.38
Camera 1	Front to back	Medium	85	20.58
Camera 1	Diagonally	Medium	100	23.34
Camera 1	Left to Right	Fast	70	17.70
Camera 1	Front to back	Fast	70	17.40
Camera 1	Diagonally	Fast	75	18.60
Camera 2	Left to Right	Slow	600	30.00
Camera 2	Front to back	Slow	480	24.00
Camera 2	Diagonally	Slow	360	31.20
Camera 2	Left to Right	Medium	480	18.00
Camera 2	Front to back	Medium	360	24.00
Camera 2	Diagonally	Medium	480	18.00
Camera 2	Left to Right	Fast	480	24.00
Camera 2	Front to back	Fast	360	18.00
Camera 2	Diagonally	Fast	335	16.80

5.2   Number of Frames Value Determination for Recording

The purpose of this experiment was to determine an optional number of frames to be stored after a single classification. This experiment was done with two different size (pixel) cameras. One camera had high resolution, approximately 16 MP and the second was a 2 MP camera. In the experiment, a person is moved across a camera with different speeds e.g., slow, medium, and fast and its time and number of frames are recorded (Table 5). The optimal value of N found in this experiment is **270** number of frames and **23** seconds after taking the average of all frames and time taken.

5.3   Model Tuning

In the YOLOv5 model there is a tradeoff between the detection speed and accuracy of detected object. The purpose of this experiment is to find the optimal detection speed for this system with minimum or no reduction in accuracy. Increasing the speed may result to save up to 80% of the time taken to detect objects at the cost of a slight reduction of accuracy. The detection speeds are flash, normal, fast, faster, and fastest. The observations are given in Table 6. We select the YOLOv5 model with a detection speed Fast for our application.

5.4   Baseline Comparison

We compare our solution (SVSS) with two baseline approaches 1) Continuous Object Detection (COD) approach - every frame is classified in real-time and 2) Motion Detection and Classification (MDC) approach - frames are classified only when motion is detected. In Table 7, we measure the CPU cost using the task manager of the local machine and the Python library Psutil [31].

Table 6. Comparison of Detection Speeds, Time, and Accuracy.

Detection Speed	Detection Time (s)	Accuracy
Normal	3.1	99.99%
Fast	1.8	90%
Faster	0.60	70%
Fastest	0.33	52.4%
Flash	0.2	25%

Table 7. Computational Cost Comparison.

System	Model	COD	MDC	SVS Sys
Task Manager (Minimum percentage)	Flash	15.1%	5.4%	3.1%
Task Manager (Average percentage)	Flash	42.9%	15.3%	9.9%
Task Manager (Maximum percentage)	Flash	57.6%	30.7%	29.1%
Psutil Library (Minimum percentage)	Flash	16%	10.3%	6.6%
Psutil Library (Average percentage)	Flash	35.8%	24%	15.6%
Psutil Library (Maximum percentage)	Flash	71%	24.4%	41.6%
Task Manager (Minimum percentage)	Normal	74.7%	22.1%	22.1%
Task Manager (Average percentage)	Normal	80.0%	43.5%	35.1%
Task Manager (Maximum percentage)	Normal	92.1%	81.2%	78.8%
Psutil Library (Minimum percentage)	Normal	31.6%	6.2%	5.8%
Psutil Library (Average percentage)	Normal	96.2%	26.6%	14.3%

We compare the CPU consumption for continuous fifty seconds and the results (Fig. 3) shows consistent improvement of the proposed model over the baselines. The COD remains at peak all the time and MDC remains on peak more frequently. In contrast, the proposed system touches the peak rarely and operates on low CPU consumption most of the time.

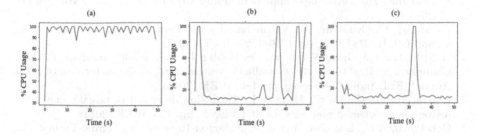

Fig. 3. CPU Consumption Graph for 50 s

6   Conclusion

The Smart Video Surveillance System (SVS System) is developed to overcome the issues and problems related to surveillance. As existing surveillance systems hold many issues like monitoring problems, issues in browsing and searching, cost of storage, no on-time notification, and high computation power consumption in case of continuous classification. The proposed system is one solution for all these issues. SVS System has five main components Motion Detection, Object Change Detection, Object Detection and Classification, Storage Service, and Notification Service. The motion Detection component is responsible for detecting motion in the captured frame. The object Change Detection component is responsible for detecting change, add or elimination of object(s) in consecutive frames. The object Detection and Classification component is responsible for object detection and predicting its label. The Storage Service is responsible for storing videos when specific conditions are met and maintaining information regarding each video recorded. Finally, Notification Service is responsible for sending notifications on the user's cell phone. The testing results show its performance in real scenarios. The optimizations in the algorithm have improved the overall system's performance using features like Motion Detection, Change Object Detection and Object Detection and Classification. In addition to this, it reduces the painful efforts of searching for a particular object in the library of recorded videos by using optimizations in video storage and notification service. Finally, the presented SVS System offers unique features in searching for a particular object and on-time notification on targeted object detection.

References

1. DVR Storage Calculator for Analog Security Cameras. Supercircuits (2020), https://www.supercircuits.com/resources/tools/security-dvr-storage-calculator, Accessed 20 Mar 2023

2. Ahn, H., Cho, H.-J.: Research of multi-object detection and tracking using machine learning based on knowledge for video surveillance system. Pers. Ubiquit. Comput. **26**(2), 385–394 (2019). https://doi.org/10.1007/s00779-019-01296-z
3. Alsmirat, M., Sarhan, N.J.: Intelligent optimization for automated video surveillance at the edge: a cross-layer approach. Simul. Model. Pract. Theory **105**, 102171 (2020)
4. Basavaraj, G., Kusagur, A.: Vision based surveillance system for detection of human fall. In: RTEICT, pp. 1516–1520. IEEE (2017)
5. Bradski, G.: The OpenCV Library. Dr. Dobb's Journal of Software Tools (2000)
6. Chandana, S.: Real time video surveillance system using motion detection. In: 2011 Annual IEEE India Conference, pp. 1–6. IEEE (2011)
7. Chitra, M., Geetha, M.K., Menaka, L.: Occlusion detection in visual scene using histogram of oriented gradients. In: ICEVENT, pp. 1–5. IEEE (2013)
8. Cob-Parro, A.C., Losada-Gutiérrez, C., Marrón-Romera, M., Gardel-Vicente, A., Bravo-Muñoz, I.: Smart video surveillance system based on edge computing. Sensors **21**(9), 2958 (2021)
9. Daigavane, P., Bajaj, P.R., Daigavane, M.: Vehicle detection and neural network application for vehicle classification. In: 2011 International Conference on Computational Intelligence and Communication Networks, pp. 758–762. IEEE (2011)
10. Dedeoğlu, Y.: Moving object detection, tracking and classification for smart video surveillance. Ph.D. thesis, Bilkent Universitesi (Turkey) (2004)
11. Fang, L., Meng, Z., Chen, C., Hui, Q.: Smart motion detection surveillance system. In: International Conference on Education Technology and Computer, pp. 171–175. IEEE (2009)
12. Fang, Y., Guo, X., Chen, K., Zhou, Z., Ye, Q.: Accurate and automated detection of surface knots on sawn timbers using YOLO-V5 model. BioResources **16**(3), 5390 (2021)
13. Feiran, F., Ming, F., Huamin, Y.: Temporal difference method based on positive and negative energy distribution in moving objects detection. In: IST, pp. 1–5. IEEE (2017)
14. Ji, P., Kim, Y., Yang, Y., Kim, Y.S.: Face occlusion detection using skin color ratio and LBP features for intelligent video surveillance systems. In: FedCSIS, pp. 253–259. IEEE (2016)
15. Jocher, G., et al.: ultralytics/yolov5: v3.1 - Bug Fixes and Performance Improvements (2020). https://doi.org/10.5281/zenodo.4154370
16. Ju, J., Ku, B., Kim, D., Song, T., Han, D.K., Ko, H.: Online multi-person tracking for intelligent video surveillance systems. In: ICCE, pp. 345–346. IEEE (2015)
17. Kalirajan, K., Sudha, M.: Moving object detection for video surveillance. Sci. World J. **2015** (2015)
18. Kim, K., Davis, L.S.: Object detection and tracking for intelligent video surveillance, pp. 265–288. Multimedia Analysis, Processing and Communications pp (2011)
19. Kruegle, H.: CCTV Surveillance: Video practices and technology. Elsevier (2011)
20. Liu, W., Liao, S., Hu, W.: Perceiving motion from dynamic memory for vehicle detection in surveillance videos. IEEE Trans. Circuits Syst. Video Technol. **29**(12), 3558–3567 (2019)
21. Liu, Y., Li, Z., Xiong, H., Gao, X., Wu, J.: Understanding of internal clustering validation measures. In: ICDM, pp. 911–916. IEEE (2010)
22. Luo, H., Liu, J., Fang, W., Love, P.E., Yu, Q., Lu, Z.: Real-time smart video surveillance to manage safety: a case study of a transport mega-project. Adv. Eng. Inform. **45**, 101100 (2020)

23. Miao, Z., Zou, S., Li, Y., Zhang, X., Wang, J., He, M.: Intelligent video surveillance system based on moving object detection and tracking. DEStech Trans. Eng. Technol. Res. **11**, 2016 (2016)
24. Mishra, A.A., Srinivasa, G.: Automated detection of fighting styles using localized action features. In: ICISC. pp. 1385–1389. IEEE (2018)
25. Nikouei, S.Y., Xu, R., Nagothu, D., Chen, Y., Aved, A., Blasch, E.: Real-time index authentication for event-oriented surveillance video query using blockchain. In: ISC2, pp. 1–8. IEEE (2018)
26. Paul: Video Resolution VS. Frames Per Second. Thinpig-media (2019), https:// thinpigmedia.com/blog/decisions-decisions-video-resolution-vs-frames-per-second
27. Pramanik, A., Sarkar, S., Maiti, J.: A real-time video surveillance system for traffic pre-events detection. Accid. Anal. Prev. **154**, 106019 (2021)
28. Qureshi, F.Z., Terzopoulos, D.: Surveillance in virtual reality: System design and multi-camera control. In: CVPR, pp. 1–8. IEEE (2007)
29. Rai, M., Husain, A.A., Maity, T., Yadav, R.K., Neves, A.: Advance intelligent video surveillance system (AIVSS): a future aspect. Intell. Video Surveill. **37** (2019)
30. Redmon, J., Divvala, S., Girshick, R., Farhadi, A.: You only look once: unified, real-time object detection. In: CVPR, pp. 779–788 (2016)
31. Rodola, G.: Psutil package: a cross-platform library for retrieving information on running processes and system utilization. Google Scholar (2016)
32. Salahat, E., Saleh, H., Mohammad, B., Al-Qutayri, M., Sluzek, A., Ismail, M.: Automated real-time video surveillance algorithms for SOC implementation: A survey. In: ICECS, pp. 82–83. IEEE (2013)
33. Sase, P.S., Bhandari, S.H.: Human fall detection using depth videos. In: SPIN, pp. 546–549. IEEE (2018)
34. Shafie, A., Ali, M., Hafiz, F., Ali, R.M.: Smart video surveillance system for vehicle detection and traffic flow control. J. Eng. Sci. Technol. **6**(4), 469–480 (2011)
35. Singla, N.: Motion detection based on frame difference method. Int. J. Inf. Comput. Technol. **4**(15), 1559–1565 (2014)
36. SuganyaDevi, K., Malmurugan, N., Manikandan, M.: Object motion detection in video frames using background frame matching. Int. J. Comput. Trends Technol **4**, 1928–1931 (2013)
37. Tuan, M.C., Chen, S.L.: Fully pipelined VLSI architecture of a real-time block-based object detector for intelligent video surveillance systems. In: ICIS, pp. 149–154. IEEE (2015)
38. Wang, R., Tsai, W.T., He, J., Liu, C., Li, Q., Deng, E.: A video surveillance system based on permissioned blockchains and edge computing. In: BigComp, pp. 1–6. IEEE (2019)
39. Wang, Z., Zhao, Y., Zhang, J., Guo, Y.: Research on motion detection of video surveillance system. In: 2010 3rd International Congress on Image and Signal Processing, vol. 1, pp. 193–197. IEEE (2010)
40. Xu, J.: A deep learning approach to building an intelligent video surveillance system. Multimedia Tool Appl. **80**(4), 5495–5515 (2021)
41. Yoon, C.S., Jung, H.S., Park, J.W., Lee, H.G., Yun, C.H., Lee, Y.W.: A cloud-based utopia smart video surveillance system for smart cities. Appl. Sci. **10**(18), 6572 (2020)
42. Zhang, S., et al.: Pedestrian search in surveillance videos by learning discriminative deep features. Neurocomputing **283**, 120–128 (2018)
43. Zhou, Z., Yu, H., Shi, H.: Optimization of wireless video surveillance system for smart campus based on internet of things. IEEE Access **8**, 136434–136448 (2020)

Enhancing the Museum Experience: A Gamified Approach of an Interactive Installation in the Industrial Museum of Hermoupolis

Athina Bosta⬭ and Modestos Stavrakis⁽⊠⁾ ⬭

Department of Product and Systems Design Engineering, University of the Aegean, 84100
Syros, Greece
modestos@aegean.gr

Abstract. This paper explores the role of interactive installations in contributing to the reuse of archived knowledge and motivating visitors' appreciation and value for cultural heritage. It also examines how gamification techniques can be employed to afford playful experiences in an educational approach within museum settings, integrating information and enabling visitors to explore industrial cultural heritage in a more engaging way. The paper presents a case study focused on the creation of an interactive installation at the Industrial Museum of Hermoupolis in Syros, Greece, utilising a non-interactive exhibit, specifically the water pump machine. The introduction provides an overview of the importance of Hermoupolis' cultural heritage, presents the Industrial Museum of Hermoupolis, and outlines the objectives of the project. Then it discusses the design phases that have been followed towards the implementation of the interactive installation. These phases include the Research and Inquiry, the Conceptual Design, and the Prototyping. Specific emphasis is given to formulating the visitor's experience of the installation by combining the historical content, the interactive elements, the physical objects and the gamified elements. In the following sections, the paper presents the design processes towards the implementation of a working prototype and the evaluation phase. The paper concludes with a summary of the implications of the project, emphasising the importance of integrating user experience and interaction design with cultural content in designing interactive installations.

Keywords: interactive installation · gamification · industrial cultural heritage · user experience

1 Introduction

Interactive installations play a pivotal role in fostering engaging museum experiences. These installations enable visitors to transcend the traditional practice of solely focusing on the information presented in museum displays. Instead, they actively participate in museum activities through a hands-on approach, thereby enriching their overall experience [1]. Installations are exploring new museum visit possibilities, forming an appealing and enjoyable environment for a broader audience. Also, they aim to capture

T. Guarda et al. (Eds.): ARTIIS 2023, CCIS 1935, pp. 118–132, 2024.
https://doi.org/10.1007/978-3-031-48858-0_10

visitors' attention and interest to convey historical knowledge into an action-based experience, promoting a more immersive approach to history and cultural context learning [2]. In this paper, the design team aims to create an interactive installation of an exhibit that follows a traditional museum collection presentation format featuring physical artifacts and accompanying informational labels. The exhibit in question, often overlooked, necessitates a focus on conducting research into its historical significance and context, including the manufacturer and owner/factory, while concurrently identifying elements of industrial heritage within interactive installations. More specifically, the design team will concentrate its efforts on engaging visitors in an educational museum activity, utilising gamification elements to enhance their experience. This will involve integrating information about the exhibit, a water pump machine, and its factory environment. Consequently, the installation will feature a model, specifically a 3D printed replica of the exhibit, and a combination of physical and digital artifacts to facilitate interaction. The installation will also illustrate the operation of the water pump and provide insight into the historical and cultural context of the period. This includes details about the factory, its workers, and their working conditions, conveyed through either printed or projected multimedia content. Consequently, some key questions arise regarding how the interactive interactions can effectively incorporate gamification techniques to adeptly communicate and convey the multifaceted aspects of this significant industrial heritage and how the historical content of an exhibit is able to shape the structure of an interactive installation.

1.1 Historic Background

The city of Hermoupolis, located in Syros, Greece, assumed the role of the capital of the Cyclades region in 1833, coinciding with the establishment of the Greek state at that time. Throughout the 19th century, Hermoupolis emerged as a pioneering city, spearheading advancements in trade, shipping, shipbuilding, and industry. It ranked as the second most populous city, after Athens, and its port claimed the distinction of being Greece's primary port. Hermoupolis swiftly became the central hub for transit trade in the eastern Mediterranean, bolstered by the island's enterprising entrepreneurs who established a remarkably reliable banking and credit system. However, the subsequent decline of Hermoupolis' economic prosperity ensued with the ascent of alternative commercial, industrial, and transit centers like Athens, Piraeus, and Patras [3].

The Industrial Museum of Hermoupolis has an interesting exhibit collection that records the history of its industrial development while gradually describing the creation of the city itself and its different socio-economic classes. More specifically, the Museum includes in its collection architectural plans, vintage photographs from citizens' archives, books, documents, maps, machinery, and tools from factories and small-scale businesses that emerged in the area over the last two centuries. In fact, the Museum facilities used to be an old factory, which was known as the Vratsanos Factory (pasta factory established in 1898) or the Katsimanti Factory, which operated as a dye factory until the onset of World War II [4].

Although many efforts have been made to create interactive installations about the industrial heritage of Syros (i-Wall [4], Threads [5], Interactive Experience Journey [6], Loom [7], Ex Machina Museum Kit [8]) cultural diffusion still remains essential as many exhibits are being ignored by museum visitors due to the lack of interest for them and the typical museum experience.

1.2 Research and Inquiry

The study of the selected exhibit was the initial step in understanding the content of the installation. The research team chose the double-acting reciprocating piston water pump from the museum's exhibition, identified by its collection number 128. This pump transferred the water flowing inside it, in an enclosed space, through the repetitive movement of a mechanical component known as the piston. The exhibit showcased a double-acting water pump, where water was compressed from both sides of the piston during the suction and discharge phases [10]. According to the museum's archived documentation pertaining to this specific exhibit, the water pump served two distinct functions within the industrial factory. Initially, it was employed as a general water supply mechanism, facilitating the distribution of brackish water throughout the factory via a central hydraulics network that featured interconnections with a well. However, when the city of Hermoupolis established its own water supply network, the factory transitioned to utilising this newly available resource, rendering the pump obsolete as the primary water supply. Consequently, the pump underwent a transformation and was repurposed in accordance with the fire safety regulations of the factory during that era. It assumed the role of an emergency fire pump, intended to be activated in case of fire incidents in the factory. To facilitate its operation in such critical situations, the emergency pump was equipped with an oil engine that was exclusively dedicated to powering it. Notably, this engine was positioned adjacent to the pump and served the singular purpose of supporting its emergency firefighting function [4] (Image 1).

Image 1. The Water Pump Exhibit

In addition, the researchers collected information about the pump's Factory and its manufacturers, in order to gain insights into its industrial context. The pump belonged to a spinning mill named: "PROODOS" of the textile industry, founded in 1910 by the general partnership:" I. & P VARDAKAS - SPATHIS - SETERIS". The factory was managed mainly by the members of the Vardakas family until the end of its operation in 1985. The factory type changed over time, from a spinning mill to a cotton mill, infiltrating into the cotton industry. The Vardakas family was involved with philanthropy, offering financial support to various institutions such as the Syros Hospital which was named after the family (Vardakeio), the local church of Three Holy Hierarchs, and the Agia Varvara orphanage. Moreover, the water pump was constructed in the Barbeta machine shop, which was the second largest after Neorion Shipyards. The machine shops represented one of the most important aspects of Hermoupolis' industrial sectors and used to sell and repair a variety of machinery to local factories and businesses. During the First World War, the Barbeta machine shop carried out repairs to Greece's allies' warships, bringing enormous economic benefits to its company. During the Second World War, it ceased its operation, but afterward, it was reopened, until its acquisition in 1953 by the Rethymni brothers [11].

The design team further explored the working conditions prevalent during the historical period, as they form a crucial aspect of the installation's contextual content. The late 19th to 20th century marked a challenging and harsh era, characterised by the inhumane treatment of workers within workplaces. For these reasons, the first strikes in Syros emerged around 1879, as workers were resolute in asserting their rights and pressing for improved conditions from their employers. One notable example is the strike undertaken by the Shipyard and Tannery Carpenters Association in 1886. According to a local magazine from that year, the workers aimed to reduce their work shifts to a maximum of twelve hours, eliminate unpaid work on Sundays, and ensure payments in the national currency, drachmas. It was common practice for employers to make payments in foreign currencies to avoid covering the difference resulting from currency conversion. This strike serves as an illustration of the workers' determination to fight for their rights. Although the Greek state began demonstrating concern over the regulation of working conditions around 1914, numerous issues persisted. These challenges included workplace accidents, child labour, mistreatment of workers, restrictions on joining labour unions, and more. It was not until September 1983, when labour legislation was introduced, that a five-day working schedule with eight-hour shifts was mandated. Prior to that, workplace conditions were largely influenced and determined solely by the whims and personal preferences of individual employers [10].

Upon completing research on the water pump exhibit and its historical context, the design team proceeded to explore the potential of gamification in configuring and designing the interactive installations, considering their connection to industrial heritage. Firstly, it is important to recognise that cultural site visits are social occasions in which visitors assume the roles of interpreters and creators of meaning, engaging with complex information and acquiring knowledge about cultural heritage [12]. In recent years, a wide array of technologies, including Information and Communication Technologies (ICT), Virtual Reality (VR), Augmented Reality (AR), and more, have been extensively integrated into cultural heritage settings. These technologies present incredible opportunities to enhance the experiential value for visitors and provide them with diverse possibilities to interact with cultural activities [13]. Gamification plays a significant role in augmenting the user experience by introducing game design elements, such as narrative, level design, mechanics, and physical objects, into non-gaming contexts. By integrating these elements into interactive installations, gamification offers a means to enrich and enhance the overall visitor experience. This approach not only fosters engagement but also enables visitors to have a more immersive and participatory encounter with the industrial heritage being presented [14].

Concurrently, there emerged a need to rejuvenate and preserve historical industrial elements that encapsulated memories of the past, representing the vestiges of human activities such as labour, technology, production, product distribution, facilities, and equipment. These elements, freed from the constraints of beauty and aesthetics, became the focal point of expanding exhibition collections dedicated to industrial heritage, which were safeguarded and conserved. These developments spurred discussions regarding the identification and differentiation of the past and present, and the determination of what should be preserved, engaging in critical deliberations [15]. It became essential to acknowledge that industrial heritage constituted recent and invaluable evidence of urban development and the progress of human society over the past two decades [16].

The integration of gamification techniques within the context of an industrial museum context provides opportunities for interaction between the visitors and non-interactive exhibits. This approach facilitates the provision of digital artefacts and user interfaces, leading to the creation of new interpretations and meanings from the visitors' perspective [16]. As a result, industrial heritage is increasingly enriched by innovative technological resources that can, in turn, encourage individuals to recognise the necessity and importance of historic preservation and thus promote a deeper understanding and appreciation of the significance of industrial cultural heritage in shaping human collective history.

2   Related Work

The selection of interactive installations related to the industrial heritage that utilise some gamification elements provides introspection about the available design approaches in this field. According to our taxonomic criteria the installations reviewed follow the pattern below: a) the theme of each installation is related to the industrial heritage, b) the installation is located either in a museum or in a related site to an industrial heritage exhibition (on-site installation), and c) the user experience includes either multimedia content or learning activities or a combination of both. Among others the most relevant installations that fulfil these criteria include, the Trabant "P601" driving simulation of the DDR Museum [17], the Sensory route of the Industrial Gas Museum [18], and the Assembly Line of the Industrimuseet [19].

The interactive installation of the Trabant "P601" vehicle with collection number 1003144 at the Museum of the German Democratic Republic (Deutsche Demokratische Republik) in Berlin (Germany), also known as the DDR Museum is a driving simulation activity within a real Trabant model. Visitors have the opportunity to drive in a 60,000-square-metre virtual world representing the neighbourhoods in the German Democratic Republic. At the time, the Trabant brand was the most popular choice of vehicle, making the model "P601" a symbol of everyday life. As part of the interactive experience, visitors are able to interact with the Trabant "P601" vehicle within the installation. They can open the car door, take a seat in the driver's position, and use the pedals, including the accelerator, brake, and steering wheel. This setup resembles the familiar controls found in racing games, allowing visitors to drive the vehicle within the simulation. Notably, the windshield of the car serves as a dynamic display screen, incorporating projection mapping technology to provide the driver with digital navigation information, projecting it directly onto the windscreen to enhance the realism of the driving experience.

Additionally, the installation features printed material on the rear cabin windows, providing information about the importance of the Trabant "P601" car. This aspect of the installation promotes an understanding of the social life within the cultural context of the German Democratic Republic, specifically emphasising the experience of driving through different neighbourhoods. By exploring the industrial heritage represented by the Trabant "P601," the installation offers visitors an educational opportunity to personally witness the driving experience and gain knowledge about the specific car model [17].

The Sensory route of the Industrial Gas Museum in Athens (Greece) offers a cultural walk inside the premises of the old factory facilities. It is an alternative visitor experience, carried out through specific interaction points (boxes) within the typical visitor's route. Yellow boxes of different dimensions and content have been placed in seven out of thirteen points of interest of the walk, through which visitors are invited to discover the history of the site by triggering their senses including sight, smell, touch, taste, and hearing. The boxes differ both in material and method of information presentation, as well as in the structure and technological equipment they utilise, depending on the room they are located. The interactions within the Sensory route at the Industrial Gas Museum vary based on the content. Visitors may encounter sounds representing characteristic factory noises, grasp objects like coke, feel simulated heat, smell scents evoking past aromas from the Gazi area, or observe boxes analyzing industrial equipment. The Sensory route offers a treasure-hunting-like experience, where visitors navigate the museum area using on-site maps that guide them along the designated path. In conclusion, this interactive journey provides a comprehensive exploration of both tangible and intangible aspects of the industrial heritage, immersing visitors in a unique and engaging museum experience [18].

Also, the Assembly Line of the Industrimuseet, the industrial museum in Horsens (Denmark) aims to highlight the working conditions and the required skills of the workers in a ball bearings supply line. More specifically, the Assembly line is an activity in which two teams are formed in order to compete with each other in assembling the ball bearings. The team that completes first the assembling wins. The installation is fully equipped with its own facilities, which include different workstations depending on the phase of the assembly process. The participants can choose the individual parts of the bearing and assembly them correctly on the metal tray following the video instructions on the screen above the workstation. This interactive installation forms a visitor experience that captures the interest of the participants, motivating them to join in an activity that represents an industrial environment of the past. In this way, a hands-on experience is created in which visitors understand assembly processes and relationships on a production line, and finally the demands and needs of the actual factory's personnel [19].

To sum up, the above-mentioned interactive installations use either original devices, i.e. the real machines of industrial history, or mockups representing the operation of a real system and its process, promoting direct contact between visitors and the installation. Participants are motivated to participate in an activity that turns theoretical knowledge into practice. In addition, augmentation through technological equipment helps to revive historical elements and maintain the attention and interest of visitors by offering a variety of stimuli that converge with reality (historical context). At the same time, it is understood that the aim of the installations is to bring events, processes, and general historical elements back to the present day, from industrial history, using game elements, involving visitors in an activity of exploration and discovery of both the content and the installation.

3 Methodology

The interactive installation was designed and developed according to the methodology that the Interactive System Design Lab of the Department of Product and System Design Engineering at the University of the Aegean, introduced in: "Teaching HCI with a Studio Approach: Lessons Learnt" [20]. The methodology is often used in a design studio course and thus is divided into five specific phases, a) Introduction to the course and sensitisation, b) Research and inquiry, c) Conceptual design, d) Technical tests and prototyping, and e) Evaluation. Of course, only four of them are involved in the design and development of the installation, as the first (Introduction to the course and sensitisation) is excluded because it is an introductory phase of the educational process of the course.

During the Research and Inquiry phase, the design team focused on gaining knowledge of the selected context, including the historical background, exhibit characteristics, and the role of gamification in installations. This involved studying articles and bibliographic sources, as well as conducting field visits when deemed beneficial. In the Conceptual Design phase, the team aimed to formulate the main idea and visual representation of the completed project or installation. Various design tools, procedures, or methods were utilised based on the project's specific needs and requirements. The subsequent phase, Technical Tests and Prototyping, involved experimenting with technological equipment and software such as Arduino, projection mapping, and video editing. The goal was to create a prototype that aligned with Conceptual Design. Evaluation was a crucial stage in understanding the strengths, weaknesses, and potential issues of the designed system, during a pilot demonstration in the Industrial Museum of Hermoupolis. The type of evaluation, such as Heuristic Evaluation, was influenced by the stage and fidelity of the produced prototype, whether it was low or high fidelity. It is important to note that these phases could occur concurrently or begin before the previous phase was fully completed. For instance, the Research and Inquiry phase could continue while the team embarked on Conceptual Design and started experimenting with preferred technologies. Similarly, during the finalisation of the prototype, the team could simultaneously organise the evaluation plan once the prototype's form was clearly defined [20].

4 Conceptual Design

The Conceptual Design phase encompassed several stages to develop a comprehensive user experience that emphasised the connection between Hermoupolis' industrial heritage, physical artefacts, and interactions. Initially, a concise description of the installation was crafted to define the project's objectives, target group, design requirements, and constraints. Subsequently, brainstorming sessions were conducted to generate a pool of ideas, from which three initial concepts emerged. The design team then organised meetings to gather feedback, comments, concerns, and suggestions for improvement and changes to the three concepts. These inputs were meticulously documented and analysed to arrive at a final installation structure that best fulfilled the project's vision. Concurrently, the team finalised the installation's aesthetics, ensuring a cohesive expression of its identity across all physical and digital elements.

The interactive installation was based on explaining the function of the exhibit, utilising the historical context of the water pump (employees of the Barbeta Factory) to trigger educational animations that integrated information for users who are intrigued in learning more about the various aspects of the exhibits by progressively increasing their visiting duration. As a result, the installation included physical and digital components, forming a tabletop activity. The physical parts consisted of a 3D printed mockup of the water pump, a control panel responsible for the reciprocating movement of the connecting rod, employee cards (game cards), and the gameboard, which served as the main surface presenting text-based information (printed material) about the factory's history. The digital components consisted of animated videos projected onto the gameboard. To outline the structure of the installation, a Mind Mapping technique was initially employed [21] (Fig. 1).

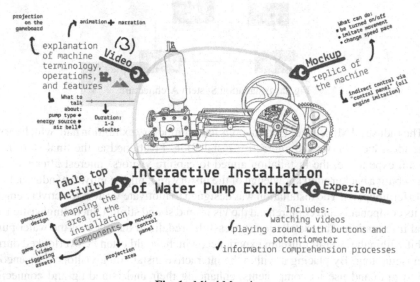

Fig. 1. Mind Mapping

More specifically, on the gameboard, the mockup of the water pump, the control panel, employee cards, and technological equipment were placed. The technological equipment consisted of a projector and an Arduino circuit, which included a motor to achieve the reciprocating movement of the connecting rod, panel interaction switches, and an RFID card reader. The water pump mockup, which was designed and printed by the teaching and technical staff member Mr. Nikolaos Politopoulos of the Department of Product and System Design Engineering, had the capability to be switched on/off and change the speed of the connecting rod movement using a toggle switch and a poten-tiometer. Additionally, the installation featured three employee cards, each measuring 9 cm × 5.5 cm, connected to a corresponding token in the form of an RFID IC key tag. These cards represented specific employees of the Factory, including an engineer, a technician, and a worker. They conveyed the employees' opinions about the working conditions, establishing a connection between the installation and the industrial era of the past. Each token corresponded to an animated video that provided information about different aspects, including the meaning of a double-acting water pump, the functioning of the reciprocating movement, and the usage of the airlock. Finally, the installation included a projection area where explanatory videos were presented. These videos were triggered when an employee card with its corresponding token was placed on the top of the card case holder (Fig. 2).

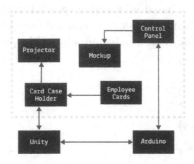

Fig. 2. Installation System Architecture

The Industrial Museum of Hermoupolis has a temporary exhibition hall, which served as the ideal location for the interactive installation. Positioned as the final stop in the museum experience, the installation aimed to capture visitors' interest after they had already built a background knowledge of the history and, importantly, the industrial sec-tor of Hermoupolis. The installation was designed to motivate visitors to actively engage with its components and comprehend the visual and sound stimuli, including written and verbal information. The installation successfully redefined the place of the water pump exhibit within the overall museum experience, which would often be overlooked during the museum tour. By placing it within the interactive installation, visitors were encour-aged to grab and use its components, enhancing their understanding and connection to the exhibit. To gather insights about visitors' engagement with the installation, a User Journey Map was created, providing a retrospective view of their experiences and interactions throughout the journey [21] (Fig. 3).

The installation incorporated game design elements to shape both its components and the overall user experience. These elements created a sense of interaction and engagement akin to a board game. The physical and digital pieces within the installation collectively formed components that could be tracked on the central board, resembling the layout of a board game. The installation encouraged participants to explore and discover in a non-linear manner, allowing visitors to choose their own path of interaction. Whether

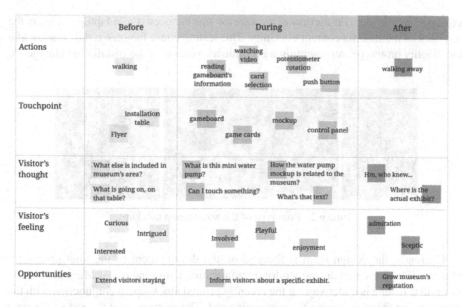

	Before	During	After
Actions	walking	watching video potentiometer rotation reading gameboard's information card selection push button	walking away
Touchpoint	installation table Flyer	gameboard mockup game cards control panel	
Visitor's thought	What else is included in museum's area? What is going on, on that table?	What is this mini water pump? How the water pump mockup is related to the museum? Can I touch something? What's that text?	Hm, who knew... Where is the actual exhibit?
Visitor's feeling	Curious Intrigued Interested	Playful Involved enjoyment	admiration Sceptic
Opportunities	Extend visitors staying	Inform visitors about a specific exhibit.	Grow museum's reputation

Fig. 3. User Journey Map

they chose to watch a video, play with the control panel, or continue reading the game-board's information, there was no prescribed sequence of steps. The installation provided directions to visitors without explicitly instructing them on what to do, promoting inter-action progression through exploration. Game design elements such as character and level design were involved in the installation. Each employee card represented a historic figure from the past, such as an actual engineer from the Barbeta Factory, who narrated their knowledge about the water pump operation. The animated videos were tailored to the personality of the selected figures, enhancing the storytelling experience. In essence, the installation embraced the concept of an open-structured world board game, creating a touchpoint that connected visitors to the Barbeta Factory and offered a unique and immersive experience.

4.1 Technical Tests and Prototyping

During the technical testing phase, the primary focus was on developing a circuit capa-ble of achieving the desired movements of the model, including the connecting rod movement, speed adjustment, and overall activation and deactivation of the pump oper-ation. Additionally, the identification of tokens corresponding to each employee card was addressed. To accomplish these requirements, the hardware components utilised included Arduino Uno, a potentiometer, a pushbutton, a toggle switch, a MG996R Servo Motor, a stepper motor, an RFID reader, and tokens. Various additional items such as jumper wires, appropriate motor drivers, and resistors were also employed for testing purposes. Subsequently, the testing process extended to establishing a connection between Arduino and Unity. This involved ensuring that the RFID reader could send a signal (e.g., a char array or string) to Unity, enabling the identification of the video requested by the user. Furthermore, a projector was connected to a laptop to assess the playback of multimedia content via Unity. This testing phase facilitated the creation of a low-fidelity prototype, representing a preliminary version of the installation (Image 2).

Image 2. Prototype of the water pump mockup

Currently, the design team is focused on the development of the final prototype, which will be presented during a pilot demonstration at the Industrial Museum of Hermoupolis. Testing is underway for the recently printed mock-up, in conjunction with the motor responsible for moving the connecting rod. The movement of the rod is achieved through a crankshaft system connected to the Arduino-controlled motor via a timing belt loop. Simultaneously, the team is working on editing the animated videos that will be incorporated into the installation. The first animation illustrates the concept of the double-acting pump, showcasing the water's path through the valves and the movement of the piston. The second video provides information on the airlock, emphasising its role in maintaining the liquid flow and pressure conditions within the pump. Lastly, the third video delves into the analysis of converting the motor's rotary motion into reciprocating motion. Additionally, the team is finalising the graphics for the game board and employee cards. These components contain descriptive information about the factory, contributing to the overall experience of the installation (Fig. 4).

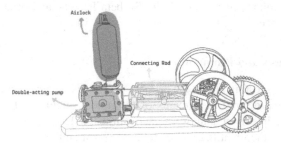

Fig. 4. The video topics of the prototype

5 Evaluation

The installation adopted an open structure resembling a board game concept, as previously mentioned in the conceptual design, a heuristic evaluation was deemed suitable. This evaluation method involved qualitative inspection of usability, wherein five usability experts engaged in negotiation and discussion to determine the degree to which the designed system adhered to commonly accepted principles [19]. The conduct of a heuristic evaluation was expected to provide valuable insights into the usability and overall effectiveness of the installation [22].

The heuristic evaluation process was organised at the Industrial Museum of Hermoupolis and involved two stages. Firstly, individual inspections were conducted in which a total of 17 findings were recorded. Every usability expert assigned each finding to one of the ten (10) heuristics and documented their opinion by explaining its importance. The heuristics were: 1) visibility of system status, 2) match between system and the real world, 3) user control and freedom, 4) consistency and standards, 5) error prevention, 6) recognition rather than recall, 7) flexibility and efficiency of use, 8) aesthetic and minimalist design, 9) help users recognise, diagnose and recover from errors, and 10) help and documentation. Before the individual inspections, the usability experts were fully informed about the operation of the evaluated system. They were provided with the design documentation, hardware, and software infrastructure to ensure a comprehensive understanding of the system. Additionally, the design team furnished a list of tasks that the usability experts should perform during the evaluation. However, it is important to note that the experts were encouraged to exercise their own initiative and propose additional tasks that they deemed relevant, thereby allowing for a more comprehensive evaluation process [22]. The task list of the heuristic inspection was the following:

1. Turn on the water pump.
2. Increase the speed of the rod.
3. Read the details of at least two employee cards.
4. Watched at least two videos.
5. Identify which factory the pump belonged to.
6. Identify when the factory was founded.

During the second stage, a group session was facilitated, involving all the usability experts who participated in the individual inspections during the previous stage. The purpose of this session was to consolidate their findings and generate a single evaluation report. The report documented the outcomes of the categorisation process, which involved grouping the findings based on their nature and relevance. Additionally, the findings were ranked in order of significance or severity, highlighting the most critical issues. The group engaged in discussions to analyse and interpret the findings, providing commentary on each identified problem or issue encountered during the users' interaction with the installation and concluded to 8 findings [22]. The usability experts were required to adhere to a specific classification method to assess the severity of usability findings. Each finding was assigned a numerical value ranging from 0 to 4, indicating its level of severity. [23]. The numbers corresponded to the magnitude of the problem created to the user and have the following meanings: a) 0: false alarm, b) 1: cosmetic, c) 2: minor, d) 3: major and d) 4: usability catastrophe.

Consequently, the report was required to encompass specific elements derived from the entire evaluation process. The evaluation report is summarised below presenting each finding by name, in order of severity and with a brief description:

A) Low sound volume (usability catastrophe): Related to heuristic 4, low video sound due to other guests, B) Instructions presentation (major): Related to heuristic 8, the plethora of instructions creates an extravagant composition, C) Cognitive work-load (major): Related to heuristic 6, the intended connection between videos-employee cards-general insights creates a continuous state of information recall, D) Control panel interaction (major): Related to heuristic 1, the panel fails to inform the user how it connects with the water pump conceptually and how it operates, E) Installation and Museum integration (minor): Related to heuristic 10, highlight the importance of the exhibit selection (why the water pump and not another exhibit), F) Language style (minor): Related to heuristic 2, the installation needs a smoother user integration into the experience, G) Employee card structure (cosmetic): Related to heuristic 5, make the employee card a singular and independent object (token removal) and H) Gameboard size (false alarm): Related to heuristic 8, the installation space is too small.

6 Conclusions

The structure of interactive installations can be enhanced by incorporating elements from the field of game design. By engaging visitors in educational and entertaining experiences, these installations can effectively highlight the significance of industrial heritage, which serves as a reflection of urban development and the evolution of society in recent human history. Tabletop board games offer a valuable foundation for the physical artefacts within an installation and serve as a means to connect interactions with cultural content. Furthermore, the collection and curation of historical content plays a crucial role in the design of interactive installations, as they identify features and characteristics that contribute to the construction of both the physical and digital environments.

This paper presents a proposal that expands the thinking process surrounding the design of interactive installations, emphasising the connection between interaction, physical/digital objects, and information related to the industrial history of a city. Through the conceptual design, the design concept for the implementation of an interactive installation at the Industrial Museum of Hermoupolis was introduced, along with the forthcoming steps to be taken by the design team, such as the evaluation phase.

Acknowledgements and Funding. This research was funded by the Research e-Infrastructure "Aegean Interregional Digital Transformation in Culture and Tourism" {Code Number MIS 5047046} which is implemented within the framework of the "Regional Excellence" Action of the Operational Program "Competitiveness, Entrepreneurship and Innovation". The action was co-funded by the European Regional Development Fund (ERDF) and the Greek State [Partnership Agreement 2014–2020].

References

1. Hornecker, E., Stifter, M.: Learning from interactive museum installations about interaction design for public settings. In: Proceedings of the 18th Australia conference on Computer-Human Interaction: Design: Activities, Artefacts and Environments, in OZCHI 2006, pp. 135–142. Association for Computing Machinery, New York, NY, USA (2006). https://doi.org/10.1145/1228175.1228201
2. Pallud, J.: Impact of interactive technologies on stimulating learning experiences in a museum. Inf. Manage. **54**(4), 465–478 (2017). https://doi.org/10.1016/j.im.2016.10.004
3. A. Κόκκου and I. Τραυλός, Ερμούπολη. Εμπορική Τράπεζα Ελλάδος (2001). https://www.politeianet.gr/books/traulos-ioannis-emporiki-trapeza-ellados-ermoupoli-180965. Accessed 5 June 2023
4. Βιομηχανικό Μουσείο Ερμούπολης - Κέντρο Τεχνικού Πολιτισμού. http://www.ketepo.gr/el/%ce%bd%ce%ad%ce%b1%ce%b1. Accessed 5 June 2023
5. Gkiti, C., et al.: i-Wall: a low-cost interactive wall for enhancing visitor experience and promoting industrial heritage in museums. In: Ioannides , M., et al. (eds.) Digital Heritage. Progress in Cultural Heritage: Documentation, Preservation, and Protection, LNCS, pp. 90–100. Springer, Cham (2018). https://doi.org/10.1007/978-3-030-01762-0_8
6. Panopoulou, E., et al.: Threads: a digital storytelling multi-stage installation on industrial heritage. In: Ioannides, M., (eds.) Digital Heritage. Progress in Cultural Heritage: Documentation, Preservation, and Protection. LNCS, pp. 457–469. Springer, Cham (2018). https://doi.org/10.1007/978-3-030-01762-0_40
7. Gaitanou, M., et al.: Design of an interactive experience journey in a renovated industrial heritage site. In: Ioannides, M. (eds.) Digital Heritage. Progress in Cultural Heritage: Documentation, Preservation, and Protection, pp. 150–161. LNCS. Springer, Cham (2018). https://doi.org/10.1007/978-3-030-01762-0_13
8. Dimitropoulos, A., et al.: The loom: interactive weaving through a tangible installation with digital feedback. In: Ioannides , M. (ed.) Digital Cultural Heritage: Final Conference of the Marie Skłodowska-Curie Initial Training Network for Digital Cultural Heritage, ITN-DCH 2017, Olimje, Slovenia, 23–25 May 2017, Revised Selected Papers, LNCS, pp. 199–210. Springer, Cham (2018). https://doi.org/10.1007/978-3-319-75826-8_17
9. Bosta, A., Katsakioris, D., Nikolarakis, A., Koutsabasis, P., Vosinakis, S., Stavrakis, M.: Ex machina: an interactive museum kit for supporting educational processes in industrial heritage museums. In: Ioannides, M., Fink, E., Cantoni, L., Champion, E. (eds.) Digital Heritage. Progress in Cultural Heritage: Documentation, Preservation, and Protection: 8th International Conference, EuroMed 2020, Virtual Event, November 2–5, 2020, Revised Selected Papers, pp. 438–449. Springer International Publishing, Cham (2021). https://doi.org/10.1007/978-3-030-73043-7_36
10. Δάγκινη, I.Κ., Γλύκα, A.I.: Αντλίες. Ίδρυμα Ευγενίδου (2016)
11. Μαρκουλής, A.: Η κλωστοϋφαντουργία στην Σύρα από τον 19ο στον 20ο αιώνα. Δήμος Ερμούπολης (2008)
12. Macdonald, S.: Interconnecting: museum visiting and exhibition design. CoDesign 3(sup1), 149–162 (2007). https://doi.org/10.1080/15710880701311502
13. Cesaria, F., Cucinelli, A.M., De Prezzo, G., Spada, I.: Gamification in cultural heritage: a tangible user interface game for learning about local heritage. In: Kremers, H. (ed.) Digital Cultural Heritage, pp. 411–422. Springer International Publishing, Cham (2020). https://doi.org/10.1007/978-3-030-15200-0_28
14. Deterding, S., Dixon, D., Khaled, R., Nacke, L.: From game design elements to gamefulness: defining 'gamification. In: Proceedings of the 15th International Academic MindTrek Conference: Envisioning Future Media Environments, in MindTrek 2011, pp. 9–15. Association

for Computing Machinery, New York, NY, USA (2011). https://doi.org/10.1145/2181037.2181040

15. "Industrial Heritage: A New Cultural Issue | EHNE (2023). https://ehne.fr/en/encyclopedia/themes/arts-in-europe/monument/industrial-heritage-a-new-cultural-issue. Accessed 5 June 2023

16. Hain, V., Löffler, R., Zajíček, V.: Interdisciplinary cooperation in the virtual presentation of industrial heritage development. Procedia Eng. **161**, 2030–2035 (2016). https://doi.org/10.1016/j.proeng.2016.08.798

17. DDR Museum, Berlin's Interactive Museum (2016). https://www.ddr-museum.de/en. Accessed 5 June 2023

18. Βιομηχανικό Μουσείο Φωταερίου - ΒΜΦ. https://gasmuseum.gr/. Accessed 5 June 2023

19. Industrimuseet. https://industrimuseet.dk/. Accessed 5 June 2023

20. Koutsabasis, P., Vosinakis, S., Stavrakis, M., Kyriakoulakos, P.: Teaching HCI with a studio approach: lessons learnt. In: Proceedings of the 22nd Pan-Hellenic Conference on Informatics, in PCI 2018, pp. 282–287. Association for Computing Machinery, New York, NY, USA (2018). https://doi.org/10.1145/3291533.3291561

21. Martin, B., Hanington, B., Hanington, B.M.: Universal Methods of Design: 100 Ways to Research Complex Problems, Develop Innovative Ideas, and Design Effective Solutions. Rockport Publishers (2012)

22. Π. Κουτσαμπάσης, Αξιολόγηση διαδραστικών συστημάτων με επίκεντρο τον χρήστη (2016). http://repository.kallipos.gr/handle/11419/2765. Accessed 5 June 2023

23. Nielsen, J., Mack, R.L. (eds.): Usability Inspection Methods. Wiley, New York (1994)

Need for Quality Auditing for Screening Computational Methods in Clinical Data Analysis, Including Revise PRISMA Protocols for Cross-Disciplinary Literature Reviews

Julia Sidorova[✉] and Juan Jose Lozano

Centro de Investigación Biomédica en Red Enfermedades Hepáticas y Digestivas (CIBEREHD),
Madrid, Spain
julia.a.sidorova@gmail.com

Abstract. Deep learning (DL) is a leading paradigm in ML, which recently has brought huge improvements in benchmarks and provided principally new functionalities. The shift towards the deep extends the horizons in seemingly every field of clinical and bioinformatics analysis. Computational platform are exposed to a great volume of new methods promising improvements. Yet, there is a trade-off between the number of man/hours and the degree to which cutting edge advances in methodology are integrated into the routine procedure. Understanding why many of the new shiny methods published in the CS literature are not suitable to be applied in clinical research and making an explicit checklist would be of practical help. For example, when it comes to survival analysis for omics and clinico-pathological variables, despite a rapidly growing number of architectures recently proposed, if one excludes image processing, the gain in efficiency and general benefits are somewhat unclear, recent reviews do not make a great emphasis on the deep paradigm either, and clinicians hardly ever use those. The consequences of these misunderstandings, which affects a number of published articles, results in the fact that the proposed methods are not attractive enough to enter applications. The example with the survival analysis motivates the need for computational platforms to work on the recommendations regarding (1) which methods should be considered as apt for a consideration to be integrated into the analysis practice for primary research articles, and (2) which literature reviews on cross-disciplinary topics are worth considering.

Keywords: survival analysis · deep learning · C-index · quality auditing · PRISMA

1 Introduction

Given the rapid advances in deep learning, for the sake of efficiency of the analysis in mission critical research, new algorithms need to be rapidly integrated into the routine clinical analysis (Sidorova, Lozano 2022a, b). There exists a known set of "regulations" regarding how machine learning must be used (Cabitza, Campagner 2021) resulting

T. Guarda et al. (Eds.): ARTIIS 2023, CCIS 1935, pp. 133–142, 2024.
https://doi.org/10.1007/978-3-031-48858-0_11

from understanding persistent errors in practical studies, as included into a checklist for the authors e.g. in the journal of Bioinformatics, but to our best knowledge there is no similar document regarding new computational methods that are to become candidates to be used in the clinical analysis. Without explicit guidelines regarding how "to separate the wheat from the chaff", computational centers need to invest time and effort into setting up the new pipelines. The protocol should save an error to the extent possible. Unfortunately, taking a publication in a premium computational journal as a suitability indication does not work, because as we will see below the objectives and criteria for success by developers are not exactly as those by practitioner. We also voice a concern regarding the PRISMA protocols (McKenzie 2021) for systematic reviews for cross disciplinary topics. For illustrative purposes, we take the topic of survival analysis based on DL.

Let us review the basics of the survival analysis to set up a technical framework for our discussion. The Cox proportional hazards (CoxPH) model (Cox 1972) for survival analysis is a well studied topic in statistics with mission critical applications in the clinical data analysis, but not so well understood by computer scientists despite the fact that a body of modern research in survival analysis now lies in deep learning. The main characteristic of the underlying mathematical problem, is that the variable of interest, Y, the time until an event (e.g. death), is attributed with an important complication of *censoring*, namely, the true event times are typically not known for all patients, because the follow up is not long enough for the event to happen, or the patient leaves the study before its termination. Due to censoring it is not correct to treat the problem as a regression. For each individual there is a true survival time T and a true censoring time C, at which the patient drops out of the study or the study ends, and

$$Y = min(T, C).$$

The status indicator is available for every observation: $\delta = 1$, if the event time is observed, and $\delta = 0$, if censoring time is observed. Furthermore, every data point has a vector of p features associated to it, also termed as attributes or covariates. The objective is to predict the true survival time T, while modeling it as a function of covariates. The (potentially stringent) proportional hazard assumption states that the hazard function has the form of

$$h(t|x_i) = h_0(t)exp(x_{i1}\beta_1 + x_{i2}\beta_2 + \ldots + x_{ip}\beta_p),$$

where $h_0(t)$ is a constant, called the basic hazard and no assumption is made about its functional form. The diminishing with time probability of surviving is expressed via the decreasing survival function $S(t) = Pr(T > t)$. The Kaplan-Meir is the estimator of the survival curve. For example, Fig. 1 results from learning the separation boundary between two groups of patients: those at high-risk and those with moderate risk, i.e. defining the biomarker with a sufficiently high C-index, and then plotting the $S(t)$ of the two groups. A formal test for the equality of two survival curves is the log-rank test. The CoxPH is a quite flexible modeling of the relationship between risk and covariates, robust to some violations of the initial assumptions. The conditions under which CoxPH can be correctly used are verified via statistical tests, and when unmet, other methods are recommendable, for example, see (Kleinbaum, Klein 2012) for classical extensions or the emerging deep survival literature for DL-based alternatives (Sidorova, Lozano under review).

In trend with other fields of data science, the expectations from the DL-based survival is that it shatters benchmarks with neural networks (Higher C-index). In the context of modern hardware and flexible software frameworks, the research community revisited the idea of Faraggi-Simon (Faraggi, Simon 1995] to approximate the risk hazard $h(x)$ directly with a NN, which looked promising since some potentially limiting assumptions of the CoxPH would be relaxed. The old failure to outperform CoxPH was explained with the lack of infrastructure and the under-developed theoretical apparatus. The arguments for success included:

1. Cox is linear and therefore can not learn nonlinear relations between the attributes (Huang et al. 2019; Kim et al. 2020), while there is the inherent capability of NN for efficient modeling of high-level interactions between the covariates (Katzman et al. 2018; Yang et al. 2019; Huang et al. 2019; Ching et al. 2016),
2. CoxPH relies on strong parametric assumptions that are often violated (Lee et al. 2018),
3. the desire to avoid the feature selection step (Katzman et al. 2018; Yang et al. 2019) that would lead to primitive modeling with a subsequent loss of information coded by the discarded attributes.

The primary research articles contain a spectrum of solutions ranging from a simple feed-forward network as in the first work reconsidering the idea of Faraggi and Simon (Fig. 1) to quite complex networks including a stand alone coding or classification problem, – gradually reflecting the advances in DL. When it comes to statisticcal journals, the recent quality reviews of the survival analysis do not put much emphasis on the DL-based methods, e.g. (Salerno, Li 2023), and (Lee, Lim 2019) both only briefly describe very few deep methodologies, and instead focus on the important topic of regularization and competing/semi-competing risks. Such lack of coverage can be explained with the proportional impact of the methods in real-life analysis. Despite a "Dictionary" of deep architectures was compiled with the uniform graphical representation of the main ideas and brief description of the methods (Sidorova, Lozano, under review), it comes with a series of warnings and a rather big emphasis on future work rather than on an intermediate applicability and superiority of the deep paradigm in survival, where one of the reasons why the ideas gain the grounds very slowly lie in the misconceptions regarding the success metric (typically C-index). The two statements below are insufficient as a motivation for the integration of a new method in the routine analysis:

I. "The proposed method outperforms with C-index of CoxPH with 0.05 and reaches 0.65"(Statement 1) and
II. C-index has not revealed any improvement over CoxPH but a statistically significant improvement has been detected via another metric (Statement 2).

The overly optimistic view is reflected in an *application-oriented* journal (Deepa, Gunavahi 2022) (with the correcting note submitted to the same journal (Sidorova, Lozano under review)), to which it should be added that the primary research that it cites was carried out according to the state of the art practices and published at premium venues, as well as the systematic review was designed according to PRISMA. There is a methodological reason why the flaw crept in a cross-disciplinary review: from technical sciences to biophysics and molecular biology.

The rest of the article is organized as follows. Section 2 addresses the listed above misconceptions from the published research regarding the assessment of new algorithms for survival analysis based in DL. Section 3 discusses what is to be blamed for the misinterpretation and what can be done to save similar errors in the future. A PRISMA extension is suggested. Section 4 draws conclusions on the need for explicit set of criteria for the new methods before they can be recommended in clinical data analysis.

2 Success Metrics for Survival Analysis

The central success metric in the survival analysis is the C-index, which estimates the probability that for a random pair of individuals the predicted survival times have the same ordering as their true survival times. $C = 0.5$ is the average C-index of a random model, whereas $C = 1$ corresponds to the perfect ranking of event times, and high values of $C > 0.8$ are desired to prove the validity of a new clinical biomarker. There is an intimate relation between the area under ROC curve (AUC) and the C-index (Heagerty, Zheng 2005; Antolini et al. 2005).

2.1 Example: Misconception Regarding the Values of the Success Value in the Survival Analysis

Regarding Statement 1, unfortunately, in biomarker research typically high values of $C > 0.8$ are desired to prove the validity of a new clinical biomarker. Consider a parallel to the prediction task: one would not be willing to accept a predictive model for a binary classification with ROC of 0.6 as a sufficiently strong biomarker to be included as a test in clinical routine. Therefore, we suggest to rise 0.5 to 0.8, for the newly proposed method to be practically valid to the a practitioner.

Although the above seems to be intuitive, as can be seen in Table 1 below, the same idea seems to be adhered in the computer science literature, where the vast majority of the proposed new architectures report rather low C-indices as long as they are greater or equal to the C-index of the CoxPH with the only exception highlighted with the bold font. The datasets SUPPORT, METABRIC, Rot&GBSD are summarized in (Kwamme et al. 2019), and the TCGA stands for the Cancer Genome Atlas (Grossman et al. 2016). The datasets are open access, which facilitates the comparison of the methods. Yet, a step is still missing to demonstrate that the proposed methods can be of practical benefit.

3. Given no improvement in C-index, with the same motivation of questionable practical benefit, an improvement detectable via a different success metric should not serve as a justification of the superiority of the method. Unless the semantics of the application implies the conditions under which the C-index can not be used.

Practitioners are left unsure with regard to the deep alternative to survival. Some articles with new clinical findings state that they are aware of these advanced deep survival methods but apologetically decline using them or describe their benefits in the Future Work. The algorithms below (DeepSurv, SALMON, and VAE-Cox) include the methods of survival analysis based on the DL that were subjectively appealing to

Table 1. C-indices for the validation of the DL-based architectures.

Study	Dataset	C-index
DeepSurv Katzman et al. (2018)	SUPPORT, METABRIC, Rot&GBSD	0.62 – 0.68
Cox-CC-Time Kvamme et al. (2019)	SUPPORT, METABRIC, Rot&GBSD	0.62 – 0.67
DeepHit Lee et al. (2018)	METABRIC	0.69
Concatenation autoencoders Tong et al. (2020)	Breast cancer data (BRCA) from TCGA, modalities: gene expression, miRNA, DNA metilation, and copy number variations	0.64
VAE-Cox (Kim et al. 2020)	10 data sets from TCGA, those with at least 50 deaths, gene expression	$C = 0.65$
Cox-PASNet (Hao et al. 2018)	GBM from TCGA, gene expression	$C = 0.64$
SurvivalNet Yosefi et al. (2017)	GBM, BRCA, KIPAN from TCGA with different set of features: 1) 17K gene expression features, and 2) the set including 3–400 clinicopathological attributes, mutations, gene- and chromosome arm-level copy number variations, and protein expression	**$C > 0.8$**

us: mathematical rigor, a large citation count, the treatment of the problem in the way needed, e.g. the interpretation and visualization mechanisms, etc.

1) Despite DeepSurv (Katzman et al. 2019) being a highly cited article in the literature devoted to the development in deep survival methodology (approaching 1K citations, according to Google Scholar in March 2023), less than five of them report the uses of the (parts of the) methodology in the routine clinical analysis: either directly as a method e.g., or taking a part of it with e.g. (Sahu et al. 2023).

2) In late 2022-early 2023 we have found no uses in clinical routine of SALMON (Huang et al. 2019), and yet the authors of several articles state that they are aware of this method and could have applied it, e.g. (Hu et al. 2019).

3) VAE-Cox (Kim et al. 2020) was not used in clinical studies at the time of the manuscript submission.

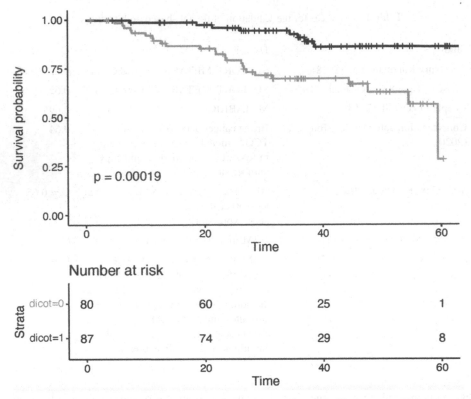

Fig. 1. The KM survival curves for the high-risk (red) and low-risk (blue) groups. Below are the counts of the survived ("at risk") patients.

3 Problem with PRISMA

The misunderstanding regarding the practical utility of the deep paradigm in the survival analysis (a warning would be suitable that these methods are hardly ever used in clinical research and that almost never an absolute high value of the success metric was reported) has crept into a non-technical journal, for which the PRISMA protocol to secure the review quality was followed. The problem is that a statistically significant improvement in the success metric, e.g. 0.05, over the baseline by CoxPH, e.g. with the resulting C-index equal to 0.65, can justify a publication in a premium CS venue, yet it is not a sufficient proof that the method is beneficial to routine clinical analysis in place or together with the state of the art methods, since to prove the discriminatory capacity of a biomarker C-index of 0.8 is desired. The systematic review in question correctly summarizes that the new methods outperform CoxPH. Let us have a look at the PRISMA flow chart (Fig. 2) to locate the place of the missing block, the aim of which will be to keep a trace of the discipline of the primary research article to be able to correctly translate the conclusions between the disciplines. We call for a need of PRISMA protocol extension along the following lines.

- *For cross-disciplinary articles, check whether the objectives behind the success metrics are the same across the disciplines of the retrieved articles, otherwise provide an explicit discussion.*

E.g. for CS research the objective is to improve the baseline as a demonstration of a suitability of the proposed algorithmic design. For clinical analysis, the objective is that the method is maximally discriminative to prove a biomarker with a typically high C-index of at least 0.8.

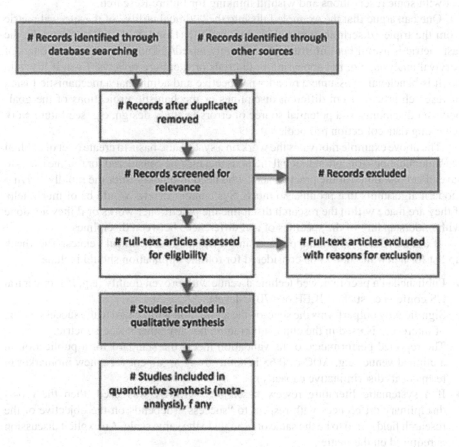

Fig. 2. The PRISMA flowchart.

Proposed Extension to PRISMA Protocol:

1. The discipline to which a primary research article belongs can be stored at the initial stage of database searching.
2. At the last block (studies included for quantitative synthesis), the articles of the same specialization should be summarized together.

3. Conclusions should be interpreted according to the research tradition within their field, and then, translated into a different discipline with an explicit discussion of the required correction/adaptation or explicitly stating no need of any change.

4 Discussion and Conclusions

The article is not aimed to promote the idea that deep survival necessarily is a dead end, moreover, in a recent article we argue for the opposite [Sidorova, Lozano, under review] yet with some reservations and wishful thinking for Future Research.

One can argue that the example falls into the "clinical utility" of the survival metric from the triple {discrimination, calibration, utility} (Hond et al. 2023). Certainly, the last metric is useful but unfortunately is largely unsed/unknown to the practitioners of survival analysis, e.g. not appearing in tutorials or literature reviews. Even if it would be. It is beneficial to assume a broader perspective and admit that a mechanistic fusion of research articles from different disciplines or mechanistic projections of the goals between disciplines is a potential source of errors in study design, e.g. see future work regarding data collection protocols.

The above example motivates the work on a systematic basis to create a set of explicit recommendations for computational methods that may be considered for routine use, – to save effort and time for the practitioners, who need to quickly filter the rapidly arriving modern algorithms that promise so much. Systematic reviews would be of much help, if they are made within the research discipline the practitioner works or if they are done with understanding of the specifics of and differences between disciplines.

If a method has no routine protocol in the main stream clinical venues. The check up list for a new method to be considered for routine application should include:

- Published at a peer reviewed technical venue with proven quality (e.g. ISI, or central CS conference such as IEEE or A/B/C-level).
- Significantly outperforms the state-of-the art method with regard to the success metric of interest as is used in the clinical literature, not any other success metric.
- The reported performance of its validation meets the standard for a publication in a clinical venue (e.g. AUC of 0.65 is not a strong argument for a new biomarker in terms of its discriminative capacity).
- If a systematic literature review based on PRISMA was used, then the cross-disciplinary differences with respect to "success" (depends on the objective of the research field) need to be the same or brought to the same scale. An explicit discussion is required on the matter.

Future Work

Unfortunately, many other subtle errors exist that make the effort invested into the application of a published and cited method results in a waste of time and effort, including the subtle differences in data collection protocols. Examples are (1) relatively easy to detect emotion expression in voice (Sidorova, Badia 2008) can be confounded with another event of interest (Sidorova et al. 2020a) such as the swing of blood glucose reflected in a vocal biomarker, (2) short-term patterns can be confounded with long-term patterns of the same disease (Sidorova et al. 2020b), and so on.

- There should be no difference between the data collection protocol in the clinical studies and the protocols adapted for the collection of data to test the algorithm, incl. The ground truth labeling. Any such minor difference must be explicitly discussed. For example, if one attempts to develop a vocal biomarker for blood glucose value, then first provide a speech sample and then read glucose value and not or vice versa. (In the case of the incorrect order, an emotion can be added to the speech sample, as the user is not entirely indifferent to one's glucose values.)

References

McKenzie, T., et al.: Statement: an updated guideline for reporting systematic reviews. BMJ **372**, 2021 (2020)

Antolini, L., et al.: A time-dependent discrimination index for survival data. Stat. Med. **24**, 3927–3944 (2005)

Cabitza, A., Campagner, A., The need to separate the wheat from the chaff in medical informatics, Introducing a comprehensive checklist for the (self) assessment of medical AI studies. Int. J. Med. Inform. **153** (2021)

Ching, T., et al, Cox-nnet: an artificial neural network method for prognosis prediction of high-thoughput omics data. PloS Comput. Biol. **14**(4) (2016)

Cox, D.R, Regression models and life-tables. J. R. Stat. Soc. Series B Methodol. **34**, 187–220 (1972)

Deepa, P., Gunavathi, C.: A systematic review on machine learning and deep learning techniques in cancer survival prediction. Progress Biophys. Molecul. Biol. **174** (2022)

Sidorova, J., Lozano, J.J.: Appendix to "A systematic review on machine learning and deep learning, under review techniques in cancer survival prediction": Validation of Survival Methods

Faraggi, D., Simon, R.: A neural network for survival data. Stat. Med. **14**(1), 72–73 (1995)

Grossman, R.L.: et al.: Toward a shared vision for cancer genomic data. N. Engl. J. Med. **375**(12), 1109–1112 (2016)

Hao, et al.: Cox-PASNet: pathway-based sparse deep neural network for survival analysis, IEEE International Conference on Bioinformatics and Biomedicine, pp. 381–386, BIBM-2018

Heagerty, P.J., Zheng, Y.: Survival model predictive accuracy and ROC curves. Biometrics **61**, 92–105 (2005)

Hu, F., et al.: A gene signature of survival prediction for kidney renal cell carcinoma by multi-omic data analysis. Int. J. Mol. Sci. **20**(22), 5720 (2019)

Huang, et al.: SALMON: survival analysis learning with multi-omics neural networks on breast cancer. Front. Genet. (2019)

Sidorova, J., Lozano, J.J.: New and classical data processing: fruit and perils, poster. CIBER (2022)

Lee, S., Lim, H.: Review of statistical methods for survival analysis using genomic data. Genom. Inform. **17**(4), e41 (2019)

Lee Ch., et al.: DeepHit: a deep learning approach to survival analysis with competing risks. In: Proceedings of 32nd AAAI Conference on Artificial Intelligence (2018)

Kim, S., et al.: Improved survival analysis by learning shared genomic information from pan-cancer data. Bioinformatics **36** (2020)

Kleinbaum, D.G., Klein, M.: Survival analysis, a self-learning text, 3rd edn. Springer, Statistics for Biology and Health (2012)

Kvamme, H., et al.: Time-to-event prediction with neural network and Cox regression. J. Mach. Learn. Res. **20** (2019)

Katzman, J., et al.: DeepSurv: personalised treatment recommender system using a Cox proportinal hazards deep neural network. BMC Med. Res. Methodol. **18**, 24 (2018)

Sahu, et al.: Discovery of targets for immune-metabolic antitumor drugs identifies estrogen-related receptor alpha. Cancer Discov. **13**(3), 672–701 (2023)

Salerno, S., Li, Y.: High-dimensional survival analysis: methods and applications. Ann. Rev. Statist. Appl. **10**, 25–49 (2023)

Sidorova, J., Lozano, J.J.: New and classical data processing: fruit and perils, jornadas Cientificas, CIBER (2022)

Sidorova, J., Lozano, J.J.: A Survey of Survival Analysis with Deep Learning: Models, Applications and Challenges. under review

[SEER, http] https://seer.cancer.gov/causespecific/

Tong, L., et al.: Deep learning based feature-level integration pf multi-omics data for breast cancer patients survival analysis. BCM Med. Informa. Dec. Mak. **20**, 225 (2020)

Yang, et al.: Identifying risk stratification associated with a cancer for overall survival by deep-learning based CoxPH. IEEE Access (7) (2019)

Yousefi, S., et al.: Predicting clinical outcomes from large scale cancer genomic profiles with deep survival models. Scientific Reports (2017)

Sidorova, J., et al.: Blood glucose estimation from voice: first review of successes and challenges. J. Voice (2020a)

Sidorova, J., et al.: Impact of diabetes mellitus on voice: a methodological commentary (2020b)

Hond, A., et al.: Perspectives of validation of clinical predictive algorithms, digital Medicine (2023)

Sidorova, J., Badia, T.: ESEDA: tool for enhanced emotion recognition and detection, Procs. AXMEDIS (2008)

Gamification in Recommendation Systems a Systematic Analysis

Agyeman Murad Taqi[1,3](✉) ⓘ, Munther Qadous[1,3] ⓘ, Mutaz Salah[1,3] ⓘ,
and Fezile Ozdamli[2,3] ⓘ

[1] Computer Information Systems, Near East University, Nicosia 1065, North Cyprus
20223090@std.neu.edu.tr
[2] Management Information Systems, Near East University, Nicosia 1065, North Cyprus
fezile.ozdamli@neu.edu.tr
[3] Computer Information Systems Research and Technology Centre, Near East University,
Mersin, Turkey

Abstract. Recommendation systems are one area where gamification has gained popularity. Gamification is a method for incorporating game design aspects into non-game environments to engage users and drive them to complete desired tasks. The systematic literature review on gamification in recommendation systems is presented in this research. The review offers insights into the most recent gamification methods, the underlying mechanisms, and how gamification affects user engagement and the success of recommendations. The review uses a methodical approach of looking for and choosing pertinent documents. The analysis covers 16 papers that were published between 2013 and 2023. According to the report, data collecting, user modeling, suggestion generation, and evaluation are just a few of the steps of recommendation systems where gamification has been used. Gamified recommendation systems incorporate game components like points, badges, leaderboards, challenges, and awards to entice and engage users. The research also demonstrates how gamification can boost recommendations' efficacy and promote user engagement. Gamification can increase user motivation, encourage exploration and learning, and provide immediate feedback to users. When they are gamified, the success of suggestions depends on the kind of recommendation task, the user type, and the context. Gamification is more effective for challenging and exploratory recommendation jobs and for users with little motivation or expertise. However, the review also highlights several problems and limitations with gamified recommendation systems. The review concluded that gamification had become a potential method for boosting user engagement and the potency of recommendations. Additional study is necessary to solve the difficulties and restrictions in gamified recommendation systems and create efficient and flexible gamification solutions.

Keywords: Gamification · Recommendation systems · User Engagement · Satisfaction · Trust · Performance

T. Guarda et al. (Eds.): ARTIIS 2023, CCIS 1935, pp. 143–153, 2024.
https://doi.org/10.1007/978-3-031-48858-0_12

1 Introduction

The advent of modernization has led to a rapid spread of information technology wherein users are faced with an increasing number of choices. In order to help with these choices, recommendation systems are introduced. Recommendation systems are algorithms that suggest what a user may like [1]. They are tools to help customers choose and purchase according to their needs and help businesses retain their customers while attracting new ones; They can, in effect, offer products based on the customers' needs and help the decision-making process by filtering out unnecessary information and prioritizing the customers' preferences [2]. Recommendation systems exploit the traces left by users to recommend a small set of items of interest to them [3].

Gamification, on the other hand, motivates greater involvement and people to reach a certain goal. Whatever the goal, be it education, investment, work promotion, or health, gamification helps the participant understand the concepts better because it is no longer a chore or a job; it has become a game that people can enjoy playing. Gamification, therefore, injects fun elements into applications and systems that might otherwise lack immediacy or relevance for users. This incentivizes users to achieve goals and helps them overcome negative associations with the system and the tasks it requires them to complete [4]. This, to a large extent, is why there is a tendency to misunderstand and confuse games and gamification. One distinctive line of difference is that games occur within a predesigned atmosphere, with set rules and conditions. This is why, no matter how complicated or serious a game might be, it is still a game. Gamification occurs in the real world, where the application of those game features can only motivate and encourage performance. It is, in essence, defined by the outward interaction it encourages. Gamification is based on achieving goals using techniques derived from games, not by using games themselves [4].

Different studies indicate that applying gamification could have positive results for the users, such as students having better learning outcomes, the rise of users' participation in fitness courses, or the increase in the efficacy of persuasive health strategies [5]. Gamification is, therefore, an effective tool to motivate behaviour change.

A critical look at both recommendations and gamification shows that both require end users for success. The fundamental purpose of any recommendation system, for example, is to filter information according to user preferences, which is why the involvement of end users is one of the most important factors in the effectiveness of recommender algorithms. The strategies are not always about improving algorithms but getting end users' involvement and collaboration to improve the system [6]. Recommendation seeks the best output for the end user, and gamification seeks to influence the output of the end user, a standout approach to improving user experience [7]. It relies on people making choices based on what other people recommend [8]. Gamification techniques can present solutions for users to transparently and voluntarily collaborate for recommender systems to deliver more relevant results.

Therefore, this project seeks to determine whether a blend of both tools can produce better motivation and engagement results; whether introducing game design elements into recommender systems can overcome motivation difficulties and promote engagement.

Using secondary data, this study will analyze the following research questions:

RQ1. What will be the outcome of incorporating gamification elements into recommendation systems?

RQ2. Will the blend improve user engagement, satisfaction, and trust in the system, ultimately leading to better system performance?

2 Methodology

2.1 Research Design

The authors ensured that tasks were methodically created and provided at each stage of the study as this research constitutes a systematic literature review. For this systematic review, the PRISMA(Preferred Reporting Items for Systematic Reviews and Meta-Analyses) selection procedure was applied [9]. The screening process is graphically depicted in the PRISMA flow diagram, which is why we selected it. Before making the selection process explicit by outlining decisions made at various stages of the systematic review, it first tallies the number of papers found.

2.2 Search Strategy

The systematic investigation used two important scholarly databases in the research field: IEEE Xplore, and SCOPUS. The following keywords and homonyms were adopted during the search process in the datasets ("Recommendation systems") AND ("Gamification" OR "Gamified" OR "game elements" OR "dynamics" OR "Game mechanics" AND ("User engagement" OR "Satisfaction" OR "Trust" OR "Advantages" OR "opportunities" OR "Challenges" OR "Disadvantages" OR "Performance"). All searches were performed between 2013 and 2023, including journal and conference papers with English titles.

Inclusion and Exclusion Criteria

Including and exclusion criteria guarantees that the searched articles are pertinent to the research goal.

The criteria determined are given in Table 1.

With (390) articles, the screening process for articles began. The Scopus database yielded 257 publications in response to the initial search, and the IEEE Xplore database returned 133 hits for articles. After reviewing the inclusion and exclusion criteria, 180 articles from the ScienceDirect database and 85 from IEEE Xplore were accessed. The screening procedure began by removing four duplicate articles because they were present in both databases. The writers independently assessed titles and abstracts about inclusion and exclusion criteria. After screening, inclusion criteria were applied to the abstracts (n = 261). One hundred forty articles have been removed because they were out of place with the subject.

Additionally, 105 articles were eliminated after screening full papers since they did not directly connect to the issue, and some of the studies were only presented in English at the abstract level. Unrelated articles, those whose full text could not be accessed, and those whose abstracts were only available in English were excluded. Finally, 16 studies satisfied the criteria for inclusion. The PRISMA flow diagram (Fig. 1) detailed the systematic literature review procedure.

Table 1. Inclusion/Exclusion criteria

Inclusion criteria	Exclusion criteria
Articles are written in the English language	Articles not written in the English language Full text is not available online. (not open access)
Articles with the research done	Any duplicated research articles
Research published between 2013–2022	Review articles and editorial materials, book chapter
Available within the two databases, IEEE Xplore and ScienceDirect	Articles not related to keywords or topics
Open Access Articles	

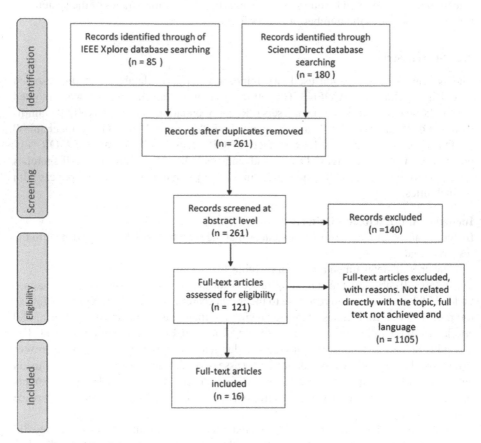

Fig. 1. The flow of information through the different phases of systematic review

2.3 Quality Assessment

To improve the total score of this planned publication study, the authors carefully read through the assessment requirements. Every selection method and criterion employed in the study was done with an eye toward the study's goals and objectives. The study was developed with care and adequate resource management.

2.4 Data Extraction

In the data extraction process for the study's PRISMA, 16 studies were identified, and the information collected from these studies included the following elements.

- Article/Citations
- Gamification/Recommendation Elements
- Key findings

3 Results

3.1 Incorporating Gamification Elements into Recommendation Systems

Recent studies have shown much interest in incorporating gamification components into recommendation algorithms. Gamification is a viable strategy to improve recommendation systems since it improves problem-solving, encourages learning, and explores user motivation.

Gamification's main goals are to support problem-solving, promote learning, and investigate user motivation. This implies that gamification can be used to improve recommendation systems by involving users and encouraging them to participate with the system.

Gamification elements such as points and rewards, progress tracking, challenges and competitions. It can be integrated into the core recommendation systems to provide incentives, track user progress and introduce competitive elements that enhance user engagement [10].

Nuanmeesri examines the incorporation of gamification elements into recommendation systems for adaptive tourism [11]. By addressing the challenges faced in tourism development. Particularly in emerging cities. Gamification approaches are explored as means to improve the standard of products and services in the tourism industry; focusing on the development of an adaptive tourism recommendation algorithm, it is suggested that recommendation systems are a key component. To utilize and enhance the tourism experience.

Using an intelligent experiment-based rehabilitation system is another way to add gamification components to a recommendation system. That uses a recommendation mechanism. The recommender system examines user interactions and usage history to choose a fresh gamified workout unique to each patient. This shows that recommendation algorithms make personalizing a rehabilitation experience based on user preferences and progress possible [12].

Nikolakis et al. developed a two-level collaborative filtering strategy in the context of industrial processes [13]. This strategy tries to improve the suggestion process by optimizing information content dissemination to shop floor+ operators. This suggests that suggestion systems are essential for improving the efficacy and efficiency of industrial activities. The study by the authors also emphasizes the necessity for self-actualization and self-fulfilment at work. This need is intended to be met by the suggested cognitive system, which strives to close the talent gap and meet the changing production requirements. The idea of self-fulfilment and self-actualization suggests that gamification approaches could engage and drive operators in their work, even when specific gamification components are not mentioned explicitly.

Adaptive Learning Path Recommendation Systems (ALPRS): ALPRS aims to provide personalized learning recommendations to students based on adaptive learning paths; the system incorporates the Fuzzy Delphi Method (FDM) to identify essential factors in learning content, the Fuzzy Interpretive Structural Model (ISM) to establish an adaptive learning path hierarchical structure, and repertory grid technology (RGT) to assess the effects of recommender element attributes, ALPRS outperforms traditional learning course guided recommendation mechanisms, resulting in better learning outcomes and higher user satisfaction scores [14].

Lavoué et al. emphasized tailoring gaming elements to learners' profiles to create personalized learning experiences [15]. By employing recommendation techniques, the adaptation process ensures that gaming features are customized to individual learners' preferences. Although specific details about these elements are not provided in this article, they will likely include gamification components such as leaderboards, badges, points, challenges, rewards, and feedback systems. These elements are carefully designed to enhance learner engagement and motivation within the learning environment.

Tailoring Process in Personalized Gamification by Rodrigues et al., highlights the need to consider both user characteristics and contextual characteristics in the tailoring process of personalized gamification [16]. User characteristics encompass demographic information and game-related preferences, while contextual characteristics include the learning activity type and geographic location. By combining these features, gamification designs can be defined to cater to individual users' specific needs and preferences.

Recognizing the potential benefits of gamification, Mostafa & Elbarawy suggests incorporating gamification tools into the job matching model [17]. These tools motivate candidates to study and engage in daily work activities, enhancing their learning path and career development. By introducing game-like elements and incentives, candidates can be encouraged to actively participate and pursue continuous learning within their chosen career field.

3.2 The Impact of Gamification-Recommendation System Blend on User Perceptions and System Performance

The effects of integrating gamification components with recommendation systems on user perceptions and system performance have been the subject of numerous research, and it has produced positive results.

In the study by Tsay et al., gamification elements were introduced in a Personal and Professional Development (PPD) course, including leaderboards, progress monitoring, challenges and quests, personalized suggestions, adaptive learning routes, and collaborative filtering [18]. The results showed that the gamified system considerably increased student performance compared to the conventional, non-gamified distribution technique, the gamified system considerably increased student performance.

Another researchers proposed a gamified method of word-of-mouth recommendations to increase client sales [2]. The gamification components used were leaderboards, challenges and goals, points and awards, badges and achievements, progress tracking, and a system for word-of-mouth recommendations. According to the research, the gamified system increased client purchases and unique visits to the e-commerce website.

A resarcher explored the gamification of a postgraduate distance education course taught in a social virtual reality environment [19]. The gamification elements incorporated quests, surprise elements, points, levels, badges, and design principles that promoted choice and agency. The findings indicated that gamification enhanced student engagement and active participation in the course. Prabowo et al. investigated the impact of gamification elements, such as a point system for incentives and ratings for feedback on gig workers in the ride-sharing industry [20]. The study revealed that gamification influenced the extrinsic motivation of drivers in ride-sharing applications.

Mohammad Akhriza and Dwi Mumpuni created a gamified Educator Career Promotion System (ECPS) with a recommender system to advance the careers of lecturers [21]. Some of the gamification components were a point system for incentives, the ECPS, challenges, and objectives. The study showed how the recommender system and gamified ECPS efficiently encouraged teachers in Indonesian higher education institutions to engage in more productive activities freely. The use of Linked Data and gamification approaches to dynamically build quiz games were presented [22] The characteristics were ranked using the gamified quiz recommender system according to relevancy and improved data quality. The study demonstrated how gamification might improve the creation of dynamic quiz games.

Blagov et al. examined how corporate Web 2.0 technologies were adopted and used gamification techniques for fitness. Motivation and rewards, fitness gamification, points and competitiveness, and the originality of the knowledge shared and developed were some of the gamification components used. The results showed that adding gamification components inspired by fitness gamification initiatives dramatically increased the adoption and use of business Web 2.0 solutions [23].

Sotirakou and Mourlas focus on designing a gamified News Reader application for mobile devices [24]. The study explores both recommendation system elements and gamification system elements. Regarding the recommendation system, the article discusses the role of recommendation systems in the News Reader application, personalized news recommendations techniques, user preferences and behaviour consideration, and evaluation methods for assessing the effectiveness of the recommendation system. In terms of gamification, the article highlights the specific game elements used in the application, the integration of gamification to enhance user engagement, and examples of gamification techniques employed, such as points, badges, leaderboards, challenges, and rewards. The findings suggest that the gamified News Reader application increases user engagement, motivation, and digital news consumption compared to a non-gamified news reader.

Overall, these studies demonstrate that integrating gamification elements into recommendation systems can positively impact user engagement, performance, motivation, and system adoption. The specific gamification elements employed varied across studies but commonly included points and rewards, leaderboards, challenges, progress tracking, personalized recommendations, and adaptive learning paths. The successful implementation of gamification in recommendation systems suggests its potential for enhancing user experiences and system effectiveness in various domains.

4 Discussion

The systematic literature review results indicate that the incorporation of gamification elements into recommendation systems has garnered significant attention in recent studies. Gamification offers a viable strategy to improve recommendation systems by enhancing problem-solving, encouraging learning, and exploring user motivation. The main goals of gamification, namely supporting problem-solving, promoting learning, and investigating user motivation, align well with the objectives of recommendation systems.

One approach to integrating gamification into recommendation systems is by incorporating gamification elements such as points and rewards, progress tracking, challenges, and competitions directly into the core recommendation algorithms [10]. This integration provides incentives for users, tracks their progress, and introduces competitive elements that enhance user engagement. For instance, Nuanmeesri explores using gamification elements in adaptive tourism recommendation systems to improve the quality of products and services in the tourism industry [11]. By emphasizing the role of recommendation systems, the study highlights the potential for gamification to enhance the tourism experience.

Another way to incorporate gamification into recommendation systems is through intelligent experiment-based rehabilitation systems. González-González et al. demonstrate how recommendation mechanisms can be utilized to personalize rehabilitation experiences for each patient based on their preferences and progress [12]. The recommender system selects tailored gamified workouts by analyzing user interactions and usage history, leading to a more engaging and personalized rehabilitation experience.

The impact of the gamification-recommendation system blend extends beyond traditional domains. Nikolakis et al. propose a two-level collaborative filtering strategy in the context of industrial processes to optimize the suggestion process and improve the efficacy and efficiency of industrial activities [13]. While gamification components are not explicitly mentioned, the authors highlight the importance of self-fulfilment and self-actualization at work, indicating that gamification approaches can engage and drive operators in their tasks.

In education, adaptive learning path recommendation systems (ALPRS) leverage gamification elements to provide personalized learning recommendations to students. Su et al. demonstrate that ALPRS outperforms traditional learning course-guided recommendation mechanisms, leading to improved learning outcomes and higher user satisfaction scores [14]. Lavoué et al. also emphasize the importance of tailoring gamification elements to learners' profiles to create personalized learning experiences, enhancing learner engagement and motivation within the learning environment [15].

The successful integration of gamification and recommendation system elements has also been observed in e-commerce, gig work, lecturer career advancement, quiz games, and corporate Web 2.0 systems. Mostafa & Elbarawy suggest incorporating gamification tools into job-matching models to motivate candidates and enhance their learning and career development [17]. This approach encourages candidates to participate and engage in their work activities actively. Moreover, studies demonstrate the positive impact of gamification on client sales, student engagement, gig worker motivation, lecturer career advancement, quiz game creation, and corporate Web 2.0 technology adoption and use, respectively.

Implementing gamification components into recommendation systems has demonstrated positive results in several fields [2, 19, 21–23]. The specific gamification elements employed varied across studies but commonly included points and rewards, leaderboards, challenges, progress tracking, personalized recommendations, and adaptive learning paths. These elements enhance user engagement, performance, motivation, and system adoption. The successful implementation of gamification in recommendation systems suggests its potential for improving user experiences and system effectiveness across different contexts.

However, it is worth noting that further research is needed to explore the optimal design and implementation of gamification elements in recommendation systems. The effectiveness of specific gamification components, their impact on long-term user engagement and behaviour change, and potential challenges and ethical considerations associated with gamification should be carefully examined. Future studies can also delve into the customization of gamification elements based on user characteristics and contextual factors to create more personalized and engaging experiences.

The findings of this systematic literature review illustrate the positive impact of incorporating gamification elements into recommendation systems. In many domains, gamification can increase user engagement, motivation, performance, and system adoption. Recommendation systems can offer individualized and interesting experiences by utilizing gamification techniques, enhancing user pleasure, learning, and problem-solving. More investigation and development in this field may result in the developing of user-centric, more efficient recommendation systems that use gamification.

5 Conclusion

Our systematic literature review concludes that combining gamification components and recommendation systems produces intriguing results. Gamification is a tactic that addresses problem-solving, learning, and user motivation while enhancing user engagement, motivation, and performance. Gamification elements, including leaderboards, challenges, points, prizes, and personalized suggestions, have been successfully included to enhance user experiences and system effectiveness.

Numerous settings, including adaptive tourism, rehabilitation, industrial processes, education, e-commerce, gig work, career progression, quiz games, and corporate environments, have been studied concerning the incorporation of gamification in recommendation systems. These studies have shown the beneficial effects of gamification on system adoption, sales, motivation, and learning outcomes.

Adaptive learning routes, leaderboards, challenges, progress tracking, and points and incentives were among the aspects that were frequently used in research, even though the precise gamification elements used varied. These components have helped recommendation systems improve user experiences, performance, and motivation.

More research is required to maximize the design and application of gamification components in recommendation systems. Investigating the efficacy of certain gamification elements, long-term user engagement, behaviour modification, and ethical issues is crucial. Gamification features can be tailored based on user traits and contextual factors to provide more interesting and personalized experiences. Therefore, adding gamification components to recommendation systems can enhance user satisfaction, educational results, and system efficiency. Constructing user-centric, effective recommendation systems that take advantage of gamification through further research and development in this area is possible.

References

1. Milano, S., Taddeo, M., Floridi, L.: Recommender systems and their ethical challenges. AI Soc. **35**(4), 957–967 (2020). https://doi.org/10.1007/s00146-020-00950-y
2. Hajarian, M., Hemmati, S.: A gamified word of mouth recommendation system for increasing customer purchase. In: 2020 4th International Conference on Smart City, Internet of Things and Applications (SCIOT), pp. 7–11 (2020). https://doi.org/10.1109/SCIOT50840.2020.9250209
3. Lonjarret, C., Auburtin, R., Robardet, C., Plantevit, M.: Sequential recommendation with metric models based on frequent sequences. DATA Min. Knowl. Discov. **35**(3), 1087–1133 (2021). https://doi.org/10.1007/s10618-021-00744-w
4. Christians, G.: The Origins and Future of Gamification. University of South Carolina (2018)
5. Vasconcelos, G., Oliveira, W., Santos, A.C., Hamari, J.: ReGammend: a method for personalized recommendation of gamification designs. In: Proceedings of the 6th International GamiFIN Conference, pp. 85–94 (2022). https://ceur-ws.org/Vol-3147/paper9.pdf
6. Galí, J.M.: Improving Recommender Systems with Gamification. Gecon (2016). https://gecon.es/gamification-recommender-systems/. Accessed 27 July 2023
7. Santos, A.C.G., et al.: The relationship between user types and gamification designs. User Model. User-adapt. Interact. **31**(5), 907–940 (2021). https://doi.org/10.1007/s11257-021-09300-z
8. Tondello, G.F., Orji, R., Nacke, L.E.: Recommender systems for personalized gamification. In: Adjunct Publication of the 25th Conference on User Modeling, Adaptation and Personalization, pp. 425–430 (2017). https://doi.org/10.1145/3099023.3099114
9. Moher, D., Liberati, A., Tetzlaff, J., Altman, D.G.: Preferred reporting items for systematic reviews and meta-analyses: the PRISMA statement. BMJ **339**(jul21 1), b2535–b2535 (2009). https://doi.org/10.1136/bmj.b2535
10. Cechetti, N.P., Bellei, E.A., Biduski, D., Rodriguez, J.P.M., Roman, M.K., De Marchi, A.C.B.: Developing and implementing a gamification method to improve user engagement: a case study with an m-Health application for hypertension monitoring. Telemat. Inform. **41**, 126–138 (2019). https://doi.org/10.1016/j.tele.2019.04.007
11. Nuanmeesri, S.: Development of community tourism enhancement in emerging cities using gamification and adaptive tourism recommendation. J. King Saud Univ. Comput. Inform. Sci. **34**(10), 8549–8563 (2022). https://doi.org/10.1016/j.jksuci.2021.04.007
12. González-González, C.S., Toledo-Delgado, P.A., Muñoz-Cruz, V., Torres-Carrion, P.V.: Serious games for rehabilitation: Gestural interaction in personalized gamified exercises through a recommender system. J. Biomed. Inform. **97**, 103266 (2019). https://doi.org/10.1016/j.jbi.2019.103266

13. Nikolakis, N., Siaterlis, G., Alexopoulos, K.: A machine learning approach for improved shop-floor operator support using a two-level collaborative filtering and gamification features. Procedia CIRP **93**, 455–460 (2020). https://doi.org/10.1016/j.procir.2020.05.160

14. Su, C.-H., Fan, K.-K., Su, P.-Y.: A intelligent Gamifying learning recommender system integrated with learning styles and Kelly repertory grid technology. In: 2016 International Conference on Applied System Innovation (ICASI), pp. 1–4 (2016). https://doi.org/10.1109/ICASI.2016.7539768

15. Lavoue, E., Monterrat, B., Desmarais, M., George, S.: Adaptive gamification for learning environments. IEEE Trans. Learn. Technol. **12**(1), 16–28 (2019). https://doi.org/10.1109/TLT.2018.2823710

16. Rodrigues, L., Toda, A.M., Oliveira, W., Palomino, P.T., Vassileva, J., Isotani, S.: Automating gamification personalization to the user and beyond. IEEE Trans. Learn. Technol. **15**(2), 199–212 (2022). https://doi.org/10.1109/TLT.2022.3162409

17. Mostafa, L., Elbarawy, A.M.: Enhance job candidate learning path using gamification. In: 2018 28th International Conference on Computer Theory and Applications (ICCTA), pp. 88–93 (2018). https://doi.org/10.1109/ICCTA45985.2018.9499189

18. Tsay, C.H.-H., Kofinas, A., Luo, J.: Enhancing student learning experience with technology-mediated gamification: an empirical study. Comput. Educ. **121**, 1–17 (2018). https://doi.org/10.1016/j.compedu.2018.01.009

19. Mystakidis, S.: Distance education gamification in social virtual reality: a case study on student engagement. In: 2020 11th International Conference on Information, Intelligence, Systems and Applications IISA, pp. 1–6 (2020). https://doi.org/10.1109/IISA50023.2020.9284417

20. Prabowo, R., Sucahyo, Y.G., Gandhi, A., Ruldeviyani, Y.: Does gamification motivate gig workers? a critical issue in ride-sharing industries. In: 2019 International Conference on Advanced Computer Science and information Systems (ICACSIS), pp. 343–348 (2019). https://doi.org/10.1109/ICACSIS47736.2019.8979938

21. Mohammad Akhriza, T., Dwi Mumpuni, I.: Gamification of the lecturer career promotion system with a recommender system. In: 2020 Fifth International Conference on Informatics and Computing (ICIC), pp. 1–8 (2020). https://doi.org/10.1109/ICIC50835.2020.9288541

22. Parekh, A., Shah, N., Varshney, L., Shah, N., Dsilva, M.: Heuristic generation of dynamic quiz game using linked data and gamfication. In: 2016 International Conference on Inventive Computation Technologies (ICICT), pp. 1–6 (2016). https://doi.org/10.1109/INVENTIVE.2016.7824905

23. Blagov, E., Simeonova, B., Bogolyubov, P.: Motivating the adoption and usage of corporate web 2.0 systems using fitness gamification practices. In: 2013 IEEE 15th Conference on Business Informatics, pp. 420–427 (2013). https://doi.org/10.1109/CBI.2013.68

24. Sotirakou, C., Mourlas, C.: Designing a gamified News Reader for mobile devices. In: 2015 International Conference on Interactive Mobile Communication Technologies and Learning (IMCL), pp. 332–337 (2015). https://doi.org/10.1109/IMCTL.2015.7359614

Object Projection from $\mathbb{R}^4$ to $\mathbb{R}^3$ in Bachelor's Degree with GeoGebra

Judith K. Jiménez-Vilcherrez[1], Robert Ipanaqué-Chero[2(✉)],
Ricardo Velezmoro-León[2], Marcela F. Velásquez-Fernández[2],
Rolando E. Ipanaqué-Silva[2], and César Silva-More[2]

[1] Universidad Tecnológica Del Perú, Av. Vice Cdra 1-Costado Real Plaza,
Piura, Peru
C19863@utp.edu.pe
[2] Universidad Nacional de Piura, Urb. Miraflores s/n, Piura, Castilla, Peru
{ripanaquec,rvelezmorol,fvelasquezf,ripanaques,csilvam}@unp.edu.pe

Abstract. Projecting objects from $\mathbb{R}^3$ to $\mathbb{R}^2$ is a subject deeply studied
since the dawn of civilization; so much so, that all software that includes
graphing tools show flat objects (on a flat screen) as if they were in
three-dimensional space. Currently, there are various studies regarding
the projection of objects from $\mathbb{R}^4$ to $\mathbb{R}^3$ and their visualization. This
paper describes various Dynamic Worksheets developed in the dynamic
mathematics software GeoGebra that visualize the projection of the unit
hypersphere and the unit "complex circumference" from $\mathbb{R}^4$ to $\mathbb{R}^3$, having as reference Pohlke-Schwarz theorem and some concepts of linear
algebra. These Dynamic Worksheets will be delivered to the students
of the Differential Geometry course of the Mathematics Program at the
Universidad Nacional de Piura. Some of the examples to be developed
in the classroom are shown and described.

Keywords: Pohlke-Schwarz Theorem with GeoGebra · Projections
with GeoGebra · Differential Geometry with GeoGebra · Complex
Functions with GeoGebra

1 Introduction

Projecting objects from $\mathbb{R}^3$ to $\mathbb{R}^2$ is a subject deeply studied since the dawn of
civilization. The various cave paintings attest to the desire of human beings to
capture scenes around them on two-dimensional surfaces [4,5]. In fact, currently
all the software that include tools for graphing include commands that show
flat objects (on a flat screen) as if they were in three-dimensional space [6,9–
11,13,15,25]. Currently, there are various studies regarding the projection of
objects from $\mathbb{R}^4$ to $\mathbb{R}^3$ and their visualization [1–3,7,14,17,18,21–23,26–28].
However, no research has been found that relates such projections to the dynamic
mathematics software GeoGebra [24].

T. Guarda et al. (Eds.): ARTIIS 2023, CCIS 1935, pp. 154–168, 2024.
https://doi.org/10.1007/978-3-031-48858-0_13

In this paper, various Dynamic Worksheets [19] developed in GeoGebra are described in which projections of various mathematical objects are displayed from $\mathbb{R}^4$ to $\mathbb{R}^3$ (points, vectors, curves, surfaces, and solids). To achieve these visualizations, the projection of the canonical vectors of $\mathbb{R}^4$ on $\mathbb{R}^3$ is established, based on Pohlke-Schwarz theorem [20], and then makes use of some concepts of linear algebra to establish the analytical expressions of the submersion associated with the aforementioned projection of the canonical vectors.

The Dynamic Worksheets obtained in this research were provided to the students of the Differential Geometry course at the Mathematics Program in the Universidad Nacional de Piura. These students are in the 7th Term. Some of the examples developed in the classroom are shown and described in this paper.

This paper is structured as follows: Sect. 2 introduces the basic concepts related to Pohlke-Schwarz theorem, an extension of it, and the formal definitions of curve, surface, and solid. Then, Sect. 3 provides examples of patch images on the circumference and sphere (unitaries). Then in Sect. 4 the projection to be used in this work is defined. Next, in Sect. 5, examples of images of proper patches on the hypersphere and the "complex circumference" are provided (unitaries). To culminate, the essential conclusions of this paper are included in Sect. 6.

2 Basic Concepts

2.1 Mathematical Preliminaries

Theorem 1 (Pohlke-Schwarz theorem). *Given three lines in a 3D space that are mutually perpendicular, they have the same length and a common origin; they can be projected parallel to 2D space as three lines of any length that form different angles. [20] (see Fig. 1).*

Since Pohlke-Schwarz theorem was stated and proved, the idea of projections has expanded. This is summarized in the following theorem [8, 16].

Theorem 2 *Given four lines in a 4D space that are mutually perpendicular, they have the same length and a common origin; they can be projected parallel to 3D space as four lines of any length that form different angles. (see Fig. 2).*

Definition 1. *A patch of coordinates* $\mathbf{x} : D \to \mathbb{R}^n$ *is a differentiable function with domain in D (open set) of $\mathbb{R}^m$ and range in $\mathbb{R}^n$.*

The range of $\mathbf{x}$ is a smooth m-dimensional subset of $\mathbb{R}^n$. Additionally, $\mathbf{x}$ is required to be one-to-one and its inverse to be continuous (This last condition guarantees that $\mathbf{x}$ has the properties of a proper patch.) [12].

Definition 2. *A C subset of $\mathbb{R}^n$, $n > 0$, is a curve in $\mathbb{R}^n$ when $\forall \mathbf{p} \in C, \exists \mathbf{x} : D \subset \mathbb{R} \to C/\mathcal{N}_\delta(\mathbf{p}) \subset \mathbf{x}(D)$; where $\mathbf{x}$ is a proper patch.*

Definition 3. *A M subset of $\mathbb{R}^n$, $n > 1$, is a surface in $\mathbb{R}^n$ when $\forall \mathbf{p} \in M, \exists \mathbf{x} : D \subset \mathbb{R}^2 \to M/\mathcal{N}_\delta(\mathbf{p}) \subset \mathbf{x}(D)$; where $\mathbf{x}$ is a proper patch.*

Definition 4. *A N subset of $\mathbb{R}^n$, $n > 2$, is a solid in $\mathbb{R}^n$ when $\forall \mathbf{p} \in N, \exists \mathbf{x} : D \subset \mathbb{R}^3 \to N/\mathcal{N}_\delta(\mathbf{p}) \subset \mathbf{x}(D)$; where $\mathbf{x}$ is a proper patch.*

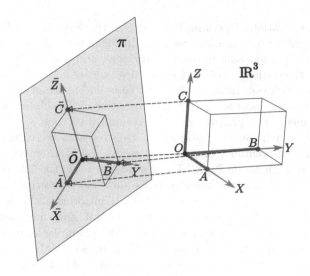

Fig. 1. Three lines of the same length and perpendicular to each other (OA, OB, and OC) projected in parallel onto three lines ($\bar{O}\bar{A}$, $\bar{O}\bar{B}$, and $\bar{O}\bar{C}$) in the π plane.

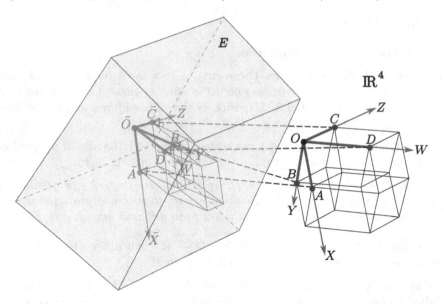

Fig. 2. Four lines of the same length and perpendicular to each other (OA, OB, OC, and OD) projected in parallel onto four lines ($\bar{O}\bar{A}$, $\bar{O}\bar{B}$, and $\bar{O}\bar{C}$) in the E space.

3   Previous Examples

3.1   Unit Circumference

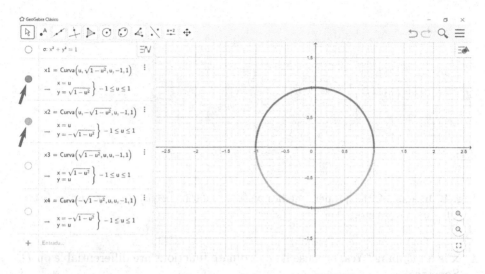

Fig. 3. Images of the proper patches $\mathbf{x}_1(u) = (u, \sqrt{1-u^2})$ (blue) and $\mathbf{x}_2(u) = (u, -\sqrt{1-u^2})$ (red).

Next, it will be verified that unit circumference σ in $\mathbb{R}^2$ is a curve. By definition, σ is made up of all points whose distance from the origin is one unit, or equivalently, all those points $\mathbf{p}$ that satisfy

$$\|\mathbf{p}\| = (p_1^2 + p_2^2)^{1/2} = 1 \,.$$

From this equality it follows that

$$p_2 = \pm\sqrt{1 - p_1^2} \tag{1}$$

$$p_1 = \pm\sqrt{1 - p_2^2} \tag{2}$$

To check Definition 2, it will suffice to define a suitable patch that covers all the points that are in the region of the positive y of σ. The points $\mathbf{p}$ in σ, with positive ordinate, can be expressed by the equality $\mathbf{p} = (p_1, p_2) = (p1, \sqrt{1 - p_1^2})$ (See Eq. 1). Based on this result, it is possible to define the function $\mathbf{x} : D \to \mathbb{R}^2$ such that

$$\mathbf{x}(u) = \left(u, \sqrt{1 - u^2}\right), \ D : \{u \in \mathbb{R} \,|\, u^2 < 1\} \,.$$

The answers to the following questions allow us to determine whether $\mathbf{x}$ is a proper patch.

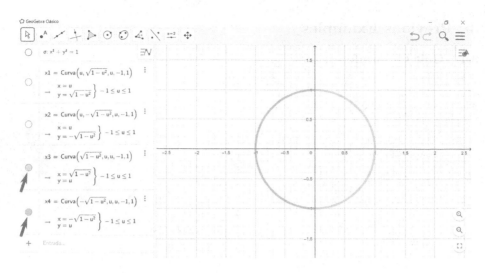

Fig. 4. Images of the proper patches $\mathbf{x}_3(u) = \left(\sqrt{1-u^2}, u\right)$ (cyan) and $\mathbf{x}_4(u) = \left(-\sqrt{1-u^2}, u\right)$ (green).

1. $\mathbf{x}$ is a mapping? Yes, because its coordinate functions are differentiable on D. Specifically

$$\frac{d}{du}u = 1, \ \frac{d}{du}\sqrt{1-u^2} = -\frac{u}{\sqrt{1-u^2}}.$$

2. $\mathbf{x}$ is regular? Yes, because the rank of it Jacobian matrix

$$\left(1 - \frac{u}{\sqrt{1-u^2}}\right)$$

at each point is 1 (domain dimension).
3. $\mathbf{x}$ is a proper patch? Yes, because the inverse function $\mathbf{x}^{-1} : \mathbf{x}(D) \to D$ such that

$$\mathbf{x}^{-1}(p_1, p_2) = p_1$$

is continuous.

Therefore, $\mathbf{x}$, thus defined, is a proper patch.

From the other equalities of Eqs. 1 and 2 we can, in a strictly analogous way, define three more proper patches, and thus verify, by Definition 2, that σ is a curve.

Figures 3 and 4 show the images of the proper patches that completely cover the circumference.

3.2 Unit Sphere

Next, it will be verified that unit sphere Σ in $\mathbb{R}^3$ is a surface. By definition, Σ is made up of all points whose distance from the origin is one unit, or equivalently, all those points $\mathbf{p}$ that satisfy

$$\|\mathbf{p}\| = (p_1^2 + p_2^2 + p_3^2)^{1/2} = 1.$$

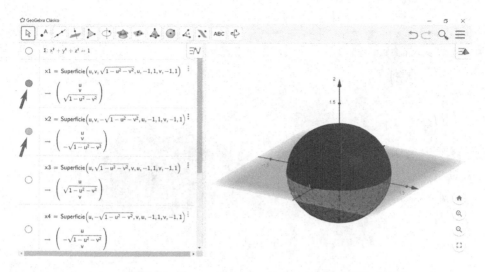

Fig. 5. Images of the proper patches $\mathbf{x}_1(u,v) = (u,v,\sqrt{1-u^2-v^2})$ (blue) and $\mathbf{x}_2(u,v) = (u,v,-\sqrt{1-u^2-v^2})$ (red).

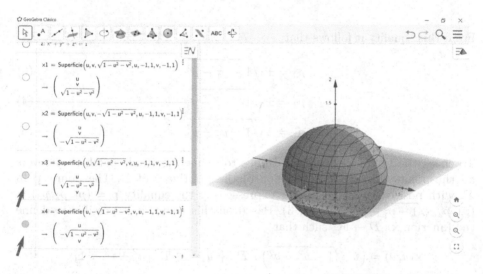

Fig. 6. Images of the proper patches $\mathbf{x}_3(u,v) = (u,\sqrt{1-u^2-v^2},v)$ (cyan) and $\mathbf{x}_4(u,v) = (u,-\sqrt{1-u^2-v^2},v)$ (green).

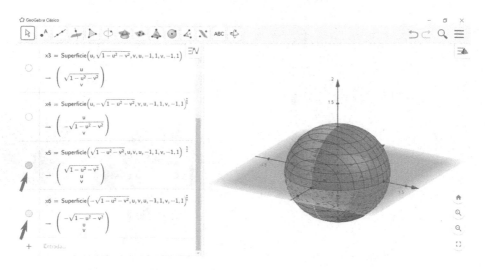

Fig. 7. Images of the proper patches $\mathbf{x}_5(u,v) = \left(\sqrt{1-u^2-v^2}, u, v\right)$ (orange) and $\mathbf{x}_6(u,v) = \left(-\sqrt{1-u^2-v^2}, u, v\right)$ (yellow).

From this equality it follows that

$$p_3 = \pm\sqrt{1 - p_1^2 - p_2^2} \tag{3}$$

$$p_2 = \pm\sqrt{1 - p_1^2 - p_3^2} \tag{4}$$

$$p_1 = \pm\sqrt{1 - p_2^2 - p_3^2} \tag{5}$$

To check the Definition 3, it will suffice to define a suitable patch that covers all the points that are in the region of the positive z of Σ. The points $\mathbf{p}$ in Σ, with positive ordinate, can be expressed by the equality $\mathbf{p} = (p_1, p_2, p_3) = (p1, p_2, \sqrt{1 - p_1^2 - p_2^2})$ (See Eq. 3). Based on this result, it is possible to define the function $\mathbf{x} : D \to \mathbb{R}^3$ such that

$$\mathbf{x}(u,v) = \left(u, \sqrt{1 - u^2 - v^2}\right), \quad D : \{(u,v) \in \mathbb{R}^2 \,|\, u^2 + v^2 < 1\}.$$

The answers to the following questions allow us to determine whether $\mathbf{x}$ is a proper patch.

1. $\mathbf{x}$ is a mapping? Yes, because its coordinate functions are differentiable on D. Specifically

$$\tfrac{\partial}{\partial u} u = 1, \ \tfrac{\partial}{\partial u} v = 0, \ \tfrac{\partial}{\partial u}\sqrt{1 - u^2 - v^2} = -\frac{u}{\sqrt{1-u^2-v^2}},$$

$$\tfrac{\partial}{\partial v} u = 0, \ \tfrac{\partial}{\partial v} v = 1, \ \tfrac{\partial}{\partial v}\sqrt{1 - u^2 - v^2} = -\frac{v}{\sqrt{1-u^2-v^2}}.$$

2. $\mathbf{x}$ is regular? Yes, because the rank of it Jacobian matrix

$$\begin{pmatrix} 1 & 0 & -\frac{u}{\sqrt{1-u^2-v^2}} \\ 0 & 1 & -\frac{v}{\sqrt{1-u^2-v^2}} \end{pmatrix}$$

at each point is 2 (domain dimension).

3. $\mathbf{x}$ is a proper patch? Yes, because the inverse function $\mathbf{x}^{-1} : \mathbf{x}(D) \to D$ such that

$$\mathbf{x}^{-1}(p_1, p_2, p_3) = (p_1, p_2)$$

is continuous.

Therefore, $\mathbf{x}$, thus defined, is a proper patch.

From the other equalities of Eqs. 3, 4, and 5 we can, in a strictly analogous way, define five more proper patches, and thus verify, by Definition 3, that Σ is a surface.

Figures 5, 6, and 7 show the images of the proper patches that completely cover the sphere.

4   Projection from $\mathbb{R}^4$ to $\mathbb{R}^3$

Based on [18], in this paper, we will use the projection $\mathbf{p} : \mathbb{R}^4 \to \mathbb{R}^3$ that satisfies the following

$$\mathbf{p}\left(\vec{i}\right) = -\frac{1}{\sqrt{3}}\left(\vec{e}_1 + \vec{e}_2 + \vec{e}_3\right) = \left(-\frac{1}{\sqrt{3}}, -\frac{1}{\sqrt{3}}, -\frac{1}{\sqrt{3}}\right), \mathbf{p}\left(\vec{j}\right) = \vec{e}_1 = (1, 0, 0),$$

$$\mathbf{p}\left(\vec{k}\right) = \vec{e}_2 = (0, 1, 0), \mathbf{p}\left(\vec{l}\right) = \vec{e}_3 = (0, 0, 1).$$

Let $P(x, y, z, w)$ be an arbitrary point of $\mathbb{R}^4$ then the projection of point P is the point $P' = \left(-\frac{x}{\sqrt{3}} + y, -\frac{x}{\sqrt{3}} + z, -\frac{x}{\sqrt{3}} + w\right)$ of $\mathbb{R}^3$.

5   Illustrative Examples

5.1   Unit Hypersphere

Next, it will be verified that unit sphere H in $\mathbb{R}^4$ is a surface. By definition, H is made up of all points whose distance from the origin is one unit, or equivalently, all those points $\mathbf{p}$ that satisfy

$$\|\mathbf{p}\| = (p_1^2 + p_2^2 + p_3^2 + p_4^2)^{1/2} = 1.$$

From this equality it follows that

$$p_4 = \pm\sqrt{1 - p_1^2 - p_2^2 - p_3^2} \tag{6}$$

$$p_3 = \pm\sqrt{1 - p_1^2 - p_2^2 - p_4^2} \tag{7}$$

$$p_2 = \pm\sqrt{1 - p_1^2 - p_3^2 - p_4^2} \tag{8}$$

$$p_1 = \pm\sqrt{1 - p_2^2 - p_3^2 - p_4^2} \tag{9}$$

To check the Definition 4, it will suffice to define a suitable patch that covers all the points that are in the region of the positive w of H. The points $\mathbf{p}$ in H, with positive ordinate, can be expressed by the equality $\mathbf{p} = (p_1, p_2, p_3, p_4) = (p1, p_2, p_3, \sqrt{1 - p_1^2 - p_2^2 - p_3^2})$ (See Eq. 6). Based on this result, it is possible to define the function $\mathbf{x} : D \to \mathbb{R}^4$ such that

$$\mathbf{x}(u, v, w) = \left(u, v, \sqrt{1 - u^2 - v^2 - w^2}\right), \quad D : \{(u, v, w) \in \mathbb{R}^3 \,|\, u^2 + v^2 + w^2 < 1\}.$$

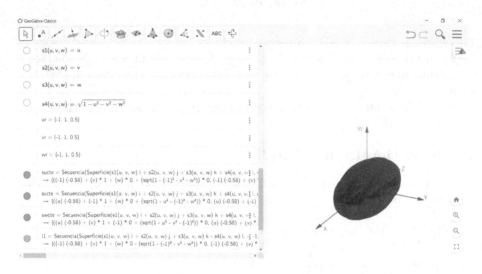

Fig. 8. Images of the proper patches $\mathbf{x}_1(u, v, w) = \left(u, v, w, \sqrt{1 - u^2 - v^2 - w^2}\right)$ (blue) and $\mathbf{x}_2(u, v, w) = \left(u, v, w, -\sqrt{1 - u^2 - v^2 - w^2}\right)$ (red). (Color figure online)

The answers to the following questions allow us to determine whether $\mathbf{x}$ is a proper patch.

1. $\mathbf{x}$ is a mapping? Yes, because its coordinate functions are differentiable on D. Specifically

$$\frac{\partial}{\partial u}u = 1, \quad \frac{\partial}{\partial u}v = 0, \quad \frac{\partial}{\partial u}w = 0, \quad \frac{\partial}{\partial u}\sqrt{1 - u^2 - v^2 - w^2} = -\frac{u}{\sqrt{1 - u^2 - v^2 - w^2}},$$

$$\frac{\partial}{\partial v}u = 0, \quad \frac{\partial}{\partial v}v = 1, \quad \frac{\partial}{\partial w}v = 0, \quad \frac{\partial}{\partial v}\sqrt{1 - u^2 - v^2 - w^2} = -\frac{v}{\sqrt{1 - u^2 - v^2 - w^2}}.$$

$$\frac{\partial}{\partial w}u = 0, \quad \frac{\partial}{\partial w}v = 0, \quad \frac{\partial}{\partial w}w = 1, \quad \frac{\partial}{\partial w}\sqrt{1 - u^2 - v^2 - w^2} = -\frac{w}{\sqrt{1 - u^2 - v^2 - w^2}}.$$

2. $\mathbf{x}$ is regular? Yes, because the rank of it Jacobian matrix

$$\begin{pmatrix} 1 & 0 & 0 & -\frac{u}{\sqrt{1 - u^2 - v^2 - w^2}} \\ 0 & 1 & 0 & -\frac{v}{\sqrt{1 - u^2 - v^2 - w^2}} \\ 0 & 0 & 1 & -\frac{w}{\sqrt{1 - u^2 - v^2 - w^2}} \end{pmatrix}$$

at each point is 3 (domain dimension).

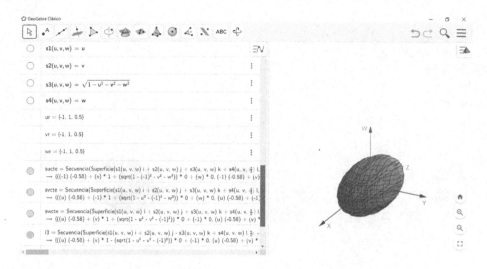

Fig. 9. Images of the proper patches $\mathbf{x}_3(u,v) = \left(u, v, \sqrt{1-u^2-v^2-w^2}, w\right)$ (cyan) and $\mathbf{x}_4(u,v) = \left(u, -\sqrt{1-u^2-v^2-w^2}, w\right)$ (green). (Color figure online)

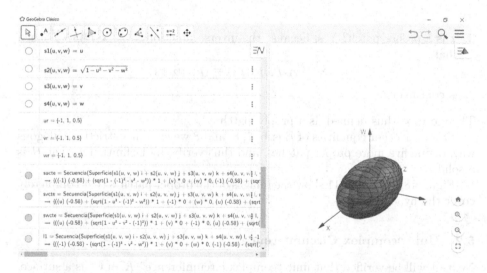

Fig. 10. Images of the proper patches $\mathbf{x}_5(u,v,w) = \left(u, \sqrt{1-u^2-v^2-w^2}, v, w\right)$ (orange) and $\mathbf{x}_6(u,v,w) = \left(u, -\sqrt{1-u^2-v^2-w^2}, v, w\right)$ (yellow). (Color figure online)

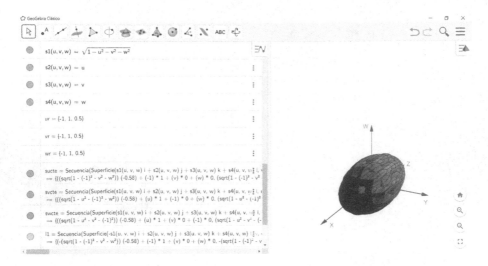

Fig. 11. Images of the proper patches $\mathbf{x}_5(u,v,w) = \left(\sqrt{1-u^2-v^2-w^2}, u, v, w\right)$ (violet) and $\mathbf{x}_6(u,v,w) = \left(-\sqrt{1-u^2-v^2-w^2}, u, v, w\right)$ (pink). (Color figure online)

3. $\mathbf{x}$ is a proper patch? Yes, because the inverse function $\mathbf{x}^{-1} : \mathbf{x}(D) \to D$ such that

$$\mathbf{x}^{-1}(p_1, p_2, p_3, p_4) = (p_1, p_2, p_3)$$

is continuous.

Therefore, $\mathbf{x}$, thus defined, is a proper patch.

From the other equalities of Eqs. 6, 7, 8, and 8 we can, in a strictly analogous way, define five more proper patches, and thus verify, by Definition 4, that H is a solid.

Figures 8, 9, 10, and 11 show the images of the proper patches that completely cover the hypersphere.

5.2   Unit "complex Circumference"

Next, it will be verified that unit "complex circumference" K in $\mathbb{C}^2$ is a surface. By definition, K is made up of all points whose distance from the origin is one unit, or equivalently, all those points $\mathbf{p}$ that satisfy

$$\|\mathbf{p}\| = (p_1^2 + p_2^2)^{1/2} = 1. \tag{10}$$

Let $p_1 = a + ib$ and $p_2 = \alpha + i\beta$ be; with $a, b, \alpha, \beta \in \mathbb{R}$. Replacing in 10 we have

$$(a + ib)^2 + (\alpha + i\beta)^2 = 1,$$

$$(a^2 - b^2 + \alpha^2 - \beta^2) + 2i(ab + \alpha\beta) = 1. \tag{11}$$

After equating the real and imaginary part of 11 we get

$$\begin{cases} a^2 - b^2 + \alpha^2 - \beta^2 & = 1\,, \\ ab + \alpha\beta & = 0\,. \end{cases}$$

After multiplying the first equation by α^2 and operating, taking into account the second equation, it turns out

$$\alpha^2 + (a^2 - b^2 - 1)\alpha^2 - a^2b^2 = 0\,.$$

So

$$\alpha = \pm f(a,b) = \pm \sqrt{\dfrac{\sqrt{(a^2 - b^2 - 1)^2 + 4a^2b^2} - (a^2 - b^2 - 1)}{2}}$$

and

$$\beta = \mp g(a,b) = \mp ab \sqrt{\dfrac{2}{\sqrt{(a^2 - b^2 - 1)^2 + 4a^2b^2} - (a^2 - b^2 - 1)}}\,.$$

Based on this result we define the function $\mathbf{x} : D \to \mathbb{R}^4$ such that

$$\mathbf{x}_1(u,v) = (u, v, f(u,v), -g(u,v))\,, \quad D : \{(u,v) \in \mathbb{R}^2 | v \neq 0 \vee -1 < u < 1\}\,.$$

The answers to the following questions allow us to determine whether $\mathbf{x}$ is a proper patch.

1. $\mathbf{x}$ is a mapping? Yes, because its coordinate functions are differentiable on D.
2. $\mathbf{x}$ is regular? Yes, because the rank of it Jacobian matrix

$$\begin{pmatrix} 1 & 0 & \frac{\partial f}{\partial u} & -\frac{\partial g}{\partial u} \\ 0 & 1 & \frac{\partial f}{\partial v} & -\frac{\partial g}{\partial v} \end{pmatrix}$$

at each point is 2 (domain dimension).
3. $\mathbf{x}$ is a proper patch? Yes, because the inverse function $\mathbf{x}^{-1} : \mathbf{x}(D) \to D$ such that

$$\mathbf{x}^{-1}(p_1, p_2, p_3, p_4) = (p_1, p_2)$$

is continuous.

Therefore, $\mathbf{x}$, thus defined, is a proper patch.

Similarly it is proved that

$$\mathbf{x}_2(u,v) = (u, v, -f(u,v), g(u,v))\,, \quad D : \{(u,v) \in \mathbb{R}^2 | v \neq 0 \vee -1 < u < 1\}\,,$$

$$\mathbf{x}_3(u,v) = (f(u,v), -g(u,v), u, v)\,, \quad D : \{(u,v) \in \mathbb{R}^2 | v \neq 0 \vee -1 < u < 1\}\,,$$

and

$$\mathbf{x}_4(u,v) = (-f(u,v), g(u,v), u, v)\,, \quad D : \{(u,v) \in \mathbb{R}^2 | v \neq 0 \vee -1 < u < 1\}$$

are proper patches. Thus it's verified, by Definition 3, that K is a surface.

Figures 12 and 13 show the images of the proper patches that completely cover the "complex circumference".

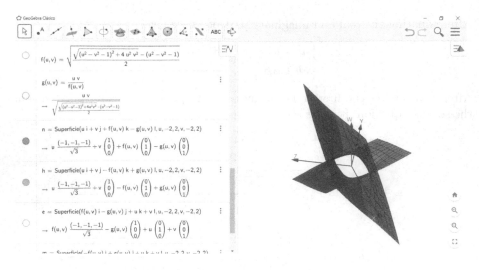

Fig. 12. Images of the proper patches $\mathbf{x}_1(u) = (u, v, f(u,v), -g(u,v))$ (blue) and $\mathbf{x}_2(u,v) = (u, v, -f(u,v), g(u,v))$ (red). (Color figure online)

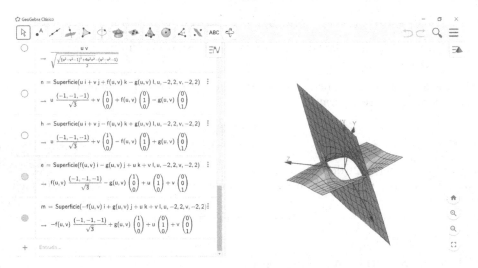

Fig. 13. Images of the proper patches $\mathbf{x}_3(u,v) = (f(u,v), -g(u,v), u, v)$ (cyan) and $\mathbf{x}_4(u,v) = (-f(u,v), g(u,v), u, v)$ (green). (Color figure online)

6   Conclusions

In this paper, several Dynamic Worksheets developed in the dynamic mathematics software GeoGebra were described in which projections of various mathematical objects from $\mathbb{R}^4$ to $\mathbb{R}^3$ were visualized, based on Pohlke-Schwarz theorem and some concepts of linear algebra. These Dynamic Worksheets were delivered to the students of the Differential Geometry course of the Mathematics Program of the Universidad Nacional de Piura. Some of the examples developed in the classroom are shown and described. In this way, we have introduced a computer tool that can be used not only for undergraduate Differential Geometry courses but also for postgraduate courses. Even teachers and instructors can benefit from this tool, as our own experience has shown us. For example, we can propose to our students to verify whether or not a subset of $\mathbb{R}^4$ satisfies the definition of surface or solid, as the case may be, and to perform the geometric interpretation of its results.

Acknowledgments. We are grateful to Markus Hohenwarter, creator of GeoGebra, and to the peer reviewers who made helpful suggestions.

References

1. Arroyo, K., et al.: Visualising higher-dimensional space-time and space-scale objects as projections to $\mathbb{R}^3$. PeerJ Comput. Sci. **3**, e123 (2017). https://doi.org/10.7717/peerj-cs.123
2. Banchoff, T.F.: Beyond the Third Dimension: Geometry, Computer Graphics, and Higher Dimensions. W. H. Freeman & Company, Scientific American Library Series (1990)
3. Brandel, Sylvain: 4D Objects for Animation: Immersion on Virtual Reality, 9th Virtual Reality International Conference, Laval, France, 1–5 (2007)
4. Fraguas, A.: El arte rupestre prehistórico de África nororiental: nuevas teorías y metodologías. CSIC - CSIC Press (2009)
5. Gruffroy, J.: El arte rupestre del antiguo Perú. Institut français d'études andines, https://horizon.documentation.ird.fr/exl-doc/pleins_textes/divers11-03/010019462.pdf (2015)
6. GeoGebra Homepage, https://www.geogebra.org. Accessed 24 Aug 2021
7. Hoffmann, C.M., Jianhua, Z.: Visualization of Surfaces in Four-Dimensional Space. Computer Science Technical Reports, Paper 814 (1990)
8. Lindgren, C.E., Slaby, S.M.: Four dimensional descriptive geometry. McGraw-Hill, NY (1968)
9. Maplesoft Homepage, https://www.maplesoft.com. Accessed 24 Aug 2021
10. MatLab Homepage, https://es.mathworks.com/products/matlab.html. Accessed 24 Aug 2021
11. Maxima Homepage, https://maxima.sourceforge.io. Accessed 24 Aug 2021
12. O'Neill, B.: Rev. 2nd ed. Academic Press, California (1990)Elementary differential geometry
13. Sage Homepage, https://www.sagemath.org. Accessed 24 Aug 2021
14. Sakai, Y., Hashimoto, S.: Interactive four-dimensional space visualization using five-dimensional homogeneous processing for intuitive understanding. Inf. Media Technol. **2**(1), 574–591 (2007)
15. Scilab Homepage, https://www.scilab.org. Accessed 24 Aug 2021
16. Schreiber, P.: Generalized descriptive geometry. J. Geom. Graph. **6**(1), 37–59 (2002)
17. Séquin, C.H.: 3D Visualization Models of the Regular Polytopes in Four and Higher Dimensions. In: Bridges 2002, pp. 37–48. Towson, Maryland, USA (2002)

18. Sobrino, E.E., Ipanaqué, R., Velezmoro, R., Mechato, J.A.: New Package in *Maxima* to Build Axonometric Projections from $\mathbb{R}^4$ to $\mathbb{R}^3$ and Visualize Objects Immersed in $\mathbb{R}^4$. In: Gervasi, O., et al. (eds.) ICCSA 2020. LNCS, vol. 12255, pp. 837–851. Springer, Cham (2020). https://doi.org/10.1007/978-3-030-58820-5_60
19. Stahl, G.: Adventures in Dynamic Geometry. Lulu.com (2015)
20. Schwarz, H. A.: Elementarer Beweis des Pohlkeschen Fundamentalsatzes der Axonometrie. Crelle's J. **63**, 309–3014 (1864)
21. Velezmoro, R., Ipanaqué, R., Mechato, J.A.: A Mathematica Package for Visualizing Objects Inmersed in $\mathbb{R}^4$. In: Misra, S., et al. (eds.) ICCSA 2019. LNCS, vol. 11624, pp. 479–493. Springer, Cham (2019). https://doi.org/10.1007/978-3-030-24311-1_35
22. Volkert, K.: On models for visualizing four-dimensional figures. Math. Intell. **39**(2), 27–35 (2017). https://doi.org/10.1007/s00283-016-9699-1
23. Wang, W. M. et al.: Interactive Exploration of 4D Geometry with Volumetric Halos. The Eurographics Association (2013)
24. Winkowska-Nowak, K.: What is GeoGebra?, https://www.geogebra.org/m/drtbnjmu. Accessed 30 Sep 2021
25. Wolfram Mathematica Homepage, https://www.wolfram.com/mathematica/?source=frontpage-carousel. Accessed 24 Aug 2021
26. Wuyts, G.: Wugi's QBComplex, http://home.scarlet.be/wugi/qbComplex.html. Accessed 30 Sep 2021
27. Xiaoqi, Y.: New Directions in Four-Dimensional Mathematical Visualization. School of Computer Engineering, Game Lab (2015)
28. Zhou, J.: Visualization of Four Dimensional Space and Its Applications. D. Phil. Thesis, Department of Computer Science Technical Reports. Paper 922 (1991)

Efficacy of Blended Learning in the Teaching of Basic Surgical Skills in Medical Students at a Public University in Peru Between 2018 and 2022

Maritza D. Placencia-Medina[1] , María A. Valcárcel-Saldaña[1] ,
Christian Nole-Álvarez[1] , Isabel Mendoza-Correa[1] ,
María E. Muñoz Zambrano[1] , Javier Silva-Valencia[2] , Julián Villarreal-Valerio[1] ,
Carlos H. Contreras-Pizarro[1,3](✉) , and Anel J. Roca-Béjar[1]

[1] Grupo de Investigación "Educación Médica", Universidad Nacional Mayor de San Marcos, Lima, Perú
carlos.contreras2@unmsm.edu.pe

[2] Unidad de Telesalud, Universidad Nacional Mayor de San Marcos, Lima, Peru

[3] Sociedad Científica de San Fernando, Universidad Nacional Mayor de San Marcos, Lima, Peru

Abstract. The objective of the research was to evaluate the efficacy of a Blended learning (B-learning) intervention to improve basic surgical skills in human medicine students at a public university in Lima, Peru. A quasi-experimental pretest/posttest study was carried out among enrolled in the Surgery course at Universidad Nacional Mayor de San Marcos (Peru). The achievement of basic surgical skills related to biosafety, tying, and suturing using simulators of low to intermediate complexity were evaluated. The McNemar´s and Kruskal-Wallis test were used for result analysis. The results showed that the intervention improved biosafety surgical skills (including handwashing, clothing, glove usage), as well as knot-making and suturings (p < 0.05). Observation revealed challenges with fine psychomotor skills and ergonomic risk factors. Interviews yielded positive reactions, significant learning, and motivation for continuous learning. Left-handed students reported serious procedural difficulties, indicating a need for more targeted training. Teachers provided audiovisual materials contributing to the achievement of basic surgical skills. The incorporation of b-learning into the learning process in basic surgical techniques significantly increase students' skills. Further refinement of the model for left-handed students and ongoing training for teachers in virtual material design is necessary.

Keywords: Clinical Competence · B-Learning · Efficacy · General Surgery · Educational Technology

T. Guarda et al. (Eds.): ARTIIS 2023, CCIS 1935, pp. 169–181, 2024.
https://doi.org/10.1007/978-3-031-48858-0_14

1 Introduction

The teaching of surgery in medical school represents a critical period during which essential surgical skills are imparted to any physician in training [1], and it can influence their aspirations for a surgical [2]. Traditionally, a model has been followed in which experienced professionals teach students individually or in small groups [3], often within the context of an operating room. A disadvantage of this approach is that student learning can be limited by different factors, including instructor availability and complexity of surgical procedures [3].

Therefore, it falls upon medical schools to use a learning methodology that facilitates the training of various technical, cognitive and/or behavioral skills. This approach should establish a secure learning environment that does not compromise patient safety or lead to ethical and legal dilemmas. Additionally, the chosen methodology should be adapted to the diverse learning needs of each student [4].

One of the methodologies employed for teaching surgery is Blended Learning (B-learning), which combines both online (asynchronous) and face-to-face (synchronous) learning. This approach has demonstrated significant benefits in terms of knowledge acquisition, particularly when compared to traditional learning methods within the health area [5]. Notably, this methodology has generated a significant increase in accurate diagnoses, skills, and student´s affinity for this approach [6]. Another innovation like live streaming of surgical procedures conducted in the operating room, has shown promise as an alternative or complement to traditional face-to-face teaching [7].

In Peru, the National University of San Marcos pioneered the initial application of B-learning to strengthen basic surgical skills, addressing the challenge posed by a high student enrollment in 2018 [8].This learning approach incorporated a hybrid assessment system, providing training to both teachers and students in utilizing virtual resources for educational materials. The model contemplated successful events as well as potential critical scenarios, leveraging online resources for positive student feedback [8].

In 2019, improvements were introduced to the educational model including pre-class evaluations; furthermore, then in 2022, revisions were made to the assessment tools for gauging basic surgical skills. The present study seeks to evaluate the effectiveness of the B-learning-based educational model in enhancing surgical skills among students pursuing human medicine at a public university in Lima, Peru.

2 Materials and Methods

Study Design and Population

Quasi-experimental study. The population was made up of medical students from the Universidad Nacional Mayor de San Marcos (UNMSM) in Lima, Peru, during the years 2018, 2019 and 2022.

The General Surgery course at UNMSM is a compulsory theoretical-practical subject comprising ten learning units. The curriculum features an Operative Technique unit spanning 16 weeks, with classes conducted at the Institute of Experimental Surgery within the Faculty of Medicine of the UNMSM. For this study, the population included three cohorts of medical students, comprising 212 participants in 2018, 100 in 2019, and

72 in 2022. Importantly, classes in the years 2020 and 2021 were conducted online due to the COVID-19 pandemic.

Participation in the study was extended to all enrolled students of both. Data was collected from those students who gave their consent to participate in the study. The accessibility of the population was facilitated by the unified learning environment they had and the specific class schedules. Exclusions comprised students who withdrew from the course or did not attend more than 30% of scheduled practical activities.

The control group consisted of students from the 2017 cohort who undertook the Operative Technique course using the traditional face-to-face teaching approach. This cohort did not undergo competency-based evaluations or utilize checklists for assessing individual basic surgical skill.

Variables and Measurement
The assessment of basic surgical skill encompassed biosafety measures, including hand washing, donning gloves and proper attire, as well as proficiency in suturing and knot-making. Each skill was evaluated using a checklist that was validated by the instructors of the Operative Technique learning unit. Scores ranged from 0 to 20. Students with a score greater than 14 were considered competent.

Academic performance was assessed as a numerical variable, measured through the vigesimal grading system of the theoretical and practical component of the Operative Technique unit (with theory accounting for 40% and practice for 60%). Students achieving a final grade greater than 14 were considered approved.

Description of the Intervention
The intervention, designed for educational purposes with Blended learning covered the following areas:

1. Integration of virtual and face-to-face activities. This aspect of the intervention began in 2018 by establishing a virtual classroom on the Moodle 3.0 platform dedicated to the Operative Technique subject (https://unmsm.online/medicina/loginepme dicinahumana/). Within this virtual space, recorded theoretical lectures, teacher-created procedure demonstration videos, discussion forums and consultation channels, as well as a repository of relevant literature for both teacher and student were made available (see Fig. 1). Additionally, a designated area allowed students to upload they own recorded the videos of procedures from multiple angles (see Fig. 2). Teachers underwent training to effectively utilize the virtual classroom and develop virtual materials, including practice guides and assessment tools such as rubrics and checklists.

2. Preparation of checklists for student evaluation. Comprehensive checklists were prepared for assess student´s proficiency in biosafety protocols, knot making and suturing techniques. These checklists aimed to establish a standardized evaluation process that encompasses cognitive, procedural, and attitudinal aspects in the evidence of achievement. Checklists are available in: https://drive.google.com/file/d/13ajY2jsD-pR75WE b4Sa3bofsqPuaXbnL/view?usp=sharing.

In 2019, the educational model was further refined, but with less changes, including the incorporation of pre-class assessment preceding each theory session. In 2022, new teachers were hired and trained to adopt the same approach, considering that some

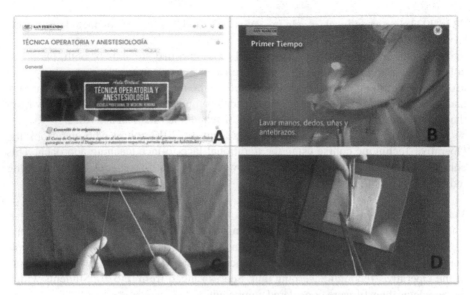

Fig. 1. A: Main interface of the virtual classroom B: Demonstrative video of hand washing C: Demonstrative video of knot with two hands D: Demonstrative video of suture

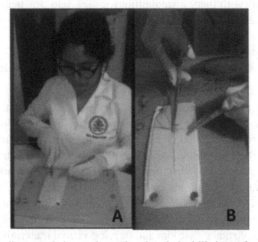

Fig. 2. Recordings made by students showing their skills in performing sutures.

teachers who had participated in 2018 and 2019 had left. Additionally, a validation of the checklists used to assess basic surgical skills was conducted with the new teaching staff.

Procedures in Qualitative Research
Simultaneously with the implementation, an observation and interview technique was carried out, guided by a team member with expertise in qualitative research. The approach used was phenomenological, which seeks to explore the life experiences of people

regarding a certain event. According to Husserl [9], this paradigm aims to explain the nature and veracity of the phenomena from the perspective of each subject.

The focus of the observation centered on the behavioral manifestations among the research participants, which, in the context of education, is important to analyze and interpret [10]. Both motor and verbal skills were considered as the unit of analysis. Together with another member of the team, they observed students during face-to-face practice sessions for basic suturing procedures, as well as the recordings made by the instructor.

In 2019, 10 students and 5 teachers participated. The sample size was done iteratively based on how the information emerged during field work, eventually reaching the saturation point. This observation extended over a period of 16 weeks, totaling 96 h (equivalent to 4 h per week). This timeframe allowed for the establishment of the finding´s plausibility criteria concerning the experiences of the individuals under study [11].

Finally, semi-structured interviews were also carried in 2019 to complement the objective of the investigation. Based on Kirkpatrick's model [12], which established the usefulness of link learning evaluation to student satisfaction and the acquired skills, the following questions were asked: How did you feel in relation to the implementation of B-Learning as a part of the course? To what extent did the educational model lead to improvements in your ir knowledge, skills and attitudes?

Statistical Analysis

Statistical analysis was carried out using the IBM SPSS Statistics V. 24.0 software. For descriptive analysis we determined the absolute and relative frequencies of categorical variables. To assess the change in the achievement of basic surgical skills, we employed the McNemar´s test.

Data normality analysis was performed using the quantile-quantile plot, and the Kruskal-Wallis test was used to assess whether there were significant differences between the scores of the theoretical and practical components with the teaching method. The analysis of the obtained performance was carried out comparing it with the qualifications from the year 2017 for the respective comparisons. The significance level was established at 0.05.

Ethical Aspects

This study was approved by the Institutional Ethics Committee of the Faculty of Human Medicine at Universidad Nacional Mayor de San Marcos (Approval Number: 1825). Student participation was both anonymous and voluntary. An informed consent form was prepared, which explained that the decision not to participate would not influence their grades.

3   Results

A total of 384 students participated in the study, with 212 in 2018, 100 in 2019 and 72 in 2022. Among them 65.4% were male and 34.6% female. No student withdrew from the course. During the year 2018, the increases in the percentage of proficient students after the intervention were significant in all areas (see Table 1).

Table 1. Number and percentage of students competent in basic surgical skills, in the years 2018, 2019 and 2022.

Assessments**	2018(n = 212)		2019(n = 100)		2022(n = 72)	
	Pre n (%)	Post n (%)	Pre n (%)	Post n (%)	Pre n (%)	Post n (%)
Hand washing[1]	148 (69.8%)	206 (97.2%)*	67 (67.0%)	100 (100%)	63 (87.5%)	63 (87.5%)
Gown placement[1]	164 (77.4%)	204 (96.2%)*	97 (97.0%)	100 (100%)	70 (97.2%)	70 (97.2%)
Donning gloves[1]	155 (73.1%)	203 (95.8%)*	98 (98.0%)	100 (100%)	66 (91.7%)	66 (91.7%)
Knot making[2]	155 (73.1%)	203 (95.8%)*	88 (88.0%)	94 (94.0%)	63 (87.5%)	63 (87.5%)
Making sutures[2]	186 (87.7%)	207 (97.6%)*	99 (99.0%)	100 (100%)	66 (91.7%)	66 (91.7%)

[1]Biosecurity
[2]Knots and sutures
* McNemar´s test. Statistically significant difference at 5% significance level
** In the year prior to the start of the intervention (2017), no competency was carried out

Regarding the performance of the students in the subject, it was compared based on the group of students who received traditional teaching (2017). The results show that the intervention, in its application in 2018, was significant for the theoretical (see Table 2) and practical (see Table 3) components, and the resulting final grade (see Table 4).

Table 2. Qualification of the theoretical component according to the B-learning didactic strategy in the students of Operative Technique, UNMSM.

Year	n	Theoretical grades		
		mean ± SD	Median ± IQR	p-value†
2017	148		5.6 ± 1.20	0.01*
2018	212		6.19 ± 1.31	
2019	100		6.69 ± 0.90	
2022	72	6.32 ± 0.61		

†Kruskal-Wallis test
* Statistically significant difference at 5% significance level

Simultaneously it was carried out the technique of observation and interviews (Fig. 3). Being a thoughtful, planned and intentional observation, the fortuitous factors found in the course practices were considered, such as recurring patterns of support

Table 3. Qualification of the practical component according to the B-learning didactic strategy in the students of Operative Technique, UNMSM.

Year	n	Practical grades	
		Median ± IQR	p-value†
2017	148	9.96 ± 0.60	
2018	212	10.36 ± 0.73	0.01*
2019	100	10.85 ± 0.89	
2022	72	10.20 ± 0.86	
Total	532		

†Kruskal-Wallis test
*Statistically significant difference at 5% significance level

Table 4. Final qualification according to the B-learning didactic strategy in the students of Operative Technique, UNMSM.

Year	n	Final note		p-value†
		mean ± SD	Median ± IQR	
2017	148	15.45 ± 1.12		0.01*
2018	212		16.58 ± 1.81	
2019	100		17.54 ± 1.49	
2022	72	16.49 ± 1.13		
Total	532			

†Kruskal-Wallis test
*Statistically significant difference at 5% significance level

among the members of the groups assigned by each work table, verifying a lot of pressure imposed by themselves to carry out practice in the best way, for the development of skills and abilities in the various techniques, to maintain and/or improve your weighted average. Likewise, it was possible to observe that the size of the students was varied and extreme, which caused certain difficulties when preparing the work table for a certain technique to be executed (Fig. 3), it was uncomfortable for some and adequate for others, it should be noted that they had ergonomic tables and could vary the height according to their needs, doing so caused a delay in completing its rotation. It was evidenced that in certain students there was lack of coordination in activities that required a fine clamp, they had to practice repeatedly due to the lack of skill at that level. There was in the groups of left-handed young students what demanded greater concentration, since the demonstrations were with examples for right-handed people and the teacher in charge had the ability to demonstrate it as if he were left-handed. Within the group there were students with laterality problems, which causes a disorganization in their fine motor planning required in the course. They were very willing to carry out their practices following the model of the video-recording of the instructor teacher. Most of the teachers were attentive in the development of the technique by their assigned students. It was possible to observe six designated teachers and three practice teachers who transmitted confidence to the students to resolve doubts, speaking confidently and fluently about the topic to be developed. The verbal level of the students was good in the majority.

After the semi-structured interviews, the following categories were obtained:

Liking Reactions

Female students were the ones who participated the most in answering the questions provided. They expressed that they were pleased to find support information in the virtual classroom to reinforce their knowledge and clear up any doubts about the instrumental procedures taught in face-to-face classes. He was also pleased by the easy access and the fact that his learning could take place in a flexible way.

- *When something is not clear to us, we go to the virtual classroom and review the videos that are there from the classes. (Sam).*
- *I think it is a great support to reinforce the course. (Leti).*
- *In the virtual classroom we find the course ordered according to the topics of the syllabus. (Juan).*
- *I think it's cool. (Susan).*

Meaningful-Combined Learning (Face-to-Face-Virtual)

The participants stated that B-Learning improved their knowledge and interest in the different topics developed in the subject, information acquired through the video tutorials, clinical cases of virtual patients, scientific articles, complementing the face-to-face classes, allowing them to select the content on the Moodle platform about some theoretical knowledge of a disease, surgical procedures or other higher cognitive functions.

- *It is the only course that we have everything in order and that does comply with the syllabus". (Lalo).*
- *I am happy with the course, I am learning. (Rita).*

Perceptions of Teachers About the Educational Intervention

In the same way, we proceeded to understand the perceptions of teachers about the educational intervention. The testimonials regarding B-learning were:

- *Each time the virtual classroom was friendlier for me. (Teacher A).*
- *At first I didn't even know how to enter the virtual classroom, I was afraid. (Teacher B).*
- *Points to improve? I would say, more commitment on our part. (Teacher C).*
- *Motivated attitude to continue with the virtual classroom, I say. (Teacher D).*
- *Now I can make forums in the virtual classroom. (Teacher E).*
- *Review easily assigned tasks. (Teacher F).*
- *I think that measuring the achievement of course competencies achieved by the students would serve to validate the intervention model. (Teacher H).*

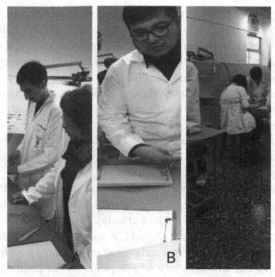

Fig. 3. Students during the practical classes of Operative Technique, year 2019. **A and B**. Teachers attentive to the development of the skills of tying knots with low complexity simulators by the students. **C**. Inadequate posture of the students maintained during practice

4 Discussion

The present study aimed to evaluate the effectiveness of the B-learning educational model in imparting basic surgical skills. The findings clearly indicate that its application during the years 2018, 2019 and 2022 led to an increase in the number of students demonstrating competency in basic surgical skills. While significant differences were only found in 2018, it is important to consider the potential explanatory factor of heterogeneous numbers of students across the 3 application years.

The effectiveness of B-learning has been demonstrated in previous studies. A meta-analysis conducted in 2019 concluded that B-learning effectively improved the knowledge of nursing students [13]. In the study carried out by Moon et al. [14], the application of B-learning in a cardiopulmonary resuscitation (CPR) program was found to effectively enhance the knowledge and attitudes of nursing students. Furthermore, the study by Chen et al. [15] revealed a significant improvement in average test scores of the laboratory for laboratory courses through the utilization of B-learning, in comparison to the traditional learning method.

To the best of our knowledge, we could not find prior studies that used the B-learning methodology in basic surgical skills with simulators of different complexity (low, medium and higher complexity), which highlights the originality of the study carried out and the flexibility in the use of any of these simulators where the student must be prepared to obtain the same results or close data [8].

The utilization of checklists for assessing each of the surgical skills is a noteworthy factor. Its implementation has demonstrated potential benefits, particularly in intensive and highly complex procedures in humans that involve multiple steps. The use of cheklists contributed to fostering coherence and precision in executing specific tasks [16]. Recently, a study focused on enhancing teaching outcomes in surgical skills employed a competency and performance checklist, resulting in increased competency, performance, and student satisfaction within the course [16].

In addition, the creation of demonstrative videos that were accessible prior to the face-to-face sessions emerge as a pivotal element contributing to the achievement of the learning objectives. This methodology has been used to teach a variety of surgical skills [17, 18]. A program that comprised a total of 12 video tutorials addressing instruments usage, suturing and knot making, demonstrated that students significantly improved their surgical familiarity, knowledge and competence [3].

From the analysis of the interviews, it is evident that both students and teachers perceive the implementation of B-learning positively, which is also consistent with other investigations in the surgical area; such as training in maxillofacial surgery [19] and spinal surgery [20]. Zambrano G. et al. [21], reported that a significant majority of Medicine students found practice with standardized or simulated patient to be conductive to knowledge integration. In their study, 95.8% (45 of 47) of responded perceived this strategy as useful for developing communication skills [21]. Likewise, in the study by Oliveros [22], it is evident that after the implementation of a specialty program in Anesthesiology under the B-learning model allowed to make the reading content and the learning load more flexible so as not to exceed the dedication time of 10 h per week, showing great benefit for the feedback of information and self-learning. In a systematic review and meta-analysis [23], authors point out that the success of the platform would be related to the commitment of students in their free time.

Considering medical education as a process of constant change and innovation using information and communication technologies, the strengthening of skills in operative techniques has been determined in compliance with biosafety standards in surgery and the results obtained are similar to other research carried out in a laparoscopic anastomosis course where a statistically significant improvement of 80.5% was observed in all the parameters of the procedure (94.8% residents vs. 67.3% specialists) [24]. Likewise, it has also been shown that the use of simulations and virtual training through educational videos on compliance with biosafety standards and surgical skills have been feasible and equally effective as face-to-face [24].

B-learning allows teaching to be individualized, adapting it to the learning needs of each student and allows training technical, cognitive or behavioral skills [25], as well as determining the correct position to perform them, the ability of the hands (left and right) to harmonize their best skills, teamwork and the development of a professional who complies with basic biosafety standards in a surgical environment, making the right knot and suture for each patient, learning and recognizing the satisfaction and needs of the actors main: the student and the teacher facilitator [3, 19].

The present study should be interpreted considering some limitations. First, it is noteworthy that all the equipment purchased (materials, real estate) was aimed at the right-handed population. Consequently, left-handed students encountered difficulties during the intervention, particularly related to ergonomics (an important factor for the development of these skills in clinical practice) [26, 27]. This fact highlights an area for innovation in subsequent studies. Second, a limiting factor was the level of interaction between teachers and student, especially in cases where both have little or no experience in applying this model. Addressing this, induction and preparatory training for the facilitating teacher becomes important, alongside the engagement of an instructive team with experience and knowledge of this model. This approach encourages active participation in forums, and even from an early educational stage, it becomes essential to enhance personal and investigative skills [28, 29].

In conclusion, the B-learning model implemented in UNMSM during the years 2018, 2019 and 2022 for teaching basic surgical techniques have demonstrated a significant increase in the students' skills. To further enhance, it is necessary to complement the model for left-handed students, include the ergonomic considerations, and provide continue training for teachers in the design and management of virtual materials.

Acknowledgments. To the students, teachers, administrative staff and authorities of the Vicerrectorado de Investigación y Posgrado, UNMSM (VRIP-UNMSM). The research was part of the project A19010022, year 2019, approved and financed by the VRIP-UNMSM.

References

1. Down, B., Morris, S., Kulkarni, S., Mohiuddin, K.: Effectiveness of a multisession combined near-peer and faculty-led surgical skills course on self-perceived ability to perform basic surgical skills. Ann. Med. Surg. **57**, 153–156 (2020). https://doi.org/10.1016/j.amsu.2020.07.045

2. Peel, J.K., Schlachta, C.M., Alkhamesi, N.A.: A systematic review of the factors affecting choice of surgery as a career. Can. J. Surg. **61**(1), 58–67 (2018). https://doi.org/10.1503/cjs.008217

3. Kumins, N.H., Qin, V.L., Driscoll, E.C., Morrow, K.L., Kashyap, V.S., Ning, A.Y., et al.: Computer-based video training is effective in teaching basic surgical skills to novices without faculty involvement using a self-directed, sequential and incremental program. Am. J. Surg. **221**(4), 780–787 (2021). https://doi.org/10.1016/j.amjsurg.2020.08.011

4. Ruiz-Gómez, J.L., Martín-Parra, J.I., González-Noriega, M., Redondo-Figuero, C.G., Manuel-Palazuelos, J.C.: Simulation as a surgical teaching model. Cir. Esp. (English Ed) **96**(1), 12–17 (2018). https://doi.org/10.1016/j.ciresp.2017.09.005

5. Vallée, A., Blacher, J., Cariou, A., Sorbets, E.: Blended learning compared to traditional learning in medical education: systematic review and meta-analysis. J. Med. Internet Res. **22**(8), e16504 (2020). https://doi.org/10.2196/16504

6. Funke, K., Bonrath, E., Mardin, W.A., Becker, J.C., Haier, J., Senninger, N., et al.: Blended learning in surgery using the Immedea Simulator. Langenbecks Arch. Surg. **398**(2), 335–340 (2013). https://doi.org/10.1007/s00423-012-0987-8

7. van Bonn, S.M., Grajek, J.S., Schneider, A., Oberhoffner, T., Mlynski, R., Weiss, N.M.: Interactive live-stream surgery contributes to surgical education in the context of contact restrictions. Eur. Arch. Otorhinolaryngol. **279**(6), 2865–2871 (2022). https://doi.org/10.1007/s00405-021-06994-0

8. Placencia Medina, M.D., Valencia, J.S., Valcárcel Saldaña, M.A., Somocurcio Vilchez, J.G., Carreño Escobedo, J.R., Villarreal Valerio, J.A, et al.: Primera experiencia de Blended-learning para fortalecer habilidades quirúrgicas básicas en estudiantes de Medicina Humana de una Universidad Nacional en Perú. En Callaos, J., Horne, E.J., Martinez Lopez, B., Sanchez, A. (eds.), CISCI 2019 - Decima Octava Conferencia Iberoamericana en Sistemas, Cibernetica e Informatica 2019, vol.2, pp. 71–76. International Institute of Informatics and Systemics, IIIS

9. Waldenfels, B.: Phenomenology of experience in Edmund Husserl. Arete **29**(2), 409–426 (2017). https://doi.org/10.18800/earring.201702.008

10. Piza Burgos, N.D., Amaiquema Márquez, F.A., Beltrán Baquerizo, G.E.: Methods and techniques in qualitative research. Some necessary precisions. Conrad **15**(70), 455–459 (2019)

11. Reeves, S., Peller, J., Goldman, J., Kitto, S. Ethnography in qualitative educational research: AMEE Guide No. 80. Med. Teacher **35**(8), e1365–e1379 (2013). https://doi.org/10.3109/014 2159X.2013.804977

12. Gaxiola-García, M.A., Kushida-Contreras, B.H., Sánchez-Mendiola, M.: Teaching surgical skills: relevant educational theories (second part). Res. Med. Educ. **11**(42), 95–105 (2022). https://doi.org/10.22201/fm.20075057e.2022.42.22433

13. Gagnon, M.P., Gagnon. J., Desmartis, M., Njoya, M.: The impact of blended teaching on knowledge, satisfaction, and self-directed learning in nursing undergraduates: a randomized, controlled trial. Nurs. Educ. Perspect **34**(6), 377–382 (2013). https://doi.org/10.5480/10-459

14. Moon, H., Hyun, H.S.: Nursing students' knowledge, attitude, self-efficacy in blended learning of cardiopulmonary resuscitation: a randomized controlled trial. BMC Med. Educ. **19**, 414 (2019). https://doi.org/10.1186/s12909-019-1848-8

15. Chen, J., Zhou, J., Wang, Y., Qi, G., Xia, C., Mo, G., et al.: Blended learning in basic medical laboratory courses improves medical students' abilities in self-learning, understanding, and problem solving. Adv. Physiol. Educ. **44**(1), 9–14 (2020). https://doi.org/10.1152/advan.000 76.201

16. Luo, P., et al.: A WeChat-based competence and performance checklist in basic surgical skills course for military medical acade-my undergraduates. BMC Med. Educ. **22**(1), 858 (2022). https://doi.org/10.1186/s12909-022-03939-x

17. Vaughn, C.J., Kim, E., O'Sullivan, P., et al.: Peer video review and feedback improve performance in basic surgical skills. Am. J. Surg. **211**, 355–360 (2016). https://doi.org/10.1016/j. amjsurg.2015.08.034

18. Wright, A.S., McKenzie, J., Tsigonis, A., Jensen, A.R., Figueredo, E.J., Kim, S., et al.: A structured self-directed basic skills curriculum results in improved technical performance in the absence of expert faculty teaching. Surgery **151**, 808–814 (2012). https://doi.org/10.1016/j.surg.2012.03.018

19. Bock, A., Modabber, A., Kniha, K., Lemos, M., Rafai, N., Hölzle, F.: Blended learning modules for lectures on oral and maxillofacial surgery. Br. J. Oral Maxillofac. Surg. **56**(10), 956–961 (2018). https://doi.org/10.1016/j.bjoms.2018.10.281

20. Acaroglu, E., Assous, M., Bransford, R., Dal Oglio Da Rocha, LG., Falavigna, A., France, J.: Evaluation of blended online learning in three spinal surgery educational courses. J. Eur. CME **11**(1), 2014042 (2022). https://doi.org/10.1080/21614083.2021.2014042

21. Zambrano Sánchez, G., Montedesoca Coloma, L., Morales López, T., Tarupi Montenegro, W.: Medical students' perception of the use of simulated patients as a strategy for training in comprehensive patient management. Educ. Medica **21**(2), 123–126 (2020). https://doi.org/10.1016/j.edumed.2018.08.004

22. Oliveros, A., Mertz, V., Corvetto, M., Delfino, A., De La Fuente, R.: Transformación de los contenidos teóricos del programa de especialidad de anestesiología en un diplomado de formato b-learning. Investigación en Educación Médica **4**(14), e14 (2015). https://doi.org/10.1016/S2007-5057(15)30053-3

23. Liu, Q., Peng, W., Zhang, F., Hu, R., Li, Y., Yan, W.: The effectiveness of blended learning in health professions: systematic review and meta-analysis. J. Med. Internet Res. **18**(1), e2 (2016). https://doi.org/10.2196/jmir.4807

24. Martinez, E.T., Martin, J.I., Magadan. C., Lopez, A., Fernandez, R., Regaño, S., et al.: Influence of previous experience on the benefits of laparoscopic surgical training based on simulation. Cir. Esp. **97** (6), 314–319 (2019). https://doi.org/10.1016/j.cireng.2019.06.001

25. León Ferrufino, F., Varas Cohen, J., Buckel Schaffner, E., Crovari Eulufi, F., Pimentel Müller, F., Martínez Castillo, J., et al.: Simulation in laparoscopic surgery. Cir. Esp. **93**(1), 4–11 (2015). https://doi.org/10.1016/j.ciresp.2014.02.011

26. Betsch, D., Gjerde, H., Lewis, D., Tresidder, R., Gupta, R.R.: Ergonomics in the operating room: it doesn't hurt to think about it, but it may hurt not to! Can. J. Ophthalmol. **55**(3 Suppl 1), 17–21 (2020). https://doi.org/10.1016/j.jcjo.2020.04.004

27. Catanzarite, T., Tan-Kim, J., Whitcomb, E.L., Menefee, S.: Ergonomics in surgery: a review. Female Pelvic Med. Reconstr. Surg. **24**(1), 1–12 (2018). https://doi.org/10.1097/SPV.0000000000000456. PMID: 28914699

28. Vázquez-Reyes, J.M., Rodríguez-Guillén, J.H., Cortés-Algara, A., González-Ramírez, P.A., Millán-Hernández, M.: Ten tips for future medical specialty professors. FEM **22**(5), 245–326 (2019). https://doi.org/10.33588/fem.225.1019

29. González-Rubio, R., Latasa Zamalloa, P., Aginagalde Llorente, A.H., Peremiquel-Trillas, P., Ruiz-Montero, R., Gullón, P., et al.: Competencias para Medicina Preventiva y Salud Pública: propuestas tras un proceso comparativo y participativo. Educ Medica **22**(2), S62–S69 (2021). https://doi.org/10.1016/j.edumed.2019.09.004

Technological Solution to Optimize Outpatient Waiting Time for Medical Care Between Multiple Private Healthcare Institutions – A Preliminary Research

Cesar Castro-Velásquez[✉][iD], Wendy Barrera-Barrera[iD], Daniel Burga-Durango[iD], and Jimmy Armas-Aguirre[iD]

Universidad Peruana de Ciencias Aplicadas (UPC), Lima San Isidro 15076, Peru
u201511066@upc.edu.pe

Abstract. This article proposes a technological solution that allows optimizing the outpatient waiting time for medical care among private health care providers using React Native as a multiplatform tool, since it facilitates the creation of user interfaces efficiently and has one of the most significant numbers of contributors for any repository on GitHub, and the use of Microsoft Azure as a cloud platform due to the fact that it provides the security, privacy and integrity requirements demanded by the Peruvian Ministry of Health (MINSA). This proposal allows users to schedule their medical appointments in a private health institution according to their needs through the following phases: 1) Capture and storage of personal data, 2) Capture of search parameters, and 3) Scheduling of medical appointments. The preliminary case study of the proposal was carried out by collecting a sample of 60 patients, aged between 17 and 65 years of both sexes, who booked medical appointments in an outpatient specialty. The results were compared with the data collected in the SUSALUD user satisfaction survey and with our own survey conducted prior to the solution's implementation. This study effectively optimized medical care waiting time by 54.5%. However, this article contains the preliminary phase of this research. Therefore, it should be considered for future research and address upcoming studies in this critical area.

Keywords: Outpatient waiting time · medical appointment · Appointment scheduling

1 Introduction

Waiting time is an indicator of healthcare services quality that directly influences a patient's primary care [1]. According to Cao et al., there are two types of outpatients' waiting time: waiting before consultation and waiting after consultation. Time waiting before consultation has taken more interest in studies, which is divided into waiting time for scheduling and waiting time for consultation [2].

© The Author(s), under exclusive license to Springer Nature Switzerland AG 2024
T. Guarda et al. (Eds.): ARTIIS 2023, CCIS 1935, pp. 182–192, 2024.
https://doi.org/10.1007/978-3-031-48858-0_15

In Peru, long waiting time for consultation in health care institutions is limited by the number of medical resources and their available time slots. According to the Organization for Economic Cooperation and Development (OECD), Peru has 12.8 doctors for every 10,000 inhabitants; being considered well below the average of 33 per 10,000 recommended by the institution [3]. Due to limited medical resources and available time slots, SUSALUD reported that outpatients wait on average 6 days to receive medical care in private healthcare institutions [4]. Long waiting times not only cause outpatient dissatisfaction but also make timely access to medical services not provided to patients requiring immediate treatment, which will cause their health to progressively deteriorate due to delay in the service [5].

Recent research has proven the benefits of online systems based on medical appointment scheduling. The solution not only focuses on providing patients with the ability to have real-time information to book a medical appointment, but also helps medical centers reduce patients' waiting time for medical care [6].

This article proposes the development of a mobile solution that allows users to book an appointment in outpatient care according to medical specialty, date, location, and health insurance. Since shift availability is limited per health center, which makes waiting time longer, the proposal will be connected to different private hospital services that will provide real-time information on available shifts. As a result, users will have more appointment options and the ability to choose them according to their needs. This mobile solution is expected to optimize the waiting time from the appointment until the medical service is completed, to improve the quality of care for users.

This article is organized as follows. First, a brief discussion of solutions similar to the proposal is given followed by an explanation of the technologies used. Then, the development process is presented, which includes the analysis, design, and deployment of the mobile solution. Finally, the article concludes with the explanation of the validation process, the metrics used, and the discussion of the preliminary results obtained through the case study.

2 Literature Review

2.1 Appointment Scheduling Systems

Habibi et al. proposed an appointment scheduling system, which was implemented in private hospitals that did not have an online system. The solution had a web and mobile version of the system; and it was based on three end-users: secretaries, doctors, and patients. The first two used the system to manage medical appointments and the third used the mobile solution to book appointments [7]. On the other hand, a different solution researched is ZocDoc, which provides patients with the ability to search for appointments from different health care providers based on their health insurance and location area. The system evaluation results stated that it provides higher access to available appointments since 17 of the 20 cities surveyed in the USA presented available medical appointments within the next three days [8]. In Turkey, a centralized doctor's appointment system (CDAS), was also implemented. The system aims to simplify the scheduling of appointments by citizens in all hospitals operating under the Ministry. Inal evaluated the CDAS's usability where it became evident the need to simplify the application's interface for users. Furthermore, due to the importance of the e-government implementation, emphasis was placed on increasing performance and efficiency so as not to decrease the total productivity of public health centers [9].

The functionalities and characteristics of medical appointment scheduling systems were identified from the solutions researched; these are presented in the following table (Table 1).

Table 1. Features of Medical Appointment Scheduling Systems.

N°	Features	References
1	Search by calendar	[1, 8]
2	Online medical appointment booking/scheduling	[1, 6–9]
3	Doctor search filter	[1, 7–9]
4	Patient registration form	[1, 6, 8]
5	Cancel/reschedule appointments	[1, 6, 7]
6	Reminders or alarms	[1, 6]
7	Forms and recommendations according to symptoms	[1, 6]
8	Messaging with doctors	[6]
9	Qualification to doctors	[8]
10	Search by health insurance	[8]
11	Search by location	[8]
12	Access policies	[10, 11]

Concerning the patient registration form, Yang et al., in their study of the features of medical appointment scheduling systems in Taiwan, mention that the ID number was the most required item (98.5%) on the forms followed by the year and date of birth (88.6%) [6].

Regarding the access policy for scheduling appointments, Ahmadi et al. present three types of policies: traditional access, open access and hybrid access. The first provides patients with the ability to schedule their medical appointments in advance, while the open access policy allows for same-day scheduling. Finally, hybrid access provides patients with both same-day and day-ahead scheduling capabilities. It is also considered an access policy when patients book a same-day or next-day appointment. [10]. According to Cho et al., the open access policy allows doctors to treat more patients; however, the traditional policy gives doctors more control over their schedule and the ability to limit overtime [11].

Web-based medical appointment services are classified in SaaS and patented. SaaS or software as a service is cloud-based and is provided and maintained by healthcare IT companies such as ZocDoc and InQuicker, through a paid subscription. In addition, the patented systems are implemented and managed by each health center. The two types of systems are integrated into the healthcare providers' websites [1].

Finally, it is important to focus on user preferences in the development of medical appointment scheduling systems. Ahmadi et al. mention that preferences will depend on each patient according to the appointment day and the doctor offered by health care providers [10]. Table 2 shows the benefits of implementing an appointment scheduling system in a health center.

Table 2. Benefits of Implementing a Medical Appointment Scheduling System

N°	Benefits	References
1	Decrease of waiting time	[1, 7, 8]
2	Decrease of no-show rate	[1, 7, 8]
3	Increase in user satisfaction	[1, 7, 8]
4	Available shifts	[8]

2.2 Cross-Platform Development Tools Evaluation

Developers want to cover more users, and cross-platform development tools help developing the application, only once, for both Android and iOS operating systems at a lower cost [12]. It was decided to use the React Native tool as a cross-platform tool, as it facilitates the creation of user interfaces efficiently and has one of the largest amounts of contributors for any repository in GitHub [13]; therefore, the code, support, and documentation [14] will assist in the development of the interface. The performance of React native is suitable for the development of the proposed solution [15].

2.3 Cloud Platform Evaluation

Cloud Computing provides services for applications, platforms, network servers, among others, through technological resources [16]. New startups focus on Cloud projects and services such as PaaS (Platform as Service). These systems are DevOps (development and operations) environments that provide efficient tools for the creation and support of cloud applications [17]. Therefore, as the project results in the development of a mobile solution, the technological platform to use will be "Platform as Service" (PaaS).

From the cloud platforms analyzed in Table 3, Microsoft Azure was selected because it provides the necessary tools for the protection of sensitive health user data, including the security and privacy requirements requested by the Peruvian Ministry of Health (MINSA) [18]. Microsoft Azure platform provides Key Vault to control access to APIS keys granted by clinics, SSL/TLS certifications for the protection of confidential information sent between two servers and to prevent attacks by cybercriminals or unauthorized modification of the data being transferred.

Table 3. Cloud Platforms

N°	Platform	Description
1	Google Cloud Platform	The platform is used to create solutions through technology stored in the cloud, as well as to use integration services, which provide a control flow to perform work in relation to the actual processing occurring within the data flow [18]
2	AWS Elastic Beanstalk	It is a service for the implementation and scale of services, and web application development with the programming languages Java, .NET, PHP, Python, Ruby, and Docker on servers such as Apache, Passenger, etc. The platform allows to upload your project and will automatically manage the implementation, automatic scaling, up to monitoring the state of the application [19]
3	Microsoft Azure	Microsoft Azure is designed to support the full life cycle of web solutions such as mobile build, test, deployment, management, and upgrade. This platform has two main components: application files and configuration files. Azure handles all the work of operating systems, as their whole approach is the creation of a quality application for its end users [20]

3 Proposed Technological Solution

Limited medical resources and scheduled availability cause outpatients to wait an average of 6 days to receive medical attention in private health institutions. To improve user access and quality of medical care, a technological solution is proposed to optimize outpatient waiting time from appointment scheduling to medical service fulfillment. Recent research has shown that online systems based on medical appointment scheduling help medical centers reduce patients' waiting time for medical care [6]. The technological solution will be based on the open-access or next-day policy, which allows patients to book their appointment for the same day they request it or for the day after. This policy is optimal because it is feasible for the type of user the solution focuses on, which are outpatients who require appointments on an urgent basis [10]. Unlike traditional systems where limited appointment options are offered, our solution will consume web services from different healthcare facilities. The solution is based on the ZocDoc system which, by having different healthcare providers, provides greater access to available appointments [8]; which will help optimize waiting time. As part of the solution's features, users will have the ability to schedule an appointment based on medical specialty, date, location, and insurance. The mobile solution proposes the functionalities presented in Table 4.

3.1 Phases of Mobile Solution

The mobile solution focuses on the medical appointment scheduling phase for patients in an outpatient care medical specialty. The phases implemented within the mobile application will be presented below.

Table 4. Mobile Solution Functionality

Heading level	Functionality	Actor
1	User registration	Patient
2	Log in	Patient
3	Personal data management	Patient
4	Search available medical appointments	Patient
5	Schedule medical appointments	Patient
6	Notify medical appointment scheduled	Patient
7	Display private hospital location	Patient
8	List medical appointments	Patient
9	Display appointment detail	Patient
10	Visualize private hospital	Patient
11	Call private hospital	Patient
12	Reschedule medical appointment	Patient
13	Cancel medical appointment	Patient
14	Add patient	Patient
15	View patient	Patient

Capture and Storage of Personal Data. First, patients register their email and password to be able to log in. Then, they must complete a form in the mobile application to fill out their data such as name, surname, ID number, date of birth, and telephone. This data will be stored in the database and used to transfer the data to the private hospital, where the patient will be treated.

Capture Search Parameters. For this phase, patients must fill out the parameters of medical specialty, date, location, and medical insurance, needed to search available appointments. These parameters will be sent through web services, which will send back to the mobile application the available appointments information obtained from private hospitals services.

Medical Appointment Scheduling. Once the available appointments are obtained, patients must select the available shift that suits their needs. Then, they must define who will attend the appointment; since there is the option of being able to add a family member as a patient. Finally, with the patient already defined, the medical appointment is booked.

3.2 Integration Architecture

The proposed architecture allows interaction between the components of the server hosted in Microsoft Azure, the services of external private hospitals, and the mobile application. The user interface, developed in React Native, that works with both Android and iOS operating systems, is part of the presentation layer that users interact with. Through the user interface, they can search for medical appointments using clinic web services and communicate with the business and data layer of the application itself hosted in Azure. First, the business layer contains the logic that will allow the application data to be recorded. With service interfaces, business functionality will be available to the presentation layer. The business components, together with workflows and entities, provide the core functionality of the application and ensure that the business needs can be optimally managed. Second, in the data layer, accesses to the application data are managed through Azure Database for MySQL to perform the physical storage and retrieval of data through the business layer request. Both business and data layers are supported by the security layer, which is divided into three submodules: authentication, authorization, and security mechanisms [22]. Authentication to identify the user according to their credentials, authorization for access control and permissions according to the roles defined in the application, and the security mechanisms that ensure the integrity and confidentiality of the data obtained from the use of security options granted by the Azure platform. The security layer is implemented based on the security directives and policies established by the Peruvian government for the treatment of personal data related to health or personal health [23]. These policies include the Personal Data Protection Law (N° 29733), which establishes principles and requirements for the treatment of personal data, the National Information Security Policy (PNSI) which establishes the objectives and guidelines for the protection of information, and the Digital Security Framework of the Peruvian State (MSED) which establishes the minimum standards of information security for the entities of the Peruvian State including private health clinics. Likewise, for transferring data between the user interface (UI) and the back-end server we use protocols such as HTTPS and WebSocket. This ensures that data can be sent and received in real-time, without having to wait for the server to respond to a query (Fig. 1).

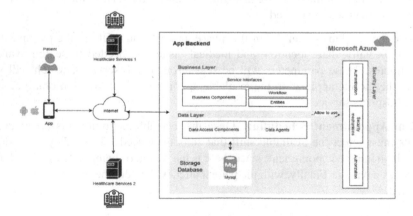

Fig. 1. Integration Architecture of the solution

4 Case Study

4.1 Scenario

The mobile solution was validated by effective procedures and patients scheduling medical appointments in outpatient clinics. To validate the results, samples were taken from 60 patients, ranging from 17 to 65 years old, of both genders. For the tests, two private clinic services were simulated in which shifts from 8:00 to 10:00 a.m. were considered already scheduled, so that no shifts were available in that time interval. It should be taken into consideration that patients chose the medical appointment of their preference and that the medical specialties considered in both simulated healthcare centers were the following: cardiology, gynecology, traumatology, pediatrics, ophthalmology, dentistry, internal medicine, dermatology, otorhinolaryngology, oncology, and gastroenterology. For this scenario, the impact of rescheduling medical appointments was not taken into consideration.

The present study was conducted in May 2020 during the global COVID-19 pandemic; therefore, due to the safety of our participants and compliance with local health regulations, the validation and clinical data obtained had to be simulated.

4.2 Implementation

The implementation was carried out on smartphones with Android operating system, which had internet access to carry out the case study.

Testing in the Mobile Application. The mobile application was provided for the patient to perform the scheduling process, which consisted of user registration, recording personal data, consulting available appointments, and scheduling the medical appointment. As patients performed the tests, they measured the time it took to complete the scheduling process.

Data Storage. The results and perceptions of the scheduling process were compiled through a survey available in https://bit.ly/3cQc2Fv. It included questions about scheduling time and waiting time for medical care by using the application.

Testing Analysis of Indicators. Indicators obtained from the medical appointment scheduling process, before and after the implementation of the proposed mobile solution were analyzed, which are the following:

Average Waiting Time for Medical Care. Interval of time patients wait for medical care; from the time the appointment is scheduled/booked.

Average Scheduling Time. Interval of time that users take to schedule the medical appointment.

Table 5 presents the indicators before the implementation of the proposal according to information provided by the Health Services User Satisfaction Survey [4]. First, there is a delay in the booking process causing it to take approximately 57 min for a patient to obtain a medical appointment. This varies significantly from the medical appointment booking methods available; either by phone call, mobile/web application, or in person.

Table 5. Indicators Before the implementation of the proposal

N°	Indicators	Measure
1	Average waiting time for medical care	144 h (6 days)
2	Average scheduling time	57 min

Adding to the time mentioned, the patient waits 144 h (about 6 days) to receive in-clinic care due to the limited number of appointments for care, which often do not coincide with the patient's availability.

Results. With the data obtained from the Survey of the Medical Appointment Scheduling Process, the following formula was used to obtain the average waiting time for medical care and scheduling time.

$$\overline{X} = \frac{\sum_{i=1}^{n} x_i}{n} \tag{1}$$

The indicators in Table 5 were compared with the collected data from the case study to calculate the percentage of optimization obtained with the implementation of the technology solution.

Table 6. Case Study Indicators

N°	Indicators	Measure	Optimization
1	Average waiting time for medical care	80 h	54.5%
2	Average scheduling time	6 min	89.49%

The average and the percentage of optimization for each indicator is shown in Table 6. Regarding the indicator "Average waiting time for medical care", with the use of the proposed mobile application, patients wait an average of 80 h (about 3 and a half days). As a result, it was calculated that the waiting time decreased by 64 h (54.5%).

In addition, in the indicator "Average appointment scheduling time," with the use of the proposed mobile application, patients took an average of 6 min to schedule a medical appointment. Therefore, the scheduling time decreased by 51 min (89.48%) (Fig. 2).

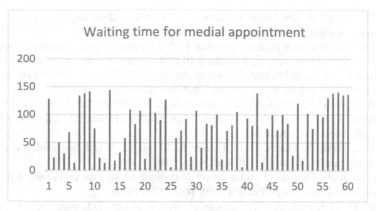

Fig. 2. Waiting time for medical appointment

5 Conclusions

This article highlights the feasibility of using a mobile solution to optimize outpatient waiting time and medical appointment booking time in private clinics. According to the evaluation of cloud computing platforms in Table 3, we used Microsoft Azure due to the tools required for the protection of sensitive user information and the React Native framework due to the ease of mobile application development using the chosen cloud platform.

The preliminary results show that patients only wait 80 h (about 3 and a half days) on average for their medical appointment, unlike the traditional appointment scheduling process where patients wait 144 h (about 6 days). It represents a considerable decrease of 54.5%. Therefore, with optimization patients gain timely access to health services, resulting in the successful treatment of their diseases or health conditions. Additionally, the time for scheduling appointments is reduced by 51 min (89.48%).

It is important to mention that private healthcare institutions also benefit from the proposed solution as they can optimize resources and make better use of time to focus on providing specialized medical care for patients, which is their primary objective. With the proposal, the institutions will have a channel where they can get new patients and build loyalty with existing ones, which implies higher incomes and an increase in their brand value.

Although this article contains the preliminary phase of this research, it should be kept in mind for future studies. By having real data from private clinics for extraction of available appointments and, taking into account the auto-scaling feature provided by Azure, the accuracy and efficiency of outpatient waiting time for medical care can be improved.

References

1. Zhao, P., Yoo, I., Lavoie, J., Lavoie, B.J., Simoes, E.: Web-based medical appointment systems: a systematic review. J. Med. Internet Res. **19**(4), e134 (2017)

2. Cao, W., et al.: A web-based appointment system to reduce waiting for outpatients: a retrospective study. BMC Health Serv. Res. **11**(1) (2011)
3. Gestión Perú tiene 12.8 médicos por cada 10,000 habitantes, muy abajo de países OCDE. https://gestion.pe/peru/peru-12-8-medicos-10-000-habitantes-abajo-paises-ocde-236346-noticia/#:~:text=Per%C3%BA%20cuenta%20con%2012.8%20m%C3%A9dicos,Minsa)%20de%20la%20Cooperaci%C3%B3n%20Italiana. Accessed 04 June 2023
4. SUSALUD Encuesta Nacional de Satisfacción de Usuario en Salud. http://portal.susalud.gob.pe/wp-content/uploads/archivo/encuesta-sat-nac/2016/PRESENTACION-SUSALUD-2016.pdf. Accessed 04 June 2023
5. Vidal, T., Rocha, S., Harzheim, E., Hauser, L., Tesser, C.: Scheduling models and primary health care quality. Revista de Saúde Pública (2019)
6. Yang, C., et al.: Features of online hospital appointment systems in Taiwan: a nationwide survey. Int. J. Environ. Res. Public Health **16**(2), 171 (2019)
7. Habibi, M., Mohammadabadi, F., Tabesh, H., Vakili-Arki, H.: Scheduling system on evaluation metrics of outpatient scheduling system: a before-after multicenter study. J. Med. Syst. (2019)
8. Kurtzman, W., Keshav, A., Satish, P., Patel, S.: Scheduling primary care appointments online: differences in availability based on health insurance. Healthcare (2018)
9. Inal, Y.: Heuristic-based user interface evaluation of the mobile centralized doctor appointment system. Electron. Libr. (2019)
10. Ahmadi-Javid, A., Jalali, Z., Klassen, J.: Outpatient appointment systems in healthcare: a review of optimization studies. Eur. J. Oper. Res. (2017)
11. Cho, D., Cattani, K.: The patient patient: the performance of traditional versus open-access scheduling policies. Decis. Sci. (2018)
12. Ciman, M., Gaggi, O.: An empirical analysis of energy consumption of cross-platform frameworks for mobile development. Pervasive Mob. Comput. (2017)
13. React Native. https://reactnative.dev/. Accessed 11 Apr 2020
14. Rieger, C., Majchrzak, A.: Towards the definitive evaluation framework for cross-platform app development approaches. J. Syst. Softw. (2019)
15. Biørn-Hansen, A., Grønli, T.-M., Ghinea, G.: Animations in cross-platform mobile applications: an evaluation of tools. Metr. Perform. Sens. (2019)
16. Alshwaier, A.: A new trend for e-learning in KSA using educational clouds. Adv. Comput. Int. J. (2012)
17. Li, Z., Zhang, Y., Liu, Y.: Towards a full-stack devops environment (platform-as-a-service) for cloud-hosted applications. Tsinghua Sci. Technol. (2017)
18. MINSA Directiva Administrativa que establece el tratamiento de los datos personales relacionados con la salud o datos personales en Salud. http://bvs.minsa.gob.pe/local/MINSA/5118.pdf. Accessed 04 June 2023
19. Google Descripción general de Google Cloud Platform. https://cloud.google.com/docs/overview. Accessed 11 Apr 2020
20. Amazon AWS Elastic Beanstalk. https://aws.amazon.com/es/elasticbeanstalk/. Accessed 11 June 2020
21. Microsoft What is Azure? https://azure.microsoft.com/en-us/overview/what-is-azure/. Accessed 11 June 2020
22. Tummers, J., Tobi, H., Catal, C., Tekinerdogan, B.: Designing a reference architecture for health information systems. BMC Med. Inform. Decis. Mak. **21**(1) (2021)
23. Ministerio de Salud: Directiva administrativa que establece el tratamiento de los datos personales relacionados con la salud o datos personales en salud. Oficina General de Tecnologías de la Información, Lima, Peru (2020)

Learning for the Empowerment of High School Girl Students

Manuel Delzo-Zurita[✉], Diego Pickman-Montoya, Daniel Burga, and David Mauricio

Universidad Peruana de Ciencias Aplicadas, Santiago de Surco, 15023 Lima, Perú
u410089@upc.edu.pe

Abstract. There is a gender gap between men and women, this is manifested in gender violence and social injustice. An alternative to reduce this gap is female empowerment through learning. This study proposes an IT model for the empowerment of girls in high school education, which is based on Moodle and includes six modules (Administrator, Instructional Team, Mentor, Girl, Learning Tools and Empowerment Test). The proposed model was implemented in a system called EmpowerMe that includes the tools digital library, chatbot, webinar and a game-based learning platform. EmpowerMe was validated through a case study over eight student girls in Huancayo, Perú. The results in the case study show that after two sessions of 1.5 h each, the girls' empowerment improves by 4.18% with the application, in contrast to the traditional method, which improves by 2%, and the usability and satisfaction evaluation show that the EmpowerMe system is rated with an average of 4.43 out of 5 points, obtaining high marks regarding usability, content management, follow-up and user satisfaction.

Keywords: Female empowerment · learning tools · moodle

1 Introduction

Globally, there is a gender gap between men and women, 70% in European countries and 50% in American countries [1], which is manifested in gender violence and social injustice. One out of every three women has experienced violence by a family member or spouse [2], 69% of trafficked persons are women and 5% of these are girls [3].

An alternative to reduce the gender gap is the empowerment of women and girls through learning content that gives them leadership and independence, to know their rights, prevent acts of violence, and know how to report them. Among the efforts for female empowerment are collective intelligence to teach concepts of information and communications technology [4], the construction of individual capacities regarding empowerment [5], pedagogical strategies such as Right To Play to educate children and girls with problems of violence [6], self-help models for collaborative learning in different cultures 38, social education for disabled women [7], prevention of abuse towards young women and older adults [8], the education for women's empowerment in rural India [9, 10]. One effort for female empowerment is the study by [11] that points out that education contributes to female entrepreneurship.

T. Guarda et al. (Eds.): ARTIIS 2023, CCIS 1935, pp. 193–208, 2024.
https://doi.org/10.1007/978-3-031-48858-0_16

Two aspects are important in female empowerment: educational models and technological tools. Educational models address empowerment from an educational perspective, focusing on high school education. On the other hand, technological tools help to improve skills, knowledge, and participation in social media and networks [12]. However, the various empowerment tools are not focused on girls and adolescents in the high school stage, since, according to UNICEF, in 2015, a considerable percentage of the population are school-age children and adolescents in several developing countries [13].

This study proposes a technological platform to assist in the process of empowerment of girls in high school, providing tools and appropriate educational content so that they can acquire and increase their leadership skills, entrepreneurship, sex education, among others, based on the open source Moodle platform. To measure empowerment, a quantitative instrument is used with questions focused on female empowerment.

This paper is organized into five sections. In Sect. 2, the state of the art on learning applications that contribute to women's empowerment is presented. The e-learning model of the technological proposal and its implementation are described in Sect. 3, respectively. Section 4 describes the validation process. Finally, Sect. 5 shows the conclusions.

2   State of the Art: Learning Systems for Women's Empowerment

The researched literature offers support tools for the process of female empowerment, thus providing alternatives to improve women's knowledge and empowerment at the intellectual level.

Learning management systems (LMS) are defined as software used to create and manage content and environments for online learning, providing an automated and simple way to educate a group of people [14]. In the case of female empowerment, LMSs have been identified that, for the most part, consider an adult age group and rarely a school-age group.

First, the social networks of Facebook and Twitter are useful for data collection when planning to learn about community problems in a society [15]. Secondly, these networks such as Instagram can be used to disseminate educational content by posting pictures to promote good habits in women [16]. Third, systems can focus on e-learning by employing digital storytelling for learning, providing stories and experiences to communities that have a high macho influence [17]. Fourth, to enhance empowerment and provide tools for female entrepreneurship, there are digital financial services that associate women as a key part of society, offering advice on basic financial education to societies with restrictions for women [18]. Fifth, there is the system related to the dissemination of improved and timely information on causes and possible effects after abnormal Pap test results, which affects women who must undergo treatment and need to be empowered to face the healing process [19]. Sixth, there is the PRISMA tool, which provides an innovative and attractive way to access female empowerment content focused on learning and to access health content [20]. Seventh, the European Network for Women in Leadership platform presents a space for professionals to exchange ideas and develop best practices according to their talent [21]. Eighth, The WIE Suite project is a community for women leaders and creators where they can share experiences of success and support among other women

[22]. Ninth, the He For She program belonging to UN Women seeks to generate solidarity for gender equality in all people, equally involving men in communities, families and businesses [23]. Tenth, the SheLeader project is developed by women and companies that contribute to generating a platform for empowerment [24]. Eleventh, the Black Girl in OM project creates a space for Afro-descendant women to have access to content and experiences totally designed for them [25]. Twelfth, the Empower Women program is dedicated to helping women reach their full economic potential, they also inspire both men and women to be activists for gender equality [26].

3 E-Learning MEG

3.1 MEG Model

We propose MEG (Model for Empowerment in Girls), an IT e-learning model to assist in the empowerment process for high school girls, which includes six modules (administrator, instructional team, learning tools, empowerment test, mentor and girl) and three roles (instructional team, mentor and girl) (see Fig. 1).

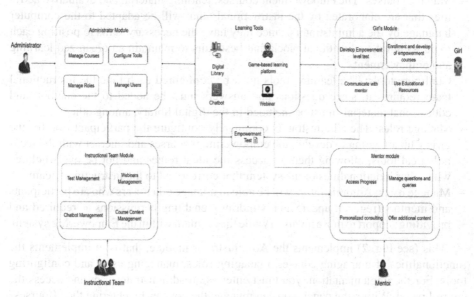

Fig. 1. E-Learning MEG

First, the Administrator manages courses, tools, roles and users. Secondly, the Instructional Team manages the test, chatbot, webinars and the content of the courses so that the girl and the tutor can make use of the platform. Likewise, the instructional team will develop a test to define what level of empowerment the girl is at, by using an instrument that will allow measuring empowerment and knowing her level (high, medium and low). For the present research, the "Instrument for measuring women's empowerment"

[27] was used. Thirdly, the girl develops the Empowerment Test and enrolls in the available courses, according to the level of empowerment achieved, communicates doubts to the mentor and uses the other educational resources. Fourthly, the Mentor accesses the girl's progress to validate doubts and queries, as well as to generate personalized advice and offer additional content in the digital library, if necessary. Fifthly, the learning tools included are a chatbot, webinar, digital library and a game-based learning platform all managed from Moodle.

3.2 Implementation

The following is a description of the EmpowerMe system (acronym from Empower and Me) implemented by MEG E-Learning to support the empowerment process of high school girls. EmpowerMe has been built on the LMS Moodle, because it has functionalities that allow easy integration with other technological tools, and it consists of five modules that are explained below.

Administrator module. This module is in charge of managing the accounts of the other users, course management, management of the tools integrated to the system, etc.:

– Manage courses: The empowerment courses, learning material and evaluative activities that are elaborated by the instructional team will be adapted to the computer language by the administrators, since they have the necessary skills to position each topic within the educational block that best suits to maintain an organized learning and empowerment.
– Configure tools: The learning tools must be configured each time the instructional team requires it, since questions and answers must be added to the chatbot, and educational materials must be included in the digital library, among others.
– Manage roles: The administrators completely configure the participant role for the girls who are going to develop the empowerment courses and interact with the technological tools, allowing them to access the ideal routes and not be overwhelmed with other functionalities of the system that correspond to the instructional team.
– Manage users: Administrators will be able to manage other users who are participants and mentors (register, update and withdraw), enabling permissions as required and providing support to those involved while they remain within the EmpowerMe system.

This (see Fig. 2) implements the Administrator module, that is, it implements the functionalities of managing courses, managing roles, managing users and configuring tools. For the implementation, you must enter as an administrator user and access the control panel. Within the panel, you can manage the courses by entering the "Courses" tab where different options are available for them. Likewise, to manage roles and users, you must enter the "Users" tab within the configuration. In this tab, users can be created, edited or deleted, as well as the roles of each of them. On the other hand, configuring tools is done by entering each course where you will find the option "Add activity or resource" with which you can add the necessary tools for its development.

Instructional team module. Through this module, the instructional team is in charge of managing the content, system activities and resources needed for each topic of the empowerment process. Will be able to manage the following:

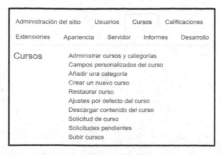

Fig. 2. Administrative management interface

- Manage test: Supervise the application of the empowerment test and suggest courses to increase and reinforce skills. The instructional team is in charge of developing the empowerment test for defining levels using an instrument for this purpose.
- Manage webinars: Develop virtual sessions on topics and courses. In this way, girls have access to a teaching done directly by a professional at a defined time and can access the broadcast of the virtual session. The Google Meet tool was selected to set up the sessions, due to its quick integration with Google Services tools.
- Manage chatbot: In an educational environment, this tool can help to clarify the doubts that girls may have after reading about a complex topic, making the existence of a mentor 24 h a day not indispensable, but the chatbot would be present to solve the most common doubts that a girl may present, leaving the most punctual ones to the mentors in their schedule of answers.
- Manage course content: Develop empowering content, evaluative and developmental activities for the girls.

This (see Fig. 3) allows the enabling and configuration of the interfaces that incorporate the technological tools for learning within Moodle, thus maintaining the educational blocks of the empowerment courses. The mentors are empowered to customize the courses within the system, adding activities and resources to each segment that requires it. In this way, you can choose from a varied group of elements to further nurture the girl's education.

Mentor module. Through this module, the mentor take care of each group of girls according to their level of empowerment, also will be able to manage the following:

- Access progress: Visualize in real time the progress of the girl in her enrolled courses and take actions or support strategies for the girl according to the level of progress that she presents.
- Manage doubts and queries: Through the chatbot, which was previously configured with the answers to the most frequent questions, the participant can communicate with the mentor, through email, also the mentor can use the webinar tool to resolve these doubts and queries, either in a group or personally.
- Personalized advice: The system offers the functionality of personalized advice that is based on the progress, doubts and queries of each girl, being able to devise better strategies for learning.

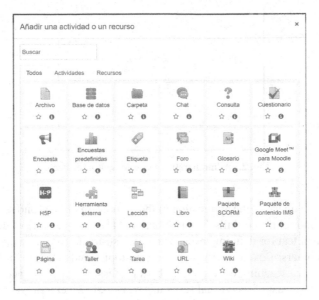

Fig. 3. Instructional team management interface

- Offer additional content: After the participant has used the course resources and these are not enough to complete the course satisfactorily, the mentor has the functionality of offering additional content, so she will have more course content that will allow her to have a better understanding of the course in the digital library.

This (see Fig. 4) allows the mentor to evaluate and measure the performance and progress of the girls in their empowerment process, through evaluation instruments, where questions are structured so that the girls reinforce what they have learned in the course lessons. In addition, the mentor will be able to view the grades of the girls' enrolled courses, in order to carry out reinforcement sessions (in cases of low grades) or award reward badges (in cases of high grades).

Girl's module. Through this module, the girl will be able to access the different courses that are enabled on the platform, also will be able to do the following:

- Develop empowerment level test: The girl must make use of the functionality of the system that allows the development of the empowerment level test. Carrying out this test allows the instructions team to know the current level of empowerment of the girl and thus offer the courses according to that level.
- Enroll in and develop empowerment courses: The girl will be able to visualize the courses she can enroll in and thus improve her empowerment level.
- Communicate with the mentor: The girl will be able to communicate with the mentor to clear her doubts or make inquiries about the topics or contents proposed by the mentor for each course.
- Use educational resources: The girl will have educational resources such as digital library, webinars, chatbot and game-based learning platform available to her to develop the courses she is enrolled in.

Fig. 4. Mentor accessing progress interface

This (see Fig. 5) is focused on the development of activities and the learning of the educational content established by the instructional team and mentor for the girls. The activities that the girl must carry out and all the lessons that you must learn to progress in the process of female empowerment could be shown in the system. Additionally, girls, mentors, and the instructional team can look at the courses they have been enrolled in to develop or manage their educational content.

Empowerment test. The instructional team will develop a test to define the level of empowerment of the girl, through the use of an instrument that will allow measuring empowerment and knowing her level (high, medium and low).

Learning tools. EmpowerMe integrates the Chatbot (see Fig. 6A), previously configured and connected to the Moodle database, with which the girls can make additional courses and consultations that can be incorporated at the decision of the mentors. Likewise, the game-based learning platform called Kahoot (see Fig. 6B) has been incorporated through EmpowerMe's institutional email, where mentors can log into the Kahoot platform to design their empowerment educational content in a more dynamic way, generate the web link and add it as a resource in Moodle within the desired course. In addition, the Google Meet webinar tool (see Fig. 6C) allows for synchronous and asynchronous video conferencing sessions, so that both students present at the defined times and those who cannot be present can learn through the tool and their mentors. Finally, EmpowerMe includes a digital library as a tool to provide the girls with manuals, documents, presentations and other materials uploaded to the system by their mentors to complement what they have learned during the empowerment sessions.

Fig. 5. Enrolled course interface

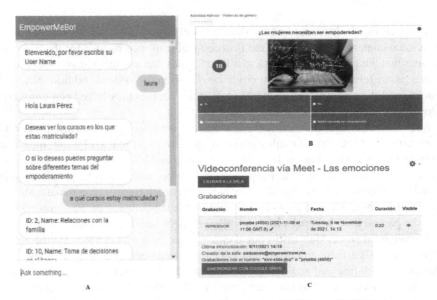

Fig. 6. EmpowerMe Tool: A) Chatbot support; B) Kahoot; C) Webinar

3.3 Architecture

The physical architecture (see Fig. 7) shows that the actors interact from their local machines via the Internet with the system services that are located in the cloud (Google Cloud) for full availability, where the two servers needed to store EmpowerMe are hosted: applications and web. The Webinar tool, the Chatbot, the Digital Library and the game-oriented learning platform are managed through the application server administrator to integrate with the Moodle-based empowerment content manager, forming the EmpowerMe proposal. Each tool is referred to as a service because of the qualities and functions that each tool possesses to communicate with the platform and be of use to the instructional team, mentors and girls.

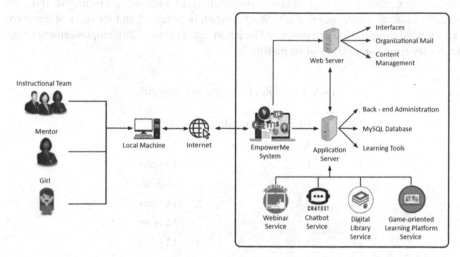

Fig. 7. EmpowerMe physical architecture

Likewise, (see Fig. 8) shows the logical architecture, which shows the components of the platform that are accessible through the local computer via the web page. This web platform is accessed through the local machines themselves and connects to the server where the functionalities of the components applied in the system are hosted to be used for each actor, which are accessible due to the interfaces and the access control managed by competent users to their respective functionalities.

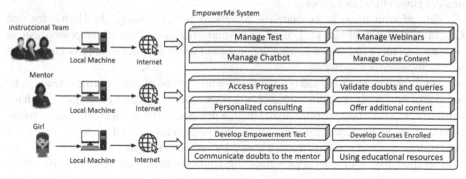

Fig. 8. EmpowerMe logical architecture

4   Case Validation

4.1   Case Study

Eight girls between the ages of thirteen and fifteen who are studying at the high school level in different schools, all of whom also study at a pre-university academy located in Huancayo, Peru, participated (see Table 1). In Peru, school studies are divided into primary (six grades) and high school (five grades). In addition, according to INEI on gender violence, it indicates that 63.2% of women between 15 and 49 years of age have experienced cases of violence produced by a partner or partner [28], empowerment being necessary from early stages of formation.

Table 1. Profiles of the participating girls.

ID	High School Grade	Age
P1	4.°	15 years
P2	1.°	13 years
P3	1.°	13 years
P4	3.°	14 years
P5	3.°	14 years
P6	1.°	13 years
P7	4.°	15 years
P8	2.°	13 years

EmpowerMe implementation. EmpowerMe was presented to the psychologist specialized in empowerment who works as a tutor in an academy. He was then trained for one hour virtually, so that he prepared the material for an empowerment course of two sessions of 1.5 h each, covering various topics such as participatory empowerment, recklessness, external influences, risk factors, etc. In addition, he prepared question and answer games through Kahoot.

Validation metrics. To evaluate the results of the case study, the Hernandez and Garcia empowerment test [27], used in several studies in Peru on empowerment in women, including [29–31], was used; it consists of thirty-four questions that encompass seven empowerment factors.

Traditional method. Nowadays, the traditional method of empowerment tends to be long talks in schools or events such as congresses where real cases of women who have achieved empowerment are presented. Under a perspective of intellectual empowerment or social recognition, women seek autonomy in general as well as to eradicate the denigrating acts and demerits that are posed by societies that are still sexist to this day. This method does not focus on girls since these talks or events are generally given from adolescence onwards.

Experiment. The eight girls were grouped into groups of four, called G1 and G2. The training was conducted in two sessions of 1.5 h each, both in one week, and at its culmination the empowerment test was applied. Both groups will take the empowerment course in the traditional way through videoconferencing and the assistance of an empowerment specialist. In addition, the G2 group, unlike the G1 group, uses EmpowerMe, i.e. the use of tools such as Chatbot, digital library, Webinar and game-based learning platform.

Results. The results show that the initial average of empowerment of groups G1 and G2 was 99.5 points, and, at the end of the course using the traditional method (see Fig. 9A), this increased on average by two points, while using EmpowerMe (see Fig. 9B) it increased by 6.25, that is, there was an improvement with respect to the traditional method.

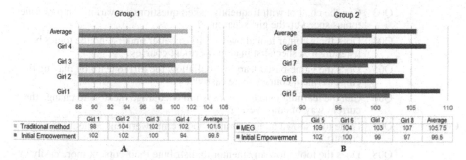

Fig. 9. Level of empowerment: A) According to the traditional method; B) Using the system

4.2 Usability and Satisfaction

Participants. Seven collegiate psychologists participated, who assumed the roles of mentor and instructional team, three of them work in schools, two in non-profit organizations, and two as independent, all of them with experience of more than six years in projects and initiatives of empowerment of children, adolescents and young people (see Table 2), also, in some technological tools for empowerment.

Table 2. Characteristics of the participating psychologists

ID	Gender	Experience in empowerment	Labor Center
P1	Female	8 years	Charity
P2	Female	7 years	Non-Governmental Organization
P3	Female	10 years	Psychologist at school
P4	Female	7 years	Independent psychologist
P5	Male	15 years	Psychologist at school
P6	Male	10 years	Psychologist at school
P7	Male	7 years	Independent psychologist

Validation instrument. A questionnaire was developed using Google Forms consisting of twenty questions divided into four sections (see Table 3): usability, content, monitoring (empowerment progress) and satisfaction. In addition, for each question, 5 response alternatives are presented according to the Likert scale (1: Strongly disagree; 2: Disagree; 3: Neither agree nor disagree; 4: Agree; 5: Strongly agree).

Table 3. Questionnaire to evaluate EmpowerMe

Dimension	ID	Question
Usability	Q01	Do the four tools presented in EmpowerMe contribute to improving the girl's learning?
	Q02	Do the four tools presented in EmpowerMe help improve the way girls are empowered?
	Q03	Can the chatbot with frequently asked questions on various empowerment topics speed up the girl's learning?
	Q04	Does the webinar tool allow the girl to better understand the topics by listening to a specialist in empowerment courses?
	Q05	Does the game-based learning tool allow the girl to learn by playing the empowerment courses more easily?
	Q06	Can the learning management system encourage mentors to change their current way of empowering?
Content	Q07	Is the tool shown as an option to boost empowerment content across the country?
	Q08	Does the tool allow any mentor to distribute their content more easily?
	Q09	Is the tool useful to create activities and communicate with my girls?
	Q10	Does the digital library within EmpowerMe allow the girl to more easily access any empowering content you create for learning?
Follow-up	Q11	Does the tool show a faster way to track girls' progress?
	Q12	Does the webinar tool allow girls to follow up more directly on their empowerment?
	Q13	Is accessing academic information and reviewing the girl's progress in the system easy and effective?
Satisfaction	Q14	As a mentor, is the use of system functionalities understandable?
	Q15	Are the design themes and graphics used attractive with respect to the content displayed?
	Q16	Does the system allow understandable and orderly navigation?
	Q17	Does the visualization of questionnaires, together with their results, allow us to better understand the level of progress with respect to the empowerment courses?
	Q18	Does EmpowerMe allow data capture of girls in the process of empowerment?
	Q19	Does EmpowerMe help the mentor make better decisions in the empowerment process?
	Q20	Is the mentor satisfied with the empowerment system?

Experiment. A 1.5-h videoconference was held with 2 to 3 psychologists at a time to present EmpowerMe, its purpose, functionalities, and advantages. Access to the system was given and activities were carried out (course management, participant management, evaluation management, question banks for the chatbot) of the mentor and the instructional team that were repeated by the psychologists. During the presentation, questions from the specialists were answered. At the end of the presentation, the usability and satisfaction questionnaire was applied, previously sent to their personal emails.

Results. The results of the EmpowerMe evaluation questionnaire (see Table 4) show a very high average rating (not less than 4.43 out of 5) regarding usability, content, follow-up, and satisfaction. In usability, it scored high for learning acceleration (Q03), and scored very high on the other questions, i.e. improving learning (Q01), improving empowerment (Q02), allowing the girl to better understand topics by listening to a specialist (Q04), and encourages mentors to change their current way of empowering (Q05). In content, a very high rating was obtained in all questions, i.e., it promotes empowering content (Q07), facilitates content distribution (Q08), is useful for creating activities and advising girls (Q09) and shows simplicity to access any empowering content through the digital library (Q10). In the follow-up, very high marks were obtained for each of the questions, i.e., the system (Q11) and the webinar (Q12) allow easy and effective progress monitoring (Q13). Finally, in satisfaction, a very high rating was obtained regarding the use of the system's functionalities (Q14), the graphic interfaces and design are attractive for the content displayed (Q15), the orderly and clear navigation (Q16), the agility in the visualization of questionnaires and their results (Q17), the improvement in girls' data capture (Q18), support for the mentor to make better decisions in the empowerment process (Q19) and compliance with the system (Q20).

Table 4. Results on the educational empowerment capacity of EmpowerMe and its usability

Dimension	Id	Specialists0							Average	
		E1	E2	E3	E4	E5	E6	E7		
Usability	Q01	5	5	4	5	3	5	5	4.57	4.50
	Q02	4	5	4	5	3	5	5	4.43	
	Q03	5	4	4	4	2	5	5	4.14	
	Q04	5	5	4	5	3	5	5	4.57	
	Q05	5	5	4	5	4	5	5	4.71	
	Q06	5	4	4	5	4	5	5	4.57	
Content	Q07	4	5	4	5	3	5	5	4.43	4.57
	Q08	5	5	4	5	3	5	5	4.57	
	Q09	5	4	5	5	3	5	5	4.57	
	Q10	5	5	5	5	3	5	5	4.71	
Follow-up	Q11	5	4	5	5	2	5	5	4.43	4.43
	Q12	5	4	5	5	2	4	5	4.29	
	Q13	5	5	5	5	2	5	5	4.57	
Satisfaction	Q14	5	5	4	5	5	5	4	4.71	4.73
	Q15	4	4	5	5	4	4	4	4.29	
	Q16	5	5	5	5	5	5	4	4.86	
	Q17	5	5	5	5	4	5	5	4.86	
	Q18	5	5	5	5	4	5	5	4.86	
	Q19	5	5	5	5	4	5	5	4.86	
	Q20	5	5	4	5	4	5	5	4.71	

5 Conclusions

MEG (Model for Empowerment in Girls), an IT e-learning model has been designed to assist in the empowerment process for girls in high school education, which includes five modules (instructional team, tools, empowerment test, mentor and girl) and three roles (instructional team, mentor and girl). MEG was implemented as a system called EmpowerMe, which is based on the Moodle LMS and integrates digital library, chatbot, webinar and game-based learning platforms. The results of the case study with eight girls point out that the empowerment process using EmpowerMe improves, significantly, the level of empowerment with respect to traditional teaching, showing after two class sessions an average score 105.75 points on a Hernandez and Garcia [27] scale of 135, four points higher than the average of traditional teaching. On the other hand, the results of the usability, content, follow-up and satisfaction survey applied to 7 psychologists with experience in female empowerment show a very high rating, with an average rating of no less than 4.4 out of 5. These results are limited to the perception of the respondents. As future work we intend to develop an adaptive version of EmpowerMe according to the level of empowerment, this because several studies show that adaptability makes students learn effectively [32].

Acknowledgment. The authors would like to thank the Universidad Peruana de Ciencias Aplicadas (UPC) for funding this research and the psychologists and girls who participated in this study.

References

1. World Economic Forum: Global Gender Gap report 2020. Switzerland: World Economic Forum (2020). https://www3.weforum.org/docs/WEF_GGGR_2020.pdf. Accessed 13 Oct 2021
2. García, N.: Cifras y datos de violencia de género en el mundo (2020). https://ayudaenaccion.org/ong/blog/mujer/violencia-genero-cifras/. Accessed 13 Oct 2021
3. UNODC: Más del 30% de las víctimas de trata de personas son menores de edad, según Informe Global de la UNODC (2021). https://www.unodc.org/peruandecuador/es/noticias/2021/ms-del-30-de-vctimas-de-trata-de-personas-son-menores-de-edad--segn-informe-global-de-la-unodc.html?testme. Accessed 9 Oct 2021
4. Meza, J., Jimenez, A., Mendoza, K., Vaca-Cardenas, L.: Collective intelligence education, enhancing the collaborative learning. In: 2018 International Conference on eDemocracy & eGovernment (ICEDEG), pp. 24–30 (2018). https://doi.org/10.1109/ICEDEG.2018.8372324
5. Eger, C., Miller, G., Scarles, C.: Gender and capacity building: a multi-layered study of empowerment. World Dev. **106**, 207–219 (2018). https://doi.org/10.1016/j.worlddev.2018.01.024
6. Moodle: Open-source learning platform (2022). https://moodle.org/?lang=es. Accessed 05 May 2022
7. Rajni: Gender and disability: dual marginalization. Indian J. Gend. Stud. **27**(3), 410–419 (2020). https://doi.org/10.1177/0971521520939285
8. Estebsari, F., et al.: Design and implementation of an empowerment model to prevent elder abuse: a randomized controlled trial. Clin. Interv. Aging **13**, 669–679 (2018). https://doi.org/10.2147/CIA.S158097

9. Otelsberg, J., Akshay, N., Bhavani, R.R.: Issues in the user interface design of a content rich vocational training application for digitally illiterate users. World Acad. Sci. Eng. Technol. Int. J. Soc. Behav. Educ. Econ. Bus. Ind. Eng. **7**(10), 2684–2689 (2013). https://doi.org/10. 5281/zenodo.1088242

10. Sheshadri, S., Coley, C., Devanathan, S., Rao, B.: Towards synergistic women's empowerment transformative learning framework for TVET in rural India. J. Vocat. Educ. Train. **1**, 1–23 (2020). https://doi.org/10.1080/13636820.2020.1834438

11. Cabrera, E.M., Mauricio, D.: Factors affecting the success of women's entrepreneurship: a review of literature. Int. J. Gend. Entrep. **9**(1), 31–65 (2017). https://doi.org/10.1108/IJGE-01-2016-0001

12. del Prete, A., Gisbert Cervera, M., Camacho Martí, M.D.M.: Las tic como herramienta de empoderamiento para el colectivo de mujeres mayores. The case of the region of montsià (Catalonia). Pixel-Bit Revista de Medios y Educación **43**, 37–50 (2013). https://doi.org/10. 12795/pixelbit.2013.i43.03

13. UNICEF: Una aproximación a la situación de adolescentes y jóvenes en América Latina y El Caribe (2015). https://www.unicef.org/lac/sites/unicef.org.lac/files/2018-04/UNICEF_Sit uacion_de_Adolescentes__y_Jovenes_en_LAC_junio2105.pdf. Accessed 8 Oct 2021

14. Vidal, M., Rodríguez, R., Martínez, G.: Learning management systems. Educ. Med. Super **28**(3) (2014). http://scielo.sld.cu/scielo.php?script=sci_arttext&pid=S0864-214120140003 00019#:~:text=UnSistemadeGesti%C3%B3ndel,demaneraf%C3%A1cilyautomatizada

15. Shockley, B., Lari, N., El-Maghraby, E., Al-Ansari, A., Hassan, M.: Social media usage and support for women in community leadership: evidence from Qatar. Women's Stud. Int. Forum (2020). https://doi.org/10.1016/j.wsif.2020.102374

16. Camacho-Miñano, M., Maclsaac, S., Rich, E.: Postfeminist biopedagogies of Instagram young women learning about bodies, health and fitness. Sport Educ. Soc. **24**(6), 651–664 (2019). https://doi.org/10.1080/13573322.2019.1613975

17. Rouhani, L.: Using digital storytelling as a source of empowerment for rural women in Benin. Gend. Dev. **27**(3), 573–586 (2019). https://doi.org/10.1080/13552074.2019.1664140

18. Hendriks, S.: The role of financial inclusion in driving women's economic empowerment. Dev. Pract. **29**(8), 1029–1038 (2019). https://doi.org/10.1080/09614524.2019.1660308

19. Reychav, I., Parush, A., McHaney, R., Hazan, M., Moshonov, R.: The use of mobile technology in waiting rooms to leverage women's empowerment: a conceptual context. Health Inform. J. **24**(3), 277–292 (2018). https://doi.org/10.1177/1460458216671561

20. Mackey, A., Petrucka, P.: Technology as the key to women's empowerment: a scoping review. BMC Women's Health **21**(1), 78 (2021). https://doi.org/10.1186/s12905-021-01225-4

21. WIL Europe (s.f.). https://www.wileurope.org/. Accessed 3 Feb 2022

22. The WIE Suite is a community for women leaders and creators (s.f.). https://www.thewie suite.com/. Accessed 3 Feb 2022

23. HeForShe | Global Solidarity Movement for Gender Equality | HeForShe (s.f.) https://www. heforshe.org/en. Accessed 3 Feb 2022

24. SheLeader: SheLeader (s.f.). https://sheleader.eu/web/es. Accessed 31 Jan 2022

25. Black Girl In Om: Black Girl In Om (s.f.). https://www.blackgirlinom.com. Accessed 3 Feb 2022

26. Empower Women: EmpowerWomen (s.f.). https://www.empowerwomen.org/en. Accessed 31 Jan 2022

27. Hernandez Sanchez, J., García Falconi, R.: Instrumento para medir el empoderamiento de la mujer, 1st edn. Universidad Juaréz Autónoma de Tabasco, Tabasco, México (2008). http:// cedoc.inmujeres.gob.mx/documentos_download/101158.pdf. Accessed 8 Oct 2021

28. INEI: 63 de cada 100 mujeres de 15 a 49 años de edad fue víctima de violencia familiar alguna vez en su vida por parte del esposo o compañero (2019). https://m.inei.gob.pe/pre nsa/noticias/63-de-cada-100-mujeres-de-15-a-49-anos-de-edad-fue-victima-de-violencia-familiar-alguna-vez-en-su-vida-por-parte-del-esposo-o-companero-11940/. Accessed 5 Oct 2021

29. Sandoval, M.: Propiedades psicométricas del "Cuestionario para la medición de empoderamiento en mujeres" que pertenecen a organizaciones de base de la provincia de Sullana de la ciudad de Piura. Grad dissertation. Fac Psy. Universidad Peruana Cayetano Heredia, Lima, Perú (2021). https://hdl.handle.net/20.500.12866/10033

30. Navas, H., Malpartida, A., Carranza, R.: Identidad de género y empoderamiento femenino en las habitantes de la asociación de vecinos Quinta Elena, 2020. Apuntes Universitarios **11**(3), 331–347 (2021). https://doi.org/10.17162/au.v11i3.709

31. Rojas, R., Vilca, E.: Empoderamiento de mujeres quechuahablantes e hispanohablantes líderes en organizaciones sociales de base en la región Huancavelica. Grad dissertation. Fac Sci Commun. Universidad Nacional del Centro del Perú, Huancayo, Perú (2021). https://reposi torio.uncp.edu.pe/handle/20.500.12894/7107

32. Mazon-Fierro, M., Mauricio, D.: Usabilidad del e-learning y usabilidad del e-learning adaptativo: una revisión de la literatura. Int. J. Hum. Factores Ergon. **9**(1), 1–31 (2022). https://doi.org/10.1504/IJHFE.2022.120472

Intelligent System Comparing Clustering Algorithms to Recommend Sales Strategies

Gianella Arévalo-Huaman, Jose Vallejos-Huaman, and Daniel Burga-Durango[✉]

Universidad Peruana de Ciencias Aplicadas (UPC), Lima San Isidro 15076, Peru
{u2016C716,u201622094,pcsidbur}@upc.edu.pe

Abstract. The context of the pandemic has accelerated the growth of electronic commerce in recent years. Consequently, there is intense competition among companies to boost sales and achieve success in a market environment where the failure rate stands at 80%. Motivated by this reason, an Intelligent System is proposed to recommend a sales campaign strategy within an e-commerce platform, automating the analysis of customer data by employing machine learning algorithms to segment (K-means) customers into groups based on their information. Additionally, the system recommends (Decision Tree) a specific sales strategy for each group. Therefore, the objective of this study is to analyze all the relevant aspects that arise in the relationship between an e-commerce business and its customers, as well as the effectiveness of generating strategies based on specific groups through Customer Segmentation. As a result, the system achieved a significant increase in Web Traffic, Click-through Rate, and Sales Revenue by 14%, 5%, and 10%, respectively, indicating a monetary growth and improved engagement after the utilization of our tool.

Keywords: Customer Segmentation · E-commerce · K-means · Marketing Strategies

1 Introduction

According to [1], it is estimated that 85% of e-commerce businesses with an investment of less than 10,000 euros fail to surpass two years of activity. The expenditure in ecommerce increased by 44% in 2020, with a similar trend in 2021, as reported by Forbes in www. elmundo.es [2]. However, the initiative of new companies entering the market in such a competitive context result in 90% of them failing within the first 4 months. To reduce the risk of user loss and strengthen their trust in products within an e-commerce platform, customer analysis should be conducted using techniques such as clustering to understand users and their needs, exploring potential customer groups [3].

In [3], the authors suggest that e-commerce platforms have the capacity to collect a large amount of data daily, which should be utilized for analyzing customer behavior and creating products for different groups of potential users. However, [4] mentions that for data to become an important resource for a company, it must be effectively utilized; otherwise, it can become a burden. This involves the utilization of technologies

T. Guarda et al. (Eds.): ARTIIS 2023, CCIS 1935, pp. 209–219, 2024.
https://doi.org/10.1007/978-3-031-48858-0_17

such as artificial intelligence, statistics, and databases, among others [4]. Consequently, smaller e-commerce companies find themselves in a disadvantaged position as they lack specialized technology and data analysis teams to compete with larger companies.

Therefore, aligned to [5], this study proposes a System that enables the generation of Sales Campaign Strategies for each customer segment in the e-commerce platform. To achieve this, the more precise Clustering algorithm will be used to classify customers for retail e-commerce, choosing between k-means and Hierarchical Clustering based on the collected company data. Then, these data will be fed into the Decision Tree algorithm to generate personalized sales strategies that the company can apply in their marketing plan, aiming to improve their performance in the market [6].

2 Related Work

In [7], a class model was developed to segment customers into groups and classify them based on their income. This proposal provided access to key information for maintaining good customer relationships and evaluating them in the long term [7]. The segmentation was based on identifying customer groups using characteristics of their own behavior. It was discussed how the obtained results could be relevant for implementing a loyalty program and improving future studies that also address customer quality and lifestyle as an additional variable, combining survey data and purchase history.

In [8], research was conducted to find patterns of customer behavior using data mining techniques and the support of the K-Means clustering algorithm to identify the best-selling products and the payment method used. RapidMiner was used to facilitate the use of necessary tools for analysis, and the Davies-Bouldin index (DBI) was used to evaluate the quality of the segmentation algorithm.

In [9], data mining was employed to discover patterns in customer behavior. It was found that the best-selling products belonged to category 503–505 and that the most used payment method was credit. It is important to adapt to changes in the virtual market and personalize strategies to achieve better results in audience relationships.

In [10], the authors proposes a comprehensive and simplified system from data pre-processing to visualization, suitable for small businesses. This system identifies the popularity of each product over a period and targets potential customers based on that information. The purpose of customer segmentation is to divide the user base into smaller groups that can be targeted with specialized content and offers. Customer segmentation allows businesses to efficiently target each specific group of customers. The study implements customer segmentation using a hierarchical clustering algorithm with a small dataset. Additionally, a credit card dataset is utilized. The agglomerative hierarchical clustering method is performed using the hclust function from the Cluster package in R. The study concludes with the authors' perspective. However, it is noted that this method can be slow and hardware-dependent.

3   Method

3.1   Algorithm Comparison

To compare the K-means and HC algorithms, we conducted a benchmarking process. We used two tables (Table 1 and Table 2) to evaluate the algorithms in terms of scalability and five other dimensions based on e-commerce sales datasets, both public and private. Then, we compared the results in Table 3 to determine the accuracy of each algorithm in customer segmentation. We used this information to develop an effective customer segmentation system.

Table 1. Algorithm Benchmarking.

Criteria	Hierarchical Clustering	K-Means
Initial condition	No	Yes
Final condition	Regular	Accurate
Random value	Not required	Numeric attribute
Impact on the size of the datasets	Regular	Good
Granularity	Flexible	K and starting point
Dynamic data management	No	Yes
Implementation	Simple	Simple

Table 2. Algorithm Benchmarking.

Criteria	%	Hierarchical Clustering		K-Means	
		Score	Results	Score	Results
Initial condition	10%	0	0	1	0.1
Final condition	15%	0	0	1	0.15
Random value	10%	1	0.1	0	0
Impact on the size of the datasets	25%	0	0	1	0.25
Granularity	10%	1	0.1	0	0
Dynamic data management	20%	0	0	1	0.2
Implementation	10%	1	0.1	1	0.1
TOTAL	100%		**0.3**		**0.8**

In Table 1, we evaluated the algorithms across five different dimensions. In Table 2, we assigned weights to each dimension to identify which one had the greatest impact on customer segmentation. Based on the results obtained in these two tables, we determined that K-means was the best algorithm for our project.

Table 3. Comparative Table of Cluster Accuracy for K-means and HC.

Datasets	K-Means	Hierarchical Clustering
Dataset 1	0.420	0.145
Dataset 2	0.456	0.409
Dataset 3	0.532	0.129
Dataset 4	0.603	0.257
Dataset 5	0.131	0.051

Finally, in Table 3, we display the results of the accuracy comparison between K-means and HC across five different companies. The results indicate that K-means achieved higher accuracy than HC in the division of 4 customer clusters. This information was crucial for selecting the appropriate algorithm for our customer segmentation application.

3.2 Decision-Making Algorithm

In the second stage of executing our solution, a decision tree algorithm was used to establish the best sales strategy for the e-commerce platform for each of the customer clusters generated as the output of the K-means segmentation algorithm. The algorithm implementation was based on creating a supervised learning model, which requires a labeled dataset from which the created model can make the correct decision based on what it has learned.

In our project, the decision was made to create a column called "Strategy," which was used as the label to determine the most accurate value. Therefore, we used the clusters created in the previous step, which have average characteristics of the customers belonging to each cluster, as the input for the decision tree algorithm. This way, the algorithm can determine the most suitable strategy to apply. To accomplish this, it was necessary to gather a dataset of 200 clusters to train the decision tree with specific strategies labeled in the designated column based on the characteristics of each cluster. We had the professional support of a marketing specialist who helped us label the best strategy.

In this manner, the intelligent system can provide the company with precise and personalized sales strategies, which contributes to improving its performance in the market and increasing profitability [4].

3.3 Tool Implementation

Once the K-means algorithm has been selected as the preferred approach for segmenting customers of small e-commerce businesses, an intelligent system was developed to generate personalized sales campaign strategies for each customer segment identified in the e-commerce platform using the data collected by the company. To classify retail customers, the K-means clustering algorithm will be employed. Then, this data will be fed into a decision tree algorithm to generate customized sales strategies that the company can apply in its marketing plan with the aim of improving its performance in the market.

The logical structure of the system consists of various layers: client, access, presentation, business, and data. First, the client layer is established, where the web browser plays a fundamental role as a means of communication with the user. To achieve successful connection, it is essential to have an internet gateway located in the access layer. The presentation and business layers are adjacent to the access layer and are encapsulated in the service provided by Azure Web App, where our solution will be deployed. The presentation layer focuses on the visual aspect and user interface of our platform, being the visible point of contact for the user. On the other hand, the business layer hosts all the necessary logic to carry out the functionalities of our solution. As for data storage, we propose directing the data generated by our intelligent system to an external cloud database using the Azure Database PostgreSQL service, which is in a separate layer called the Data Layer.

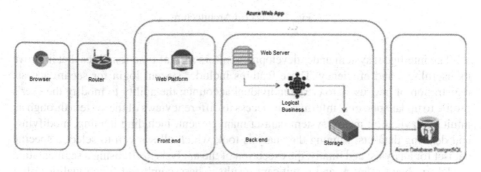

Fig. 1. Logical Architecture

The proposed physical architecture outlines how the connection will be established between the user, in this case, a marketing employee of an e-commerce business, and our solution. It also details the necessary technologies for the proper development of the intelligent system.

The user's connection will be made through a laptop or desktop computer, either via a Wi-Fi or direct Ethernet connection. Once the user has internet access, they can access our platform deployed on the Azure Web App service.

The technology distribution is divided into two sections: the front-end part of our platform, where direct visual interaction with the user will be established. For this, we will use HTML, CSS, and JavaScript, and enhance the user experience using Angular, taking advantage of its facilities for implementing modules and views.

In the back-end part, the main language will be Python, along with the Django framework, to carry out the necessary logical functionalities in the development of our algorithms and data storage. For data storage and connection with the external Azure Database PostgreSQL service, we will utilize the SQLAlchemy library, which will facilitate the creation of the data model and transactional rules to be applied in our solution.

For the creation and development of the clustering algorithms, we will employ the scikit-learn library, which offers various functions related to major clustering algorithms and simplifies their implementation.

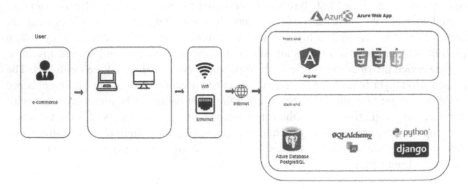

Fig. 2. Physical Architecture

The intelligent system under development offers a set of functionalities that improve its usefulness and efficiency. These features include: system login for secure access; registration of new users to create individual accounts; the ability to modify the user's profile to update personal information; access to different views of the system through an intuitive navigation menu; system dataset management, including loading, modifying, and deleting datasets; running the analysis tool, which allows you to select a specific dataset for analysis; and finally, the execution of the analysis itself, using a segmentation model to obtain relevant and significant results. These combined functionalities offer users a complete and efficient experience when using the intelligent system. The success of the development of these functionalities can be seen in Figures 1, 2 and 3 of the tool (Figs. 4 and 5).

4 Validation

The selected e-commerce company carried out a comprehensive evaluation of our platform and its key features over an approximate period of 1 month. The objective of this process was to obtain quantifiable results that can be compared with historical data, in order to validate any observed variations after using our tool [11]. In this way, the aim is to determine how our solution can support the growth of an e-commerce business by effectively leveraging customer data and providing effective support in that regard. The success or failure in e-commerce will depend on the positive response to the established indicators [12].

Fig. 3. Login

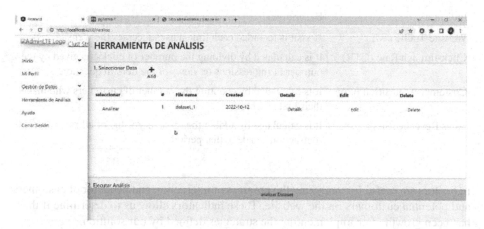

Fig. 4. Dataset Loading

4.1 Evaluation Indicators

The validation of the results obtained after the company has used our service will serve as support to evaluate four relevant indicators that contribute to improving business growth and increasing productivity. This validation will also help prevent the inclusion of the company in the alarming failure rate that prevails among small e-commerce businesses (Table 4).

The proposed indicators encompass several key aspects to evaluate the performance and growth of an e-commerce business. These indicators include Web Traffic, Click-through Rate, Customer Acquisition, and Sales Revenue. Both the visit and page click

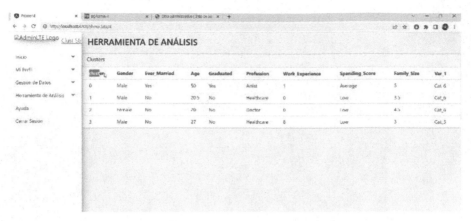

Fig. 5. Dataset Analysis and Cluster Results

Table 4. Evaluation Indicators.

Indicator	Description
Website Traffic (WT)	A visit is recorded each time a user accesses the website
Click-through Rate (CTR)	It is calculated by dividing the number of clicks received by the number of impressions or views of the item in question
Customer Acquisition (CA)	It is calculated by counting the number of customers who make their first purchase
Sales Revenue (SR)	It is calculated by adding the monetary value of all sales transactions made in that period

indicators are useful for analyzing the progress of interaction and behavior of customers and potential customers on the website. These indicators allow us to determine if there has been growth after implementing the strategies defined by our solution.

Additionally, it is important to consider that increased interaction can lead to the conversion of potential customers into actual customers. This aspect will also be evaluated to measure growth in the buyer base. Lastly, the primary indicator to observe will be the increase in sales through the platform, as this will provide a substantial outcome on the growth of the e-commerce business.

In summary, the selected indicators such as page visits, new customers, page clicks, and sales are fundamental elements to evaluate the growth and success of the e-commerce business. These indicators will provide us with a comprehensive view of performance and allow us to measure the impact of the implemented strategies on e-commerce growth.

4.2 Pre-implementation State

To validate the obtained results, it is necessary to have access to the historical information of the e-commerce business related to our indicators, in order to make a comparison and determine if there has been an improvement and growth with the use of our tool. The selected company uses Shopify as the platform for website management and organization, along with Google Analytics for page interaction ratios, which has facilitated the extraction of various metrics related to their customers, generated in their information panel of both tools. These metrics have been aligned with our indicators, including Web Traffic, Click-through Rate, Customer Acquisition, and Sales Revenue. The comparison will be performed using data from the last six months, prior to the implementation of our solution, as shown in Table 5.

Table 5. Six-Month Metrics per Indicator.

Indic	Dec	Jan	Feb	Mar	Apr	May
WT	406	356	363	322	337	340
CTR	1766	1758	1769	1651	1712	1680
CA	10	7	8	3	1	3
SR	S/4.756,89	S/4.449,49	S/4.410,50	S/4.268,36	S/3.916,89	S/4.131,67

Then, Formula 1 will be used to assess the variation of these indicators over the 6-month study period.

$$VarWatWon = \frac{results\ ffor\ the\ month_a - results\ ffor\ the\ month_{a-1}}{results\ ffor\ the\ month_{a-1}} \tag{1}$$

In formula (1), "a" is the index of the month being evaluated and "a − 1" is the index of the previous month.

4.3 Pos-implementation State

With the objective of evaluating the indicators, an estimated period of 1 month (4 weeks) was established during which a weekly marketing plan was implemented based on the recommendations provided by our platform. This plan sought to obtain results that reflected the impact and benefits of our solution on the potential development of the electronic commerce business and to compare the growth percentages between the previous months without the use of the tool, compared to the growth of the latter. Month. Once the 1-month period was over, we proceeded to evaluate the results of the four key indicators (WT, CTR, CA and SR). We made a comparison between the values prior to the implementation of the solution and the values after the application of the strategies recommended by our system. To carry out this comparison, we considered the results of one month prior to the use of the tool in comparison with the results obtained using our tool.

Next, we define the formula used to determine the variation in the indicators and that gives us an objective answer about the growth or not of the indicators:

$$VarWatWon = \frac{scenario\ wwssth\ tool - no\ tool\ scenario}{no-tool\ scenario} \tag{2}$$

5   Results

The metrics from the e-commerce Shopify platform were collected, and the results of the 4 indicators were analyzed considering the periods mentioned in Table 6 (Table 7).

Table 6. Sampling Periods.

Range	Period
1 month before	15/04/2023–14/05/2023
1 month after	15/05/2023–14/06/2023

Table 7. Two-Month Metrics per Indicator.

Indicator	May (no tool)	Jun (with tool)
WT	340	420
CTR	1680	1781
CA	3	4
SR	S/.4131,67	S/.4557,49

We applied Formula 1 and Formula 2 to evaluate a comparison of both scenarios for each of the indicators.

Table 8. Indicators Variation.

Indicator	Previous scenario	Current scenario
WT	4,73%	14,41%
CTR	1,21%	5,95%
CA	25,85%	33,33%
SR	0.94%	10.31%

Table 8 displays the Variation of the 4 indicators (WT, CTR, CA, and SR), showing a comparison of the average growth before the use of the tool, contrasted with the growth of the metrics with the use of our solution. This allows for a more objective and effective comparison of the percentages.

6   Conclusions

The analysis of the results concludes that there is a significant increase in web traffic, click-through rate, and total sales compared to the previous scenario where the tool was not used and marketing strategies were not planned based on data. It is important to consider that December, January, and February are the months with the highest sales in the year. Despite these factors, it is evident that the use of the proposed solution allows for the growth of the indicators. It is also important to highlight that there is a notable increase in sales in monetary terms, despite the implementation of discounts and promotions on the products.

In conclusion, the sales strategies recommended by the tool have positively influenced the company both in monetary terms and in engagement.

References

1. We Need To Talk About E-Commerce: Too Many Digital Brands Are Failing, And We Need New Tools To Help Keep Founders On Track. https://www.forbes.com/sites/forbestechco uncil/2021/07/22/we-need-to-talk-about-e-com-merce-too-many-digital-brands-are-failing-and-we-need-new-tools-to-help-keep-founders-on-track/?sh=736f25871c9c. Accessed 21 Apr 2023
2. La burbuja de las tiendas 'online': el 85% cierra antes de cumplir 2 años. https://www.elm undo.es/comunidad-valen-ciana/2016/05/21/57401de422601d252e8b4589.html. Accessed 21 Apr 2023
3. Zhang, B., Wang, L., Li, Y.: Precision marketing method of e-commerce platform based on clustering algorithm. Complexity **2021**, Article no. 5538677, 10 p. (2021). https://doi.org/10.1155/2021/5538677
4. Fang, C., Liu, H.: Research and application of improved clustering algorithm in retail customer classification. Symmetry 13(10), 1789 (2021). https://doi.org/10.3390/sym13101789
5. Zhan, M., Gao, H., Liu, H., Peng, Y., Lu, D., Zhu, H.: Identifying market structure to monitor product competition using a consumer-behavior-based intelligence model. Asia Pac. J. Mark. Logist. **33**(1), 99–123 (2020). https://doi.org/10.1108/APJML-08-2019-0497
6. Lam, H.Y., Tsang, Y.P., Wu, C.H., et al.: Data analytics and the P2P cloud: an integrated model for strategy formulation based on customer behaviour. Peer Peer Netw. Appl. **14**, 2600–2617 (2021). https://doi.org/10.1007/s12083-020-00960-z
7. Shen, B.: E-commerce customer segmentation via unsupervised machine learning. In: The 2nd International Conference on Computing and Data Science (CONF-CDS 2021), pp. 1–7. Association for Computing Machinery, New York, Article no. 45 (2021). https://doi.org/10.1145/3448734.3450775
8. Punhani, R., Arora, V.P.S., Sabitha, S., Kumar Shukla, V.: Application of clustering algorithm for effective customer segmentation in e-commerce. In: 2021 International Conference on Computational Intelligence and Knowledge Economy (ICCIKE), Dubai, United Arab Emirates, pp. 149–154 (2021). https://doi.org/10.1109/ICCIKE51210.2021.9410713
9. Zhou, J., Wei, J., Xu, B.: Customer segmentation by web content mining. J. Retail. Consum. Serv. **61**, 02588 (2021). ISSN 0969-6989. https://doi.org/10.1016/j.jretconser.2021.102588
10. Hung, P.D., Lien, N.T.T., Ngoc, N.D.: Customer segmentation using hierarchical agglomerative clustering. In: Proceedings of the 2nd International Conference on Information Science and Systems (ICISS 2019), pp. 33–37. Association for Computing Machinery, New York (2019). https://doi.org/10.1145/3322645.3322677
11. Alvarez Intriago, V., Agreda Fernández, L., Cevallos Gamboa, A.: Análisis de la estrategia de marketing digital mediante herramientas de analítica web. Investigatio (7), 81–97 (2021). https://doi.org/10.31095/investigatio.2016.7.5
12. Fernández-Planells, A.: Guía para la definición y creación de sitios web de calidad: evaluación y análisis comparativo a través del análisis experto. Revista Española De Documentación Científica **39**(4), e158. Recuperado a partir de (2016). https://redc.revistas.csic.es/in-dex.php/redc/article/view/962

Digitizing Musical Skills in Elementary School with the Use of Instagram

Almudena Álvarez-Castro Lamolda[iD] and Jorge Rafael González-Teodoro[✉][iD]

Universidad Isabel I, Burgos, Spain
Jorgerafael.gonzalez@ui1.es

Abstract. This paper examines the implementation of digital tools, specifically Instagram, to enhance musical competencies in primary education. The introduction of the LOGSE in 1990 brought positive changes to music education in schools, making it a mandatory subject at all educational stages. Moreover, specialized music teachers were introduced. Currently, under the LOMLOE, the Music subject is integrated with Visual Arts, forming a single area known as Artistic Education. This integration poses challenges in terms of curriculum development, evaluation criteria, content, and key competencies.

In contrast, according to a 2019 UNESCO report than other countries allocate significantly more time to music education within their school schedules. This approach has been shown to facilitate the development of important cognitive, creative, and social skills. Despite the high interest in music, a significant percentage of individuals lack formal music training. While many people listen to music regularly, only a small fraction can play an instrument or sing in a choir.

Addressing this gap, this intervention proposal aims to help students acquire musical competencies through motivating activities, specifically focusing on learning music notation through a melodic instrument (xylophone) using new technologies and social media platforms such as Instagram. The proposed intervention adopts a Flipped Classroom methodology. The intervention includes the creation of interactive tutorials using the Genially platform, allowing students to learn to interpret conventional music notation for instrumental songs on the xylophone. In conclusion, this intervention proposal aims to address the lack of musical competencies among students by leveraging digital tools and social media platforms.

Keywords: Digitization · Musical competences · Primary education · Instagram and flipped classroom

1 Introduction

In 1990, the LOGSE (General Law of the Educational System at Spain) was implemented in our education system. This new law brought a positive change in terms of Music Education in schools, as music became a mandatory subject at all educational stages. Additionally, the role of specialized music teachers was established.

T. Guarda et al. (Eds.): ARTIIS 2023, CCIS 1935, pp. 220–229, 2024.
https://doi.org/10.1007/978-3-031-48858-0_18

Currently, under the LOMLOE (Organic Law for the Modification of the LOE), the Music subject is integrated with Visual Arts, forming a single area called Artistic Education. This situation results in a combined grading system for these areas, with curriculum elements such as evaluation criteria, content, and key competencies not being developed in a more specific manner. Moreover, the allocated time for both areas together is one hour and thirty minutes per week, with each educational institution responsible for distributing this time between the two areas. In contrast, a 2019 UNESCO report titled "Rethinking Education: Towards a Global Common Good?" [1] states that other countries such as Denmark, Finland, France, Iceland, Norway, Sweden, and Switzerland allocate a significant amount of time in their school schedules for music education, as it has been proven to help students develop important cognitive, creative, and social skills.

Another UNESCO report [2] from 2021 analyzes the role of artistic and cultural education worldwide. This report mentions that some countries, including Norway, Finland, Australia, and New Zealand, have included artistic and cultural education more solidly in their curricula compared to others.

As evident from one of the latest surveys conducted by the Spanish Ministry of Culture and Sports on cultural habits and practices in Spain [3] during the 2021–2022 period, 64.7% of respondents reported listening to music daily, surpassing activities such as reading or using the internet for leisure purposes. However, as shown in the following figure, only 6.5% claimed to know how to play a musical instrument, and merely 1% participated in a choir. Therefore, while listening to music is a common habit, acquiring proper musical knowledge without adequate training remains a challenge.

According to the 2018 PISA report, Spain ranked low in terms of extracurricular creative activities related to music and art offered by schools in selected countries. Although a PISA report was conducted in 2022, the results have not yet been released. Considering these reports and the current state of music education in the country, a significant portion of students complete their schooling with limited knowledge of music. When referring to musical knowledge, it pertains to the ability to interpret musical language using an instrument, which is the minimum foundation, albeit insufficient, to consider someone as having musical competencies. Similarly, just as a person who lacks basic mathematical operations such as addition, subtraction, multiplication, and division can be deemed mathematically incompetent, or a student who completes compulsory education without the ability to write, read, and comprehend language can be considered illiterate, a similar situation frequently occurs in music education. In conclusion, based on the aforementioned factors, this intervention proposal aims to assist students in acquiring musical competencies through motivating activities, specifically focusing on the acquisition of musical language using a melodic instrument, facilitated by the use of new technologies and social media platforms such as Instagram.

1.1 Problem Statement

Considering the justification presented, an intervention proposal will be provided to help students develop musical competencies through the implementation of the Flipped Classroom methodology, also known as reverse teaching or inverted classroom. With this methodology, the role of the teacher changes. Rather than primarily delivering information orally, the teacher assumes functions to guide and support students, prioritizing their intellectual development and fostering autonomy, higher-level critical thinking, and enhanced creativity [4].

The proposal involves creating two tutorials using the Genially tool [5] by the teacher, enabling students to interpret conventional music notation for instrumental songs on the xylophone. Which is a platform that allows the creation of visual content such as images, infographics, and presentations, among others. The tool also provides interactive features and animations that enhance student engagement. Through the use of this instrument, which will better capture the attention of students and motivate them, they can more easily acquire the desired musical competencies.

The didactic proposal is based on two tutorials. These tutorials will feature a xylophone with colored plates, with each plate corresponding to a musical note. Additionally, students will be able to play the plates of the xylophone while following along with the song. Each tutorial will focus on a different song, namely the "Himno de Andalucía" (Andalusian Anthem), which will be performed in the schoolyard to commemorate a specific event, and "Shakira: Bzrp Music Session," chosen to motivate students given the popularity of the song. The reasons for using this instrument are as follows:

- It is easy to learn and does not require advanced musical training.
- It is a melodic instrument that allows for the removal of plates not used in a specific song.
- It develops coordination and dexterity, requiring good coordination between the hands and fingers.
- It promotes collaboration, as it can be played in a group setting.
- It improves focus and attention, benefiting children in other areas of their lives.

These Genially tutorials will be shared with students through social media, specifically Instagram, where there will be a feedback loop between the teacher and the students. [6] argue that social media platforms serve as resources for digital literacy, reinforcing competencies, skills, and abilities while providing meaningful and formative learning experiences.

Instagram is one of the most widely used social media platforms among young people and has experienced significant growth worldwide. It allows users to upload photos and videos with various filters, frames, and colors, and share them with their contacts. This approach aims to motivate and engage students, while considering the advantages and disadvantages that may arise [7].

1.2 Objectives

- General Objectives (G.O.)

GO. Develop an educational intervention proposal through the Flipped Classroom methodology, utilizing social media platforms like Instagram, to enable primary school students to develop various musical competencies.

- Specific Objectives (S.O.)

SO1. Highlight the main challenges in the Music subject within educational institutions.
SO2: Investigate the use of the Flipped Classroom methodology in the Music subject.

SO3. Share the Genially instrument tutorials to be utilized by other educational institutions.

SO4. Demonstrate the benefits of using social media platforms like Instagram in the educational context.

- Learning Objectives (L.O.)

The following objectives are related to the Evaluation Criteria outlined in the Order of January 15, 2021, which develops the curriculum for the Primary Education stage in the Autonomous Community of Andalusia:

LO1. Independently and in groups, interpret a simple composition through a melodic instrument such as the xylophone.

Evaluation Criterion: EC.03. Plan, design, and perform simple compositions individually or in groups using voice or instruments, incorporating musical procedures of repetition, variation, and contrast, assuming responsibility in group performance and respecting the contributions of others and the person leading the performance.

LO2. Utilize social media platforms like Instagram to enhance motivation in the interpretation of instrumental musical pieces.

Evaluation Criterion: EC.03.14. Explore and use audiovisual media and computer resources for information search, creation of musical pieces, and sound design for images and dramatic representations.

By addressing these objectives, the proposed intervention aims to bridge the gap in musical competencies among students by utilizing engaging activities, specifically focused on acquiring musical language through a melodic instrument, facilitated by the use of new technologies and social media platforms like Instagram.

2 Theorical Framework

The theoretical framework for this research revolves around several key concepts related to music education, social media, and the Flipped Classroom methodology. This section will provide a brief overview of each concept and its relevance to the proposed intervention.

Music Education:

Music education plays a crucial role in fostering students' cognitive, creative, and social development. It encompasses various aspects, including musical literacy, instrumental and vocal skills, music appreciation, and cultural understanding. Research has shown the positive impact of music education on students' academic performance, cognitive abilities, and overall well-being [8]. However, the implementation and effectiveness of music education programs can vary across different educational systems and countries.

Social Media:

Social media platforms have gained immense popularity and become an integral part of the lives of young people. They offer opportunities for communication, collaboration, self-expression, and content sharing. Instagram, in particular, has emerged as a widely-used social media platform, known for its visual-centric nature and interactive features. Studies have explored the potential of social media in education, highlighting its ability to enhance student engagement, facilitate collaborative learning, and promote creativity [9].

Flipped Classroom:

The Flipped Classroom methodology, also known as reverse teaching or inverted classroom, involves reversing the traditional learning process. In a Flipped Classroom model, students are introduced to new content outside the classroom through pre-recorded videos, readings, or online resources. Classroom time is then dedicated to collaborative activities, discussions, and application of knowledge with the guidance of the teacher. Research has indicated the potential of the Flipped Classroom approach to improve student engagement, deepen understanding, and promote active learning [10].

Genially:

Genially is an interactive content creation tool that enables educators to design visually appealing and interactive materials, such as presentations, infographics, and tutorials. Its features allow for the integration of multimedia elements, animations, and interactive components, making it a versatile tool for engaging students and promoting active learning. Genially has been recognized for its potential in creating interactive learning experiences and fostering student creativity [11].

2.1 State of the Art

With the advent of new technologies, new educational methodologies and a multitude of resources have been developed, facilitating and improving the teaching-learning process. One such methodology is the "flipped classroom," in which students take on a more active role. They solidify their understanding, foster diversity in the classroom, experience deep and lasting learning, and exhibit increased motivation. In the flipped classroom model, students first watch a video at home and then apply the knowledge gained in class. To implement this methodology, it is crucial to create the materials that students need to review at home. Videos play a significant role in conveying the desired content and competencies for students' acquisition [12, 13].

To assess the effectiveness of the flipped classroom approach, it is important to analyze the obtained results. This involves collecting information about the process and outcomes using various data collection techniques and instruments. Analyzing these results allows for an assessment of the effectiveness of implementing the flipped classroom methodology in the teaching-learning process.

The implementation of the flipped classroom methodology requires the use of different digital tools that enable students to work from home. Among these tools, Chromebook stands out as a digital tool with various applications that facilitate learning based on specific subject areas, such as developing digital competencies. Each application within Chromebook focuses on different aspects, adapting to the unique characteristics of each subject area [14].

By employing the flipped classroom methodology, students' musical competencies can be expanded, as they can work on challenging areas from home. Moreover, this work significantly complements the classroom activities, and the use of digital tools encourages collaborative learning among students.

Considering the positive impact of digital tools on competency development and the current popularity of social media platforms among primary school students, it is essential to assess the level of digital literacy students acquire through their use. One study demonstrates that young people have the capacity to develop skills for accessing, understanding, drawing conclusions, communicating, and creating content, thereby demonstrating their ability for self-learning and competency development.Some social media platforms, such as TikTok, are used in music education to motivate students. This application can be utilized for activities such as song creation and improvisation, music theory, body expression, listening skills, and instrumental practice. Due to the widespread use of social media platforms, including Instagram and TikTok, and the increased use of electronic devices, students are more engaged in projects that involve the social media platforms they use daily for leisure [14].

The popularity and widespread use of Instagram among young people, from late primary school to higher education, make it a tool that fosters student motivation. Students are familiar with this platform, and it appeals to their interests. Furthermore, through Instagram, they can explore realities that they may not encounter daily, which broadens their understanding of various topics [15].

3   Music-Based Didactic Proposal

The proposed didactic proposal consists of eight sessions aimed at developing digital skills and musical competencies through a variety of activities and methodologies. Each session has specific objectives, competencies to be addressed, activities, resources, and unique aspects. Let's explore each session in detail.

Session 1: Introduction and Presentation of the Didactic Unit

In this session, the main elements of musical language are introduced. Students engage in a cooperative brainstorming activity to assess their prior knowledge. The Plickers app is used for an initial assessment, providing valuable insights into the students' understanding of the subject matter.

Session 2: Musical Figures

The focus of this session is an in-depth exploration of rhythmic elements in music. Video presentations are utilized to introduce various rhythmic figures, accompanied by the use of a music notation app. A group activity is conducted to create a digital mind map that visually represents and connects different musical figures.

Session 3: Musical Notes

This session delves into the melodic elements of music. Students individually explore note names and colors using a Genially presentation, which facilitates a visual and interactive learning experience. To reinforce their understanding, a group activity is conducted using Boomwhackers, allowing students to play musical notes together.

Session 4: Xylophone

The xylophone is introduced as a musical instrument in this session. Students engage in individual practice using a digital xylophone app, providing them with a platform to familiarize themselves with the instrument's nuances. The session culminates in a group practice and recording of a simple melody using xylophones and percussion instruments, fostering teamwork and musical expression (See Fig. 1 and 2).

Session 5: Social Media: Instagram

This session explores the utilization of Instagram as a social media platform. Students create individual Instagram profiles dedicated to music-related content. They actively participate in a group activity where they share videos of their xylophone performances, employing specific hashtags to enhance visibility and engagement.

Session 6: Group Instrumental Practice and Recording

Collaboration takes center stage in this session as students engage in group instrumental practice. Using xylophones, percussion instruments, and a metronome, they practice a graduation song. Individual performances are recorded using tablets, and the recordings are then uploaded and shared on Instagram, fostering a sense of accomplishment and showcasing their musical progress.

Session 7: Recording, Uploading, and School Performance

Students work in pairs to record their individual performances, ensuring a high-quality audiovisual representation. They proceed to upload their recordings to Instagram, adding relevant hashtags to facilitate easy searchability and feedback. Furthermore, as a group, they perform the Andalusian Anthem during school recess, celebrating their collective musical achievements.

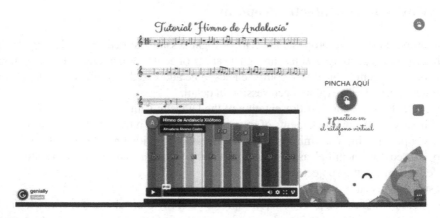

Fig. 1. Screen shoot of the genially tutorial

Session 8: Graduation Song

The final session revolves around the preparation of a graduation song using xylophones. Employing a flipped classroom approach, students engage in individual and small group practice to perfect their performance. The culmination of their efforts is a final performance of the graduation song during the graduation ceremony, providing a memorable and gratifying musical experience.

Throughout these eight sessions, students acquire digital skills, develop their musical competencies, and foster creativity and collaboration. The integration of technology, social media platforms, and musical instruments enhances their learning experience, making it engaging, interactive, and relevant to their lives.

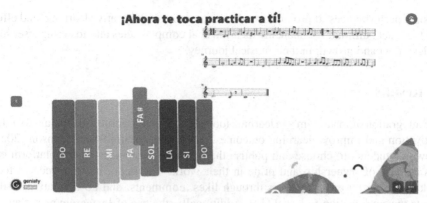

Fig. 2. Screen shoot of the genially application

4 Instagram Based Evaluation

The main objective of this research is to utilize Instagram as a self-assessment tool for students, allowing them to choose their best recording for publication on the social media platform. Additionally, it enables peer evaluation through comments and feedback provided by classmates on the shared videos. Furthermore, the teacher plays a vital role in evaluating the students' performances through the video submissions published on Instagram.

By incorporating Instagram as a platform for self-assessment, students are empowered to take ownership of their learning process. They have the opportunity to review their recorded performances, analyze their strengths and areas for improvement, and select the recording that best represents their musical abilities. This process of self-reflection and self-evaluation promotes critical thinking and self-awareness, as students actively engage in assessing their own progress.

Moreover, Instagram provides a platform for co-evaluation among classmates. As students share their videos on Instagram, their peers have the opportunity to watch, listen, and provide constructive feedback through comments and likes. This collaborative aspect of co-evaluation fosters a supportive and interactive learning environment, where students can learn from each other, offer suggestions, and appreciate one another's musical talents.

Lastly, the teacher assumes the role of an evaluator by assessing the students' performances based on the videos published on Instagram. By watching the recordings, the teacher can provide valuable feedback, highlighting areas of improvement, acknowledging strengths, and offering guidance for further development. The teacher's evaluation serves as a comprehensive assessment that complements the self-assessment and co-evaluation processes, providing a well-rounded evaluation of the students' musical progress.

Overall, the utilization of Instagram as a platform for self-assessment, co-evaluation, and teacher evaluation offers a dynamic and interactive approach to assessing students' musical performances. It promotes student autonomy, collaborative learning, and effective feedback, ultimately enhancing their musical competencies and fostering a sense of achievement and growth in their musical journey.

5 Results

The integration of Instagram as a learning tool has shown to significantly enhance student motivation and improve learning outcomes. According to Smith and Johnson (2020), allowing students to choose and publish their best performances on the platform creates a sense of ownership and pride in their work. The opportunity to receive feedback and recognition from peers through likes, comments, and co-evaluation further boosts their motivation to Excel [16]. Additionally, the use of Instagram as a platform for self-reflection and self-assessment promotes metacognitive skills, as students critically evaluate their own performances before sharing them [17]. This process not only enhances their understanding of musical concepts but also encourages self-improvement and growth. Overall, the incorporation of Instagram in the learning process creates an authentic and engaging learning environment, resulting in heightened student motivation and improved learning outcomes [18].

6 Conclusions

In conclusion, the proposed didactic proposal outlined in this chat focuses on developing digital skills and musical competencies through eight sessions. Each session incorporates various activities and methodologies to engage students in active learning and promote their understanding of musical elements.

The use of digital tools such as Plickers, Genially, Mindmeister, and Instagram adds an interactive and innovative dimension to the learning process. These tools enable selfassessment, co-evaluation, and teacher evaluation, allowing students to reflect on their progress, receive feedback from peers, and benefit from the guidance of the teacher.

The integration of technology, such as digital xylophone apps and the Micro:bit metronome, expands the possibilities for practicing and exploring musical concepts. It offers students a more immersive and hands-on experience while fostering their creativity and musical expression.

The cooperative and collaborative activities implemented throughout the sessions promote teamwork, communication, and peer learning. The brainstorming sessions, group discussions, and group instrumental practice encourage students to exchange ideas, support each other, and develop important social and interpersonal skills.

Furthermore, the inclusion of real-world applications, such as recording and sharing performances on Instagram, enhances students' motivation and engagement. It provides them with opportunities to showcase their musical abilities, receive recognition from their peers, and develop a sense of pride and accomplishment.

Overall, this didactic proposal emphasizes student-centered learning, where students actively participate in their own musical development. It integrates technology, cooperative learning, and real-world applications to create a dynamic and interactive learning environment that nurtures students' digital skills, musical competencies, and overall growth.

By implementing this proposal, educators can foster a love for music, enhance students' musical understanding, and prepare them for the digital age, equipping them with the necessary skills and knowledge to thrive in the modern world.

References

1. UNESCO: Rethinking Education: Towards a Global Common Good? (2019). https://unesdoc. unesco.org/ark:/48223/pf0000374465
2. UNESCO: Creative and Cultural Education at a Glance (2021). https://unesdoc.unesco.org/ ark:/48223/pf0000374937
3. Ministerio de Cultura y Deporte: Hábitos y Prácticas Culturales en España. (Ministry of Culture and Sports website) (2022)
4. Lorente, L.: Flipped Classroom: Nuevas Metodologías para la Enseñanza del Inglés en Educación Primaria. Universidad Nacional de Educación a Distancia (UNED), Madrid, Spain (2017)
5. Infod: Infod – Genially (2021). https://www.infod.it/it/tools/genially
6. Belmonte, A.M., Tusa, F.: Social networking sites: a resource for teaching and learning in universities. Revista Latinoamericana de Tecnología Educativa 9(1), 33–41 (2010)
7. García-Ruiz, R., Pinto-Molina, M., Beltrán Llavador, F.J.: Instagram and youth. Conceptual framework and intervention proposals in education. Int. J. Educ. Technol. High. Educ. 17(1), 1–16 (2020)
8. Hallam, S.: The power of music: its impact on the intellectual, social, and personal development of children and young people. Int. J. Music Educ. 33(3), 269–289 (2015)
9. Junco, R., Heiberger, G., Loken, E.: The effect of Twitter on college student ngagement and grades. J. Comput. Assist. Learn. 27(2), 119–132 (2011)
10. Bishop, J.L., Verleger, M.A.: The flipped classroom: a survey of the research. In: ASEE National Conference Proceedings, Atlanta, GA (2013)
11. Ruiz-Palomino, P., Molero, F., León, C., García-Morales Fernanda, M.: Social media as educational tool: is it the right time for Instagram in the classroom? In: Proceedings of the First Annual ACM Conference on Learning at Scale, pp. 353–354 (2010)
12. Manca, S., Ranieri, M.: Is It a tool suitable for learning? A critical review of the literature on Facebook as a technology-enhanced learning environment. J. Comput. Assist. Learn. 32(2), 139–151 (2016)
13. Fernández, C.: Integrating social networks in the classroom: a study of the potential of TikTok for music education. J. Music Technol. Educ. 15(1), 5–19 (2022)
14. NPD Group: Classroom digital Chromebooks are #1 selling device for K-12 schools in the U.S., according to the NPD Group. https://www.npd.com/wps/portal/npd/us/news/press-rel eases/2013
15. Smith, A., Johnson, B.: Enhancing student motivation through social media: a case study of instagram in the classroom. J. Educ. Technol. 37(2), 157–172 (2020)
16. García, J., López, E., Fernández, A.: Social networks in music education: the potential of instagram as a learning tool. Int. J. Music Educ. 36(3), 436–449 (2018)
17. Brown, K., Miller, K.: The role of self-reflection and self-assessment in music learning. Music Educ. Res. 21(3), 286–300 (2019)
18. Lee, H., Chen, J.: Exploring the use of instagram in music education: perspectives from students and teachers. J. Res. Music Educ. 69(1), 5–26 (2021)

Control of Type 1 and 2 Diabetes in Middle-Aged Individuals at Private Clinics in Metropolitan Lima: A Technological Solution Based on Wearables and IoT

Diego Zapata, Sofia Bravo, and Juan-Pablo Mansilla$^{(\boxtimes)}$ (ID)

Univ. Peruana de Ciencias Aplicadas, Lima, Peru
{u201812085,u201815877}@upc.edu.pe, juan.mansilla@upc.pe

Abstract. The control of type 1 and type 2 diabetes in individuals aged 55 to 64 seeks a non-invasive alternative for continuous monitoring of blood glucose levels. In Peru, there is poor accessibility for data collection within the monitoring of this disease due to economic resources and lack of technical support. Therefore, a technological solution is proposed that integrates the use of IoT and wearable technologies, such as smartwatches, to collect and monitor real-time heart rate data, integrating the Google Fit API as our data source. This solution aims to strengthen and improve the quality of the managed data in order to facilitate the treatment of diabetic patients. The solution was validated with 20 users, of which 15 were diabetic patients and the remaining 5 were endocrinologists. For this process, they registered in the application, used it for a certain period of time to collect sufficient data, and filled out a satisfaction survey. The results obtained show that a satisfaction rate of over 75% was achieved, indicating that this technological solution allows for more accurate and continuous monitoring, facilitating self-management for patients and providing real-time information to physicians for control purposes.

Keywords: Internet of Things (IoT) · wearables · diabetes · glucose · continuous monitoring · heart rate

1 Introduction

Diabetes is a serious chronic disease that occurs when the pancreas does not produce enough insulin for the body or when the body cannot effectively use the insulin it produces. According to the National Center for Chronic Disease Prevention and Health Promotion (2022) [1], there are different types of diabetes: type 1 diabetes, which is caused by an autoimmune reaction where the body mistakenly attacks itself, resulting in the inability to produce insulin and requiring daily insulin injections. This type of diabetes typically occurs in children, adolescents, and young adults, but there are also cases in older adults,

T. Guarda et al. (Eds.): ARTIIS 2023, CCIS 1935, pp. 230–242, 2024.
https://doi.org/10.1007/978-3-031-48858-0_19

affecting approximately 5 to 10% of patients. Type 2 diabetes occurs when the body does not use insulin properly, preventing the maintenance of normal blood sugar levels. It is more common and affects over 90 to 95% of patients, often occurring in middle-aged individuals or those who are overweight.

Currently, in Peru, there is a Diabetes Surveillance System, which is a tool of great importance for the control of this disease. However, to date, it still has deficiencies in data collection (MINSA, 2021) [2], thus affecting continuous monitoring. Consequently, there is limited frequent use of such solutions aimed at facilitating patient treatments. By harnessing the power of IoT and wearables technology, the goal is to strengthen and improve the quality of data managed by the system.

Various research studies propose contributions to diabetes control. For example, Garcia et al. (2020) [7] implemented an IoT-based algorithm for constructing historical readings to prevent diabetic complications, which notified patients when their values deviated from those defined by the World Health Organization (WHO). Other studies suggest self-management of glucose levels using visualization tools through deep learning and wearables capable of measuring hypoglycemia and hyperglycemia, significantly reducing the root mean square error (RMSE) (Zhu, Taiyu et al., 2022) [5]. Additionally, non-invasive techniques using Raspberry Pi with dermal sensors were examined and compared to blood analysis, resulting in an accuracy of 90.32% (Alarcón-Paredes, Antonio et al., 2019) [3]. Furthermore, fog computing and frameworks have been used to continuously monitor glucose levels, showing high precision and a continuous device duration of 157 h, establishing a decision-making technique (Nguyen Gia, Tuan et al., 2019; Aldaej, Abdulaziz, 2022) [4].

The proposed solution aims to address diabetes control by providing a non-invasive alternative. Through the use of wearables, the patient's health status can be continuously monitored. Additionally, this proposal aims to encompass the ongoing assistance of patients to medical centers, benefiting them in terms of time and money saved on travel to their healthcare facility.

This article proposes a technological solution for the control of type 1 and type 2 diabetes in people aged 55 to 64, using IoT-based portable devices. By using a smart watch and a mobile application, the patient's heart rate can be collected and, with the integration of the Google Fit API, we can interpret the hemoglobin levels and then have an approximate glucose level, with this the assigned doctor You can register it and see it in real time without the need for an appointment in person at the medical center, and with which you can make decisions based on the results obtained, thus optimizing the flow of medical care.

This work is organized into 5 sections. Section 2 discusses previous research related to the use of IoT and wearable technologies for continuous monitoring of individuals. Section 3 presents the methodology used for data connectivity and synchronization. Section 4 presents the case validations. Finally, in Sect. 5, conclusions and ideas for further research are presented.

2   Related Works

Some continuous glucose monitoring solutions using IoT technology are presented below. These are divided into three categories:

The first category encompasses diabetes monitoring solutions, for example: In the work of Cappon et al. (2019) [8], the creation of a category iCGM (integrated continuous glucose monitoring system) and integrated continuous glucose monitoring systems are presented to achieve better data control in the management of diabetes. The study by Bruttomesso D. et al. (2022) [9] recognize the benefits of real-time continuous glucose monitoring (rtCGM) and rapid glucose monitoring (FGM) systems, such as their storage capacity for glycemic control for weeks to months. It concludes by validating a consistent approach for use in clinical diabetes care. Likewise, Muhammad, A. (2020) [10] demonstrates that optical and electrochemical glucose monitoring sensors can function under physiological conditions, which provides insights into future prospects for the development of new glucose monitoring sensors. in blood.

The study by Azbeg, K. et al. (2022) [11] presents a secure healthcare system called BlockMedCare, which combines IoT medical devices and blockchain technology. It is designed to collect data from patients and share it with the medical team, allowing remote monitoring of patients, especially in the case of chronic diseases that require regular monitoring. Sousa, A. et al. (2021) [12] offers a platform capable of generating visual information that is easy to analyze and alerting the physician if any value measured by the patient is outside the established limits. They implement a system that collects real-time readings taken by the patient and provides the physician with a larger sample of data, allowing analysis of damaging factors in patient treatment. Real-time data collection allows for better patient diagnosis and treatment. Lastly, the new health paradigm called SMEAD by Saravanan, M. et al. (2018) [13] develops a safe comprehensive care system for people with diabetes, which includes wearable devices to monitor various parameters and predict the condition of patients. You can provide information on how data captured by these devices can be transmitted and stored in a cloud using mobile phones as gateways.

The second category refers to the non-invasive techniques that have been implemented to control diabetes, for example: The study by Hanna et al. (2022) [14] highlights advances in new body-adapted electromagnetic sensors for instantaneous, continuous, and wireless detection of glucose variations in the bloodstream, especially for patients experiencing hypoglycemia or hyperglycemia. In the work of Alarcón-Paredes et al. (2019) [3], a non-invasive technological solution is proposed for the continuous monitoring of blood glucose levels in people with diabetes, using IoT. Its objective is to explore the perspective of non-invasive glucose monitoring systems. A good example is the research by Tate, A et al. (2020) [15] highlighting significant differences between consumer devices (wrist activity trackers), medical devices, and technologies not yet considered clinical trial devices. Also the method proposed by Rosen, K et al. (2022) [16] suggests an alternative for detection of type 2 diabetes by ultrasound of the shoulder deltoid muscle, which is a sensitive and strong predictor of type 2 diabetes diagnosis. The work of Rajesh Kumar J et al. (2019) [17] aims to provide accurate readings and generate alerts to prevent adverse events by using IoT devices to measure extreme fluctuations in blood sugar levels. Finally, the research by Baghelani M et al. (2020) [18]reports on high-sensitivity non-invasive sensors for real-time glucose monitoring. The structure consists of a chipless tag sensor that is attached to the skin with a tape and takes readings by integrating with a smart watch.

By last category we have the works related to the integration of IoT devices for glucose monitoring, for example: The work of Sankhala, D. et al. (2022) [19] presents a modern, non-invasive sweat platform technology capable of measuring and reporting human sweat glucose concentrations on the surface using a capture probe. It provides continuous monitoring of glucose levels and explores how this system can be integrated into people's daily activities. In addition, for patients with this condition, the results of continuous monitoring can be stored on a cloud server and accessed by the patients themselves. In the study by Pavleen, K. et al. (2019) [20], a real-time health monitoring system that uses IoT infrastructure and cloud computing is presented. It combines techniques, procedures and data to improve the service and treatment of diseases using IoT as a technology to interconnect mobile devices and provide adequate care. As in the work of Nguyen, G. (2019) [4], a fog-assisted IoT system is presented to monitor blood glucose levels. This new system can monitor body temperature, including data such as humidity and air quality, and observe the movements that patients make. It also offers services like push notification and local storage. The closed-loop system that combines an insulin pump with continuous glucose monitoring, developed by Mannava Srinivasa (2022) [21], ensures accurate and complete capture of critical data for diabetes management. This is important as it allows fast queries of large data sets regardless of size. Also in the study by Rhayem, A. et al. (2021) [22] a decision-making process called Measure-Event-Risk-Treatment-Alert (M-E-R-T-A) is proposed, which considers the entire process of remote diagnosis of the patient. This work provides an analysis of the measures that can be taken for the patient, detects possible future health problems, predicts the risk of complications, suggests the appropriate treatment and provides information for control. The work of Fernández-Caramés, T. et al. (2019) [25] implements a solution using smartphones to collect CGM blood glucose values, detailing the steps taken for data collection using smartphones.Rahman, R. et al. (2017) [26] presents research focused on wearable health monitoring, making it easier to control diabetes levels using breath analysis and IoT technology. This research contributes to the future implementation of new alternatives for diabetes management using a greater number of portable devices.

Muneer, U. et al. (2021) [25] proposes a machine learning-based approach for the classification, early identification and prediction of diabetes using algorithms based on MultiLayer Perceptron (MLP) and Long-Short Term Memory (LSTM) to deep learning in diabetes prediction. The work of Abdulaziz, A. (2022) [6] aims to propose a cloud-inspired health framework to regulate diabetes levels in patients by monitoring, predicting and controlling the risk of diabetes in real time. remote diabetic patients based on physiological factors. conditions. The study by Kato, S. et al. (2020) [26] evaluates the effects of intensive healthcare guidance using IoT among employees of Japanese companies with early-stage type 2 diabetes. Deploy a portable monitoring system and remote health guidance for intensive lifestyle intervention. Likewise, the model proposed by Valenzuela, F. et al. (2020) [7] suggest an IoT-based glucose monitoring algorithm to prevent diabetes complications. It uses previous measurements to evaluate them over time, calculate averages and trends, resulting in a prognosis for the patient. The study by Kobayashi, T. et al. (2019) [27] provides automated feedback messages that convey health parameters and a smartphone-based self-management support system, which can interact with patient inputs in real time.

3   Proposal of Technological Solution

The present study proposes a technological solution called "Gluetrack" (an acronym for Glucose and Tracking) for the control of type I and II diabetes, integrating IoT technology and wearables capable of non-invasively and real-time measuring the patient's heart rate. Along with the integration of Google Fit, we can collect various metrics. This project consists of two modules: Patient and Doctor. The use of Google Fit is employed as it allows for multiple metrics such as heart rate, blood pressure, and glucose with the connection to wearables capable of effectively and increasingly reliably measuring these parameters (Stutz, 2023) [28]. This use of technology is known as "EHealth."

Figure 1 illustrates how this solution interacts with the stakeholders.

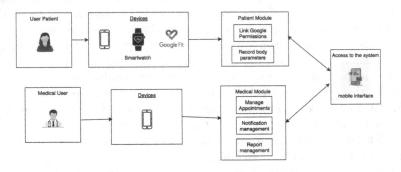

Fig. 1. Stakeholders diagram

The patient will be able to view their latest measurement in real-time, as well as generate a daily, weekly, or monthly report of their measurements. On the other hand, the specialist doctor will be able to monitor each of their assigned patients, as well as schedule appointments with each of them.

3.1 Modules

Next, the registration, measurement, appointments, and notifications modules will be presented, which will be used for the validation of the project with the use of wearables.

Figure 2 shows the registration module, where if the user is a patient, they will need to add a permission validation with Google to synchronize the data in the application. On the other hand, the doctor will need to register their information to have their functional account.

Fig. 2. Registration module

Figure 3 shows the heart rate reports module that displays the measurements from the patient's wearable. These measurements can be filtered on a daily, weekly, and monthly basis. Additionally, it features a chat function that allows for a doctor-patient conversation thread at the bottom.

Fig. 3. Heart Rate Reports Module

Figure 4 displays the Scheduled Appointments module, where the doctor has the ability to create and delete appointments as desired.

Fig. 4. Appointments module.

In Fig. 5, the notifications module is displayed, which will be accessible to the doctor, and it also includes the functionality of alerting the phone when an abnormal frequency is detected.

Fig. 5. Notifications module

3.2   Arquitecture

This solution implements IoT technology along with wearables, which connects its functions through Azure cloud service, managing all the data from the modules and querying it through Google Fit API with account permissions. It collects all the metrics from the patients through the wearables, as shown in Fig. 6.

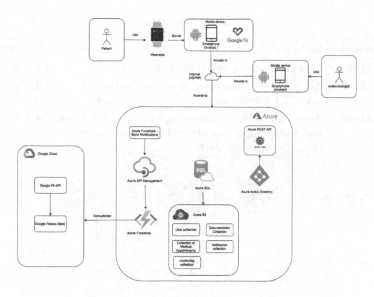

Fig. 6. Description of architecture components

4   Validation and Results

4.1   Validation Process

The validation process with endocrinologists and patients was carried out as follows. Fifteen patient users filled out a consent form, created an account in the mobile application, linked their Google account to synchronize the data, and configured their smartwatches to collect data for a period of one month. They then filled out a satisfaction form. For the endocrinologists, the functionality of the application was validated with five users. They created their respective accounts in the application and used its features, after which they filled out an expert satisfaction form and a consent document. The validation flow will be shown in Fig. 7.

The objectives are as follows:

- Verify the functionality of the application and how it facilitates disease management.
- Validate that the 3 proposed indicators are achieved.
- Validate the efficiency of the As Is and To Be processes.

Table 1. Indicator

Identifier	Indicator	Objective
IND01	User satisfaction rate greater than 75%	OE1
IND02	Achieve a user-perceived speed percentage of over 75% for the application environments	OE2
IND03	Attain an efficiency percentage of over 75% when registering appointments and frequency values through the application	OE3

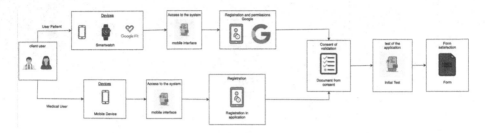

Fig. 7. Validation Process

A form was presented with a series of questions related to Satisfaction, Speed, and Efficiency, based on the usage provided by the users (Table 1).

Validation Form. For this validation, the total percentage will be determined based on the responses regarding the functioning provided by the users. To do so, "Google Forms" will be used as the tool for creating the form with the questions and level 1–5 alternatives. For the patient, we used https://forms.gle/b5WyY pXdtfFAQ9ra7, and for the doctor, we used https://forms.gle/bCtcGpw6aBtz R3N69.

The surveys were organized into three sections. The first section evaluated the users' satisfaction with the application and whether they would recommend it (5 questions). The second section assessed the speed of response times of the application (5 questions). The third section evaluated the efficiency in data accuracy and immediate alerts (4 questions).

The Likert scale was used to evaluate the sections of satisfaction, speed, and efficiency, with five points ranging from: 1 "Strongly Disagree", 2 "Disagree", 3 "Neutral", 4 "Agree", and 5 "Strongly Agree".

4.2 Results

The results obtained from the satisfaction surveys will now be presented, along with an average that should surpass 75%. As shown in Fig. 8, the results obtained from the patients who validated the functionality of the application are displayed. It can be seen that the percentage obtained meets the established threshold.

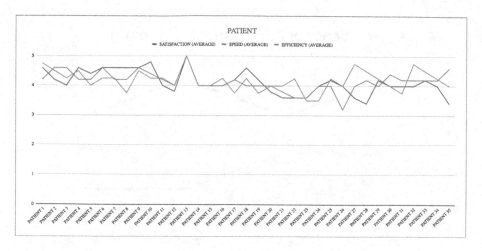

Fig. 8. Percentage of Patient Results

Also, as can be seen in Fig. 9, the results obtained by the specialists (Endocrinologists) who validated the functionality of the application are shown, and it can be seen that the obtained percentage meets the established criteria.

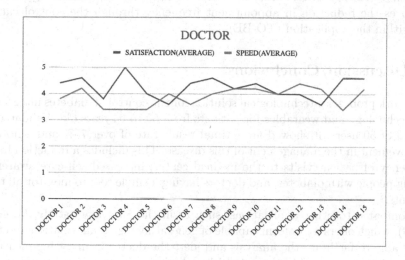

Fig. 9. Percentage of Medical Results

Finally, improvement tests were validated in comparison with the current treatment of the disease. In Fig. 10, the number of times one of our evaluated patients goes to appointments in 1 month was compared.

Based on an average taken with validated users, it is evident that prior to the one-month trial of the application, scheduled appointments had a fairly high

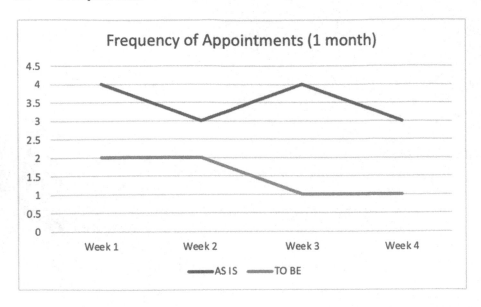

Fig. 10. Frequency of Appointments per Week in 1 month

frequency (AS-IS). Afterwards, it is evident how the application significantly improves the reduction in appointment frequency through the control carried out within the application (TO-BE).

5   Discussion/Conclusions

This work proposes a technological solution for the control of diabetes integrating IoT technology and wearables for patients from 55 to 64 years old. Validated by a total of 50 users, it showed an optimal result rate of over 75% and a notable improvement in the management of this disease. This includes a reduction in the frequency of patient visits to the medical center, increased self-care awareness among people with diabetes, and doctors having a single tool to monitor all their patients.

Compared to other applications, such as in the Saravanan study, M. et al. (2018), which offers a platform capable of generating visual information and thus being able to facilitate the analysis and alert the doctor if any value measured by the patient is outside the established limits; ours offers real-time doctor-patient interconnectivity, along with a non-invasive alternative to 24/7 monitoring, improving communication efficiency and providing more comprehensive measurements, respectively.

For future work, we aim to expand the measurement possibilities by including additional variables such as sweat measurement and the integration of electronic scales to automatically synchronize weight data. This will broaden the monitoring spectrum, providing the assigned physician with even more real-time data.

References

1. Centro Nacional para la Prevención de Enfermedades Crónicas y Promoción de la Salud. (2022). Centros para el Control y la Prevención de Enfermedades. Available at: https://www.cdc.gov/diabetes/spanish/basics/diabetes.html. Accessed 20 Aug 2023
2. MINSA. (2021). Epidemiologia de la diabetes en el Perú. Available at: https://www.dge.gob.pe/portalnuevo/wp-content/uploads/2022/01/Unidad-I-Tema-1-Epidemiologia-de-la-diabetes_pub.pdf. Accessed 20 Aug 2023
3. Alarcón-Paredes, A., et al.: An IoT-Based Non-Invasive Glucose Level Monitoring System Using Raspberry Pi. Appl. Sci. **9**, 3046 (2019). https://doi.org/10.3390/app9153046
4. Nguyen, T., et al.: Energy efficient fog-assisted IoT system for monitoring diabetic patients with cardiovascular disease. Future Gener. Comput. Syst. **93**, 198–211 (2019). https://doi.org/10.1016/j.future.2018.10.029)
5. Zhu, T., et al.: Enhancing self-management in type 1 diabetes with wearables and deep learning. Digital Med. **78** (2022). https://doi.org/10.1038/s41746-022-00626-5
6. Abdulaziz, A.: IoT-inspired smart healthcare framework for diabetic patients: fog computing initiative. Int. J. Innov. Comput. Inf. Control **18**, 917–939 (2022). https://doi.org/10.24507/ijicic.18.03.917
7. Valenzuela, F., et al.: An IoT-based glucose monitoring algorithm to prevent diabetes complications. Appl. Sci. **10**, 921 (2020). https://doi.org/10.3390/app10030921
8. Cappon, G., et al.: Continuous glucose monitoring sensors for diabetes management: a review of technologies and applications. Diabetes Metab. J. **43**, 383–397 (2019). https://doi.org/10.4093/dmj.2019.0121
9. Bruttomesso, D., et al.: The use of real time continuous glucose monitoring or flash glucose monitoring in the management of diabetes: A consensus view of Italian diabetes experts using the Delphi method. Nutr. Metab. Cardiova. Dis. **29**, 421–431 (2019). https://doi.org/10.1016/j.numecd.2019.01.018
10. Muhammad, A., et al.: Recent advances of electrochemical and optical enzyme-free glucose sensors operating at physiological conditions. Biosens. Bioelectron. **165**, 112331 (2020). https://doi.org/10.1016/j.bios.2020.112331
11. Azbeg, K., et al.: BlockMedCare: a healthcare system based on IoT, Blockchain and IPFS for data management security. Egypt. Inf. J. 23, 329–343 (2022). https://doi.org/10.1016/j.eij.2022.02.004
12. Sousa, A., et al.: mHealth: monitoring platform for diabetes patients. Proc. Comput. Sci. **184**, 911–916 (2021). https://doi.org/10.1016/j.procs.2021.03.113
13. Saravanan, M., et al.: SMEAD: a secured mobile enabled assisting device for diabetics monitoring. IEEE, pp. 1–6 (2018). https://doi.org/10.1109/ANTS.2017.8384099
14. Hanna, J., et al.: Wearable fexible body matched electromagnetic sensors for personalized non-invasive glucose monitoring, Sci. Rep. **12**, 14885 (2022). https://doi.org/10.1038/s41598-022-19251-z
15. Tate, A., Rao, G.: Activity trackers, wearables, noninvasive technologies for early detection, and management of cardiometabolic risks. Int. J. Biomed. 10, 189–197 (2020). https://doi.org/10.21103/Article10(3)_RA2
16. Rosen, K., et al.: The sonographic quantitative assessment of the deltoid muscle to detect type 2 diabetes mellitus: a potential noninvasive and sensitive screening

method. BMC Endocr. Disord. **22**, 193 (2022). https://doi.org/10.1186/s12902-022-01107-2

17. Rajesh, C., et al.: VLSI design of intelligent, Self-monitored and managed, Strip-free, Non-invasive device for Diabetes mellitus patients to improve Glycemic control using IoT. Proc. Comput. Sci. **163**, 157350 (2019). https://doi.org/10.1016/j.procs.2019.12.093

18. Baghelani, M., et al.: invasive continuous-time glucose monitoring system using a chipless printable sensor based on split ring microwave resonators. Sci. Rep. **10**, 12980 (2020). https://doi.org/10.1038/s41598-020-69547-1

19. Sankhala, D., et al.: A machine learning-based on-demand sweat glucose reporting platform. Sci. Rep. **12**, 2442 (2022). https://doi.org/10.1038/s41598-022-06434-x

20. Kaur, P., et al.: A healthcare monitoring system using random forest and internet of things (IoT), Multimedia Tool Appl. **78** (2019). https://doi.org/10.1007/s11042-019-7327-8

21. Srinivasa, M., et al.: A novel Internet of Things (IoT)-enabled platform for patients with type 1 diabetes. Appl. Nanosci. (2021). https://doi.org/10.1007/s13204-021-02110-0

22. Rhayem, A., et al.: A semantic-enabled and context-aware monitoring system for the internet of medical things. Expert Syst. **38**, e12629 (2021). https://doi.org/10.1111/exsy.12629

23. Fernández-Caramés, T., et al.: Enabling the internet of mobile crowdsourcing health things: a mobile fog computing, blockchain and IoT based continuous glucose monitoring system for diabetes mellitus research and care. **19**, 3319 (2019). https://doi.org/10.3390/s19153319

24. Rahman, R., et al.: IoT-based personal health care monitoring device for diabetic patients. IEEE, pp.168–173 (2017). https://doi.org/10.1109/ISCAIE.2017.8074971

25. Muneer, U., et al.: Machine learning based diabetes classification and prediction for healthcare applications. J. Healthcare Eng. 9930985 (2021). https://doi.org/10.1155/2021/9930985

26. Kato, S., et al.: Effectiveness of lifestyle intervention using the internet of things system for individuals with early type 2 diabetes mellitus. Internal Med. **59**, 45–53 (2020). https://doi.org/10.2169/internalmedicine.3150-19

27. Kobayashi, T., et al.: Automated feedback messages with shichifukujin characters using IoT system-improved glycemic control in people with diabetes: a prospective, multicenter randomized controlled trial. J. Diabetes Sci. Technol. **13**, 796-798 (2019). https://doi.org/10.1177/1932296819851785

28. Stutz, M.: Wearables are electronic devices that are placed on the body and allow different variables that monitor the health of the user to be measured (2023). Available at: https://www.iprofesional.com/health-tech/375953-que-ventajas-tienen-los-wearables-para-la-salud

Easy-Programming: Towards a Web Collaborating Algorithmic and Programming Aid for Early Apprentices

Ricardo Vardasca[1,2]($\boxtimes$) , Duarte Silva[1], Joao Fonseca[1], Marco Tereso[1] ,
Fernando Bento[1,3] , and Domingos Martinho[1]

[1] ISLA Santarem, Rua Teixeira Guedes 31, 2000-029 Santarem, Portugal
ricardo.vardasca@islasantarem.pt
[2] INEGI, Universidade do Porto, Rua Dr. Roberto Frias 400, 4200-465 Porto, Portugal
[3] ISTAR, ISCTE-IUL, Av. Prof. Aníbal Bettencourt 9, 1600-189 Lisbon, Portugal

Abstract. Science, Technology, Engineering and Mathematics (STEM) undergraduate students must develop problem solving skills through algorithmic and
programming learning. There are several tools available to aid them in this process
but none in a web collaborative environment that can be used for e-learning accommodating the three methods available for that development: code, flowchart, and
pseudocode. It is aim of this research to outline the existing tools and their features, and to propose a new web based collaborative tool accommodating the main
features found. An architecture, technological infrastructure, database structure,
requirements definition, UML use case and class diagrams and a user interface
were proposed. New STEM undergraduate students can develop a solid foundation in algorithmic thinking, problem-solving skills, and the ability to effectively
communicate and collaborate with others, establishing the foundations for their
success in specific fields.

Keywords: Algorithms · collaboration tool · flowcharts · programming learning

1 Introduction

In today's rapidly evolving technological landscape, the importance of algorithmic and
programming skills cannot be overstated, especially in the context of an academic degree.
As the world becomes increasingly digitized, Science, Technology, Engineering and
Mathematics (STEM) graduates are at the forefront of driving innovation and solving
complex problems through the application of computational thinking. The ability to
understand, design, and implement algorithms and programming logic is a foundational
skillset that plays a vital role in a STEM academic and professional journey [1–4].

Early exposure to algorithmic and programming skills during an academic STEM
degree provides students with a solid foundation for tackling real-world challenges.
Examples of those skills include problem-solving and logical thinking, efficiency and
optimization, interdisciplinary collaboration, innovation and creativity, and adaptability
and futureproofing [1–4].

© The Author(s), under exclusive license to Springer Nature Switzerland AG 2024
T. Guarda et al. (Eds.): ARTIIS 2023, CCIS 1935, pp. 243–254, 2024.
https://doi.org/10.1007/978-3-031-48858-0_20

Learning algorithmic and programming skills cultivates a structured and analytical approach to problem-solving. STEM professionals encounter intricate problems that require breaking them down into smaller, manageable components. By understanding algorithms, students can devise systematic solutions, identify patterns, and apply logical thinking to efficiently solve complex problems [1–4].

Algorithms lie at the core of developing efficient and optimized solutions. Through learning early algorithmic skills, STEM students acquire the ability to evaluate the time and space complexities of different approaches. This knowledge empowers them to design algorithms that streamline processes, reduce resource consumption, and optimize system performance, ultimately contributing to enhanced solutions [5].

STEM projects often involve collaboration across various disciplines. Algorithmic and programming skills serve as a common language, enabling effective communication and collaboration among peers from different backgrounds. When peers possess a shared understanding of algorithms and programming concepts, it becomes easier to collaborate on designing and implementing solutions, leading to more integrated and comprehensive project outcomes [5].

Algorithmic and programming skills provide the foundation for innovation and creativity in engineering. Armed with the ability to develop custom algorithms, students can devise novel solutions to complex problems, explore unconventional approaches, and think outside the box. This creative thinking, combined with technical proficiency, allows students to propose groundbreaking solutions, drive technological advancements, and make a lasting impact on society [1–5].

The rapid advancement of technology requires students to be adaptable and future-proof their skillsets. Algorithmic and programming skills provide a strong foundation for learning new programming languages, frameworks, and technologies. By mastering the fundamentals early in their academic journey, STEM students develop a solid base from which they can easily adapt to emerging technologies and stay relevant in a rapidly evolving industry [5].

Learning algorithmic and programming skills at an early stage of an academic STEM degree is of paramount importance. These skills foster critical thinking, problem-solving abilities, and interdisciplinary collaboration. By equipping students with a strong foundation in algorithms and programming, educational institutions can empower future engineers to tackle complex challenges, drive innovation, and make meaningful contributions to the field of engineering. The subsequent sections will delve into specific approaches and methodologies to effectively integrate algorithmic and programming education into degrees curriculum [1–4].

Algorithms can be learned in three different ways, with which they can be represented, they are pseudocode (a formal language between natural and a programming language), flowchart (graphical representation) or by code in an explicit programming language. The perception of each of these forms depends on everyone, being easier for some in one way and more difficult for others in another. Deep down, they are all complementary and allow a different view of a solution to a problem [6, 7].

The aim of this research is to identify the existing collaborative tools to support algorithmic learning, identifying the innovative characteristics and based on them to propose a tool that consolidates them for future implementation in an e-Learning environment.

2 Existing Tools

There are several tools available to support algorithmic and programming language learning. These tools are designed to provide learners with a practical and interactive environment to acquire and practice algorithmic and programming skills. Examples of those tools include Integrated Development Environments (IDEs), Online Coding Platforms, Code Editors, Online Learning Platforms, Documentation and Reference Materials, Community Forums and Q&A Platforms and Educational Coding Games. These tools offer a range of resources and interactive experiences to support learners in their algorithmic and programming language journey. Depending on individual preferences and learning styles, learners can explore and utilize these tools to enhance their programming skills and gain practical experience.

At basic and secondary education students are starting to become familiarized with tools devoted to algorithmic thinking, examples of these tools are Scratch, Blocky and Flowgorithm [8–11]. Scratch is a visual programming language developed by the MIT Media Lab. It features a block-based interface where users can drag and snap together code blocks to create animations, games, and interactive stories. Scratch is widely used to introduce programming concepts to beginners, especially children, in a fun and intuitive way. Blockly is a web-based visual programming editor created by Google. It provides a similar block-based interface like Scratch but offers more flexibility and extensibility. Blockly supports multiple programming languages, allowing learners to transition from visual coding to text-based coding. It is often used as a foundation for other visual programming environments. Flowgorithm is a visual programming tool designed specifically for teaching algorithmic thinking and flowchart-based programming. It allows users to create flowcharts to represent algorithms and control structures. Flowgorithm supports multiple programming languages and can generate code from the flowcharts [8–11].

At Table 1 a comparison between these tools is shown according to complexity, supported programming languages, allowing customization and available community and resources. Scratch is more oriented towards beginners and Flowgorithm to a more advanced users, being Blocky in between, the Scratch has its own programming language limiting the user development towards others, the other two support the most used. Flowgorithm, due to be based in flowcharts is very rigid and the two other options are customizable until a certain point. In terms of community, Scrach has a large one and plenty of resources, for the other tools the community is small and the resources scarce.

For more mature students there are other tools available such as Visual Alg, Portugol (in three versions: IDE, Studio and Online), Algorithmi, SICAS, COLLEGE, OOP-Admin and Progranimate.

VisuAlgo [12] is an online platform that provides visualizations for various algorithms and data structures. It covers a wide range of topics, including sorting, searching, graph algorithms, and dynamic programming. Users can choose an algorithm, input their data, and interactively step through the visualization to understand the algorithm's behavior.

Portugol [13–15] is a pseudocode-based programming language and tool that is widely used for teaching and learning programming concepts. It is specifically designed for beginners and serves as a steppingstone to learning actual programming languages.

It comes in three versions: IDE (provides features such as code editing, compilation, and execution), Studio (local instance of IDE, can run offline) and Online (web-based platform that allows you to write, compile, and execute programs directly in a web browser).

Table 1. Programming reasoning learning graphical authoring tools comparison

Tool	Complexity	Programming languages	Customization	Community & Resources
Scratch	Beginner-oriented	Limited (own)	Customizable	Large
Blocky	Simple and flexible	JavaScript, Python, PhP, Lua	Customizable	Small
Flowgorithm	More complex	C#, C++, Java, JavaScript, Lua, Perl, Python, Ruby, Swift, Visual Basic	Rigid	Small

Algorithmi [16] is an application aid for programming learners, which has as goal to help them to overcome their learning barriers, it can use pseudocode and code of several programming languages, allowing conversion between them.

Interactive system for algorithm development and simulation (SICAS) [17] is a basic procedural programming learning tool for concepts such as selection or repetition, its goal is to improve problem solving abilities using those concepts.

COLLEGE [18], also known as Real Time Collaborative Programming system that allows remotely distributed programmers to work concurrently and collaboratively in the same programming task.

OOP-Anim [19] is a support tool that allows students animate and simulate small Java programs, it aims to support student learning, through execution simulation and errors detection.

Progranimate [20, 21] is a simplified development environment that uses dynamic structured flowchart program construction, can generate code in several languages and provides an animated execution.

A comparison between the outlined algorithmic learning tools according to features such as web orientation, having flowchart support, having pseudocode support, having a code editor, having a depurator, providing a program structure, having a variable inspector, accommodating a chat, providing a set o examples, providing automatic evaluation and programming languages support is given at Table 2.

From that comparison, one two tools provide web environment, the most provided feature is the incorporation of a code editor and a depurator, followed by a variable inspector, being scarcer the support to pseudocode and flowchart, provision of examples, and rarer a chat and automatic evaluation. In terms of programming languages, the most supported is Java.

From this evaluation there is no web solution providing pseudocode, flowchart and any language code support with a code editor and depurator available to aid early algorithmic and programming learners.

Table 2. Comparison of algorithmic tools for more mature users.

Tool	a)	b)	c)	d)	e)	f)	g)	h)	i)	j)	k)
Visual Alg	X		X	X	X		X		X		Pascal
Portugol IDE		X	X	X	X		X				
Portugol Studio				X	X	X	X		X		
Portugol Online	X		X	X					X		
Algorithmi		X	X	X	X	X	X		X		C, Java, Python
SICAS		X		X	X		X		X		
COLLEGE				X	X	X	X	X			
OOP-Anim				X	X		X				Java
Progranimate				X	X	X	X		X	X	Java, Visual Basic

a) Web oriented, b) Flowchart support, c) Pseudocode support, d) Code editor, e) Depurator, f) Program structure, g) Variable inspector, h) Chat, i) Provision of examples, j) Automatic evaluation and k) Programming languages.

3   Proposed Tool Modelling

Based on the verified opportunity of lack of a collaborative web tool to support the learning of algorithms and programming language, a proposal will be elaborated based on a definition of architecture, technological infrastructure, database Entity-Relationship diagram, requirements analysis, UML modulation of use cases and classes and finally, it is proposed a user interface.

The proposed architecture for the Easy Programming collaborative tool is Model-View-Controller (MVC), which is a software architecture pattern commonly used in the development of web applications. It separates the application logic into three interconnected components: the Model, the View, and the Controller. The Model represents the application's data and business logic. The View is responsible for the presentation layer of the application. The Controller acts as the intermediary between the Model and the View. The MVC enforces a clear separation between the different aspects of the application, allowing code reutilization, easy maintenance, testability, and scalability. Due to its benefits and is supported by many popular frameworks and technologies [22].

In terms of technological infrastructure (see Fig. 1), the Easy Programming application is expected to run at the client in a web browser support by a JavaScript framework (e.g. angular.js or react.js), which provides interfaces, components, directives and services to the application, that connects with a remote server through a REST API and on the server side there is a database repository supporting the application server.

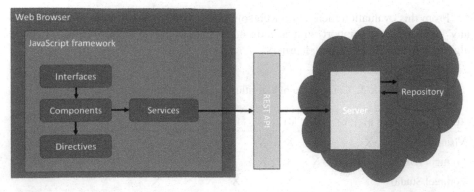

Fig. 1. The technological infrastructure for the proposed Easy Programming application.

The database in the repository (see Fig. 2) will have at least three tables: user, exercise, and solution. The relationship between user and exercise is Many-to-Many being option from the user side, and the relationship between exercise and solution is One-to-Many.

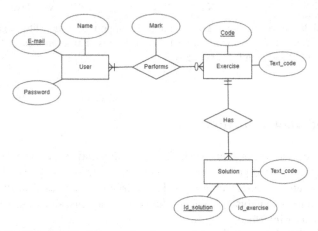

Fig. 2. The Entity-Relationship diagram for the repository of the proposed Easy Programming application.

The identified requirements for the proposed Easy Programming tool are:
Functional Requirements:

- User Registration and Authentication, allow users to create accounts, log in, and manage their profiles.
- Pseudocode Editor, provide an interactive editor that allows users to write, edit, and save pseudocode.
- Flowchart Editor, implement a visual editor that enables users to create, modify, and save flowcharts.
- Code Editor, include a code editor with syntax highlighting and code completion for writing and editing programming code.

- Code Execution, integrate a code execution engine that can run code written in various programming languages and provide immediate feedback on the output or errors.
- Algorithm Visualization, incorporate features to visually represent algorithms and their execution steps.
- Problem-Solving Exercises, offer a collection of algorithmic problems or exercises for users to practice and apply their algorithmic skills.
- Progress Tracking, track and display user progress, including completed exercises, achievements, and performance metrics.
- Social Features, enable users to share their pseudocode, flowcharts, and code with others, provide feedback, and engage in discussions.
- Collaborative Learning, support collaborative learning by allowing users to work together on solving problems or reviewing algorithms.
- Learning Resources, provide additional learning resources such as tutorials, reference materials, and examples related to algorithms and problem-solving.

  Non-Functional Requirements:

- Usability, to ensure that the system is intuitive, easy to navigate, and provides a user-friendly interface.
- Performance, optimize the system to handle concurrent users, execute code efficiently, and provide real-time feedback.
- Scalability, design the system to handle increasing user loads and accommodate future growth.
- Reliability, ensure the system is stable, available, and resilient to failures or disruptions.
- Security, implement proper security measures to protect user data, prevent unauthorized access, and handle potential vulnerabilities.
- Compatibility, ensure the system works well across different web browsers, devices, and operating systems.
- Accessibility, design the system to be accessible to users with disabilities, adhering to relevant accessibility guidelines.
- Maintainability, develop the system using modular and maintainable code, allowing for easy updates, bug fixes, and future enhancements.
- Data Privacy, adhere to privacy regulations and safeguard user data by implementing appropriate data protection measures.
- Integration, allow for integration with other systems or platforms, such as learning management systems or external APIs for additional functionality.

A simple UML use case diagram (see Fig. 3) would have a Lecturer that needs to login, create a new exercise, a new solution to that exercise or a set of solutions, check students' grades and be able to chat with students to support them, at the end of his interaction he should be able to logout. A student would be able to login, solve an exercise, check grade, change to flowchart or code, or change again to pseudocode, create a new exercise, or logout.

To allow the development of the proposed easy programming tool in an object-oriented approach, a simple UML class diagram is proposed (Fig. 4), it has five classes: user, exercise, exercise-student (to store the mark), exercise_code, exercise_flowchart

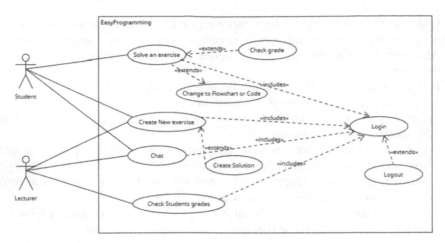

Fig. 3. A simple UML use case diagram for the proposed Easy Programming application.

and exercise_solution. A user can perform several exercises, an exercise may have a grade to a student, an exercise must have a correspondent code and flowchart and may have one or more solutions.

For aiding the user interface designer, the proposed main interface for the Easy Programming tool is presented in the Fig. 5, when the user logs in it will display its name and the interface is split in three sections with more option over the username button, such as run, check grade, chat, add solution, add new exercise, view student grades, change programming language and logout. The three areas on the main screen are: on the left the pseudocode, at the middle the flowchart and at the right the code of the specified programming language.

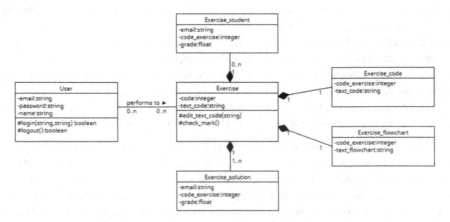

Fig. 4. A simple UML class diagram for the proposed Easy Programming application.

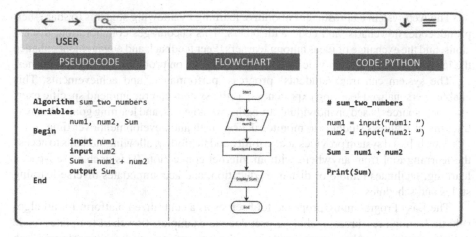

Fig. 5. Proposed user interface for the proposed Easy Programming application.

4 Discussion

There are several advantages of having a collaborative web system for an integrated algorithmic learning tool that incorporates pseudocode, flowcharts, and code, such as: enhanced learning experience, visual representation, language agnostic, seamless transition from design to implementation, immediate feedback and error analysis, collaborative learning and discussion, progress tracking and personalization, accessible and flexible learning, and a centralized learning resource.

The integration of pseudocode, flowcharts, and code provides a comprehensive learning experience. Students can understand algorithms at different levels of abstraction, from high-level problem-solving using pseudocode and flowcharts to low-level implementation using code. This holistic approach helps in developing a deep understanding of algorithmic concepts.

Pseudocode and flowcharts offer visual representations of algorithms, making them easier to understand and analyze. Visual aids help students grasp complex algorithms and their execution flow, enhancing their algorithmic thinking and problem-solving skills.

A web system that supports pseudocode, flowcharts, and code is language-agnostic. This allows students to focus on algorithmic principles rather than being tied to a specific programming language. It prepares them to adapt to different programming languages and environments, which is particularly valuable in the rapidly evolving field of computer science.

The integration of pseudocode, flowcharts, and code facilitates a smooth transition from algorithm design to implementation. Students can start by designing algorithms using pseudocode and flowcharts, and then directly translate them into code. This helps in bridging the gap between problem-solving and coding skills.

With code execution integrated into the system, students can receive immediate feedback on their code's correctness and output. This allows for instant error detection and analysis, helping students identify and understand common mistakes, debug their code, and improve their problem-solving skills.

The web system can foster collaborative learning by allowing students to share their pseudocode, flowcharts, and code with others. This encourages collaboration, discussions, and the exchange of ideas among learners. Peer feedback and engagement enhance the learning process and provide different perspectives on problem-solving approaches.

The system can track students' progress, performance, and achievements. This enables personalized learning experiences, as the system can recommend specific exercises or resources based on individual strengths, weaknesses, and learning goals. Progress tracking also allows students to monitor their growth and development over time.

A web-based system provides accessibility and flexibility, allowing students to access the learning tool from anywhere with an internet connection. This enables self-paced learning, facilitates remote or distance education, and accommodates diverse learning styles and schedules.

The Easy Programming proposed tool serves as a centralized platform for all algorithmic learning resources, including pseudocode examples, flowchart templates, code samples, and interactive exercises. This organized and comprehensive resource hub supports efficient learning and reduces the need for students to search for scattered materials.

Overall, a web system for integrated algorithmic learning offers a multifaceted and interactive learning environment that promotes effective algorithmic understanding, problem-solving skills, collaboration, and personalized learning experiences.

5 Conclusion

This research has identified the existing collaborative tools to support algorithmic learning, and their innovative characteristics, with such information a proposal of a collaborative e-Learning environment tool for algorithmic and programming skills learning was outlined with architecture, technological infrastructure, database structure, requirements definition, UML use case and class diagrams and a user interface.

An integrated algorithmic learning tool that incorporates pseudocode, flowcharts, and code can be highly beneficial for new STEM (Science, Technology, Engineering, and Mathematics) undergraduate students for several reasons, such as: conceptual understanding, transitional support, algorithmic thinking, error identification and debugging, collaboration and communication.

The next phase in this research project will be to develop, test and integrate the outlined features into a fully functional pilot to be used with first year students and evolve from there to a study support tool.

By integrating pseudocode, flowcharts, and code in the learning process, new STEM undergraduate students can develop a solid foundation in algorithmic thinking, problem-solving skills, and the ability to effectively communicate and collaborate with others. These skills are crucial for success in STEM disciplines and provide a strong basis for further learning and specialization in their respective fields.

References

1. Prinsloo, G.J., Helleveeg, C.: The integration of algorithmic thinking in undergraduate information systems courses. Int. J. Educ. Technol. High. Educ. **15**(1), 1–24 (2018)

2. Guerra, S.R., Reis, C.R.: Algorithmic problem-solving in undergraduate computer science education: a systematic literature review. Comput. Sci. Educ. **28**(4), 284–316 (2018)
3. Sanders, K.: Algorithmic thinking and computational problem solving. Commun. ACM **59**(8), 33–34 (2016)
4. Körner, T.: Algorithms for Undergraduate Students. Cambridge University Press, Cambridge (2016)
5. Mehta, D., Gupta, S.: Algorithmic thinking and problem-solving skills: an integral part of computer science education. In: Proceedings of the 49th ACM Technical Symposium on Computer Science Education, p. 1076 (2018)
6. Andrzejewska, M., Stolińska, A.: Do structured flowcharts outperform pseudocode? Evidence from eye movements. IEEE Access **10**, 132965–132975 (2022)
7. Cormen, T.H., Leiserson, C.E., Rivest, R.L., Stein, C.: Introduction to Algorithms. MIT Press, Cambridge (2022)
8. Fagerlund, J., Häkkinen, P., Vesisenaho, M., Viiri, J.: Computational thinking in programming with Scratch in primary schools: a systematic review. Comput. Appl. Eng. Educ. **29**(1), 12–28 (2021)
9. Weintrop, D., Shepherd, D.C., Francis, P., Franklin, D.: Blockly goes to work: block-based programming for industrial robots. In: 2017 IEEE Blocks and Beyond Workshop (B&B), pp. 29–36 (2017)
10. Gajewski, R.R., Smyrnova-Trybulska, E.: Algorithms, programming, flowcharts and flowgorithm. E-Learn. Smart Learn. Environ. Prep. New Gener. Spec., 393–408 (2018)
11. Cook, D.D.: Flowgorithm: principles for teaching introductory programming using flowcharts. In: Proceedings of American Society of Engineering Education Pacific Southwest Conference (ASEE/PSW), pp. 158–167 (2015)
12. Borba, F.H., Marchi, M.I., Rehfeldt, M.J.H.: Utilização do Software VisuAlg no Ensino da Lógica de Programação. Revista de Ensino, Educação e Ciências Humanas **22**(3), 295–304 (2021)
13. Manso, A., Oliveira, L., Marques, C.: Portugol IDE–Uma ferramenta para o ensino de programação. In: PAEE'2009—Project Approaches in Engineering Education—Guimaraes (2009)
14. Noschang, L.F., Pelz, F., de Jesus, E., Raabe, A.: Portugol studio: Uma ide para iniciantes em programaçao. In: Anais do XXII SBC Workshop sobre Educação em Computação, pp. 1–10 (2014)
15. Silva, D.G.S., Silva, D.G.S., Soussa, M.R.B.: Portugol WebStudio: IDE Online de Desenvolvimento em Portugol como instrumento de ensino-aprendizagem. Ensino e Tecnologia em Revista **6**(1), 16–30 (2022)
16. Manso, A., Marques, C.G., Santos, P., Lopes, L., Guedes, R.: Algorithmi IDE-Integrated learning environment for the teaching and learning of algorithmics. In: 2019 IEEE International Symposium on Computers in Education (SIIE), pp. 1–6 (2019)
17. Gomes, A., Mendes, A.J.: SICAS: interactive system for algorithm development and simulation. Comput. Educ. Towards Interconnected Soc., 159–166 (2001)
18. Bravo, C., Redondo, M.A., Ortega, M.: Aprendizaje en grupo de la programación mediante técnicas de colaboración distribuida en tiempo real. In: Proceedings of V Congreso Interacción Persona Ordenador, Lleida, Spain, pp. 351–357 (2004)
19. Santos, A., Gomes, A., Mendes, A.J.: Integrating new technologies and existing tools to promote programming learning. Algorithms **3**(2), 183–196 (2010)
20. Scott, A., Watkins, M., McPhee, D.: E-learning for novice programmers; a dynamic visualisation and problem solving tool. In: 2008 3rd IEEE International Conference on Information and Communication Technologies: From Theory to Applications, pp. 1–6 (2008)

21. Scott, A., Watkins, M., McPhee, D.: A step back from coding–an online environment and pedagogy for novice programmers. In: Proceedings of the 11th Java in the Internet Curriculum Conference, pp. 35–41. The Higher Education Academy, London Metropolitan University (2007)
22. Dey, T.: A comparative analysis on modeling and implementing with MVC architecture. Int. J. Comput. Appl. 1, 44–49 (2011)

Scheme of the Software Engineering Elements that Are Part of the Development of eHealth-Oriented Models and Frameworks

Sandra Gutierrez-Rios[1,2](✉) , Clifton Clunie[1,2] ,
and Miguel Vargas-Lombardo[1,2,3]

[1] Universidad Tecnológica de Panamá, FISC, Ciudad de Panamá, Panama City, Panama
sandra.gutierrez@utp.ac.pa
[2] Universidad Tecnológica de Panamá, CIDITIC, GISES, Ciudad de Panamá, Panama City, Panama
[3] Tecnología e Innovación, SNI-SENACYT Sistema Nacional de Investigación-Secretaria Nacional de Ciencia, Clayton, Ciudad del Saber Edif.205, 0816-02852 Panama City, Panama

Abstract. When developing models or frameworks in electronic health, known as eHealth, they must consider a variety of essential characteristics for their optimal functioning; however, identifying these characteristics is complicated because health processes, especially those directed at health care, are very diverse. Therefore, the objective of the research is to identify the most used characteristics in the development of frameworks or models for eHealth, to determine which are the ones that have had the greatest relevance and thus offer a general extract of the essential components in the design of eHealth-oriented models or frameworks. The set of evidence shows as a result the essential characteristics to develop models and frameworks in the eHealth field, such as: optimal management of documentation based on semantic terminology, adoption or management of ontologies, application of IT governance standards, quality and health, safety and privacy, functional and quality requirements, among others. Based on what has been observed, it is concluded that by identifying the main characteristics that any model or framework developed for eHealth must have, it allows the researcher or developer to have a clearer vision of what these types of systems should consider creating an architectural structure. More solid, formal and quality in the context of eHealth.

Keywords: QoS · software · ehealth · development · frameworks · IT

1 Introduction

Prevention and control of health are one of the most important aspects worldwide [1] and that is why, in the scientific community, there is a large volume of studies directed to this area. In addition, many of these investigations are oriented to health care, since, by offering adequate care in a timely manner, the individual and community health of a population can be prevented and controlled with better alternatives. To this end, many health institutions have implemented Information and Communication Technologies (ICTs)

© The Author(s), under exclusive license to Springer Nature Switzerland AG 2024
T. Guarda et al. (Eds.): ARTIIS 2023, CCIS 1935, pp. 255–266, 2024.
https://doi.org/10.1007/978-3-031-48858-0_21

[2]. In the various health processes related to patient care, known as eHealth, since these technologies offer optimal alternatives for the study and analysis of the health condition of each country. However, many institutions have now conceived to give a deeper and more formal meaning to the set of technological systems that are developed in the health context, and for this purpose, they have established the development of models and/or frameworks that provide a solid and unified basis on which all system developers or developers can base themselves to create the different health-oriented systems. Based on the, through research aims to identify the fundamental components and/or characteristics for the design of the models and/or frameworks that have been developed to know the main characteristics that govern all of them and, in this way, to identify and establish the software engineering principles that they have in common. This document is composed as follows: the second chapter describes the generalities regarding eHealth, the third chapter details the challenges of designing eHealth models and frameworks as well as the most important characteristics involved in their development, the fourth chapter shows the main elements of software engineering present in eHealth models and frameworks, and Sects. 4 and 5 show the conclusions derived from the research as well as the scientific references used to support this study.

2 Background

From the earliest implementations of telemedicine fundamentals in the 1960s [3–5] to the present day, there has been an exponential advance in information systems, specifically oriented to healthcare. This is for the constant development of electronic devices, improvements in communications and the large amount of data generated every day have significantly affected contemporary health care systems.

Now, to go into detail it is necessary to understand what with the use of ICT technologies in the field of health, which is known as eHealth/Digital Health (digital transformation), the World Health Organization (WHO) defines it as "the use of Information and Communication Technologies (ICT) for health" [6]. On the other hand, the European Commission defines it as: "the use of modern information and communication technologies to meet the needs of citizens, patients, health professionals, health care providers, as well as policy makers [7, 8]; and the authors [3] refer to the term eHealth as "the use of emerging information and communication technologies to improve or enable health and health care". In other words, electronic health is the adoption of Information and Communication Technologies (ICTs) in health care processes, which enable health professionals to have a better knowledge of existing needs that lead to an improvement in health care and prevention.

All this with the aim of offering a better quality of care, monitoring and control of the patient's health. In addition, eHealth-oriented tools can improve the quality of health care delivery [9] and patient safety [10, 11] by providing all healthcare professionals with access to relevant information and patient records across locations and time zones [12–16]. In this way, eHealth contributes to greater efficiency and effectiveness by avoiding the duplication of diagnostic procedures, in addition to minimizing manual processes such as the preparation of handwritten records [17].

Added to this, eHealth can intensify the coordination and care processes between all parts of the healthcare system which are interested in changes to the treatment process, benefiting patients, especially those with complex chronic diseases [1, 12, 18, 19].

In addition, these improvements in the quality of health system processes will reduce costs in the medium and long term. Thus, eHealth is a crucial element in advancing healthcare reforms to improve quality and costs accompanied by the development of software systems for the public health system [1, 14].

In particular, the use of eHealth has experienced tremendous growth in Latin America and the world; and software services are now implemented as an integral point to support and sustain the challenge of healthcare delivery, patient safety, efficient process management and clinical decision making; as well as interoperability with other public health system processes [1, 2, 20, 21] thereby reducing rising healthcare costs, supporting research, and improving patient care.

This is because, the potential of eHealth goes beyond supporting the burdened healthcare system; it can also contribute to health-related behavior modification, facilitate communication between distinct levels of processes and improve healthcare accessibility [3, 20, 22, 23].

In other words, eHealth provides instantaneous access to patient records [21], interactive learning environments capable of receiving a record amount of information continuously and immediately; and access to immediate quality medical care for those who may underserved by the public health systems [3, 12, 14].

As a result, the skyrocketing cost of medical care [2] and insufficient workforce [21] have driven the paradigm shift in healthcare, especially with regard to chronic disease hospital management, disease monitoring, general population wellness and care in rural areas, with more emphasis on efficient patient-centered healthcare management where the patient is located [24]. However, patient-centered health management implies that the patient's entire environment shares responsibility for the care and individual attention of the sick patient within the public health system.

Therefore, the tools needed to obtain this contain electronic records, devices with sensors to collect information, optimized communication and involvement of health care staff, and presentation with clinical details through patient information and physicians [25]; leading to the need to apply linked and modernized ICT structures in the healthcare processes [26]. Consequently, with population growth the demand for quality healthcare services is necessary, in conjunction with technological advances in ICT and other; major economic changes and social and cultural changes, driving the need for healthcare entities to integrate information and communication technologies (ICT) into the service delivery systems of the public health sectors [27].

However, the difficult and complex nature of healthcare environment, the abundance of clinical data and the incompatibility between data and lack of unified eHealth system [19, 27, 28] makes it necessary to design models and frameworks that provide the basis for a health-oriented architecture involving all aspects of health, as described in the following section.

3   Models and Frameworks in eHealth

When analyzing eHealth systems and identifying areas for continuous improvement, an in-depth study of software components and artifacts is required within a holistic structure based on models and frameworks for eHealth systems development; being aware of interactive software environments patients and healthcare providers can use with a high level of ease [20, 24].

Therefore, with the purpose of improving processes in healthcare, the scientific community has conducted scientific projects based on the design and construction of architectural models and frameworks in the healthcare context, as described below:

The authors in [29], the requirements to develop an Information Responsibility Framework (IAF) in responsible eHealth (AeH) systems that implement AI protocols are studied; In its conception, an extended IAF model was implemented and validated, which characterized four types of users: the user owner of the data (that is, the patients), the users of the data (that is, health professionals, doctors, nurses, etc.). And others) who use health information for legitimate purposes, data users who misuse the information, and a central health authority (HA) government agency, for the purpose of integrating the IAF into an existing electronic health record system.

In contrast, the proposed structural model for quality requirements described in [30] is developed with a simple but effective method to support requirements engineering and software quality assurance throughout the life cycle of an EHR service and was developed as part of an extensive research project that began in 2007 with the goal of supporting transnational quality certification of EHR services.

Therefore, the model prepared by [30] is part of a general framework and it consists of four basic components: quality objectives, generic requirements, implementations, and metrics; these components presented in terms of the content they represent and their sensitivity to changes during the lifetime of a service.

On the other hand, in [31] an integrative cognitive, theoretical and methodological analytical framework of Chan-Kaufman is presented to elucidate the nature of literacy barriers in eHealth, and to develop tailored solutions to the problem; the analysis of this framework differs from other frameworks in the objectives which are developed with a diagnostic approach rather than a screening tool. However, a major difficulty with this framework is the methodology which requires substantial training. From another point of view, the authors of [32] develop an eHeatlh architecture based on Zachman's model which provides a taxonomy for information describing the implementation of ICT and HIS in the real world.

This eHealth model proposed [32] presents the requirements for current and future ICT and health information systems. It examines the requirements in terms of health-care needs, current system, system project implementer and hardware requirements. In turn, the eHealth architectural model [32] product of the model also defines the dynamic capability as linking the health system to integrate others, create new services and reconfigure internal and external management competencies to meet innovative technology challenges.

For its part, in the article [33] the authors present the KONFIDO approach that is building on and extending the OpenNCP results based on a sound holistic approach to security at a systemic level, in order to increase trust and security of eHealth data exchange, as well as to increase awareness of security issues among the cross- border healthcare communityacrossEurope; further more, it is designed and implemented as a toolkit composed of different services and tools whose combination can be used to address a wide range of possible eHealth scenarios.

Meanwhile, the authors [34] propose an eHealth approach to manage and distribute information in Ambient Assisted Living (AAL) environments to the cloud, using a software architecture with semantic features, which includes processing of sensed data using QoC parameters for timely assessment and data transport using SDN, the latter allowing the context of the information to be delivered in a flexible way to provide clinical data of differentiated quality.

However, the proposed case study focused only on monitoring and delivery of clinical data from the AAL environment to the cloud. On the contrary, in [35] a theoretical model for quality of experience (QoE) management in eHealth service delivery was proposed, it was created with the adoption of an ontology and an innovative architecture that offers many details and that is designed to provide services aware of the context on the Internet and which consisted of building a knowledge base (KB) with semantic formalism so that the AI mechanism of the proposed architecture could learn experience users (UX) while using the service, using knowledge of the KB; and the QoE knowledge representation model was incorporated into a service delivery platform oriented to user needs.

In contrast, [2] presents a new eHealth model for implementation that aims to obtain the benefits of cloud computing (information availability, security, and privacy) based on ontology chains. On the other hand, in [16] an interface created between the content of the laws and regulations in the field of eHealth and the requirements that can developed in the technology and processes associated with eHealth.

However, the development of models and frameworks in the healthcare context present relevant challenges that make their design, development, and implementation more complex, as described below.

3.1 Challenges

The advantages of successful eHealth services involve a decrease in demand for basic resources while increasing productivity [36, 37]. However, the complexity of the health-care environment. However, due to the complexity of the healthcare environment in the world, the large amount of clinical data in the medical context, and the incompatibility of databases and information systems in eHealth [38] create challenges in presenting an efficient and attractive eHealth model and/or framework that encompasses all these elements [2, 31]. Given the need to implement health technologies, different countries around the world have adopted eHealth initiatives. However, despite WHO support many initiatives have been subject to poor implementation, high resistance to change by health service managers, budget shortfalls, and the acquisition of information systems and services incapable of clinically informing the patient medical environment and support decision-making [2, 3]. This is because the eHealth information systems acquired by the countries and their governments do not meet the software quality requirements or eHealth standards to support work processes within the health system [5, 12, 13, 32, 36].

Added to this, the growth of the world population and especially in Latin America generates an enormous amount of clinical data without formats or standards, which entails the acquisition and use of information systems that do not facilitate the proper management of information, do not only for the patient, but also for the health personnel who offer medical care; aspect of this complex due to the lack of technology to access patients promptly [22].

Consequently, due to the large volumes of data, the sensitive information managed and the nature of the application context, the development of healthcare systems is complex [28], which forces requirements engineers and those involved in the implementation eHealth applications to have significant and specific knowledge of the healthcare domain targeted by the software [18, 32, 39, 40]. In addition to possessing the necessary knowledge and skills to conduct a correct software requirement engineering and thus design models and frameworks with specific and effective solutions in the health context [18, 31, 32, 39].

3.2 Features

As mentioned above, it is important to understand what are the main components that are part of the design of any model or framework in the field of health, which is why Table 1 describes the main features present in eHealth models and frameworks.

4 Elements of Software Engineering in Models and Frameworks for eHealth

Based on the characteristics described in Table 1, Fig. 1 shows the main software engineering principles that have considered in the development of eHealth- oriented models and frameworks. Within this perspective, it can be observed that the basis of these systems is an adequate analysis of the functional requirements and quality, which may vary depending on the country where it is applied, as well as the types of standards used to analyze these requirements. In addition to this, it is very important to point out that these systems must be developed with standards, policies and certifications in IT governance, eHealth, and software quality, all of which are evaluated through QoS, QoE and QoC metrics.

Therefore, all these principles must be present in eHealth systems, which involve everything from medical records to predictive analytics. However, to fulfill this purpose, these systems must be compatible in such a way that a high level of interoperability is achieved; and in this way, the result of good interoperability implies that the data obtained in the exchange are stored in a private cloud that allows to take advantage of the different Cloud Computing service models, such as IaaS, PaaS, SaaS; together with the benefits offered by Big Data to present quality information to the different actors involved in the health sector. On the other hand, it is important to point out that the documentation of the model or framework should be explicit to promote semantic formalism, making use of ontologies that allow a better understanding of these systems and enable the literacy of eHealth environments.

Table 1.   Characteristics of Models and Frameworks in the eHealth Context.

Reference	Publication	· Feature
[40]	A framework for eHealth readiness of dietitians	· Adaptability · Continuous support · Compatibility between systems · Communication between interested parties · Interoperability, security, privacy and confidentiality · Access to and financing of IT infrastructure · Terminology and process standards
[27]	An integrated, holistic model for an eHealth system: A national Implementation approach and a new cloud-based security model	· Next generation network infrastructure · Independent layered architecture · eHealth standards and policies · It adopts strategic or governance, tactical and operational management levels · eHealth Private Cloud (IaaS, SaaS, PaaS) · Role-based access control · Availability of information · Security
[35]	A conceptual model for quality of experience management to provide Context-aware eHealth services	· SDN approach Layered network structure (management, control and data) · Multiple network applications to manage QoE during the use of a service · Adoption of ontology, semantic formalism · Knowledge base queries and inferences · SDN core controller and generic modules · QoS metrics for traffic engineering decisions · Virtual private network using encryption and authentication protocols · Context information with fine granularity
[34]	A health context management and distribution approach in AAL Environments	· Data processing · Semantic formalism · QoC parameters · Data transport with SDN

(continued)

Table 1. (*continued*)

Reference	Publication	· Feature
[41]	Semantic interoperability and pattern classification for a service-oriented architecture in pregnancy care	· Development of archetypes based on the openEHR standard · Use of ontologies · Use of safety standards · Interoperability management
[33]	An Open NCP-based Solution for Secure eHealth Data Exchange	· Service-oriented paradigm · Security of eHealth data exchange · HL7 standards · General information about the patient · Medical summary · List of current medication · Electronic prescriptions · Basic architecture blocks: query, retrieve and report · Authentication system based on ideas · Data exchange · Different communication channels · Participation of heterogeneous devices · High level of modularity
[32]	eHealth integration and interoperability issues: towards a solution through enterprise architecture	· Integrate, build and reconfigure internal and external competencies · Changing environments · Vertical and horizontal integration of health management · Interoperability between information systems. Use of ISO 15704 standard

However, it is essential to point out that security and privacy must be present in all aspects of these systems, as well as usability principles. From the analysis of the essential characteristics present in the development of models and frameworks for eHealth previously described, important conclusions were reached, which are presented below.

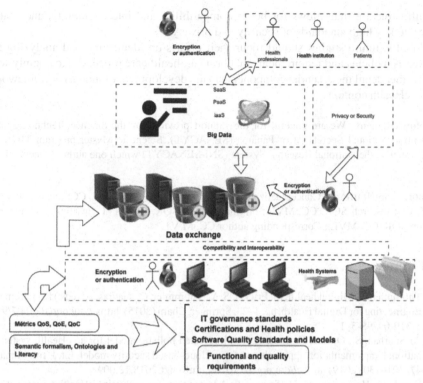

Fig. 1. Scheme of the software engineering elements that are part of the development of eHealth-oriented models and frameworks.

5 Conclusions

The concept of eHealth refers to the use of information and communication technologies in the improvement of health processes and is of immense importance because it allows government entities, health professionals and patients to know the risk factors present in the population and thus implement better prevention and health care plans.

Consequently, the models and frameworks that have been developed in eHealth seek to provide a solid and formal basis for researchers and developers of health- oriented systems; However, these models and frameworks vary according to various factors such as: country of application, health standards and regulations dictated by the country, types of health regulations and/or policies, and software engineering development standards.

On the other hand, the characteristics present in the development of eHealth models and frameworks describe a set of elements that involve regulatory aspects, as well as quality and safety. However, each of these investigations highlights the importance of knowing the environment in which it is to be implemented to obtain better results.

In addition to this, the software engineering principles that support the basis of the design of models and frameworks for an eHealth architecture involve good documentation, standards, regulations, and policies, as well as the proper management of an infrastructure that allows for better compatibility and interoperability, and that is supported by high standards of security and privacy.

Finally, future studies should focus their efforts on identifying and analyzing the standards, policies and requirements that best suit healthcare processes, to comply with and further detail the essential components in the development of models or frameworks in the eHealth context.

Acknowledgment. We are grateful for the support provided by the Science, Technology and Innovation National Secretariat of Panama (SENACYT), Scientific Master program TIC-UTP FISC-2019, to the National Research System (SNI-SENACYT) which one author is member.

Authors Contribution. Conceptualization SQR, CC; methodology SQR, CC; for- mal analysis SQR, CC; research SQR, CC, MVL.; original-writing SQR, CC, MVL.; writing— review and edition SQR, CC, MVL.; Corresponding author CC, M.V.L.

References

1. Thümmler, C.: Digital health. In: Fricker, S.A., Thümmler, C., Gavras, A. (eds.) Requirements Engineering for Digital Health, pp. 1–23. Springer, Cham (2015). https://doi.org/10.1007/978-3-319-09798-5_1
2. Al-Sharhan, S., Omran, E., Lari, K.: An integrated holistic model for an eHealth system: a national implementation approach and a new cloud-based security model. Int. J. Inf. Manage. **47**, 121–130 (2019). https://doi.org/10.1016/j.ijinfomgt.2018.12.009
3. Dansky, K.H., Thompson, D., Sanner, T.: A framework for evaluating eHealth research. Eval. Program Plann. **29**, 397–404 (2006). https://doi.org/10.1016/j.evalprogplan.2006.08.009
4. Leitner, G., Hitz, M., Holzinger, A.: Technical Expertise and Its Influence on the Acceptance of Future Medical Technologies: What Is Influencing What to Which Extent. (2010). https://doi.org/10.1007/978-3-642-16607-5
5. De, I., Díez, T.: Systematic Review about QoS and QoE in Telemedicine and eHealth Services and Applications. (2018)
6. WHO Executive Board: eHealth: Report by the Secretariat (Executive Board EB115/39 115th Session, Provisional agenda item 4.13), pp. 1–6 (2004)
7. Comisión Europea: Comunicación de la Comisión al Consejo, al Parlamento Europeo, al Comité Económico y Social Europeo y al Comité de las Regiones. Plan de acción sobre la salud electrónica 2012–2020: atención sanitaria innovadora para el siglo XXI {SWD(2012) 413 final} {SW. D. Of. las Comunidades Eur. COM(2012), pp. 1–17 (2012)
8. Barbabella, F., Melchiorre, M.G., Papa, R., Lamura, G.: How can eHealth improve care for people with multimorbidity in Europe? Health Systems and Policy Analysis (2016)
9. Oh, H., Rizo, C., Enkin, M., Jadad, A.: What is eHealth?: a systematic review of published definitions. World Hosp. Health Serv. **41**, 32–40 (2005)
10. Edemacu, K., Park, H.K., Jang, B., Kim, J.W.: Privacy provision in collaborative ehealth with attribute-based encryption: survey challenges and future directions. IEEE Access **7**, 89614–89636 (2019). https://doi.org/10.1109/access.2019.2925390
11. Jahan, S., Chowdhury, M.: Security and Privacy Protection for eHealth Data **878**, 197–205 (2018). https://doi.org/10.1007/978-3-319-94421-0
12. De Pietro, C., Francetic, I.: E-health in Switzerland: The laborious adoption of the federal law on electronic health records (EHR) and health information ex- change (HIE) networks. Health Policy (New. York) **122**, 69–74 (2018). https://doi.org/10.1016/j.healthpol.2017.11.005

13. Ouhbi, S., Fernández-Alemán, J.L., Carrillo-de-Gea, J.M., Toval, A., Idri, A.: E-health internationalization requirements for audit purposes. Comput. Methods Programs Biomed. **144**, 49–60 (2017). https://doi.org/10.1016/j.cmpb.2017.03.014

14. Baumel, A., Birnbaum, M.L., Sucala, M.: A systematic review and taxonomy of published quality criteria related to the evaluation of user-facing eHealth programs. J. Med. Syst. 41 (2017). https://doi.org/10.1007/s10916-017-0776-6

15. Kluge, E.H.W.: Health information professionals in a global eHealth world: ethical and legal arguments for the international certification and accreditation of health information professionals. Int. J. Med. Inform. **97**, 261–265 (2017). https://doi.org/10.1016/j.ijmedinf.2016.10.020

16. Purtova, N., Kosta, E., Koops, B.-J.: Laws and Regulations for Digital Health. In: Fricker, S.A., Thümmler, C., Gavras, A. (eds.) Requirements Engineering for Digital Health, pp. 47–74. Springer, Cham (2015). https://doi.org/10.1007/978-3-319-09798-5_3

17. Natsiavas, P., et al.: Identification of barriers and facilitators for eHealth acceptance: the KONFIDO study. IFMBE Proc. **66**, 81–85 (2018). https://doi.org/10.1007/978-981-10-7419-6_14

18. Fricker, S.A., Grau, R., Zwingli, A.: Requirements engineering: best practice. In: Fricker, S.A., Thümmler, C., Gavras, A. (eds.) Requirements Engineering for Digital Health, pp. 25–46. Springer, Cham (2015). https://doi.org/10.1007/978-3-319-09798-5_2

19. Swiatek, P., Schauer, P., Kokot, A., Demkiewicz, M.: Platform for building eHealth streaming services (2013). https://doi.org/10.1109/healthcom.2013.6720632

20. Maunder, K., Walton, K., Williams, P., Ferguson, M., Beck, E.: A framework for eHealth readiness of dietitians. Int. J. Med. Inform. **115**, 43–52 (2018). https://doi.org/10.1016/j.ijmedinf.2018.04.002

21. Pape, M.A. et al.: Developing an HMIS architecture framework to support a national health care eHealth strategy reform: a case study from Morocco developing an HMIS architecture framework to support a national health care eHealth strategy reform: a case study from Morocco 8604 (2017). https://doi.org/10.1080/23288604.2017.1265041

22. Aanestad, M., Grisot, M., Hanseth, O., Vassilakopoulou, P.: Information Infrastructures for eHealth. Inf. Infrastructures within Eur. Heal. Care. 25–33 (2017). https://doi.org/10.1007/978-3-319-51020-0

23. Alonso, S.G., Arambarri, J., López-Coronado, M., de la Torre Díez, I.: Proposing new blockchain challenges in eHealth. J. Med. Syst. **43**, 64 (2019). https://doi.org/10.1007/s10916-019-1195-7

24. Al-Thani, D., Monteiro, S., Tamil, L.S.: Design for eHealth and telehealth (2020). https://doi.org/10.1016/b978-0-12-816427-3.00004-x

25. Koren, A., Jurcevic, M., Huljenic, D.: Requirements and challenges in integration of aggregated personal health data for inclusion into formal electronic health records (EHR) (2019). https://doi.org/10.23919/smagrimet.2019.8720389

26. Statti, A., Martinez Madrid, N.: Requirements analysis for user interfaces in mobile eHealth applications (2017). https://doi.org/10.1007/978-3-319-56154-7_57

27. Al-Sharhan, S., Omran, E., Lari, K.: An integrated holistic model for an eHealth system: a national implementation approach and a new cloud-based security model. Int. J. Inf. Manage. **47**, 121–130 (2019). https://doi.org/10.1016/j.ijinfomgt.2018.12.009

28. Kabukye, J.K., de Keizer, N., Cornet, R.: Elicitation and prioritization of requirements for electronic health records for oncology in low resource settings: a concept mapping study. Int. J. Med. Inform. **135**, 104055 (2020). https://doi.org/10.1016/j.ijmedinf.2019.104055

29. Grunwel, D., Sahama, T.: Delegation of access in an information accountability framework for eHealth. ACM Int. Conf. Proceeding Ser. 01–05-Febr (2016). https://doi.org/10.1145/2843043.2843383

30. Hoerbst, A., Ammenwerth, E.: A structural model for quality requirements regarding electronic health records - State of the art and first concepts. In: Proceedings of the 2009 ICSE Work Software Engineering Health Care, SEHC 2009. 34–41 (2009). https://doi.org/10.1109/SEHC.2009.5069604

31. Patel, V.L., Arocha, J.F., Ancker, J.S.: eHealth Literacy as a Mediator of Health Behaviors. Presented at the (2017). https://doi.org/10.1007/978-3-319-51732-2

32. Adenuga, O.A., Kekwaletswe, R.M., Coleman, A.: EHealth integration and interoperability issues: towards a solution through enterprise architecture. Heal. Inf. Sci. Syst. **3**, 1–8 (2015). https://doi.org/10.1186/s13755-015-0009-7

33. Staffa, M., et al.: An OpenNCP-based Solution for Secure eHealth Data Exchange. J. Netw. Comput. Appl. 116, 65–85 (2018). https://doi.org/10.1016/j.jnca.2018.05.012

34. Da Silva, M.P., et al.: An eHealth context management and distribution approach in AAL environments. In: Proceedings - IEEE Symposium Computing Medical System 2016-Augus, pp. 169–174 (2016). https://doi.org/10.1109/CBMS.2016.15

35. da Silva, M.P., Gonçalves, A.L., Dantas, M.A.R.: A conceptual model for quality of experience management to provide context-aware eHealth services. Futur. Gener. Comput. Syst. **101**, 1041–1061 (2019). https://doi.org/10.1016/j.future.2019.07.033

36. Badran, M.F.: eHealth in Egypt: the demand-side perspective of implementing electronic health records. Telecomm. Policy. **43**, 576–594 (2019). https://doi.org/10.1016/j.telpol.2019.01.003

37. Alonso, S.G., de la Torre Díez, I., Zapiraín, B.G.: Predictive, personalized, preventive and participatory (4P) medicine applied to telemedicine and eHealth in the literature. J. Med. Syst. **43** (2019). https://doi.org/10.1007/s10916-019-1279-4

38. Stefan, G., Hoffmann, M.: Identifying security requirements and privacy concerns in digital health applications. In: Fricker, S.A., Thummler, C., Gavras, A. (eds.) Requirements Engineering for Digital Health, pp. 133–154. Springer, Cham (2015). https://doi.org/10.1007/978-3-319-09798-5_7

39. Fricker, S.A., Thummler, C., Gavras, A.: Requirements Engineering for Digital Health. Springer, Cham (2015). https://doi.org/10.1007/978-3-319-09798-5

40. Moreira, M.W.L., Rodrigues, J.J.P.C., Sangaiah, A.K., Al-Muhtadi, J., Korotaev, V.: Semantic interoperability and pattern classification for a service-oriented architecture in pregnancy care. Futur. Gener. Comput. Syst. **89**, 137–147 (2018). https://doi.org/10.1016/j.future.2018.04.031

41. Herrera, M., Moraga, M.A., Caballero, I., Calero, C.: Quality in use model for Web Portals (QiUWeP). In: Daniel, F., Facca, F.M. (eds.) ICWE 2010. LNCS, vol. 6385, pp. 91–101. Springer, Heidelberg (2010). https://doi.org/10.1007/978-3-642-16985-4_9

Reliable Reputation-Based Event Detection in V2V Networks

Vincenzo Agate[✉], Alessandra De Paola, Giuseppe Lo Re, and Antonio Virga

Department of Engineering, University of Palermo, Palermo, Italy
{vincenzo.agate,alessandra.depaola,giuseppe.lore,antonio.virga01}@unipa.it

Abstract. Technological advances in automotive and vehicle-to-vehicle communication paradigms promise the implementation of increasingly advanced services to make driving safer and more aware of events such as traffic congestion and road hazards. The detection and dissemination of reliable information about road events is of paramount importance to avoid unpleasant and potentially dangerous situations caused by the dissemination of false messages from unreliable or intentionally tampered vehicles. This paper proposes an event detection system based on reliable data dissemination, exploiting a fully distributed reputation and trust mechanism. Experiments conducted on a dataset containing realistic vehicle tracks on real-world maps demonstrate the system's ability to withstand the presence of up to 30% of attackers orchestrated to propagate false events without significant performance degradation.

Keywords: VANET · V2V · reputation management · reputation · trust

1 Introduction

Vehicle-to-Vehicle (V2V) and Vehicle-to-Infrastructure (V2I) communications are fundamental components of Intelligent Transport Systems (ITS) in order to improve quality of service (QoS), such as safety and efficiency of vehicle traffic [1,2]. These two VANET communication paradigms, despite their profound differences, aim to enable advanced services such as congestion analysis, traffic management, collision avoidance, cooperative driving and comfort/infotainment applications [3,4]. In V2I, the interaction between vehicles is based on the presence of a static infrastructure, so communication takes place between the on-board units (OBUs) installed in the vehicles and the roadside units (RSUs) that are part of the static infrastructure. The need for this infrastructure is the main limitation of this paradigm, as it may not always be present due to multiple reasons, including environmental impact or excessive cost.

Therefore, it is of utmost importance to explore efficient and reliable solution to guarantee advanced services in V2V scenarios. One of the main challenges in this scenario is to ensure the reliability of communications, which can be affected by various physical factors such as vehicle speed, high traffic density

T. Guarda et al. (Eds.): ARTIIS 2023, CCIS 1935, pp. 267–281, 2024.
https://doi.org/10.1007/978-3-031-48858-0_22

and the presence of physical obstacles. Many works in the literature attempt to solve this problem through the design of efficient data dissemination protocols [5]. However, this approach is not sufficient, as in a fully distributed environment [6], without any control over the quality of the data exchanged, false information could be disseminated due to sensor errors or opportunistically falsified by malicious nodes participating in the network. For these reasons, trust and reputation become essential in assessing the reliability of received data and network nodes [7,8]. Nevertheless, existing reputation management systems are inadequate for scenarios such as vehicular networks due to the high mobility of nodes and the need to process trust assessment requests in a timely manner to maintain network operations [9].

This paper proposes a V2V communication model based on a one-way population protocol [10], which uses a reputation management system to give more importance to data sent by trusted users and thus improve the overall QoI [11]. The solution proposed here is resistant to attacks by malicious users organised in groups acting simultaneously to damage the system. The remainder of the paper is organized as follows. Related work is outlined in Sect. 2. The proposed architecture is described in Sect. 3, focusing on the most important aspects of the data dissemination protocol and the reputation model. The experimental evaluation is presented in Sect. 4 and, finally, some conclusions are drawn in Sect. 5.

2   Background

VANETs consist of a large number of vehicles that cooperate by exchanging information. This cooperation is useful for the improvement of road safety, comfort and infotainment services. In this context, a major problem is the handling of unreliable data, i.e. data collected from vehicles that have inaccurate or noisy sensors or, in the worst case, deliberately display malicious behaviour (e.g. sending false information to the system to compromise the service). In traditional distributed scenarios, trust and reputation management techniques have been increasingly used to manage untrusted users or unreliable data [12–14]. Typically, such mechanisms take into account the history of previous transactions between users to assess the reliability of newly disseminated information [15]. Given the variety of application scenarios in which RMSs can be deployed, as well as the multitude of behaviors that agents can implement, many research efforts have focused on realizing simulation software for vulnerability assessment of RMSs [11]. In VANETs, due to the high speed of moving nodes and the dynamic nature of vehicular networks, the application of reputation management systems presents further challenges.

2.1   Related Work

The authors of [16] propose a trust model that uses direct trust based on factors such as Packet Delivery Rate (PDR) and Average Delivery Delay (ADD). These factors, which indicate physical characteristics of network communications and links, are used indirectly to calculate a node's trust. In [17], an attack-resistant trust management (ART) scheme is proposed to assess the trustworthiness of nodes and messages in VANETs. Data reliability is estimated on the basis of data collected from multiple vehicles. The reliability of a node is measured by combining the estimated probability that it performs its functions and the probability that its recommendations are reliable. The authors of [18] propose REPLACE, a reliable recommendation scheme based on the trustworthiness of the platooning service, which is a driving model in which vehicles with common goals move cooperatively. The ultimate goal of REPLACE is to recommend a reliable platoon leader to coordinate the platooning service. This model uses a centralised reputation system to calculate scores using user feedback. To mitigate the potential impact of feedback from malicious nodes, the authors propose an iterative filtering algorithm. The security of the proposed system is based on cryptographic techniques such as public key cryptography and session key agreement between vehicles and RSUs. However, as with most centralised trust management mechanisms that exploit cryptographic techniques, a pre-existing static infrastructure is required.

The work described in [19] proposes a framework for estimating traffic density, calculating trust between entities, detecting malicious nodes and disseminating this information in a network. Malicious vehicles are excluded from the network using different trust metrics, e.g. MSW-based trust, event-based trust, direct and indirect trust. The dissemination mechanism involves a periodic exchange of global trust values by adding new fields to beacon messages. The main limitation of this work is that the authors assume that malicious vehicles always exhibit dishonest behavior, but this may not be likely in a real-world setting.

A recent work proposed in [20] exploits clustering techniques for electing a cluster head (CH) responsible for sending dissemination of trusted information in the network. Unfortunately, the main drawback of this approach is the possibility of electing dishonest CHs when the majority of nodes are dishonest [21]. An extensive discussion of the most recent work in which communication is driven by trust in VANETs can be found in [22].

Unlike other works proposed in the recent literature which base the QoS control mechanism on a trusted infrastructure or on entities that may not always be available, in the proposed approach the communication is realized in a completely distributed way through a population protocol in which information about events is disclosed only after being suitably filtered by a reputation module. The reputation mechanism exploits both the information acquired directly through the sensory layer and the reported information appropriately weighted, thanks to a layered architecture.

3   The Multi-Layer Vehicular Architecture

The system proposed here is designed according to a multilayer architecture, as depicted in Fig. 1, consisting of three layers. Starting from the bottom of the

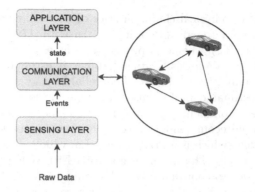

Fig. 1. The multi-layer architecture of the system.

figure and going up, the three layers are the Sensing Layer (SL), the Communication Layer (CL), and the Application Layer (AL).

The *Sensing Layer* is responsible for the detection of events that may occur while the vehicle is in motion. This recognition phase is achieved through the interaction between the vehicle's sensors (e.g. cameras, proximity sensors, accelerometers, gyroscopes, air quality sensors, GPS, etc.) and the environment. The collected raw data is processed by a data fusion module that detects and classifies events encountered as the vehicle moves, such as potholes, traffic, road construction, traffic accidents, etc. It is worth noting that if the system were to base its services solely on the information produced by the Sensing Layer, each vehicle would only be aware of the environmental phenomena close to it, and the quality of the information would not be protected against sensor malfunctions. When the Sensing Layer detects an event using the vehicle sensors, it generates a representation for the Communication Layer. The Communication Layer receives this event data through an interface and can then process, filter, and include it in the list of relevant events it handles. The interface helps to keep the two layers separate and independent, reducing coupling between different parts of the system.

The purpose of the *Communication Layer* is to cooperate with other vehicles to disseminate information on the network and enable a distributed event detection mechanism [23–25]. Through this cooperation, vehicles can become aware of events that are not in their vicinity and well in advance, allowing them to plan appropriate actions to achieve their goals; furthermore, obtaining information from multiple sources on the same event would help improve detection accuracy. To overcome the limitation of realising such distributed cooperation without an external communication infrastructure, the Communication Layer adopts a communication protocol based on the Population Protocol paradigm, originally designed for distributed networks whose sensors are characterised by limited resources, and which allows the population of nodes to converge on a shared view of certain information. While a distributed event detection algorithm based on information dissemination offers the advantages just discussed,

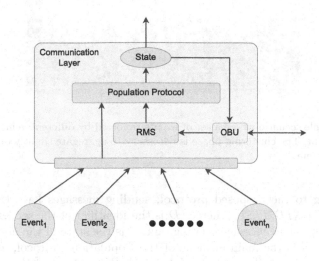

Fig. 2. Overview of the Communication Layer.

it also opens the way for possible attack scenarios, such as the dissemination of false events. In order to face this problem, the Communication Layer is also responsible for filter the received messages using a reputation model to keep the knowledge base updated with reliable information. The details of the Communication Layer implementation are discussed in the following of this section.

Finally, the *Application Layer*, using the list of events generated by the lower layers, provides specific services aimed at improving the user experience (such as reporting incidents nearby, etc.). The Application Layer receives the list of events detected by other vehicles, through the Communication Layer, and uses this information to identify relevant events in the user's proximity (e.g. traffic accidents) and to make suggestions for improving the route. It can also provide feedback to the Communication Layer. The Application Layer can also exploit the trust values of the events deduced from the Communication Layer to modulate the services provided to the end user.

The Communication Layer, schematically illustrated in Fig. 2, maintains an internal state, which summarises events detected or deduced from messages received from other vehicles. This state is communicated to other vehicles through the On-Board Units (OBUs) that also collect incoming messages. The received messages are filtered according to a reputation model and the resulting information contributes to update the state according to the rules of the proposed population protocol.

3.1   State Model

Following the Population Protocol (PP) model, each vehicle, sends its state to all vehicles with which it interacts. This sending occurs regularly and involves vehicles within the communication range of the source vehicle.

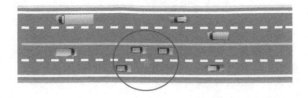

Fig. 3. Example scenario where a set of events reported by different vehicles refer to a single real event. The clustering phase is necessary to aggregate slightly different views within the system.

According to the proposed protocol, sending messages have the following structure: $M = \{ID, T, S\}$, where, ID is the identifier of the sender node, T is the timestamp of the message sending, and S is the state of the node.

The state S is the main element of the Population Protocol, and contains all the information to be exchanged between the nodes, i.e. the events to be disseminated. S is defined as follows: $S = \{E_L, F_L, flag\}$. The state consists of two lists and a flag. The first list, E_L, contains events considered reliable by the sender, which may be either those generated by the detection layer or those added to the knowledge base as a result of interactions with neighbouring nodes. The second list, F_L, contains the list of events that the node considers to be false, which may have been communicated by malicious or untrustworthy users. Finally, $flag$ is a binary field used by the PP to determine whether the state it is processing is an internal state, i.e. generated by the lowest level of the architecture, or an external state deduced from received messages.

Given n events and called the set of events $E = \{e_1, e_2, \ldots, e_n\}$, the following property holds on both lists: $E_L, F_L \subset E$ with $E_L \cap F_L = \emptyset$.

Moreover, each event $\{e_i\}_{i=1,\ldots,n}$ consists of:

$$e_i = \begin{cases} C_i & \text{class of the recognized event} \\ (X_i, Y_i) & \text{geographical coordinates} \\ T_i & \text{timestamp of event} \\ ID_v & \text{ID of the vehicle } v \end{cases} \tag{1}$$

where the X_i, Y_i variables are the GPS coordinates, estimated by GPS sensors.

3.2 Reputation Model

The Reputation Management Subsystem (RMS) is responsible for estimating the level of trust in events reported by neighbouring vehicles and the reputation of those vehicles. The RMS performs four key phases, detailed in the following: the aggregation of events (I), the local event trust calculation (II), the estimation of node reputations (III), the calculation of the trust of received events (IV).

Aggregation of Events. The first step performed by the RMS is the clustering of events according to their geographical coordinates and class C_i. This first step is useful for aggregating perceived events with slightly different geographical locations, e.g. due to noise in the detection, but which identify the same actual event. For a better understanding of the problem addressed, see Fig. 3, which represents a scenario in which several detections of the same event are broadcast from different vehicles. The clustering of these reported events makes it possible to treat them as a single actual event, rather than considering them as different events. Clustering is performed through the DBSCAN algorithm. This algorithm was chosen because, unlike other algorithms, it can find clusters of any shape and does not require that the number of clusters is known in advance. Its operation is governed by two parameters, *eps* and *MinPts*, representing respectively the maximum distance between two points belonging to the same cluster and the minimum size of a cluster. Since the topology of the network is dynamic and the nodes are not uniformly distributed, the event aggregation described here adopts $MinPts = 1$ in order to avoid that events located at the least trafficked points, detected by a limited number of nodes, being classified as noise points. The *eps* parameter is set by considering the maximum distance at which the sensors, on-board the vehicles, are able to obtain the raw measurements as a reference value, plus a tolerance margin of 10% of its value as a fair trade-off to prevent the presence of cluster merging or fragmentation.

Local Trust of Events. After the clustering phase, the RMS calculates the local trust of each aggregated event. During this phase, events are distinguished by considering the identifiers assigned by the clustering algorithm, named $cluster_{id}$. The trust value, for each event, is determined through the following equation:

$$f(e_i) = \frac{m(e_i) - k(e_i)}{n}, \tag{2}$$

with $m(e_i), k(e_i) \subset [0, n]$ and $0 < m(e_i) + k(e_i) \leq n$.

The value $f(e_i)$ represents the trust value assigned to the i-th event, $m(e_i)$ is the number of nodes that consider the i-th event as trustworthy (i.e., e_i is contained in the E_L list), while $k(e_i)$ is to the number of nodes that consider the i-th event as untrustworthy, (i.e., e_i is contained in the F_L list). Finally n is the number of nodes that participated in the communication in the last time interval. $f(e_i)$ has values in the $[-1, 1]$ interval.

Node Reputation. The next step aims to calculate the reputation of the vehicles with which one has interacted, by exploiting the trust values of individual events $f(e_i)$ obtained from previous step. Assuming that the time window of stored data is W, for each node at time t, messages received from time $t - W + 1$ to time t are kept in memory. To evaluate the reputation of the j-th node, the model uses the history of received messages. The trust of each received message is computed as follows:

$$F_M(M_j^k) = \frac{\sum\limits_{e_i \in M_j^k} f(e_i)}{|M_j^k|}, 0 < j < w, \tag{3}$$

where M_j^k represents for the j-th message, received by the k-th node.

Once the trust values for each message are obtained, the reputation of the node k, named $R(x_k)$, is obtained by averaging the trust values of its messages. This averaging is done by means of the exponential weighted moving average ($EWMA$), which has proven to be the most effective, as shown by experimental evaluation:

$$R(x_k^t) = \alpha * F_M(M_j^k) + (1 - \alpha) * R(x_k^{t-1}) \tag{4}$$

Trust of Received Events. Once the reputation values of the sending nodes have been calculated, the RMS evaluates the trust values for the events contained in the messages received at the current step, so as to send the events received from the OBU with their respective trust values to the PP. The trust $F(e_i)$ of the i-th event is calculated through the following equation:

$$F(e_i) = \frac{\sum_{k \in K} R(x_k^t) - \sum_{z \in Z} R(x_z^t)}{n}, \tag{5}$$

where x_k are the nodes that reported that the event e_i was reliable, while x_z reported the opposite and $n = |K| + |Z|$.

3.3   Diffusion Model

The PP module is responsible for keeping the vehicle state updated with information obtained both during communication with neighboring nodes and with events obtained from the lower SL layer. The PP proposed here is of the one-way type [10], because unlike the basic PP, where the update of states occurs only after the synchronization of two agents (i.e., after both have exchanged states), in the considered scenario, the update occurs upon receipt of a message, after it has been processed by the previous modules. This feature is well suited to VANETs, where node mobility and other phenomena that typically affect wireless communications, such as fading, can adversely affect the symmetry of communications.

The input parameters of the Population Protocol proposed here are:

- the alphabet of possible initial values Σ, which has only the null symbol ϵ so that the input function ι initializes the state of each node to a base configuration common to each node.

$$S : \iota(\epsilon) = \{E_L, F_E, flag\} \; where \; E_L, F_E = \emptyset \; \& \; flag = 0 \tag{6}$$

- the output function ω that given as input a state S returns the sets of events e_i contained in the two lists.
- the transition function δ that updates the list of the receiving node.

The transition function, is defined as:

$$\delta(S_i, S_j) = (S_i', S_j'), \tag{7}$$

where S_i and S_j are the states of the receiving and sending nodes, respectively, before the update, and S'_i and S'_j are the states after the update. Since the proposed PP is one-way, the state of the sender node is not updated and only the state of the receiver node is updated. The update of S'_i occurs differently depending on the value of the variable $flag$ in the processed State. If the value of $flag$ is $false$, the state to be processed is internal, i.e. it comes from the Sensing Layer of the vehicle itself. In this case, the events si not associated with a trust value and is considered trusted. Consequently, the $\delta(\cdot)$ function includes the event to the next state S'_i. Instead, if the value of $flag$ is $true$, the state S_j is received from another node participating in the communication. In this case, $\delta(\cdot)$ parses the events contained in the state with their respective trust values, adopting different behavior depending on the obtained value.

Assuming two threshold values θ_h and θ_l, representing respectively the event trust threshold above which an event is deemed trustworthy and the threshold below which an event is deemed untrustworthy, and denoting by e_k^j the k-th event of state S_j, the policy to be followed falls into one of the following cases:

- if $F(e_k^j) \geq \theta_h$, and $e_k \not\subset S_i$, the received event is unknown and its trust value is greater than the threshold θ_h, so the event is considered trustworthy and is added to the list E_L of S_i;
- if $F(e_k^j) \leq \theta_l$, and $e_k \not\subset S_i$, the received event is unknown and its trust value is less than the threshold θ_l, then the event is considered untrustworthy and added to the list F_E of S_i;
- if $F(e_k^j) \geq \theta_h$, and $e_k \subset E_L$ of S_i, or $F(e_k^j) \leq \theta_l$, and $e_k \subset F_L$ of S_i, the received event is known and is in the correct list. If the newly received event is more recent, the system updates the corresponding timestamp and the event provider's ID;
- if $F(e_k^j) \geq \theta_h$, and $e_k \subset F_L$ of S_i, or $F(e_k^j) \leq \theta_l$, and $e_k \subset E_L$ of S_i, the received event is known and is in the wrong list. As a result, the event is removed and placed back on the correct list, unless it conflicts with knowledge derived from direct experience, which always overrides referred information.
- if $\theta_l < F(e_k^j) < \theta_h$ and $e_k \not\subset S_i$, event e_k is ignored because the trust value of the received event did not reach the appropriate threshold for determining trustworthiness;
- if $\theta_l < F(e_k^j) < \theta_h$ and $e_k \subset S_i$, the event was known with certainty, regardless of whether it was on the list of reliable events or not. Since the event is now uncertain, it is removed from the list it is on, unless it conflicts with knowledge derived from direct experience, which always overrides referred information.

4   Experimental Evaluation

This section shows the results of the experimental evaluation of the proposed solution, demonstrating that it is adequate for the dissemination of events useful in V2V scenarios, and it is also resilient to the presence of security attacks from nodes opportunistically organized to damage the system.

Fig. 4. Map of the test area.

Fig. 5. Map of the roads in the test area. (Color figure online)

4.1 Simulation Environment

Experiments were carried out using the open source VEINS [26] framework based on two simulators, SUMO [27] which is a road traffic simulation suite, and OMNET++ [28] a C++-based simulation library suitable for creating network simulators. The proposed model can be used in a variety of road scenarios, regardless of network topology. The experiments described were performed in urban environments simulated from real maps.

4.2 Experimental Setting

The simulation dataset was generated through the OpenStreetMap tool and covers an area of the university campus of the city of Palermo. A portion of the map is shown in Fig. 4, and the size of the work area is $12\ Km(Colorfigureonline)^2$.

In order to make communication more realistic, obstacles such as buildings were added in the dataset with SUMO's *polyconvert* script. Each vehicle has a communication radius equal to 100 m and the frequency for message exchanging is 5 Hz. In addition, the maximum useful distance for event recognition was set to 3 m for each node and the vehicle speeds in the map depend on the speed limits imposed by roads ranging from 7 m/s to 13 m/s. In Fig. 5, yellow colored markers represent the events of interest for the scenario considered here (e.g. accident, construction site etc.). The locations of the events were chosen from all possible intersections of the roads, extracting them according to a Gaussian distribution with mean 0 and variance 1. Each simulation was performed for the duration of one hour. To evaluate the effectiveness of the model, different types of averages were used for calculating node reputation namely weighted arithmetic mean (WAM), geometric mean (GM) and exponential weighted moving average (EWMA).

Model of Malicious Agents. A set of malicious vehicles is generated together with the other vehicles. They are evenly distributed in the map, so that the spread of the malicious information can occur from multiple outbreaks.

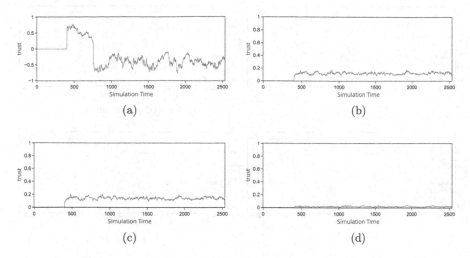

Fig. 6. Average trust values of false events computed adopting only local trust (a) or adopting the reputation model, where the reputation update rule uses weighted average (b), geometric mean (c) or exponential weighted moving average (d).

An attacker's behaviour consists of adding deliberately incorrect information to his state, such as false events that are not present in the map, or claiming that real events are false [29]. The attacker communicate such false information together with other truthful information, in order to maintaing a high value for its reputation. The simulations were performed by including in the network a percentage of malicious node between 5% and 30%. The attacks start at simulation time 400. Since the range of possible trust values is $[-1, 1]$, such interval is divided in the following three regions: trusted, untrusted, and uncertain region. The thresholds values to discriminate an event as trusted or untrusted were set at $\theta_h = 0,33$ and $\theta_l = -0,33$.

4.3 Experimental Results

The first experiment described in this section aims to asses the system's ability to correctly react to the presence of malicious nodes and to evaluate the classification capabilities under different and increasing attack conditions.

The Fig. 6 shows the trust trend of a fake event over time, considering first the use of local trust and then the complete reputation system with indirect feedback weighted by reputation values. In particular, it can be seen in the top right-hand graph that the use of direct trust alone is inadequate. Without considering the vehicle reputation, the false event assumes a positive trust value, at least at the beginning of the simulation, and this allows the false information to spread among the vehicles. In this case, the vehicles consider an event reliable, even if reported by unreliable vehicles, until they have direct feedback

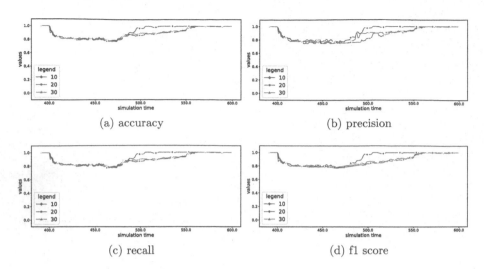

(a) accuracy   (b) precision

(c) recall   (d) f1 score

Fig. 7. Trend of the model's evaluation metrics as the number of attacking nodes varied. The EWMA average is adopted to updated the node reputation.

on the authenticity of the event. Figures 6-b-c-d illustrate how the proposed system, which exploits vehicle reputation, makes it possible to correct assess trust even during the fake event. In the graphs it is clearly visible how the trend of the event trust, is correctly considered below the θ_h threshold, and recognized by the system as a malicious event. Furthermore, the type of average used in estimating vehicle reputation has a significant impact on the trust value. The best performance is achieved by using EWMA, which proves to be the most effective in reacting in a timely manner to changes in neighbouring behaviour. Since malicious event detection can be viewed as a binary classification problem, where an event can be either true or false [30], the performance of the proposed system is evaluated through the following metrics: *accuracy*, that is the ratio of correct predictions to all predictions made, *precision*, which is the ratio of correct positive predictions to all positive predictions made, *recall*, which is the ratio of correct positive predictions to all predictions that must be positive, and *f1_score*, which is the harmonic mean between *precision* and *recall*. The weighted definition of these metrics have been adopted in order to address the strong imbalance between the class of real events and the class of malicious events. Figure 7 shows the trend of the considered metrics for the first 600 s of the simulation. After this time instant, the trend of the evaluation metrics stabilizes without showing any significant changes. Such metrics refer to scenarios where the presence of attackers is equal to 10%, 20%, and 30% of the good nodes, respectively. The trend of all the curves shows almost stable and maximum trend up to time step 400. From this moment on, a significant but moderate decrease can be observed due to the beginning of the attack phase. The attack consists in spreading information about false events. Surprisingly, the proposed system is able to identify and isolate the malicious information and limit its spread in

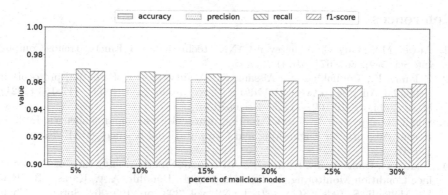

Fig. 8. System performance as the percentage of attackers on the network changes.

about 100 s. Note how the number of attacking nodes affects the time it takes for the four metrics to return to optimal levels. The more the percentage of attacking nodes increases, the longer the metric returns to 1. Finally, the cumulative value of the considered metrics, as the percentage of attacking nodes varies from 5% to 30% in increments of 5%, is shown in Fig. 8. The scale shows the values in the range between 0.9 and 1.0 to better appreciate the variations. As seen from the graph, the metrics have slightly decreased as the number of attackers has increased. This can be seen from the percentage change of the F1-score, which has decreased from 1.04%. Despite the significant increase in the number of attackers, the system continues to perform reasonably well, indicating that the system is able to maintain its performance.

5   Conclusion

This paper proposes a reliable event detection and dissemination scheme for VANET based on population protocols and reputation management. In the proposed scheme, the reliability of events and nodes is evaluated using two separate metrics, local event trust and node reputation, respectively. Local event trust is used to evaluate the reliability of events received by vehicles in the network. Furthermore, node reputation indicates how trustworthy the nodes within the VANETs are. In the proposed system, reputation management is fully distributed on the vehicles and does not depend on the network topology and the density of RSUs distributed in the network. In order to validate and evaluate the performance of the system, several experiments were conducted, which showed that our solution can withstand up to 30% of attackers generating false events and organizing into cliques to make the attack more effective, without significant performance degradation.

Acknowledgment. This research is partially funded by the S6 Project (PO FESR Sicilia 2014/2020).

References

1. Anwer, M.S., Guy, C.: A survey of VANET technologies. J. Emerg. Trends Comput. Inf. Sci. **5**(9), 661–671 (2014)
2. Belamri, F., Boulfekhar, S., Aissani, D.: A survey on QoS routing protocols in Vehicular Ad Hoc Network (VANET). Telecommun. Syst. **78**(1), 117–153 (2021). https://doi.org/10.1007/s11235-021-00797-8
3. Singh, S., Agrawal, S.: VANET routing protocols: issues and challenges. In: 2014 Recent Advances in Engineering and Computational Sciences (RAECS), pp. 1–5 (2014)
4. Agate, V., Concone, F., Ferraro, P.: A Resilient Smart Architecture for Road Surface Condition Monitoring. In: Ben Ahmed, M., Boudhir, A.A., Karas, I.R., Jain, V., Mellouli, S. (eds.) SCA 2021. LNNS, vol. 393, pp. 199–209. Springer, Cham (2022). https://doi.org/10.1007/978-3-030-94191-8_16
5. Nadeem, T., Shankar, P., Iftode, L.: A comparative study of data dissemination models for VANETs. In: 2006 Third Annual International Conference on Mobile and Ubiquitous Systems: Networking & Services, pp. 1–10. IEEE (2006)
6. Timilsina, A., Khamesi, A.R., Agate, V., Silvestri, S.: A reinforcement learning approach for user preference-aware energy sharing systems. IEEE Trans. Green Commun. Networking 5, 1138–1153 (2021)
7. Agate, V., De Paola, A., Lo Re, G., Morana, M.: A platform for the evaluation of distributed reputation algorithms. In: 2018 IEEE/ACM 22nd International Symposium on Distributed Simulation and Real Time Applications (DS-RT), pp. 1–8. IEEE (2018)
8. Huang, X., Yu, R., Kang, J., Zhang, Y.: Distributed reputation management for secure and efficient vehicular edge computing and networks. IEEE Access **5**, 25408–25420 (2017)
9. Kerrache, C.A., Calafate, C.T., Cano, J.C., Lagraa, N., Manzoni, P.: Trust management for vehicular networks: an adversary-oriented overview. IEEE Access **4**, 9293–9307 (2016)
10. Aspnes, J., Ruppert, E.: An introduction to population protocols. Middleware for Network Eccentric and Mobile Applications pp. 97–120 (2009). https://doi.org/10.1007/978-3-540-89707-1_5
11. Agate, V., De Paola, A., Lo Re, G., Morana, M.: A simulation software for the evaluation of vulnerabilities in reputation management systems. ACM Trans. Comput. Syst. (TOCS) **37**(1–4), 1–30 (2021)
12. Agate, V., De Paola, A., Lo Re, G., Morana, M.: Vulnerability evaluation of distributed reputation management systems. In: InfQ 2016 - New Frontiers in Quantitative Methods in Informatics, pp. 1–8. ICST, ICST, Brussels, Belgium (2016)
13. Crapanzano, C., Milazzo, F., De Paola, A., Lo Re, G.: Reputation management for distributed service-oriented architectures. In: 2010 Fourth IEEE International Conference on Self-Adaptive and Self-Organizing Systems Workshop, pp. 160–165. IEEE (2010)
14. Agate, V., De Paola, A., Lo Re, G., Morana, M.: DRESS: a distributed RMS evaluation simulation software. Int. J. Intell. Inf. Technol. (IJIIT) **16**(3), 1–18 (2020)
15. Agate, V., De Paola, A., Gaglio, S., Lo Re, G., Morana, M.: A framework for parallel assessment of reputation management systems. In: Proceedings of the 17th International Conference on Computer Systems and Technologies 2016, pp. 121–128 (2016)

16. Tan, S., Li, X., Dong, Q.: A trust management system for securing data plane of ad-hoc networks. IEEE Trans. Veh. Technol. **65**(9), 7579–7592 (2015)
17. Li, W., Song, H.: Art: an attack-resistant trust management scheme for securing vehicular ad hoc networks. IEEE Trans. Intell. Transp. Syst. **17**(4), 960–969 (2015)
18. Hu, H., Lu, R., Zhang, Z., Shao, J.: Replace: A reliable trust-based platoon service recommendation scheme in VANET. IEEE Trans. Veh. Technol. **66**(2), 1786–1797 (2016)
19. Kerrache, C.A., Lagraa, N., Calafate, C.T., Cano, J.C., Manzoni, P.: T-VNets: a novel trust architecture for vehicular networks using the standardized messaging services of ETSI its. Comput. Commun. **93**, 68–83 (2016)
20. Mahmood, A., Butler, B., Zhang, W.E., Sheng, Q.Z., Siddiqui, S.A.: A hybrid trust management heuristic for vanets. In: 2019 IEEE International Conference on Pervasive Computing and Communications Workshops (PerCom Workshops), pp. 748–752 (2019)
21. Ahmad, F., Kurugollu, F., Kerrache, C.A., Sezer, S., Liu, L.: NOTRINO: a novel hybrid trust management scheme for internet-of-vehicles. IEEE Trans. Veh. Technol. **70**(9), 9244–9257 (2021)
22. Hussain, R., Lee, J., Zeadally, S.: Trust in VANET: a survey of current solutions and future research opportunities. IEEE Trans. Intell. Transp. Syst. **22**(5), 2553–2571 (2020)
23. Bordonaro, A., Concone, F., De Paola, A., Lo Re, G., Das, S.K.: Modeling efficient and effective communications in vanet through population protocols. In: 2021 IEEE International Conference on Smart Computing (SMARTCOMP), pp. 305–310 (2021)
24. Agate, V., Ferraro, P., Gaglio, S.: A cognitive architecture for ambient intelligence systems. In: AIC, pp. 52–58 (2018)
25. Bordonaro, A., De Paola, A., Lo Re, G.: VPP: a communication schema for population protocols in VANET. In: 2021 20th International Conference on Ubiquitous Computing and Communications (IUCC/CIT/DSCI/SmartCNS), pp. 11–18 (2021)
26. Sommer, C., German, R., Dressler, F.: Bidirectionally coupled network and road traffic simulation for improved IVC analysis. IEEE Trans. Mobile Comput. (TMC) **10**(1), 3–15 (2011)
27. Lopez, P.A., et al.: Microscopic traffic simulation using sumo. In: 2018 21st International Conference on Intelligent Transportation Systems (ITSC), pp. 2575–2582. IEEE (2018)
28. Varga, A., Hornig, R.: An overview of the OMnet++ simulation environment. In: 1st International ICST Conference on Simulation Tools and Techniques for Communications, Networks and Systems (2010)
29. Agate, V., De Paola, A., Lo Re, G., Morana, M.: A simulation framework for evaluating distributed reputation management systems. In: Distributed Computing and Artificial Intelligence, 13th International Conference. AISC, vol. 474, pp. 247–254. Springer, Cham (2016). https://doi.org/10.1007/978-3-319-40162-1_27
30. Khatri, N., Lee, S., Mateen, A., Nam, S.Y.: Event message clustering algorithm for selection of majority message in VANETs. IEEE Access **11**, 14621–14635 (2023)

New Open Access Interactive Multifunctional Database Management System for Research of Biological Terminology: Technical Solutions

Karina Šķirmante[1](✉) ⓘ, Gints Jasmonts[1] ⓘ, Roberts Ervīns Ziediņš[1] ⓘ,
Silga Sviķe[1] ⓘ, and Arturs Stalažs[2] ⓘ

[1] Ventspils University of Applied Sciences, Inženieru iela 101a, Ventspils LV-3601, Latvia
`karina.krinkele@venta.lv`
[2] Institute of Horticulture, Graudu iela 1, Cerini, Krimunu pagasts,
Dobeles novads LV-3701, Latvia

Abstract. Terminology work requires a lot of manual processing, especially extracting data from materials that have not been digitized, so more efficient solutions and tools are necessary to improve the efficiency of the research. Since 2021, a team of terminologists, translators, researchers, information system developers worked together, during which the new open-access interactive multifunctional information management system was designed and developed for data storage and a wide range of statistical and search options especially for language research purposes and comparative multilingual studies in linguistics. The information system consists of multiple modules, which are successfully designed and developed and have been effectively used by researchers during the period of August 2021—July 2023 for entering, collection and retrieval data for special lexis research.

Keywords: Design and development of information system · terminology · data collection

1 Introduction

1.1 State of Art

In some research areas, the lack of appropriate wide usage electronic tools and databases still slows down the practical research in contrastive linguistics, especially when it comes to large groups of special lexis with many synonyms, such as the names of plants or animals. It should be noted that special lexis and terminology is often an issue not only for lexicographers and translators, but also for people in other professions whose work involves this terminology, for instance journalists, content creators, teachers and students [1]. Many scholars usually create their own glossaries and term bases using Computer Assisted Translation tools (e.g. Memsource, SDL Trados Studio) or simply in Word files or Excel worksheets to collect linguistic information for their studies. Incidentally, most of the scientific data remains in personal computers and is not available to a wider public, especially for international researchers, linguists, terminologists and translators,

T. Guarda et al. (Eds.): ARTIIS 2023, CCIS 1935, pp. 282–296, 2024.
https://doi.org/10.1007/978-3-031-48858-0_23

therefore the results of initial studies are not verifiable, research is not repeatable, and it cannot be compared to more recent studies, as information sources from previous research are usually not known.

There are databases which are dedicated to scientific names of organisms, but the coverage of the local names of organisms is minor. For example, the World's Flora Online [2] as 'an open-access web-based compendium of the world's 400,000 species of vascular plants and mosses' or all animal names e.g. Additionally, the Plants of the World Online database [3] offers a wealth of accurate information, making it highly valuable for scientific research. This database includes an extensive collection of synonyms and comprehensive species coverage, encompassing an impressive 1,423,000 scientific names of plants worldwide. All Animals A-Z List [4] which allows to search animal names by starting letter (in English), by scientific name, by class, location etc., but such electronic database would also be needed with the local names of organisms, which would be useful for terminology research and translators and experts in the field. There are several IT solutions that collect local names of organisms in Latvian, for example, Skosmos [5], however, this resource is more suitable for researchers in library science because researchers need the full set of designations for a given taxon to obtain data such as frequency of use, track changes or to clarify the accepted scientific or local name. There are different term bases and encyclopedias for Latvian as well but they are either not renewed, are small or contain only the names of the local flora [6].

This study is part of a larger project and the aim of the particular paper is to describe development process, characterize problems and solutions for creation of the open-access interactive multifunctional database management system (hereinafter—IMDS) which provides data storage and a wide range of statistical and search options especially for language research purposes and comparative multilingual studies in linguistics and terminology. The system will be published at the end of the year 2023 as Biolexipedia under the domain Bioleksipedija.lv. Biolexipedia is a blend word that consists of three words merged into one. It comes from the parts of words from Greek *bios* meaning 'life', from English *lexis* meaning 'the vocabulary of a particular field' and 'pedia' (from a back-formation of encyclopedia) meaning a specialized encyclopedia of biology vocabulary. Biolexipedia is planned as an universal repository of biological vocabulary, especially names of organisms.

It should be noted that the developed system may later be used for collection and research of other systems. The objectives of the IMDS development process are: 1) creation of a novel solution with a wide range of statistical and search possibilities suitable for language research and public use worldwide; 2) description of the initial linguistic and terminological research possibilities by using organism names as the lexical model field.

The IMDS solution provides statistical data for the usage of organism names, as well as automatically provides the different meanings of homonyms. From the viewpoint of language heritage, a vast number of organism name records will allow recognition of which names have already disappeared from daily usage, and which are close to disappearing because they are not included in specialized sources. A large amount of lexical background information from the IMDS gives the possibility to track back the timeline and the earliest publications to when particular new names were established.

These diachronic studies will allow researchers to compare how the old and the new names are used; and whether and when the new names possibly start dominating over the old ones. Section 3 gives an insight into some research possibilities for which the system may be used for.

1.2 Implementation of the Project

Previous mentioned activities are implemented during project 'Smart complex of information systems of specialized biology lexis for the research and preservation of linguistic diversity' which objectives are: 1) Creation of a novel system encompassing previously mentioned requirements; 2) Characterisation of a new IMDS by using organism names as the lexical model field. To verify the possibilities of newly created research database, more than 149,000 entries of names of different organisms (mainly in Latvian, additionally also in English, German, Russian, as well as in Estonian, Lithuanian, Polish etc.) are collected on the basis of excerpts from different publications (more than 8,470 bibliography units are used). Organism names cover all organism kingdoms, with current focus on plants, although animal and disease names are also included. Names of organisms are excerpted from different printed and electronic publications (scientific and popular scientific sources, dictionaries, specialized textbooks etc.).

2 Design of the IMDS

2.1 Overview of Used Technologies and IMDS Architecture

A team of researchers and system developers have worked together to design and develop the open-source web tool IMDS which is an effective solution for the research on special lexis of biology and related fields. In order to design the IMDS it was important to develop an application programming interface (API) driven information system to provide a successful web information system where the front-end can consist of multiple solutions and be used simultaneously. In this case, IMDS was designed as a two-part system with 1) the back-end which is primarily developed using Java programming language and a popular framework called Spring Framework [7]; 2) the front-end as single-page application (SPA) using React JavaScript libraries. This back-end and front-end design requires delivering effective communication between back-end servers and front-end application and for this action, Representational State Transfer (REST) was used. REST technology provides transmission of JavaScript Object Notation (JSON) requests and responses, and it allows to easily create an API for server client communication, by creating constant endpoints using Spring Framework controllers' classes.

The main objective of using Java as the back-end programming language—is that it is a high-performance, object-oriented, threaded, open source, platform-independent general purpose programming language. Although it is considered interpreted, it is also compiled, and uses a technique called Just-In-Time, which compiles and makes optimizations during run time. Spring framework is based on Java, and it simplifies the development process, as it comes with built-in annotations that can map functions as necessary. IMDS includes multiple sub-frameworks of Spring framework, for example, predefined framework for security—Spring Security and predefined framework for data usage—Spring Data Java Persistence Application Programming Interface (JPA). IMDS was developed using Spring Model-View-Controller (MVC) [8] pattern with additional service implementation for the system business functionality. The front-end of the IMDS is developed using SPA technology, which helps to make the application mobile friendly and generally usable on any device. SPA is also typically faster than multiple page applications, as their scripts are only loaded once during the lifespan of the application. ReactJS's technology was selected as front-end main technology because of ReactJS effectiveness, performance and popularity in the last three years [9] and research of the possible used technologies showed that there is effective synergy between Spring framework and ReactJS in multiple large scale IT projects. For data management, three database systems were used 1) MySQL database system was used for the storage of the IMDS data collection and non- hierarchical linkages. MySQL [10] is one of the top database engines, as it is efficient and easy to use. It guarantees constant uptime, which is critical for a web-based system. MySQL is also free and open-source, and it is possible to connect using Spring Data JPA framework using interfaces of repositories. 2) Mongo DB database system was used to obtain hierarchical linkages between scientific names of organisms. MongoDB [11] is a source-available cross-platform document-oriented database program and it allows us to organize data using tree data structure. 3) Redis database was used in large data caching of IMDS. Redis [12] is an open source (BSD licensed), in-memory data structure store, used as a database, cache, and message broker. An architecture of the IMDS is shown in Fig. 1.

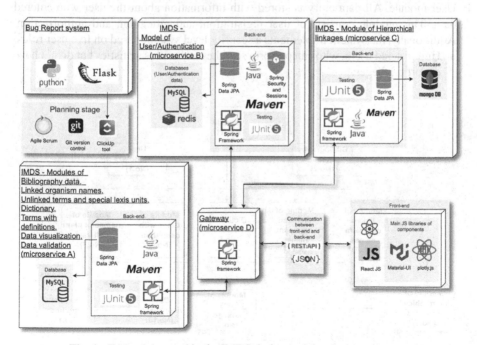

Fig. 1. Technology used in the IMDS design and development process.

IMDS design and development process was organized using Agile method Scrum, where software design and development activities were split into 2 weeks exercises called Sprints. The ClickUp tool was used for developing task management. GitHub was used for the version control and management of the IMDS code and GitHub Actions—as a continuous deployment pipeline—was used for automatization multiple processes of development workflow, for example testing and finding the vulnerabilities of the IMDS. IMDS testing was organized using the Junit framework to test model classes, validations, services, repositories, and Jest to test front-end components.

As an IMDS sub-system the new 'Bug reporting web system' was developed using the Flask framework and Python programming language. Bug reporting system is integrated with the ClickUp project of the IMDS where all development tasks are managed. IMDS users can create bug reports in the developed Bug system and the reports automatically are integrated as new tickets in the ClickUp project of the IMDS and programmers are informed about identified bugs.

At the first phase, the IMDS has been published on the internal server of Ventspils University of Applied Sciences, but the final version of IMDS will be developed as public open-access web system.

2.2 Overview of IMDS Modules and Data Layer

The developed IMDS consists of multiple modules which are mutually connected (see Fig. 2):

1. User module. All data entry is stored with information about the user who entered data. This module consists of user registration, authentication, and authorization. Additionally, the system implements a security level system based on five user roles:
   a. Unregistered users, who can perform searches and access statistics but do not have export privileges.

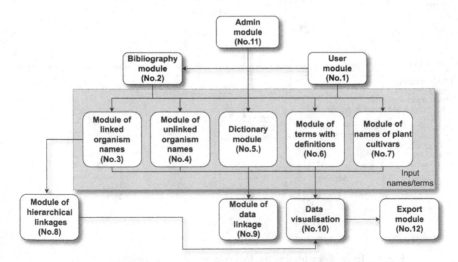

Fig. 2. Final version of modules for the IMDS

b. First-level registered users, who have all the capabilities of the previous role and can also export data.

c. Second-level registered users, who possess all the capabilities of the previous roles and can input data into the system for specific publications but are restricted from editing or deleting data entered by others.

d. Third-level registered users, who are qualified professionals with expertise and credentials to ensure IMDS's integrity through data validation.

e Admin user which is responsible for system administration tasks.

2. Bibliography module. All lexeme information is linked to the bibliographical information. This module provides the ability to store all publication data: monographs, journals, proceedings and papers with linked additional information, for example, publisher, ISBN, alternative title, place, Digital Object Identifier (DOI), authors, etc. In this case, it was important: 1) that the bibliographic source is correctly linked with the specific excerpted unit; 2) to organize the collection of such publication data, which will allow further provision of an appropriate reference to the source of information in the database. In this case, it was important to ensure that only papers, monographs, series of monographs and their parts can be used as a bibliography source for the organism name, species or term linkage. It was done using Java inheritance and polymorphism possibilities. (see Fig. 3).

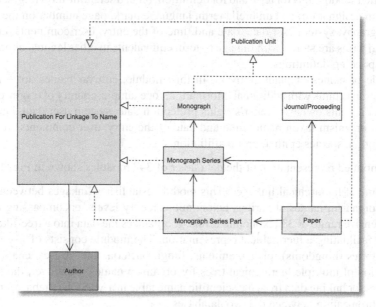

Fig. 3. The simplified Unified Modeling Language (UML) class diagram of the module of bibliography

3. Module of linked organism names. There are three types of organism names entered in this module—scientific name, local name, and names of diseases caused by organisms (since the names of organisms can also be the names of diseases). In this module, the linkage between the organism name and bibliography unit is stored with additional

information, for example, language mark, page number on the source bibliography, system user data, date and time, user comments. Also, the linkage between the root element and other names of organisms in the same linkage group is carried out in this module. In this case, multiple many-to-many tables were developed.

4. Module of unlinked terms and special lexis units. In this module, the linkage between a specific organism name (not linked to other languages) and bibliography unit is stored with additional information, for example, language mark, page number on the source bibliography, system user data, date and time, user comments. There are no linkages between other organism names.

5. Dictionary module. It is for lexemes of different languages that are not related to the scientific name of organisms and where entries are linked to specific bibliography units with additional information, for example, part of speech, gender, number, language mark, page number on the bibliographic source, system user data, date and time of the entry, user comments. Dictionary entries are linked together if there is a terminological or linguistic connection between them. This module also provides links to synonyms of the same language, if the scientific name of the organisms is not used in the original publication used for data collection in the database.

6. Module of terms and definitions. In this module, terms with their corresponding definitions are linked to specific bibliography units with definitions, for example, identified subdomains for term and for definition, related scientific term (e.g. scientific or Latin designation) and umbrella term, language mark, page number on the source bibliography, system user data, date and time of the entry, user comments, etc. The entered terms are stored with linkage to term equivalents in other languages and their corresponding definitions.

7. Module of names of plant cultivars. In this module, cultivar names are linked to bibliography units with additional information, for example, country of origin, cultivar breeder's rights owner, breeder's rights protection date, system user data, language, related organism taxon name, time and date of the entry, user comments, cultivar's description, species epithet, group affiliation, etc.

A simplified representation of the data layer of 3–7 modules shown in Fig. 4.

8. Module of hierarchical linkages. This module establishes linkages between scientific organism names at various taxonomic category levels, encompassing a comprehensive range of 33 taxonomic levels. It organizes the data into a tree-like structure, facilitating a hierarchical representation. The module consists of five distinct categories (kingdoms): plants, animals, fungi, bacteria, and viruses, enabling the creation of multiple hierarchical trees for organism names. Moreover, the module allows for linking data from the scientific name table in a MySQL database, ensuring synchronization between the two databases.

9. Module of data linkage. In this module, the linking of scientific names entered in Module 8 with the excerpt from different publications will be ensured and controlled. This will ensure that regardless of spelling differences, scientific names will be linked to the appropriate and correctly spelled names.

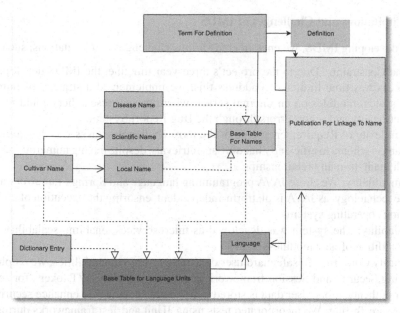

Fig. 4. The simplified UML class diagram of the names of organisms, plant cultivars names, dictionary words and terms with definitions

10. Data visualization. This is a module for information filtering and retrieving from the databases of the developed IMDS. Results are reproduced in multiple ways, for example, in graphs, plots of time series, word clouds, tables, etc. (see Fig. 6, Fig. 7, Fig. 8 and Fig. 9).

11. Admin Module. In this module, users with higher-level privileges have the ability to edit and delete associated organism names, scientific names, author first names and last names, etc. Additionally, they can approve user requests for input at a higher level.

12. Export Module. This is an additional module to complement the data visualization (No.10) module. With the help of this module, information about the searched name can be easily exported to an Excel spreadsheet for further research. The exported data is presented in a tabular format, organized into multiple sheets, each providing valuable insights. For example:

    a. Basic Information: This sheet contains data with the global comment for the name, the searched name, all found name linkages, including their name, language, group, and the number of publications. It also includes statistics with publication years and a histogram of publications within a specific time period. Additionally, users have the option to view detailed information about the publications.

    b. Data from Module No. 3 to Module No. 7: These sheets include information retrieved from various modules, together with bibliography details, language, comments, and corresponding page numbers.

2.3 Limitations and Challenges of IMDS

When developing IMDS, we encountered various challenges and limitations, such as:

1. Time Constraints: Due to the project's three-year timeline, the IMDS development process was time-limited. To address this, we implemented a strategy of publishing system modules on an internal server, where project researchers could test the functionality and report errors through the Bug Report System.
2. Complexity of Requirements: One of the most challenging tasks was designing the database schema to efficiently handle data retrievals, despite having numerous records with many-to-many relationships.
3. Compatibility: We chose JAVA programming language and Spring Framework as the core technology, as JAVA is platform-independent, ensuring the execution of code on various operating systems.
4. Scalability: The system was developed as microservices, enabling scalability with the addition of new modules.
5. Security Concerns: To safeguard user data and prevent vulnerabilities, we employed Spring Security and Session framework in conjunction with JWT tokens for secure user authentication. User data is stored in a separate database to enhance security.
6. Software Testing: We incorporated tests using JUnit and Jest frameworks during the IMDS development process to ensure software reliability.
7. User Acceptance: The system was developed in close collaboration with terminologists, translators and linguists, considering their requirements and customizing the user interface for specific researchers in the field.
8. Technical limitations (a few examples):
   a. the complexity of the data model arises due to intricate linkages between organism names, both horizontally through publications and vertically through a hierarchical tree (see optimization in Sect. 2.3);
   b. the system currently supports internationalization only for Latvian and English languages, considering the development scope and time constraints;
   c. there is a need to synchronize scientific names between two databases - MongoDB, where they are stored hierarchically, and MySQL, where they are associated with specific publications and other names. This is ensured by developing an additional synchronization Python script that runs once a day;
   d. now, the system imposes a simultaneous 30-connection limit with MySQL;
   e. data is extracted from the frontend to the backend using sessions, commonly employing batch sizes ranging from 100 to 1000 records. If necessary, this batch size can be further increased to accommodate larger data sets, up to a maximum of 10,000 records per batch.

By addressing these challenges and limitations, we aimed to create a robust and user-friendly IMDS system that meets the needs of its users effectively.

2.4 Optimization of the IMDS Performance of Big Data Retrieval

The main challenging factor was to design the opportunity to save organism name linkage to other organism names in one specific bibliography and to retrieve all linked objects as fast as possible. The IMDS system has been used for almost two years and in the most advanced case scenario so far, there are multiple cases where 49 names of organisms are linked together. Overall, a histogram of linkages counts is shown in Fig. 5.

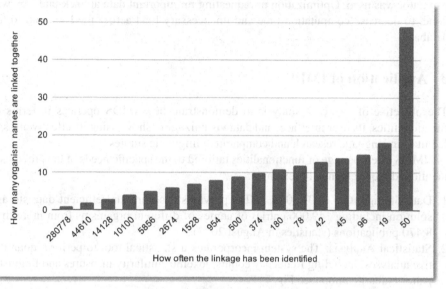

Fig. 5. The histogram depicts the linkage between organism names, showcasing the variability in how frequently particular organism names are linked with other names within one group.

The @ManyToMany Spring annotation was used for linkage storage of the same type of object, but Spring Data JPA retrieval process was very slow, because the Spring Data JPA usage not only filters and retrieves data from the database, but also loads processed data into the collection using many-to-many linkage and organizes them. Currently, the number of the linkages per bibliography unit is in range from 1 to 10,006 (avg). In the advanced-case scenario, when 10,006 names of organisms are linked to one specific publication, there were problems retrieving data from the database in optimal time using Spring Data JPA. The chosen solution was to manage data filtering and retrieving with MySQL database procedures instead of usage of the Spring Data JPA framework. More than thirty database procedures in the database side and relevant interfaces in the back-end side were created for data filter functionality, thus improving the retrieval of linked names of organisms more than ten times. To optimize data transfer from the back-end to the front-end, the data was split per page, where five linkage groups were organized in each page. Each linkage group may contain a different number of linkages. Although, in the usage of database procedures, it was necessary to use a self-developed paginator, instead of Spring Pagination. To optimize data retrieval from the database, advanced

Spring Data JPA methods were also used. In this case, specifications with builder criteria were applied to process results of the API requests dynamically. Specifications allow the usage of pre-stored query parts that can be combined at runtime in different combinations. To ensure the speed of data transfer between front-end and back-end of the IMDS, the Data Transfer Object (DTO) classes were created including necessary data for the specific controller endpoint, thus ensuring more optimized bandwidth throughput and IMDS performance. Also, the IMDS was designed not to use multiple requests, which may be required to gather all the data to render a view on the front-end side. In this case, paginator was used. Optimization of requesting unimportant data at back-end side was done, to decrease computation time and unnecessary load across the back-end to the database.

3 Application of IMDS

The objective of this case study is to demonstrate how IMDS operates in terms of functionalities, its user interface, and data visualization, showcasing its effectiveness in facilitating language research and comparative linguistic studies.

IMDS offers a range of functionalities tailored to the specific needs of the previously mentioned requirements, for example:

1. Data Storage: On 12.07.2023, IMDS provides a secure and efficient data storage solution including 149,000 entries of names of different organisms from more than 8,470 publications (statistics in August 2023).
2. Statistical Analysis: The system incorporates a statistical tool to perform quantitative analyses, including frequency counts, lexeme similarity measures and linguistic pattern identification (see Fig. 7).
3. Multilingual Search: IMDS supports advanced search options, enabling researchers to retrieve specific entries across multiple languages, facilitating cross-linguistic comparisons (see Fig. 6 on the right side).
4. Comparative Studies: IMDS allows researchers to conduct in-depth comparative analyses, identifying linguistic patterns and variations among different languages (see Fig. 6 and Fig. 8). It is possible to compare multiple definitions of terms for linguistic and translation studies (see Fig. 9) [13].

The next example shows the *Quercus robur* species name in Latvian 'parastais ozols', 'common oak' in English. This name is referenced in 140 publications from 1950 to 2023.

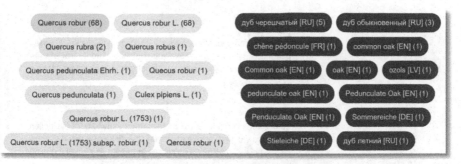

Fig. 6. On the left, there are all linked scientific names of 'parastais ozols', along with the corresponding frequency of mentions in IMDS. On the right, there are linked local names of 'parastais ozols' with the option to view the frequency of mentions in IMDS for each linked name. Additionally, language filters can be applied to refine the search and analysis.

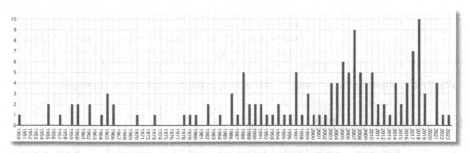

Fig. 7. Timelines depicting the usage of the searched species name 'parastais ozols' within publications covered by IMDS

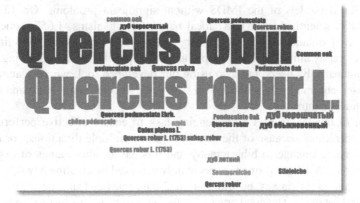

Fig. 8. Word cloud depicting the searched species name 'parastais ozols' within publications covered by IMDS.

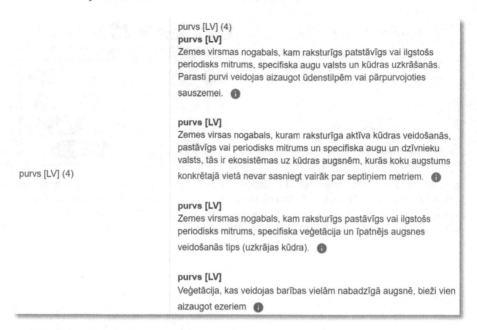

purvs [LV] (4)

purvs [LV] (4)
purvs [LV]
Zemes virsmas nogabals, kam raksturīgs patstāvīgs vai ilgstošs
periodisks mitrums, specifiska augu valsts un kūdras uzkrāšanās.
Parasti purvi veidojas aizaugot ūdenstilpēm vai pārpurvojoties
sauszemei.

purvs [LV]
Zemes virsas nogabals, kuram raksturīga aktīva kūdras veidošanās,
pastāvīgs vai periodisks mitrums un specifiska augu un dzīvnieku
valsts, tās ir ekosistēmas uz kūdras augsnēm, kurās koku augstums
konkrētajā vietā nevar sasniegt vairāk par septiņiem metriem.

purvs [LV]
Zemes virsmas nogabals, kam raksturīgs pastāvīgs vai ilgstošs
periodisks mitrums, specifiska veģetācija un īpatnējs augsnes
veidošanās tips (uzkrājas kūdra).

purvs [LV]
Veģetācija, kas veidojas barības vielām nabadzīgā augsnē, bieži vien
aizaugot ezeriem

Fig. 9. Definitions extracted from the IMDS system for the term 'purvs' (in English 'bog').

4 Conclusion and Future Work

Since 2021, linguists, terminologists, translators and IT specialists have been working together to design the IMDS during the implementation of the Project 'Smart complex of information systems of specialized biology lexis for the research and preservation of linguistic diversity'. After almost twenty four months, members of the grant have used developed models of the IMDS without significant problems. On 12.07.2023, overall 62,836 scientific and 81,137 local names of organisms, 1,657 names of diseases caused by organisms, 2,996 dictionary words, 403 terms and 361,598 linkages in 8,471 bibliography units (656 monographs and 7,815 papers) are stored during this time not only manually by users, but also using our developed tool, where scanned books are processed automatically with Optical Character Recognition (OCR) and language recognition algorithms [14].

Design of the IMDS was a challenging task to ensure effective performance in all IMDS operations because of the data linkages in multiple directions, for example, organisms' name linkage to bibliography and linkage to other names of organisms). Optimization of IMDS performance was mainly achieved by creating MySQL database procedures and DTO classes, ensuring optimal data transfer from the front-end to the back-end and database. The good practice to increase web system performance is to split functionality in two parts—back-end and front-end and run each system on individual hardware. In this case, IMDS back-end was developed using Java and Spring Framework and front-end—using ReactJS.

As part of system enhancements, search optimization can be implemented using a machine learning algorithm, for example, Word2vec [15] which is a technique for natural language processing (NLP) that utilizes a neural network model to learn word associations from a large corpus of text. Once trained, such a model can detect synonymous words or suggest additional words for a partial sentence. Currently, the Levenshtein algorithm [16] is used for searching similar lexemes, but its performance could be optimized.

The use of old printed books remains crucial for studying organism names in the past and their transformation through ages. This data collection could increase the importance of IMDS data repository. We developed a methodology [17] for digitizing Old Latvian Orthography using the Tesseract machine learning algorithm, with the main focus on G. H. Kawall's book 'Dieva radījumi pasaulē' (God's Creatures in the World), published in 1860 and translated from German into Latvian. Our digitization process achieved an approximate accuracy of 83%. However, manual verification is still required before integrating this data collection into IMDS. The optimization of model training can be continued. In the future, it would be necessary to involve volunteers to continue entering data into the system. Data input from printed and not digitized books in the Old Orthography is definitely needed in order to implement historical studies and to trace the very first publication of different organism names.

Acknowledgements. This research has been funded by the Latvian Council of Science, project 'Smart complex of information systems of specialized biology lexis for the research and preservation of linguistic diversity', No. Lzp-2020/1-0179.

References

1. Rudziša, V.: Ekvivalences problēmas juridisko tekstu tulkojumos. [Equivalence Problems in Translations of Legal Texts]. In: Aktuālas tendences terminoloģijas teorijā un praksē. Rakstu krājums. Sast. I. Pūtele. [Topical Trends in the Theory and Practice of the Terminology, Collection of the Articles, Pūtele, I. (ed.)] Rīga: LU Latviešu valodas institūts, pp. 17–27 (2013)
2. World Flora Online. http://www.worldfloraonline.org. Accessed 06 Aug 2023
3. Plants of the World Online. https://powo.science.kew.org/. Accessed 06 Aug 2023
4. All Animals A-Z List. https://a-z-animals.com/animals/. Accessed 06 Aug 2023
5. Skosmos, NLL subject authority ontology ('LNB tematisko priekšmetu ontoloģija' in Latvian). https://dati.lnb.lv/onto/nllsh/en/page/LNC10-000047992. Accessed 06 Aug 2023
6. Stalažs, A., Šķirmante, K., Sviķe, S., Jasmonts, G., Ziediņš, R.E.: Experience of design and development of a new open access interactive multifunctional database management system for special lexis of biology. Studies about Languages/Kalbų studijos **42**, 52–67 (2023). https://doi.org/10.5755/j01.sal.1.42.33107
7. Lui, M., Gray, M., Chan, A., Long, J.: Introduction to core spring framework. In: Pro Spring Integration. Apress, Berkeley, CA (2011). https://doi.org/10.1007/978-1-4302-3346-6_3
8. Singh, A., Piyush, C., Singh, K., Singh, A.: Formulating an MVC framework for web development in JAVA, pp. 926–929 (2018). https://doi.org/10.1109/ICOEI.2018.8553746
9. Mukthapuram, R.: Analysis of Component Libraries for ReactJS. IARJSET. **8**, 43–46 (2021). https://doi.org/10.17148/IARJSET.2021.8607
10. Győrödi, C., Dumşe-Burescu, D., Zmaranda, D., Győrödi, R., Gabor, G., Pecherle, G.: Performance analysis of NoSQL and relational databases with CouchDB and MySQL for application's data storage. Appl. Sci. (2020). https://doi.org/10.3390/app10238524

11. Győrödi, C.A., Dumşe-Burescu, D.V., Zmaranda, D.R., Győrödi, R.Ş: A comparative study of MongoDB and document-based MySQL for big data application data management. Big Data Cogn. Comput. **6**, 49 (2022). https://doi.org/10.3390/bdcc6020049

12. Chen, S., Tang, X., Wang, H., Zhao, H., Guo, M.: Towards scalable and reliable in-memory storage system: a case study with Redis, 1660–1667 (2016). https://doi.org/10.1109/TrustCom.2016.0255

13. Ozola-Ozoliņa, L., Sviķe, S.: Latvian environmental term *purvs*: problems and solutions in Latvian-English-Latvian translations of helonyms. Studies about Languages/Kalbų studijos, **42**, 80–92 (2023). https://doi.org/10.5755/j01.sal.1.42.33113

14. Jasmonts, G., Sviķe, S., Šķirmante, K.: New information extracting and analysis methdology for the terminology research purposes: the field of biology. In: CEUR Workshop Proceedings, vol. 3160. IRCDL 2022: 18th Italian Research Conference on Digital Libraries (2022). https://ceur-ws.org/Vol-3160/paper2.pdf

15. Mikolov, T., Chen, K., Corrado, G.S., Dean, J.: Efficient estimation of word representations in vector space. In: Proceedings of Workshop at ICLR (2013)

16. Haldar, R., Mukhopadhyay, D.: Levenshtein distance technique in dictionary lookup methods: an improved approach. In: Computing Research Repository – CORR https://doi.org/10.48550/arXiv.1101.1232 (2011)

17. Šķirmante, K., Jasmonts, G., Sviķe, S.: Digitisation of Printed Books in Old Latvian Orthography for the Preservation and Sustainability of Cultural Heritage: Workflow and Methodology Digital Humanities in the Nordic & Baltic Countries (DHNB2023): Sustainability, Environment, Community, Data March 8–10 (2023)

An Optimization Model for the Placement of Mobile Stroke Units

Saeid Amouzad Mahdiraji[1]([✉]), Muhammad Adil Abid[1], Johan Holmgren[1],
Radu-Casian Mihailescu[1], Fabian Lorig[1], and Jesper Petersson[2,3]

[1] Malmö University, Bassänggatan 2, 21119 Malmö, Sweden
{saeid.amouzad-mahdiraji,muhammad.adil-abid,johan.holmgren,
radu.c.mihailescu,fabian.lorig}@mau.se
[2] Skåne University Hospital, Fritz Bauersgatan 5, 21428 Malmö, Sweden
jesper.petersson@skane.se
[3] Lund University, Entrégatan 7, 22242 Lund, Sweden

Abstract. Mobile Stroke Units (MSUs) are specialized ambulances that can diagnose and treat stroke patients; hence, reducing the time to treatment for stroke patients. Optimal placement of MSUs in a geographic region enables to maximize access to treatment for stroke patients. We contribute a mathematical model to optimally place MSUs in a geographic region. The objective function of the model takes the tradeoff perspective, balancing between the efficiency and equity perspectives for the MSU placement. Solving the optimization problem enables to optimize the placement of MSUs for the chosen tradeoff between the efficiency and equity perspectives. We applied the model to the Blekinge and Kronoberg counties of Sweden to illustrate the applicability of our model. The experimental findings show both the correctness of the suggested model and the benefits of placing MSUs in the considered regions.

Keywords: Optimization · MILP · Time to Treatment · Mobile Stroke Unit (MSU) · MSU Placement

1 Introduction

A stroke refers to when a blood clot or a bleeding interrupts the blood circulation inside the brain, and stroke is a main global reason for death and permanent disability [1]. There are three main stroke types, each requiring specific treatment. To assure providing the correct stroke treatment, a computed tomography (CT) scan is required to identify which type of stroke the patient is suffering. Ischemic strokes are most common, and they occur when blood clot(s) impede blood circulation in the brain. Treatment for ischemic stroke patients typically involves thrombolysis and, in specific cases, thrombectomy.

Early treatment is known to be crucial for the successful recovery of stroke patients [2]. However, it is often difficult to treat stroke patients immediately since the patient typically cannot be diagnosed and treated until the ambulance delivers him/her to an acute hospital.

T. Guarda et al. (Eds.): ARTIIS 2023, CCIS 1935, pp. 297–310, 2024.
https://doi.org/10.1007/978-3-031-48858-0_24

One effective way to decrease the time to treatment for stroke patients involves the utilization of Mobile Stroke Units (MSUs). An MSU is a specialized ambulance equipped with advanced medical equipment, including a CT scanner, that enables the ambulance personnel to diagnose and administer thrombolysis on stroke patients while the patient is still in the MSU. As a result, MSUs have the potential to reduce the time to treatment by eliminating the time required for the transportation and diagnosis of the patient at the hospital. However, due to the high operational expenses associated with MSUs, only a limited number of MSUs can be placed in a geographic region. Therefore, when introducing MSUs, it becomes essential to strategically place them in order to provide a timely service for residents living in a region.

There are a number of studies focusing on identifying the optimal locations for placing MSU(s) within a region to enhance stroke care. These studies mainly explore two perspectives regarding where to place MSUs: efficiency and equity. The term efficiency refers to placing MSUs so that they provide access to treatment in the shortest possible time for most patients in a region, for example, in urban areas [3, 4]. Equity emphasizes the placement of MSUs in a manner that ensures equal access to healthcare services regardless of the geographic location of the patients, for example, in rural areas [5]. Phan et al. [3] introduce a data-driven approach that utilizes the Google application programming interface to determine the best possible placement for an MSU within the Sydney area. Rhudy Jr. et al. [4] use geospatial analysis to optimize service delivery for stroke patients in Memphis by studying the distribution of an MSU throughout the city. Dahllöf et al. [6] propose an expected value optimization approach to determine the best placement for an MSU in Sweden's Skåne county, aiming to assess the potential advantages of placing an MSU for urban and rural residents respectively. Amouzad Mahdiraji et al. [7] utilize an exhaustive search approach to optimally place MSUs in southern Sweden with the aim of balancing the efficiency and equity perspectives for the placement of MSUs.

The aim of the current study is to introduce a mathematical optimization model in the form of a mixed integer linear programming (MILP) model to identify the best locations of MSUs within a geographic region. Mathematical optimization has been demonstrated to be an effective technique to solve complex problems in a wide range of domains, such as emergency medical services (EMS). Due to the computational complexity of emergency vehicle placement problems, it is vital to build efficient mathematical models to represent the key characteristics of the MSU placement problem. However, no existing research directly addresses the mathematical formulation of the MSU placement problem. The objective function of the presented MILP model expresses a tradeoff between the efficiency and equity perspectives, aiming to provide maximum population coverage as well as equal service for the inhabitants of a region; however, considering the chosen tradeoff between the two perspectives. A scenario study is conducted in two counties of southern Sweden to show the correctness and advantages of our proposed model, where we solve the model to identify the optimal placements for different numbers of MSUs.

The subsequent sections of the paper are outlined as follows. We review the related work in Sect. 2. In Sect. 3, we present the MSU placement problem with a tradeoff between the efficiency and equity perspectives. In Sect. 4, we present our optimization model for the described problem. The scenario study is presented in Sect. 5, which is followed by an analysis of experimental results and a discussion. Eventually, we conclude the paper in Sect. 6.

2 Related Work

Previous studies in EMS use MILP for problems related to ambulance routing and placement, ambulance fleet allocation, crew scheduling, and resource allocation, ultimately leading to better patient outcomes and resource utilization [8]. As an example, Tavakoli et al. [9] propose a mathematical model for the strategic placement of ambulances, aiming to improve the response time of EMS in Fayetteville, North Carolina. Røislien et al. [10] use mathematical modeling to explore the optimal locations for air ambulance sites in Norway. Their approach utilizes high-resolution population data to estimate the number of required sites to provide service within 30 and 45 min for different shares of the population. Leknes et al. [11] present a MILP model to address the strategic and tactical problems of placing ambulance sites in heterogeneous regions. The authors examined the model in an urban-rural area in Norway. Akdoğan et al. [12] utilize queuing theory and a MILP model to locate emergency vehicles on fully connected networks. The MILP model aims to reduce the average response time of EMS according to an approximate queuing model.

In another study, Tlili et al. [13] propose a mathematical model to improve EMS transportation during disaster situations. The authors use a genetic algorithm for the ambulance routing problem to reduce time-sensitive treatment delays during urgent situations involving congested traffic compounds. Acuna et al. [14] contribute an ambulance placement optimization model to decrease patients' waiting times, time to treatment, and emergency department overcrowding in a county in Florida. The model considers disparities and fairness in placing ambulance services to emergency departments. Wan S. et al. [15] use a 0–1 MILP model to represent the location of distribution centers in massive emergencies, applied in a case study of earthquake response logistics in Chengdu, China. The proposed bi-objective model considers both the total transportation cost and the coverage level of emergency supplies.

While numerous research studies focus on the mathematical modeling of ambulance location problems, no previous study explicitly contributes to the mathematical formulation of the MSU placement problem. To address this gap, in this paper, we present a MILP model to represent the MSU placement problem.

3 MSU Placement Problem

As mentioned earlier, when placing MSU(s) in a geographic region, we need to take the impacts of the MSU locations into account to assure that the inhabitants of different parts of a region receive maximum benefit. In this section, we describe the MSU placement problem and how MSUs can be placed in a region considering the tradeoff between the efficiency and equity perspectives.

In our companion study [7], we demonstrate how different placements of MSUs would impact individuals living in different parts of a region. In particular, we propose an objective function that could be used in an optimization model to tradeoff between the efficiency and equity perspectives, and hence, allows placing MSUs so that most people living in a region are expected to receive more equitable service and shorter time to treatment. In addition, we employ the concept of the expected time to treatment to capture the value of the corresponding measure for each perspective. It should be noted that the expected time to treatment for a stroke patient denotes the expected time until the patient gets treatment either at a hospital or inside an MSU. In a previous study [16], we present how to calculate the expected time to treatment for patients in different subregions of a geographic region, considering that both a regular ambulance and an MSU can be dispatched.

The efficiency perspective refers to placing MSUs in a region to ensure a higher proportion of the population is expected to receive treatment at an earlier time. Using this perspective, the MSUs are placed close to highly populated regions, that is, in or near the urban areas. The efficiency perspective can be measured by the weighted average time to treatment (WATT). The expected time to treatment for individuals located in each subregion of a larger region is multiplied by the share of stroke cases expected to take place in the corresponding subregion; the sum of these values yields the WATT. We can use the WATT as an objective function in an optimization model for the MSU placement problem that considers the efficiency perspective.

The equity perspective refers to placing MSUs where the people who live far from the medical centers (for example, hospitals) benefit most, that is, people living in or close to rural areas. The range measure can be utilized to model the equity perspective, aiming to minimize the time difference between the expected times to treatment for patients who are located in different subregions of the studied region. The focus of an optimization problem corresponding to the equity perspective is to identify the MSU placements that minimize range.

In our companion study [7], we also introduce a tradeoff function that is established based on the WATT and range. It is shown that the tradeoff function enables to balance between the efficiency and equity perspectives to optimally place MSUs. In an optimization problem for placing MSUs in a region, the tradeoff perspective aims to find the locations of MSUs that minimize the tradeoff function.

It should be highlighted that in the formulated optimization problem, we only consider, for each perspective, the placement of MSUs in the existing ambulance sites in a geographic region.

4   Optimization Model

We here present our MILP model, which represents the key characteristics of the MSU placement problem. Our optimization model aims to minimize the tradeoff function that enables to identify the optimal locations for MSU(s) that can provide highly equitable service and reduced time to treatment for residents within a region.

We let $I = \{1, \ldots, m\}$ denote the index set over ambulances sites, where m is the total number of ambulance sites, and N is the number of MSUs to place. The aim is to place a fixed number of MSUs at the existing ambulance sites in a geographic region. It is assumed that there is always at least one regular ambulance available at each ambulance site. We also assume that there is always an ambulance or an MSU available for dispatch when it is required, and that the placed MSU(s) have no limitation concerning driving distance, and that they can provide service throughout the whole region.

We further assume that the studied region is divided into a non-overlapping set of subregions, denoted by $R = \{1, \ldots, n\}$, where n is the total number of subregions. We also assume that all inhabitants located in subregion $r \in R$ are in the same location, for example, in the centroid of r.

We let t_r^{RA} be the shortest time to treatment using a regular ambulance located in any ambulance site $i \in I$ for subregion $r \in R$, t_{ir}^{MSU} be the expected time to treatment for a patient located in subregion $r \in R$ using an MSU located in site $i \in I$, and Q_r be the share of stroke incidents within the studies region that is expected to take place in subregion $r \in R$ ($\sum_{r \in R} Q_r = 1$). Please note that the t_r^{RA}:s ($r \in R$), t_{ir}^{MSU}:s ($i \in I$, $r \in R$), and Q_r:s ($r \in R$) are input parameters, and hence can be calculated beforehand.

In order to formulate the MILP model, we need the following decision variables:

- $x_i \in \{0, 1\}$, ($i \in I$) is a binary decision variable such that:

$$x_i = \begin{cases} 1 \text{ if there is an MSU in site } i \in I, \\ 0 \text{ Otherwise.} \end{cases} \tag{1}$$

- y_{ir}^{MSU} is the expected time to treatment for a patient in subregion $r \in R$ using an MSU in site $i \in I$. This variable is assigned a large value, M, if there is no MSU placed in site $i \in I$.
- y_r^{MSU} is the shortest expected time to treatment for a patient in subregion $r \in R$ using any of the placed MSUs.
- y_r is the shortest expected time to treatment for a patient in subregion $r \in R$ using either an MSU or a regular ambulance.
- u^{max} is the longest expected time to treatment for any subregion $r \in R$.
- u^{min} is the shortest expected time to treatment for any subregion $r \in R$.

The tradeoff function z, presented in Eq. (2), is the objective function for our MILP model. The objective function has two components: the first one is the WATT as a measure for the efficiency perspective, and the second one is the range (time difference between subregions with the shortest and longest expected time to treatments) as a measure for the equity perspective.

$$\min z = \sum_{r=1}^{R} (1 - w) y_r Q_r + w \left(u^{max} - u^{min} \right), \tag{2}$$

In Eq. (2), $w \in [0, 1]$ is the weight employed to control the effects of the efficiency and equity perspectives. For example, we here assume $w = 0.5$ to let each of the terms have an equal impact on the tradeoff function.

The optimal solution of our model is subject to the following constraints:

$$y_{ir}^{MSU} = x_i t_{ir}^{MSU} + M (1 - x_i), i \in I, r \in R, \tag{3}$$

$$y_r^{MSU} = \min_{i \in I} \left\{ y_{ir}^{MSU} \right\}, i \in I, r \in R, \tag{4}$$

$$y_r = \min \left\{ y_r^{MSU}, t_r^{RA} \right\}, r \in R, \tag{5}$$

$$u^{max} \geq y_r, r \in R, \tag{6}$$

$$u^{min} \leq y_r, r \in R, \tag{7}$$

$$\sum_{i \in I} x_i = N. \tag{8}$$

We use constraint sets (3)-(5) to obtain the values of the y_r, which is the shortest expected time to treatment for any subregion $r \in R$ using either an MSU or a regular ambulance. The constraint in Eq. (3) assigns t_{ir}^{MSU} to y_{ir}^{MSU} if there is an MSU available in site i for a patient in subregion r. However, if no MSU is located in site i, it instead assigns a large value M to the y_{ir}^{MSU}. M, which is a parameter in our optimization model, is a sufficiently large constant value. For example, M can be set to any value larger than the longest expected time to treatment for any subregion r and any ambulance site i, that is, $M > \max_{r \in R} t_r^{RA}$.

The constraint in Eq. (4) takes the minimum over the expected times to treatment for the possible MSU locations. The minimum operation is used to assign the shortest expected time to treatment using an MSU for a patient in subregion r. In the optimization model, the constraint $y_r^{MSU} = \min_{i \in I}\{y_{ir}^{MSU}\} = \min\{y_{1r}^{MSU}, \ldots, y_{mr}^{MSU}\}$ is modeled as an ordered sequence of $(|I| - 1)$ minimum operations, each having two components. For this purpose, we introduce a set of positive help variables p_{ir}^{MSU}, $i \in \{1, \ldots, |I| - 1\}, r \in R$, which are used in the following way:

$$p_{1r}^{MSU} = min\left\{y_{1r}^{MSU}, y_{2r}^{MSU}\right\}, \tag{9}$$

$$p_{2r}^{MSU} = min\left\{p_{1r}^{MSU}, y_{3r}^{MSU}\right\},$$

$$\ldots$$

$$p_{(\lceil I \rceil - 1)r}^{MSU} = min\left\{p_{(\lceil I \rceil - 2)r}^{MSU}, y_{|I|r}^{MSU}\right\}.$$

In turn, each of these $(|I| - 1)$ minimum operations are represented using six constraints in our optimization model.

To model each of the minimum operations (including two components), we also need one binary variable. We let binary help variable s_{ir}^{MSU}, $i \in \{1, \ldots, |I| - 1\}, r \in R$ be used in the i:th minimum operation in this sequence for subregion r.

The first of the minimum operations $p_{1r}^{MSU} = min\{y_{1r}^{MSU}, y_{2r}^{MSU}\}$, determining the minimum between y_{1r}^{MSU} and y_{2r}^{MSU} is modeled using the following (six) constraints.

$$y_{2r}^{MSU} - y_{1r}^{MSU} \leq M s_{1r}^{MSU}, \tag{10}$$

$$y_{1r}^{MSU} - y_{2r}^{MSU} \leq M\left(1 - s_{1r}^{MSU}\right),$$

$$p_{1r}^{MSU} \leq y_{1r}^{MSU},$$

$$p_{1r}^{MSU} \leq y_{2r}^{MSU},$$

$$p_{1r}^{MSU} \geq y_{1r}^{MSU} - M\left(1 - s_{1r}^{MSU}\right),$$

$$p_{1r}^{MSU} \geq y_{2r}^{MSU} - Ms_{1r}^{MSU}$$

The i:th $(2 \leq i \leq |I| - 1)$ of the minimum operations $p_{ir}^{MSU} = min\left\{p_{(i-1)r}^{MSU}, y_{(i+1)r}^{MSU}\right\}$, determining the minimum between $p_{(i-1)r}^{MSU}$ and $y_{(i+1)r}^{MSU}$, is modeled using the following (six) constraints. Please note that there are in total $|I| - 2$ such constraint sets for each subregion r.

$$y_{(i+1)r}^{MSU} - p_{(i-1)r}^{MSU} \leq Ms_{ir}^{MSU}, \tag{11}$$

$$p_{(i-1)r}^{MSU} - y_{(i+1)r}^{MSU} \leq M\left(1 - s_{ir}^{MSU}\right),$$

$$p_{ir}^{MSU} \leq p_{(i-1)r}^{MSU},$$

$$p_{ir}^{MSU} \leq y_{(i+1)r}^{MSU},$$

$$p_{ir}^{MSU} \geq p_{(i-1)r}^{MSU} - M\left(1 - s_{ir}^{MSU}\right),$$

$$p_{ir}^{MSU} \geq y_{(i+1)r}^{MSU} - Ms_{ir}^{MSU}.$$

Then, we use the constraint in Eq. (12) (one for each $r \in R$) to acquire y_r^{MSU}. Please note that this constraint is needed in order to be consistent with the constraint set (11).

$$y_r^{MSU} = p_{(|I|-1)r}^{MSU}, r \in R. \tag{12}$$

The constraint $y_r = min\left\{y_r^{MSU}, t_r^{RA}\right\}$ shown in Eq. (5) captures the minimum value between y_r^{MSU} and t_r^{RA} for the patients located in subregion r. In the optimization model, this constraint is modeled using the following six constraints, where $v_r, r \in R$ is a binary help variable:

$$y_r^{MSU} - t_r^{RA} \leq Mv_r, r \in R, \tag{13}$$

$$t_r^{RA} - y_r^{MSU} \leq M(1 - v_r), r \in R,$$

$$y_r \leq t_r^{RA}, r \in R,$$

$$y_r \leq y_r^{MSU}, r \in R,$$

$$y_r \geq t_r^{RA} - M(1 - v_r), r \in R,$$

$$y_r \geq y_r^{MSU} - Mv_r, r \in R.$$

The constraints $u^{max} \geq y_r$ and $u^{min} \leq y_r$ in Eqs. (6) and (7) capture the longest and shortest expected time to treatment for any subregion r and for any MSU in site i. The value of $u^{max} - u^{min}$ in the objective function, see Eq. (2), refers to the range measure.

Finally, the constraint $\sum_{i \in I} x_i = N$ defined by Eq. (8) specifies the number of MSUs to be placed in a region.

5 Scenario Study

In this section, we describe the application of our proposed optimization model to two counties in southern Sweden. We then describe the experimental results.

5.1 Scenario Description

To evaluate the efficacy of the presented optimization model, we apply it to the Blekinge and Kronoberg counties of Sweden, which are parts of Sweden's southern healthcare region (SHR). The SHR covers an area of 16,622 km^2 and encompasses four counties: Skåne, Blekinge, Halland, and Kronoberg. The SHR has 49 municipalities, and its population was 1,687,000 in 2018. In Sweden, over 21,000 stroke incidents occur annually, with 3,900 cases reported in SHR [17]. In SHR, there are 39 ambulance sites and 13 acute hospitals equipped with CT scanners. Using the standard solvers, for example, Gurobi, we realized that it would be difficult to solve the model for large problem instances, that is, the entire SHR. Therefore, we decided to test the model with two counties of SHR. Table 1 represents the demographic and geographic statistics for each county of SHR. Figure 1 shows an overview of SHR, where each green triangle (referred to by a specific circled number) and each purple circle corresponds to an ambulance site and an acute hospital, respectively. The borders of the Blekinge and Kronoberg counties are represented in red and blue, respectively. As shown in Fig. 1, the ambulance sites in Blekinge are in Karlshamn (id: 15), Karlskrona (id: 16), Olofström (id: 26), Ronneby (id: 29), and Sölvesborg (id: 30), and ambulance sites in Kronoberg are in Älmhult (id: 1), Alvesta (id: 3), Lenhovda (id: 21), Lessebo (id: 22), Ljungby (id: 23), Markaryd (id: 25), Tingsryd (id: 34), and Växjö (id: 36).

We considered the same input data and assumptions as we did in our companion study [7]. In particular, we utilized the demographic data and stroke data for 2018 collected from Statistics Sweden [18] and Sweden's southern healthcare region committee [19], respectively. In our data, each county of SHR was divided into a set of non-overlapping subregions, each equaling to 1×1 km^2 and indicated by $r \in R$ so that the union of all subregions $\bigcup_{r \in R} r$ equals to the corresponding county of SHR. The demographic data included the number of inhabitants for each subregion $r \in R$ and each of the 21 assumed age groups, that is $\{[0, 4), [4, 8), \ldots, [95, 99), [100, \infty)\}$. In addition, the stroke data included the number of stroke cases for each age group in each county of SHR. Using the provided data, we calculated Q_r, indicated in Sect. 4, for each subregion $r \in R$, obtained by dividing the expected number of stroke cases in subregion r by the total expected number of stroke cases in the SHR.

Table 1. Demographic and geographic data of each county of SHR.

County	Population	Number of municipalities	Number of subregions	Number of ambulance sites	Number of hospitals
Blekinge	134,188	5	1,959	5	2
Halland	133,025	3	1,603	4	1
Kronoberg	198,903	8	4,233	8	2
Skåne	1,221,074	33	8,827	22	8

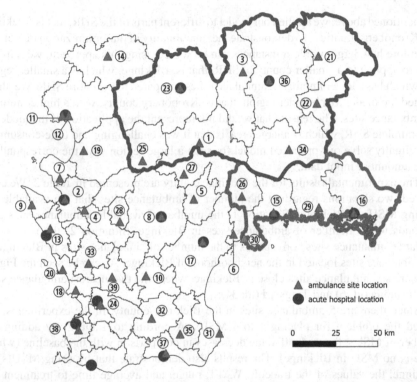

Fig. 1. Overview of the Sweden's southern healthcare Sweden (SHR). The purple circles and green triangles show the locations of acute hospitals and ambulance sites, respectively. The circled numbers indicate the corresponding ambulance site IDs. The borders of the Blekinge and Kronoberg counties are shown in red and blue, respectively. (Color figure online)

In the scenario study, we aimed to identify the optimal locations of different numbers of MSUs in either Blekinge or Kronoberg using the proposed optimization model. In the experiments, we took into consideration that every ambulance site within the region could potentially serve as a location for placing an MSU. In addition, for all experiments, we measured the results using only the expected time to treatment. We also compared the experimental results of placing MSU(s) with the experimental results of the baseline, representing the current situation in the SHR, where there are only regular ambulances across all 39 ambulance sites in the SHR.

We solved the problem in Gurobi[1] 10.0.0, which uses the barrier and simplex algorithms to solve continuous relaxations of mixed-integer models and continuous models. In all experiments, we solved the described problem using the barrier and simplex algorithms. All of the code was written in Jupyter Notebook using Python on a computer with 32-gigabyte memory (RAM) and a Core(TM) i7-8650U CPU 1.90 gigahertz Intel(R) processor.

5.2 Experimental Results

As mentioned above, we applied our model to different parts of the SHR, that is, Blekinge and Kronoberg counties. To demonstrate the functionality of our optimization model and to explore how large problem instances can be solved using this approach, we initially tried to apply it to a smaller county of SHR, that is, Blekinge, which is a smaller region and which has a lower number of ambulance sites compared to the entire SHR. We, then, applied the model to a broader region, that is, Kroboberg county, with a higher number of ambulance sites. The reason that we did not represent the application of the model to the complete SHR, which is a large area, is that it was challenging and time-consuming to optimally solve our proposed model for such a large region with the corresponding large amount of input data.

The experimental results for the Blekinge county are presented in Table 2. We considered two situations regarding the number of ambulance sites that are available for placing MSUs in Blekinge: Situation 1) the number of available ambulance sites corresponds to the number of ambulance sites in Blekinge; Situation 2) the number of available ambulance sites corresponds to the number of ambulance sites in Blekinge + all ambulance sites located in the neighborhood of Blekinge. As can be seen the Fig. 1, there are six ambulance sites close to Blekinge, where the two nearest ambulance sites are Bromölla (id: 6) and Tingsryd (id: 34).

Since there are 5 ambulance sites in the Blekinge county, in the experiments, we solved the problem for placing 1 to 4 MSUs. According to Table 2, by adding the number of MSUs, the tradeoff value decreases in comparison with the baseline (where there is no MSU in Blekinge). The results also demonstrate that by using MSU(s) in Blekinge, the values of the tradeoff, WATT, range, and average time to treatment are expected to decrease compared to the baseline. In particular, by placing two MSUs in Blekinge, it is possible to make the treatment available within an hour for all inhabitants living in Blekinge.

When we solved the problem considering Situation 1 (only ambulance sites in Blekinge), the Simplex and Barrier algorithms produced the same results for each MSU placement. For Situation 1, we pointed out the minimum execution time between Simplex and Barrier in Table 2.

For Situation 2, where we considered 11 ambulance sites (5 ambulance sites in Blekinge and 6 neighborhood ambulance sites), the Gurobi solver using the Simplex algorithm had difficulty in solving the problem for placing of 1 to 4 MSUs. We instead

---

[1] Available: https://www.gurobi.com.

decided to only consider the 2 nearest ambulance sites to the existing ambulance sites of Blekinge and perform the experiments with 7 ambulance sites, shown in the third row of each MSU placement in Table 2. However, using the Barrier algorithm, Gurobi could solve the problem considering 11 ambulance sites in a feasible amount of time. According to the Gurobi documentation[2], the reason is probably that the Barrier algorithm is more efficient for complex models with large size. The results of the Barrier algorithm for Situation 2 are presented in parentheses in the third row for each MSU placement.

Table 2. Experimental results for the Blekinge county. NoAAS: number of available ambulance sites for placing MSUs; NoM: number of MSUs to place in the county; algorithm: algorithm used to solve the problem; MSU IDs: found optimal MSU site IDs, denoted by numbers within the square brackets; Ex. Time: Execution time (in seconds); Tr.: objective function corresponding to tradeoff value (in hour); Ra.: range (in hours); ATT: average time to treatment (in hour); WATT: weighted average time to treatment (in hour); and ES: exhaustive search.

NoAAS	NoM	Algorithm	MSU IDs	Ex. Time	Tr.	Ra.	WATT	ATT
Baseline	-	-	-	-	1.39	1.44	1.34	1.61
5 & 11	1	ES	[29]	-	1.09	1.16	1.01	1.11
5	1	Simplex & Barrier	[29]	22	1.09	1.16	1.01	1.11
7 (11)	1	Simplex (Barrier)	[29]	42 (45)	1.09	1.16	1.01	1.11
5 & 11	2	ES	[15,16]	-	0.87	0.89	0.84	0.97
5	2	Simplex & Barrier	[15,16]	572	0.87	0.89	0.84	0.97
7 (11)	2	Simplex (Barrier)	[15,16]	978 (1008)	0.87	0.89	0.84	0.97
5	3	ES	[15,16,29]	-	0.81	0.83	0.79	0.93
5	3	Simplex & Barrier	[15,16,29]	466	0.81	0.83	0.79	0.93
7 (11)	3	Simplex (Barrier)	[15,16,34]	1243 (1127)	0.82	0.79	0.84	0.95
11	3	ES	[15,16,34]	-	0.82	0.79	0.84	0.95
5	4	ES	[15,16,26,29]	-	0.78	0.81	0.75	0.89
5	4	Simplex & Barrier	[15,16,26,29]	24	0.78	0.81	0.75	0.89
7 (11)	4	Simplex (Barrier)	[15,16,26,34]	1003 (995)	0.81	0.81	0.80	0.91
11	4	ES	[15,16,26,34]	-	0.81	0.81	0.80	0.91

In Table 2, the comparison of the results of Situation 1 and Situation 2 shows that the identified MSU locations are equal when placing 1 and 2 MSUs. However, the identified MSU locations are different when placing 3 and 4 MSUs, where the corresponding tradeoff values of Situation 1 are smaller than Situation 2.

---

[2] Available: https://www.gurobi.com/documentation/

According to Table 2, in Situation 1 and Situation 2, the highest execution times are recorded when placing 2 MSUs (572 s) and 3 MSUs (1243 s for Simplex and 1127 s for Barrier), respectively.

In order to verify the optimal solutions and optimal objective function values obtained using our optimization model, we compared the output of our model with the exhaustive search, proposed in our companion paper [7], for placing 1, 2, 3, and 4 MSUs in Blekinge, presented in Table 2. In all MSU placements and Situations, the identified solutions and objective function values are the same both for our proposed model and for the exhaustive search.

Table 3. Experimental results for the Kronoberg county. The abbreviations are the same as in Table 2.

NoAAS	NoM	Algorithm	MSU IDs	Ex. Time	Tr.	Ra.	WATT	ATT
Baseline	-	-	-	-	1.65	1.84	1.45	1.78
8	1	ES	[3]	-	1.32	1.53	1.11	1.31
8	1	Simplex (Barrier)	[3]	2195 (133)	1.32	1.53	1.11	1.31
8	2	ES	[23,36]	-	1.09	1.24	0.94	1.13
8	2	Simplex	[23,36]	2667	1.09	1.24	0.94	1.13
8	3	ES	[21,23,36]	-	1.01	1.10	0.91	1.10
8	3	Simplex	[21,23,36]	3481	1.01	1.10	0.91	1.10
8	4	ES	[21,23,34,36]	-	0.99	1.10	0.87	1.02
8	4	Simplex	[21,23,34,36]	4099	0.99	1.10	0.87	1.02
8	5	ES	[21,23,25,34,36]	-	0.97	1.10	0.83	0.98
8	5	Simplex	[21,23,25,34,36]	2340	0.97	1.10	0.83	0.98

In Table 3, we present the results of applying our model to the Kronberg county. In the experiments, we assumed that only ambulance sites in Kronberg can be used for placing MSUs. Considering the complexity of solving the model, we, further, assumed that it is relevant to solve the problem of placing 1 to 5 MSUs in Kronoberg.

According to Table 3, by adding the number of MSUs, the tradeoff value decreases in comparison with the baseline (where there is no MSU in Kronoberg). In Table 3, the results also show that by placing MSU(s) in Kronoberg, the values of the tradeoff, WATT, range, and average time to treatment are expected to reduce compared to the baseline. Especially, placing 5 MSUs in Kronoberg would potentially provide treatment within an hour for all inhabitants living there.

It can be observed in Table 3 that when we solve the problem of placing one MSU in Kronoberg, the Simplex and Barrier algorithms produce the same results. However, when placing more than one MSU in Kronoberg, the Barrier algorithm had difficulties in finding feasible solutions for placing 2 to 5 MSUs. Alternatively, using the Simplex algorithm, Gurobi could solve the problem for different numbers of MSUs within a feasible amount of time. As mentioned above, the reason appears to be that the Barrier algorithm tends to be quicker when handling large complex models, but it exhibits greater numerical sensitivity. On the other hand, the simplex algorithm is generally less affected by numerical issues. According to Table 3, the highest execution time (4099 s) is recorded when placing 4 MSUs in Kronoberg.

Similar to Table 2, we compared the output of the presented optimization model with the exhaustive search for placing different numbers of MSUs in Kronoberg, presented in Table 3. As can be seen for all MSU placements, the identified solutions and objective function values are the same both for our proposed model and for the exhaustive search.

From the conducted experiments, we could explore to what extent large problem instances can be solved using our optimization model, and in that way, we could learn about the limits of using the Gurobi solver to solve the described problem.

6 Conclusions

We have presented a MILP model for the optimal placement of MSUs in a geographic region. The objective function of our optimization model is a tradeoff function proposed in our prior study [7], used to tradeoff the equity and efficiency perspectives for the MSU placement problem while aiming to provide shorter time to treatment and equal service for residents living in a region. To evaluate our optimization model, we conducted a scenario study to place MSUs in the Blekinge and Kronoberg counties of Sweden. Applying the model to smaller counties provided us the opportunity to assess the model's functionality and performance on a more manageable scale before scaling it up to larger problem instances. In the presented model, the time needed to identify an optimal solution for the given problem instances indicated the complexity of the MSU placement problem. The experimental results, supported by the results of the exhaustive search approach presented in previous research [7], indicated that the proposed optimization model is able to find the optimal MSU locations concerning the defined objective function and constraints. The results of the experiments also showed that using our proposed optimization model for the MSU placement problem enabled to cut down the expected time to treatment for most residents compared to the baseline. From the experimental results, we concluded that by placing 2 and 5 MSUs in Blekinge and Kronoberg, respectively, it is likely to achieve access to treatment within an hour for all inhabitants living there, which is often considered an important goal.

The focus of the current paper was on validating the correctness of the proposed optimization model and illustrating the possible idea of placing MSU(s) in a region using the tradeoff perspective. As mentioned above, solving large problem instances, for example, the SHR, is computationally expensive, in particular for standard optimization solvers. For future work, we plan to investigate the use of heuristics to solve large problem instances within a reasonable time frame.

Acknowledgment. This work was partially supported by the Kamprad Family Foundation for Entrepreneurship, Research & Charity, Sweden's Southern Regional Healthcare Committee, and the Wallenberg AI, Autonomous Systems and Software Program – Humanities and Society (WASP-HS), funded by the Marianne and Marcus Wallenberg Foundation.

References

1. World Stroke Organization (2019) Facts and figures about stroke. https://www.world-stroke. org/world-stroke-day-campaign/why-strokematters/learn-about-stroke/
2. Ebinger, M., et al.: Effect of the use of ambulance-based thrombolysis on time to thrombolysis in acute ischemic stroke: a randomized clinical trial. JAMA **311**(16), 1622–1631 (2014)
3. Phan, T.G., Beare, R., Srikanth, V., Ma, H.: Googling location for Mobile Stroke Unit hub in metropolitan Sydney. Front. Neurol. **10**, 810 (2019)
4. Rhudy, J.P., Jr., et al.: Geospatial visualization of mobile stroke unit dispatches: a method to optimize service performance. Intervent. Neurol. **7**(6), 464–470 (2018)
5. Mathur, S., Walter, S., Grunwald, I.Q., Helwig, S.A., Lesmeister, M., Fassbender, K.: Improving prehospital stroke services in rural and underserved settings with mobile stroke units. Frontiers in Neurology 10 (2019)
6. Dahllöf, O., Hofwimmer, F., Holmgren, J., Petersson, J.: Optimal placement of Mobile Stroke Units considering the perspectives of equality and efficiency. Procedia Comput. Sci **141**, 311–318 (2018)
7. Mahdiraji, S.A., Holmgren, J., Mihailescu, R.-C., Petersson, J.: An optimization model for the tradeoff between efficiency and equity for mobile stroke unit placement. In: Chen, Y.-W., Tanaka, S., Howlett, R.J., Jain, L.C. (eds.) Innovation in Medicine and Healthcare. SIST, vol. 242, pp. 183–193. Springer, Singapore (2021). https://doi.org/10.1007/978-981-16-3013-2_15
8. Bélanger, V., Ruiz, A., Soriano, P.: Recent optimization models and trends in location, relocation, and dispatching of emergency medical vehicles. Eur. J. Oper. Res. **272**(1), 1–23 (2019)
9. Tavakoli, A., Lightner, C.: Implementing a mathematical model for locating EMS vehicles in Fayetteville. NC. Comput. Oper. Res. **31**(9), 1549–1563 (2004)
10. Røislien, J., van den Berg, P.L., Lindner, T., Zakariassen, E., Aardal, K., van Essen, J.T.: Exploring optimal air ambulance base locations in Norway using advanced mathematical modelling. Inj. Prev. **23**(1), 10–15 (2017)
11. Leknes, H., Aartun, E.S., Andersson, H., Christiansen, M., Granberg, T.A.: Strategic ambulance location for heterogeneous regions. Eur. J. Oper. Res. **260**(1), 122–133 (2017)
12. Akdoğan, M.A., Bayındır, Z.P., Iyigun, C.: Locating emergency vehicles with an approximate queuing model and a meta-heuristic solution approach. Transp. Res. Part C: Emerg. Technol. **90**, 134–155 (2018)
13. Tlili, T., Abidi, S., Krichen, S.: A mathematical model for efficient emergency transportation in a disaster situation. Am. J. Emerg. Med. **36**(9), 1585–1590 (2018)
14. Acuna, J.A., Zayas-Castro, J.L., Charkhgard, H.: Ambulance allocation optimization model for the overcrowding problem in US emergency departments: a case study in Florida. Socioecon. Plann. Sci. **71**, 100747 (2020)
15. Wan, S., Chen, Z., Dong, J.: Bibjective trapezoidal fuzzy mixed integer linear programased distribution center location decision for largecale emergencies. Appl. Soft Comput. **110**, 107757 (2021)
16. Amouzad Mahdiraji, S., Dahllöf, O., Hofwimmer, F., Holmgren, J., Mihailescu, R.-C., Petersson, J.: Mobile stroke units for acute stroke care in the south of Sweden. Cogent Eng. **00** (2021). https://doi.org/10.1080/23311916.2021.1874084.
17. The Swedish Stroke Register. Stroke registrations (2020). https://www.riksstroke.org/sve/for skning-statistikoch-verksamhetsutveckling/statistik/registreringar/. Accessed 20 Dec 2020
18. Statistics Sweden (2018) demographic data 2018. https://www.scb.se. last accessed 2018/07/10
19. Sweden's Southern Regional Health Care Committee (2018) stroke data 2018. https://sodras jukvardsregionen.se/. Accessed 10 July 2018

Data Intelligence

Leveraging Large Language Models for Literature Review Tasks - A Case Study Using ChatGPT

Robert Zimmermann[1]([envelope]) [iD], Marina Staab[1] [iD], Mehran Nasseri[1,2] [iD],
and Patrick Brandtner[1,2] [iD]

[1] University of Applied Sciences Upper Austria, 4400 Steyr, Austria
{robert.zimmermann,marina.staab,mehran.nasseri,
patrick.brandtner}@fh-steyr.at
[2] Josef Ressel Centre PREVAIL, 4400 Steyr, Austria

Abstract. Literature reviews constitute an indispensable component of research endeavors; however, they often prove laborious and time-intensive. This study explores the potential of ChatGPT, a prominent large-scale language model, to facilitate the literature review process. By contrasting outcomes from a manual literature review with those achieved using ChatGPT, we ascertain the accuracy of ChatGPT's responses. Our findings indicate that ChatGPT aids researchers in swiftly perusing vast and heterogeneous collections of scientific publications, enabling them to extract pertinent information related to their research topic with an overall accuracy of 70%. Moreover, we demonstrate that ChatGPT offers a more economical and expeditious means of achieving this level of accuracy compared to human researchers. Nevertheless, we conclude that although ChatGPT exhibits promise in generating a rapid and cost-effective general overview of a subject, it presently falls short of generating a comprehensive literature overview requisite for scientific applications. Lastly, we propose avenues for future research to enhance the performance and utility of ChatGPT as a literature review assistant.

Keywords: Large Language Model · Literature Review · ChatGPT · Use Case

1 Introduction

Literature reviews represent a crucial part of any research project, as they help to identify existing knowledge gaps, synthesize relevant information, and formulate research questions and hypotheses [1]. However, literature reviews can also be a challenging and time-consuming task, as researchers often have to deal with a large amount of literature sources and complex topics.

Large language models (LLMs) are a type of artificial neural networks that can generate natural language texts based on a given input or context [2, 3]. LLMs have shown remarkable performance in various natural language processing (NLP) tasks, such as text classification, question answering, and text generation [4–7]. However, LLMs face challenges concerning their ethical and social impacts (e.g., generating harmful, biased,

T. Guarda et al. (Eds.): ARTIIS 2023, CCIS 1935, pp. 313–323, 2024.
https://doi.org/10.1007/978-3-031-48858-0_25

or wrong content). Also, their evaluation and interpretation in terms of measuring their quality and reliability is lacking [8, 9].

In this regard, the application of LLMs for literature review has not been extensively explored. Thus, in this paper, we use ChatGPT, a LLM designed by OpenAI [10], to perform a literature review by asking questions about the content of a set of papers. By doing so, we want to answer the following research question:

RQ: How can ChatGPT support researchers to conduct a literature review?

The rest of this paper is structured as follows: Sect. 2 presents the related work on LLMs and a literature review on how LLMs have been applied for conducting literature reviews. Section 3 describes the methodology of our approach, including the data collection, prompt definition, model architecture, and evaluation methods. Section 4 presents the results of our use case, and Sect. 5 discusses the implication of the gained results and highlights the limitations of our approach. Section 6 concludes the paper and suggests directions for future work.

2 Background

This section presents a general overview about LLMs as well as a literature review about previous approaches that used LLMs for conducting a literature review.

2.1 Large Language Models

LLMs are a type of artificial intelligence models that can generate natural language texts based on a given input or context [11]. As such, they have greatly enhanced the capabilities of systems to process and manipulate text for various purposes [12].

LLMs have evolved from early natural language processing techniques (NLPs) and have achieved remarkable improvements [13]. In contrast to NLPs, LLMs are typically characterized by their enormous size, often spanning tens of gigabytes, and are trained on massive text corpora that can reach up to the petabyte scale [12].

Besides the sheer size, another important component of LLM is the transformer architecture introduced by [14]. The authors proposed several key innovations, such as multi-head attention, positional encoding, layer normalization, and residual connections. These innovations enabled transformers to capture long-range dependencies and context more effectively, while also benefiting from increased scalability and training efficiency. The authors demonstrated the superiority of the transformer architecture through its performance on machine translation tasks, paving the way for the development of subsequent large language models based on the transformer framework such as BERT [11], RoBERTa [15], and T5 [16]. OpenAI's GPT series, including GPT-2 [4], GPT-3 [13], and GPT-4 [17] further expanded the capabilities of LLMs, showcasing their potential as multitask learners, few-shot learners and zero-shot learners [4, 13, 18].

The increase in size and the introduction of the transformer architecture led to the successful application of LLMs domains, in various domains such as: "Generation" (producing new text based on a given input or context) [4, 6, 18], "Open QA" (answering questions by searching through a text corpus) [13, 15, 19], "Closed QA" (answering questions that require a specific, factual answer) [11, 20], "Brainstorming" (generating numerous ideas in a short period of time) [21–23], "Chatting" (interacting with users through natural language queries and responses) [4, 24, 25], "Rewrite" (changing the wording or structure of a text while retaining its meaning) [26–28], "Classification" (categorizing text-based data into predefined groups or classes) [11, 26, 29], and "Extract" (identifying and extracting relevant information from unstructured text data) [11, 30–32].

However, LLMs also pose many challenges and limitations that need to be addressed. One of the main challenges are the ethical and social implications of LLMs, such as their potential to generate misleading or harmful content, their bias and fairness issues, and their environmental impact [9]. Another challenge is the evaluation and interpretation of LLMs, such as how to measure their quality and reliability, how to explain their reasoning and decisions, and how to ensure their accountability and transparency [8].

2.2 Application of Large Language Models for Literature Review

To review the state-of-the-art in the application of LLMs in the task of conducting a literature review, we conducted a literature review following [1] in May 2023. The literature review focused on research outcomes and applications, with the goal to find previous use case in which LLMs have been applied to conduct, or to help to conduct, a literature review. We took a neutral perspective for general scholars. The literature search was conducted using the "Scopus" and "Dimensions" database, as the combination of those databases has shown to cover an extensive coverage of scientific literature [33]. The following search string was applied:

TITLE-ABS-KEY (("Large language model" OR "LLM" OR "LLMs" OR "chatgpt") AND "Literature Review").

The search revealed eleven papers in the Scopus database and 48 papers in the Dimensions database. After joining both searches and filtering for duplicates and papers not written in English, 48 papers remained. To ensure scientific rigor, we removed all preprints from this selection, leaving 30 papers. For these papers, title and abstract were screened if they used ChatGPT to support in the task of conducting a literature review. Four papers contained such information, and their key findings concerning the use of ChatGPT for conducting a literature review are presented in the following.

In [34] the authors discuss the ethical and practical issues of using ChatGPT in the research process, especially for conducting a literature review. They argue that using ChatGPT for this purpose is unethical, as it violates the responsibility and accountability of the authors conducting a literature review. In addition, they show that using ChatGPT is impractical, as it generates many non-existent or incorrect papers when given a general prompt in the field of medicine. They conclude that ChatGPT is not reliable or trustworthy for the research process and advise against using it.

In [35] the authors conducted a literature review with the help of ChatGPT. They utilized ChatGPT as a tool to extract and synthesize the key themes from the relevant literature. Following this process, the output of ChatGPT was rigorously validated by the authors against the original articles. The authors state that this approach allowed them to use the capabilities of ChatGPT in the review process while maintaining human oversight for quality and interpretation. However, they did not state to which extent ChatGPT was able to help, or to which extent they had to correct it. Besides that, the review discusses the potential applications of ChatGPT in medical education, scientific research, medical writing, and diagnostic decision-making, as well as the ethical concerns and challenges associated with its use. The review suggests that more research and evaluation are needed to ensure the optimal and responsible use of ChatGPT in healthcare domains.

In [36] the authors aim to explore the application and impact of ChatGPT, in academic research and writing. The authors demonstrate a practical example of using ChatGPT to generate ideas and to write a literature review on the topic of artificial intelligence (AI) in higher education. To do so, they asked ChatGPT to write a complete literature review about the "adoption of Artificial Intelligence (AI) in higher education" with APA-style in-text citations and references. ChatGPT was able to generate an adequate text, however, similar to [35], the generated references could not be found by the authors and were thus considered fictional. Thus, the authors suggest that researchers should be cautious and critical when using ChatGPT or other LLMs in academic research or publishing, and call for the establishment of ethical guidelines for the appropriate use of these tools.

In [37] the authors used ChatGPT, to generate novel ideas for systematic reviews in the domain of cosmetic surgery. They asked ChatGPT to find novel topics for which no systematic literature review has been conducted and evaluated its accuracy by comparing its suggestions with a thorough literature review carried out by humans for each topic. They found that ChatGPT was able to find such topics with an accuracy of 55%. Thus, they argue that ChatGPT contributes to the formation of evidence-based research. However, they also point out that ChatGPT can put authors at an increased risk of plagiarism and therefore should be used with care. In addition, the authors identified three additional areas where ChatGPT could be beneficial. These were patient consultations and patient support, as ChatGPT could provide personalized and informative communication to patients and potential patients, as well as marketing, as it can generate content very easily.

In summary, it becomes evident that previous literature on the topic of how ChatGPT might conduct or help to conduct literature reviews is scarce. Previous research [34, 36] either tried to let ChatGPT conduct a literature review on its own, with limited success as the literature stated by ChatGPT did not exist. Or they used it to generate ideas for new literature reviews, with limited success (55% accuracy) [37]. Only in [35] the researchers used ChatGPT to support their research as they let ChatGPT extract and synthesize the key themes from the relevant literature. However, they did not state how effective ChatGPT was in this process. Therefore, we argue that literature is lacking a thorough analysis of how ChatGPT performs in the typical literature review task of identifying relevant literature in a specific literature search.

3   Method

To analyze how ChatGPT can assist in the task of literature review, the following experimental setting was defined.

First, we conducted a literature review with the objective of identifying relevant scholarly works that examine the prediction of sales in the retail sector in the context of the Covid-19 pandemic using machine learning techniques. To carry out this task, we utilized the Scopus database in March 2023 and applied a predefined search query. The search query was restricted to journal articles and conference proceedings published in English.:

TITLE-ABS-KEY ((covid OR coronavirus OR "corona virus" OR covid-19 OR pandemic) AND (retail OR sales OR purchase OR turnover OR revenue OR basket) AND (prediction OR predict OR "Machine Learning" OR forecast* OR forecasting OR "Neural Network" OR "Deep learning")) AND (LIMIT-TO (DOCTYPE, "ar") OR LIMIT-TO (DOCTYPE, "cp")) AND (LIMIT-TO (LANGUAGE, "English")).

This led to 585 search results. To enrich these results and gradually narrow down the relevant papers, their title and abstract were evaluated by two experienced researchers who examined the following questions (Q) consecutively, continuing the evaluation of a particular paper only if the answer to questions Q1 to Q4 was "Yes":

- Q1: Does the abstract contain information about how Covid-19 impacted retail?
- Q2: Does the abstract contain information regarding the impact of Covid-19 on sales?
- Q3: Was machine learning used to predict something in this paper?
- Q4: Was machine learning used to predict the influence from Covid-19 on sales?
- Q5: Which machine learning methods were used?
- Q6: In which country was the research conducted?

Second, we used ChatGPT to perform the same analysis. For this, we converted the previously mentioned questions into prompts, following best practices [38] and the OpenAI guidelines [39], aiming for clarity and simplicity in our prompts. Our prompts have two components. The first component is the query or instruction that specifies the desired output from the model. The second component is the data that the model needs to process to produce the output. We used the OpenAI API in Python and the GPT-3.5 Turbo model [40] from this API to implement the title and abstract of each paper and asked the API to return the result as a JSON string. We chose the GPT-3.5 Turbo model for our analysis as it is the best performing GPT model available for everyone [40]. Due to token limitations, and for having better performance, we processed each paper individually by feeding one paper to the model in each request until we completed the processing of all papers in our dataset. The general prompt can be seen in the following:

```
//Component 1://
I want you to act like a researcher.
I will give you the ID, title and an abstract of a paper
and you must answer the following questions.
Print your result in a json string including 'Paper ID',
'Q1', 'Q2', 'Q3', 'Q4', 'Q5', 'Q6',.
Just print a json string nothing else.
Q1 - "Does the abstract contain information about how
Covid-19 impacted retail? Answer with only yes or no."
Q2 - "Does the abstract contain information regarding the
impact of Covid-19 on sales? Answer with only yes or no."
Q3 - "Was machine learning used to predict something in
this paper? Answer with only yes or no."
Q4 - "Was machine learning used to predict the influence
from Covid-19 on sales? Answer with only yes or no."
Q5 - "Which machine learning methods were used?"
Q6 - "In which country was the research conducted?"

//Component 2://
This is the ID: [PAPER ID]
This is the Title: [Paper Title]
This is the Abstract [Paper Abstract]
```

Third, we compared the answers given by ChatGPT with our assessment made during the consecutive literature review by checking if ChatGPT's answers exactly matched our answers (Q1-Q4, Q6), or contained the correct information (Q5). Partial matches (Q5) were considered as incorrect.

4 Results

Table 1 shows the performance of ChatGPT in conducting literature review for the six previously formulated questions. For each question, we report the number and percentage of papers for which ChatGPT's answer matched our answer (Match) and for which ChatGPT's answer did not match our answer (No Match). We also report the total number of papers evaluated for each question (N Total).

The results indicate that ChatGPT achieved a high accuracy rate for most questions, except for Q4 (*"Was machine learning used to predict the influence from Covid-19 on Sales?"*), which had the lowest match percentage of 54%. The highest match percentage was obtained for Q6 (*"In which country was the research conducted?"*), which had 92% of papers matched. The overall match percentage for all questions was 70%. It should also be mentioned that the analysis of the 585 papers took ChatGPT 2.5 h and did cost 0.86 USD. In comparison, it took the two experienced researchers each approximately 40 h to conduct the same review.

Table 1. ChatGPT performance conducting literature review

Question	N		%		N Total
	Match	No Match	Match	No Match	
Q1 *"Does the abstract contain information about how Covid-19 impacted retail?"*	417	168	71%	29%	585
Q2 *"Does the abstract contain information regarding the impact of Covid-19 on sales?"*	72	36	67%	33%	108
Q3 *"Was machine learning used to predict something in this paper?"*	42	20	68%	32%	62
Q4 *"Was machine learning used to predict the influence from Covid-19 on sales?"*	20	17	54%	46%	37
Q5 *"Which machine learning methods were used?"*	17	7	71%	29%	24
Q6 *"In which country was the research conducted?"*	22	2	92%	8%	24
Total	**590**	**250**	**70%**	**30%**	

5 Discussion

Regarding the formulated research question (*RQ: How can ChatGPT support* researchers to conduct a literature review?), our findings have several implications.

As demonstrated by the high overall accuracy (70%) and speed (2.5 h) of ChatGPT, we suggest that ChatGPT can help researchers to quickly scan through large and diverse datasets of scientific publications and find relevant information for their research topic. However, we want to point out that even though 70% can be regarded as high accuracy for a quick overview, it is not enough to conduct comprehensive reviews. However, when considering the time invested (2.5 h) and the associated costs (0.86 USD) of utilizing ChatGPT in comparison to the substantial time investment (80 h) and labor costs incurred by human researchers, it prompts us to question the feasibility of exclusively relying on manual literature reviews. From a scientific perspective, this can clearly be answered with yes, as the goal of science should always be to generate highly accurate results. However, from a business perspective, it can be argued that a 70% accuracy might be enough for most business-related use cases if achieving the missing 30% generate immensely more costs.

In summary, we argue that in comparison to previous research [34, 36] we could demonstrate that if asked the correct questions, ChatGPT can indeed support researchers in conducting literature review, especially in the initial stage of conducting a literature review. In this regard, and in comparison to [35], we could also demonstrate the accuracy of ChatGPT when performing literature review is about 70%.

However, our findings also have some limitations that need to be acknowledged. First, our findings are based on the specific research topic of predicting the influence of Covid-19 on sales in retail using machine learning. Therefore, our findings may not be generalizable to other research topics or domains. As such, ChatGPT's performance may vary depending on the complexity and specificity of the research topic, as well as the quality and quantity of the data sources. Also, our findings are based on a limited set of questions that we used to screen the papers. Therefore, our findings may not capture all the aspects or dimensions of literature review. Also, ChatGPT's performance may vary depending on the complexity of the proposed question and the diversity and ambiguity of the possible answers. In this regard, it must also be noted that the proposed questions Q1-Q4 can be viewed as binary classification problems (yes/no), which we evaluated using error rates to measure the accuracy of ChatGPT. This approach works best if the dataset contains balanced data. However, our dataset is slightly biased and, depending on the question, either contains more "Yeses" or more "Noes" (Q1: Yes $= 18.46\%$; Q2: Yes $= 57.41\%$; Q3: Yes $= 59.68\%$; Q4: Yes $= 64.86\%$). Nevertheless, as our dataset is biased in both directions, and we receive comparable error rates for all the questions, we regard this bias as minimal. Despite this, it must be noted that the sample size for Q1-3 is higher compared to Q4-6, thus potentially producing more robust results for Q1-3 It must also be mentioned that we gave ChatGPT only the title and abstract of a paper to answer the formulated questions as we were limited by the current token limitation of ChatGPT. Thus, the results might also improve if ChatGPT would be provided with the complete papers instead. Also, it can be pointed out that we only used the pre-trained LLM ChatGPT for our analysis, as it is easily accessible for everyone. However, other LLM (e.g., BLOOM [41], LLaMa [42]) offer the opportunity to be fine-tuned with specific text. Thus, these models might offer even better results if they are properly trained with scientific texts. At last, our findings are based on a comparison with our own manual literature review. Therefore, our findings may be influenced by our own subjective judgment and analysis.

6   Conclusion

In this study, we explored how the LLM ChatGPT, can assist in the task of literature review. We compared the results of a manual literature review with those obtained by ChatGPT for a specific research topic: predicting the influence of Covid-19 on sales in retail using machine learning. We conclude that ChatGPT can support researchers to scan and evaluate literature by providing relatively accurate answers if provided with specific questions. However, we also conclude that comprehensive literature reviews currently cannot be conducted using ChatGPT, as its accuracy is still too low. Nevertheless, ChatGPT offers high cost and time reductions, which might be interesting points in the business area.

We suggested the following directions for future work to improve the performance and usefulness of ChatGPT as an assistant for literature review. Foremost, we suggest that more experiments with different research topics and domains should be conducted, to test the robustness and generalizability of ChatGPT as an assistant for literature review. We also suggest using different data sources and databases to test the adaptability and scalability of ChatGPT. In addition, we suggest using more complex questions to evaluate literature in order to test the comprehensiveness and granularity of ChatGPT as an assistant for literature review. Also, future research should investigate if the accuracy of ChatGPT, in supporting literature review, can be improved if ChatGPT is provided with not only title and abstract but a complete paper. Lastly, it would also be interesting to compare the accuracy of ChatGPT with the accuracy of LLM specifically trained on scientific texts.

Acknowledgments. This research has been funded by both the Government of Upper Austria as part of the research grant Logistikum.Retail and by the Christian Doppler Gesellschaft as part of the Josef Ressel Centre PREVAIL.

References

1. vom Brocke, J., et al.: Reconstructing the giant: on the importance of rigour in documenting the literature search process. In: ECIS 2009 Proceedings (2009)
2. Jozefowicz, R., Vinyals, O., Schuster, M., Shazeer, N., Wu, Y.: Exploring the limits of language modeling. arXiv (2016)
3. Uszkoreit, J.: Transformer: A Novel Neural Network Architecture for Language Understanding – Google AI Blog (2017). https://ai.googleblog.com/2017/08/transformer-novel-neural-network.html
4. Radford, A., Wu, J., Child, R., Luan, D., Amodei, D., Sutskever, I.: Language models are unsupervised multitask learners, 1–9 (2019)
5. Ouyang, L., et al.: Training language models to follow instructions with human feedback. Adv. Neural. Inf. Process. Syst. **35**, 27730–27744 (2022)
6. Zhang, S., et al.: OPT: open pre-trained transformer language models. arXiv
7. Chakrabarty, T., Padmakumar, V., He, H.: Help me write a poem: instruction tuning as a vehicle for collaborative poetry writing. In: Proceedings of the 2022 Conference on Empirical Methods in Natural Language Processing, pp. 6848–6863 (2022)
8. Weidinger, L., et al.: Ethical and social risks of harm from Language Models (2021)
9. Weidinger, L., et al.: Taxonomy of risks posed by language models. In: 2022 ACM Conference on Fairness, Accountability, and Transparency, New York, NY, USA, pp. 214–229. ACM (2022). https://doi.org/10.1145/3531146.3533088
10. OpenAI: Introducing ChatGPT (2023). https://openai.com/blog/chatgpt
11. Devlin, J., Chang, M.-W., Lee, K., Toutanova, K.: BERT: pre-training of deep bidirectional transformers for language understanding. In: Proceedings of the 2019 Conference of the North American Chapter of the Association for Computational Linguistics: Human Language Technologies, pp. 4171–4186 (2019). https://doi.org/10.18653/v1/N19-1423
12. Leippold, M.: Thus spoke GPT-3: interviewing a large-language model on climate finance. Financ. Res. Lett. **53**, 103617 (2023). https://doi.org/10.1016/j.frl.2022.103617
13. Brown, T.B., et al.: Language Models are Few-Shot Learners (2020)
14. Vaswani, A., et al.: Attention is all you need. In: Advances in Neural Information Processing Systems, pp. 5998–6008 (2017). https://doi.org/10.48550/arXiv.1706.03762
15. Liu, Y., et al.: RoBERTa: a robustly optimized BERT pretraining approach. arXiv (2019)
16. Raffel, C., et al.: Exploring the limits of transfer learning with a unified text-to-text transformer. J. Mach. Learn. Res. **2020**, 5485–5551 (2020). https://doi.org/10.5555/3455716.3455856

17. OpenAI: GPT-4 Technical Report (2023)
18. Kojima, T., Gu, S.S., Reid, M., Matsuo, Y., Iwasawa, Y.: Large Language Models are Zero-Shot Reasoners (2022)
19. Snæbjarnarson, V., Einarsson, H.: Cross-Lingual QA as a Stepping Stone for Monolingual Open QA in Icelandic. Proceedings of the Workshop on Multilingual Information Access (MIA), vol. , 29–36 (2022). doi: https://doi.org/10.18653/v1/2022.mia-1.4
20. Gao, T., Xia, L.,Yu, D. (eds.): Fine-tuning pre-trained language model with multi-level adaptive learning rates for answer selection, vol. (2019)
21. DeRosa, D.M., Lepsinger, R.: Virtual Team Success: A Practical Guide for Working and Learning from Distance. Wiley (2010)
22. Hosseini-Asl, E., Asadi, S., Asemi, A., Lavangani, M.A.Z.: Neural text generation for idea generation: the case of brainstorming. Int. J. Hum.-Comput. Stud. **151** (2021)
23. Palomaki, J., Kytola, A., Vatanen, T.: Collaborative idea generation with a language model. In: Proceedings of the 2021 CHI Conference on Human Factors in Computing Systems, vol. 1–12 (2021)
24. Valvoda, J., Fang, Y., Vandyke, D.: Prompting for a conversation: how to control a dialog model? In: Proceedings of the Second Workshop on When Creative AI Meets Conversational AI, pp. 1–8 (2022)
25. Zeng, Y., Nie, J.-Y.: Open-Domain Dialogue Generation Based on Pre-trained Language Models
26. Li, D., You, J., Funakoshi, K., Okumura, M.: A-TIP: attribute-aware text Infilling via Pre-trained language model. In: Proceedings of the 29th International Conference on Computational Linguistics, pp. 5857–5869 (2022)
27. Rahali, A., Akhloufi, M.A.: End-to-End transformer-based models in textual-based NLP. AI **4**, 54–110 (2023). https://doi.org/10.3390/ai4010004
28. Ziegler, D.M., et al.: Fine-tuning language models from human preferences (2020). https://doi.org/10.48550/arXiv.1909.08593
29. Jiang, X., Liang, Y., Chen, W., Duan, N.: XLM-K: improving cross-lingual language model pre-training with multilingual knowledge. AAAI **36**, 10840–10848 (2022). https://doi.org/10.1609/aaai.v36i10.21330
30. Dunn, A., et al.: Structured information extraction from complex scientific text with fine-tuned large language models (2022)
31. Wu, T., Shiri, F., Kang, J., Qi, G., Haffari, G., Li, Y.-F.: KC-GEE: knowledge-based conditioning for generative event extraction (2022)
32. Santosh, T.Y.S.S., Chakraborty, P., Dutta, S., Sanyal, D.K., Das, P.P.: Joint entity and relation extraction from scientific documents: role of linguistic information and entity types (2021). https://ceur-ws.org/Vol-3004/paper2.pdf
33. Singh, V.K., Singh, P., Karmakar, M., Leta, J., Mayr, P.: The journal coverage of Web of science, Scopus and dimensions: a comparative analysis. Scientometrics **126**, 5113–5142 (2021). https://doi.org/10.1007/s11192-021-03948-5
34. Haman, M., Školník, M.: Using ChatGPT to conduct a literature review. Accountab. Res. 1–3 (2023). https://doi.org/10.1080/08989621.2023.2185514
35. Temsah, O., et al.: Overview of early ChatGPT's presence in medical literature: insights from a hybrid literature review by ChatGPT and human experts. Cureus **15**, e37281 (2023). https://doi.org/10.7759/cureus.37281
36. Rahman, M., Terano, H.J.R., Rahman, N., Salamzadeh, A., Rahaman, S.: ChatGPT and academic research: a review and recommendations based on practical examples. J. Educ. Mngt. Dev. Stud. **3**, 1–12 (2023). https://doi.org/10.52631/jemds.v3i1.175
37. Gupta, R., et al.: Expanding cosmetic plastic surgery research using ChatGPT. Aesthetic Surgery J. (2023). https://doi.org/10.1093/asj/sjad069

38. Ouyang, L., et al.: Training language models to follow instructions with human feedback
39. OpenAI: Best practices for prompt engineering with OpenAI API (2023). https://help.openai.com/en/articles/6654000-best-practices-for-prompt-engineering-with-openai-api
40. OpenAI: Models (2023). https://platform.openai.com/docs/models/overview
41. BigScience Workshop: BLOOM. Hugging Face (2022)
42. Touvron, H., et al.: LLaMA: Open and Efficient Foundation Language Models (2023)

Environmental Impact of Food Products: A Data Analysis Approach Using HJ-Biplot and Clustering

Johanna Vinueza-Cajas[✉][ID], Stadyn Román-Niemes[ID], Isidro R. Amaro[ID], and Saba Infante[ID]

Yachay Tech University, Hacienda San José, Urcuquí 100119, Ecuador
{johanna.vinueza,stadyn.roman,iamaro,sinfante}@yachaytech.edu.ec

Abstract. In recent decades, the impact of human activities on the environment has been worsened, and one of the causes is the food industry and its methods, which produce scarcity and overconsumption of resources. Thus, it is essential to determine and measure the environmental impact of food products by collecting data and employing appropriate statistical methods. Multivariate statistical methods allow us to analyze phenomena in a broader and more refined way, with Biplots and clustering as two of the most important. In this work, we use HJ-Biplot and k-means clustering in order to analyze data about the environmental impact of food products. The resulting plots and values show that, in general, meat products tend to impact the air and soil, plant-based products tend to affect water reserves and flow, and products that are not firmly connected to the previously mentioned categories have a lesser impact on resources. The results are consistent with the process of production or acquisition of these food products, providing valuable insights into the extent of their environmental impact.

Keywords: Data analysis · Food products · HJ-Biplot · Cluster analysis

1 Introduction

One of the major causes that have contributed to environmental degradation worldwide is the dietary choice and production practices, causing damage to land-based and water-based ecological systems, exhausting freshwater reserves, and accelerating climate change [19]. Consequently, it has become threatened to achieve the Sustainable Development Goals. For a better understanding, food production through agriculture has several negative environmental impacts. Firstly, it is responsible for emitting approximately 30% of global greenhouse gases (GHGs). In addition, it occupies around 40% of the Earth's land, contributes to nutrient pollution that significantly disrupts ecosystems and water quality, and accounts for nearly 70% of the Earth's freshwater withdrawals from rivers, reservoirs, and groundwater [3]. These are just a few examples of the detrimental effects that agricultural food production has on the environment.

T. Guarda et al. (Eds.): ARTIIS 2023, CCIS 1935, pp. 324–338, 2024.
https://doi.org/10.1007/978-3-031-48858-0_26

This research focuses on studying food products using HJ-Biplot and clustering as multivariate statistical techniques to enhance the decision-making process and more effectively recognize the various aspects of environmental effects. We analyze the impact of 211 food products composed of multiple ingredients through multivariate statistical methods because they allow us to represent complex data more efficiently and interpretably.

This paper is organized as follows: Sect. 2 provides the materials and methods describing the data and multivariate statistic methods such as HJ-Biplot and cluster analysis. Section 3 shows the results and discussion of cluster and HJ-Biplot analysis, including the goodness of fit, quality of representation, and projections. Finally, we present the conclusions of this study in Sect. 4.

2   Materials and Methods

2.1   Data Description

In this work, we considered a dataset that quantifies the environmental impact of food products across retailers in the United Kingdom and Ireland. It was retrieved from the source Our World in Data [23]. This source provided food products and variables contributing to environmental pollution, which interests us. Those indicators are greenhouse gas emissions, land use, scarcity-weighted water, freshwater withdrawals, and eutrophication-five variables in total.

The data set consists of 211 observations of food products categorized as beverages, fruits, vegetables, and nuts; cereals and bread; snacks; desserts; kitchen accessories; prepared foods; dairy, egg, meat, and plant-based alternatives. Our study is focused on quantifying the impacts of food products of multiple ingredients than those with individual commodities.

We will consider five variables and known indicators to analyze the products' environmental impact. A description [23] of these they are given below

1. Greenhouse gas emissions (per kg of food product): Emissions are measured in carbon dioxide equivalents (CO_2 eq). It refers to non-CO_2 gases weighted by the warming they cause over a 100-year timescale. Represented as **V1** in plots.
2. Land use (per kg of food product): Land use is measured in meters squared (m^2) per kilogram of a given food product. Represented as **V2** in plots.
3. Eutrophication (per kg of food product): Eutrophying emissions represent runoff of excess nutrients into the surrounding environment and waterways, which affect and pollute ecosystems. They are measured in grams of phosphate equivalents (PO_4 eq). Represented as **V3** in plots.
4. Scarcity-weighted water use (per kg of food product): Scarcity-weighted water use represents Freshwater use weighted by local water scarcity. It is measured in liters per kilogram of a food product. Represented as **V4** in plots.
5. Freshwater withdrawals (per kg of food product): Freshwater withdrawals are measured in liters per kilogram. Represented as **V5** in plots.

2.2 HJ-Biplot

Multivariate techniques can be used to analyze high-dimensional data matrices for both individuals and variables. One of the primary objectives is to decrease the dimensionality so that the data projection is onto an optimal subspace [17]. For that reason, Biplot methods have emerged as a valuable statistical technique for depicting both variables and individuals within a shared coordinate framework [4]. Gabriel developed biplot methods as statistical techniques [8], which provide a graphic representation of the structure of matrix data $Y_{m \times n}$ under a reduced subspace dimension in a manner that can be visually interpretable.

For a better understanding, this technique consists of expressing any data matrix $Y_{m \times n}$ as the product of two matrices A with dimensions $m \times s$ and as well as B with dimension $s \times n$. A Biplot is a graphical representation of a matrix $Y_{m \times n}$ that combines the display of m rows of matrix A and n columns of matrix B in a single figure. If we choose an element y_{ij} of Y, it can be written as the inner product of $a_i^T b_j$ where $a_1, ..., a_m$ are the rows markets of A and $b_1, ..., b_n$ are the columns markets of B, obtaining as result $Y = AB^T$. Hence, the data matrix Y is composed of m individuals and n variables.

Matrices A and B are typically obtained through the singular value decomposition (SVD) of matrix Y which is defined as:

$$Y = AB^T = UDV^T, \tag{1}$$

where U is the matrix whose column vectors represent the eigenvalues of YY^T. D is a diagonal matrix corresponding to the singular values, and V is a matrix whose column vectors represent the eigenvalues of Y^TY [13].

The HJ Biplot is a particular case of classical Biplots, including the JK and GH Biplots. The GH-Biplot analyses the relationships between the columns as well as higher quality of representation such that $A = U$ and $B = VD$ [13]. On the other hand, JK-Biplot analyses the similarity between the rows with a higher quality of representation in which $A = UD$ and $B = V$ [27].

As an extension of the classical Biplots, Galindo [30] proposed HJ-Biplot which is mainly based on maximizing the quality of representation of the rows and columns in the low dimensional space, for which $A = UD$ and $B = VD$. To illustrate the steps of the HJ-Biplot, we have them summarized in Fig. 1.

In the current work, we illustrate the use of the HJ-Biplot method in order to explain the relationship between the four indicators of environmental impact (columns) and the food products (rows), emphasizing the guidelines of the HJ-Biplot to interpret the results adequately. For a better understanding, we have illustrated the interpretation of the HJ- Biplot in Fig. 2.

We provide a brief description of the main guidelines for interpreting a HJ-Biplot.

1. The difference between points representing the row markets a_m approximate the similarity between the associated individuals. While closer individuals to each other, they are more similar. Hence, it will allow us to introduce the concept of clusters of individuals [4].

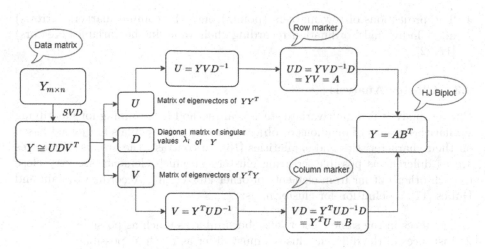

Fig. 1. Scheme of HJ-Biplot. From [1,21].

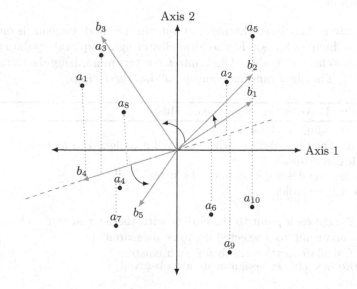

Fig. 2. Geometric interpretation of HJ-Biplot. Source: [1,17].

2. For column marker b_m, the length of arrows is interpreted as the variance of the variable. Moreover, the cosine of the angle between arrows represents their correlation between variables. Acute angles indicate that variables positively correlate [5]. Obtuse angles represent negative correlations, while right angles suggest uncorrelated variables [5,17].

3. In order to know the relationships between individuals and variables, it can be interpreted using scalar products, specifically through the orthogonal projections of row markers (points) onto the column markets (vectors) [17,22].

4. The projections of row markers (points) onto the column markers (arrows) allow individuals' ordination regarding their value in the variables (vectors) [17, 22].

2.3 Cluster Analysis

Cluster analysis is a multivariate statistical method for grouping for identifying similarities groups of invidious or objects, in which individuals are joined based on their characteristics and similarities [16]. In contrast, the groups themselves are as different as possible, creating clusters in which elements are very close to each other but far from elements of other clusters [6]. According to Jain and Dubes [11], a definition for clustering is:

1. Instances in the same cluster must be similar as much as possible.
2. Instances in the different clusters must differ as much as possible.
3. Measurement for similarity and dissimilarity must be clear and have a practical meaning.

Clusters were calculated through the k-means method. k-means is one of the most used techniques for non-hierarchical clustering in exploratory data analysis [1] that allows classifying a set of data into k clusters minimizing the intra-cluster distance [18]. The algorithm for k-means follows these steps:

Algorithm 1: Algorithm for k-means clustering.

Input   : Complete dataset
Output: The same dataset with each point assigned to a cluster
Function *K-Means*:
  Choose the desired k number of clusters.
  Select k centroids.
  do
      Assign each point to the cluster with the nearest centroid according to a selected distance measurement.
      Calculate new centroids for each cluster.
    while new cluster assignments are observed;
end

2.4 Determination of the Best k

Different methods exist for finding the best k value for k-means clustering. One of the most used methods is silhouette analysis [24], which is a graphical technique for evaluating the similarity of an object to the other objects in the same cluster and to the objects in other clusters. The silhouette coefficient is calculated for each sample and ranges from -1 to 1, where a coefficient close to 1 indicates that the sample is well-matched to its own cluster [25]. A coefficient close to -1 indicates that the sample is more similar to a different cluster [26]. The optimal number of clusters is the one that results in the highest average silhouette coefficient.

Another common method is the Bayesian Information Criterion (BIC) [7], which is used to evaluate the goodness of fit of a model. BIC is a trade-off between the goodness of fit of the model (measured by the likelihood) and the complexity of the model (measured by the number of parameters) [2,15]. The BIC penalizes models with more parameters, as they are more likely to overfit the data. Thus, the optimal number of clusters is the one that results in the lowest BIC.

Finally, another common method chosen for this work is the elbow method [12]. The elbow method is based on the within-cluster sum of squared distances (WCSS), which measures the similarity of the data points within a cluster [14]. The idea behind the elbow method is to run the k-means algorithm for a range of k values and plot the WCSS for each k value. As the number of clusters increases, the WCSS will decrease, but at some point, the decrease will become less significant as the number of clusters increases. The point at which the decrease in WCSS begins to level off is referred to as the "elbow" of the plot, and the number of clusters at this point is considered the optimal value for k [14].

3   Results and Discussion

This section presents and discusses the results from the HJ-Biplot and Clustering. Moreover, to verify if the graphical results are interpretable, we first evaluate the goodness of fit and the quality of representation of variables and individuals.

3.1   Elbow Method

The determination of the best k value for the dataset we used was done using the factoextra[1] and cluster[2] libraries of R [20]. After processing the k values and plotting them accordingly to their WCSS, the resulting plot was Fig. 3. As can be seen, the optimal number of clusters is 3, as it is the "elbow" of the plot.

3.2   Clustering and HJ-Biplot Analysis

Figure 4 shows the HJ- Biplot and clustering generated by the data. These graphics were carried out by the program Multibiplot [29] and represented 91.71% of variance. Accordingly, to the primary dataset, the individuals that belong to Cluster 2 are mainly vegetables or plant-origin products. These products are located near and around the vectors V_4 and V_5 of the HJ-Biplot corresponding to water consumption: freshwater withdrawals per kilogram and scarcity-weighted water use per kilogram, with the highest consumption individuals (according to their orthogonal projections onto the vectors) being almonds and almond butter.

---

[1] https://cran.r-project.org/package=factoextra.
[2] https://cran.r-project.org/package=cluster.

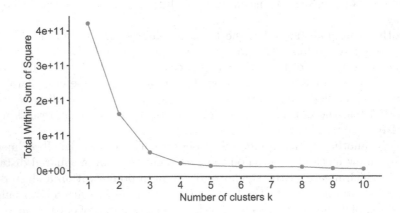

Fig. 3. Plot of the WCSS for $k = 1$ to $k = 10$

It is consistent, as plant-origin products require significant amounts of water to grow and be produced. According to the University of Massachusetts [28], This can give us insight into the overall water consumption of plant-origin products and their environmental impact.

Moreover, we can analyze the nature of the variables V_4 and V_5. As we can see in the main plot (See Fig. 4), the vectors corresponding to freshwater withdrawals per kilogram and scarcity-weighted water use per kilogram are relatively close to each other. Thus the angle between them is lesser than 90°C which means that the cosine of the angle is high, i.e., getting an acute angle, and the correlation between those variables is positive, meaning that food products that have an impact in one variable are also going to have an effect in the other. Next is the third cluster. This cluster is the smallest and contains individuals of animal origin, concretely, meat-based food products. In this case, the products impact the variables greenhouse gas emissions per kilogram, land use per kilogram, and eutrophication per kilogram, with beef steak being the highest consumption individual (according to its orthogonal projection onto the vectors). It is also consistent with reality, as meat-based products require water and significant land areas for breeding and farming. Using land for livestock accounts for 70% of the EU's agricultural land [31]. Additionally, livestock farming (along with other types of animal farming) generates greenhouse gas emissions into the atmosphere, contributing to about 12-17% of greenhouse emissions in Europe [31], and about 18% globally [10], along with the maintenance of the crops used to feed the animals.

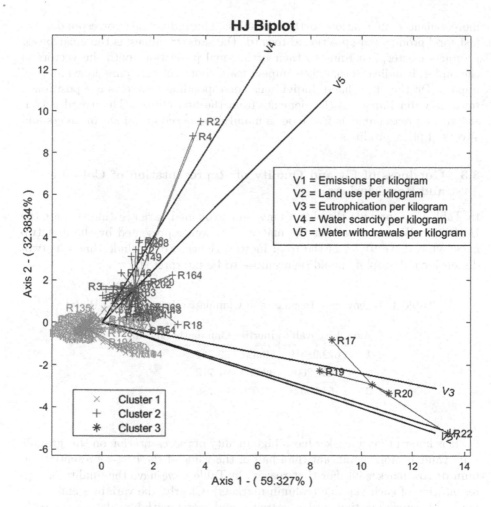

Fig. 4. HJ Biplot and clustering

Regarding the HJ-Biplot analysis of the variables, the vectors corresponding to gas emissions per kilogram and land use per kilogram are very close to each other, which, analogous to the previous interpretation, means that the correlation between both variables is very high. It means that the products with high land use also have increased greenhouse gas emissions and illustrate how both environmental impacts are very similar and generally happen together. Additionally, these two variables are less close to the eutrophication per kilogram variable, meaning that their relationship and presence in this product is not as strong but is part of the impact that those products create nonetheless.

Finally, Cluster 1 groups the remaining individuals, which are not as strongly plant or meat-based as the rest. This cluster mainly comprises pasta, sweets, and more processed food which is the most populated cluster, and its individuals are more balanced in relation to the variables. The individuals corresponding to fast food products are positioned towards the same variables as the meat-based products cluster, according to their orthogonal projections onto the vectors of the biplot. It indicates that their impact leans more onto gas emissions and land impact. On the other hand, individuals corresponding to sweets are positioned towards water impact as the elements from the first cluster. This trend is consistent and reasonable as fast food is mainly composed of animal products and sweets of plant products.

3.3   Goodness of Fit and Quality of Representation of Column and Row Markers

In Table 1, we provide the eigenvalues and explained variance (inertia) for the HJ-Biplot. We can note that the matrix Y is well represented by the first two axes, which have 91.7% of the total inertia. Hence, we conclude that this two-dimensional data plot should be accurate to be interpreted.

Table 1. Eigenvalues, Inertias, and Cumulative Inertias of HJ-Biplot

Axis	Eigenvalue	Inertia	Cumulative Inertia
1	622.93319	59.327	59.327
2	340.02600	32.383	91.710
3	53.30028	5.076	96.786

It is known that a marker has a high quality of representation on this graphic if its value is more significant than half of the value of the best-represented column or row marker [9]. For that reason, in Table 2, we have the quality of representation of each variable (column markets). Clearly, the variables emissions, land use, eutrophication, water scarcity, and water withdrawals are correctly interpreted because each of them presents a high-quality of representation (See Fig. 5).

Table 2. Quality of representation for variables (Cumulative Contributions)

Variables (per kilogram)	Dim 1	Dim 2	Dim 3
Emissions	82.70	94.94	96.54
Land use	79.11	92.07	98.12
Eutrophication	79.62	84.21	98.18
Water scarcity	18.36	93.58	96.09
Water withdrawals	36.84	93.75	95.01

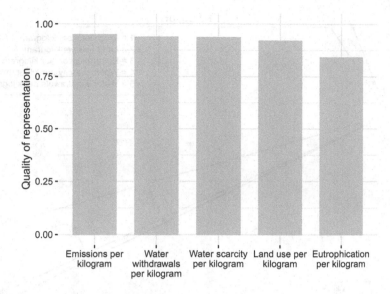

Fig. 5. Quality of representation of five variables

Furthermore, the quality of representation (cumulative contributions) for the row markets has not been included here since it is an extended list of individuals. However, we have obtained the following results as follows: Quality of representation of individuals which shows that the most of individuals present a high quality of representation.

3.4   HJ-Biplots with Projections onto the Variables

Developing projections onto the variables of interest could provide essential information to help us recognize and clarify the most relevant phenomena through HJ-Biplot. This section discusses two projections of the variables V_2 and V_3.

1. **Representation of HJ-Biplot of Cluster 3 with projection onto the variable V_2**

   As shown in Fig. 6, the individuals in Cluster 3 correspond to meat-based food products such as beef burgers, beef meatballs, beef mince, and beef steak. These individuals were projected onto the variable V_2, the land use per kilogram. We can note that the variable V_1 has more variance among the variables V_2 and V_3. On the other hand, the variables V_2 and V_1 show us a positive high correlation. We observe that the larger Euclidean distance between individuals of cluster 3 is $R17$ and $R22$, and the smallest distance is obtained between $R17$ and $R19$. The projection of individuals onto variable V_3 represents the relationship between one variable and individuals. We can say that the individual $R22$ presents the largest value of the variable V_2, followed by $R20$, $R19$, and $R17$. In the case of individual $R17$, it represents the smallest value of the variable V_2.

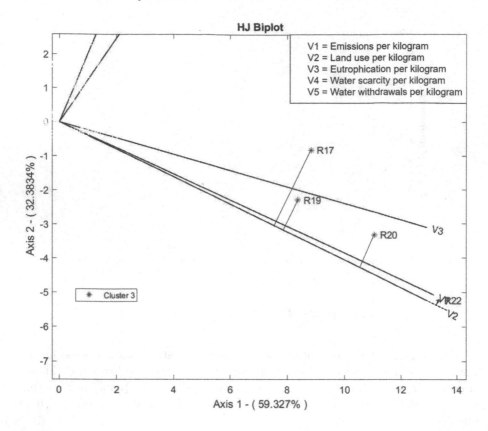

Fig. 6. Projection of individuals of cluster 3 onto V2

2. **Representation of HJ-Biplot of one individual of each Cluster with projection onto the variable V_3**

For this analysis, we have considered one individual from each cluster. The individual $R164$ corresponds to prawns, $R20$ beef mince, and $R104$ instant coffee. Those individuals were projected onto the variable V_3 eutrophication per kilogram. In Fig. 7, the beef mince represents the largest value on the variable V_3, followed by instant coffee and prawns. Instant coffee belongs to cluster 3, which corresponds to processed food. In the same way, prawns belong to Cluster 2, which are vegetables and plant-origin products and others.

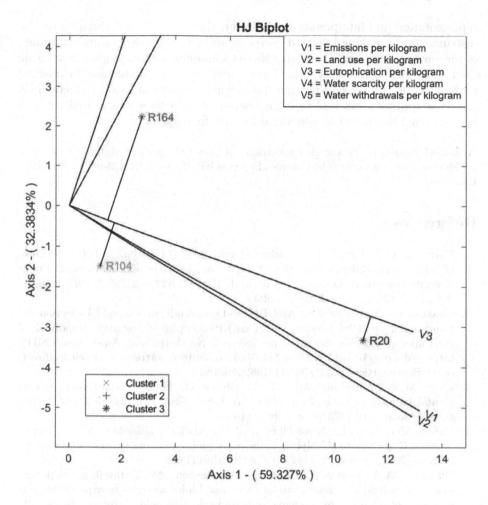

Fig. 7. Projections onto V3

4   Conclusions

In conclusion, using HJ Biplot and k-means clustering enabled us to visualize and analyze the environmental impact of the food groups and how that impact differed between groups. The findings from the HJ-Biplot provide evidence that plant-based products have the greatest impact on water reserves and ecological equilibrium, leading to resource hoarding and provoking scarcity. Conversely, meat products have the most impact on the air and land they use, using great lengths of land for their production and generating high greenhouse gas emissions. Although the data was readily available, interpreting it required substantial effort. However, applying multivariate techniques considerably enhanced the analysis, making the relationship between individuals and their impact more visible and comprehensible. Thus, multivariate techniques are helpful for data representation and interpretation. Moreover, these statistical techniques can be instrumental in making informed decisions and gaining a deeper understanding of the current situation. By utilizing these techniques, we can propose a strategic plan in the local community to implement new measures to enhance the positive environmental impact and mitigate the negative effects of food products. This strategic approach can lead to more sustainable practices and contribute to a healthier and more environmentally conscious food system.

Acknowledgment. This work was carried out under the project Statistical Methods for Modeling data generated by Complex Systems REGINV- MATH23-04, Yachay Tech University.

References

1. Carrasco, G., Molina, J.L., Patino-Alonso, M.C., Castillo, M.D.C., Vicente-Galindo, M.P., Galindo-Villardón, M.P.: Water quality evaluation through a multivariate statistical HJ-biplot approach. J. Hydrol. **577**, 123993 (2019). https://doi.org/10.1016/j.jhydrol.2019.123993
2. Chakrabarti, A., Ghosh, J.K.: AIC, BIC and recent advances in model selection. In: Bandyopadhyay, P.S., Forster, M.R. (eds.) Philosophy of Statistics, Handbook of the Philosophy of Science, vol. 7, pp. 583–605. North-Holland, Amsterdam (2011). https://doi.org/10.1016/B978-0-444-51862-0.50018-6. https://www.sciencedirect.com/science/article/pii/B9780444518620500186
3. Clark, M.A., Springmann, M., Hill, J., Tilman, D.: Multiple health and environmental impacts of foods. Proc. Natl. Acad. Sci. USA **116**, 23357–23362 (2019). https://doi.org/10.1073/pnas.1906908116
4. Cubilla-Montilla, M., Nieto-Librero, A.B., Galindo-Villardón, M.P., Torres-Cubilla, C.A.: Sparse HJ biplot: a new methodology via elastic net. Mathematics **9**, 1298 (2021). https://doi.org/10.3390/math9111298
5. Díaz-Faes, A.A., Costas, R., Galindo, M.P., Bordons, M.: Unravelling the performance of individual scholars: use of canonical biplot analysis to explore the performance of scientists by academic rank and scientific field. J. Inform. **9**, 722–733 (2015). https://doi.org/10.1016/j.joi.2015.04.006
6. Dongkuan, X., Ying-jie, T.: A comprehensive survey of clustering algorithms. Annal. Data Sci. **2**, 165–193 (2015)
7. Fraley, C., Raftery, A.E.: Model-based clustering, discriminant analysis, and density estimation. J. Am. Statist. Assoc. **97**(458), 611–631 (2002). https://doi.org/10.1198/016214502760047131
8. Gabriel, K.R.: The biplot graphic display of matrices with application to principal component analysis (1971). http://biomet.oxfordjournals.org/
9. González Cabrera, J., Fidalgo Martínez, M., Martín Mateos, E., Vicente Tavera, S.: Study of the evolution of air pollution in salamanca (spain) along a five-year period (1994-1998) using HJ-biplot simultaneous representation analysis. Environ. Modell. Softw. **21**(1), 61–68 (2006). https://doi.org/10.1016/j.envsoft.2004.10.009. https://www.sciencedirect.com/science/article/pii/S1364815204002713
10. Herrero, M., et al.: Livestock and greenhouse gas emissions: the importance of getting the numbers right. Animal Feed Sci. Technol. **166**, 779–782 (2011). https://doi.org/10.1016/j.anifeedsci.2011.04.083

11. Jain, A.K., Dubes, R.C.: Algorithms for clustering data. Prentice-Hall, Inc. (1988)
12. Kaufman, L., Rousseeuw, P.: Finding groups in data: an introduction to cluster analysis (1990). https://doi.org/10.2307/2532178
13. Martínez-Regalado, J.A., Murillo-Avalos, C.L., Vicente-Galindo, P., Jiménez-Hernández, M., Vicente-Villardón, J.L.: Using HJ-biplot and external logistic biplot as machine learning methods for corporate social responsibility practices for sustainable development. Mathematics **9**, 2572 (2021). https://doi.org/10.3390/math9202572
14. Marutho, D., Hendra Handaka, S., Wijaya, E., Muljono: The determination of cluster number at k-mean using elbow method and purity evaluation on headline news. In: 2018 International Seminar on Application for Technology of Information and Communication, pp. 533–538 (2018). https://doi.org/10.1109/ISEMANTIC.2018.8549751
15. Narisetty, N.N.: Chapter 4 - Bayesian model selection for high-dimensional data. In: Srinivasa Rao, A.S., Rao, C. (eds.) Principles and Methods for Data Science, Handbook of Statistics, vol. 43, pp. 207–248. Elsevier (2020). https://doi.org/10.1016/bs.host.2019.08.001. https://www.sciencedirect.com/science/article/pii/S0169716119300380
16. Punitha, S.C., Nathiya, G., Punithavalli.: An analytical study on behavior of clusters using EM and K-Means algorithm. Data Min. Knowl. Eng. **1**(6) (2009). issn: 0974 – 9578, http://www.ciitresearch.org/dl/index.php/dmke/article/view/DMKE092009003
17. Nieto, A.B., Galindo, M.P., Leiva, V., Vicente-Galindo, P.: Una metodología para biplots basada en bootstrapping con r. Revista Colombiana de Estadistica **37**, 367–397 (2014). https://doi.org/10.15446/rce.v37n2spe.47944
18. Omran, M., Engelbrecht, A., Salman, A.: An overview of clustering methods. Intell. Data Anal. **11**, 583–605 (2007). https://doi.org/10.3233/IDA-2007-11602
19. Poore, J., Nemecek, T.: Reducing food's environmental impacts through producers and consumers. http://science.sciencemag.org/
20. R Core Team: R: A Language and Environment for Statistical Computing. R Foundation for Statistical Computing, Vienna, Austria (2020). https://www.R-project.org/
21. Rafi Muhammad, A., Surya Wardhani, N.W., Iriany, A., Lestantyo, P.: Robust fast minimum covariance determinant elastic net HJ biplot analysis for mapping cabbage yields in Malang. Math. Statist. Eng. Appl. **71**(4), 1159–1167 (2022)
22. Riera-Segura, L., Tapia-Riera, G., Amaro, I.R., Infante, S., Marin-Calispa, H.: HJ-biplot and clustering to analyze the COVID-19 vaccination process of American and European countries. In: Narváez, F.R., Proaño, J., Morillo, P., Vallejo, D., González Montoya, D., Díaz, G.M. (eds.) SmartTech-IC 2021. CCIS, vol. 1532, pp. 383–397. Springer, Cham (2022). https://doi.org/10.1007/978-3-030-99170-8_28
23. Ritchie, H., Roser, M.: Environmental impacts of food production. Our World in Data (2020), https://ourworldindata.org/environmental-impacts-of-food
24. Rousseeuw, P.J.: Silhouettes: a graphical aid to the interpretation and validation of cluster analysis. J. Computat. Appl. Math. **20**, 53–65 (1987). https://doi.org/10.1016/0377-0427(87)90125-7. https://www.sciencedirect.com/science/article/pii/0377042787901257
25. Shahapure, K.R., Nicholas, C.: Cluster quality analysis using silhouette score. In: 2020 IEEE 7th International Conference on Data Science and Advanced Analytics (DSAA), pp. 747–748 (2020). https://doi.org/10.1109/DSAA49011.2020.00096

26. Shutaywi, M., Kachouie, N.N.: Silhouette analysis for performance evaluation in machine learning with applications to clustering. Entropy **23**(6), e23060759 (2021). https://doi.org/10.3390/e23060759. https://www.mdpi.com/1099-4300/23/6/759

27. Tenesaca-Chillogallo, F., Amaro, I.R.: COVID-19 data analysis using HJ-biplot method: a study case. Bionatura **6**, 1778–1784 (2021). https://doi.org/10.21931/RB/2021.06.02.18

28. University of Massachusetts: irrigating vegetable crops. https://ag.umass.edu/vegetable/fact-sheets/irrigating-vegetable-crops (2016)

29. Vicente-Villardón, J.: MULTBIPLOT: a package for multivariate analysis using biplots. Departamento de Estadística, Universidad de Salamanca (2010). https://biplot.usal.es/ClassicalBiplot/index.html

30. Villardón, M.P.G.: Una alternativa de representación simultánea: HJ-biplot. Qüestiió: quaderns d'estadística i investigació operativa, pp. 13–23 (1986)

31. Weishaupt, A., Ekardt, F., Garske, B., Stubenrauch, J., Wieding, J.: Land use, livestock, quantity governance, and economic instruments-sustainability beyond big livestock herds and fossil fuels. Sustainability **12**(5), 2053 (2020). https://doi.org/10.3390/su12052053. https://www.mdpi.com/2071-1050/12/5/2053

WS-YOLO: An Agronomical and Computer Vision-Based Framework to Detect Drought Stress in Lettuce Seedlings Using IR Imaging and YOLOv8

Sebastian Wolter-Salas[1] (ID), Paulo Canessa[2,3] (ID), Reinaldo Campos-Vargas[4] (ID),
Maria Cecilia Opazo[5] (ID), Romina V. Sepulveda[1(✉)] (ID), and Daniel Aguayo[6]

[1] Center for Bioinformatics and Integrative Biology, Facultad de Ciencias de la Vida,
Universidad Andrés Bello, Av. República 330, 8370186 Santiago, Chile
romina.sepulveda@unab.cl
[2] Centro de Biotecnología Vegetal, Facultad de Ciencias de la Vida, Universidad Andrés Bello,
Av. República 330, 8370186 Santiago, Chile
[3] ANID–Millennium Science Initiative–Millennium Institute for Integrative Biology (iBIO),
Av. Libertador Bernardo O'Higgins 340, 7500565 Santiago, Chile
[4] Centro de Estudios Postcosecha, Facultad de Ciencias Agronómicas, Universidad de Chile,
Av. Santa Rosa 11315, 8831314 Santiago, Chile
[5] Instituto de Ciencias Naturales, Facultad de Medicina Veterinaria y Agronomía, Universidad
de Las Américas, Av. Manuel Montt 948, 7500000 Santiago, Chile
[6] Instituto de Tecnología para la Innovación en Salud y Bienestar, Facultad de Ingeniería,
Universidad Andrés Bello, Quillota 980, 2531015 Viña del Mar, Chile

Abstract. Lettuce (*Lactuca sativa* L.) is highly susceptible to drought and water deficits, resulting in lower crop yields, unharvested areas, reduced crop health and quality. To address this, we developed a High-Throughput Phenotyping platform using Deep Learning and infrared images to detect stress stages in lettuce seedlings, which could help to apply real-time agronomical decisions from data using variable rate irrigation systems. Accordingly, a comprehensive database comprising infrared images of lettuce grown under drought-induced stress conditions was built. In order to capture the required data, we deployed a Raspberry Pi robot to autonomously collect infrared images of lettuce seedlings during an 8-day drought stress experiment. This resulted in the generation of a database containing 2119 images through augmentation. Leveraging this data, a YOLOv8 model was trained (WS-YOLO), employing instance segmentation for accurate stress level detection. The results demonstrated the efficacy of our approach, with WS-YOLO achieving a mean Average Precision (mAP) of 93.62% and an F1 score of 89.31%. Particularly, high efficiency in early stress detection was achieved, being a critical factor for improving food security through timely interventions. Therefore, our proposed High-Throughput Phenotyping platform holds the potential for high-yield lettuce breeding, enabling early stress detection and supporting informed decision-making to mitigate losses. This interdisciplinary approach highlights the potential of AI-driven solutions in addressing pressing challenges in food production and sustainability. This work contributes to the field of precision agricultural

© The Author(s), under exclusive license to Springer Nature Switzerland AG 2024
T. Guarda et al. (Eds.): ARTIIS 2023, CCIS 1935, pp. 339–351, 2024.
https://doi.org/10.1007/978-3-031-48858-0_27

technology, providing opportunities for further research and implementation of cutting-edge Deep Learning techniques for stress detection in crops.

Keywords: Digital Agriculture · Computer Vision · High-Throughput Phenotyping

1 Introduction

Nowadays, the agricultural sector has been severely affected by water shortages affecting horticultural production. The effects of water stress on horticultural crops can induce physiological stress in plants, leading to stunted growth, diminished produce quality, and increased susceptibility to pests and diseases (Molina-Montenegro et al., 2011; Knepper y Mou, 2015; Kumar et al. 2021). The resulting water scarcity has significantly affected lettuce (*Lactuca sativa* L.) an extensively cultivated leafy vegetable, requiring an adequate water supply for optimal growth and quality. Lettuce stands as one of the most extensively cultivated leafy vegetables globally, encompassing a cultivation area of 1.3 million hectares and yielding approximately 29 million tons (Kim et al. 2016; Chen et al. 2019). Various cultivation methods are employed for lettuce, including hydroponic systems, greenhouses, and plant factories, while open-field cultivation remains prevalent (Donoso 2021). However, decreased water availability necessitates appropriate water management practices, influencing irrigation strategies and crop performance. Due to the water-intensive nature of lettuce cultivation, it is especially susceptible to water stress (Kumar et al. 2021). Optimal irrigation management during the seedling stage is closely linked to future productivity and the provision of healthy, uniform seedlings, thereby impacting the overall yield of horticultural crops (Shin *et al.* 2021). In seedling farms, the determination of irrigation management predominantly relies upon cultivation techniques and the visual discernment of the crop manager (Chen et al. 2014; Yang et al. 2020). Nonetheless, deficient and subjective cultivation methods yield undesirable consequences, including escalated labour and temporal requirements.

In the context of water scarcity, the incorporation of Artificial Intelligence (AI) methodologies, specifically Deep Learning (DL), holds the potential for improving the well-being of vegetable crops, such as lettuce (Das Choudhury et al. 2019). DL algorithms excel at analyzing large volumes of data and extracting meaningful patterns, which can aid in optimizing irrigation management, predicting crop water needs, and improving resource-use efficiency (Cheng et al. 2020; Xiao *et al.* 2022; Gill et al. 2022). By leveraging the power of DL, it is possible to create predictive models that incorporate various environmental and crop-specific parameters to optimize irrigation scheduling, thereby reducing water usage and ensuring optimal plant growth (Kamarudin et al. 2021). In addition, DL algorithms can aid in the early detection and identification of plant stress symptoms caused by a lack of water, allowing for prompt intervention and mitigating yield losses (Kamarudin and Ismail 2022). For example, by analyzing Infrared (IR) imagery, these algorithms can detect minute changes in the observed phenotype, allowing for the early detection of crop stress phenotypes (Paulo et al. 2023). This early detection enables producers to implement targeted irrigation strategies, optimize resource allocation, and mitigate the adverse effects of water stress on crop health and yield (Islam and Yamane 2021; Chen et al. 2014). Thus, the precise and effective identification of stress-induced characteristics is imperative for the progression of our understanding of plant reactions to environmental stressors and the development of practical mitigation approaches.

DL models, such as YOLO, have become prominent in the field of automated and High-Throughput Phenotyping (HTP) (Buzzy et al. 2020; Zhang and Li 2022; Cardellicchio et al. 2023; Xu et al. 2023). YOLO is a sophisticated object detection and instance segmentation model that utilizes deep neural networks to identify and precisely locate objects within images (Song et al. 2021). The cutting-edge architecture has exhibited exceptional efficacy in diverse Computer Vision (CV) assignments (Chen et al. 2021). Using YOLO in plant science has significantly transformed phenotyping, providing a potent approach for automating stress-related phenotype identification and measurement (Chen et al. 2021, Xu et al. 2023). Through the process of training YOLO on extensive collections of plant images, the model can acquire the ability to identify and precisely locate stress symptoms (Mota-Delfin et al. 2022). Its real-time processing capability enables rapid analysis of large-scale datasets, facilitating HTP (James et al. 2022). This speed is critical for real-time monitoring of plant responses to stress and allows for timely interventions to mitigate damage and optimize crop management. Detailed knowledge of stress patterns in a plant population can guide targeted breeding tasks and precise agricultural interventions.

1.1 Related Work

In recent years, there have been notable advancements in the field of crop phenotyping through the utilization of CV and DL approaches (Wang and Su 2022; Jiand and Li 2020; Chandra et al. 2020; Li et al. 2020). Particularly, instance segmentation refines the classic object detection task by identifying individual object instances and segmenting them pixel-wise. Recent studies have investigated the utilization of YOLO models in order to perform instance segmentation and object detection tasks specifically for plant phenotyping.

In recent studies conducted by Khalid et al. (2023) and Qiu *et al.* (2022), a comparable methodology was employed, wherein numerous YOLO models were utilized for the timely identification of pests and illnesses in the field of agriculture. The primary objective of the research conducted by Khalid et al. (2023) is to discern and classify thistle caterpillars, red beetles, and citrus psylla pests. This was achieved through the utilization of a dataset of 9875 images, which were acquired under different lighting conditions. The YOLOv8 model demonstrates superior performance in the detection of tiny pests, surpassing prior studies with a mean Average Precision (mAP) of 84.7% and an average loss of 0.7939. Similarly, Rong et al. (2023) present a visual methodology for efficient point cloud processing of tomato organs, essential for automated crop management. The method involves segmenting tomato organs using instance segmentation and a strategy that utilizes point cloud constraints to match the organs. YOLOv5-4D detects the region of interest on tomatoes, achieving a mAP of 0.953, being slightly more accurate than the native YOLOv8 model. The proposed point cloud constraint-based search method effectively matches tomato organs in 3D space, yielding an 86.7%

success rate in multiple real scenarios. However, the utilization of YOLOv5 in the agricultural sector, particularly in crop phenotype research, has gained significant traction and reached a level of maturity (Kong et al. 2023). Liu et al. (2023) proposed Small-YOLOv5 for automatically identifying the growth period of rice, which is crucial for producing high-yield and high-quality rice. The Small-YOLOv5 approach utilizes MobileNetV3 as the backbone feature extraction network, resulting in smaller model size and fewer parameters, thus improving the detection speed. Experimental results demonstrate that Small-YOLOv5 outperforms other popular lightweight models, achieving a 98.7% mAP value at a threshold of 0.5 and a 94.7% mAP at a threshold range of 0.5 to 0.95. Moreover, Small-YOLOv5 significantly reduces the model parameters and volume. This is still project-dependent, as the work of Blekos et al. (2023) achieves the second-highest bounding box accuracy using YOLOv8 for grape maturity estimations utilizing their custom dataset of 2500 images. This result outperforms all YOLO versions, with an 11% accuracy margin compared to YOLOv3.

Previous studies in this domain have not explored the application of YOLO for this purpose in lettuce. The closest related research is the work of Wang et al. (2023), which shares similarities but focuses on microscopic imaging of stomatal opening and closure. This excellent investigation has limitations, mainly in data acquisition and in the stage of abiotic stress. However, in our study, an IR camera is utilized to capture a complete frontal view of the entire plant. This approach eliminates the need for costly microscopic cameras and allows the use of ground drones for phenotyping purposes, enhancing water usage through the early detection of water stress. Herein we develop an HTP platform for the early detection of drought stress in lettuce using the DL model YOLOv8 by IR imaging. Accordingly, we developed an autonomous platform to generate a database that comprehends the different levels of stress that can affect lettuce over an extended period of water deficit. This database was used to train a YOLOv8 model that successfully from IR images lettuces exposed to different water stress levels. This development can be used to build novel strategies for efficient water use based on automatic stress detection.

2 Methodology

2.1 Plant Material and Experimental Conditions

In order to define the state of water stress, it is necessary to grow lettuce seedlings. Lettuce seedlings (*Lactuca sativa* L. var. Capitata (L.) Janchen) were grown in a greenhouse under a controlled environment and irrigation. The lettuce seedlings were grown up to 10 days after the appearance of their true leaves continuing to the experimental phase. In this phase water was not administered to the experimental group for 8 days, maintaining a control group with normal water administration. A total of 72 individuals corresponded to the control group, meanwhile, 60 individuals corresponded to the experimental group.

2.2 Database Collection

The water deficit stress level was defined using the morphological state of the lettuce seedlings. Based on this, an autonomous robot (named as High-Performance

Autonomous Phenotyper, HPAP) with a camera capable of detecting and capturing digital images of lettuce seedlings in motion was built using Arduino. The images were using the Camera Module 2 Pi NoIR with a Sony IMX219 8-megapixel sensor and calibrated with OpenCV library using Python. In addition, 3 ultrasound sensor modules connected to the Raspberry Pi 3B were connected via a prototyping board and used to census the distance of its surroundings and make decisions on its trajectory automatically and correctively. HPAP is programmed to stay between 12 to 14 cm (cm) away from the surface where the lettuce seedlings are located, so if it is outside the threshold, it can correct its trajectory to maintain the proximity margin (Fig. 1).

2.3 Stress Detection

The stress detection was assessed using YOLOv8 instance segmentation using a total of 2119 images (named Water Stress - YOLO, or WS-YOLO). The image resolution used was 640×480 pixels. The image annotation was automated using Supervision and fine-tuned Segment Anything Model (SAM) model using 4 states: 'healthy lettuce', 'lettuce with mild stress', 'lettuce with moderate stress' and 'lettuce with severe stress' based on the morphological characteristics and literature. The control group was annotated as 'healthy' as long as it did not show symptoms of water stress. Lettuces were annotated as 'moderately stressed' when they exhibited the first symptoms of water stress, such as slight wilting of the leaves and reduced turgor. In the case of 'severe stress' (or plant death) lettuces were annotated when they had traits such as wilting, reduced leaf area, leaf decay and loss of biomass. Finally, 'mild' (or early) stressed plants belonging to the experimental group (without irrigation) were annotated when they exhibited no stress symptoms since day 1. This was corroborated in the literature (see Discussion). Furthermore, the dataset was augmented by applying a horizontal flip, crop with a minimum zoom of 13% and a maximum zoom of 50%, rotation of 20°, saturation of 20%, exposure of 15%, and up to 5% pixel noise. The dataset was divided into training, validation, and test sets (70:20:10). The hyperparameters used in WS-YOLO model were defined to achieve a trade-off between the precision of the model and its computational efficiency. A batch size of 6 was used, resulting in good training times while preserving model stability. Additionally, an initial learning rate of $1*10^5$ was implemented using 'AdamW' optimizer during 25 epochs. The incorporation of momentum of 0.85 and weight decay of $1*10^M$ was implemented to expedite convergence and forestall overfitting. The PyTorch DL framework was utilized to implement the WS-YOLO model, which underwent training on a Windows System equipped with a 14-core Intel i5 CPU and an NVIDIA RTX 3070 Ti graphics card. The pre-trained model used was YOLOv8x-seg.

2.4 Model Evaluation

The efficacy of the performed experiments on the WS-YOLO model was evaluated using Precision, Recall, F1-score, and Mean Average Precision (mAP) of 50% and between 50 and 95% of the Intersection over Union (IoU) as the evaluation metrics. The methodology for calculating is presented in the Eqs. (1–4). The abbreviations of these equations are:

True positive (TP), False Positive (FP), False Negative (FN) and Average Precision (AP).

$$\textbf{Precision} = \frac{TP}{TP + FP} \tag{1}$$

$$\textbf{Recall} = \frac{TP}{TP + FN} \tag{2}$$

$$F1 = \frac{2 * \text{Precision} * \text{Recall}}{\text{Precision} + \text{Recall}} \tag{3}$$

$$\textbf{mAP} = \frac{1}{n} \sum_{k=1}^{k=n} AP_k \tag{4}$$

3   Results and Discussion

The trained WS-YOLO model successfully detects the experimentally-defined stress levels of lettuce seedlings. The model was evaluated using Precision, Recall, F1-score, mAP (50%), and mAP (50–95%) of the lettuce image analysis for evaluating the performance and effectiveness. Table 1 displays the experimental outcomes.

Table 1. WS-YOLO performance.

Statistics	Values (%)
Precision	90.63
Recall	88.08
F1	89.31
mAP (50%)	93.62
mAP (50–95%)	74.07

The calculated precision shows that 90.63% of the instances predicted by the model are correct. This high precision value indicates a low false positive rate for this model. Furthermore, the recall value indicates that the model correctly identified 88.08% of real instances. This observation suggests a significant level of recall, indicating that the model exhibits a low rate of false negatives (Fig. 2). The F1 score is the harmonic mean of precision and recall, providing a balanced measure of both metrics. With an F1 score of 89.31%, this model has a good balance between precision and recall, obtaining the best score with 0.593 confidence (Fig. 3). The mAP at an IoU threshold of 50% measures the average precision across different segmented categories. A score of 93.62% indicates that the model achieves a high precision-recall tradeoff on average across the segmented categories. This result indicates good overall performance. The mAP assessed across a range of IoU thresholds from 50% to 95% provides a more stringent evaluation. The model demonstrates satisfactory performance in terms of precision and recall throughout a broader spectrum of IoU thresholds, albeit slightly lower than the mAP at 50%, with a value of 74.07%.

With respect to other plant phenotyping research, the values presented in this study are within good parameters. In example, the work conducted by Lin et al. (2023) introduces YOLO-Tobacco, an improved YOLOX-Tiny network designed for detecting fungal-induced diseases. This network achieved a detection accuracy of 80.45% AP, a recall of 69.27%, a precision of 86.25%, and an F1-score of 0.7683. Although these results are slightly lower compared to our findings (Table 1), this discrepancy may be attributed to the limited number of images used for model training. Conversely, Wang and He (2021) utilized the YOLOv5s model to successfully detect apple fruitlets before fruit thinning. Their study yielded favourable outcomes by employing a dataset containing 3165 images, resulting in a recall of 87.6%, precision of 95.8%, and an F1-score of 91.5%. In contrast to the previous example, these results surpass those achieved by the WS-YOLO model. Similarly, Isaac *et al.* (2023) employed the YOLOv5 model to detect cotton bolls. Their research achieved a precision of 0.84, a recall of 0.99, and an F1-score of 0.904 by utilizing a dataset comprising 9000 images. Therefore, obtaining a larger image dataset is essential for attaining improved results.

The WS-YOLO model visualization (Fig. 4) was carried out to view the segmented and detected lettuces with their stress levels across the experiment duration. According to our experimental design, the model successfully segmented healthy lettuces on day 8. This consistency is maintained throughout the experiment. In turn, Fig. 3 shows evidence of the detection of mild stress in lettuce during day 2.

Mild water stress was detected on the second day using IR images, which provide different information compared to conventional images. Numerous phenotypic alterations, such as changes in biomass, are often observable following stress treatment, although certain changes, like water content dynamics, are less obvious or subtle to discern without specialized instruments. Previous studies have mentioned that IR images would be particularly effective for analyzing water stress (Berger et al. 2010; Munns et al. 2010; Chen et al. 2014). IR cameras possess high spectral sensitivity, capturing wavelengths between 400 and 1000 nm. This range allows for capturing information about leaf width, which is influenced by their water content (Fahlgren et al. 2015). Specifically, wavelengths between 700 and 1000 nm exhibit higher reflectance in plant tissues compared to visible light, whose reflection is affected by leaf thickness (Ma et al. 2022). Osco et al. (2019) effectively identified physiological alterations resulting from water stress by employing hyperspectral imaging. Furthermore, they employed artificial neural network algorithms to classify the obtained images on the initial day of the experiment. Additionally, Basahi *et al.* (2014) determined a decrease in the relative water content in lettuce after 2 days of water stress. Moreover, the study conducted by Knepper and Mou (2015) supports this observation, reporting similar findings in three distinct lettuce varieties. Notably, only one of these strains exhibited a significant reduction in the relative water content of its leaves upon the initial day of drought stress induction. Based on this, it can be inferred that lettuce begins to experience water stress within a few days of initiating the experimental phase. Accordingly, on the fourth day, the model detected the first signs of wilting in the leaves of lettuce subjected to water stress (Fig. 4). Leaf wilting, as a morphological trait of stress, is caused by the loss of turgidity in the leaves, which eventually yields due to a lack of cellular elasticity (Seleiman et al. 2021). This finding aligns with the study conducted by Shin *et al.* 2020, where similar leaf morphology was detected on the sixth day. However, it is important to consider that environmental differences and variations in lettuce strains may influence these observations. As discussed earlier, stress begins to manifest early depending on the resistance of the specific strain. Additionally, it is worth noting that not all lettuce plants in Fig. 4 exhibit moderate stress. Some lettuce plants do not show notable morphological characteristics of this stress, which may be attributed to genetic differences. These differences can result in slightly more resistant lettuce plants compared to others in response to drought stress (Lafta *et al.* 2021; Park et al. 2021). By the eighth day of water stress, a complete leaf drooping is observed, with reduced leaf area and length, indicating severe stress or plant death. This condition is attributed to the low soil moisture content and insufficient physiological responses to cope with advanced water stress.

The novelty of our study resides in the integration of CV techniques to tackle the difficult task of detecting early stress in crops with a vision of inexpensive agronomic management. Although previous work explored the use of CV methods to determine plant phenotypes, the use of the YOLOv8 (WS-YOLO) model to assess stress levels in lettuce by IR cameras, to our knowledge, is unprecedented. This innovative approach leverages YOLOv8's segmentation capabilities, allowing for precise identification and characterization of stress-induced phenotypic changes through IR imaging with good accuracy. In addition, the creation of a comprehensive database of IR images obtained through automated data collection of the Raspberry Pi robot expands the range of alternatives for data collection for similar research studies. As a result, our research innovates by combining the most advanced DL techniques with automated IR data collection, leading to alternatives for precision irrigation, food safety and sustainability.

While there have been notable advancements in crop phenotyping and instance segmentation using YOLO-based models, there remain challenges in handling diverse environmental conditions, scale variations, and occlusions in crop images. Our study has revealed promising findings regarding the use of YOLOv8 for stress detection in lettuce. However, there are several areas that warrant further investigation in future research. Firstly, it would be beneficial to expand the application of this approach to different crop species to assess its generalizability and effectiveness. Water stress caused by drought is already causing issues in the cultivation of various leafy vegetables (Khalid et al. 2022). Additionally, an intriguing avenue for future research involves incorporating temporal dynamics into the model. This would involve training the WS-YOLO model on sequential imagery, enabling real-time stress monitoring throughout the entire lifecycle of a crop. Additionally, considering the ever-evolving landscape of deep learning architectures, it would be valuable for future studies to evaluate the performance of emerging and older models and architectures in comparison to WS-YOLO. This could potentially lead to even higher levels of accuracy in stress detection. Finally, it is necessary to assess the phenotypic state using omics techniques. This has the potential to enhance the classification and robustness of this study.

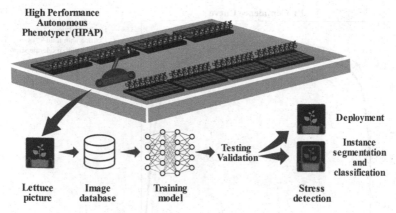

Fig. 1. Experimental design for WS-YOLO development.

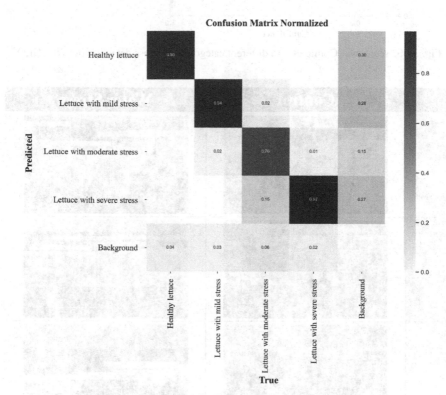

Fig. 2. Normalized Confusion Matrix of WS-YOLO.

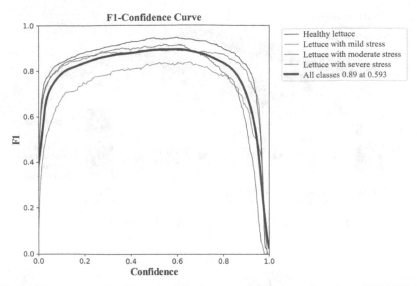

Fig. 3. F1 score over Confidence in different categories of stress detection of WS-YOLO.

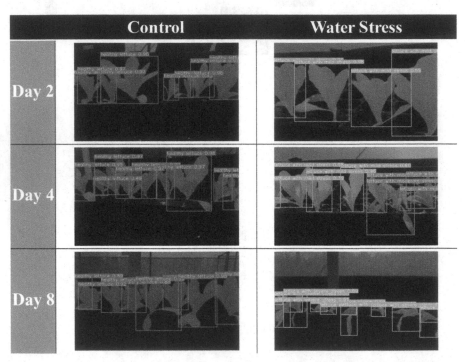

Fig. 4. WS-YOLO detection on Control and Water Stress group through the duration of the experiment.

4 Conclusion and Future Perspectives

This research contributes to the field of agricultural technology and stress detection in lettuce. By introducing a novel HTP platform that leverages DL, Robotics, and CV, the study addresses the critical challenge of early stress detection through IR imaging in lettuce, crucial for ensuring food security and mitigating yield losses. The application of WS-YOLO model with instance segmentation demonstrates promising results, achieving a mAP of 93.62% and an F1 score of 89.31%. These findings showcase the efficacy and potential of AI-driven solutions in tackling pressing challenges in food production and sustainability. Moreover, the creation of a comprehensive database of IR images through autonomous data collection further enriches the scientific knowledge base and opens opportunities for further research in cutting-edge DL techniques for stress detection in crops.

Nonetheless, effectively demonstrating water stress in lettuce through experimental analysis is crucial. This approach would provide greater robustness in phenotype detection and enable the characterization of the physiology of this lettuce strain.

Acknowledgement. This research was funded by ANID BECAS/DOCTORADO NACIONAL (2023) 21231516 (S.W.S.), ANID/FONDECYT 1200260 (R.C.V.), FONDEF ID19I10160 (D.A.), Proyecto interno UDLA DI-08/22 (C.O.), ANID/Millennium Science Initiative Program ICN17_022 and ANID/FONDECYT 1190611 (P.C.).

References

Basahi, J.: Effects of Enhanced UV-B Radiation and Drought Stress on Photosynthetic Performance of Lettuce (*Lactuca sativa* L. Romaine) Plants. Ann. Res. Rev. Biol. **4**, 1739–1756 (2014)

Berger, B., Parent, B., Tester, M.: High-throughput shoot imaging to study drought responses. J. Exp. Bot. **61**, 3519–3528 (2010)

Blekos, A., et al.: A grape dataset for instance segmentation and maturity estimation. Agronomy **13**, 1995 (2023)

Buzzy, M., Thesma, V., Davoodi, M., Mohammadpour Velni, J.: Real-time plant leaf counting using deep object detection networks. Sensors **20**, 6896 (2020)

Cardellicchio, A., et al.: Detection of tomato plant phenotyping traits using YOLOv5-based single stage detectors. Comput. Electron. Agric.. Electron. Agric. **207**, 107757 (2023)

Chandra, A.L., Desai, S.V., Guo, W., Balasubramanian, V.N.: Computer Vision with Deep Learning for Plant Phenotyping in Agriculture: A Survey. arXiv 1–26 (2020). https://doi.org/10.48550/arXiv.2006.11391

Chen, D., et al.: Dissecting the phenotypic components of crop plant growth and drought responses based on high-throughput image analysis. Plant Cell **26**, 4636–4655 (2014)

Chen, W., Zhang, J., Guo, B., Wei, Q., Zhu, Z.: An apple detection method based on Des-YOLO v4 algorithm for harvesting robots in complex environment. Math. Probl. Eng.Probl. Eng. **2021**, 1–12 (2021)

Chen, Z., et al.: Assessing the performance of different irrigation systems on lettuce (*Lactuca sativa* L.) in the greenhouse. PLOS ONE **14**, e0209329 (2019)

Cheng, Q., Zhang, S., Bo, S., Chen, D., Zhang, H.: Augmented reality dynamic image recognition technology based on deep learning algorithm. IEEE Access **8**, 137370–137384 (2020)

Das Choudhury, S., Samal, A., Awada, T.: Leveraging image analysis for high-throughput plant phenotyping. Front. Plant Sci. 10 (2019)

Donoso, G.: Management of water resources in agriculture in chile and its challenges. Int. J. Agric. Natural Resources 48, 171–185 (2021)

Fahlgren, N., Gehan, M.A., Baxter, I.: Lights, camera, action: high-throughput plant phenotyping is ready for a close-up. Curr. Opin. Plant Biol.. Opin. Plant Biol. 24, 93–99 (2015)

Gill, T., Gill, S.K., Saini, D.K., Chopra, Y., de Koff, J.P., Sandhu, K.S.: A comprehensive review of high throughput phenotyping and machine learning for plant stress phenotyping. Phenomics 2, 156–183 (2022)

Islam, M.P., Yamane, T.: HortNet417v1—a deep-learning architecture for the automatic detection of pot-cultivated peach plant water stress. Sensors 21, 7924 (2021)

James, K.M.F., Sargent, D.J., Whitehouse, A., Cielniak, G.: High-throughput phenotyping for breeding targets—Current status and future directions of strawberry trait automation. Plants, People, Planet 4, 432–443 (2022)

Kamarudin, M.H., Ismail, Z.H.: Lightweight deep CNN models for identifying drought stressed plant. IOP Conf. Ser. Earth Environ. Sci. 1091, 012043 (2022)

Kamarudin, M.H., Ismail, Z.H., Saidi, N.B.: Deep learning sensor fusion in plant water stress assessment: a comprehensive review. Appl. Sci. 11, 1403 (2021)

Khalid, M.F., et al.: Alleviation of drought and salt stress in vegetables: crop responses and mitigation strategies. Plant Growth Regul.Regul. 99, 177–194 (2022)

Khalid, S., Oqaibi, H.M., Aqib, M., Hafeez, Y.: Small pests detection in field crops using deep learning object detection. Sustainability 15, 6815 (2023)

Kim, M. J., Moon, Y., Tou, J. C., Mou, B., Waterland, N.L.: Nutritional value, bioactive compounds and health benefits of lettuce (Lactuca sativa L.). J. Food Composition Anal. 49, 19–34 (2016)

Knepper, C., Mou, B.: Semi-high throughput screening for potential drought-tolerance in lettuce (lactuca sativa) germplasm collections. J. Vis. Exp. 98, 1–6 (2015)

Kong, S., Li, J., Zhai, Y., Gao, Z., Zhou, Y., Xu, Y.: Real-time detection of crops with dense planting using deep learning at seedling stage. Agronomy 13, 1503 (2023)

Kumar, P., Eriksen, R. L., Simko, I., Mou, B.: Molecular mapping of water-stress responsive genomic loci in lettuce (Lactuca spp.) using kinetics Chlorophyll fluorescence, hyperspectral imaging and machine learning. Front. Genetics 12 (2021)

Lafta, A., Sandoya, G., Mou, B.: Genetic variation and genotype by environment interaction for heat tolerance in crisphead lettuce. HortScience 56, 126–135 (2021)

Li, Z., Guo, R., Li, M., Chen, Y., Li, G.: A review of computer vision technologies for plant phenotyping. Comput. Electron. Agric.. Electron. Agric. 176, 105672 (2020)

Lin, J., et al.: Improved YOLOX-Tiny network for detection of tobacco brown spot disease. Front. Plant Sci. 14 (2023)

Liu, K., Wang, J., Zhang, K., Chen, M., Zhao, H., Liao, J.: A lightweight recognition method for rice growth period based on improved YOLOv5s. Sensors 23, 6738 (2023)

Ma, Z., et al.: A review on sensing technologies for high-throughput plant phenotyping. IEEE Open J. Instr. Measure. 1, 1–21 (2022)

Mota-Delfin, C., López-Canteñs, G. de J., López-Cruz, I.L., Romantchik-Kriuchkova, E., Olguín-Rojas, J.C.: Detection and counting of corn plants in the presence of weeds with convolutional neural networks. Remote Sensing 14, 4892 (2022)

Munns, R., James, R.A., Sirault, X.R.R., Furbank, R.T., Jones, H.G.: New phenotyping methods for screening wheat and barley for beneficial responses to water deficit. J. Exp. Bot. 61, 3499–3507 (2010)

Osco, L.P., et al.: Modeling hyperspectral response of water-stress induced lettuce plants using artificial neural networks. Remote Sensing 11, 2797 (2019)

Park, S., Kumar, P., Shi, A., Mou, B.: Population genetics and genome-wide association studies provide insights into the influence of selective breeding on genetic variation in lettuce. The Plant Genome **14** (2021)

de Paulo, R.L., Garcia, A.P., Umezu, C.K., de Camargo, A.P., Soares, F.T., Albiero, D.: Water stress index detection using a low-cost infrared sensor and excess green image processing. Sensors **23**, 1318 (2023)

Qiu, R.-Z., et al.: An automatic identification system for citrus greening disease (Huanglongbing) using a YOLO convolutional neural network. Frontiers in Plant Science **13** (2022)

Rong, J., Yang, Y., Zheng, X., Wang, S., Yuan, T., Wang, P.: Three-Dimensional Plant Pivotal Organs Photogrammetry on Cherry Tomatoes Using an Instance Segmentation Method and a Spatial Constraint Search Strategy. (2023). https://doi.org/10.2139/ssrn.4482155

Seleiman, M.F., et al.: Drought stress impacts on plants and different approaches to alleviate its adverse effects. Plants **10**, 259 (2021)

Song, P., Wang, J., Guo, X., Yang, W., Zhao, C.: High-throughput phenotyping: breaking through the bottleneck in future crop breeding. Crop J. **9**, 633–645 (2021)

Wang, D., He, D.: Channel pruned YOLO V5s-based deep learning approach for rapid and accurate apple fruitlet detection before fruit thinning. Biosys. Eng.. Eng. **210**, 271–281 (2021)

Wang, J., Renninger, H., Ma, Q., Jin, S.: StoManager1: An Enhanced, Automated, and High-throughput Tool to Measure Leaf Stomata and Guard Cell Metrics Using Empirical and Theoretical Algorithms. *arXiv* 1–15 (2023). https://doi.org/10.48550/arXiv.2304.10450

Wang, Y., et al.: Insights into the stabilization of landfill by assessing the diversity and dynamic succession of bacterial community and its associated bio-metabolic process. Sci. Total. Environ. **768**, 145466 (2021)

Wang, Y.-H., Su, W.-H.: Convolutional neural networks in computer vision for grain crop phenotyping: a review. Agronomy **12**, 2659 (2022)

Xiao, Q., Bai, X., Zhang, C., He, Y.: Advanced high-throughput plant phenotyping techniques for genome-wide association studies: a review. J. Adv. Res. **35**, 215–230 (2022)

Xu, J., Yao, J., Zhai, H., Li, Q., Xu, Q., Xiang, Y., Liu, Y., Liu, T., Ma, H., Mao, Y., Wu, F., Wang, Q., Feng, X., Mu, J. & Lu, Y. TrichomeYOLO: A Neural Network for Automatic Maize Trichome Counting. *Plant Phenomics* **5,** (2023)

Yang, W., et al.: Crop phenomics and high-throughput phenotyping: past decades, current challenges, and future perspectives. Mol. Plant **13**, 187–214 (2020)

Zhang, P., Li, D.: YOLO-VOLO-LS: a novel method for variety identification of early lettuce seedlings. Front. Plant Sci. **13** (2022)

Deep Learning Model for the Recognition of Its Environment of an Intelligent System

Jesús Ocaña[1]([⊠]) [ID], Guillermo Miñan[1] [ID], Luis Chauca[1] [ID], Víctor Ancajima[2] [ID], and Luis Leiva[3]

[1] Universidad Tecnológica del Perú, Km 424 Panamericana Norte - Calle 56, Chimbote, Perú
{c25777,c20342,jchauca}@utp.edu.pe
[2] Universidad Católica Los Ángeles de Chimbote. Jr, Tumbes 247, Chimbote, Perú
vancajimam@uladech.edu.pe
[3] Universidad Nacional del Santa., Av., Pacifico 508 Urb. Buenos Aires – Nvo., Chimbote, Perú
lleiva@uns.edu.pe

Abstract. This research project consisted in the design of an Artificial Neural Network with Deep Learning for an intelligent system, they were installed twelve sensors ultrasonic HC-SR04, which ones detected and learned all kinds of obstacles, such as: walls, tables, chairs and others. The methodology used was the concurrent design has five phases: the first the conceptual plan was carried out, the second a kinematic study, the third a dynamic study, the fourth a mechanical project and finally the simulation of the system. Artificial Neural Networks were designed with Deep Learning and trained with the Backpropagation algorithm. The ANN was programmed and recorded in the Arduino Mega 2560 module. All the corresponding simulations were carried out, it was verified that the ultrasonic sensors have sent the signal to the Artificial Neural Network with deep learning and they carried out a learning of their environment, they were also checked the displacement of the mobile robot resulting in the desired performance. In conclusion, the proposed design was achieved and it was simulated with all kinds of events, in addition it was verified that Artificial Neural Networks with deep learning can detect and learn from all the obstacles that are in their environment.

Keywords: Deep Learning · Artificial neural networks · mobile robot · security

1 Introduction

The detection of walls, tables, chairs and other objects by robots continues to be one of the exploration matters in the robotics sector, all these mentioned objects have different dimensions. Therefore, the identification of walls, tables, chairs and, among other things, it is fundamental due to the variety of shapes that the object has. For example, understanding the detection of different objects could promote the autonomy of robots. Determining the locations of objects and crossing narrow spaces can help wheelchair automation and locomotion work is completely independent of robots [1]. To solve this problem, they were used ANN with deep learning.

Deep learning is an issue that is becoming increasingly relevant in the field of artificial intelligence (AI). Being a subclass of machine learning, deep learning is the science of training artificial neural networks on very large data. Deep neural networks (DNN) manage to have hundreds of millions of data [2, 3], which accepts difficult application configuration such as non-linear operation. They elaborate a compressed abstraction of the situation from the information provided by the sensors, which are frequently located in the robots [4]. However, various developments have gradually changed the non-linear operation, what is currently called deep learning.

An Artificial neural network, therefore, at all times has an input layer, an output layer and contains hidden layers. The definition of Deep Learning begins by employing a number of hidden layers in artificial neural networks [5].

Artificial neural networks in the 1980s, were used with much welcome to the automatic robot [6].

Hinton presented a training procedure that demonstrated that multilayered artificial neural networks are efficient [7]. The emergence of this technology led to an attraction to this deep learning research at an unprecedented speed [8].

Deep learning has advanced in image verification systems [9] and has also focused on controlling handwriting recognition zones [10], video recognition [11], image verification [12], verification biomedical imaging [13–15]. It has also achieved superhuman accuracy in various image identification participations [9, 16, 17]. Researchers are more frequently studying deep learning algorithms [18]. Possibly the speed or skill will be a next success where the machines will begin to express the human domain. If it is true, deep neural networks will be the type of learning that will dominate in the future.

Deep learning algorithms have been implemented in the computer system, and developed in the humanoid robot models. Currently learning algorithms claim human cognitive aptitude and help the use of robots in frequent environments. Within these algorithms are the Convolutional Neural Networks (CNNs), which have proven to be excellent in object recognition, location and detection projects, becoming more effective in terms of accuracy in the execution of these activities [19].

Robotics is not restricted to just running and walking like humans, robot education is also found, in mobile movement in pedestrian environments, automated container/shelf gathering, combat robot reset, overhaul and repair of automated aircraft, sending robots in high-risk areas and others [20–22].

As antecedent, is mentioned Enciso [23] in his research project "Design of an autonomous navigation system for mobile robots using sensor fusion and neuro-fuzzy controllers", he reached the following conclusion: autonomous navigation was simulated using the algorithm of Developed control and location by sensor fusion for the model of a car-type mobile robot, ultimately checking the good performance of the system. The results obtained during the development of the investigations show that the designed navigation system is perfectly applicable in real situations and can be adapted to various scenarios.

Burak y Kaya [24] denominada "Comparison of deep learning techniques for detection of doors in indoor environments", llegó a la siguiente conclusión que intentó exhibir la capacidad de la construcción de aprendizaje profundo fundamentado en puntos para las dificultades de detección de puertas. Sus logros se fundamentan en la longitud y el ángulo entre los marcos de la puerta y la ubicación del sensor.

In the investigation by Joaquín, Cristian, Luis and David [25] called "Performance Evaluation of Convolutional Networks on Heterogeneous Architectures for Applications in Autonomous Robotics", they obtained the following conclusion that despite the development of deep learning prototypes in the conventional computer system of humanoid robots, the duration of the process in the course of object recognition are forced by the high computational cost required by types of deep learning such as Artificial Neural Networks.

This research project aims to design an Artificial Neural Network with Deep Learning for recognition its environment by a security guard mobile robot. It was modeled with twelve HC-SR04 ultrasonic sensors, Artificial Neural Networks with deep learning were used and for training the backpropagation algorithm, to record the ANN with deep learning described, the Arduino Mega 2560 module was used.

It was concluded that the proposed model was verified with the simulations, verifying that Artificial Neural Networks with deep learning learn and corroborating the response time of the system, providing an effective result for future development.

2   Materials and Methods

The research design was non-experimental and a descriptive-propositive type, which a mobile robot with Artificial Neural Network with Deep Learning was designed and described for the recognition of its environment; considering that the investigation was of a transactional type, since the collection of information was carried out in a single circumstance.

The methodology used for this research is the concurrent design [26], which consists of five phases:

Conceptual Design. In this first phase, the requirements and technical specifications of the components to be used were analyzed, as well as the frame, dimensions, travel and operating time of the mobile robot.

Kinematic Analysis. In this phase, the analysis of the movement of the mobile robot was carried out, for which the differential type mobile robot was proposed and for recognition of its environment, twelve HC-SR04 ultrasonic sensors were chosen, strategically installed in the mobile robot.

Dynamic Analysis. In this phase, the dynamic part of the mobile robot was analyzed, which allowed the choice of motors, the design of the system that controls the robot, the training of Artificial Neural Networks with Deep Learning.

Mechanical Design. In this phase, kinematics and dynamics were integrated and the different stages that make up the methodology were listed, based on the creation of projects and the development of electronic circuits.

Simulation Tests. In this last stage, the simulation of the system was carried out with the Proteus 8 Professional program and the code developed is the Arduino IDE program, all the tests were also carried out with Neural Networks with Deep Learning. This simulation made it possible to verify the expected operation of the system.

3   Proposed Mode

Control System Circuit. In this stage, the Arduino Mega 2560 was used, with twelve HC-SR04 Ultrasonic sensors. Artificial Neural Networks were also trained with Deep Learning, using the Backpropagation algorithm.

The 12 HC-SR04 ultrasonic sensors are distributed in the mobile robot in this way: 2 sensors are looking at the floor, which verify that there is no hole or other similar, 4 ultrasonic sensors are installed in front at 20 cm from the floor, to detect small objects and the legs of chairs or tables, 2 ultrasonic sensors are also installed in front 50 cm from the floor, which detect high objects, 2 sensors are installed on the right side and 2 sensors are installed on the left of the robot (Fig. 1).

The following Table shows the 12 ultrasonic sensors, activation of the motors and the movement it performs.

Table 1 shows the 12 sensors that are distributed as S1, S2, S3, S4, S5, S6, S7, S8, S9, S10, S11 and S12. The first M1 engine and the second M2 engine are not considered the M3 engine and M4 engine, because they have the same functionality as the M1 and M2 engines. The table only shows 12 combinations, in total there are 144 combinations that the Artificial Neural Network was trained with Deep Learning.

The proposed neural network architecture is a backpropagation of two hidden layers, due to the amount of data to be input.

There is no specific formula to determine the number of neurons to use, but some approximate rules have been used that are recommended to be used to assign the number of neurons that the hidden layer will have.

Calculation of the ratio between the input neuron and the output neuron.

$$R = \left(\frac{IN}{ON} \right)^{\frac{1}{3}} \tag{1}$$

R: Ratio
IN: Input Neuron $= 12$ neurons
ON: Output Neuron $= 4$ neurons

$$R = \left(\frac{12}{4} \right)^{\frac{1}{3}}$$

$$R = 1.44$$

Calculation of the First layer

$$C_1 = ON * R^2 \tag{2}$$

$$C_1 = 4 * (1.44)^2$$

$$C_1 = 8 \ neurons$$

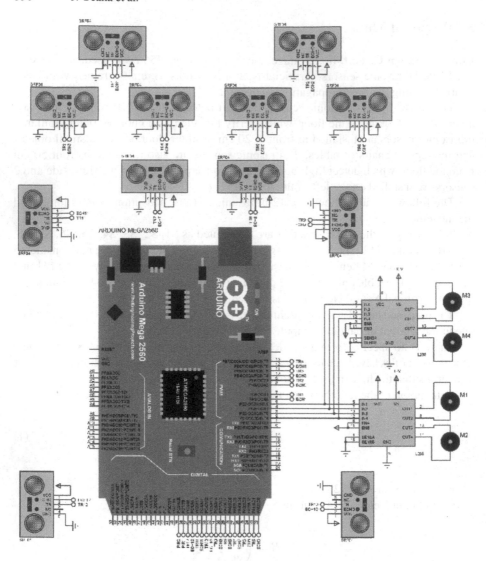

Fig. 1. Control circuit.

Table 1. The truth table of the sensors and activation of the motors

S. Floor		S. Forward				S. Stop		S. Left		S. Right		Motor		displacement
Detect floor		Detect left		Detect Right		Detect stop		Detect left		Detect right				
S1	S2	S3	S4	S5	S6	S7	S8	S9	S10	S11	S12	M1	M2	
0	0	0	0	0	0	0	0	0	0	0	0	1	0	1	0	go forward
1	1	0	0	0	0	0	0	0	0	0	0	0	1	0	1	go back
0	0	1	1	0	0	0	0	0	0	0	0	1	0	0	1	right side
0	0	0	0	1	1	0	0	0	0	0	0	0	1	1	0	left
0	0	1	1	1	1	0	0	0	0	0	0	0	1	1	0	left
0	0	1	1	1	1	1	1	0	0	0	0	0	1	1	0	left
0	0	1	1	1	1	1	1	1	1	0	0	1	0	0	1	right side
0	0	1	1	1	1	1	1	0	0	1	1	0	1	1	0	left
0	0	0	0	0	0	1	1	0	0	0	0	1	0	0	1	right side
0	0	0	0	0	0	0	0	1	1	1	1	1	0	1	0	go forward
0	0	1	1	1	1	0	0	1	1	1	1	0	1	0	1	go back
0	0	1	1	1	1	1	1	1	1	1	1	0	1	0	1	go back

Calculation of the Second layer

$$C_1 = ON * R \tag{3}$$

$$C_1 = 4 * 1.44$$

$$C_1 = 6\,neurons$$

The design of the Artificial Neural Network is composed of 12 input neurons, the first hidden layer contains 8 neurons, the second hidden layer contains 6 neurons, and the output consists of 4 neurons. These output neurons are the ones that controlled the motors, the O1 and O2 neuron controlled the M1 motor, the O3 and O4 neuron controlled the M2 motor. It was trained with the Backpropagation algorithm (Fig. 2).

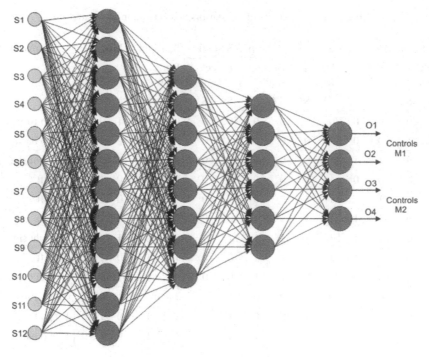

Fig. 2. Deep learning design

Training the Neural Network with the Backpropagation algorithm in Matlab. For the simulation, the Matlab NNTool neural network tool was used. The Matlab NNTool allows to create, train and simulate this type of Artificial Neural Network (RNA) [27] (Fig. 3).

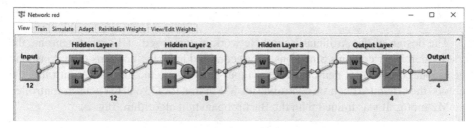

Fig. 3. Training deep learning in Matlab

In the previous figure you can see the result after training, to show this result we have made as 8 Train Network, it shows us the training, the validation, the test and all, giving R = 1 as the optimal response, indicating that the ANN have learned correctly.

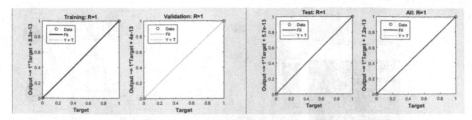

Fig. 4. ANN training result.

4 Results

The code with the neural networks was recorded on the Arduino Mega 2560, the outputs of the ultrasonic sensors were checked in binary form, for example, the two sensors that are looking at the floor verify that there is no hole or other similar, it was coded on the Arduino IDE in this way, if the distance is greater than 15 cm it will send "1" and if there are no gaps it will send "0" to the Artificial Neural Network, of the other ultrasonic sensors, 4 ultrasonic sensors are installed in front 20 cm from the floor, 2 ultrasonic sensors are also installed in front at 50 cm from the floor. The remaining 10 ultrasonic sensors were coded in this way, if there is no object at 20 cm it will send "0" and if there is an object close to 20 cm it will send "1" to the Artificial Neural Network. For the verification of the data input to the Artificial neural network, the Proteus Virtual terminal was placed.

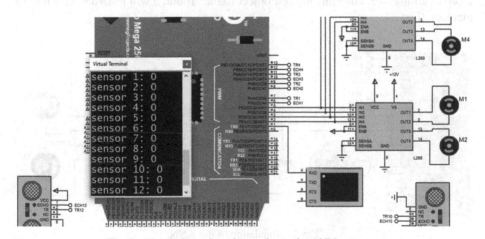

Fig. 5. Simulation when the entries to the ANN are zero.

In Fig. 4 it can be seen that all the sensors send Zeros to the ANN, that means that there is no obstacle and the mobile robot must move forward.

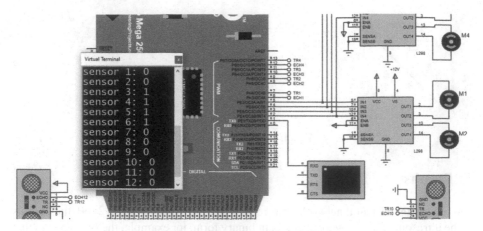

Fig. 6. Simulation of the ANN.

In Fig. 5 it can be seen that 4 sensors S3, S4, S5 and S6, which are in the front, at the bottom have detected a small object, and the sensors that are 50 cm away have not detected anything, this tells us shows the robot moves to the left. All the simulation tests were carried out and verified with Table 1.

Mobile Robot Displacement Tests

The simulation tests carried out by the control of the artificial neural networks with Deep Learning, was efficient, any new object found around it will learn and save it in its memory (Fig. 7).

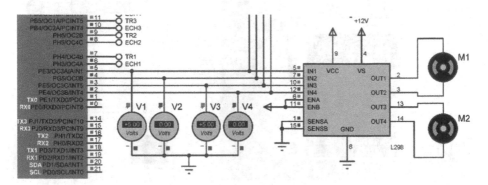

Fig. 7. Simulation of the ANN.

Figure 6 shows the data from the neural network is sent to the motor controller; In order to check the displacement of the robot, voltmeters were placed between the Arduino Mega and the motor controller. The voltage values obtained correspond to the displacement of the mobile robot, the figure shows V1 = 5V, V2 = 0V, V3 = 5V and V4 = 0V, these values correspond in binary 1 – 0 for a motor and 1 – 0 for the another motor, therefore, the robot will move forward. In this way, the movements of the mobile robot in all directions were verified.

Table 2. Result of simulation tests with ANN

Salida de la RNA				V1 Voltios	V2 Voltios	V3 Voltios	V4 Voltios	Motion
1	0	1	0	5	0	5	0	Avanza
0	1	1	0	0	5	5	0	Left
1	0	0	1	5	0	0	5	Right
0	1	0	1	0	5	0	5	go back
0	0	0	0	0	0	0	0	Stop

Table 2 shows the voltage of the four voltmeters called V1, V2, V3 and V4, connected to the motor controller; the 5V voltage corresponds to the value "1" in binary and the 0V voltage corresponds to "0" in binary. In the simulation we check that the values sent by the ANN 1 0 1 0, this means that no ultrasonic sensor is activated, the ANN sends a signal to the motor driver and the mobile robot will move forward. The values sent by the ANN 0 1 1 0, this means that it has detected an object to the right, the ANN sends a signal to the motor driver and the mobile robot heads to the left, likewise all the displacements of the mobile robot.

5 Discussion

Enciso [23], maintain in their research work "Design of an autonomous navigation system for mobile robots using sensor fusion and neuro-fuzzy controllers", points out that autonomous navigation was simulated using the developed control algorithm and localization by fusion of sensors for the model of a car-type mobile robot, ultimately verifying the good performance of the system. The results obtained during the development of the research show that the designed navigation system is perfectly applicable in real situations and can be adapted to various scenarios. In this research, a displacement system with Artificial Neural Networks was chosen in Deep Learning and for this, twelve HC-SR04 ultrasonic sensors were installed on the mobile robot. Ultrasonic sensors with obstacles were simulated, resulting in a displacement system perfectly applicable in real situations.

They also allow us to corroborate, as de Burak and Kaya [24] called "Comparison of deep learning techniques for detection of doors in indoor environments", indicating that in this research, he tried to show the capacity of deep learning architectures based on the difficulties of door detection, taking into account the length and angle between the door frames and the location of the sensors. In this investigation, it was possible to implement twelve HC-SR04 ultrasonic sensors, strategically installed to detect all kinds of obstacles, such as walls, tables, chairs and other objects.

On the other hand, in the research by Joaquín, Cristian, Luis and David [25] called "Performance Evaluation of Convolutional Networks on Heterogeneous Architectures for Applications in Autonomous Robotics", they point out that despite the development of deep learning prototypes using software, The duration of the process in the course of object recognition are forced by the high computational cost required by types of deep learning such as Artificial Neural Networks. In this investigation, it was possible to design the ANN with Deep Learning and the operation of the HC-SR04 ultrasonic sensors was verified, to detect all the objects in its environment, this sensor was used because it is low cost.

6 Discussion

Based on the proposed design, the movement of the mobile robot was simulated with Artificial Neural Networks with Deep Learning and the robot could be located through the distribution of twelve HC-SR04 ultrasonic sensors, verifying the proper functioning of the system, showing that the designed movement is perfectly adaptable in real spaces and can be applied to different scenarios.

The tests of the recognition system of all kinds of obstacles from walls, tables, chairs and other objects were carried out, and the mobile robot with Artificial Neural Networks in Deep Learning, responded appropriately for the different movements, go forward, stop, left, right and goes back, correctly checking the operation of the system, resulting in the expected operation.

It was possible to design the Artificial Neural Network with Deep Learning and it was trained with the Backpropagation algorithm, the operation of the HC-SR04 ultrasonic sensors was verified, detecting all the objects in its environment, this sensor was used because it was cheap.

Therefore, this research can be a reference to correctly identify all types of obstacles in any environment.

References

1. Kakillioglu, B., Ozcan, K., Velipasalar, S.: Doorway detection for autonomous indoor navigation of unmanned vehicles. In: IEEE International Conference on Image Processing (ICIP), pp. 3837–3841 (2016)
2. LeCun, Y., Bengio, Y., Hinton, G.: Deep learning. Nature 521(7553), 436–444 (2015)
3. Jordan, M., Mitchell, T.: Machine learning: arends, perspectives, and prospects. Science 349(6245), 255–260 (2015)
4. Böhmer, W., Springenberg, J., Boedecker, J., et al.: Autonomous learning of state representations for control: an emerging field aims to autonomously learn state representations for reinforcement learning agents from their real-world sensor observations. KI-Künstliche Intelligenz 29(4), 353–362 (2015)
5. Artificial Neural Networks: What are they and how are they trained? https://www.xeridia.com/blog/redes-neuronales-artificiales-que-son-y-como-se-entrenan-parte-i. Accessed 11 Apr 2023
6. Miyamoto, H., Kawato, M., Setoyama, T., Suzuki, R.: Feedback-error-learning neural network for trajectory control of a robotic manipulator. Neural Netw.Netw. 1(3), 251–265 (1998)

7. Hinton, G., Osindero, S., The, Y.: A fast learning algorithm for deep belief nets. Neural Comput.Comput. **18**(7), 1527–1554 (2006)
8. Dean, J., Corrado, G., Monga, R., et al.: Large scale distributed deep networks. Advances in Neural Information Process. Syst. 25 (2012)
9. Schmidhuber, J.: Deep learning in neural networks: an overview. Neural Netw.Netw. **6**(1), 85–117 (2015)
10. Graves, A., Liwicki, M., Fernández, S., et al.: A novel connectionist system for unconstrained handwriting recognition. IEEE Trans. Pattern Anal. Mach. Intell. **31**(5), 855–868 (2009)
11. Yang, M., Ji, S., Xu, W., et al.: Detecting human actions in surveillance videos. TREC Video Retrieval Evaluation Workshop (2009)
12. Lin, M., Chen, Q., Yan, S.: Network in network. https://arxiv.org/abs/1312.4400. Accessed 21 Mar 2023
13. Ciresan, D., Giusti, A., Gambardella, L., et al.: Deep neural networks segment neuronal membranes in electron microscopy images. Advances in Neural Information Processing Sys 25 (2012)
14. Roux, L., Racoceanu, D., Lomenie, N., et al.: Mitosis detection in breast cancer histological images an ICPR 2012 contest. J. Pathol. Inform. **4**(8) (2013)
15. Cireşan, D., Giusti, A., Gambardella, L., et al.: Mitosis detection in breast cancer histology images with deep neural networks. In: Mori, K., Sakuma, I., Sato, Y., Barillot, C., Navab, N. (eds.) Medical Image Computing and Computer-Assisted Intervention–MICCAI. Springer, Heidelberg (2013). https://doi.org/10.1007/978-3-642-40763-5_51
16. Cireşan, D., Meier, U., Masci, J., et al.: A committee of neural networks for traffic sign classification. Neural Networks (IJCNN). Int. Joint Conf. on 1918–1921 (2011)
17. Ciresan, D., Meier, U., Schmidhuber, J.: Multi-column deep neural networks for image classification. In: 2012 IEEE Conference on Computer Vision and Pattern Recognition (CVPR), pp. 3642–3649 (2012)
18. André, A., Paula, C., Maribel, C.: Using deep learning language models as scaffolding tools in interpretive research. Contemporary Administration Magaz. **27**(3), 1–11 (2023)
19. Sermanet, P., Eigen, D., Zhang, X., Mathieu, M., Fergus, R., Le Cun, Y.: Integrated recognition, localization and detection using convolutional networks. https://arxiv.org/abs/1312.6229. Accessed 10 May 2023
20. World Technology Evaluation Center, Inc. International Assessment of Research and Development in Robotics. Baltimore, MD, USA (2006)
21. A roadmap for US robotics: from internet to robotics, edition (2016)
22. DARPA Robotics Challenge. http://www.darpa.mil/program/darpa-robotics-challenge. Accessed 15 Apr 2023
23. Enciso, L.: Design of an autonomous navigation system for mobile robots using sensor fusion and neuro-fuzzy controllers, M.S. thesis, Pontifical Catholic University of Peru, Lima, (2015)
24. Burak, K., Kaya, T.: Comparison of deep learning techniques for detection of doors in indoor environments. ESOGU Eng. Arch. Fac. **29**(3), 396–412 (2021)
25. Joaquín, G., Cristian, A., Luis, C., David, M.: Performance evaluation of convolutional networks on heterogeneous architectures for applications in autonomous robotics. TecnoLógicas **25**(53), 2170–2022 (2022)
26. Sabater, J. Martínez, J.: Teaching guide for the design of service robots, Editors: Jaime Martínez Verdú/José María Sabater Navarro, Spain (2012)
27. César, R., Jhon, J., Julian, F.: Character recognition by means of an artificial neural network. Dialnet **14**(1), 30–39 (2009)

Steels Classification Based on Micrographic Morphological and Texture Features Using Decision Tree Algorithm

Yamina Boutiche[✉][iD] and Naima Ouali[iD]

Research Center in Industrial Technologies CRTI, ex CSC, P.O.Box 64, 16014
Algiers,
Cheraga, Algeria
{y.boutiche,n.ouali}@crti.dz
http://www.crti.dz

Abstract. In materials science, the microstructure which defines the inner structure of a material is particularly important. The material micrographic image (microstructure) is obtained by different methods and provides various informations about the material. The main focus of the present paper is the classification of steels based on the analysis of their microstructure images.

This work is subdivided into two stages. The first one is about the construction of a small dataset that contains 90 micrographs belonging to the three distinct steel classes. The second stage is about the image processing proposed algorithm that mainly incorporates three modules: the segmentation to extract grains morphological features, texture analysis employing Local Oriented Optimal Pattern (LOOP), and the Decision Tree algorithm for the classification. Our algorithm classifies microstructures into one of three grades (Carbon, Austenitic and Duplex stainless) with greater than 90% accuracy.

Keywords: Decision tree · Microscopic images · Microstructure characterization · Morphological features · Steel classification · Texture analysis

1 Introduction

Steels are the most important materials used in industry, as oil refineries, chemical industry, power engineering industry and petrochemical domains, because of their excellent mechanical properties [1,2]. Based on their chemical compositions, steels can be categorized into four groups: Carbon, Alloys, Stainless and Tool steels. The steel microstructures have different appearances, influenced by alloying elements, rolling process, cooling rates, heat treatment and further post-treatments [3]. These manufacture processes induce various microstructures, with different micro-constituents such as ferrite, cementite, austenite, pearlite,

T. Guarda et al. (Eds.): ARTIIS 2023, CCIS 1935, pp. 364–374, 2024.
https://doi.org/10.1007/978-3-031-48858-0_29

bainite and martensite. The steel performances is highly depend on the distribution, shape and size of phases in the microstructures [3]. Carbon group is the most important commercial steel alloy; it exhibits a ferrite/ pearlite microstructure. Duplex stainless steels (DSS) are dual phases, comprise equivalent proportions of ferrite (α) and austenite (γ) and exhibit excellent integration of mechanical and corrosion properties [4]. Austenitic alloys are mono phase with austenitic matrix.

Traditionally, steel microstructures are classified by comparing the microscopy images with reference series. Especially for steel and its complex microstructures, the comparison with reference series is strongly dependent on the expert's subjective opinion. Furthermore, it is tedious and time consuming task [5].

Recently, computer vision and image processing have great applications in materials science where many works are devoted to automatize some important tasks [5]. According to the study in [6] those works can be mainly subdivided on two groups:

(i) **Image processing techniques** that are based on the properties of the image itself (such color intensity, shape, texture). The segmentation step is crucial in this approach for further processing such as the morphological parameter computations that helps to quantitatively describing each microstructures. The simplicity, efficiency and accessibility of this approach have made it ideal candidate to be part of many works. For example, image thresholding was used in [7,8], Region Growing in [9,10], and Variational models in level set framework in [11,12]. as the material micrographic images exhibit repeated local patterns, the texture analysis technique is employed as descriptors. In this context, authors in [13] used Local binary descriptor and several combinations of morphological parameters in support vector machine (SVM) to classify the microstructure components (martensite, pearlite and bainite). They concluded that the texture features showed fewer correlations with each other, which is one of the great advantages over the other two parameter groups.

(ii) **Learning-based approach** that is based on learning a model from the data to be treated. Nowadays, it is widely introduced in micrographic analysis. In [14] authors classified the 13CrMo4-5 steel damages, using the geometrical coefficients resulting from the SEM digital images and their classification methodology uses artificial neural networks (ANN). S. M. Azimi et al. [15] worked on microstructural classification of low Carbone steel by Deep Learning method, with 93.94% classification accuracy. In the study of Vitalii et al. [16], authors have developed an algorithm to automate metallographic metals analysis based on artificial intelligence technologies. Beskopylny et al. [17] applied a method based on non-destructive test, to evaluate the indentation characteristics that correlate with the material properties to classify steel grades. The main contributions of this paper are:

1. **The image processing stage** describes an algorithm that aims to classify three steel classes based on their micrographic images. To achieve such goal several steps are considered: (i) The images are prepossessed then segmented

to extract the MGs, (ii) the MG morphological is described base on its shape features (orientation, circularity, elongation) and phase rate (iii) The Local Oriented Optimal Pattern (LOOP) is used to describe the microstructure texture. (iiii) The extracted features are fed to the Decision Tree (DT) algorithm to classify the input image onto the corresponding grade.

2. **Metallic Materials Dtataset** we propose, for this study, a new small dataset that contains 90 microstructure images of three steel grades (austenitic, carbon, and duplex stainless). The steel samples performing and image acquisitions (using the light optical microscope Nikon-Eclipse) were done at the Mechanics and Materials Development laboratory of Research Center in Industrial Technologies -CRTI- https://www.crti.dz/. The dataset is available in public domain github platform, Microstructure Images for Metallic Materials at https://github.com/Yamina77/Microst. Images_MetallicMaterialsDataset

2   Material and Dataset

The materials analyzed for this study were acquired from the industry machinery elements. The three types of steel are mainly used to fabricate typical products, as tubes, pipes, plates for pressure vessels, boilers and piping procedures. The different specimens were identified as $S1$, $S2$ and $S3$, to refer to Austenite steel, Carbone steel, and Stainless steel, respectively. The samples were prepared with an established procedure, providing high surface quality. First, specimens with a 20×20 mm^2 square surface were cut from the received plates. The obtained samples were then, prepared for metallography by a conventional polishing, on turning disks with grinding papers of different grit size in six steps ($P320$, $P500$, $P800$, $P1000$, $P1200$, and $P2400$). The last polishing was performed by adding an alumina standard suspension onto the rotating disk to obtain a mirror surfaces. The polished samples were washed with ethanol and dried with air; a subsequent etching with adequate chemical reagent is performed to reveal the different microstructures.

The images acquisition was done by the means of a light optical microscope (Nikon-Eclipse), equipped with objective lenses and camera for maximum optical resolution. The images are saved in .JPG format, with different observation scales (20 μm, 50 μm, 100 μm), and resolutions (640×480, 2560×1920). In this work, a total of 90 images are used that are regrouped in three folders according to their grade (30 images for carbon steel, 30 images for Stainless steals, and 30 images for Austenite).

3   Proposed Materiel Classification Model

Through the above mentioned discussion in Sect. 1, we propose the framework shown in Fig. 1 where the classification is based on both grain's morphology features and texture analysis using local binary pattern. Mainly the model includes three steps where the following subsection details each one.

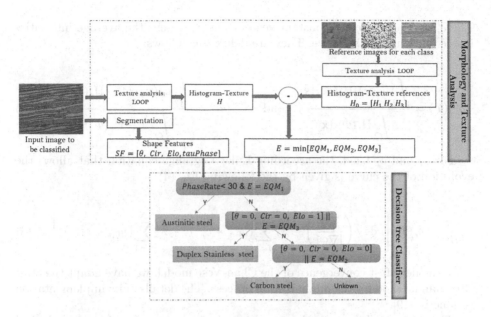

Fig. 1. Micrographic identification based on Morphology and texture in decision tree classifier

3.1 Segmentation and Morphological Features Computation

The segmentation is the crucial step in this task. In this work, we have used the Chan-Vese in level set framework optimized via Split Bregman method for fast convergence. The Chan and Vese [18] constructed the energy functional by minimizing the square error between the gray value and the mean value of the pixel points inside and outside the curve.

$$
\begin{aligned}
F^{PCVV}\left(c_i^{in}, c_i^{out}, \Phi\right) = \nu &\int_\Omega |\nabla \mathrm{H}_\epsilon(\Phi)| \mathbf{dx} \\
&+ \int_\Omega \frac{1}{N} \sum_{i=1}^N \lambda_i^{in}(u_{0,i}(\mathbf{x}) - c_i^{in})^2 \mathrm{H}_\epsilon(\Phi) \ \mathbf{dx} \\
&+ \int_\Omega \frac{1}{N} \sum_{i=1}^N \lambda_i^{out}(u_{0,i}(\mathbf{x}) - c_i^{out})^2 (1 - \mathrm{H}_\epsilon(\Phi)) \ \mathbf{dx}
\end{aligned}
\tag{1}
$$

where $i = 1, \ldots N$ represents the ith channel of the original image u_0, generally $N = 3$ for color images. λ^{in} and λ^{out} are constant vectors that penalize energy inside and outside curve in each channel i.

$$
H_\epsilon(\mathbf{x}) = \frac{1}{2}\left[1 + \frac{2}{\pi}\mathtt{arctan}\left(\frac{\mathbf{z}}{\epsilon}\right)\right], \quad \text{and} \quad \delta_\epsilon(\mathbf{x}) = \frac{1}{\pi}\frac{\epsilon}{\epsilon^2 + z^2}; \qquad z \in \mathrm{R}.
\tag{2}
$$

The c_i^{in} and c_i^{out} are the constant vectors that represent the average intensities inside and outside the curve. They are defined as follows:

$$c^{in}(\Phi) = \frac{\int_\Omega u_0(\mathbf{x}))H_\epsilon(\Phi)d\mathbf{x}}{\int_\Omega H_\epsilon(\Phi)d\mathbf{x}}, \quad \text{and} \quad c^{out}(\Phi) = \frac{\int_\Omega u_0(\mathbf{x}))\,(1 - H_\epsilon(\Phi))\,d\mathbf{x}}{\int_\Omega (1 - H_\epsilon(\Phi))\,d\mathbf{x}}. \quad (3)$$

For c_1 and c_2 fixed, the according Euler-Lagrange equation that allows the evolution of the curve is given by the following Eq. (4)

$$\frac{\partial \Phi}{\partial t} = \delta_\epsilon(\Phi)\left[\nu \text{div}\left(\frac{\nabla\Phi}{|\nabla\Phi|}\right) - \lambda_1 \sum_{i=1}^{N}(u_{0,i} - c_i^{in})^2 + \lambda_2 \sum_{i=1}^{N}(u_{0,i} - c_i^{out})^2\right]. \quad (4)$$

To achieve fast convergence of the Chan-Vese model, we have adapt the Split Bregman method for the minimization process. The details of its implementation is done in [19].

The segmented image is then used to calculate a set of grain morphological features that allows describing the structural of microstructure. In our work, we have chosen four morphological features so that each one give a best grain characterization as follows:

- **Phase Fraction** that is computed as the percent of the phase surface divided by the total image surface. In the case of austinitic grade this feature is very low since it is a monphase steel.
- **Elongation** *Elo* **and Orientation** θ: those features describe well the duplex steel, where phases are longer and flattened than in other steels (austinitic and carbon).
- **Circularity** *Cir*: this feature is used to caracterise the carbon's phases.

3.2 Texture Analysis

Local binary descriptors have been shown to be effective encoders of repeated local patterns for robust discrimination in several visual recognition tasks [20]. In literature exist a large variety of texture descriptors that are derived from the first and popular one named Local Binary Pattern LBP [20]. In the present work, we use the Local Oriented Optimal Pattern (LOOP) [21] that was introduced to overcomes the disadvantages of classic LBP.

Let i_c be the image intensity I at pixel (x_c, y_c) and i_n $(n = 0, 1, \ldots, 7)$ be the intensity of a pixel in the 3×3 neighborhood of i_c excluding the center pixel $i_c = (x_c, y_c)$. Also, the 8 responses of the Kirsch masks noted by m_n corresponding to pixels with intensity i_n, $(n = 0, \ldots, 7)$. Each of these pixels are assigned an exponential w_n (a digit between 0 and 7) according to the rank of the magnitude of m_n among the 8 Kirsch mask outputs. Then the LOOP value for the pixel (x_c, y_c) is given by [21]

$$LOOP(x_c, y_c) = \sum_{n=0}^{7} s(i_n - i_c).2^{w_n} \qquad (5)$$

where

$$s(\mathbf{x}) = \begin{cases} 1 \ if & \mathbf{x} \geq 0 \\ 0 & otherwise \end{cases} \qquad (6)$$

As reported in [21] the LOOP descriptor has many advantages (i) encodes rotation invariance into the main formulation, (ii) negates the empirical assignment of the value of the parameter k in a variety of local binary descriptors (iii) less susceptible to noise than the traditional LBP operator, (iiii) LOOP allows gains in time complexity.

Three images are randomly selected from each grade to be used as reference for it. Let H_{aust}, H_{carb}, and H_{duplex} be the histograms of the resulting LOOP images for austinitic, carbon and duplex, respectively. Let H be the histogram of the image to be classified. The Mean Square Error MSE is then computed for each grade as follows

$$MSE_i = \frac{1}{D}(H - H_i)^2, \quad i = \text{aust, carb, duplex} \qquad (7)$$

where D is the length of H. Such the image is classed to the grade that corresponds to the minimum average squared distance between the H and reference H_i.

3.3 Microstructure Identification Based on Morphological and LOOP Descriptor in Decision Tree

The framework of the decision tree based method for microstructure identification is shown in the second bloc in Fig. 1. It is proposed through the following analysis. The class of austinitic steels is characterized by a monphase structure thereby the phase rate is small. Consequently the identification of this class is the combination between the austinitic local binary descriptor and fraction phase.

The grains, in duplex class, are horizontally laminated, thereso this class is strongly described by a very weak orientation, non circularity and large elongation shape features such its morphology parameters are set to $[\theta = false, Cir = false, Elo = true]$, incorporate with texture descriptor.

The carbon steel class generally has polygonal grains, such it is classified based on circularity and elongation morphology parameters associated to the LOOP descriptor with Or logic operation.

4   Experimental Evaluations and Discussion

In this section, we present comparisons of the steel micrographic images segmentation using the proposed morphological-local binary pattern model against some widely used methods. Furthermore, the evaluation is performed to show the advantages of combining the morphological and local texture computation to increase the classification accuracy. In addition, all experiments are done on the dataset described in Sect. 2.

The algorithm is implemented using Matlab2018a, on a computer equipped with CPU $Intel(R)$ $Core$ (TM) $i7 - 10700FCPU@2.90GHz$ and $16,0\,Go$ of RAM. Furthermore, for all experiments the level set is automatically initialized to a rectangle binary function, where $\Phi = +1$ inside curve and $\Phi = 0$ outside (as shown in the first raw of Fig. 2(a)).

The experiment in Fig. 2 shows the first bloc outcomes for an example of Duplex stainless image displayed in first raw and column. The curve initialization is represented, via yellow solid line on the image domain, in the second column and the corresponding level set on last column. The second row represents, from the left to the right the convergence of curve (solid yellow line), the level set at the convergence and the binary segmented image, respectively. The last row shows the LOOP image and its histogram. The algorithm performs well the

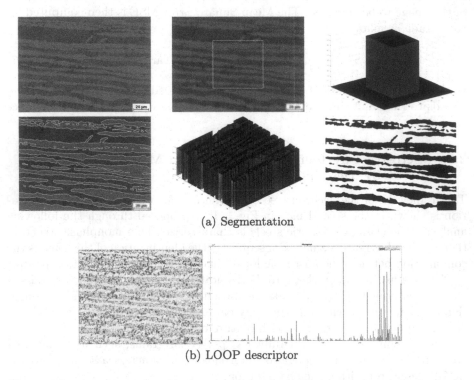

(a) Segmentation

(b) LOOP descriptor

Fig. 2. Demonstration example where input image, in first row, refers to duplex stainless micostructure. The second row presents the segmentation bloc: from the left to right initial zero level set function (yellow line), the convergence of this function, and the segmented image. The third row shows the LOOP image and corresponding histogram.

segmentation where the two phase in the microstructure are correctly extracted. In addition, The LOOP image exhibits exceedingly the pattern in the image.

4.1   Segmentation Performance Compared with the Other Methods

The morphological parameters are directly computed from the segmented image, thereby it is primordial to use algorithm able to deal with high performance on microstructures. In this subsection, we compare the segmentation results using proposed method with some widely used methods. The first row of Fig. 3 displays, an arbitrary selected images from each considered material grades. The second, third and fourth rows show the segmentation results for three class of methods, as follows:

- Thresholding methods represented by Ridler algorithm and Kapur algorithm;
- Clustering methods represented by kmeans and fuzzy kmeans (FCM);
- Variationnal (or active contours) methods represented by Local Binary Fitting Energy LBF model [22] and the Picewise Constant Chan-Vese (PC) model optimized using Split Bregman method (adopted in our work).

As the Austenitic grade is a monphase steel, the segmented image should be one region. This is obtained by Ridler, kmeans and PC algorithms. However, Kapur, FCM and LBF have extracted two regions. The carbon is a biphase steel, its microstructure is characterized by small two regions. A good performance are obtained using Kapur, FCM and PC methods. The PC model out performs all others methods in the case of the Duplex steel grade, where the two regions are correctly extracted.

4.2   Classification Performance Evaluation

The classification in our work is performed using the classic decision tree algorithm, where there is no learning stage (see Sect. 3). To evaluate the classification rate of proposed algorithm with and without combination of features, we use the accuracy rate formulation done in Eq. 8. The obtained values are displayed on Table 1. These results shows clearly the importance of the combination between morphological and texture features to classify steels microstructures, specially for the carbon and duplex grades where accuracy is 100% and 93.33%, respectively.

$$Acc = \frac{\text{Number of correct predictions}}{\text{Overall number of predictions}} \tag{8}$$

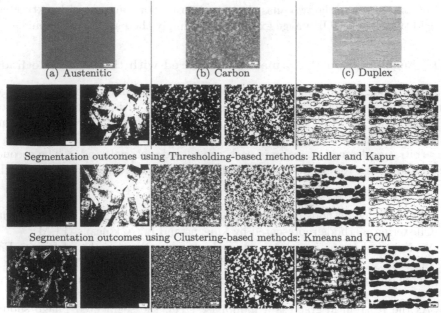

Fig. 3. Testing of the segmentation outcomes on three images for the three grades. The first row: the original images. The 2nd to $4^{t}h$ rows represents obtained binary segmentation using Thresholding-based methods, Clustering-based methods and Variational-based methods.

Table 1. Classification accuracies obtained for each grade in the three cases.

	Austenitic steel (30 images)	Carbon steel (30 images)	Duplex steel (30 images)
Classification base on texture and morphology			
Acc(%)	**90.00%**	100%	**93.33%**
Classification base on morphological only			
Acc(%)	36.66%	90.00%	86.67%
Classification base on texture only			
Acc(%)	86.67%	76.67%	76.67%

5   Conclusion

The proposed image analysis algorithm involves image segmentation, morphological feature extraction, and local texture pattern synthesis. The obtained set of parameters are incorporated in a decision tree algorithm to classify the input image to its corresponding steel grade (Carbon, Austenitic and Duplex stainless). The developed method allows to determine the grade and steel quantitative parameters (ratio Ferrite/Perlite, grain amount, etc.), that are very useful for metallurgy.

The proposed method was shown a higher accuracy using the combination of morphological and texture features compared to using them separately. However, the study was done on small dataset thereby it can not be generalized. In addition, a comparative study with the state-of-art methods should be done. Both of these points are the goals of further work.

References

1. Tasan, C., et al.: An overview of dual-phase steels: advances in microstructure-oriented processing and micromechanically guided design. Annu. Rev. Mater. Res. **45**(1), 391–431 (2015). https://doi.org/10.1146/annurev-matsci-070214-021103
2. Khedkar, P., Motagi, R., Mahajan, P., Makwana, G.A.: Review on advance high strength steels. Int. J. Curr. Eng. Technol. Special Iss. **6**, 240–243 (2016)
3. Barralis, J., Maeder, G.: Précis de métallurgie: elaboration structures propriétés et normalisation, AFNOR-Nathan
4. Ouali, N., Cheniti, B., Belkessa, B., Maamache, B., Kouba, R., Hakem, M.: Influence of isothermal aging in LDX 2101 duplex stainless steel on the microstructure and local properties. Int. J. Adv. Manuf. Technol. **116**, 1881–1893 (2021). https://doi.org/10.1007/s00170-021-07515-3
5. Gola, J., et al.: Advanced microstructure classification by data mining methods. Comput. Mater. Sci. **148**, 324–335 (2018). https://doi.org/10.1016/j.commatsci.2018.03.004
6. Luengo, J., et al.: A tutorial on the segmentation of metallographic images: taxonomy, new MetalDAM dataset, deep learning-based ensemble model, experimental analysis and challenges. Inform. Fusion **78**, 232–253 (2022). https://doi.org/10.1016/j.inffus.2021.09.018
7. Kim, D., et al.: Image segmentation for FIB-SEM serial sectioning of a Si/C-Graphite composite anode microstructure based on preprocessing and global thresholding. Microsc. Microanal. **25**(5), 1139–1154 (2019). https://doi.org/10.1017/S1431927619014752
8. Lievers, W., Pilkey, A.: An evaluation of global thresholding techniques for the automatic image segmentation of automotive aluminum sheet alloys. Mater. Sci. Eng., A **381**(1), 134–142 (2004). https://doi.org/10.1016/j.msea.2004.04.002
9. Cheng, Z., Wang, J.: Improved region growing method for image segmentation of three-phase materials. Powder Technol. **368**, 80–89 (2020). https://doi.org/10.1016/j.powtec.2020.04.032
10. Campbell, A., Murray, P., Yakushina, E., Marshall, S., Ion, W.: New methods for automatic quantification of microstructural features using digital image processing. Mater. Des. **141**, 395–406 (2018). https://doi.org/10.1016/j.matdes.2017.12.049
11. Jørgensen, P., Hansen, K., Larsen, R., Bowen, J.: A framework for automatic segmentation in three dimensions of microstructural tomography data. Ultramicroscopy **110**(3), 216–228 (2010). https://doi.org/10.1016/j.ultramic.2009.11.013
12. Ramou, N., Chetih, N., Boutiche, Y., Rabah, A.: Automatic image segmentation for material microstructure characterization by optical microscopy. Informatica (Slovenia) **44**(3), 367–372 (2020). https://doi.org/10.31449/inf.v44i3.3034
13. Gola, J., et al.: Objective microstructure classification by support vector machine (SVM) using a combination of morphological parameters and textural features for low carbon steels. Comput. Mater. Sci. **160**, 186–196 (2019). https://doi.org/10.1016/j.commatsci.2019.01.006

14. Dobrzański, J., Sroka, M.: Automatic classification of the 13CrMo4-5 steel worked in creep conditions. J. Achiev. Mater. Manuf. Eng. **29**, 147–150 (2008)
15. Azimi, S.M., Britz, D., Engstler, M., et al.: Advanced steel microstructural classification by deep learning methods. Sci. Rep. 2128 (2018). https://doi.org/10.1038/s41598-018-20037-5
16. Emelianov, V., Zhilenkov, A., Chernyi, S., Zinchenko, A., Zinchenko, E.: Application of artificial intelligence technologies in metallographic analysis for quality assessment in the shipbuilding industry. Heliyon **8**(8), e10002 (2022). https://doi.org/10.1016/j.heliyon.2022.e10002
17. Beskopylny, A., Lyapin, A., Anysz, H., Meskhi, B., Veremeenko, A., Mozgovoy, A.: Artificial neural networks in classification of steel grades based on non-destructive tests. Materials **13**, 2445 (2020). https://doi.org/10.3390/ma13112445
18. Chan, T.F., Sandberg, B., Vese, L.A.: Active contours without edges for vector-valued images. J. Vis. Commun. Image Represent. **11**(2), 130–141 (2000). https://doi.org/10.1006/jvci.1999.0442
19. Yunyun, Y., Yi, Z., Boying, W.: Split Bregman method for minimization of fast multiphase image segmentation model for inhomogeneous images. J. Optim. Theory Appl. **166**, 285–305 (2015). https://doi.org/10.1006/jvci.1999.0442
20. Ojala, T., Pietikainen, M., Harwood, D.: Performance evaluation of texture measures with classification based on Kullback discrimination of distributions. In: Proceedings of 12th International Conference on Pattern Recognition, vol. 1, pp. 582–585 (1994). https://doi.org/10.1109/ICPR.1994.576366
21. Chakraborti, T., McCane, B., Mills, S., Pal, U.: Loop descriptor: local optimal-oriented pattern. IEEE Signal Process. Lett. **25**(5), 635–639 (2018). https://doi.org/10.1109/LSP.2018.2817176
22. Li, C., Kao, C.-Y., Gore, J.C., Ding, Z.: Implicit active contours driven by local binary fitting energy. In: IEEE Conference on Computer Vision and Pattern Recognition, vol. 2007, pp. 1–7 (2007). https://doi.org/10.1109/CVPR.2007.383014

Amazlem: The First Amazigh Lemmatizer

Rkia Bani[1]([✉]) [iD], Samir Amri[2] [iD], Lahbib Zenkouar[1] [iD], and Zouahir Guennoun[1] [iD]

[1] Smart Communication Research Team (SCRT), Mohammadia School of Engineering (EMI),
Mohammed V University, Rabat, Morocco
`rkiabani@research.emi.ac.ma`
[2] Department of Computer Science and Mathematics, ENSAM School of Engineering, Moulay
Ismail University, Meknes, Morocco

Abstract. Natural language processing has become the center of research, not only, in rich languages but also in low resourced ones. In this perspective and to enrich Amazigh as an under-resourced language, we present in this paper, Amazlem, the first lemmatizing system for Amazigh language. This system takes as input, sentences in Amazigh language and outputs the lemma of each word in the sentences. The approach considered in the realization of this system is based on the rules from the Amazigh language grammar. These rules include the formation of nouns and verbs in Amazigh language. Starting from the word even without knowing its morphological syntax, the system returns the lemma of the word by matching it in a dictionary. Amazlem uses two lemmatization algorithms, one for nouns and the other for verbs. Due to the absence of a labeled corpus of lemma, we validate this approach by labeling a dataset of 10000 words from an existing Amazigh corpus for part-of-speech tagging and the results reaches 85, 5%.

Keywords: Amazigh language · Lemmatization · computational linguistic · Natural Language processing

1 Introduction

The expansion of digital text in the world is changing enormously the processing of the human language, and low resources languages aren't an exception. From information retrieval to sentiment analysis, lemmatization is a crucial tool for natural language processing (NLP) and understanding. Unlike the well-known languages such as French and English, Amazigh language is an extremely low resourced language and the number of NLP research in the field is very low compared to the other languages. Thus, lemmatization of Amazigh language is not yet studied beside one research in the field. This is why we present this paper, as a first detailed rule-based lemmatization approach for Amazigh language.

Nowadays, particularly, in Morocco, the Amazigh language receives its part of intention as a basic axe in the culture of the country [1, 2]. Starting with the creation of an official spelling [3], a standard Unicode [4, 5] and a keyboard with linguistic structures has been established [6, 7]. In terms of natural language processing of the Amazigh

T. Guarda et al. (Eds.): ARTIIS 2023, CCIS 1935, pp. 375–385, 2024.
https://doi.org/10.1007/978-3-031-48858-0_30

language, researchers have started to develop the automation of this language in the last decade. Any project in the natural language processing starts from the basic tools but essentials like part-of-speech tagging [8, 9] and named-entity-recognition [10]. However, with the scarcity of annotated Amazigh datasets, developing Amazigh natural language processing encounters difficulty. Especially for the one that we present in this paper, as a first lemmatizer for the Amazigh language.

1.1 Amazigh Language

Amazigh, often called Berber, is a language that belongs to the Hamito-Semitic "Afro-Asiatic" languages [11]. It is spoken in Morocco, Algeria, Tunisia, Libya, and Siwa (an Egyptian oasis), in addition to some communities in parts of Niger and Mali. Amazigh language is a mixture of dialects that were not considered a national standard in any of the cited countries above.

However, the increasing sense of identity among the Amazigh speakers motivates them to wish that their language and culture could be enriched and developed. As a result, some Maghreb institutions have been created, such as the Royal Institute of Amazigh Culture (IRCAM) in Morocco, and the high commission of Amazigh in Algeria. In Morocco, not only the Amazigh language has been introduced in mass media but also established in the educational system in cooperation with the concerned ministry. In addition to this achievement, a dedicated tv channel for Amazigh has been launched in March 2010.

1.2 Amazigh Script

The standardization of Amazigh has considered the linguistic diversity. As for the alphabet, Tifinagh has been chosen to be the standard system of writing Amazigh for a many historical reasons. IRCAM has kept only the relevant phonemes for Tamazight which are 33, 31 are coded in Unicode plus a modifier letter to form $\mathsf{X}^\cdot(g^w)$ and $\mathsf{K}^\cdot(k^w)$. Those phonetic units include:

- 27
  consonants including: the labials (X , Θ , C), dentals ($+$, $\wedge$, E , E , I , O , Q , W), the alveolars ($\odot$, X , $\oslash$, $\ast$), the palatals (C , I), the velar (K , X), the labiovelars ($\mathsf{K}^\cdot$, $\mathsf{X}^\cdot$), the uvular's (E , X , H), the pharyngeals ($\wedge$, H)and the laryngeal (Φ).
- 2 semi-consonants: S and U
- 4 vowels: three full vowels $\circ$, E , S and neutral vowel (or schwa) S.

1.3 Amazigh Morphology

Amazigh language is morphologically rich and complex due to its inflections including infixation, suffixation and prefixation. There are different morphosyntactic categories including noun, verb, pronoun, preposition, and adverb [12]. To understand the Amazigh grammar, we present a small introduction of those morphosyntactic categories.

- Noun

A noun is a lexical unit obtained from a root and a scheme. It could be simple such as "ⴰⵔⴱⴰ"('arba', kid), composite like "ⴱⵓⵄⴰⵔⵉ"('buεari', forest Gard) or derived such as "ⴰⵙⵍⵎⴰⴷ"('aslmad', teacher). Nouns range from gender ("ⴰⵏⴰⵥⵓⵕ"for masculine artist, "ⵜⴰⵏⴰⵥⵓⵕⵜ"for feminine artist), number (singular "ⴰⵍⵖⵎ"='camel', plural "ⵉⵍⵖⵎⴰⵏ"= camels) and case (free case: " ⴰⴷⵍⵉⵙ"='book', annexed case: "ⵓⴷⵍⵉⵙ").

- Verb

The verb in Amazigh language appears in two forms: simple form ("ⴰⴳⵎ":'draw water', " ⴰⴳⵍ": 'hang') and derived form ("ⵜⵜⵡⴰⴳⵎ", "ⵜⵜⵡⴰⴳⵍ"). In both cases, the verb is conjugated in four themes: aorist, positive accomplished, negative accomplished and unaccomplished. Either simple or derived, they receive the same verbal desinence or person indices. They are employed according to the themes using one of the aspectual particles: ⴰⴷ, ⵔⴰⴷ, ⴷⴰ, ⵍⴰ, ⴰⵔ, ⴰⵣⵣ.

- Pronoun

Pronouns are every unit susceptible to replace a noun or nominal group. In Amazigh language, there are several pronouns: personal, possessive, demonstrative, interrogative and undefined.

- Adverb

Adverb class is heterogeneous, some have nominal origin ("ⴰⴼⵍⵍⴰ": up, "ⴰⵎⵎⴰⵙ": center) and others results of the association of noun or adverb with prepositions ("ⵙ ⵡⴰⴷⴷⴰⵢ": above, " ⵖⵔ ⵙⴷⴰⵜ", in front). In general, we class adverbs according their semantic. Hence, we discern adverbs of place, of time, of quality and of manner.

2 Related Works

The lemmatization process is solved using three different approaches, the rule-based approach, the statistical-probabilistic approach, and finally the hybrid one that combines the two precedent approaches. Thus, the first stemming algorithm was rule based and introduced by Lovins [13], then Porter improves this algorithm [14] to become the popular stemming algorithm especially for English. This algorithm relays on removing commoner morphological and inflectional endings from words. In [15], they presented MADA + TOKAN multitask natural language processing that includes lemmatization.

The most used lemmatizing techniques are based on editing binary trees. Like in German language, [16] developed Lemming that uses a log-linear model that jointly models lemmatization and part-of-speech tagging. This methodology has been tested in [17] for English, Bulgarian, Sloven, and Czech which provided good results. With the development of machine learning techniques specifically neural networks, researchers are interested increasingly in applicating those techniques to lemmatization. In [18], they treated the context-sensitive lemmatization using bidirectional-gated-recurrent networks. Moreover, with the advent of encoder-decoder architecture and aspiring from neural machine translation, in [19], they presented Lematus, a system that learns context-sensitive lemmatization.

However, Amazigh language as a low resourced language, doesn't yet have a lemmatizing system. Research on natural language processing of this language is recent. Also, it is about part-of-speech tagging problematic, named entity recognition [20] and morphological analysis [21]. In [22], they proposed a stemming and lemmatizing model for information retrieval with a 56% precision.

3   Proposed Methodology

In this work, we present a rule-based approach of lemmatization for Amazigh language processing and understanding. We have used two algorithms of lemmatization, one for nouns and the other for verbs based on Amazigh grammar [12, 23] with a verification in a dictionary. We have done this work throw different steps, starting from collecting the data, preprocessing it then feeding it to the algorithm as shown in Fig. 1.

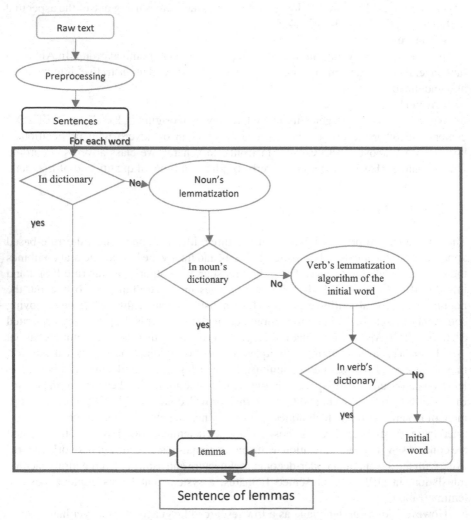

Fig. 1. Lemmatizing system architecture

After the text has been tokenized, the token is checked in a general dictionary of Amazigh language. If it exists, then it will be returned directly. If not, it will be fed to the noun's lemmatization algorithm first. If the result exists in dictionary of nouns, it will be returned. If not, the token will be fed to the verb's lemmatization algorithm, then check if the result is in the verb's dictionary, the result will be returned. If not, the token will be returned.

3.1 Noun's Lemmatization

In the Amazigh language, nouns could be sorted according to their gender, number, and case. To obtain the dictionary form of the noun, we start with special forms to general forms. Special form means the form that is evident to belong to a special type of nouns such as feminine. And general form is a type of nouns that have different possible roots like masculine plural. Using the Amazigh grammar, we sort the noun's algorithm to these multiple rules. We should mention that adjectives have the same proprieties of nouns, so this algorithm is applicable for them also. Table 1 presents the different rules for nouns formation elaborated to an algorithm, dictN is a dictionary of Amazigh nouns. Note that, ■■■could be two or more Amazigh letter and ■ is one letter.

Starting from the rules presented in the Table 1 above, we draw up the Noun's lemmatization algorithm below, it is an algorithm aiming to find if the word has a root from the dictionary of Amazigh nouns.

Noun's lemmatization algorithm
If first character is ✝ and termination is ⵥⵜ: do Algorithm1.
Elif first character is ✝ and termination is ✝: do Algorithm2.
Elif first character is ✝: do Algorithm3.
Elif first character is ⵥ and the before last character is ⵔ: do Algorithm4.
Elif first character is ⵥ and the termination is ⵔCⵔ where C is an Amazigh consonant: do Algorithm5.
Elif first character is ⵥ and last character is ⵜ: do Algorithm6.
Elif first character is ⵜ or ⵔ or ⵁ: do algorithm7.

3.2 Verb's Lemmatization

The verb in Amazigh language, comes with two forms, simple or derived. But both forms undergo the same themes such as aorist, positive accomplished, negative accomplished and unaccomplished. To find the original form of the words, we first delete the desinence or person's indices as shown in Table 2.

There is a special desinence for participle form with ⵥ-----ⵜfor singular and -----ⵜⵥⵜfor plural.

Table3 presents the algorithms for finding the lemma form of verbs after deleting the desinence and using a dictionary of Amazigh verbs (dictV). We should mention that the aorist is called non marked, the lemma of the verb is directly obtained by deleting the desinences. Note that, ■■■could be two or more Amazigh letters and ■ is one letter.

Table 1. Rules for finding lemma for nouns.

Word's form	Algorithm
+■■■ؤا (feminine plural)	Algorithm1
	- check if ■■■ in dictN
	- no, check if +■■■ in dictN
	- no; check if +∘■■■ or +ؤ■■■ or +؛■■■ in dictN
	- no; check if +∘■■■+ or +ؤ■■■+ or +؛■■■+ in dictN
	- no, check if ∘■■■ or ؤ■■■ or ؛■■■ in dictN
	- If form is +■■■ًؤا, apply previous steps deleting ًؤا
+■■■+ (feminine)	Algorithm2: This algorithm is for transforming feminine to masculine:
	- check if +∘■■■ in dictN
	- no, check if +∘■■■ or +ؤ■■■ or +؛■■■ in dictN
	- no, check if ∘■■■ or ؤ■■■ or ؛■■■ in dictN
+■■■ (another form of feminine)	Algorithm3
	- check if +∘■■■ or +ؤ■■■ or +؛■■■ in dictN
	- no, no, check if ∘■■■ or ؤ■■■ or ؛■■■ in dictN
	- If the letter before the last one is ∘, delete it and check if the result in dictN
ؤ■■■∘■ (intern plural or bruised one)	Algorithm4
	- check if ∘■■■■ in dictN
	- no, check if ∘■■■ؤ■ in dictN
	- no, check if ∘■■■■+ in dictN
	If form is ؤ■؛■■■∘■
	- check if ∘■■■■∘■ in dictN
	- no, check if ∘■∘■■■∘■
ؤ■■■؛■∘ (intern plural or bruised one	Algorithm5
	Check if ∘■■■∘■؛ in dictN
ؤ■■■ا (plural of masculine)	Algorithm6
	- check if ■■■ in dictN
	- no, check if ∘■■■ or ؛■■■ in dictN
	If form is ؤ■■■ًا:
	- check if ؤ■■■ in dictN
	- no, check if ∘■■■ or ؛■■■ in dictN
	If form is ؤ■■■∘ًا:
	- check if ؤ■■■ in dictN
	- no, check if ∘■■■ or ؛■■■ in dictN
	If form is ؤ■■■ؤًا:
	- check if ؤ■■■ in dictN
	- no, check if ∘■■■ or ؛■■■ in dictN
	If form is ؤ■■■؟ا:
	- check if ؤ■■■ in dictN
	- no, check if ∘■■■ or ؛■■■ in dictN
	If form is ؤ■■■ +ا:
	- check if ؤ■■■ in dictN
	- no, check if ∘■■■ or ؛■■■ in dictN
ً■■■ or ؛■■■ or ؟■■■ (annexed case form)	Algorithm7
	- check if ■■■ in dictN
	- no, apply plural algorithm to ■■■

Table 2. Desinences in Amazigh language

	Masculine		Feminine	
Singular	First person	-------Ɏ	First person	-------Ɏ
	Second person	+------ Λ	Second person	+------ Λ
	Third person	Ɛ------	Third person	+------
Plural	First person	I-------	First person	I-------
	Second person	+------ Ⲉ	Second person	+----- Ⲉ+
	Third person	------I	Third person	------I+

Table 3. Rules for finding lemma for verbs.

Words after deleting desinences	algorithm
++■■■■ (Unaccomplished)	Algorithm8 - check if ■■■■ in dictV - If form is ■■o■ or ■■°■ or ■■Ⲉ■, check if ■■■ in dictV (remove before last letter) - if form is ■■oϞ or ■■°Ϟ or ■■ⲈϞ, check if ■■Ⲉ in dictV - if form is o■oϞ or o■°Ϟ or o■ⲈϞ, check if ■Ϟ in dictV - If form is ■■■o or ■■■° or ■■■Ⲉ, check if ■■■ in dictV
CC■■■■ (C as consonant) (Unaccomplished)	Algorithm9 - check if ⲈC■■■■ in dictV - if form is CC■■■o, check if ⲈC■■■o in dictV
■CC■■■ (C as consonant) (Unaccomplished)	Algorithm10 - check if ■C■■■ in dictV, - no, check if o■C■■■ or °■C■■■ or Ⲉ■C■■■ in dictV
■■■■Ⲉ or ■■■■o (Unaccomplished)	Algorithm11 - check if ■■■■ in dictV - no, check if ■■■■°

°■■■■ (Accomplished)	Algorithm12
	- check if o■■■■ in dictV
	- if form is °■■■Ⲉ or °■■■o:
	  - check if o■■■ in dictV
	  - no, check if o■■■° in dictV

Starting from the rules presented in Table 3, we draw up the Verb's lemmatization algorithm below, it is an algorithm aiming to find if the word has a root from the dictionary of Amazigh verbs.

Verb's lemmatization algorithm
After deleting the Amazigh desinence:
If the result is in the verb's dictionary, return result.
Elif the first two characters are ⵜⵜ: do Algorithm8.
Elif the first two characters are the same consonants: do Algorithm9.
Elif the second and the third character are the same consonants: do Algorithm10.
Elif the las character is ⵄ or ⵔ: do Algorithm11.
Elif the first character is ⵝ: do algorithm12.

To resume, the algorithm below represents the detailed steps to word lemmatizing algorithm used in Amazlem for Amazigh text lemmatization.

Amazigh Lemmatization Algorithm
1-Take Amazigh text as input
2-Tokenization of the text
3-Insert the text into list of words
4-Check if the word in the general Amazigh dictionary
5-Yes, return word
6-No, do noun's lemmatization algorithm
7-Check if the result in noun's dictionary
8-Yes, return result
9-No, go to verb's lemmatization algorithm
10-Check if the result in verb's dictionary
11-Yes, return result
12-No, return the initial word

4 Evaluation

The evaluation of any natural language application requires an annotated dataset. In the case of lemmatization, the annotated dataset is corpus tagged with the lemma of each word. And since the Amazigh language hasn't a dataset of the lemma, we realized our dataset for this experiment. We take a dataset annotated for part-of-speech tagging [24] as our base for work. And we enriched it by adding a lemma column for 10000 words, using the dictionary of Amazigh language to find the lemma form. Our algorithm performs 85, 5% of accuracy. The accuracy of the algorithm is calculated using this equation:

$$Accuracy = \frac{number\ of\ the\ lemma\ found\ correct}{total\ number\ of\ words}$$

Below an example of using our lemmatizing script to lemmatize a sentence in Amazigh language.

```
>>python Amazlem.py
Input: ⵉⵙⵡⵓⵔⵔⵉ ⵓⵙⵉⵏⴰⴳ ⴰⵀⴰⴷ ⵉⴳ ⵓⵏⵎⵓⴽⴽⴰⵔ ⴰ ⵢⴰⵜ ⵜⵎⵃⴷⴰ ⵍⵍⴰ ⵔⴰⴷ ⵏⵙⵙⴽⵜⵉ
ⴰⵏⵙⴰⵢ ⵏ ⵉⵍⵍⴰⵢⵔ ⵉⵜⵜⵉⵃⵉⵏ ⴳ ⵜⵙⴳⴳⵉⵡⵉⵏ ⴰⴽⴽⵡ ⵏ ⵜⵎⴰⵣⵉⵔⵜ
Output: ⵙⵡⵓⵔⵔⵉ ⴰⵙⵉⵏⴰⴳ ⴰⵀⴰⴷ ⵉⴳ ⴰⵏⵎⵓⴽⴽⴰⵔ ⴰ ⵢⴰⵜ ⵜⴰⵎⵃⴷⴰ ⵍⵍⴰ ⵔⴰⴷ
ⵙⵙⴽⵜⵉ ⴰⵏⵙⴰⵢ ⵏ ⵉⵍⵍⴰⵢⵔ ⵉⵃⵉ ⴳ ⵜⴰⵙⴳⴳⴰ ⴰⴽⴽⵡ ⵏ ⵜⴰⵎⴰⵣⵉⵔⵜ
```

Because our lemmatizing algorithm is the first for the Amazigh language, we will discuss its performance on varied sizes of dataset, as well as on the types of words.

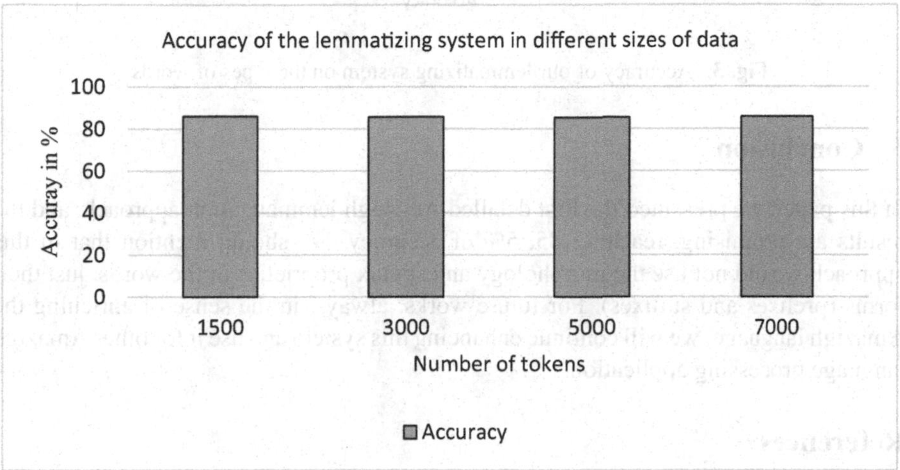

Fig. 2. Performances of our lemmatizing system on different sizes of data

As shown in Fig. 2, the accuracy of our system is relatively stable when changing the size of the dataset. As for Fig. 3, the performance of our system change depending on the grammatical class. We notice that the accuracy declines in the case of verbs. When we check some wrong results from the verb lemmatization, we notice some errors. These errors concern some verbs on third person that have the same form of some adjective like ('ⵉⵖⵓⴷⴰⵏ', 'ighudan'). Also, other varying errors in the case of derived verbs.

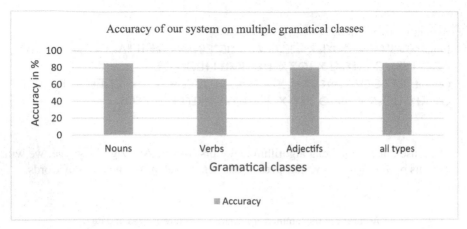

Fig. 3. Accuracy of our lemmatizing system on the types of words

5 Conclusion

In this paper, we presented the first detailed Amazigh lemmatization approach, and the results are promising, reaching 85, 5% of accuracy. We should mention that in this approach we did not use the morphology and syntax proprieties of the words, just their forms (prefixes and suffixes). For future works, always, in the sense of enriching the Amazigh language, we will continue enhancing this system and use it for other Amazigh language processing application.

References

1. Blilid, M. : La gestion de la question amazighe par l'État marocain : entre marginalisation et intégration. Sociétés plurielles (2021)
2. Nachef, L.: La langue amazighe, menaces et résistance. Revue des Études Amazighes **2**(2), 155–171 (2018)
3. Boumalk, A.: Conditions de réussite d'un aménagement efficient de l'amazighe. Ameur [dir.] **2009**, 53–61 (2009)
4. Andries, P. : Unicode 5.0 en pratique : codage des caractères et internationalisation des logiciels et des documents. Dunod (2008)
5. Zenkouar, L.: Normes des technologies de l'information pour l'ancrage de l'écriture amazighe. Etudes et documents berbères **27**(1), 159–172 (2008). https://doi.org/10.3917/edb. 027.0159
6. Ameur, M., Bouhjar, A., Boukhris, F.: Initiation à la langue amazighe. Institut Royal de la Culture Amazighe (2004)
7. Ameur, M.: Aménagement linguistique de l'amazighe : pour une approche poly-nomique. Rabat: Asinag **3**, 75–88 (2009)
8. Amri, S., Zenkouar, L., Benkhouya, R.: A comparative study on the efficiency of POS tag-ging techniques on amazigh corpus. In: Proceedings of the 2nd International Conference on Networking, Information Systems & Security, pp. 1–5 (2019)
9. Samir, A., Rkia, B., Lahbib, Z., Zouhair, G.: A machine learning approach to POS tagging case study: amazighe language. In: 2022 2nd International Conference on Innovative Research in Applied Science, Engineering and Technology (IRASET), pp. 1–4. IEEE (2022)

10. Samir, A., Lahbib, Z.: Amazigh named entity recognition: a novel approach. J. Theor. Appl. Inf. Technol. **96**(11), 3589–3599 (2018). https://doi.org/10.1007/978-3-030-11928-7_86
11. Cohen, D. : Chamito-sémitiques (langues). Encyclopædia Universalis (2007)
12. Boukhris, F., Boumalk, A., Elmoujahid, E., Souifi, H.: La nouvelle grammaire de l'amazighe, Rabat, Maroc: IRCAM (2008)
13. Lovins, J.B.: Development of a stemming algorithm. Mech. Transl. Comput. Linguistics **11**(1–2), 22–31 (1968)
14. Porter, M.F.: An algorithm for suffix stripping. Program **14**(3), 130–137 (1980). https://doi. org/10.1108/eb046814
15. Habash, N., Rambow, O., Roth, R.: MADA+ TOKAN: a toolkit for Arabic tokenization, diacritization, morphological disambiguation, POS tagging, stemming and lemmatization. In: Proceedings of the 2nd International Conference on Arabic Language Resources and Tools (MEDAR), Cairo, Egypt, vol. 41, p. 62 (2009)
16. Müller, T., Cotterell, R., Fraser, A., Schütze, H.: Joint lemmatization and morphological tagging with lemming. In: Proceedings of the 2015 Conference on Empirical Methods in Natural Language Processing, pp. 2268–2274 (2015)
17. Toutanova, K., Cherry, C.: A global model for joint lemmatization and part-of-speech prediction. In: Proceedings of the Joint Conference of the 47th Annual Meeting of the ACL and the 4th International Joint Conference on Natural Language Processing of the AFNLP, pp. 486–494 (2009)
18. Chakrabarty, A., Pandit, O.A., Garain, U.: Context sensitive lemmatization using two successive bidirectional gated recurrent networks. In: Proceedings of the 55th Annual Meeting of the Association for Computational Linguistics (Volume 1: Long Papers), pp. 1481–1491 (2017)
19. Bergmanis, T., Goldwater, S.: Context sensitive neural lemmatization with lematus. In: Proceedings of the 2018 Conference of the North American Chapter of the Association for Computational Linguistics: Human Language Technologies, Volume 1 (Long Papers), pp. 1391–1400 (2018)
20. Amri, S., Zenkouar, L., Outahajala, M.: Combination POS taggers on amazigh texts. In: 2017 3rd International Conference of Cloud Computing Technologies and Applications (CloudTech), pp. 1–6. IEEE (2017)
21. Nejme, F.Z., Boulaknadel, S., Aboutajdine, D.: AmAMorph: finite state morphological analyzer for amazighe. J. Comput. Inf. Technol. **24**(1), 91–110 (2016)
22. Samir, A., Lahbib, Z.: Stemming and lemmatization for information retrieval systems in amazigh language. In: International Conference on Big Data, Cloud and Applications, pp. 222–233. Springer, Cham (2018). https://doi.org/10.1007/978-3-319-96292-4_18
23. Laabdelaoui, R., Boumalk, A., Iazzi, E.M., Souifi, H., Ansar, K.: Manuel de conjugaison de l'amazighe. IRCAM, Rabat, Morocco (2012)
24. Amri, S., Zenkouar, L., Outahajala, M.: Build a morphosyntaxically annotated amazigh corpus. In: Proceedings of the 2nd International Conference on Big Data, Cloud and Applications, pp. 1–7 (2017)

The Method of Contextual Selection of the Functions of Cultural Heritage Objects Based on the Urban Environment Network Model

Drozhzhin Andrei[(✉)], Lavrov Igor, Loktev Egor, and Mityagin Sergey [iD]

ITMO University, Kronverksky Pr. 49, St. Petersburg 197101, Russia
drozhzhin@itmo.ru

Abstract. The article deals with the problem of managing cultural heritage. Many such objects from among the capital construction facilities have now lost their main function and are gradually being destroyed. Options for the revival of cultural heritage objects require the search for a new function for the object, which will make its operation economically profitable, and make investment attractive the object itself. However, the traditional methods used to determine a new function for objects are not always able to form suitable recommendations, since they do not systematically consider the context of the environment. This leads to the fact that many potentially investment attractive objects fall out of consideration. The paper proposes an approach to profiling the investment-attractive functional content of cultural heritage based on network modeling of the urban environment, its objects and their interaction.

Keywords: Network modeling · City graph · Cultural heritage · Investment attractiveness · Information model · Functional model · Recommendation system

1 Introduction

The article is devoted to the problem of cultural heritage management. Under the object of cultural heritage we consider real estate objects with territories historically associated with them, which arose as a result of historical events, which are of value in terms of history, architecture, urban planning, art, science, aesthetics and are evidence of civilizations, genuine sources of information about the origin and development of culture [1, 2]. Management of cultural heritage objects is carried out at several levels and is based on the choice of the optimal strategy, including options for the functional content of the object, estimates of investment volumes and a forecast of their return, as well as imposed restrictions.

The problem of managing such objects is related to the fact that traditional methods of forming management strategies often do not allow obtaining options that simultaneously ensure the investment attractiveness of the project and the preservation of its historical appearance. The average payback of investments in such facilities is 20–25 years [3,

© The Author(s), under exclusive license to Springer Nature Switzerland AG 2024
T. Guarda et al. (Eds.): ARTIIS 2023, CCIS 1935, pp. 386–399, 2024.
https://doi.org/10.1007/978-3-031-48858-0_31

4], which can rarely be considered a positive or neutral factor when making a decision regarding investment. This leads to the loss of the historical appearance and memory of the place, and in some cases to the loss of objects entirely. It is easier and cheaper for investors, even with possible fines, to demolish an object before its inclusion in the list of protection, than to work with such an object. Striking examples are the demolitions in St. Petersburg of the buildings of the St. Petersburg sports complex in 2020 and the Manege of the Finland Regiment in 2022.

At the same time, the most important factor in determining the prospects for the operation of a building is its environment. For objects of cultural heritage, a significant role is played by the entry of such an object into a historical ensemble, the presence of objects connected through historical events, cultural aspects or artistic properties. Moreover, the investment attractiveness is influenced by the content and the state of the environment in terms of choosing a new function and justifying this choice. Network models of the urban environment are one of the approaches that allow consider the relationship between objects of the urban environment and objects of cultural heritage for the formation of alternative management options. The use of this class of models makes it possible to consider the additional effects of a cultural heritage object environment, which for some objects will allow to select an investment-attractive scenario, which at the same time ensures the preservation of the historical appearance of the object.

In this paper, the authors carried out a study and proposed an approach to system modeling of scenarios for managing cultural heritage objects based on a network model of the urban environment. Experimental studies of the method were carried out on the example of the city of St. Petersburg, which is rich in cultural heritage objects, which made it possible to identify classes of objects for which the proposed methods are the most promising.

2 Problems of Cultural Heritage Preservation

Preservation of cultural heritage involves the choice of management strategies for cultural heritage sites that ensure the safety of at least the external, and at best, the structural features of the object. As a rule, buildings that are objects of cultural heritage require increased maintenance and operation costs, and the functions they perform are not always able to provide these costs. On the other hand, the restrictions imposed on the operation and reconstruction of cultural heritage objects limit the options for the possible functions of these objects. Often this leads to the implementation of strategies such as the demolition of a cultural heritage site or replacement with modern copies [5–7].

Modern urbanism recognizes the importance of cultural heritage objects as the foundation of civic consciousness [8–10], the perception of cultural identity and the emotional attitude of citizens to a place. From a cultural and historical point of view, the most optimal is the complete museumification of all objects. For this reason, there is a practice of state support for the preservation of cultural heritage sites around the world. For example, the palaces of Frederick the Great in Potsdam [11], the Louvre [12], historical monuments of Beijing [13], etc. are museumified. However, the number of objects both preserved and requiring preservation can be large and this may require significant financial costs for restoration or at least conservation of all objects [14, 15].

As a result, funding is often allocated only to status objects [16–18]. According to some estimates [19, 20] the money allocated by the state for the restoration and preservation of objects is almost 20 times less than the minimum required amount. Complex restoration and maintenance of objects in a new state will require more significant costs.

Currently architectural, legislative and economic methods of preserving cultural heritage sites are being applied. Architectural methods include the practice of preserving an object as an architectural object, issues of restoration and conservation of an object or its elements, etc. [2, 21, 22]. Legislative initiatives are aimed at amending the existing legislation of countries and supranational organizations in order to ease the bureaucratic burden faced by both states and individuals or companies that work with cultural heritage [23, 24]. Economic methods are aimed at developing approaches to increase the attractiveness of specific objects for private investors while ensuring the safety of a cultural heritage object [25–28].

This paper discusses the method of forming recommendations for the selection of optimal strategies for managing cultural heritage objects within the framework of the economic group of methods, in the current legislative conditions and without considering the details of architectural execution.

It is possible to single out the main strategies for managing cultural heritage objects [2, 29, 30], presented in Table 1..

The most preferable from the point of view of preserving the cultural identity of the place and historical memory are projects related to the restoration of the object.

The cost part is formed from a complex of works on studying the monument, restoring its appearance virtually, creating a project and, in fact, work to recreate the lost constructs, decorative elements, decoration, etc. Often such work requires approaches and materials that are not currently used in mass construction, which greatly increases the cost of the work carried out.

The income part is formed on the basis of two options for the further use of the object and their combination: after restoration, the object can continue to perform the functions for which it was originally intended (for example, housing), or become part of the tourist infrastructure (museumification). A related option is the use of a previously residential facility to house a hotel there - on the one hand, the function is preserved, on the other hand, such an object is already involved in the tourism sector.

The revenue part is determined by the following main factors:

(a) coverage of the potential audience;
(b) the availability of the facility for visiting;
(c) the capacity of the object;
(d) the artistic and historical significance of the object;
(e) object context.

The choice of strategy is made by the investor personally for each object of cultural heritage and depends both on the parameters of the object and on the possibilities and goals of the investor. For this reason, the tasks of choosing an object and choosing a control scenario should be considered.

Table 1. Cultural heritage management strategies.

№	Strategy name	Description	Expenditures	Income sources	Examples
1	Conservation	a set of measures to maintain the strength, stability and reliability of completed building structures, as well as to ensure the safety of the capital construction facility for others	- project work - protection from precipitation - protection of soils and building structures from freezing	- tourism	- Ethiopia [31] - India [32]
2	Restoration	research, survey, design and production work carried out in order to identify and preserve the historical and cultural value of a cultural heritage object	- research - project work - creation and/or strengthening of constructive - reconstruction of decorative elements - reconstruction of the lost texture	- intended use - tourism	- Zimbabwe [33] - Russia [34]
3	Renovation	strategy for adapting the object to the modern requirements	- survey work - project work - works on partial reconstruction and restoration - construction works	- intended use - new use - tourism	- China [35] - Russia [36]

3 Cultural Heritage Context Network Modeling

Improving the attractiveness of strategies related to the preservation of a cultural heritage object can be carried out by reducing the cost part and increasing the revenue part of the strategy.

Within the proposed method, the reduction in the cost part is achieved by delegating part of the costs to co-investors, which is possible when implementing an approach to combining several functions as part of one facility.

Increasing the revenue in the proposed method is provided by increasing the number of expected users of the object.

3.1 Cultural Heritage Object Information Model

The information model of a cultural heritage object is shown in Fig. 1.

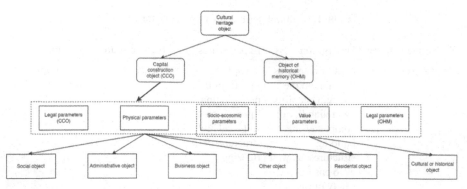

Fig. 1. Information model of a cultural heritage object

According to the model shown in Fig. 1, a cultural heritage object is a capital construction object and may include several functions depending on the scale. Each function requires space to accommodate. At the same time, places not occupied by any functions act as a potential for profiling a cultural heritage object under the objectives of the chosen strategy.

Objects of cultural heritage may have an adjacent territory, which relates directly to the object and a zone of contextual influence, which depends on the scale of the object and is perceived as the "neighborhood" of the object.

The parameters of the cultural heritage object are presented in Table 2..

Table 2. Cultural heritage object parameters

№	Parameters group	Parameters examples
1	Legal parameters as an object of capital construction	Object owner, intended purpose, operating mode etc.
2	Physical parameters	Environment, constructive, engineering support, site area, area of premises, safety etc.
3	Socio-economic parameters	Cost per square meter, availability, functionality etc.
4	Value characteristics	Cultural significance, historical significance etc.
5	Legal parameters as an object of historical memory	Security zone, security elements etc.

An example of a cultural heritage site is shown in Fig. 2.

In terms of scale, cultural heritage objects can be divided into palace complexes, architectural ensembles, building complexes, detached buildings.

In terms of functional content, cultural heritage objects can be divided into objects of administrative, social, business, residential, cultural, historical and other purposes.

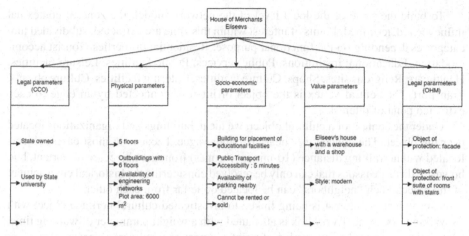

Fig. 2. Information model of a specific object of cultural heritage - the house of the merchants Eliseevs on the Birzhevaya line (St. Petersburg, Russia)

The parameters of the cultural heritage object functions are presented in Table 3..

Table 3. Cultural heritage object functions

№	Object function	Examples	Parameters
1	Social facility	An object of education, healthcare, sports, culture, etc	Accessibility, capacity etc
2	Administrative object	Placement of organizations associated with power	Capacity, square etc
3	Business object	Placement of offices of one or more companies	Accessibility, capacity, square etc
4	Residential property	Apartment building, dormitory, hotel, etc	Accessibility, capacity, square etc
5	Cultural and historical object	Museum, museumified space	Significance, accessibility
6	Object of another purpose	Industrial, religious enterprises, etc	Square

3.2 Cultural Heritage Network Information Model

The network model of cultural heritage objects is due to the presence of interrelations between cultural heritage objects and environmental objects. To explore these relationships, it is necessary to construct a model that includes a local facility level scale to explore context, and a city level model to explore clusters and degree of centralization.

To build the scale of the local level of the network model, the zone of contextual influence is determined. Points of interest within this zone are extracted, subdivided into categories depending on the functional purpose: Residential properties, Tourist accommodation, Educational institutions, Public services, Public facilities, Leisure facilities, Healthcare, Religious sites, Shops, Culture facilities, Catering facilities, Culture objects, Transport. The central vertex is the object of interest, connected by an edge to each extracted point of interest.

Under the context of a cultural object, we mean buildings and organizations located near the object. The concept of "near" is rather vague, because in most cases, objects located within walking distance (10-min isochrones) from the object are important, but, however, there are issues that can only be resolved considering the historical environment of the object. Such "neighbors" can be located quite far from each other.

Every point of interest is being linked to investigated cultural heritage object with its walking isochrone. Every link is attributed with a weight parameter of walking time. Link weights are used as evaluation of point's impact on a cultural object.

As the isochrone determines a zone of contextual impact, it's coverage may be adjusted by enwidening according to average pedestrian routes of evaluated city. Time-frame adjusting is applicable for comparison of several cultural sites for tailored results, due to amount of noise in the data.

As stated above, object context learning can be divided into three groups:

(a) ensembleness - a test for the occurrence of an object in any ensemble. It is worth separating the author's and established ensembles. In the first case, the entry of an object into the ensemble was implied by the architect (or a group of architects). In the second case, the ensemble has developed historically and is an inalienable value of the chosen territory. In both cases, the inclusion of an object in an ensemble imposes restrictions on the choice of strategies, since requires the maximum possible preservation of the current appearance, which is not always possible, for example, when opening any establishments (for example, a cafe) on the 1st floor. Any changes must fit into the existing environment.

(b) economic content of the environment - the study of services that are within walking distance from the object to understand the market. Here it is worth paying attention, firstly, to those services that already exist on the territory. For example, if 9 out of 10 points in the territory are catering, it will be quite difficult to open another one and withstand economic competition with the already established business of neighbors. And secondly, on services that are missing. For example, if there are no cafes and restaurants on the territory, this can become a promising direction. Of course, before choosing this option, you need to study related issues, for example, pedestrian traffic, etc. In addition, based on the study of existing and missing services, it is quite easy to suggest missing pairs for services that have colocation dependencies, for example, jewelry stores are most often located near stores clothes, and grocery stores often coexist with cafes [37].

(c) thematic connection - checking for the presence of neighbors associated with the object by historical figures or events, artistic features. Since thematic connectivity is interesting mainly from the point of view of object museumification and possibility to create thematic clusters, the search is not limited to the territory of walking distance:

in an agglomeration it would be more correct to study objects that are an hour away from the selected object, outside the agglomeration - the object and the neighbor must be at a distance of 4 h (conditionally a third of the daylight hours). However, it is difficult to calculate the economic potential for this option: significant objects are usually protected, and others rarely have such significant value as to create new excursion routes based on them.

The socio-economic parameters of the object and its context are beyond the scope of the current article, but are planned for consideration in the next ones.

An example of a network model of a cultural heritage site is shown in Fig. 3.

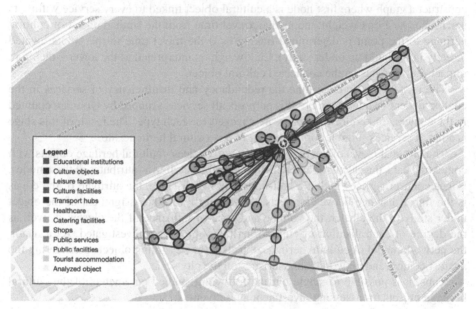

Fig. 3. Network of Specific Cultural Heritage Sites: Rumyantsev Mansion (St. Petersburg, Russia)

4 Context-Dependent Definition of Cultural Heritage Management Strategies

The attractiveness of a particular cultural heritage site for various population groups can be assessed based on a set of characteristics:

(a) the object itself: the calculated significance of the object, considering its assignment to a certain group of monuments (federal, regional or local significance);

(b) context: nearby services that are of interest to a certain group of the population act as points of attraction for this group and increase the likelihood that they will visit the object of cultural significance under consideration; at the same time, the presence of a number of services that perform the same function as this object may reduce its interest due to the presence of competition;

(c) the location of the object on the city scale: the higher the centrality of the vertex of the graph of urban objects of cultural significance and the greater the size of the cluster in which this vertex belongs, the wider its influence within the city and, accordingly, the higher its attractiveness for visitors.

5   Application of the Models for the Future Operation

At the local level of the model scale, first of all, the influence degree of each point of interest is assessed. A pedestrian isochrone is constructed and the services located within walking distance from the object under consideration are determined. This is used to construct a graph where first node is a cultural object linked to every service within its isochrone. As a link weight, the median travel time from the studied object of cultural heritage to the point is determined (taking as 0 the travel time to the points located directly in the building under study). Link weight is interpreted as the lower – the more impact a service has on the connected cultural object.

The next step is to determine the redundancy and insufficiency of services in the context under consideration. For this purpose, all services grouped by types are counted in the context, and collocation pairs are checked for each type. The result of this stage is a list of services suitable for placement in this cultural heritage site.

The city scale level of the model consists of vertices - cultural heritage objects with contextual data, the calculation of which is described earlier, as attributes of these nodes. Edges connect vertices within a half-hour walking distance, the attribute of the edges is the linear distance between objects. At the city level, the assignment of the object under study to the cluster, the volume and zone of influence of the cluster, as well as the degree of centralization of cultural heritage objects are investigated. As a result, the network model of cultural heritage objects allows profiling objects considering the nearest context and network characteristics on the city scale.

Thus, it is possible to single out the following studied parameters of the cultural heritage objects for assessing investment attractiveness:

1. **Connectivity** – number of points of interest within walking distance. Connectivity can represent an estimate of potential attendance based on nearby features.
2. **Accessibility** – the total walking distance to all points of interest associated with the cultural heritage. A shorter overall distance will mean that object is easily accessible, which could be attractive to potential investors.
3. **Diversity** – the number of different categories with the associated POIs. A higher variety may indicate a larger potential audience.
4. **Centralization** – the degree of centralization of the cultural heritage in the general network of the city. A more central object may be more attractive due to its potential visibility and importance.

Each parameter is expected to have a linear effect and can be taken into account in accordance with the following formula 1:

$$I_i = w_C \times C_i + \frac{w_A}{A_i} + w_D \times D_i + W_B \times B_i, \qquad (1)$$

where I means the investment potential of object i, w_x is the weight of the corresponding parameter, C_i means the connectivity of object i, A_i is accessibility of object i, D_i is diversity of object i, B_i is centralization parameter of object i.

However, in addition to the parameters estimated by the network model, there are also expertly estimated parameters and the general state of the cultural heritage object. It is possible to consider two such factors as "the current state" and "the historical significance". Since historical significance is a subjective parameter, it requires an expert assessment, for example, historians, urbanists, restorers.

Determination of weight coefficient values is one of the stages of Multicriteria Decision Analysis (MCDA). One of the most common methods for solving this problem, in this case, in relation to the cultural heritage objects, is the Analytic Hierarchy Process (AHP) [38], but there are a number of other methods [39]. In the general case, the methods determine how exactly expert assessments should be considered in calculating the weighting coefficients of the parameters under consideration.

In the basic case, the assessment of the cost of a cultural heritage object consists in its categorization: with low values of the investment potential indicator, the costs of maintaining or restoring it are so high that it is more expedient to demolish or leave this object unchanged. Such objects can be mothballed, since they have the potential for development with an improvement in external conditions (for example, with an increase in their transport accessibility). And high values of the indicator indicate that the costs of renovation or restoration of such an object are most appropriate.

The cost of a cultural heritage object can be determined in the following ways: "rough estimation" by ranking objects and allocating them to the cost class, or exact methods by calculating the indicator on the basis of expert evaluations. In the basic case, the assessment of the cost of a cultural heritage object consists in its categorization: when the values of the investment attractiveness indicator are low, the costs of its maintenance or restoration are so high that it is more appropriate to demolish or leave it unchanged, when the values of the indicator are medium, the restoration of the object has a certain payback risk – such objects can be mothballed because they have the potential for development when external conditions improve (for example, when their transport accessibility is increased), and higher, the cost of the restoration of an object is higher.

Accurate methods for determining the cost of the object consists in determining the values of the weighting factors by Multicriteria Decision Analysis (MCDA). These estimates can be calculated if sufficient raw data is available. One of the most common methods for solving this problem, in this case with respect to MCDA, is the Analytic Hierarchy Process (AHP) [38], but there are a number of other methods [39]. In general, the methods determine how exactly the expert assessments should be taken into account in the calculation of the weighting coefficients of the parameters under consideration. In the case of AHP, expert evaluations consist of a pairwise comparison of the indicators with each other and are written in the form of a matrix. Further, transformations are performed over the matrix of evaluations and the final values of the weights of each indicator are calculated.

Table 4. shows the calculation of the Investment Potential indicator for the cultural heritage of the Moskovsky district of St. Petersburg. The indicator weights were

Table 4. The results of calculating the Investment Potential values for the cultural heritage objects of the Moskovsky district of St. Petersburg

№	Object	Connectivity	Accessibility	Diversity	Centralization	Investment Potential
1	The Maltsev's house	445.00	1098.30	12.00	47.00	128.35
2	The management the of the St. Petersburg Carriage Works partnership	419.00	1101.49	11.00	47.00	121.60
3	The fire station	417.00	1092.65	11.00	47.00	121.10
...						
129	The guard house	331	1257.55	2	1	83.55
130	The officers' aviation school	331	1303.31	2	1	83.55
131	The barracks for employees of the Varshavsky railway station	331	1404.95	2	1	83.55

determined in consultation with experts and are defined as 0.25 for Connectivity, Accessibility, Diversity and 0.3 for centralization. We also can note that the weights should be calibrated according to the urban context: for compact cities with high population density, centralization obviously has a lesser effect than diversity (Fig. 4).

Thus, as a result of the analysis in this district, 3 objects were identified with the highest value of the calculated indicator of more than 120.

For the Moskovsky district, this level can be interpreted as the maximum value of investment attractiveness for an object for choosing a managing strategy, depending on the expediency for potential investors in its renovation. Thus, the proposed method of evaluation makes it possible to identify the most potentially investment-attractive objects in the urban landscape.

On the part of the city authorities, it is advisable to initiate procedures for the implementation of joint projects for objects with the highest rating.

Fig. 4. Network model of the Officers' Aviation School (PI = 83.55) and the Maltsev's House (PI = 128.35)

On the contrary, cultural heritage sites with the lowest rating are more likely to be unable to recoup the costs of competitive procedures, as their investment attractiveness is low. For such facilities, state management strategies should be adopted. For example, it is possible to conserve such an object if it has sufficient cultural value.

This multi-level network, once established, serves as a comprehensive tool for stakeholders, aiding them in making informed decisions about investment potential and utilization of cultural heritage objects. In a practical scenario, if a cultural heritage object is centrally located in a network dense with tourist accommodations and attractions, it might be deemed highly valuable for tourism-related ventures.

6 Conclusion

The method of profiling the functions of a cultural heritage object based on environmental factors presented in the paper makes it possible to increase the efficiency of the management of cultural heritage objects from the point of view of their preservation. The key concept in the work is the assessment of investment attractiveness since the main mechanism for the preservation of cultural heritage remains their transfer to the management of the investor.

Among the advantages of the presented method, it should be noted that it operates as a cultural heritage object as a container of several mutually reinforcing functions that jointly increase its investment attractiveness, and also takes into account factors of the urban environment. This makes it possible to increase its attractiveness without directly affecting the object through measures to transform the urban environment around, and the method can be used in the formation of budget programs.

As a debatable drawback of the method, we note that it cannot always be successfully applied to isolated or remote objects of cultural heritage.

Acknowledgments. This research is financially supported by the Russian Science Foundation, Agreement 17–71-30029 (https://rscf.ru/en/project/17-71-30029/), with co-financing of Bank Saint-Petersburg.

References

1. Logan, W.S.: Closing Pandora's Box: Human Rights Conundrums in Cultural Heritage. In: Silverman, H., Ruggles, D. (eds.) Cultural heritage and human rights, pp. 25–32. NY, Springer, New York (2007). https://doi.org/10.1007/978-0-387-71313-7_2
2. Federal Law "On objects of cultural heritage (monuments of history and culture) of the peoples of the Russian Federation", dated June 25, 2002 N 73-FZ. http://www.consultant.ru/document/cons_doc_LAW_37318/. Accessed 16 Dec 2022
3. Kudimov, I.S.: Increasing the investment attractiveness of cultural heritage objects of the Russian Federation. Property Relations in the Russian Federation **10**(229), 104–106 (2020)
4. Work plan for culture 2019–2022. Workshop on complementary funding for cultural heritage. Background paper and selected good practices - march 2021, https://eenc.eu/uploads/eenc-eu/2022/03/04/7869028db14908a0ecd4d6c4c7385b46.pdf. Accessed 22 Mar 2023
5. Shapiro, L.G.: Peculiarities of the preliminary check of the primary information about crimes connected with infringements on the objects of the cultural heritage of the Russian federation. Legal Policy and Legal Life **4**, 99–106 (2021)
6. Takaho, M.A., Bratoshevskaya, V.V.: The estimation of the demolition rationality of buildings in the architectural and historical environment. Bull. Sci. **6**(27), 181–182 (2020)
7. Polyakova, M.A.: The remake in the estate: "pro" et "contra." Herit. Modernity **3**(2), 44–53 (2020)
8. Kaminskaya, N.D., Ertman, E.V.: The formation of historical self-consciousness of the young people by means of tourism and local activities. Bull. Moscow State Univ. Cult. Arts **5**(103), 144–154 (2021)
9. Likhacheva, A.: National identity and the future of Russia: Report. Valdai, Moscow: Valdai (2014)
10. Kasatkina, S.S.: Historical and cultural heritage of Russian cities as an element of the cultural universum. the bulletin of the Omsk State Pedagogical University. Humanit. Stud. **1**(30), 21–24 (2021)
11. Bauwerk: Potsdam, Schloss "Sanssouci". https://www.deckenmalerei.eu/cedabcb8-190d-438e-9a0a-b9d44c70cde1. Accessed 20 Mar 2023
12. Les monuments de l'État. https://www.culture.gouv.fr/fr/Thematiques/Monuments-Sites/Monuments-historiques-sites-patrimoniaux/Les-monuments-historiques/Les-monuments-de-l-Etat. Accessed 20 Mar 2023
13. Bulletin of the State Council of the People's Republic of China. http://www.gov.cn/gongbao/shuju/1982/gwyb198204.pdf. Accessed 21 Mar 2023
14. Mikhailova, N.N.: Modern values of cultural heritage and new approaches to its preservation. Tradit. Appl. Arts Educ. **1**(32), 130–138 (2020)
15. Titarenko, I.N.: Preservation of the cultural heritage of historical settlements in Russia: history and modern problems. Tomsk State Univ. Bull. **450**, 177–184 (2020)
16. Brandousova, E.K.: The methods of preserving architectural traditions in the renovation of buildings and structures. Balandinsky Readings **1**(15), 16–22 (2020)
17. Karpova, E.S.: Reconstruction of historic buildings in a contemporary cultural context. Archit. Mod. Inf. Technol. **4**(57), 191–211 (2021)
18. Paliy, K.R.: On the issue of public-private partnership in the field of protection of cultural heritage of St Petersburg. Manag. Consult. **5**(125), 140–150 (2019)
19. Heritage at Risk. World report 2016–2019. On monuments and sites in danger. https://openarchive.icomos.org/id/eprint/2430/1/hr20_2016_2019.pdf. Accessed 19 Mar 2023
20. Lavrova, T.A.: The Funding the preservation of objects of historical and cultural heritage: a methodological aspect. Petersburg Econ. J. **1**, 8–14 (2013)

21. Mendoza, M.A.D., De La Hoz, E., Franco, J.E., Gómez, G.: Technologies for the preservation of cultural heritage—a systematic review of the literature. Sustainability **15**(2), 1059 (2023). https://doi.org/10.3390/su15021059

22. Ricca, M., et al.: A combined non-destructive and micro-destructive approach to solving the forensic problems in the field of cultural heritage: two case studies. Appl. Sci. **11**(6951), 1–14 (2021)

23. Reap, J.K.: Introduction: heritage legislation and management. https://built-heritage.spring eropen.com/articles/10.1186/s43238-022-00059-9. Accessed 22 Mar 2023

24. Lowthorp, L.: National intouchable heritage legislation & initiatives. https://unesdoc.unesco. org/ark:/48223/pf0000368351.locale=en. Accessed 22 Mar 2023

25. Goddard-Bowman, R.: Something old is something new: the role of heritage preservation in economic development. https://openjournals.uwaterloo.ca/index.php/pced/article/download/ 4002/4957/20684. Accessed 22 Mar 2023

26. Loulanski, T.: Cultural heritage in socio-economic development: local and global perspectives. Environments **34**(2), 51–69 (2006)

27. Marcinkowska, M.: The recovery and reconstruction of cultural heritage: the socio-economic approach. In: Hadzimuhamedovic, A. (eds.): Heritage Reconstruction and People: Integrated Recovery After Trauma, pp. 81–93, UNESCO (2021)

28. Tišma, S., Uzelac, A., Jelinčić, D.A., Franić, S., Škrtić, M.M.: Overview of social assessment methods for the economic analysis of cultural heritage investments. J. Risk Financ. Manag. **15**(8), 327 (2022). https://doi.org/10.3390/jrfm15080327

29. Rebec, K.M., Deanovic, B., Oostwege, L.: Old buildings need new ideas: holistic integration of conservation-restoration process data using heritage building information modelling. J. Cult. Herit. **55**, 30–42 (2022)

30. Van Sanford, S.: Historic building restoration, preservation, and renovation. https://encyclope dia.pub/entry/29561. Accessed 25 Mar 2023

31. Mekonnen, H., Bires, Z., Berhanu, K.: Practices and challenges of cultural heritage conservation in historical and religious heritage sites: evidence from North Shoa Zone, Amhara Region. Ethiopia. Herit. Sci. **10**(172), 1–22 (2022)

32. Roy, D., Kalidindi, S.: Critical challenges in the management of heritage conservation projects in India. J. Cult. Heritage Manag. Sustain. Dev. **7**(3), 290–307 (2017)

33. Thondhlana, P., Machiridza, L.H.: Restoration and restitution of cultural heritage, the case of the Ndebele Monarch: the post-colonial dilemma in Zimbabwe. J. Afr. Cult. Heritage Stud. **2**(1), 52–84 (2020)

34. Pastukh, O., Gray, T., Golovina, S.: Restored layers: reconstruction of historical sites and restoration of architectural heritage: the experience of the United States and Russia (case study of St. Petersburg). Archit. Eng. **5**(2), 17–24 (2020). https://doi.org/10.23968/2500-0055-2020-5-2-17-24

35. Yuan, P., Wei, X., Yu, W.: A tale of the new and the old: renovation of Yong'an Warehouse at Yangpu waterfront. Shanghai. Built heritage **5**, 1–15 (2021)

36. Bareicheva, M., Kubina, E., Daineko, L.: Redevelopment of the cultural heritage object (the case of the "Nurov's Estate"). SHS Web Conf. **128**, 1–10 (2021)

37. Time sharing of unused space: case of New York City. https://habidatum.com/projects/time-sharing-of-unused-space. Accessed 25 Mar 2023

38. Turskis, Z., Morkunaite, Z., Kutut, V.: A hybrid multiple criteria evaluation method of ranking of cultural heritage structures for renovation projects. Int. J. Strateg. Prop. Manag. **21**, 318–329 (2017)

39. Ferretti, V., Bottero, M., Mondini, G.: Decision making and cultural heritage: an application of the multi-attribute value theory for the reuse of historical buildings. J. Cult. Herit. **15**, 644–655 (2014)

Urban Lawns State Identification Method Based on Computer Vision

Roman Bezaev[1](✉) ⓘ, Sergey Mityagin[1] ⓘ, Aleksey Sokol[1] ⓘ,
Daniil Zhembrovskii[1] ⓘ, Alexander Kryukovskiy[2] ⓘ, and Irina Melnichuk[2] ⓘ

[1] ITMO University, Birzhevaya Line, 14, Saint-Petersburg, Russia
r.bezaev@gmail.com
[2] Saint-Petersburg State Forest Technical University, Novorossiyskaya Ulitsa, 28,
Saint-Petersburg, Russia

Abstract. The article discusses an approach to assessing the condition of urban lawns based on computer vision. The assessment of the condition of urban lawns is based on the identification of the composition of plant species growing on the lawn, since the species composition can characterize the state of the soil and growing conditions, as well as the characteristics of some external factors. Traditionally, the assessment of the condition of urban lawns is carried out by the method of full-scale research and requires considerable time and resources of specialists. The paper investigates the hypothesis of the possibility of automating this process using computer vision methods. To test this hypothesis, we used the YOLOv5 neural network for object recognition. The model was fine-tuned on a carefully curated dataset of lawn images that had been annotated with rectangles. The study revealed the shortcomings of the model, the most recognizable classes, as well as opportunities for development and improvement of the model. The proposed approach makes it possible to develop a large service for analyzing the state of urban green spaces.

Keywords: Computer vision · green spaces · YOLO neural network · detection of plant species

1 Introduction

Greenery plays an important role in the formation of a comfortable urban environment for people, performing several functions: biological, physiological and aesthetic. Due to active urbanization and an increase in the share of the urban population, the load on urban green spaces is rising [1, 2]. Assessment of their condition throughout the city is a necessary process for the effective functioning of the entire urban space.

The traditional approach to assessing the state of green spaces and urban lawns is to conduct regular monitoring by the method of field studies. Conducting field studies requires the involvement of specialists and allows you to get a comprehensive conclusion about the state of urban lawns.

However, it requires a lot of time, financial and labor resources to perform, and the impact of possible errors and inaccuracies in field research is high. Meanwhile, this

T. Guarda et al. (Eds.): ARTIIS 2023, CCIS 1935, pp. 400–411, 2024.
https://doi.org/10.1007/978-3-031-48858-0_32

process can be mostly automated, reducing costs and minimizing human influence on the process. In this study, we propose a method which can evaluate a state of the given lawn based on its pictures using machine learning and computer vision. Photos can be captured by drones or on the ground, then transferred to the server to run the algorithm, picking the most damaged lawn zones to be inspected by human operators.

In this way, the kind of lawn and its condition won't need to be detected by specialists. Their main task will be checking the results of the working autodetection system. Also, the necessity of transferring information from hand notes to the database becomes not relevant, because specialists can add characteristics of the lawn to the photo with detected classes.

2 The Problems of Assessing the State of Urban Lawns

The basic process of determining the condition of lawns in the city is shown below (see Fig. 1).

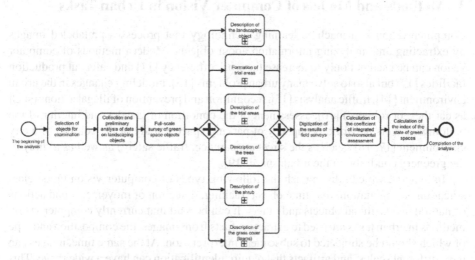

Fig. 1. The procedure for assessing the state of green spaces in the city

In general, the methodology for assessing the ecological state of green spaces includes a preparatory stage, a full-scale survey (data collection), inhouse processing of collected materials and analytical work with the results obtained (see Fig. 1). The main result of the assessment is data on the state of green spaces, which also determine the ecological situation in a particular district or city as a whole [3, 4].

At the same time, it should be noted that there are currently no general ways to assess the condition of urban lawns. The world scientific community comes up with different ways to assess the quantitative and qualitative assessment of the state of green spaces in urban space. This is due not only to the unique operating conditions of urban lawns, but also to the human factor. A specialist involved in the process of assessing the condition of urban lawns can make an assessment subjectively or based on situational factors [5].

Due to the dependence of the results of assessing the state of urban lawns on the human perception of the expert, there are approaches to automating this process. For example, there are known approaches to assessing the state of green spaces based on information from citizens [6]. Other approaches are aimed at assessing the condition based on the automation of data collection of environmental parameters, for example, the degree of humidity of the lawn using a drone, cameras, and programmable Arduino modules [7].

To date, the most popular methods of collecting data about a plot of land and lawns located on it are photographs of the site, which leads to the opportunity to use computer vision methods to analyze such data [8, 9]. The possibilities of assessing the state of green spaces using computer vision are now only being studied and gaining popularity in the research community [10]. However, the use of computer vision methods in assessing the condition of urban lawns is associated with several limitations: the need for preliminary labeling of images, the consumption of a large amount of computing power, difficulties with adding contextual data.

3   Methods and Models of Computer Vision in Urban Tasks

Computer vision is a machine learning technology that processes prelabeled images by extracting and analyzing information about objects. Modern methods of computer vision can be used not only to increase the work efficiency [11] and safety at production facilities [12] but also to solve many urban problems [13]: modeling changes in the urban environment [14], traffic analysis [15], recognition and prevention of illegal actions (such as car theft or robbery) [16], assessment of the condition of facades and interior of the buildings, streets network, occupancy of parking spaces, study of the comfort of a city environment [17, 18] (such as the street appearance, traffic safety) as well as a study of the greenery condition in the urban space [19].

In general, we can distinguish the following types of computer vision tasks: classification, segmentation, real-time object tracking, detection of movements and actions of natural and artificial objects and others. It can be said that currently computer vision methods in urban tasks are used to extract artifacts from images, the composition and type of which should be subjected to subsequent interpretation. At the same time, images can have different scales, and artifacts that require identification can have a wide range. This is very clearly manifested in the tasks of assessing the condition of lawns, which are generally represented by homogeneous photographic images. This led to the predominant use of «Deep Neural Network models» for urban tasks, which can be called neural networks with deep structures. In general, the convolutional neural network (CNN) method is the most representative model of deep learning. It has been widely applied in many applications, such as super resolution image reconstruction, image classification, face recognition, pedestrian detection, and video analysis.

Figure 2 shows that there are two different structures related to object detection methods. The first structure is regional proposals based on the traditional object detection pipeline, where it first produces regional proposals, and then classifies each proposal into different groups of objects. The second structure considers object detection as a regression of the classification problem, taking an integrated structure to obtain the final result (categories and locations) directly [20].

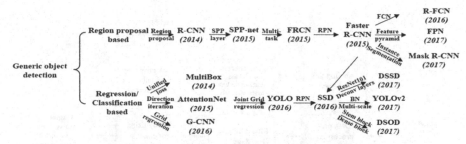

Fig. 2. Basic frameworks for object detection methods

YOLO was chosen as the method for recognizing and classifying objects. YOLO stands for «you only look once». The method was developed in 2016 by Joseph Redmon, Santosh Divvala, Ross Girshik and Ali Farhadi [21]. This algorithm requires only one direct propagation pass through the network to build predictions. This method divides the image into grids and then runs an image classification and localization algorithm on each of the grid cells. The advantage of the YOLO algorithm is that it is very fast and predicts much more accurate bounding boxes compared to other object recognition methods [22].

The current level of development of computer vision methods allows them to be used to solve various urban problems, freeing up the resources of subject specialists to work with more complex objects, but requires significant training of neural networks on many images with high-quality markup.

When working with object recognition, it is important to have enough data for training before processing any type of analysis. Note that if you prepare enough data, you can get good results with good accuracy. There are several different ways to collect data: manually from the environment or an online database from the Internet.

4   Lawn Species Detection Algorithm

We suggest using the YOLOv5 computer vision model to identify different objects in the images. The model provides images of the grass with the detected plant species in a given area.

In this way, specialists can easily determine the most common plant species present, identify areas with trampled grass or dried lawns, and suggest potential solutions to address these issues. This approach saves time that would otherwise be spent conducting field surveys and manually describing plant species.

The service, labeled data and model's weights can be found at the following link [23]. Scheme suggested method is shown higher (see Fig. 3).

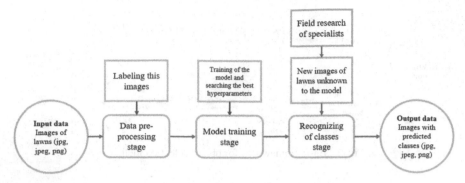

Fig. 3. Simplified model operation scheme

The proposed method consists of 3 main parts:

1. Classify uploaded images. It is necessary to designate all classes of plants in the image with a rectangular frame;
2. Model training. At this stage, hyperparameters are selected for the most accurate training of the model.
3. Uploading images to the model. After the field study, new photos are uploaded. Next, the classes of green spaces in the photo are recognized.

The main result of the method is images with selected classes that were recognized using computer vision technology.

4.1 Data Preprocessing

There were few requirements for the assessors during data labeling:

- It is desirable to label all the needed labels on each image. Since YOLO considers unlabeled objects as negative samples, this could drastically reduce the final quality.
- Objects of the same type should be similarly squared.
- Each object should be detected only once.

There were two types of images with labels prepared:

- Grass images from 1m above the ground (900 samples)
- Grass images from **UAV** 3 m and 5 m above the ground (431 samples)

The annotation was done by using the open-source annotation tool LabelImg. 12 classes of objects were labeled in total, their quantitative distribution in the input dataset is presented below (see Fig. 4).

Class Balance

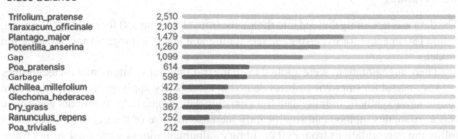

Trifolium_pratense	2,510
Taraxacum_officinale	2,103
Plantago_major	1,479
Potentilla_anserina	1,260
Gap	1,099
Poa_pratensis	614
Garbage	598
Achillea_millefolium	427
Glechoma_hederacea	388
Dry_grass	367
Ranunculus_repens	252
Poa_trivialis	212

Fig. 4. Balance of different classes

Dataset for training and testing of the model contains 1341 images, with 11309 annotations, which is 8.4 annotations per image on average. Almost every image is larger than 1024×1024. Labeling example below (see Fig. 5).

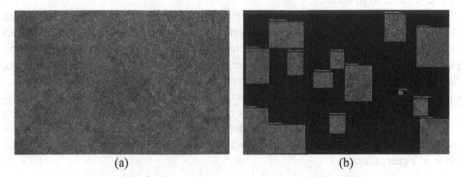

(a)   (b)

Fig. 5. (a) Image without labeling; (b) Image after labeling

The images were different sizes, so the different resizing approaches have been tried. Such as 320×320 with reflection edges, 320×320 with black edges, 640×640 crop from the center, 640×640 with reflection edges and 640×640 with black edges. It was found out experimentally that the last option works better than the others, so all the further steps will be done with 640×640 images with black edges. This type of images is better than the other, due to the inability to store multiple 1024×1024 images in the video card's memory.

In addition, auto-orientation and normalization were applied. Image normalization helps ensure that pixel values across all input images have similar and comparable ranges and ensures that the model learns representations of visual patterns from the actual pixel intensity differences rather than from the raw pixel values themselves.

4.2 Training

The data was randomly divided into three sets: train (1.1 k images) for training the model, valid (180 images) for hyper-parameters tuning and test (92 images) for evaluating the model.

Then, augmentations were applied to all the train samples. Augmentation techniques are very useful for improving object detection models. By applying augmentations, we can generate synthetic training data from existing data, which helps the model generalize better. Also, this method can significantly increase the size of the training dataset. The following augmentations from Python-library «albumentations» were used during training: Blur (p = 0.01), MedianBlur (p = 0.05), ToGray (p = 0.01), CLAHE (p = 0.03), RandomBrightnessContrast (p = 0.1), RandomGamma (p = 0.1), ImageCompression (p = 0.1), HorizontalFlip (p = 0.3), ShiftScaleRotate (p = 0.3), OpticalDistortion (p = 0.05), RandomShadow (p = 0.1), where p is a probability of applying the transform.

The model was trained on a single Nvidia GTX 980 GPU with 6 GB of memory. The GPU usage allowed to train neural networks in a quick way by processing batches of images with high speed.

The main optimized metric was mAP_0.5:0.95, where «mAP» stands for Mean Average Precision, which is calculated as the average precision across multiple object classes. It is a popular evaluation metric for object detection models. The «0.5:0.95» part refers to the range of intersection over union (IoU) thresholds used in calculating the precision. IoU is a measure of how well the predicted bounding box of an object overlaps with the ground truth bounding box.

The model was first trained for 500 epochs using the default set of hyperparameters (see Fig. 6). Then, an evolutionary algorithm was used to find the best hyperparameters over 60 generations. Finally, the model was trained for another 130 epochs using the evolved hyperparameters.

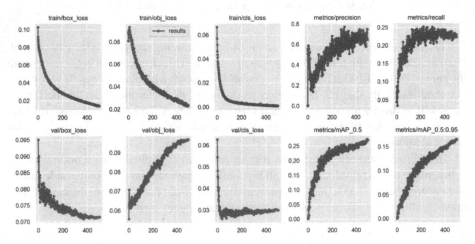

Fig. 6. Loss and metrics while first 500 training generations

We can see that the training loss is continuously decreasing, but the losses on the validation set remain almost the same, except for the box loss. However, the training continues because the metrics on the validation set are growing.

Only 60 generations of hyperparameters evolution were used due to the time consuming nature of the process, while the authors of YOLOv5 recommend making 300–500 generations. The hyperparameters don't change that much, but it seems that the momentum in the optimizer should be equal to 0.93, the learning rate should be decreased a bit to 0.09 and the weight decay should be equal to $4.7*10^{-4}$. The model with such hyperparameters was selected according to its highest mAP value.

5 Experimental Results

In order to make the inference process faster, we exported the model to the ONNX format. With the model execution time decreasing almost three times using CPU and approximately two times using GPU. The metrics of the final model are shown in Table 1, where the classes with the highest quality scores are highlighted in gray.

Based on four abovementioned metrics, the plant species Plantago Major, Trifolium Pratense, and Ranunculus Repens are recognized with the highest accuracy. This can be explained by the distinct differences in leaf shape and bright flower colors that distinguish these species apart from others. The model also performs well in detecting Dry Grass, Garbage, and Gaps due to their noticeable contrast with the surrounding greenery, making them easier to detect. However, the low metric values in most cases can be attributed to poor labeling of the data. There are instances where objects in the training images are left unlabeled when they should have been marked. Consequently, these unlabeled objects become negative samples for the model.

Table 1. Metrics for each class

Class	Precision	Recall	mAP50	mAP50–95
Average	0.627	0.254	0.285	0.188
Achillea Millefolium	0.694	0.115	0.187	0.104
Dry Grass	0.72	0.448	0.488	0.342
Glechoma Hederacea	0.687	0.086	0.0919	0.0634
Garbage	0.506	0.463	0.358	0.193
Plantago Major	0.721	0.301	0.359	0.216
Poa Pratensis	0.427	0.115	0.13	0.045
Poa Trivialis	0.474	0.111	0.227	0.0824
Gap	0.769	0.35	0.409	0.33
Ranunculus Repens	0.665	0.333	0.343	0.253
Taraxacum Officinale	0.694	0.187	0.237	0.165
Trifolium Pratense	0.709	0.393	0.44	0.369

During inference, this leads to an increase in false positives that should have been true positives. While this doesn't directly impact the recall, having a high number of false positives makes it challenging for the model to accurately identify true positives, ultimately reducing the recall rate.

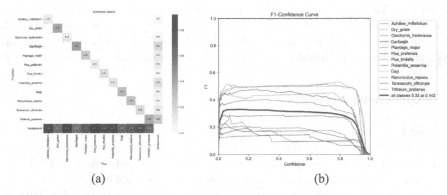

(a)   (b)

Fig. 7. (a) Confusion matrix for each class; (b) F1-Confidence Curve for each class

The confusion matrix (see Fig. 7) shows the comparison between the predicted values and the true values for different classes. The last column shows that each class has a certain number of false positives. Through empirical analysis, it has been found that in many cases these false positives are actually true positives that were missed by the assessors during the labeling process. The F1-Confidence Curve (see Fig. 7) represents the F-1 metric (the harmonic mean between precision and recall) at different confidence thresholds.

We can observe that the highest F1 score, equal to 0.33, is achieved at a threshold of 0.142, which will be used in the final model. In other words, if the model shows the probability of class assignment higher than 14.2%, we accept that class.

The comparison between the ground truth images and the detection results of the model is presented in the following figures (see Figs. 8 and 9).

(a)   (b)

Fig. 8. (a) Labeling of the original image; (b) Classes predicted by the model and those classes that it has not defined (highlighted with a blue border)

(a)   (b)

Fig. 9. (a) Labeling of the original image; (b) Classes predicted by the model and those classes that it has not defined (highlighted with a blue border)

Thousands and tens of thousands of images per class are considered necessary for good quality. In this case, the entire sample consists of 1,341 images. The experiments revealed the influence of the following factors on the model:

- The quality of photo markup for model.
- Quantitative balance of class.
- Computational power used for training.
- Count of the images of each class.

6 Discussion

Empirical evidence has shown that providing the model with photos taken from 5 m above the ground as input data is almost useless. When these photos are resized to 640×640, they become too small for the model to accurately identify the desired objects. As a result, significant progress has been made in recognizing different classes of lawn, despite the limitations of the small training sample. To address this issue, two potential solutions have been identified. First, photos can be divided into segments and fed to the model one at a time. Alternatively, GPUs with more video memory can be used to train a model capable of handling higher resolution images without losing small details due to scaling.

Our proposed method is unique, so there is no way to compare the results obtained with the available studies of other scientists. The main part of scientific articles that use computer vision to recognize plant species and states describes the results of classification of 1 plant species by pictures from a close distance, which is an example of ideal image markup. At the same time, images with 5–10 classes are used as training images for the proposed method. This makes the method under consideration and the results obtained unique.

It is worth noting that a minimum of 500 images per label is necessary for effective training according to the YOLOv5 documentation. In addition, it is important to eliminate all negative samples during the labeling process by identifying all instances of each class in the images.

Although there is potential for further development and improvement of the model, the current limitation is the lack of sufficient computing power to pursue these advances.

7 Conclusion

In summary, the YOLOv5 neural network shows promising accuracy in identifying distinct features of the lawn such as bright colors, unique leaf shapes, as well as distinguishing garbage and bald spots objects that stand out from the background. It's important to note that these findings are based on a specific dataset. The model's performance may vary as new classes are introduced or as the quantity and quality of annotated training images increases.

An important result of the study is the identification of classes whose recognition is the least accurate: Achillea Millefolium, Glechoma Hederacea, Poa Pratensis, Poa Trivialis, Taraxacum Officinale. At the moment, there are 2 ways to increase the accuracy of recognition of these classes: the formation of a training sample from photos taken from a closer distance and better marking of photos (highlighting all classes).

It is important to note that the integration of the suggested method will need fundamental changes of management of urban lawns: changing legislation, report forms, responsibilities of city department of landscaping employees. For example, the process of lawn state identification will be automatized, it results in speeding up decision making by management about the urban green programme. Additionally new tasks will appear about managing automatization of other processes and uniting all components to the whole system.

The combination of a lot of data, modern environmental solutions, and the detection model provides promising opportunities to use computer vision in urban grass analysis.

Acknowledgements. This research is financially supported by The Russian Science Foundation, Agreement №22–26-20120 (https://rscf.ru/project/22-26-20120/). Also it is financially supported by St. Petersburg Scientific Foundation in accordance with the agreement of April 14, 2022 No. 31/2022.

References

1. Haaland, C., Konijnendijk van den Bosch, C.: Challenges and strategies for urban green-space planning in cities undergoing densification: a review. Urban For. Urban Greening 14, 760–771 (2015)
2. Fuller, R.A., Gaston, K.J.: The scaling of green space coverage in European cities. Biol. Let. 5, 352–355 (2009)
3. Barnes, M.R.: Urban lawns as nature-based learning spaces. Ecopsychology. 14, 92–100 (2022)
4. Paudel, S., States, S.L.: Urban Green Spaces and sustainability: exploring the ecosystem services and disservices of grassy lawns versus floral meadows. Urban For. Urban Greening. 84, 127932 (2023)
5. Ignatieva, M., Haase, D., Dushkova, D., Haase, A.: Lawns in cities: from a globalised urban green space phenomenon to sustainable nature-based solutions. Land. 9, 73 (2020)
6. Seiferling, I., Naik, N., Ratti, C., Proulx, R.: Green streets – quantifying and mapping urban trees with street-level imagery and computer vision. Landsc. Urban Plan. 165, 93–101 (2017)
7. Marín, J., et al.: Urban Lawn Monitoring in smart city environments. J. Sens. 2018, 1–16 (2018)

8. Degerickx, J., Roberts, D.A., McFadden, J.P., Hermy, M., Somers, B.: Urban tree health assessment using airborne hyperspectral and LiDAR imagery. Int. J. Appl. Earth Obs. Geoinf. **73**, 26–38 (2018). https://doi.org/10.1016/j.jag.2018.05.021

9. Shi, J., Malik, J.: Normalized cuts and image segmentation. IEEE Trans. Pattern Anal. Mach. Intell. **22**(8), 888–905 (2000). https://doi.org/10.1109/34.868688

10. Rustamov, J., Rustamov, Z., Zaki, N.: Green space quality analysis using machine learning approaches. Sustainability. **15**, 7782 (2023)

11. Brecht, E.A., Konshina, V.N.: Application of the YOLO neural network for defect recognition. Intell. Technol. Transp. **2**(30), 41–47 (2022)

12. Filichkin, C.A., Vologdin, S.V.: Application of the YOLOv5 neural network for recognizing the presence of personal protective equipment. Intell. Syst. Prod. **2**, 61–67 (2022)

13. Ibrahim, M.R., Haworth, J., Cheng, T.: Urban-I: from urban scenes to mapping slums, transport modes, and pedestrians in cities using deep learning and computer vision. Environ. Plann. B Urban Analytics City Sci. **48**, 76–93 (2019)

14. Ibrahim, M.R., Haworth, J., Cheng, T.: Understanding cities with machine eyes: a review of deep computer vision in urban analytics. Cities **96**, 102481 (2020)

15. Messelodi, S., Modena, C.M., Zanin, M.: A computer vision system for the detection and classification of vehicles at urban road intersections. Pattern Anal. Appl. **8**, 17–31 (2005)

16. Naik, N.: Visual Urban Sensing: Understanding Cities Through Computer Vision (2017)

17. Lee, J., Kim, D., Park, J.: A machine learning and computer vision study of the environmental characteristics of streetscapes that affect pedestrian satisfaction. Sustainability. **14**, 5730 (2022)

18. Matasov, V., et al.: Covid-19 pandemic changes the recreational use of Moscow parks in space and time: outcomes from crowd-sourcing and machine learning. Urban For. Urban Greening. **83**, 127911 (2023)

19. Kajabad, E.N., Begen, P., Nizomutdinov, B., Ivanov, S.: Yolov4 for urban object detection: case of electronic inventory in St. Petersburg. In: 2021 28th Conference of Open Innovations Association (FRUCT) (2021)

20. Zhao, Z.-Q., Zheng, P., Xu, S.-T., Wu, X.: Object detection with deep learning: a review. IEEE Trans. Neural Networks Learn. Syst. **30**, 3212–3232 (2019)

21. Redmon, J., Divvala, S., Girshick, R., Farhadi, A.: You only look once: unified, real-time object detection. In: 2016 IEEE Conference on Computer Vision and Pattern Recognition (CVPR) (2016)

22. Bochkovskiy, A., Wang, C.-Y., Liao, H.-Y.M.: YOLOv4: optimal speed and accuracy of object detection. In: Computer Vision and Pattern Recognition (2020)

23. Trixdade Github. https://github.com/trixdade/Grass-Detection. Accessed 04 Jun 2023

A Behavior-Based Fuzzy Control System for Mobile Robot Navigation: Design and Assessment

Juan Pablo Vásconez[1]([✉])[iD], Mailyn Calderón-Díaz[1][iD], Inesmar C. Briceño[1][iD], Jenny M. Pantoja[1][iD], and Patricio J. Cruz[2][iD]

[1] Faculty of Engineering, Universidad Andres Bello, Santiago, Chile
{juan.vasconez,mailyn.calderon,inesmar.briceno,jenny.pantoja}@unab.cl
[2] Departamento de Automatización y Control Industrial (DACI),
Escuela Politécnica Nacional Ladrón de Guevara, 170517 Quito, Ecuador
patricio.cruz@epn.edu.ec

Abstract. Decreasing the number of robot navigation accidents due to slow robot reaction times is still an important research topic. This paper proposes a methodology based on a behavior-based fuzzy control scheme for the path planning of a simulated mobile robot. The behaviors are designed based on fuzzy logic and are integrated to switch between them when necessary during navigation in narrow and unknown environments. To test the proposed methodology, we build a simulation environment in which a mobile robot can navigate in straightforward or curved scenarios by using only a Lidar sensor and the proposed behavior-based control scheme. We tested experiment conditions for each scenario, and we evaluated the performance of the vehicle by analyzing the minimum avoidance distance from the obstacles. The simulation results demonstrate that the proposed methodology can be used for a mobile robot to react fast enough to successfully avoid obstacles when navigating in narrow and unknown environments at different velocities.

Keywords: Path planning · Mobile robot · Fuzzy logic · Behavior-based control

1 Introduction

Nowadays, there is still an increasing interest in service robots, which can be attributed to the fact these platforms are moving from industrial applications to our homes and workplaces. There is a wide range of applications where a quick response is required by a service robot, such as the hospitality industry, healthcare facilities, retail stores, elderly care, education, manufacturing and logistics, agriculture, cleaning and maintenance, entertainment, and social applications [14,16]. As technology advances, the potential for service robots continues to

Supported by Faculty of Engineering, Universidad Andres Bello, Santiago, Chile.

expand, enabling them to take on more complex tasks and operate in diverse environments. Additionally, these robotic platforms may or may not perform tasks while sharing the workspace with humans, thus having fast response times to evade obstacles and avoid accidents is key to these applications. The effectiveness of the response of a service robot to evade an obstacle will depend on its velocity, since at high velocities, a robot may or may not be able to evade an obstacle in time, which can cause economic losses and accidents. On the other hand, the efficiency with which it performs a task also depends on the robot's navigation velocity, thus analyzing the trade-off between velocity and the capacity to evade obstacles is key to the design of service robots [12].

There are two well-defined approaches that can be used to solve the problems of navigation and evasion, which are the Sense-Plan-Act (SPA) models and the Behavior-Based models [6,15]. The Sense-Plan-Act model decomposes the robot's behavior into three main stages: sensing (using sensors such as lidar, ultrasonic, and cameras), planning (trajectory generation and mapping), and acting (the robot executes the planned actions by using position, velocity, or acceleration control techniques) [6,7]. On the other hand, the Behavior-Based models, also known as the Reactive architectures, focus on creating a set of simple and reactive behaviors that interact with the environment directly [7,13]. The key difference between the SPA model and the Behavior-Based Model lies in the level of abstraction and the control structure. The SPA model is often associated with more complex systems that require higher-level decision-making and planning capabilities, that allow for more flexibility and adaptability. However, SPA models might have more delays due to the planning process. On the other hand, the Behavior-Based Model focuses on low-level reactive behaviors and their coordination, which can be simpler, as behaviors are designed to handle specific situations. The Behavior-Based Model excels in real-time responsiveness, and it is better suited for dynamic and uncertain environments where rapid reactions are crucial [6].

In a behavior-based navigation system, each behavior or module is responsible for a specific aspect of navigation, such as obstacle avoidance, path planning, waypoint tracking, and goal-seeking, among others [8]. These behaviors are designed to be relatively simple and operate independently, yet collectively contribute to the overall navigation capabilities of the robot. The coordination and integration of behaviors are typically achieved through a behavior arbitration mechanism, which determines the activation and priority of different behaviors based on their relevance and the current context. This arbitration process enables the robot to exhibit dynamic and context-dependent behavior selection, ensuring suitable responses to different situations encountered during navigation.

By combining the flexibility of behavior-based systems and the reasoning capabilities of fuzzy logic, a behavior-based fuzzy control system can allow that the mobile robot to exhibit intelligent and adaptive behavior, effectively navigating and interacting with its environment in a robust and efficient manner [2,5]. The behavior-based fuzzy control system operates in a continuous loop, continuously perceiving the environment, evaluating fuzzy rules, and updating the control signals based on the current sensor inputs. Different techniques have been developed for navigation systems applications based on behavior-based fuzzy control systems, and have presented sundry results. For example, a subsumption architecture was developed in [2]. The behaviors in this architecture are arranged in levels of priority such that when a higher-level behavior is triggered, all lower-level behaviors are suppressed. In [5], the authors have discussed the usage of motor-based approaches, which are reflexive behaviors. This work proposed the use of potential fields to specify the output of each approach. After that, a weighted summation is used to merge all of the outcomes. Other works have presented voted output results from the centralized arbitration of votes offered by independent behaviors [1,11]. Another behavior-based fuzzy control technique for mobile robot navigation based on behavioral architecture was presented in [9]. In this work, a component of command fusion and a few independent fuzzy behaviors were used to build the fuzzy behavior system. The weights given to each of the behaviors were the basis for the behavior fusion and arbitration stage. In [4,7], the authors propose several navigational behaviors to reach the goal, avoid obstacles, and get out of differently shaped unknown obstacles and walls by using different behavior arbitration fusion techniques.

From the different works found in the literature that used behavior-based fuzzy logic control for robot navigation, it has been observed that the construction of the membership functions, the creation of each behavior, and the arbitration stage are key to the correct navigation of the robot [2,5]. It has also been observed that the performance of the robot during navigation depends on the complexity of the environment or map, on the sinuosity with which the behaviors and their membership functions are incorporated, and on the correct calibration of the arbitration algorithm [4]. Although different works have been carried out regarding navigation control systems based on behaviors and fuzzy logic, there are still several problems to solve in this research area. For example, a detailed analysis of how each behavior intervenes during navigation is necessary. Likewise, an analysis of how robot velocity affects performance during navigation tasks while avoiding obstacles has not yet been carried out to date.

In this context, we propose a behavior-based fuzzy control system for mobile robot navigation in different unknown environments in order to analyze: a) how each behavior intervenes during navigation tasks in different unknown environments, and b) how the velocity affects the performance of the navigation during obstacle avoidance tasks.

2   Materials and Methods

The proposed behavior-based fuzzy control system for mobile robot navigation is presented in Fig. 1. As can be observed, the proposed architecture is conformed by a mobile robot model, environment information related to goal waypoints and obstacles, and a fuzzy behavior-based control system. Each of these stages is explained in detail below.

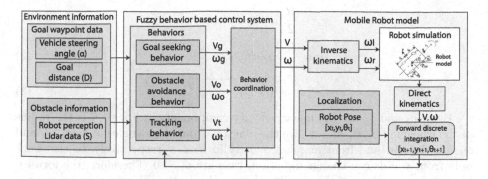

Fig. 1. Proposed architecture for the behavior-based control system for a mobile robot navigation.

2.1 Mobile Robot Model

We consider a car-like mobile robot, in which, for simplicity, we assume the Ackermann steering for the mobile robot model (see Fig. 2.a) such that the vehicle can be approximated as a two-wheel system commonly known as a bicycle model (see Fig. 2.b) [3,10].

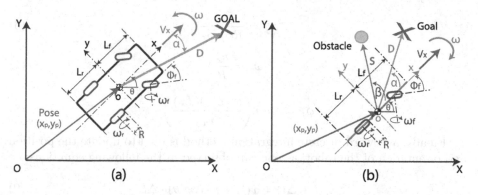

Fig. 2. Mobile robot models. a) Ackermann mobile robot model. b) Bicycle approximation for a mobile robot model.

The forward kinematics in the context of a mobile robot refers to the mathematical modeling of the robot's pose (position and orientation) $[x, y, \theta]$, and its linear and angular velocity v and ω, based on the motion of its individual wheels $(\omega_f, \omega_r, \text{ and } \phi)$. The robot's position and orientation (robot's pose) are obtained from the simulation and are represented with respect to the world coordinate system O as $[x; y; \theta]$ in meters and radians, respectively. On the other hand, the forward kinematics of the bicycle model presented in Fig. 2.b is stated as follows.

$$v_x = \frac{R}{2} \left(\omega_f cos\phi_f + \omega_r cos\phi_r \right) \tag{1}$$

$$v_y = \frac{R}{2} \left(\omega_f sin\phi_f + \omega_r sin\phi_r \right) \tag{2}$$

$$v = \sqrt{(v_x)^2 + (v_y)^2} \tag{3}$$

Here, v_x and v_y are the linear velocity components in $[m/s]$, R is the radius of the wheel in $[m]$, ϕ_r and ϕ_f are the rear and front steer angles in $[rad]$, ω_f and ω_r are the rear and front angular velocity in $[rad/s]$ respectively. In this work only front wheels can change direction, thus are $\phi_r = 0$. Therefore, the forward kinematics equations of the mobile robot to obtain the velocity components can be stated as follows.

$$v_x = \frac{R}{2} \left(\omega_f cos\phi_f \right) \tag{4}$$

$$v_y = \frac{R}{2} \left(\omega_f sin\phi_f \right) \tag{5}$$

On the contrary, for the inverse kinematic equations of the mobile robot, the inputs are the linear velocity v and the angular velocity ω, and the outputs are the front angular and rear angular velocities ω_f and ω_r, as well as the front steer angle ϕ_f, as it is detailed below.

$$\omega_f = \frac{v_x}{R cos\phi_f} \tag{6}$$

$$\omega_r = \frac{v_x}{R} \tag{7}$$

$$\phi_f = atan \left(\frac{\omega (L_f + L_r)}{v_x} \right) \tag{8}$$

Finally, a forward discrete integration method is used to update the position and orientation of the robot, as one can observed in the following equations:

$$x(t + \Delta t) = x(t) + v \cdot cos(\theta) \cdot \Delta t \tag{9}$$

$$y(t + \Delta t) = y(t) + v \cdot sin(\theta) \cdot \Delta t \tag{10}$$

$$\theta(t + \Delta t) = \theta(t) + \omega \cdot \Delta t \tag{11}$$

2.2 Environment Information

In this stage, we explain the information that can be extracted from the environment. In this regard, we can mention the goal waypoints data and the obstacles information (see Fig. 2.b). The goal waypoints data is related to the location of the waypoints that the mobile robot has to reach, thus will be used as a reference point during navigation. The angle between the front of the mobile robot and the next waypoint is α. Finally, the distance between the waypoint and the robot is D. At this stage, it is also considered the information related to the obstacles that will be found within the environment. To detect obstacles, the mobile robot uses a Lidar sensor that allows it to obtain 2D line-of-sight capabilities. In this study, we represent the orientation of each Lidar beam with the angle β. We consider that the Lidar sensor is installed pointing to the front of the robot, *i.e.* $\beta = 0°$, the Lidar beam on the right side of the robot is $\beta = -90°$, and from the left side of the robot is $\beta = 90°$. For our experiments, we only consider the following six beam measures of the Lidar $S1$ at $\beta = -90°$, $S2$ at $\beta = -60°$, $S3$ at $\beta = 0°$, $S4$ at $\beta = 30°$, $S5$ at $\beta = 60°$, $S6$ at $\beta = 90°$, since this was enough to control the navigation of the robot.

2.3 Behavior-Based Fuzzy Control

A behavior-based fuzzy control system for a mobile robot combines behavior-based navigation principles with fuzzy logic techniques to enable intelligent and adaptive robot behavior. The proposed approach involves the integration of multiple fuzzy behaviors that collectively command the robot's navigation steering and velocity [2,5,7]. The proposed fuzzy behavior-based control system for robot navigation consists of two stages: the behavior-based fuzzy modules and the behavior coordination. We explain these two stages below.

Behavior-Based Modules. The behavior-based fuzzy control system comprises multiple behavior modules, each defined by a set of fuzzy rules using fuzzy logic. Each module represents a specific behavior or task that the mobile robot should perform. In this work, we used three different behavior rules that are shown in the Fuzzy behavior based control system block of Fig. 1. These are goal-seeking behavior (see Table 1), obstacle avoidance behavior (see Table 2), and tracking behavior (see Table 3).

- Goal-seeking behavior: The goal-seeking behavior fuzzy rules are briefly explained as follows: a) If the goal is on the front, the vehicle moves forward; If the goal position is on the left side (or right) then the vehicle will turn left (or right) depending on the situation; b) If the vehicle steering angle ϕ is big (or medium or small) then the vehicle's angular velocity ω is big (or medium or small) depending on the situation; c) If the distance between the current position and the goal is near (or medium or far), the linear velocity is set to slow (or medium, fast) depending on the situation.

– Obstacle avoidance behavior: The obstacle avoidance fuzzy rules are: a) If an obstacle is on the right-front (left-front), then the vehicle turns left (right); If there is an obstacle directly on the front of the vehicle, it turns left by default; b) If the front obstacle distance is small (or medium, large), the angular velocity is big (or medium, small) and the linear velocity of the vehicle is slow (or medium, fast) depending on the situation.

– Tracking behavior: The tracking behavior fuzzy rules are briefly explained as follows: a) If a sidewalk or lane is on the left side (or right side) and the goal is on the left, the vehicle moves forward (navigates towards the goal without crashing with the wall); b) If an obstacle is on the left side (or right side) and the goal is on the right, the vehicle navigates towards the goal (moves forward without crashing with the wall); c) If the vehicle moves towards the goal, the linear velocity is fast, otherwise, the linear velocity is medium.

Table 1. Goal-seeking behavior fuzzy rules.

Goal distance (D)	velocity	α						
S	ω	NB	NM	NS	Z	PS	PM	PB
	V	Vs	Vs	Vs	Vs	Vs	Vs	Vs
M	ω	NB	NM	NS	Z	PS	PM	PB
	V	Vm	Vm	Vm	Vm	Vm	Vm	Vm
B	ω	NB	NM	NS	Z	PS	PM	PB
	V	Vf	Vf	Vf	Vf	Vf	Vf	Vf

D=goal distance, Z=zero, S=small, M=Medium,
B=big, NS=negative small, NM=negative medium,
NB=negative big, PS=positive small,
PM=Positive medium, PB=positive big,
Vs=slow velocity, Vm=medium velocity,
Vf=fast velocity.

Fuzzy Controller. Each behavior module has its own set of fuzzy rules that map sensor inputs to the right course of action. The information or expertise needed to complete the navigational tasks for robots is encoded in these rules. The structure of the fuzzy logic inference approach is illustrated in Fig. 3, and explained as follows.

– Fuzzification: It converts a set of controller inputs (crisp data) into a set of fuzzy variables (linguistic values) using the membership functions. Fuzzification is performed to represent the uncertainty and imprecision associated with the sensor data.

– Rule-base: The fuzzy rules in each behavior module are evaluated based on the fuzzified sensor inputs. At this stage, a set of if-then rules are used based on a fuzzy logic quantification of the expert's linguistic description of how to control certain situations or accomplish a particular task.

Table 2. Obstacle avoidance behavior fuzzy rules.

Goal distance (D)	velocity	S0 $\beta = -90°$	S1 $\beta = -60°$	S2 $\beta = -30°$	S3 $\beta = 0°$	S4 $\beta = 30°$	S5 $\beta = 60°$	S6 $\beta = 90°$
S	ω	PB	PB	PB	PB	NB	NB	NB
	V	Vs	Vs	Vs	Vs	Vs	Vs	Vs
M	ω	PM	PM	PM	PM	NM	NM	NM
	V	Vm	Vm	Vm	Vm	Vm	Vm	Vm
B	ω	PS	PS	PS	Z	NS	NS	NS
	V	Vf	Vf	Vf	Vf	Vf	Vf	Vf

D=goal distance, Z=zero, S=small, M=Medium, B=big, NS=negative small,
NM=negative medium, NB=negative big, PS=positive small, PM=Positive medium,
PB=positive big, Vs=slow velocity, Vm=medium velocity, Vf=fast velocity,
β=angle to the obstacle, S0 to S6 are the lidar measures.

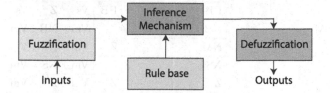

Fig. 3. The structure of the fuzzy controller.

- Inference mechanism: It emulates the expert's decision-making in interpreting and applying knowledge about how best to control different situations. This step evaluates the set of if-then rules that define the fuzzy system, identifies the rules that apply to the current situation, and computes the values of the output linguistic variables. For this, the outputs of the fuzzy rules within a behavior module are aggregated to obtain a combined control action for that specific behavior.
- Defuzzification: It converts the linguistic values resulting from the inference mechanism into crisp outputs, which represent the robot's desired action or motion. In this work, the Mamdani Defuzzification type was used to facilitate interpretation which is well suited to human input applications and has a MIMO (multiple-input and multiple-output) structure. Finally, the defuzzification method used was the centroid calculation.

The fuzzy rules used in this work depend on a set of membership functions aimed at controlling the mobile robot's velocity and steering angle. The membership functions for the inputs and outputs used in this work for the behavior-based fuzzy controller are illustrated in Fig. 4.

Behavior Coordination. At this stage, the outputs from the defuzzification step are combined using a coordination (arbitration) mechanism. This mechanism determines the final control signal that controls the mobile robot's behavior based on priority. The resulting control signal is then used to control the robot's angular and linear velocity. The behavior coordination scheme for the behavior-based fuzzy control system for mobile robot navigation is illustrated in Fig. 5.

Table 3. Tracking behavior fuzzy rules.

		S0 $\beta = -90°$		S6 $\beta = +90°$	
Goal distance (D)	Steering angle (ϕ)	ω	V	ω	V
S	NB	Z	Vm	NB	Vm
	NM	Z	Vm	NM	Vm
	NS	Z	Vm	NS	Vm
	Z	Z	Vm	Z	Vm
	PS	PS	Vs	Z	Vs
	PM	PM	Vs	Z	Vs
	PB	PB	Vs	Z	Vs
M	NB	Z	Vm	NB	Vm
	NM	Z	Vm	NM	Vm
	NS	Z	Vm	NS	Vm
	Z	Z	Vm	Z	Vm
	PS	PS	Vm	Z	Vm
	PM	PM	Vm	Z	Vm
	PB	PB	Vm	Z	Vm
B	NB	Z	Vm	NB	Vm
	NM	Z	Vm	NM	Vm
	NS	Z	Vm	NS	Vm
	Z	Z	Vm	Z	Vm
	PS	PS	Vf	Z	Vf
	PM	PM	Vf	Z	Vf
	PB	PB	Vf	Z	Vf

D=goal distance, Z=zero, S=small, M=Medium,
B=big, NS=negative small, NM=negative medium,
NB=negative big, PS=positive small,
PM=Positive medium, PB=positive big,
Vs=slow velocity, Vm=medium velocity,
Vf=fast velocity, S0 to S6 are the liDAR measures.

The first condition to accomplish is goal-seeking behavior. If the robot reaches the goal, it will stop navigation or try to go to the next goal waypoint if exist. Then, if an obstacle or a wall is found, obstacle avoidance or tracking behavior comes into play depending on the conditions and position of the obstacles.

3   Results

In this section, we present the experiments carried out based on the implementation of the proposed behavior-based fuzzy control system for mobile robot

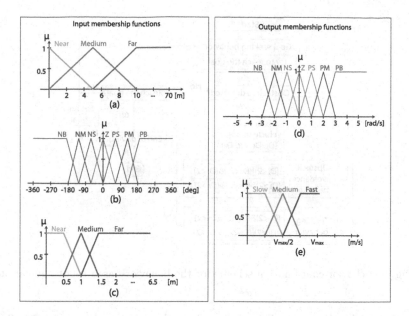

Fig. 4. Fuzzy membership functions for the input and output values of the behavior-based control scheme. a) Goal distance, b) Angle with respect to the goal α, c) Distance D to the obstacles considering sensor measures $S1$ to $S6$. d) Steering angle ϕ_f, e) mobile robot velocity module v.

navigation. For this purpose, we have built two different scenarios with obstacles. The first is a straight scenario, and the second is a curved scenario, as can be observed in Figs. 6 and 7 respectively. As can be observed, for each scenario, three different experiments were performed, one for each maximum velocity: a) max-velocity of 1 m/s, b) max-velocity of 0.75 m/s, and c) max-velocity of 0.3 m/s respectively. The navigation velocity can decrease from those points during navigation depending on the sensor measures (see Fig. 4.e). It is worth mentioning that obstacle avoidance behavior and tracking behavior enter into action when the obstacles are less than 2 m from one or more of the robot's sensors, thus the robot's maneuverability capacity will be analyzed from this point.

As can be observed on the left side in Fig. 6.a, 6.b, and 6.c, a straight scenario with obstacles was created, where the robot tries to navigate from point A to point B using the proposed behavior-bases fuzzy control system. The minimum distance from the robot to the obstacles measured during navigation can be observed within the green boxes in each case in Fig. 6.a, 6.b, and 6.c. It can be noticed that the distance from the robot to the obstacles during navigation increases as the velocity is reduced. This is because the robot's maneuverability capacity increases as the velocity decreases. For example, it is observed that in Fig. 6.a, the robot approaches up to 0.67m away from the first obstacle navigating at 1m/s, while it approaches at 1.3m and 1.92m as its velocity decreases to 0.75m/s and 0.3 m/s respectively. Similar behavior is observed for the second

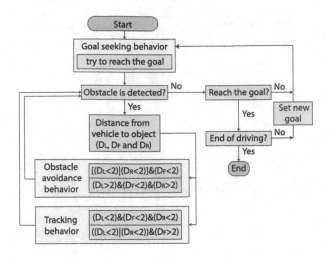

Fig. 5. Behavior coordination scheme for the behavior-based robot navigation.

obstacle found in Fig. 6.a, 6.b, and 6.c, where the robot approaches up to 2.05m, 2.6m, and 2.76m respectively during navigation. For these obstacles, the decrease in the maneuverability capacity of the robot at high speeds is not as noticeable as for the first obstacle. This is because the second obstacle barely obstructs the trajectory of the robot in all cases, while for the first obstacle, it was necessary to perform a much greater maneuver to evade said obstacle. Finally, as can be observed on the right side in Fig. 6.a, 6.b, and 6.c, the goal-seeking behavior predominates, followed by the obstacle avoidance behavior, and tracking behavior respectively. However, it is observed that the obstacle avoidance behavior is replaced by the tracking behavior as the speed decreases. This is because, at lower speeds, the robot navigates more time with obstacles to its sides, which is related to the tracking behavior.

Now we carry out the same analysis for Fig. 7. As can be observed on the left side in Fig. 7.a, 7.b, and 7.c, a curved scenario with obstacles was created, where the robot tries to navigate from point A to point B using the proposed behavior-bases fuzzy control system. The minimum distance from the robot to the obstacles measured during navigation can be observed within the green boxes in each case in Fig. 7.a, 7.b, and 7.c. It can be noticed that the distance from the robot to the obstacles during navigation increases as the velocity is reduced. This is because the robot's maneuverability capacity increases as the velocity decreases. For example, it is observed that in Fig. 7.a, the robot approaches up to 0.9m away from the first obstacle navigating at 1m/s, while it approaches at 1.1m and 1.42m as its velocity decreases to 0.75m/s and 0.3 m/s respectively. However, it is observed that this scenario does not necessarily be met for the second obstacle. As can be observed for the second obstacle found in Fig. 7.a, 7.b, and 7.c, the robot approaches up to 1.25m, 1.13m, and 1.54m respectively during navigation. For example, the robot is near the second obstacle in the case in 7.b

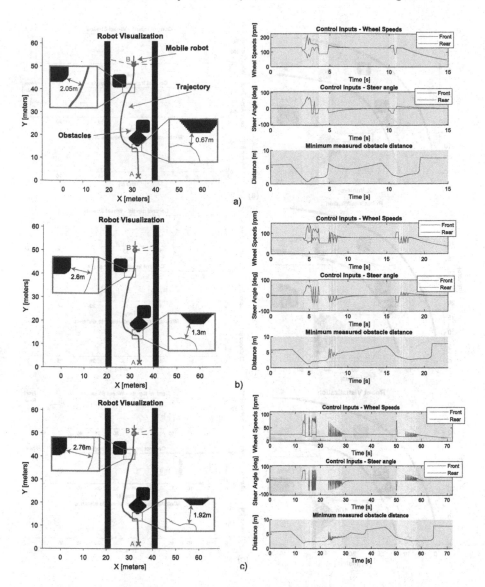

Fig. 6. Mobile robot simulation results. The images on the left represent a straight scenario and the robot navigation simulation. The images on the right represent the control signals and the minimum measured obstacle distance, in which the blue areas represent the goal-seeking behavior, the red areas represent the obstacle avoidance behavior, and the green areas represent the tracking behavior. a) max-velocity of 1 m (Color figure online)/s, b) max-velocity of 0.75 m/s, and c) max-velocity of 0.3 m/s.

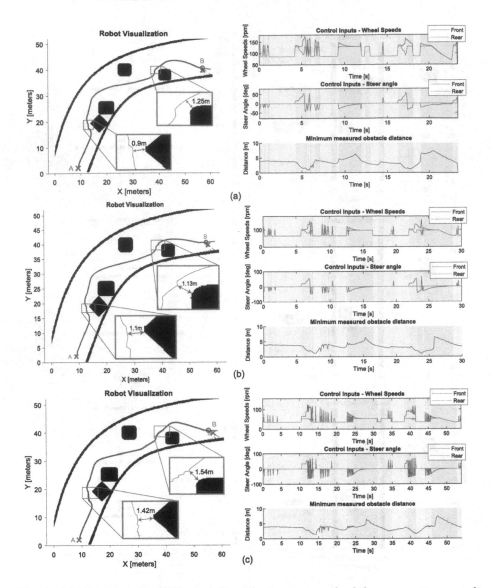

Fig. 7. Mobile robot simulation results. The images on the left represent a curved scenario and the robot navigation simulation. The images on the right represent the control signals and the minimum measured obstacle distance, in which the blue areas represent the goal-seeking behavior, the red areas represent the obstacle avoidance behavior, and the green areas represent the tracking behavior. a) max-velocity of 1 m (Color figure online)/s, b) max-velocity of 0.75 m/s, and c) max-velocity of 0.3 m/s.

compared to the case in 7.a. This occurs because the robot travels more slowly in the second case, it has more time to position itself so that it tries to reach the goal after evading the first obstacle, but this makes the robot encounter the second obstacle in a slightly difficult position compared with the first case. Nevertheless, at the lowest speed for case 7.c, the robot is able to better maneuver, and its distance to the second obstacle is 1.54m. Finally, as can be observed on the right side in Fig. 7.a, 7.b, and 7.c, the tracking behavior predominates, followed by the goal-seeking behavior, and obstacle avoidance behavior respectively. It is observed that this behavior is similar in Fig. 7.a, 7.b, and 7.c. This is because, in curved scenarios, the robot navigates more time with obstacles or walls to its sides, which is related to the tracking behavior.

4   Conclusions

In this work, we developed a behavior-based fuzzy control system for mobile robot navigation able to perform tasks in different unknown environments. Three different behavior-based modules were implemented which are related to goal-seeking, obstacle avoidance, and tracking in a straight and a curved scenario. We proposed a fuzzy controller based on membership functions that allow controlling the robot's movement by changing its linear and angular velocity depending on the environmental conditions. A behavior coordination based on high-priority behaviors was used demonstrating its effectiveness in experiments with variable velocity. We analyzed how each behavior intervenes during navigation tasks in straight and curve unknown environments and the effect of velocity on performance during obstacle avoidance tasks. The results show that the proposed system performs better at low speeds than at high speeds. Also, they showed that a behavior-based fuzzy control system for mobile robot navigation is able to perform tasks in different unknown environments reacting fast enough to avoid crashes and accidents.

Acknowledgments. The authors gratefully acknowledge the support provided by the Faculty of Engineering, Universidad Andres Bello, Santiago, Chile.

References

1. Bao, Q.y., Li, S.m., Shang, W.y., An, M.j.: A fuzzy behavior-based architecture for mobile robot navigation in unknown environments. In: 2009 International Conference on Artificial Intelligence and Computational Intelligence, vol. 2, pp. 257–261. IEEE (2009)
2. Brooks, R.A.: A robot that walks: emergent behaviors from a carefully evolved network. In: Proceedings of the Workshop on "Locomotion Control in Legged Invertebrates" on Biological Neural Networks in Invertebrate Neuroethology and Robotics (2013)
3. Corke, P., Jachimczyk, W., Pillat, R.: Mobile robot vehicles. In: Robotics, Vision and Control: Fundamental Algorithms in MATLAB®, pp. 127–160. Springer (2023). https://doi.org/10.1007/978-3-031-07262-8_4
4. Dongshu, W., Yusheng, Z., Wenjie, S.: Behavior-based hierarchical fuzzy control for mobile robot navigation in dynamic environment. In: 2011 Chinese Control and Decision Conference (CCDC), pp. 2419–2424. IEEE (2011)

5. Fatmi, A., Al Yahmadi, A., Khriji, L., Masmoudi, N.: A fuzzy logic based navigation of a mobile robot. World Acad. Sci. Eng. Technol. **2** (2008)
6. Gasparetto, A., Boscariol, P., Lanzutti, A., Vidoni, R.: Path planning and trajectory planning algorithms: a general overview. In: Carbone, G., Gomez-Bravo, F. (eds.) Motion and Operation Planning of Robotic Systems. MMS, vol. 29, pp. 3–27. Springer, Cham (2015). https://doi.org/10.1007/978-3-319-14705-5_1
7. Hong, T.S., Nakhaeinia, D., Karasfi, B.: Application of Fuzzy Logic in Mobile Robot Navigation, pp. 21–36. Fuzzy Logic-Controls, Concepts, Theories and Applications pp (2012)
8. Li, J., Ran, M., Wang, H., Xie, L.: A behavior-based mobile robot navigation method with deep reinforcement learning. Unmanned Syst. **9**(03), 201–209 (2021)
9. Mo, H., Tang, Q., Meng, L.: Behavior-based fuzzy control for mobile robot navigation. Math. Probl. Eng. **2013** (2013)
10. Novotny, G., Liu, Y., Wöber, W., Olaverri-Monreal, C.: Autonomous vehicle calibration via linear optimization. In: 2022 IEEE Intelligent Vehicles Symposium (IV), pp. 527–532. IEEE (2022)
11. Seraji, H., Howard, A.: Behavior-based robot navigation on challenging terrain: a fuzzy logic approach. IEEE Trans. Robot. Autom. **18**(3), 308–321 (2002)
12. Vásconez, J.P., et al.: Comparison of path planning methods for robot navigation in simulated agricultural environments. Procedia Comput. Sci. **220**, 898–903 (2023)
13. Vásconez, J.P., Cheein, F.A.A.: Workload and production assessment in the avocado harvesting process using human-robot collaborative strategies. Biosys. Eng. **223**, 56–77 (2022)
14. Vasconez, J.P., Carvajal, D., Cheein, F.A.: On the design of a human-robot interaction strategy for commercial vehicle driving based on human cognitive parameters. Adv. Mech. Eng. **11**(7), 1687814019862715 (2019)
15. Vasconez, J.P., Guevara, L., Cheein, F.A.: Social robot navigation based on HRI non-verbal communication: a case study on avocado harvesting. In: Proceedings of the 34th ACM/SIGAPP Symposium on Applied Computing, pp. 957–960 (2019)
16. Vasconez, J.P., Viscaino, M., Guevara, L., Cheein, F.A.: A fuzzy-based driver assistance system using human cognitive parameters and driving style information. Cogn. Syst. Res. **64**, 174–190 (2020)

Optimising a Formulated Cost Model to Minimise Labour Cost of Computer Networking Infrastructure: A Systematic Review

Richard Nana Nketsiah[1]($\boxtimes$) (iD), Richard C. Millham[1] (iD), Israel Edem Agbehadji[2,3] (iD),
Emmanuel Freeman[4] (iD), and Ayogeboh Epizitone[5] (iD)

[1] ICT and Society Research Group, Department of Information Technology, Durban University of Technology, Durban, South Africa
rnananketsiah@gmail.com, richardm1@dut.ac.za
[2] Honorary Research Associate, Faculty of Accounting and Informatics, Durban University of Technology, P.O. Box 1334, Durban 4000, South Africa
israeldel2006@gmail.com
[3] University of KwaZulu-Natal, Pietermaritzburg, South Africa
[4] Faculty of Computing and Information Systems, Ghana Communication Technology University, PMB 100, Accra North, Ghana
efreeman@gctu.edu.gh
[5] Faculty of Accounting and Informatics, Durban University of Technology, P.O. Box 1334, Durban 4000, South Africa
ayo2811@gmail.com

Abstract. Contemporary enterprises need to manage their infrastructure effectively while keeping personnel costs low to ensure profitability. Achieving this necessitates the study of employing a quantitative research approach to develop a cost model that enables companies to optimise their networking infrastructure while reducing human expenses. The study identified variables such as topologies and configuration complexities that affect labour costs and incorporated the uncovered methods for cutting labour expenses into the developed cost model. Thus, to establish the model's efficacy, the study used real-world data to validate the proposed cost model and compare it to other models. The findings indicate that the cost model can reduce labour costs in computer networking infrastructure and other areas while maintaining excellent network performance and reliability. The study highlights the issues that can impact policy and educate network practitioners. It emphasises the likelihood of developing a reliable cost model that offers financial advantages to customers. Finally, the study used a systematic approach to identify and select relevant literature from the Scopus and Web of Science databases for the research. Overall, the quantitative research approach used in this study enabled a comprehensive evaluation of cost-saving methods related to computer networking infrastructure and the development of an effective cost model that can benefit contemporary enterprises.

Keywords: Bio-inspired algorithm · Cost model · Computer networking infrastructure · Labour cost

T. Guarda et al. (Eds.): ARTIIS 2023, CCIS 1935, pp. 427–442, 2024.
https://doi.org/10.1007/978-3-031-48858-0_34

1   Introduction

In today's fast-paced and interconnected world, the computer networking infrastructure is vital for organisations to facilitate communication, data sharing, and collaboration among employees and customers [1]. Computer networking infrastructure has become an essential component of businesses and organisations in today's digital age, enabling communication and information exchange across devices locally and globally [2]. However, the costs associated with setting up, maintaining, or upgrading such infrastructure, including labour costs, are substantial, often limiting or hindering organisations attempting to establish one. Therefore, optimising a formulated cost model to minimise labour costs is essential for businesses, especially those reliant on computer networking infrastructure. Cost optimisation is a crucial aspect of business management, particularly concerning computer networking infrastructure [3].

Despite numerous challenges in establishing computer networks in organisations, reducing labour costs is a significant goal that addresses many obstacles associated with the infrastructure setup. Labour costs generally constitute a substantial portion of operating expenses in computer networking, making it crucial to find ways to minimise these costs. Consequently, optimising a formulated cost model to minimise labour costs is an important research issue worth exploring [4]. This involves developing a cost model that considers various factors contributing to labour costs in computer networking, such as the required number of employees, task completion time, necessary skill levels, hourly rates per worker, and worker benefit-related costs. Addressing these cost-related components could provide a viable solution to enhance the efficiency of computer network infrastructure. Bio-inspired algorithms have proven effective approaches for solving complex optimisation problems [5].

This study explores the various approaches and techniques used to optimise cost models in computer networking infrastructure, focusing mainly on minimising labour costs. By synthesising the findings of relevant studies, we aim to provide a comprehensive overview of the current state of knowledge in this area, identify key factors influencing the effectiveness of cost optimisation strategies, and highlight areas for future research. The insights gained from this review are expected to inform the development of more effective cost optimisation strategies for computer networking infrastructure, helping businesses reduce labour costs and improve overall efficiency. Additionally, the review holds important implications for researchers and industry professionals.

The paper structure includes the following sections: Sect. 2 presents an overview of related works, Sect. 3 introduces the materials and methods applied in this research, Sect. 4 provides an analysis and discussion, and Sect. 5 concludes the study with a summary and recommendations.

2 Literature Review

2.1 Related Literature

Introduction:

Computer networking infrastructure is a significant expense for many organisations, and optimising this cost is a critical concern [6]. Various cost models have been developed to identify the factors contributing to labour costs in computer networking infrastructure, providing a comprehensive approach tailored to the specific needs of different organisations [7]. This paper focuses on strategies to minimise labour costs in computer networking infrastructure and highlights effective cost models for achieving this goal. Labour Cost Optimisation Strategies focus on reducing expenditures and maximising profits; strategising labour cost optimisation is crucial for businesses, especially in the computer network structure.

This systematic review explores the optimisation of a formulated cost model to minimise labour costs associated with computer networking infrastructure. It highlights strategies such as outsourcing network infrastructure management, utilising automation tools and cross-training employees to reduce labour costs [8]. Long-term impacts, such as employee retention and job satisfaction, are also emphasised to ensure the chosen strategies maintain quality and employee well-being.

Factors Affecting Labour Costs in Computer Networking Infrastructure: Labour costs significantly impact the overall cost of computer networking infrastructure [9]. Researchers have identified several factors influencing labour costs in this field, including project complexity, worker expertise, available qualified workers, total workforce size, and project location [10]. Adopting automation tools and new technologies has shown promising results in reducing labour costs. This review highlights the importance of understanding these factors to develop effective cost models for computer networking infrastructure projects [11].

Formulated Cost Models: Optimising cost models is crucial for organisations aiming to reduce labour expenses and increase profitability [12]. In the field of computer networking infrastructure, where labour costs constitute a significant portion of overall expenses, researchers have proposed various cost models. These models consider device numbers, types, data traffic, network topology, equipment placement, and labour skill requirements [13]. Considering long-term costs, maintenance, and upgrades is also essential when formulating cost models. The review provides valuable insights into developing and implementing cost models, helping organisations achieve their cost optimisation goals [14].

Contributions of the Review: This comprehensive review provides an overview of the current state of research on cost modeling in computer networking infrastructure, identifies research gaps, and proposes a formulated cost model that considers factors affecting labour costs [15]. It also highlights implementation challenges, such as data availability and accuracy, and the need for skilled professionals [16]. The review emphasises potential benefits, including cost savings and better resource allocation, motivating further research and development of the cost model [17]. Additionally, the study categorises the methodology and findings in Table 1, providing a clear overview of the different categories [18].

The optimisation of a formulated cost model to minimise labour costs in computer networking infrastructure is a critical research topic. This systematic review provides valuable insights into cost modelling, labour cost optimisation strategies, factors affecting labour costs, and the benefits of using the formulated cost model. It highlights the importance of considering long-term impacts and practical implementation challenges. By addressing these areas, organisations can achieve cost savings and better resource allocation in their computer networking infrastructure projects.

Table 1. Research focus – methodology – findings table

Research Focus	Methodology	Findings
Cost Optimisation	Mathematical Modelling	These studies focused on developing mathematical models to optimise costs in computer networking infrastructure. They used optimisation techniques like linear programming, dynamic programming, and heuristic algorithms to minimise costs [19]
Labour Cost	Case Studies	These studies focused on case studies of organisations implementing cost optimisation strategies to minimise labour costs in their computer networking infrastructure [20]. They analysed the effectiveness of these strategies and identified the factors that influenced their success
Cost Optimisation	Simulation	These studies used simulation techniques to evaluate the effectiveness of different cost optimisation strategies in computer networking infrastructure [21]. They simulated different scenarios and assessed the costs associated with each scenario
Labour Cost	Survey	These studies used surveys to collect data on the labour costs associated with computer networking infrastructure. They identified the factors that influenced labour costs and the strategies organisations used to minimise them [22]
Cost Optimisation	Meta-Analysis	These studies examined existing literature on cost optimisation in computer networking infrastructure [23]. They identified the most effective strategies and the factors that influenced their effectiveness
Labour Cost	Cost-Benefit Analysis	These studies conducted a cost-benefit analysis of different cost optimisation strategies in computer networking infrastructure [24]. They evaluated the costs and benefits associated with each strategy and identified the most cost-effective strategies

Studies focusing on cost optimisation using mathematical modelling found that techniques such as linear programming, dynamic programming, and heuristic algorithms can effectively minimise costs in computer networking infrastructure [25]. Case studies on labour cost optimisation strategies identified influential factors and evaluated their effectiveness in reducing labour costs [26]. Simulation techniques were used to evaluate the effectiveness of different cost optimisation strategies in computer networking infrastructure, helping organisations identify the most effective approaches [30]. Surveys on labour costs associated with computer networking infrastructure identified influencing factors and strategies to minimise these costs. Meta-analyses of existing literature on cost optimisation in computer networking infrastructure identified effective strategies and influential factors. Cost-benefit analysis studies evaluated the costs and benefits associated with various optimisation strategies [31–34]. The evaluation process has assessed the quality and pertinence of each piece of work in relation to the research topic, and the resulting conclusions are as follows:

The study on cost optimisation using mathematical modelling is highly relevant. Using techniques such as linear programming, dynamic programming, and heuristic algorithms directly relates to minimising labour costs [28]. The quality of the study depends on the accuracy of the mathematical models and assumptions made during the optimisation process. Case studies on labour cost optimisation strategies are also highly relevant. Analysing the strategy's effectiveness and identifying influential factors is crucial in minimising labour costs in computer networking infrastructure [29]. The quality of the study relies on appropriate case selection and accurate data collection. Studies utilising simulation techniques are relevant. Evaluating the effectiveness of cost optimisation strategies through simulations helps identify the most effective approaches for minimising labour costs [27]. The quality of the study depends on accurate simulation models and assumptions. Surveys conducted on labour costs associated with computer networking infrastructure are relevant. Identifying influential factors and strategies to minimise costs is essential for formulating cost models [28]. The study's quality depends on the survey sample's accuracy and representativeness.

The meta-analysis of existing literature on cost optimisation in computer networking infrastructure is highly relevant. Identifying effective strategies and influential factors helps formulate cost models that minimise labour costs [29]. The quality of the study depends on the selection of appropriate investigations and accurate data collection. Cost-benefit analysis studies are highly relevant. Evaluating the costs and benefits associated with different optimisation strategies helps identify cost-effective approaches for minimising labour costs [30]. The quality of the study depends on accurate cost-benefit analysis and assumptions made during the analysis process.

In summary, all the studies are relevant to the research question, and their quality depends on accurate data, valid assumptions, and appropriate study selection. Overall, these studies provide valuable insights into strategies for minimising labour costs in computer networking infrastructure, which can inform the formulation of cost models for optimisation.

2.2 Identification of Gaps

Based on the information gathered from the literature, there have been a few potential gaps or inconsistencies in the literature that have been identified, including the number of years where data was not recorded. The first identified gap is a lack of information on the specific cost models used in the studies focusing on mathematical modelling and simulation techniques. Without knowing the details of these models, assessing their effectiveness and relevance to the research question is complex. The second is that studies focusing on labour cost optimisation strategies may not fully consider the impact of other costs, such as equipment and maintenance, on overall cost optimisation. It would be helpful to see how labour costs are related to these additional costs and how they can be minimised in conjunction with labour costs. Thirdly, while the studies generally provide insights into effective cost optimisation strategies, they do not necessarily address the challenges and limitations of implementing these strategies in practice. For example, some cost optimisation strategies may be challenging to implement due to organisational constraints or may not be feasible in specific contexts. Lastly, there may be potential differences in cost optimisation strategies and their effectiveness depending on the kind of computer networking infrastructures used (e.g., cloud-based vs on-premises). The studies do not specifically address this potential variability.

Addressing these gaps and inconsistencies may further improve the effectiveness and applicability of cost models for minimising labour costs in computer networking infrastructure.

3 Research Methodology

The Preferred Reporting Items for Systematic Reviews and Meta-Analyses statement's (PRISMA) flow diagram was chosen to depict the flow of information through the different phases of a systematic review. The PRISMA is a 27-item check-listed document used in enhancing systematic review write-ups [31]. It also enhances the replicability of reviews, making results from systematic reviews of diagnostic test accuracy studies more useful. The criteria used to select and analyse scholarly works on the method for minimising the labour cost of computer networking infrastructure are provided. The keywords used for searching the various databases are as follows: "cost model", "labour cost", "bio-inspired algorithm", and "computer network infrastructure".

3.1 Search Strategy

The search strategy focused on identifying relevant studies that discuss optimising a cost model for computer networking infrastructure while minimising labour costs. It thus followed a laid-down protocol, as in Table 2.

The researchers extracted data from Scopus (38) and Web of Science (34) databases. These two were chosen due to their source and integrity, reliability and compatibility with the RStudio integrated development environment (IDE) software application that the researchers selected for their analysis. The details of the refinements have been captured in the PRISMA flow chart. The review considered a period between 2002 and

Table 2. Search strategy laid-down protocol

#	Description
1	Identify main concepts: "optimisation," "cost model," "labour costs," and "computer networking infrastructure."
2	Develop a list of relevant keywords: "cost modelling," "labour cost," and "computer networking infrastructure."
3	Use Scopus and Web of Science database search engines for relevant literature
4	Refine search terms by modifying and combining them for specificity and relevance
5	Use Boolean operators (AND, OR, NOT) to combine and exclude search terms, e.g., "optimisation AND cost modelling AND labour cost AND networking infrastructure."
6	Apply limiters such as publication date, study type, and language to narrow search results

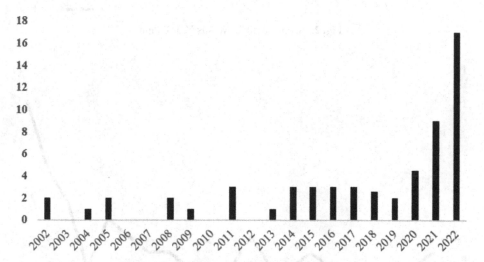

Fig. 1. Combined Scopus-Wos Article-Year graph

2022. The activity years are identified as opposed to the years of inactivity, combining records from the two separate databases of Scopus and the Web of Science, respectively, as indicated in Fig. 1.

Though 2002 to 2022 shows that it covers 21 years, Scopus had data only for 15 years, with the remaining six years having no recorded data. The missing years are not serial. They are as follows: 2003, 2006–2007, 2010, 2012, and 2018, in that order. Figure 2 identifies those years that Scopus had no data collection in relation to the number of years that it had.

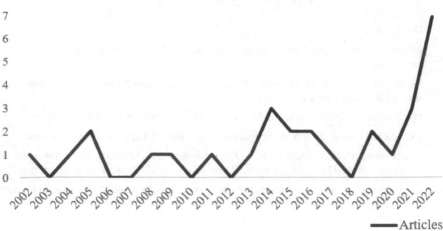

Fig. 2. Scopus Articles versus Year Graph

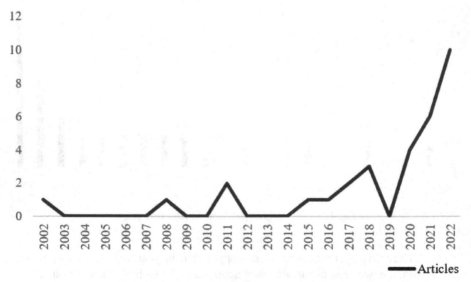

Fig. 3. Web of Science Articles versus Year graph

The Web of Science database was no exception. It had data for ten non-consecutive years, with the other eleven non-serial years also having no recorded data. The non-data registered years are 2003–2007, 2009–2010, 2012–2014, and 2019, as shown by the *article-year* graph in Fig. 3. This indicates that little research has gone into minimising labour costs. A combined total of 72 records were retrieved. After screening the titles and abstracts, full-text articles were reviewed based on inclusion and exclusion criteria. The inclusion criteria were: (1) the article must be related to the research question, (2) the article must be published in a peer-reviewed journal or conference proceedings, and

(3) the article must be written in English. The exclusion criteria were: (1) the article must not be a duplicate; (2) the article must not be a book or book chapter; and (3) the article must not be a non-peer-reviewed publication.

3.2 Screening Process

There are a number of tools for checking for duplicates, removing duplicates, and combining data from different database sources.

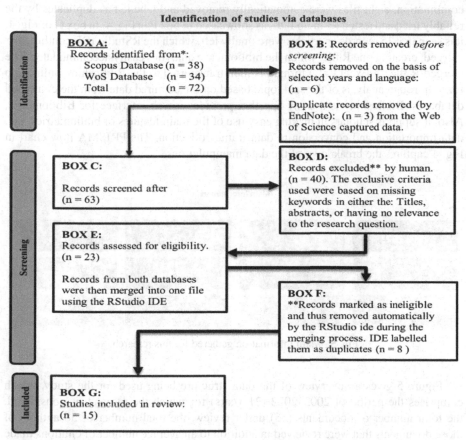

NOTE: The asterisk symbol (*), as in **Box A**, reports on the number of records identified from each database searched (rather than the total number across all databases). The double asterisk symbols (**) in **Boxes D & F**, indicate how many records were excluded by humans and how many were excluded by automation tools.

Fig. 4. Prisma Flow Diagram for the Systemic Literature Review

These include Mendeley and the RStudio integrated development environment (IDE). The initial search resulted in 72 articles, as captured in box A of Fig. 4. Six publications were removed due to the refined selection of years and language, as captured in Prisma flow chart box B in Fig. 4. Before the screening, Endnote, a citation management tool, was used to store the captured data from both databases. It was then used to check for duplicates. Three were identified and subsequently removed. Thus, nine articles were removed during the pre-screening and refinement stages. During the screening, the exclusive criteria used were missing keywords in the title, abstract, or have no relevance to the research question. After a thorough screening, 40 articles were excluded, as shown in box D of Fig. 4. Twenty-three (23) records or papers were assessed for eligibility and full-text review, as also captured in box E of Fig. 4. After that, the user-friendly RStudio interface was used to combine both the remaining extracted Scopus and Web of Science data from their respective databases into a single Excel file. After the combination, eight files were automatically removed and labelled as duplicates by the reliably tried and tested RStudio IDE, as showcased in box F in Fig. 4. In box G of Fig. 4, it is seen that 15 records or articles were finally left, which the RStudio IDE combined or merged, creating one R file, which the bibliometric analytics easily accommodates. The merged R file, in Excel (.xls) format, is then transported to the Biblioshiny online app for a thorough analysis of the said topic based on the captured data from the combined databases. Biblioshiny is a shiny app that provides a web interface for Bibliometric. Also, it supports scholars in making easy use of the main features of bibliometrics, i.e., data importation and conversion to data frame collection. The PRISMA flow chart in Fig. 4 captures the breakdown of the data manipulations.

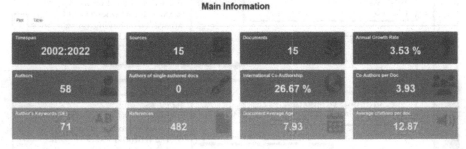

Fig. 5. Main Information gathered for this research.

Figure 5 gives an overview of the data structure being used for the study, which comprises the period of 2002–2022 (21 years) for which the research is considered, the total number of documents (15) under review, the total number of 58 authors of those documents that were reviewed in addition to an average number of citations made per document, the total number of 482 references documented, as well as the annual growth rate of citations chronicled. None of the papers under review was written by a single author, showing zero (0) co-authors per document recorded at 3.93, which, when multiplied by the 15 articles, will approximately give you the registered 58 authors.

4 Analysis and Discussion

The findings of related works provide valuable insights into how a formulated cost model can minimize labor costs in computer networking infrastructure through optimization. These studies focused on various approaches to cost optimization using mathematical modeling, simulation techniques, and cost-benefit analysis. Studies utilizing mathematical optimization techniques such as linear programming, dynamic programming, and heuristic algorithms effectively minimized costs in computer networking infrastructure. Meanwhile, case studies on labor cost optimization strategies identified key success factors and evaluated their effectiveness in reducing labor costs in this domain. Furthermore, simulation techniques proved useful for assessing the effectiveness of different cost optimization strategies, aiding organizations in identifying the most suitable approach. A meta-analysis of existing literature on cost optimization in computer networking infrastructure identified the most effective strategies and the factors influencing their success. Moreover, cost-benefit analysis studies showed that evaluating the costs and benefits associated with different optimization strategies can assist organizations in identifying the most cost-effective approach for computer networking infrastructure.

In summary, the findings from related works suggest that a cost model incorporating the practical strategies, factors, and optimization techniques identified in these studies can be applied to minimize labor costs in computer networking infrastructure.

4.1 Compare and Contrast the Methodologies and Results of the Related Works

The related works have different research focuses and methodologies, but they all aim to optimise costs and minimise labour costs in computer networking infrastructure. Here's a comparison of their methods and results, as in Table 3.

The related works demonstrate that different research methodologies can optimise costs and minimise labour costs in computer networking infrastructure. The choice of methods depends on the research focus and the research question. Each method has strengths and weaknesses, and researchers should choose the methodology that best suits their research question.

4.2 Discuss the Implications of the Findings

The implications of minimizing labour costs in computer networking infrastructure management are crucial in the pursuit of cost optimization. The escalating complexity of networking infrastructures has rendered their management and maintenance increasingly challenging and time-consuming, resulting in elevated labour costs for businesses reliant on networking technology for efficient operations.

A pivotal finding that emerges from this study is the paramount significance of automation in reducing labour costs associated with computer networking infrastructure management. As highlighted by [32], automating routine tasks such as system updates, network monitoring, and data backups can significantly curtail the demand for manual labour, concurrently augmenting operational efficiency. Automation not only saves companies substantial time and resources but also mitigates the risk of human error, a concern acknowledged by [33].

Table 3. Comparing and contrasting methodologies with relevant results of the related works.

Research Focus	Methodology	Description	Results
1	Mathematical Modelling	A quantitative approach using mathematical algorithms to create a model representing a system and optimise variables	Mathematical modelling provides an optimal solution that minimises costs
2	Case Studies	A qualitative approach analyses specific phenomenon instances to identify patterns and trends	Case studies provide a comprehensive understanding of factors influencing cost optimisation strategies' effectiveness
3	Simulation	A modelling technique that uses computer programs to simulate system behaviour under different scenarios	Simulation provides a quantitative evaluation of different cost optimisation strategies
4	Surveys	A data collection method that gathers information through questionnaires or interviews	Surveys provide a qualitative understanding of factors influencing labour costs and organisations' strategies to minimise these costs
5	Meta-Analysis	A statistical technique used for combining results of multiple studies to identify common themes or patterns	Meta-analysis helps identify common themes or patterns in multiple studies
6	Cost-Benefit Analysis	A method used to compare the costs and benefits of different strategies	Cost-benefit analysis compares the costs and benefits of different strategies

However, it is imperative to note that while automation is a powerful tool in labour cost reduction, the presence of skilled IT personnel remains indispensable. While automation diminishes the necessity for manual intervention, competent IT staff adept in network security, troubleshooting, and other critical IT skills remain pivotal in the oversight and management of the system.

Moreover, cloud-based networking solutions offer a potential avenue to minimize labour costs associated with computer networking infrastructure management. Outsourcing networking infrastructure management to proficient third-party providers, as evidenced by [34], can yield cost-effective solutions and expertise in managing intricate networking structures. Cloud-based solutions can thus provide a dual benefit of economizing labour costs while concurrently enhancing overall infrastructure management efficiency.

Decisively, the findings underscore the symbiotic relationship between automation, skilled IT personnel, and cloud-based solutions in reducing labour costs and optimizing networking infrastructure management. By integrating these strategies, businesses can potentially realize substantial reductions in labour costs and concurrently improve the efficiency of their networking infrastructure management, leading to a competitive advantage [35].

5 Conclusion

The research topic "Using a Formulated Cost Model for Optimisation to Minimise Computer Network Infrastructure Labour Cost" aims to develop a cost model to optimise the use of computer networking infrastructure and minimise labour costs associated with its management. The study focuses on formulating a mathematical model that incorporates various factors, such as the number of devices, network topology, labour costs, and operational requirements, to arrive at an optimal network configuration that minimises labour costs while meeting the required operational needs. The research involves gathering data on the current networking infrastructure and Analysing it to identify areas for improvement that can lead to cost savings. The cost model is then developed using the collected data, and its effectiveness is evaluated through simulations and case studies. The study concludes that the formulated cost model can help organisations optimise their networking infrastructure and reduce labour costs associated with its management. The cost model is a valuable tool for IT decision-makers, providing a systematic approach to network optimisation that can lead to cost savings and increased efficiency.

5.1 Recommendations

Recommendations for future research on using a formulated cost model for optimisation to minimise computer networking infrastructure labour costs:

Investigate the cost model's applicability to different types of computer networking infrastructure: While a cost model may work well for optimising labour costs in one kind of computer networking infrastructure, it may not be as effective in other types. Future research could explore whether the same cost model applies to different computer networking infrastructures, such as local area networks (LANs), wide area networks (WANs), and cloud-based networks.

Analyse the impact of labour cost optimisation on network performance: Reducing labour costs may not always result in optimal network performance. Future research could examine the relationship between labour cost optimisation and network performance and identify potential trade-offs. For example, optimising labour costs may lead to fewer resources allocated to monitoring and maintenance, which could result in increased downtime or security breaches.

Incorporate machine learning and AI into the cost model: Machine learning and AI technologies can potentially improve the accuracy and effectiveness of cost models. Future research could explore machine learning and AI algorithms to predict labour costs and optimise infrastructure maintenance schedules.

Consider the impact of external factors on labour costs: Labour costs may be influenced by external factors such as regulatory requirements, market competition, and the availability of skilled labour. Future research could investigate how these external factors impact labour costs and develop strategies to mitigate their effects.

Test the effectiveness of the cost model in real-world scenarios: The significance of a cost model for optimising labour costs in computer networking infrastructure must be tested in real-world scenarios. Future research could conduct field trials to test the accuracy and effectiveness of the cost model and identify any potential limitations or areas for improvement.

References

1. Al-Samarraie, H., Al-Shemmari, N.: The role of computer networking in organizational communication and collaboration. Int. J. Inf. Technol. Manag. 19(2–3), 193–208 (2020). https://doi.org/10.1504/IJITM.2020.10025956
2. Patel, K.K., Patel, S.M., Scholar, P.: Internet of things-IOT: definition, characteristics, architecture, enabling technologies, application \& future challenges. Int. J. Eng. Sci. Comput. 6(5) (2016)
3. Mohanty, S.P., Choppali, U., Kougianos, E.: Everything you wanted to know about smart cities: the Internet of things is the backbone. IEEE Consum. Electron. Mag. 5(3), 60–70 (2016)
4. Han, J., Xue, K., Xing, Y., et al.: Leveraging coupled BBR and adaptive packet scheduling to boost MPTCP. IEEE Trans. Wirel. Commun.Wirel. Commun. 20(11), 7555–7567 (2021). https://doi.org/10.1109/TWC.2021.3085661
5. Darwish, A.: Bio-inspired computing: Algorithms review, deep analysis, and the scope of applications. Futur Comput. Inform. J. 3(2), 231–246 (2018)
6. Cocco, L., Pinna, A., Marchesi, M.: Banking on blockchain: costs savings thanks to the blockchain technology. Futur. Internet. 9(3), 25 (2017)
7. Tran, V.P., Santoso, F., Garratt, M.A., Anavatti, S.G.: Distributed artificial neural networks-based adaptive strictly negative imaginary formation controllers for unmanned aerial vehicles in time-varying environments. IEEE Trans. Ind. Inform. 17(6), 3910–3919 (2021). https://doi.org/10.1109/TII.2020.3004600
8. Wessel, M., Serebrenik, A., Wiese, I., Steinmacher, I., Gerosa, M.A.: What to expect from code review bots on GitHub? a survey with OSS maintainers. In: Proceedings of the XXXIV Brazilian Symposium on Software Engineering, pp. 457–462 (2020)
9. Hojjati, S.N., Khodakarami, M.: Evaluation of factors affecting the adoption of smart buildings using the technology acceptance model. Int. J. Adv. Netw. Appl. 7(6), 2936 (2016)
10. Chen, H., Li, L., Chen, Y.: Explore success factors that impact artificial intelligence adoption on telecom industry in China. J. Manag. Anal. 8(1), 36–68 (2021)
11. Georgakopoulos, D., Jayaraman, P.P., Fazia, M., Villari, M., Ranjan, R.: Internet of Things and edge cloud computing roadmap for manufacturing. IEEE Cloud Comput. 3(4), 66–73 (2016)
12. Ren, W., Lian, X., Ghazinour, K.: Effective and efficient top-k query processing over incomplete data streams. Inf. Sci. (Ny). 544, 343–371 (2021). https://doi.org/10.1016/j.ins.2020.08.011
13. S. Saha, J., Sarkar, A., Dwivedi, N., Dwivedi, A.M.: Narasimhamurthy and RR. A novel revenue optimization model to address the operation and maintenance cost of a data center. 5(1), 1–23 (2016)
14. Frangopol, D.M., Liu, M.: Maintenance and management of civil infrastructure based on condition, safety, optimization, and life-cycle cost. Struct Infrastruct Syst. Published online 2019, pp. 96–108
15. Enholm, I.M., Papagiannidis, E., Mikalef, P., Krogstie, J.: Artificial intelligence and business value: a literature review. Inf. Syst. Front. 24(5), 1709–1734 (2022)

16. Björklund, M., Johansson, H.: Urban consolidation centre--a literature review, categorisation, and a future research agenda. Int. J. Phys. Distrib. Logist. Manag. Published online 2018
17. Oztemel, E., Gursev, S.: Literature review of Industry 4.0 and related technologies. J. Intell. Manuf. **31**, 127–182 (2020)
18. Bibri, S.E., Krogstie, J.: Smart sustainable cities of the future: an extensive interdisciplinary literature review. Sustain. Cities Soc. **31**, 183–212 (2017)
19. Bahlawan, H., Morini, M., Pinelli, M., Spina, P.R.: Dynamic programming based methodology for the optimization of the sizing and operation of hybrid energy plants. Appl. Therm. Eng. **160**, 113967 (2019)
20. Wamba-Taguimdje, S.L., Fosso Wamba, S., Kala Kamdjoug, J.R., Tchatchouang Wanko, C.E.: Influence of artificial intelligence (AI) on firm performance: the business value of AI-based transformation projects. Bus. Process. Manag. J. **26**(7), 1893–1924 (2020)
21. Khan, A., Umar, A.I., Shirazi, S.H., et al.: QoS-aware cost minimization strategy for AMI applications in smart grid using cloud computing. Sensors **22**(13), 4969 (2022)
22. Ngoc, S., Luc Tra, D., Thi Huynh, H.M., Nguyen, H.H.T., O'Mahony, B.: Enhancing resilience in the Covid-19 crisis: lessons from human resource management practices in Vietnam. Curr. Issues Tour. **24**(22), 3189–3205 (2021)
23. Azumah, K.K., Sørensen, L.T., Tadayoni, R.: Hybrid cloud service selection strategies: a qualitative meta-analysis. In: 2018 IEEE 7th International Conference on Adaptive Science \& Technology (ICAST), pp. 1–8 (2018)
24. Liu, J., Hu, C., Kimber, A., Wang, Z.: Uses, cost-benefit analysis, and markets of energy storage systems for electric grid applications. J. Energy Storage. **32**, 101731 (2020)
25. Santoyo-González, A., Cervelló-Pastor, C.: Latency-aware cost optimization of the service infrastructure placement in 5G networks. J. Netw. Comput. Appl.Netw. Comput. Appl. **114**, 29–37 (2018)
26. Bosona, T.: Urban freight last mile logistics—Challenges and opportunities to improve sustainability: a literature review. Sustainability **12**(21), 8769 (2020)
27. Wang, Y., Kung, L., Byrd, T.A.: Big data analytics: Understanding its capabilities and potential benefits for healthcare organizations. Technol. Forecast Soc. Change. **126**, 3–13 (2018)
28. Grant, R.M.: Contemporary Strategy Analysis. John Wiley \& Sons (2021)
29. Nguyen, T.-D., Nguyen-Quang, T., Venkatadri, U., Diallo, C., MA. Mathematical Programming Models for Fresh Fruit Supply Chain Optimization: A Review of the Literature and Emerging Trends. 2021, vol. 3, 3, 519–541 (2021)
30. Ghobakhloo, M., Fathi, M.: Corporate survival in Industry 4.0 era: the enabling role of lean-digitized manufacturing. J. Manuf. Technol. Manag. Published online 2019
31. Page, M.J., McKenzie, J.E., Bossuyt, P.M., et al.: Updating guidance for reporting systematic reviews: development of the PRISMA 2020 statement. J. Clin. Epidemiol.Epidemiol. **134**, 103–112 (2021)
32. Wollschlaeger, M., Sauter, T., Jasperneite, J.: The future of industrial communication: Automation networks in the era of the internet of things and industry 4.0. IEEE Ind Electron Mag. **11**(1), 17–27 (2017). https://doi.org/10.1109/MIE.2017.2649104
33. Raisch, S., Krakowski, S.: Artificial intelligence and management: the automation–augmentation paradox. Acad. Manag. Rev.Manag. Rev. **46**(1), 192–210 (2021)

34. Maddikunta, P.K.R., Pham, Q.V., B P, et al.: Industry 5.0: a survey on enabling technologies and potential applications. J. Ind. Inf. Integr. **26** (2022). https://doi.org/10.1016/j.jii.2021.100257
35. Dao, V., Langella, I., Carbo, J.: From green to sustainability: information technology and an integrated sustainability framework. J. Strateg. Inf. Syst.Strateg. Inf. Syst. **20**(1), 63–79 (2011)

Comparison of Solution Methods the Maximal Covering Location Problem of Public Spaces for Teenagers in the Urban Environment

Maksim Natykin[1]([✉]), Sergey Mityagin[1], Semen Budennyy[2],
and Nikita Zakharenko[2]

[1] ITMO University, Birzhevaya Line, 14, Saint Petersburg, Russia
`mvin@itmo.ru`
[2] Sber AI Lab, Moscow, Russia

Abstract. The article considers methods of solving the problem of optimal planning of public spaces, based on the approach of network modeling of the urban environment. The problematic of the work, is relevant for many modern cities, and lies in the fact that the urban environment is poorly adapted to provide quality leisure for young people. This leads to various behavioral and social deviations. At the same time, the task of planning the placement of public spaces and their profiling for the needs of young people is not trivial and is complicated by the diversity of possible functions and types of such spaces, as well as the variability of their scale. In addition, the task of choosing locations for leisure public spaces is complicated by the presence of competition, which reduces the overall effectiveness of the system of leisure for teenagers, and modern development imposes significant restrictions on their layout and functional content. The work compares the greedy algorithm and linear programming and draws conclusions about the applicability of the methods to solve the problem of optimal placement of public spaces. It allowed to optimally solve the problem of placement of public spaces under imposed internal and external constraints. The article presents the experimental research of the method and its implementation for St. Petersburg, Russia.

Keywords: Network Modeling · Urban Environment Model · Information Model · Algorithms on Graphs · Urban Neighborhood Model · Urban Centrality · Urban Neighborhood Profile

1 Introduction

Adolescence is an important period in a person's life associated with significant physical, psychological, and social changes. One important aspect of this development is the need for socialization and a sense of identity. Public spaces play an important role in providing adolescents with opportunities to connect with their peers and engage in activities that contribute to their development. At the same

T. Guarda et al. (Eds.): ARTIIS 2023, CCIS 1935, pp. 443–456, 2024.
https://doi.org/10.1007/978-3-031-48858-0_35

time, there is a problem relevant to many modern cities and lies in the fact that the urban environment is poorly adapted to provide quality recreational activities for young people. At the same time, the question of filling public spaces with services, is not regulated in any normative way. Unfortunately, location of public spaces takes place without taking into account the real demand for them and the assessment of provision [1]. This leads to various behavioral and social deviations. At the same time, the task of planning the placement of public spaces and their profiling for the needs of young people is not trivial and is complicated by the diversity of possible functions and types of such spaces, as well as the variability of their scale. In addition, the task of choosing locations for leisure public spaces is complicated by the presence of competition, which reduces the overall effectiveness of the system of leisure for teenagers, and modern development imposes significant restrictions on their layout and functional content. To solve this problem a method based on the modeling of urban environment objects with the help of network models application is offered. This approach allows us to represent a variety of youth spaces as a spatially distributed system of youth leisure activities.

The following text will describe the information model of public spaces for teenagers. In this work, the definition of public space refers to a landscaped area of the city with services of interest to teenagers, in which they realize their needs for leisure, recreation and social interaction.

Classifying public spaces by functional type and size is a great way to show their importance in shaping the city [2]. In the course of the research different world practices of public space design for teenagers were considered. As an example of public spaces for teenagers we can single out Yama in Moscow, Fremantle Esplanade Youth Plaza in Western Australia and FACTORIA JOVEN in Spain. Based on their following 4 types of spaces for adolescents were identified according to the functional profile shown in Fig. 1.

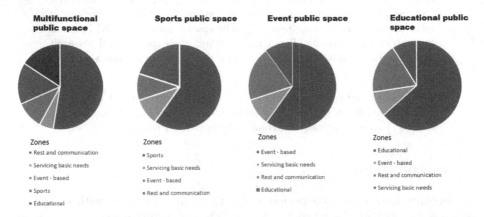

Fig. 1. Classification of the functional profile of public spaces

- **Multifunctional**. The most versatile type of space, the balance of functions is shifted in favor of relaxing outdoor recreation and social interaction between teenagers.
- **Sports**. Spaces aim to meet the needs for active leisure activities and often have the largest size. This is due to the presence of services such as a skate park or a basketball field, which require more free space than services for a relaxing holiday; the sports zone occupies approximately 50-70 percent, and the core of the sports zone is usually a sports field or a skate park.
- **Eventful**. Public space is provided for the organization of teenagers' creative or noisy leisure activities, such as musical events, open workshops, and workshops. He event-based public space should be located at a distance from residential buildings and places of quiet recreation so that conflict situations do not arise due to noise levels, as happens with the Yama public space in Moscow.
- **Educational**. A public space designed for cultural and educational events, such as workshops, seminars, open-air lectures, and exhibitions. Educational spaces should be located within walking distance from schools and places of additional education.

The factor of scale of public spaces depends on the occupied area, and can vary at three levels [3]. The level depends on the administrative-territorial unit, which is usually inhabited by such a number of adolescents, which is able to provide this space according to the normative. According to the occupied area, public spaces can be divided into three types:

- Small, occupying an area of up to 600 m2 and mainly located inside courtyards.
- Medium, with an area of 600 m2 to 1200 m2. They can serve all teenagers within one quarter.
- Large, the occupied area of which is more than 1200 m2. Public spaces of this size can provide leisure for teenagers within municipalities.

2   Background in Public Spaces Optimal Planning

The coverage location problem can be classified as the set location coverage problem (LSCP) and the maximum coverage location problem (MCLP). In a classical MCLP, it is possible to locate a number of objects in the network in such a way that the population covered is maximum. A facility covers a demand node if it is placed at a distance less than a threshold to the demand node. This predetermined threshold is often referred to as the coverage radius, which directly affects the solution.

This paper is limited in its ability to fully cover the extensive MCLP literature. Therefore, in this section we will review only some of the major contributions to the field. If you are interested in learning more, it is advisable to consult two recent reviews that provide valuable insights: the work of ReVelle and colleagues [4] and the article by Berman et al. [5].

The MCLP was first introduced by Church and ReVelle [6] in the mid-1970s, and since then many articles have been published on various aspects of the problem. For example, Moore and ReVelle [7] proposed a hierarchical approach to MCLP, Plastri and Vanhaverchek [8] investigated MCLP modeling in a competitive environment, Church and Robertson [9] and Berman et al. [10], developed gradual model covers, Alexandris and Yannikos [11] applied GIS to MCLP problems, and Yoon and Wesolowski [12] proposed a node coverage method using parallelograms. These are only a few examples from the numerous studies in this area.

The public space placement problem is an optimization problem, which is to place public spaces in a way that satisfies certain requirements and constraints. The complexity of the problem is that there are public spaces of different functional types and sizes. Also within the task, quality factors for the placement of public spaces must be considered, such as:

- External factors of the urban environment - demographics, accessibility, land use.
- Local factors of public space - size, type, inner filling.
- The mutual arrangement of public spaces - diversification, competition.

The set coverage problem is an NP-hard problem in combinatorial optimization. There are several methods for solving this problem:

- The greedy algorithm is an iterative algorithm that, at each step, selects the set that covers the largest number of uncovered elements until all elements are covered by [13].
- Linear programming is a method that formulates a set coverage problem as a linear programming problem and then solves it using linear programming methods [14].
- Genetic algorithm is an evolutionary algorithm that uses the mechanisms of natural selection and genetics to find a solution to the set coverage problem [15].
- Artificial intelligence methods can be used to apply optimization algorithms, such as machine learning algorithms, to find optimal locations for public spaces given multiple criteria and constraints.

As part of this research work, an experimental implementation of each method for solving the problem of optimal planning of public spaces for teenagers will be carried out. For each method, numerical experiments on one set of data were conducted and the results obtained were evaluated, as well as the choice of the best method for solving the problem. The conclusion will formulate conclusions about the advantages and disadvantages of each method, as well as recommendations for further research.

Traditionally, location decisions are long-term strategic decisions, so computational performance is not as important. In this paper, however, the decision to place public spaces is operational in nature. At the beginning of the time period (which is as short-term as a day), spatial planners will know the structure of demand, available space, etc. and will decide where to place a predetermined number of public spaces of 4 functional types in the planning area. In the next period of time, if the data is similar and the area has not changed we can use the same solution. Otherwise, we will have to quickly re-optimize the system and possibly open new public spaces or re-balance their functional type. For this purpose, we developed and compared three heuristics, which are described below.

3   Methods for Optimal Planning of Public Spaces

3.1   Linear Programming

Linear programming (LP) is an optimization method that can be applied in the context of this problem of optimal placement of public spaces. LP is based on mathematical modeling and optimization of a linear target function with linear constraints.

Denotations:

- n &- number of houses (iterator - i)
- m &- number of public spaces (iterator - j)
- k &- number of types of public spaces (iterator - l)
- r &- radius in which public spaces affect houses
- W &- matrix of distances from houses to public spaces
- M &- large number compared to the number of public spaces
- p &- number of public spaces that can be opened
- V &- matrix of selected locations for public spaces, binary, dimensions $(m \times k)$

Matrix of house coverage by public spaces, integer, dimensions $(n \times k)$:

$$hp(i, k) \& = \sum_{j=1}^{m} (W_j(i) * V_j(k))$$

Matrix of house coverage by public spaces, binary, dimensions $(n \times k)$:

$$Hp(i, k) : \& \begin{cases} 1, \text{ if } hp(i, k) \geq 1 \\ 0, \text{ if } hp(i, k) < 1 \end{cases}$$

Optimization function:

$$\max_{l=1}^{k} \sum_{i=1}^{n} Hp_{il}$$

Constraints:

$$\sum_{l=1}^{k} \sum_{j=1}^{m} V_{jl} \leqslant p - \text{No more than } p \text{ new public spaces are allowed.}$$

$$\sum_{l=1}^{k} V_{jl} \leqslant 1 - \text{There is only 1 type of PS in 1 place}$$

In this case, LP can be used to optimize the placement of public spaces to maximize home coverage. The linear objective function can be defined as the sum of Hp(i, k) over all i and l, where Hp(i, k) is a binary variable denoting coverage of house i by public space type k.

Constraints in LP may include:

- A constraint on the number of public spaces available: The sum of all items V by l and j must not exceed p, where p is the number of public spaces that can be opened.
- Limitation on the types of public spaces in one location: The sum of all elements V by l must not exceed 1, which means that there can be only one type of public space in one location.

Using LP, it is possible to find the optimal placement of public spaces that maximizes house coverage, given the constraints on the number and types of spaces. The problem for linear programming can be formulated as follows: there is a set of places for public spaces (PS), the PS can be several types. There is a set of houses that need to be satisfied with the PS, a house is considered satisfied with the PS of the selected type, if within a given radius from it there is an PS of the selected type.

This mathematical formulation of the problem of optimal placement of public spaces near homes provides a systematic approach to maximizing home coverage and considering constraints on the number and types of spaces. This contributes to economic efficiency, sustainable development and improved quality of life by providing convenient access to public services and creating comfortable public environments.

3.2   Greedy Algorithm

A greedy algorithm is a method for solving optimization problems in which a locally optimal solution is chosen at each step, aiming to achieve a global optimum. In the context of this problem of optimal placement of public spaces, the greedy algorithm can be used for an approximate solution. The greedy algorithm can be applied as follows:

- Start with an empty set of selected locations for public spaces.
- For each type of public space:
  1. View all available locations and select the one that provides the most coverage of homes of that type
  2. Add the selected location to the set of selected locations.
- Repeat step 2 until the maximum number of public spaces is reached or all types of spaces are accounted for.

The greedy algorithm is based on local optimization at each location selection step for a public space. It does not guarantee finding the global optimum, but it can give an approximate solution to the problem in a reasonable amount of time. However, it should be noted that in some cases the greedy algorithm may not achieve an optimal solution and other optimization methods will need to be used to solve the problem accurately. The simplicity of the algorithm makes it easy to understand, implement, and debug, and its fast execution time allows it to be used for tasks where the number of solutions is large.

For convenience, we introduce the following abbreviations: PPS - Potential public space. Consider the following bipartite graph $G = (U, V, E)$:

- $U = \{1, \ldots, n\}$ lots of PPS.
- $V = \{1, \ldots, m\}$ lots of houses that will be serviced (covered) by PPS.
- $(u, v) \in E$ an edge corresponding to walking distance from the PC $u \in U$ to home $v \in V$.
- $k(v)$ the number of teenagers living in the house $v \in V$.
- $w(u, v)$ distance(time) from PPS $u \in U$ to home $v \in V$.
- $c(u)$ the standard capacity of a PPS $u \in U$ in people $(S/2)$.
- S the area of potential public spaces.

Consider the following variables $(u \in U, v \in V)$:

$$y_u = \& \begin{cases} 1, \text{ if } u \text{ PPS open}, \\ 0, \text{ else} \end{cases}$$

$$x_v = \& \begin{cases} 1, \text{ if house } v \text{ is covered}, \\ 0, \text{ else} \end{cases}$$

4   Experimental Studies of Methods

4.1   Data and Method

The following datasets are required for the developed research methodology as presented below.

Data that is needed from the user:

1. The geo-layer with the planning area shown. The boundaries or the polygon itself can be downloaded from open information sources, for example, the Open Street maps (OSM) service or from the ITMO University digital urbanism platform.
2. A model of the settlement of teenagers by polygons of houses. Data on the settlement of a social group of teenagers inside the city in GeoJSON format with an attribute of the number of teenagers living in the house.
3. A geo-layer, including services in which teenagers are interested and polygons of recreational areas, for subsequent classification of existing public spaces.

The data that is obtained during the operation of the algorithm:

1. Existing public spaces public spaces presented. Existing public spaces public space refers to the landscaped territory of the city, which is a place for teenagers to spend their leisure time due to the proximity of services they are interested in. Existing public spaces public spaces allow us to minimize costs

due to the fact that we are not building a new public space but adding functions and services that teenagers need to the already landscaped territory. To classify potential spaces, you need a geo-layer with polygons of recreational areas and a list of services that teenagers are interested in. Based on these data, it is proposed to build buffer zones with a radius of 200 m around the services and to highlight those polygons of green zones that intersect with each other. The functional profile of a public space is classified based on the type of services with which it intersects and the size of the occupied area.

2. Geo layer, which includes polygons of vacant areas inside the city, which are many places where we can place new public spaces. The free area will be calculated using an algorithm written in the Python programming language according to the following principle:

   (a) Objects and zones that have a functional purpose and an OSM tag are cut out of the planning territory polygon: roads, buildings, green areas, shopping areas, territories of various institutions, etc.

   (b) The next step is to cut out the minimum distance from residential buildings and other structures to the planned public space in order to comply with urban planning standards.

   (c) The final stage is the cleaning of polygons whose area is less than 200 sq.m. and polygons that have geometry that is not suitable for the placement of public spaces.

3. Isachrons of the coverage area. The data is obtained using an algorithm written in the Python programming language. A pedestrian road graph is needed to construct isochrons. The graph itself can be taken from open sources of information, for example OpenStreetMap.

4. Network model of public spaces, which is a bipartite graph in GraphML format. The network nodes are divided into two types - residential buildings and potential public spaces, and the edges connecting them - walking time in minutes.

The data that the user receives at the output:

1. The result of the algorithm will be a geo-layer with polygons from a variety of potential locations, where it is best to place new public spaces.

The algorithm of the method of optimal placement of public spaces for teenagers is shown in the Fig. 2. The source data is indicated in red, the methods are indicated in blue, and the data obtained as a result of the methods are indicated in gray.

The proposed greedy algorithm and linear programming were evaluated using a real dataset based on the Vasileostrovsky district of St. Petersburg. Demand nodes are assumed of 1141 households, with the number of teenagers living in each house, with a total demand of 8946. It is assumed that the service distance coverage corresponds to the size of the public space. Public space of each type can be built on one 372 spaces that represent vacant space in the established development. Due to budget constraints, only 70 public spaces can be built.

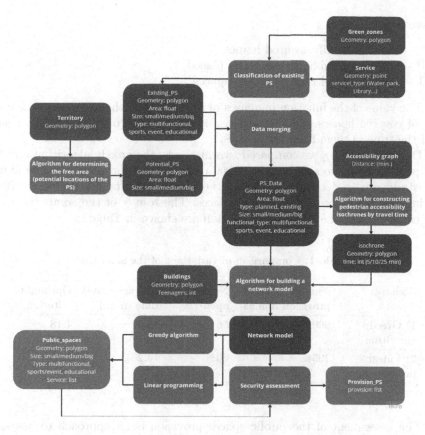

Fig. 2. High-level architecture of optimal placement of public spaces for teenagers

As a result of the data preparation steps described earlier, the network model is a bipartite graph and a radiosity matrix [16] of size n public spaces per m residences, where for each public space there is a 1 opposite the house in its service area and it is assumed that the public space can handle the load coming from the house. The load means the sum of all teenagers in the public space service area multiplied by the space standard per person. There is no standard for public space area, and the standard developed for playgrounds [17] was adapted for the task of calculating accessibility. As a result, there should be 2 square meters of public space per teenager.

4.2   Results

To assess the quality of placement of public spaces and to compare the results of the algorithms, we used the optimality criterion, which is a non-linear function, which is calculated by the formula:

$$\max \& \frac{H}{PT}$$

where:

- H - Number of fully secured homes
- P - Number of public spaces to be placed
- T - Average travel time to public spaces

The value of the function increases in proportion to the increase in the number of covered houses and the decrease in the number of placed public spaces and the time to them from the houses.

During the study, we compared two methods, the greedy algorithm and linear programming, to solve the maximal covering location problem. The aim of the study was to determine which of these methods provides better results in optimizing the placement of public spaces. The results of the comparison and the calculation of the optimality criterion are shown in Table 1:

Table 1. Comparison of variations of the algorithm

Scenario	Number of fully provision homes	Number of open PS	Average travel time (min.)	Optimality criterion
1) Greedy algorithm	900	56	13.6	1.18
2) Linear programming	1051	60	14.2	1.23

The assessment of the public spaces provision is an approach to assessing how well public spaces are accommodated in the existing urban development. The assessment is made up of the sum of the provision of all residences in the planning area. According to this, a house is considered fully provisioned if it is within the service area of all four functional types of public spaces, and they can handle the load from the house.

In the first scenario, where the greedy algorithm was used, 900 homes were fully provisioned, while 56 public spaces were open. The average travel time was 13.6 min, and the optimality criterion was 1.18. In the second scenario, where linear programming was applied, 1,051 homes were fully provisioned, with 60 public spaces open. The average travel time was 14.2 min, and the optimality criterion is equal to 1.23. Comparing the results of the two methods, we can conclude that linear programming shows slightly better results. It provides more fully provisioned houses (1,051 vs. 900), as well as more open public spaces (60 vs. 56) compared to the greedy algorithm. The average path time and optimality criterion are also slightly higher for linear programming. These results argue in favor of using linear programming in the maximum location coverage problem to achieve a more optimal resource allocation.

This analysis examines the impact of increasing the number of public spaces on percentage demand coverage. Demand coverage refers to the extent to which

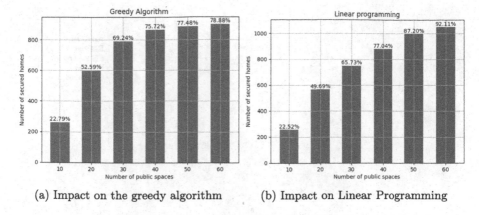

(a) Impact on the greedy algorithm   (b) Impact on Linear Programming

Fig. 3. Analysis of the impact of increasing the number of public spaces on the percentage coverage of demand

available public spaces meet the needs and demands of the population. By systematically changing the number of public spaces, we seek to understand how changes in the number of public spaces affect the overall degree of coverage. To conduct the analysis, we start with a baseline scenario, which is the placement of 10 public spaces. We then gradually increase the number of public spaces by 10 and estimate the corresponding percentage of demand coverage at each level.

Analyzing the results presented in Fig. 3, we can observe the relationship between the number of public spaces and demand coverage. As the number of public spaces increases, the percentage of demand coverage is also expected to increase. However, it is important to assess whether there is a point of diminishing returns at which further increases in the number of public spaces have a minimal impact on coverage.

Through this analysis, we can provide valuable information about the optimal number of public spaces needed to achieve the desired level of coverage. This information can guide city planners in making informed decisions about resource allocation and design of public spaces to ensure efficient use and meet community needs. The developed software implementation of the methods, available on github, allows this analysis to be performed on any design area. The final visualization of the optimal location of public spaces on the territory of Vasileostrovsky District of St. Petersburg is shown in Fig. 4.

Discussion

The objective of the study was to evaluate the quality of the placement of public spaces and to compare two algorithms: the greedy algorithm and linear programming to solve the problem of maximizing the coverage of locations. The optimization criterion used in the study was a non-linear function that takes into account the number of fully served houses, the number of public spaces

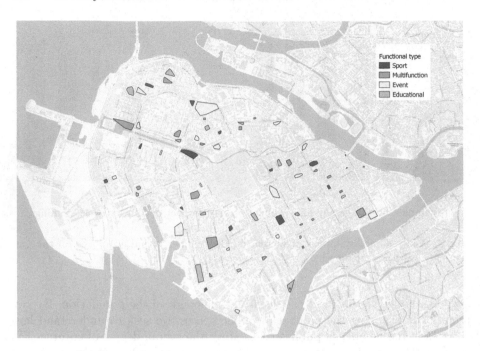

Fig. 4. Optimal placement of public spaces

placed, and the average travel time to these spaces. The results were compared based on the number of fully supplied homes, the number of public spaces provided, the average travel time, and the optimization criterion.

The results highlight the importance of applying mathematical optimization techniques in urban environmental management to determine the optimal placement of public spaces. By comparing the two algorithms, the study showed that linear programming can lead to a more balanced distribution of public spaces, providing better demand coverage while minimizing the number of open spaces and travel time for residents.

Both methods, linear programming and greedy algorithm, have their advantages and limitations. Linear programming provides a more optimal result and guarantees to find the global optimum, but requires a more complex implementation and may be less accessible to urban planners. On the other hand, the greedy algorithm is easier to understand and debug, and has high speed, making it attractive for simple problems and large data sets. However, it may not always produce optimal results and is not guaranteed to find a global optimum.

Therefore, the choice between these methods depends on the specific requirements of the task and the resources available. If speed and ease of implementation are priorities, the greedy algorithm may be preferable. However, if the best results are required and an optimal solution is guaranteed, linear programming would be a more appropriate choice, even considering its complexity.

Certain limitations may have affected the effectiveness of the study. One possible limitation could be the specific characteristics of the urban area studied, which may not fully reflect the entire context of the city. In addition, the models used in the algorithms depend on the accuracy and completeness of the available data, which may be subject to errors or inconsistencies. Finally, the study did not take into account specific demographic or socio-economic factors that may influence the actual demand for public space.

Conclusions and Future Research

This study compares two algorithms, namely the greedy algorithm and linear programming, in the context of solving the maximal covering location problem for the optimal placement of public spaces for teenagers, in order to provide residential buildings. This problem has an important practical value, because the proper placement of public spaces contributes to improving the quality of life of residents and optimizing the use of urban infrastructure.

Urban area data, taking into account land constraints and potential residential building locations, were used to conduct a comparative analysis. The greedy algorithm, known for its simplicity and efficiency, was applied to find the closest public spaces to potential locations. The goal of the greedy algorithm was to select the locations that provide the best coverage of residential buildings based on a given optimality criterion.

On the other hand, linear programming was applied to formalize the problem and find the optimal solution. Linear programming allows different constraints and target functions to be considered, including the coverage of residential buildings with the maximum number of public spaces. Using a mathematical model and linear constraints, linear programming was used to optimize the placement of public spaces leading to maximum coverage of residential buildings.

Based on the results of the calculation of the optimality criterion of the solution, it was found that linear programming provides a better result compared to the greedy algorithm. Linear programming allows all constraints and target functions of the maximum location coverage problem to be considered more accurately and systematically, resulting in optimal placement of public spaces to provide residential buildings. Thus, the results of the study confirm the advantages of using linear programming in this problem. However, the choice between these methods depends on the specific requirements of the problem and available resources. If speed of operation and simplicity of implementation are prioritized, the greedy algorithm may be preferred. If, however, the best results are required and an optimal solution is guaranteed, then linear programming would be a better choice, even given its complexity.

Future research can focus on the following aspects. First, various optimization models and algorithms can be considered for the efficient placement of public spaces, taking into account a variety of constraints and needs of different communities. Incorporating additional factors into the model, such as the influence of the type of public space on its size or the dynamic scaling of the coverage area depending on demand, may lead to more accurate and relevant results.

Acknowledgements. This research is financially supported by The Russian Science Foundation, Agreement No 22-21-20081

References

1. Rashchenko, A., Perkova, M.: The problem of development of public spaces in small towns. Vestnik of Belgorod State Technological University named after V.V. Shukhov (1), pp. 61–64 (2015)
2. Franck, K.A., Huang, T.S.: Types: Descriptive and analytic tools in public space research, pp. 209–220 (2020)
3. Carmona, M.: Principles for public space design, planning to do better. Urban Design Int. **24**, 47–59 (2019)
4. Revelle, C.S., Eiselt, H.A., Daskin, M.S.: A bibliography for some fundamental problem categories in discrete location science. Eur. J. Oper. Res. **184**(3), 817–848 (2008)
5. Berman, O., Drezner, Z., Krass, D.: Generalized coverage: new developments in covering location models. Comput. Oper. Res. **37**(10), 1675–1687 (2010)
6. Church, R., ReVelle, C.: The maximal covering location problem. In: Papers of the Regional Science Association, vol. 32, pp. 101–118. Springer, Heidelberg (1974)
7. Moore, G.C., ReVelle, C.: The hierarchical service location problem. Manage. Sci. **28**(7), 775–780 (1982)
8. Plastria, F., Vanhaverbeke, L.: Discrete models for competitive location with foresight. Comput. Oper. Res. **35**(3), 683–700 (2008)
9. Church, R.L., Roberts, K.L.: Generalized coverage models and public facility location. In: Papers of the Regional Science Association, vol. 53, pp. 117–135. Springer (1983)
10. Berman, O., Krass, D., Drezner, Z.: The gradual covering decay location problem on a network. Eur. J. Oper. Res. **151**(3), 474–480 (2003)
11. Alexandris, G., Giannikos, I.: A new model for maximal coverage exploiting gis capabilities. Eur. J. Oper. Res. **202**(2), 328–338 (2010)
12. Younies, H., Wesolowsky, G.O.: A mixed integer formulation for maximal covering by inclined parallelograms. Eur. J. Oper. Res. **159**(1), 83–94 (2004)
13. Kritter, J., Brévilliers, M., Lepagnot, J., Idoumghar, L.: On the optimal placement of cameras for surveillance and the underlying set cover problem. Appl. Soft Comput. **74**, 133–153 (2019)
14. Trevisan, L.: Stanford university— cs261: Optimization (2011)
15. Razip, H., Zakaria, N.: Genetic algorithm with approximation algorithm based initial population for the set covering problem. In: Kumar, S., Purohit, S.D., Hiranwal, S., Prasad, M. (eds.) Proceedings of International Conference on Communication and Computational Technologies. AIS, pp. 59–78. Springer, Singapore (2021). https://doi.org/10.1007/978-981-16-3246-4_6
16. Harary, F.: The determinant of the adjacency matrix of a graph. SIAM Rev. **4**(3), 202–210 (1962)
17. Zhigulina, Y., Stetsura, Y., Taranukha, E.: Basic requirements for the design of playgrounds, pp. 6847–6850 (2017)

Digital Transformation Assessment Model Based on Indicators for Operational and Organizational Readiness and Business Value

Daniela Borissova[1]([✉])[ID], Naiden Naidenov[1][ID], and Radoslav Yoshinov[2][ID]

[1] Institute of Information and Communication Technologies at the Bulgarian Academy of Sciences, 1113 Sofia, Bulgaria
{daniela.borissova,naiden.naidenov}@iict.bas.bg
[2] Laboratory of Telematics at the Bulgarian Academy of Sciences, Sofia, Bulgaria
yoshinov@cc.bas.bg

Abstract. Ongoing digital transformation plays an important role in any organization. Effective digitalization involves several levels related to technologies, processes, and users. In this regard, the assessment of the digital transformation level is of great importance. The three stages of operational and organizational readiness, as well as business value and their KPIs, are the focus of the article. For this purpose, an algorithm for evaluating digital transformation is proposed. In addition, a multi-criteria model based on KPIs is formulated, which takes into account these three main stages, through which the degree of digital transformation can be determined. A different number of measurable indicators have been identified for each of these stages. Numerical testing of the proposed model was done for a small company by using 9 KPIs for all 3 stages. The obtained results demonstrate the applicability of the proposed modeling approach for evaluating digital transformation.

Keywords: Digital transformation · Operational readiness · Organizational readiness · Business value · Multi-criteria model

1 Introduction

Digital technologies are dramatically reshaping industries, and many companies are undertaking massive change efforts to take advantage of these trends and keep up with competitors. Many businesses believe that moving to the cloud or implementing SaaS technologies to replace legacy business processes is transformative. Digital transformation is deeper because it requires digital thinking to improve business processes, streamline operations and meet customer demands. Digital transformation affects the organization as a whole, including people, processes, and technologies [1]. A recent study shows that digital transformation requires changes in employee skills that organizations need [2]. IT infrastructure and employee skill levels are important factors

T. Guarda et al. (Eds.): ARTIIS 2023, CCIS 1935, pp. 457–467, 2024.
https://doi.org/10.1007/978-3-031-48858-0_36

influencing digital transformation processes [3] The authors have shown the impact of the human and non-human components (i.e. knowledge, leadership, digital servitization, technological) of digital transformation that can either enhance it or derail it [4]. The successful integration of new technologies in organizations is directly proportional to the level of digital maturity of the organizations. Technologies already in use and digital skills are among the factors that influence an organization's level of digital maturity. The use of maturity models contributes to shaping the strategically aligned digitalization transition of companies [5]. Digital maturity level could be asses by a model that includes the following dimensions: digital strategy, partner interface, the company's processes, employees and technologies, products and services, and customer interface [6]. Digital transformation integrates not only digital technologies and solutions in every area of business and to make this possible it is also necessary for cultural and technological change. This is forcing organizations to make fundamental changes in how they operate and how deliver user experiences and benefits. Digital transformation significantly changes the ways of doing business and is a key component of a business transformation strategy [7]. It is critical to the success or failure of any transformation effort. Digitalization changes go beyond changes in simple organizational processes and tasks [8, 9]. The right technologies combined with people, processes, and operations make it possible to adapt to meet new and evolving customer needs and drive future growth and innovation. Various capabilities at different time points are needed to support organizations during digital transformation [10].

Thanks to the new digital solutions, an increase in the workforce is realized, which, on the other hand, leads to a transformation of business processes and business models [11]. It requires rearranging the processes to change the business logic and value-creation processes through sustainable business models [12, 13]. Today, there is no area where digitalization has not started to one degree or another. Therefore, it is important to propose a model for evaluating the readiness for digital transformation. Digital transformation along with digital maturity should be considered more of a continuum rather than a fixed measure and should be viewed as a flexible and dynamic concept.

The goal of digital transformation is to obtain a sufficient return on investment as a result of the implementation of new technology. This could be achieved by following a proper digital transformation program that can impact the business. Such a program should include the objectives such as the implementation of the latest technologies; cost reduction; increasing employee productivity; increasing business growth; improve customer satisfaction [14]. These goals should be implemented into the overall digital transformation plan and tracked using appropriate KPIs to ensure that the following digital transformation plan is on track. In order to achieve a successful digital transformation, it is necessary to pursue an end goal aimed at improving the overall user experience and customer satisfaction. Unlike previous work where objective and subjective indicators are used, in this article all KPIs are considered measurable [15]. Since there are no strictly established metrics to measure the digital transformation process, having a model based on measurable indicators would be a step in the right direction. Therefore, this article aims to propose a model based on groups of indicators concerning three fundamental areas, namely operational and organizational readiness and business value.

The rest of the article is organized as follows: Sect. 2 contains a description of KPIs to assess digital transformation in terms of its stages as operational and organizational readiness and business value; Sect. 3 describes the proposed multi-criteria model for evaluation of digital transformation; Sect. 4 contains the numerical application of proposed digital transformation assessment model based on groups of KPIs along with results analysis and discussion, and conclusions are drawn in Sect. 5.

2 KPIs to Assess Digital Transformation Stages – Operational Readiness, Organizational Readiness and Business Value

Key performance indicators play an essential role in determining the progress of digital transformation. There are no universal sets of KPIs for measuring digitalization progress. There isn't even a set amount of KPIs applicable to different industries but it is possible to be divided into groups of indicators related to the stages of operational readiness, organizational readiness, and business value and ROI [16] as shown in Fig. 1.

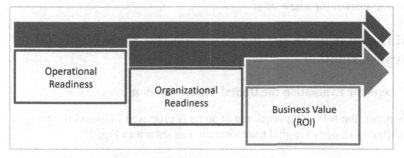

Fig. 1. Groups of KPIs to assess digital transformation

Operational Readiness is an important part of understanding how well the business processes and the technologies are aligned before go-live. Operational readiness could be defined as the ability to effectively implement, operate and maintain the systems and procedures. Various processes and practices are used to ensure that all functional and non-functional requirements, together with all operational deliverables, are performed, available and certified [17].

Organizational Readiness can be used as a measure of an organization's ability to make changes based on current conditions. It is critical to measure what percentage of the organization is fully trained in the various modules and what percentage has demonstrated competence to execute end-to-end business processes [18].

Business Value and ROI quantifies the benefits to the business and can be defined as the overall value (tangible and intangible) that investment brings to a company. The following factors could serve as a measure of tangible and intangible elements of business value: revenue; profitability; market share; brand recognition; customer loyalty; customer retention; customer satisfaction; etc.

The most common indicators related to Operational Readiness (*OpR*) are:

1) Active usage metrics that express the number of purchased licenses to the number of users who are actually using the software;
2) Technology infrastructure that shows the availability of digital systems and the number of digital points;
3) The availability of data analytics tools.

The most common indicators related to Organizational Readiness (*OrR*) are:

1) Leadership that show the number of executives engaged in digital initiatives;
2) Cybersecurity measured by metrics such as the number of cyber-attacks detected, the number of successful cyber-attacks prevented, and the time to detect and respond to cyber threats.

The most common indicators related to Business Value (*BV*) and ROI are:

1) Quantity of successfully implemented innovations;
2) Application of innovative solutions;
3) New products or services;
4) The ratio of funds received due to transformation and spent on it;
5) Time to market for a new offer.

3 Mathematical Model for Assessing the State of Digital Transformation

3.1 Stages for Evaluation the Digital Transformation

In this paper, the following sequence of steps is proposed to assess the progress of the three different stages of digital transformation as shown in Fig. 2.

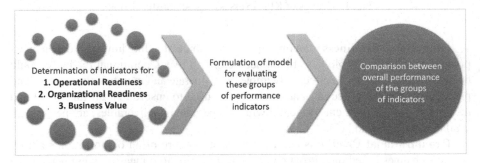

Fig. 2. Digital transformation evaluation stages

The first step concerns the definition of appropriate evaluation indicators for all three groups: (1) Operational Readiness, (2) Organizational Readiness and (3) Business Value. The second step requires the formulation of a suitable model for assessing the state of digital transformation, while the third step refers to some actions according to the results obtained.

Table 1. Indicators to measure the stages of digital transformation

Groups of KPIs	KPIs
Operational readiness	1.1. Number of purchased licenses to the number of users who are actually using the software
	1.2. Number of digital points
	1.3. Number of used analytics tools
Organizational readiness	2.1. Number of executives engaged in digital initiatives
	2.2. Number of cyber-attacks detected
	2.3. Number of successful cyber-attacks pre-vented
	2.4. Time to detect and respond to cyber threats
Business value	3.1. Number of successfully implemented innovations
	3.2. Number of applications of innovative solutions
	3.3. Number of new products or services
	3.4. The ratio of funds received due to transformation and spent on it
	3.5. Time to market for a new offer

There are no strict indicators that could be used to express these readiness stages and the following common indicators for all three groups are shown in Table 1.

Successful digital transformation requires sustainable technology adoption and one of the best KPIs to measure is the active usage of digital assets. This can be measure by comparing *the* number of licenses purchased to the number of users who are actually using the software. The operational readiness includes also indicators for available digital points and the number of used analytics tools. All of these KPIs could be measured.

The second group of KPIs related to the organizational readiness includes the following also measurable indicators: number of executives engaged in digital initiatives; the number of detected cyber-attacks; number of successful prevented cyber-attacks; and the needed time to detect and respond to cyber threats. The third group of KPIs refers to business value activities, expressed by the number of successfully implemented innovations; number of applications of innovative solutions; realized number of new products or services; the ratio between received funds due to transformation and spent on it; needed time to market for a new offer. It should be noted that it is possible to define other indicators that may not have measurable values, such as digital culture or digital skills. In this situation, it is necessary to involve the decision-maker to evaluate the effectiveness of such types of indicators. The evaluation of these indicators will be subjective and will express the point of view of a particular expert. Once the set of KPIs is determined, the proper model needs to be formulated.

3.2   Model for Assessing the State of Digital Transformation

To assess the state of digital transformation (DX), the 3 groups of indicators about 3 stages are used as described in the previous section. Maximum productivity is sought for all 3 groups. This means that it is necessary to use the following multi-criteria model to assess the state of digital transformation:

$$DX = \begin{cases} \max OpR \\ \max OrR \\ \max BV \end{cases} \qquad (1)$$

subject to

$$OpR = \sum_{i=1}^{I} w_i m_i > 0 \qquad (2)$$

$$OrR = \sum_{j=1}^{J} w_j m_j > 0 \qquad (3)$$

$$BV = \sum_{k=1}^{K} w_k m_k > 0 \qquad (4)$$

$$\sum_{i=1}^{I} w_i = 1 \qquad (5)$$

$$\sum_{j=1}^{J} w_j = 1 \qquad (6)$$

$$\sum_{k=1}^{K} w_k = 1 \qquad (7)$$

The coefficients w_i, w_j and w_k express the relative importance between indicators within each group, while m_i, m_j and m_k represent the quantity of the measurable indicators. Metrics for measurable indicators can be expressed in different units, which necessitates their normalization. That means the normalization should correspond to the same range of relative importance between indicators in the model (1)–(7). Therefore, the acceptable range for this normalization should be in the range between 0 and 1. The relations (2), (3) and (4) express the fact that all groups need to be positive, i.e. the company needs to demonstrate the performance of specific activities for the purpose of digitalization. Data normalization is essential in decision-making problems because it ensures that the resulting dimensionless units can be used to form a generalized evaluation.

Over time, the value of operational readiness measurable indicators should be increasing, as it is one of the main prerequisites for realizing digital transformation. The same applies to the second group (organizational readiness) of indicators, which show the extent to which executives are engaged in digitization activities and how well this digital data is protected. The good performance of the indicators from these two groups is a prerequisite for good performance of the indicators from the third group, related to business value.

It should be noted that in the model (1)–(7) formulated above, all indicators have to be measurable. But it is also permissible to use immeasurable indicators, the measure of which can be the rating given by an authorized person, for example, the Chief Information Officer (CIO), Chief Digital Officer (CDO), etc. CIO and CDO are among the responsible persons that need to provide the right IT infrastructure along with the right people for the digitalization of business by advanced technologies to create business value. It is assumed that the ratings about the evaluation will be in the range of 0 to 1 (or any other that need to be normalized) where a bigger value will indicate the better performance of the indicator and vice versa.

There are a variety of techniques that allow to solve multi-criteria problems such as the weighted sum method, lexicographical method, e-constraints method, etc. [19, 20]. Regardless of which one is used, the resulting Pareto optimality solution expresses the fact none of the criteria can be improved without degrading some of the others [21].

4 Numerical Application of Proposed Digital Transformation Assessment Model Based on Groups of KPIs

For the numerical testing of the proposed model (1)–(7), a CDO was asked to provide information on performance indicators. The presented metrics refer to a micro-sized company. To solve the multi-criteria model (1)–(7) the weighted sum method is used. This method was chosen because it is easy to understand. The implementation of this method requires transforming the multi-criteria objective function (1) to a single criterion function as follows:

$$max\left(w_i \left(\frac{OpR^{max} - OpR}{OpR^{max} - OpR^{min}} \right) + w_j \left(\frac{OrR^{max} - OrR}{OrR^{max} - OrR^{min}} \right) + w_k \left(\frac{BV^{max} - BV}{BV^{max} - BV^{min}} \right) \right)$$

(8)

The rest of the restrictions remains the same. Using such a normalization scheme allows obtaining dimensionless values in the interval between 0 and 1.

The minimal values for operational readiness (OpR^{min}), organizational readiness (OrR^{min}), and business value (BV^{min}) are obtained by solving consequence single-criterion tasks seeking its minimum. Analogical tasks need to be solved to get the maximal values for operational readiness (OpR^{max}), organizational readiness (OrR^{max}), and business value (BV^{max}). Once these values are known, the transformation objective function (8) subject to (2)–(7) needs to be run.

4.1 Input Data

The normalized data about the measurable indicators in groups along with weighted coefficients for their importance are shown in Table 2.

It should be noted that 3 of the KPIs are given with a value equal to zero. One of them is the "*Number of digital points*" from the Operational Readiness, while the rest two "*Number of detected cyber-attacks*" and "*Number of successful cyber-attacks prevented*" are from the Organizational Readiness. Even at this stage, it can be suggested that the particular company's digital transformation has significant security gaps.

Two cases are simulated for the importance of indicators, labeled Case-1 and Case-2. These two scenarios express different points of view with respect to prioritizing the indicators within the 3 groups (3 stages). The normalized units of measure for the indicators are made to range from 0 to 1 to be comparable to the weighted importance coefficients of the indicators according to the restrictions (5), (6), and (7).

Table 2. Normalized metrics about the indicators and weights for their importance.

KPIs	Normalized indicators	Weights for KPIs importance (Case-1)			Weights for KPIs importance (Case-2)		
	m_i, m_j, m_k	w_i	w_j	w_k	w_i	w_j	w_k
1.1. Number of purchased licenses to the number of users actually using the software	1.00	0.33			0.20		
1.2. Number of digital points	0.00	0.33			0.40		
1.3. Number of used analytics tools	0.067	0.34			0.40		
2.1. Number of executives engaged in digital initiatives	0.001		0.25			0.50	
2.2. Number of detected cyber-attacks	0.00		0.25			0.10	
2.3. Number of successful cyber-attacks prevented	0.00		0.25			0.15	
2.4. Time to detect and respond to cyber threats	1.00		0.25			0.25	
3.1. Number of successfully implemented innovations	0.002			0.20			0.15
3.2. Number of applications of innovative solutions	0.005			0.20			0.15
3.3. Number of new products or services	0.007			0.20			0.10
3.4. The ratio of funds received due to transformation and spent on it	0.010			0.20			0.40
3.5. Time to market for a new offer	1.000			0.20			0.20

The normalized input data from Table 2 and the proposed model (1)–(7), respectively the transformed objective function (8) subject to the restrictions (2)–(7) are used to formulate an optimization problem. The obtained results are illustrated and discussed in the next section.

4.2 Results Analysis and Discussion

The results of the tested two simulations (Case-1 and Case-2) with respect to prioritizing the indicators according to different points of view for the KPIs within 3 groups (respectively 3 stages) are illustrated in Fig. 3.

It can be seen (from Fig. 3) the difference in overall performance when using different weighted coefficients for the indicators – the value of 0.808 in case of equal importance of all indicators and 0.683 when some indicators are preferred over others. These values do not carry complete information about the digital transformation progress, therefore it is good to pay attention to the individual groups of indicators.

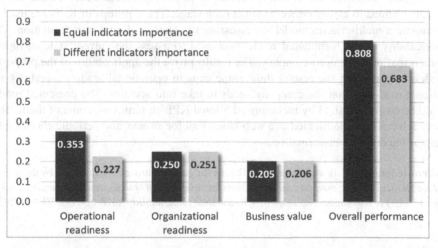

Fig. 3. Comparison of results using different weights for importance indicators

For example, in Case-1 (equal weights for KPIs) Operational Readiness has better performance with a value of 0.353 compared to Organizational Readiness (0.250) and Business Value (0.205) despite missing activities for "*Number of digital points*" and "*Number of detected cyber-attacks*" and "*Number of successful cyber-attacks prevented*".

When some indicators are favored over others as in Case-2 the results show better performance for Organizational Readiness (0.251) compared to Operational Readiness (0.227) and Business Value (0.206). In this situation, it could not expect that digital transformation will succeed because the business processes and the technologies are not well aligned before go-live.

The proposed mathematical model could be easily modified by including additional KPIs or removing some of them. There is no limitation to forming other group/s of

KPIs to measure the progress of digital transformation. In addition, it is possible to assess the current state of digital transformation in relation to only one of the groups of indicators (1) Operational Readiness, (2) Organizational Readiness, or (3) Business Value. Besides forming a different set of KPIs for different stages it is possible also to use different modeling approaches. For example, single criterion models or models based on group decision-making where the opinions of many decision-makers are taken into account.

Using such types of models, it is possible to predict digital transformation failure or success, as it focuses not only on an organization's ability to implement new technology and software but also on its people, culture, processes, etc.

5 Conclusions

The current article deals with the problems related to digital transformation. In this regard, 3 stages of digital transformation are discussed namely (1) Operational readiness, (2) Organizational readiness, and (3) Business value. Appropriate measurable indicators are defined to assess performance at each stage. These groups of KPIs are used to formulate a multi-criteria model for assessing the state of digital transformation. The applicability of the formulated model was used to assess the current state of digital transformation of a micro-company. The results prove the applicability of the proposed model. In particular, the results show some gaps in operational readiness and organizational readiness that the company needs to take into account. The presented model could be easily modified by including additional KPIs or removing some of them. This approach can be implemented as a web-based tool for an easy and periodic check of the state of the digital transformation.

Acknowledgment. This work is supported by the Bulgarian National Science Fund by the project *"Mathematical models, methods and algorithms for solving hard optimization problems to achieve high security in communications and better economic sustainability"*, KP-06-H52/7/19-11-2021.

References

1. Borissova, D., Keremedchieva, N.: Decision support approach in evaluating the parameters of books for digital manufacturing. In: Rocha, A., Ferras, C., Mendez Porras, A., Jimenez Delgado, E. (eds.) Information Technology and Systems. ICITS 2022. Lecture Notes in Networks and Systems, vol. 414 (2022). https://doi.org/10.1007/978-3-030-96293-7_16
2. Ostmeier, E., Strobel, M.: Building skills in the context of digital transformation: How industry digital maturity drives proactive skill development. J. Bus. Res. **139**, 718–730 (2022). https://doi.org/10.1016/j.jbusres.2021.09.020
3. Cirillo, V., Fanti, L., Mina, A., Ricci, A.: The adoption of digital technologies: investment, skills, work organization. Struct. Chang. Econ. Dyn.Dyn. (2023). https://doi.org/10.1016/j.strueco.2023.04.011
4. Feliciano-Cestero, M.M., Ameen, N., Kotabe, M., Paul, J., Signoret, M.: Is digital transformation threatened? a systematic literature review of the factors influencing firms' digital transformation and internationalization. J. Bus. Res. **157**, 113546 (2023). https://doi.org/10.1016/j.jbusres.2022.113546

5. Hein-Pensel, F., et al.: Maturity assessment for Industry 5.0: a review of existing maturity models. J. Manuf. Syst. **66**, 200–210 (2023). https://doi.org/10.1016/j.jmsy.2022.12.009

6. Schallmo, D.R.A., Lang, K., Hasler, D., Ehmig-Klassen, K., Williams, C.A.: An approach for a digital maturity model for SMEs based on their requirements. In: Schallmo, D.R.A., Tidd, J. (eds.) Digitalization. Management for Professionals, pp. 87–101 (2021). https://doi.org/10.1007/978-3-030-69380-0_6

7. Pfister, P., Lehmann, C.: Digital value creation in German SMEs – a return-on-investment analysis. J. Small Bus. Entrep.Entrep. (2022). https://doi.org/10.1080/08276331.2022.2037065

8. Verhoef, P.C., et al.: Digital transformation: a multidisciplinary reflection and research agenda. J. Bus. Res. **122**, 889–901 (2021). https://doi.org/10.1016/j.jbusres.2019.09.022

9. Stalmachova, K., Chinoracky, R., Strenitzerova, M.: Changes in business models caused by digital transformation and the COVID-19 pandemic and possibilities of their measurement – Case study. Sustainability **14**(1), 127 (2022). https://doi.org/10.3390/su14010127

10. Konopik, J., Jahn, C., Schuster, T., Hoßbach, N., Pflaum, A.: Mastering the digital transformation through organizational capabilities: a conceptual framework. Digital Bus. **2**(2), 100019 (2022). https://doi.org/10.1016/j.digbus.2021.100019

11. Li, X., Zhang, L., Cao, J.: Research on the mechanism of sustainable business model innovation driven by the digital platform ecosystem. J. Eng. Tech. Manage. **68**, 101738 (2023). https://doi.org/10.1016/j.jengtecman.2023.101738

12. Gebauer, H., et al.: How to convert digital offerings into revenue enhancement – conceptualizing business model dynamics through explorative case studies. Ind. Mark. Manage. **91**, 429–441 (2020). https://doi.org/10.1016/j.indmarman.2020.10.006

13. Broccardo, L., Zicari, A., Jabeen, F., Bhatti, Z.A.: How digitalization supports a sustainable business model: a literature review. Technol. Forecast. Soc. Chang. **187**, 122146 (2023). https://doi.org/10.1016/j.techfore.2022.122146

14. Periyasamy, R.: 5 key metrics to measure your digital transformation progress (2021). https://www.apty.io/blog/digital-transformation-progress/

15. Borissova, D., Dimitrova, Z., Naidenov, N., Yoshinov, R.: Integrated approach to assessing the progress of digital transformation by using multiple objective and subjective indicators. In: Guizzardi, R., Ralyté, J., Franch, X. (eds.) Research Challenges in Information Science. RCIS 2022. Lecture Notes in Business Information Processing, vol. 446, pp. 626–634 (2022). https://doi.org/10.1007/978-3-031-05760-1_37

16. Kimberling, E.: Top digital transformation KPIs and performance measures (2022). https://www.thirdstage-consulting.com/top-digital-transformation-kpis-and-performance-measures/

17. Levovnik, D., Gerbec, M.: Operational readiness for the integrated management of changes in the industrial organizations – assessment approach and results. Saf. Sci.. Sci. **107**, 119–129 (2018). https://doi.org/10.1016/j.ssci.2018.04.006

18. Weiner, B.J.: A theory of organizational readiness for change. Implementation Sci. **4**(67) (2009). https://doi.org/10.1186/1748-5908-4-67

19. Kirilov, L., Guliashki, V., Genova, K., Vassileva, M., Staykov, B.: Generalized scalarizing model GENS in DSS WebOptim. Int. J. Decision Support Syst. Technol. **5**(3), 1–11 (2013). https://doi.org/10.4018/jdsst.2013070101

20. Marler, R.T., Arora, J.S.: The weighted sum method for multi-objective optimization: new insights. Struct. Multidiscip. Optim.Optim. **41**, 853–862 (2010). https://doi.org/10.1007/s00158-009-0460-7

21. Marler, R.T., Arora, J.S.: Survey of multi-objective optimization methods for engineering. Struct. Multidiscip. Optim. **26**, 369–395 (2004). https://doi.org/10.1007/s00158-003-0368-6

Domain-Specific Sentiment Analysis of Tweets Using Machine Learning Methods

Tshephisho Joseph Sefara[✉][iD] and Mapitsi Roseline Rangata[iD]

Council for Scientific and Industrial Research, Pretoria, South Africa
{tsefara,mrangata}@csir.co.za

Abstract. Most general sentiment analysers degrade quality when tested on Tweets in the broadcast domain. This domain covers both radio and television broadcast. This paper proposes domain-specific data in the broadcast domain. Furthermore, it proposes the use of machine learning methods for the sentiment analysis of tweets in this domain. Data were collected from Twitter using Twitter application programming interfaces. The data were preprocessed, and most special characters and emoticons were not removed, as sentiment analysis involves the use of opinions and emotions which are expressed using emoticons and other characters. The data were automatically labelled using a pre-trained sentiment analyser to enable the use of supervised learning on the data. Two supervised machine learning methods, such as XGBoost and multinomial logistic regression (MLR), are trained and evaluated on the data. The performance of the models was affected by two factors; limited data and the use of a general sentiment analyser to label the data in a specific domain.

Keywords: Sentiment analysis · Machine learning · XGBoost · Logistic regression · Text classification · NLP · AI

1 Introduction

Sentiment analysis is a computational analysis in Natural Language Processing (NLP) that identifies and categorises a sentiment (people's opinion or feeling or expression) in a text about a certain event, topics or product, and others [18]. Twitter platform is one of the famous microblogging social media sites that generates a large volume of data in real time with millions of tweets posted daily, which enables researchers such as Agarwal et al. [1] to build supervised learning models to classify tweets into different categories such as positive, neutral and negative. Machine learning models such as support vector machine (SVM), naive Bayes, logistic regression, decision trees, random forest, and others are being used to create sentiment analysers. [2,7–9] created a sentiment analyser using SVM, while [20] used naive Bayes. The use of text classification using machine learning as sentiment analysis has dominated the current research approach. Ramadhan et al. [24] used logistic regression to create a sentiment analysis model. Their

T. Guarda et al. (Eds.): ARTIIS 2023, CCIS 1935, pp. 468–482, 2024.
https://doi.org/10.1007/978-3-031-48858-0_37

model was tested on different sizes of training and testing data, also on different numbers of K-fold cross-validation, where the results showed that the higher the training size, the better the performance, and the higher the K-fold the better the performance. While sentiment analysis is being carried out as a multiclass classification, Prabhat [23] created a sentiment analyser using logistic regression and naive Bayes as a binary classification where the labels are positive and negative.

Most sentiment analysers are trained for English text, only a few work has been done for other languages [14,15]. Social media data is unstructured and may contain text in different languages that Twitter may not support in terms of automatic language identification during data acquisition using Twitter APIs. Mabokela et al. [14] created a multilingual annotated sentiment data set for South African languages, including Setswana, Sepedi, and English. The authors also created an application that enables automatic labelling of sentiments in a multilingual context.

Sentiment analysis is being applied in many domains, including viewership [16], political [6], food retail [5], phone retail [10], and can be applied for customer satisfaction [25]. Most sentiment analysers work with textual data, recently [28] conducted a study on the analysis of sentiments from both textual data and speech data. The authors used supervised learning methods, such as SVM for textual data and fuzzy logic for speech data. These machine learning methods recorded good results in speech and language processing [27].

In the broadcasting domain, radio and television (TV) are one of the broadcasting services that are used for communication. In this paper, the sentiments of radio and television services are analysed to obtain the opinions and feelings of people shared on Twitter about certain services such as TV shows, TV channels, news, etc., offered in South African broadcast. There are many sentiment analysers for social networks that use general data, but such analysers are trained on general domain data and consequently degrade performance when testing in the broadcasting domain. Therefore, this paper proposes a domain-specific dataset and an analysis of the sentiment analysis models trained in the broadcasting domain using limited data acquired from Twitter.

The main contributions of this paper are as follows.

- The paper proposes models for sentiment analysis in the broadcasting domain.
- Automatic labelling of data using pre-trained model to allow analytics using supervised learning.
- Data are made available on GitHub[1].
- We publish the source code on GitHub see footnote 1 to enable benchmarking of the results.

---

[1] https://github.com/JosephSefara/Topic-Classification-of-Tweets.

This paper is organised as follows. The next section explains the background. Section 3 explains data acquisition, data processing, machine learning models, and model evaluation. Section 4 discusses the findings and analysis, while Sect. 5 concludes the paper with future work.

2   Background

This section discusses the recent applications of sentiment analysis in different domains. In the viewership domain, Malik et al. [16] performed sentiment analysis to predict viewers on streaming TV shows using Twitter data. For each TV show, the authors collected tweets using a certain keyword for a specific period. They also explored the performance of various supervised machine learning methods for the classification of sentiments from tweets about TV programmes.

In the food retail domain, El Rahman et al. [5] conducted a sentiment analysis on Twitter data to show which restaurant is popular between McDonald's and KFC. They used different supervised classification algorithms. Maxtent, as one of the explored, was a top performer for McDonald's and KFC with a four-fold cross-validation of 74% (McDonald's) and 78% of a four-fold cross-validation (KFC).

For the food supply domain, based on the public sentiments expressed on Twitter, Neogi et al. [21] conducted a sentiment analysis on India's farmer protests. Their study used a lexicon-based method; TextBlob, together with an exploration of machine learning classification methods, to evaluate public sentiment in India about farmer protests. TF-IDF was used as a feature extractor in their modelling simulation. Random Forest was one of the classifiers investigated in their study and was found to be the best performer in terms of accuracy.

In the phone retail domain, Hasan et al. [10] analysed a sentiment analysis on Twitter data related to particular phone brands to obtain sentiment to show which phone brand is popular between the iPhone and Samsung, where the authors have collected 1000 tweets. The authors explored the use of both term frequency-inverse document frequency (TF-IDF) and bag-of-words (BoW) to generate features for modelling. Their results showed that both TF-IDF and BoW improve the performance of the results, showing that the iPhone was more popular compared to Samsung devices.

In the health domain, Vijay et al. [29] analysed Twitter data related to covid-19 for sentiment classification in certain parts of India from November 2019 to May 2020 to evaluate the progression of virus spread and people's opinions based on covid-19 and the measures implemented by the government to curb virus spread. TextBlob was used in their study to analyse Twitter data obtained during that time period.

In the political domain, Elbagir et al. [6] analysed tweets from the 2016 US elections for sentiment classification to categorise tweets into 4 categories; positive, negative, neutral, highly negative, highly positive using Valence Aware Dictionary and sEntiment Reasoner (VADER) [11] and Natural Language Toolkit (NLTK). On the other hand, Joyce et al. [12] also performed sentiment analysis in the 2016 US elections for comparison of sentiment analysis approaches known as lexicon-based sentiment analysis and machine learning classifiers for sentiment. They used manual and automated labelled tweets in both approaches. Their results show that the lexicon-based sentiment analysis performed better. In their research, the author [30] analysed the 2020 US presidential election for sentiment analysis to obtain opinions on Twitter between the two candidates running for president, and also to predict the outcome of the election, five machine learning classifications were explored in the data for performance evaluation. Among the five classifiers, multilayer perceptron (MLP) was the top performer. The sentiment analysis method to extract the individual's point of view on Twitter about electricity hikes in a developed and developing country was developed by Kaur et al. [13]. In their study, they proposed a lexicon-based method known as VADER to infer sentiment polarity together with classification algorithms. TF-IDF was used for feature extraction. Four algorithms were explored for performance evaluation. Random forest and decision tree were the most successful models.

3   Methodology

In this section, we discuss the proposed architectural design, the acquired data, the exploratory analysis of the acquired data, the proposed supervised machine learning methods, and the evaluation techniques of the models.

3.1   Architectural Design

This paper proposes a method illustrated in Fig. 1 that uses a pre-trained sentiment analysis model to label the new data that are collected. Figure 1 shows the architecture of the proposed method. The first step is to acquire data from Twitter that are not labelled. We pre-process the data to remove unnecessary characters and to enhance the quality of the acquired data. We extracted the features using the TF-IDF vectoriser for each tweet. The pre-trained sentiment analyser is applied to the data to create labels. We labelled the data using the labels generated by the pre-trained sentiment analyser for each tweet. At this stage, the data are labelled and supervised learning can be applied to the labelled data. We trained machine learning methods on the labelled data and compared the performance of the trained models. We further analysed the predictions of the models using confusion matrix.

3.2   Data

The data was collected from Twitter using Twitter streaming APIs in real time. Data are collected from February 2023 for a period of 3 months. The following rules were sent to Twitter to match the tweets in real time. We did not retrieve historical Twitter data.

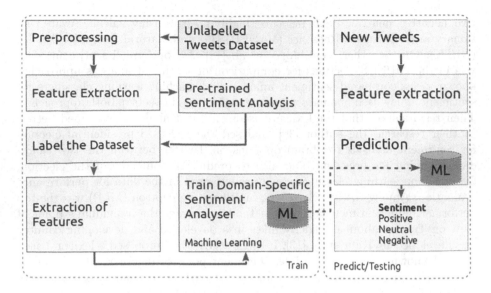

Fig. 1. Proposed architecture.

Algorithm 1. Rules used to collect tweets on Twitter APIs

1: The tweet must be original or quoted tweets not retweet.
2: The tweet must be created by a user in South Africa.
3: The tweet must be tagged with a place.
4: The geo-location of the tweet should be near a tagged place.
5: The tweet must contain one or more keywords provided to Twitter.

3.3   Exploratory Data Analysis

This section analyse the acquired data to determine the quality of the data, the relationship between the entities, the patterns within the data, and errors and anomalies. We use the following entities from the data:

- User: The account authored a tweet.
- Hashtags: The hashtags mentioned in a tweet.
- User mentions: Accounts that are mentioned in a tweet.
- Text: The actual tweet.
- Place: The geographical place where a tweet was authored.
- Date: The date and time on which a tweet was composed.

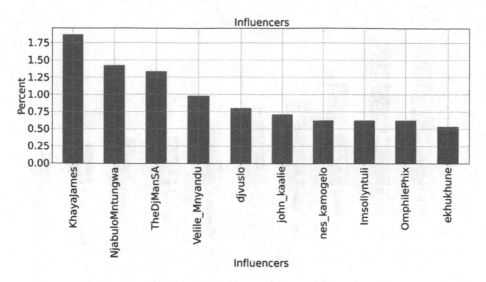

Fig. 2. Top 10 social media influencers.

The data consisted of 1125 number of tweets where some tweets are authored by same user. Figure 2 shows the top 10 most frequent social media influencers or users. This figure validates whether some users are robots or not. We validate the users with the most frequent tweets and ascertain that the users are not robots. About 173 tweets are authored by the same influencers, and 572 tweets are authored by unique influencers.

The data contained tweets generated by users in South Africa. The country name will be shared when a user does not share the actual location. Figure 3 shows the top 10 most frequent places where a tweet was authored. The first place with the most frequent tweets is South Africa followed by the following cities: Johannesburg, Pretoria, Cape Town, Sandton, Randburg, Midrand, Durban, Roodepoort, and Centurion. This figure shows that most of the tweets are authored from populated and developed cities in South Africa. The most frequent tweets are authored from 83 places, whereas other tweets are authored from 78 unique places.

The tweets may mention other users. Figure 4 shows the top 10 most frequent user mentions with *etv* being the highest followed by *DStv, METROFMSA, Official_SABC1*, and others.

Tweets may contain hashtags. Figure 5 shows the top 10 most frequent hashtags with *sabcnews* having the highest mentions followed by *DStvPrem, radio*, and others.

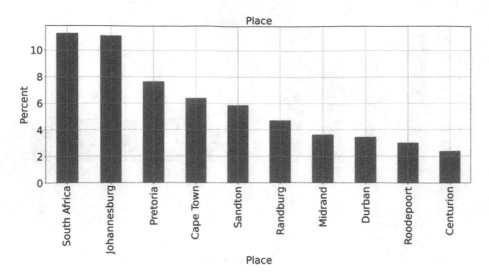

Fig. 3. Top 10 places.

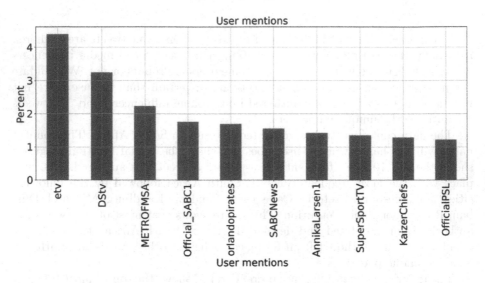

Fig. 4. Top 10 user mentions.

The tweets contain a date entity that tells when a tweet was authored. Figure 6 shows the time distribution of tweets for a 24-hour period in a day. It shows that most tweets are authored from 5:00 in the morning until 19:00 in the afternoon. Since Twitter uses GMT timezone, the local timezone for South Africa is GMT+2 which implies that most tweets are authored from 7:00 until 21:00, but around 17:00 fewer tweets are authored, this happens when most users travel from work to their homes.

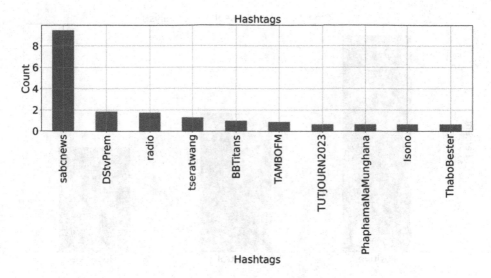

Fig. 5. Top 10 hashtags.

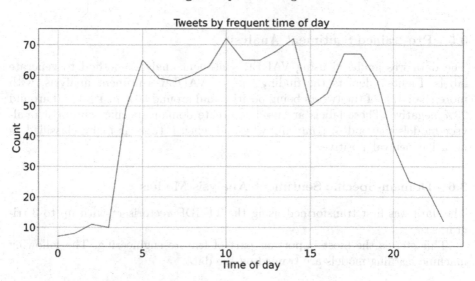

Fig. 6. Frequent tweets during 24 h time in a day.

3.4 Data Preprocessing

The data was pre-processed to validate that the tweet exists. In sentiment analysis, special characters and emoticons express emotions and meaning, which is an important feature during model building. We preserve the original tweet without removing any characters.

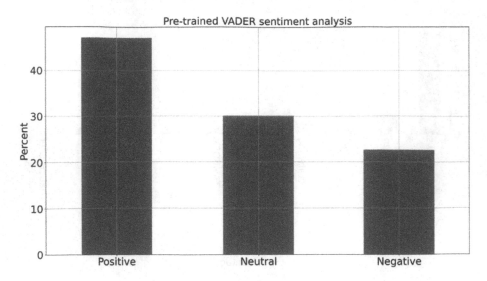

Fig. 7. Pre-trained sentiment analysis using VADER.

3.5 Pre-trained Sentiment Analysis

The data was analysed using VADER sentiment analysis method to generate labels. Figure 7 depicts the findings of the VADER sentiment analysis, with more than 47% of the tweets being positive and around 30% neutral and around 23% negative. These labels are used to create domain-specific sentiment analyser models that aid in analysing why and when a tweet is being classified as negative/neutral/positive.

3.6 Domain-Specific Sentiment Analysis Models

The data was first transformed using the TF-IDF vectoriser[2] with up to 3 trigrams.

This step is the most important part of feature engineering. The following machine learning models are trained on the data.

- **Multinomial logistic regression (MLR)**: is a supervised machine learning model that is trained on the data. MLR model can output the predictions and the importance of features.
- **XGBoost**: is an implementation of gradient-boosting decision trees that is trained on the data. XGBoost model can output the predictions and importance of features.

---

[2] https://scikit-learn.org/stable/modules/generated/sklearn.feature_extraction.text.TfidfVectorizer.html.

3.7   Evaluation

The quality performance of the machine learning models was tested using the confusion matrix, the F measure, and the accuracy metrics:

Confusion Matrix. The confusion matrix is defined as a matrix that is applied to measure the classification performance of machine learning models. This matrix is used to calculate the precision, recall, F measure, and accuracy of machine learning models. The matrix also helps to understand the accuracy of predicting each label or class. The confusion matrix is depicted in Fig. 8, where:

1. True positive (TP) is when a tweet is correctly predicted as positive,
2. False positive (FP) is when a tweet is incorrectly predicted as positive,
3. True negative (TN) is when a tweet is correctly predicted negative,
4. False negative (FN) is when a tweet is incorrectly predicted negative.

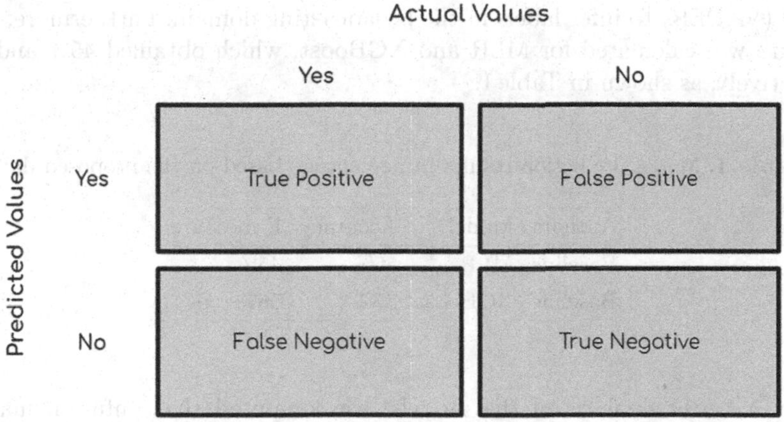

Fig. 8. Confusion matrix.

Accuracy. Accuracy is defined as the total number of correctly predicted tweets divided by the total number of tweets. Accuracy is determined as:

$$Accuracy = \frac{TN + TP}{FP + FN + TN + TP} \tag{1}$$

F Measure. F Measure is the harmonic mean of precision and recall. F Measure is defined by the following equation.

$$FMeasure = \frac{2 * TP}{2 * TP + FP + FN} \tag{2}$$

4   Results and Discussions

This section explains the findings of the domain-specific sentiment analysis models. The acquired data was splitted into 80% for building the model and the rest for testing the model. The test data were not used to build the model to allow for a proper evaluation of the models on unseen data. MLR and XGBoost were fitted on the training dataset, and most of the parameters are default. The logistic regression implemented in scikit-learn [22] was used as the first model in which the parameter *multi_ class* was set to *multinomial* to make it suitable for multiclass classification, since this type of model is well-known for binary classification. The XGBoost model implemented in [3] was used as the second model in which the parameter *objective* was set to *multi:softmax* to make it suitable for multiclass classification, as this type of model is well-known for binary classification. MLR and XGBoost obtained an accuracy of 56% and 57%, respectively. The quality of the performance of the models depends on the size of the data [19], and since our data were limited, this affected the performance of the results in this domain. Another factor that affects the accuracy is the use of a general model (VADER) to infer labels in the broadcasting domain. Furthermore, the F measure was calculated for MLR and XGBoost, which obtained 45% and 56% respectively, as shown in Table 1.

Table 1. Model prediction results in percentage based on the proposed data.

Authors	Model	Accuracy	F measure
Baseline	MLR	56%	45%
Baseline	XGBoost	57%	56%

For a better analysis of the models, we computed the confusion matrices in Fig. 9 and Fig. 10 for MLR and XGBoost, respectively. These matrices aid to understand the prediction performance for each label within the data. The models were better in predicting the positive sentiments with 49% for MLR and 34% for XGBoost. The XGBoost predicted neutral sentiment better than MLR, while MLR incorrectly predicted most of neutral and negative sentiments as positive sentiments.

This paper proposed a limited Twitter data in the specific domain (broadcasting domain) for the South African context. Models were built and generated the baseline results in this domain.

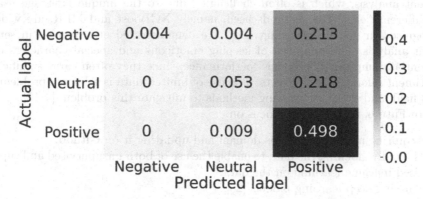

Fig. 9. MLR confusion matrix.

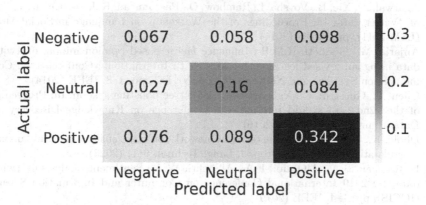

Fig. 10. XGBoost confusion matrix.

5   Conclusions and Future Work

This paper proposed the use of unlabelled data to create sentiment analysis models for a broadcasting domain. The data were labelled using a pre-trained VADER sentiment analyser to enable us to conduct supervised learning on the data. The two machine learning methods; MLR and XGBoost are trained and tested on the data. The models are evaluated using accuracy and the F measure. The models were evaluated using the confusion matrix to show the performance of each label. The results revealed that a variety of factors affected the models' performance; limited data, and using a general model to label the data that are specific to broadcasting domain.

In conclusion, the paper addresses an essential issue of domain-specific sentiment analysis, which is often challenging due to the unique language usage in different fields. The methods used, namely XGBoost and MLR, are widely recognised in machine learning and have demonstrated effectiveness in sentiment analysis. The approach of keeping emoticons and special characters can potentially improve the models' performance, since they often carry significant sentiment information in tweets. The use of limited data is a known problem in this field, and there are existing methods to mitigate this problem [4,17].

In Future, this work will focus on:

– Acquiring more data in this domain and updating it on Github.
– Manually labelling the data to enable the use of both unsupervised and supervised machine learning on the data.
– Training deep learning models [26].

References

1. Agarwal, A., Xie, B., Vovsha, I., Rambow, O., Passonneau, R.J.: Sentiment analysis of Twitter data. In: Proceedings of the Workshop on Language in Social Media (LSM 2011), pp. 30–38 (2011)
2. Anjaria, M., Guddeti, R.M.R.: Influence factor based opinion mining of Twitter data using supervised learning. In: 2014 Sixth International Conference on Communication Systems and Networks (COMSNETS), pp. 1–8. IEEE (2014)
3. Chen, T., Guestrin, C.: Xgboost: A scalable tree boosting system. In: Proceedings of the 22nd acm sigkdd International Conference on Knowledge Discovery and Data Mining, pp. 785–794 (2016)
4. Dhole, K., et al.: NL-Augmenter: a framework for task-sensitive natural language augmentation. Northern Europ. J. Lang. Technol. 9(1) (2023)
5. El Rahman, S.A., AlOtaibi, F.A., AlShehri, W.A.: Sentiment analysis of Twitter data. In: 2019 International Conference on Computer and Information Sciences (ICCIS), pp. 1–4. IEEE (2019)
6. Elbagir, S., Yang, J.: Twitter sentiment analysis using natural language toolkit and VADER sentiment. In: Proceedings of the International Multiconference of Engineers and Computer Scientists, vol. 122, p. 16 (2019)
7. Fouad, M.M., Gharib, T.F., Mashat, A.S.: Efficient Twitter sentiment analysis system with feature selection and classifier ensemble. In: Hassanien, A.E., Tolba, M.F., Elhoseny, M., Mostafa, M. (eds.) AMLTA 2018. AISC, vol. 723, pp. 516–527. Springer, Cham (2018). https://doi.org/10.1007/978-3-319-74690-6_51
8. Gautam, G., Yadav, D.: Sentiment analysis of Twitter data using machine learning approaches and semantic analysis. In: 2014 Seventh International Conference on Contemporary Computing (IC3), pp. 437–442. IEEE (2014)
9. Ghiassi, M., Skinner, J., Zimbra, D.: Twitter brand sentiment analysis: a hybrid system using n-gram analysis and dynamic artificial neural network. Expert Syst. Appl. 40(16), 6266–6282 (2013)
10. Hasan, M.R., Maliha, M., Arifuzzaman, M.: Sentiment analysis with NLP on Twitter data. In: 2019 International Conference on Computer, Communication, Chemical, Materials and Electronic Engineering (IC4ME2), pp. 1–4. IEEE (2019)

11. Hutto, C., Gilbert, E.: Vader: a parsimonious rule-based model for sentiment analysis of social media text. In: Proceedings of the International AAAI Conference on Web and Social Media, pp. 216–225 (2014)
12. Joyce, B., Deng, J.: Sentiment analysis of tweets for the 2016 US presidential election. In: 2017 IEEE MIT Undergraduate Research Technology Conference (URTC), pp. 1–4. IEEE (2017)
13. Kaur, P., Edalati, M.: Sentiment analysis on electricity Twitter posts. arXiv preprint arXiv:2206.05042 (2022)
14. Mabokela, K.R., Celik, T., Raborife, M.: Multilingual sentiment analysis for under-resourced languages: a systematic review of the landscape. IEEE Access (2022)
15. Mabokela, R., Schlippe, T.: A sentiment corpus for South African under-resourced languages in a multilingual context. In: Proceedings of the 1st Annual Meeting of the ELRA/ISCA Special Interest Group on Under-Resourced Languages, pp. 70–77 (2022)
16. Malik, H., Shakshuki, E.M., et al.: Approximating viewership of streaming TV programs using social media sentiment analysis. Procedia Comput. Sci. **198**, 94–101 (2022)
17. Marivate, V., Sefara, T.: Improving short text classification through global augmentation methods. In: Holzinger, A., Kieseberg, P., Tjoa, A.M., Weippl, E. (eds.) CD-MAKE 2020. LNCS, vol. 12279, pp. 385–399. Springer, Cham (2020). https://doi.org/10.1007/978-3-030-57321-8_21
18. Medhat, W., Hassan, A., Korashy, H.: Sentiment analysis algorithms and applications: a survey. Ain Shams Eng. J. **5**(4), 1093–1113 (2014)
19. Mokgonyane, T.B., Sefara, T.J., Manamela, M.J., Modipa, T.I.: The effects of data size on text-independent automatic speaker identification system. In: 2019 International Conference on Advances in Big Data, Computing and Data Communication Systems (icABCD), pp. 1–6. IEEE (2019)
20. Neethu, M., Rajasree, R.: Sentiment analysis in Twitter using machine learning techniques. In: 2013 Fourth International Conference on Computing, Communications and Networking Technologies (ICCCNT), pp. 1–5. IEEE (2013)
21. Neogi, A.S., Garg, K.A., Mishra, R.K., Dwivedi, Y.K.: Sentiment analysis and classification of Indian farmers' protest using Twitter data. Int. J. Inform. Manage. Data Insights **1**(2), 100019 (2021)
22. Pedregosa, F., et al.: Scikit-learn: machine learning in Python. J. Mach. Learn. Res. **12**, 2825–2830 (2011)
23. Prabhat, A., Khullar, V.: Sentiment classification on big data using naive Bayes and logistic regression. In: 2017 International Conference on Computer Communication and Informatics (ICCCI), pp. 1–5 (2017). https://doi.org/10.1109/ICCCI.2017.8117734
24. Ramadhan, W., Astri Novianty, S., Casi Setianingsih, S.: Sentiment analysis using multinomial logistic regression. In: 2017 International Conference on Control, Electronics, Renewable Energy and Communications (ICCREC), pp. 46–49 (2017). DOI: https://doi.org/10.1109/ICCEREC.2017.8226700
25. Ramirez, L.A.P., Marquez, B.Y., Magdaleno-Palencia, J.S.: Neuromarketing to discover customer satisfaction. In: Guarda, T., Portela, F., Augusto, M.F. (eds.) Advanced Research in Technologies, Information, Innovation and Sustainability, pp. 191–204. Springer, Cham (2022). https://doi.org/10.1007/978-3-031-20316-9_15
26. Sefara, T.J., Zwane, S.G., Gama, N., Sibisi, H., Senoamadi, P.N., Marivate, V.: Transformer-based machine translation for low-resourced languages embedded with

language identification. In: 2021 Conference on Information Communications Technology and Society (ICTAS), pp. 127–132. IEEE (2021)

27. Sefara, T.J., Mokgonyane, T.B.: Emotional speaker recognition based on machine and deep learning. In: 2020 2nd International Multidisciplinary Information Technology and Engineering Conference (IMITEC), pp. 1–8. IEEE (2020)

28. Vashishtha, S., Susan, S.: Inferring sentiments from supervised classification of text and speech cues using fuzzy rules. Procedia Comput. Sci. **167**, 1370–1379 (2020)

29. Vijay, T., Chawla, A., Dhanka, B., Karmakar, P.: Sentiment analysis on covid-19 Twitter data. In: 2020 5th IEEE International Conference on Recent Advances and Innovations in Engineering (ICRAIE), pp. 1–7. IEEE (2020)

30. Xia, E., Yue, H., Liu, H.: Tweet sentiment analysis of the 2020 US presidential election. In: Companion Proceedings of the Web Conference 2021, pp. 367–371 (2021)

Trends in Computer Networking Congestion Control: A Bibliometric Analysis

Richard Nana Nketsiah[1]([✉]) [iD], Israel Edem Agbehadji[2] [iD], Richard C. Millham[1] [iD], Samuel A. Iwarere[3] [iD], and Emmanuel Freeman[4] [iD]

[1] ICT and Society Research Group, Department of Information Technology, Durban University of Technology, Durban, South Africa
rnananketsiah@gmail.com
[2] Honorary Research Associate, Faculty of Accounting and Informatics, Durban University of Technology, P.O. Box 1334, Durban 4000, South Africa
[3] Department of Chemical Engineering, Faculty of Engineering, Built Environment and Information Technology, University of Pretoria, Hatfield, Pretoria 0002, South Africa
samuel.iwarere@up.ac.za
[4] Faculty of Computing and Information Systems, Ghana Communication Technology University, PMB 100, Accra North, Ghana

Abstract. Computer networking congestion control is an important area of research. This study presents a bibliometric analysis of trends in computer networking congestion control research over the past decade. A total of 1,156 papers published in top-tier networking conferences and journals were analyzed using various bibliometric techniques. The results of the analysis show that the number of publications in this field has been steadily increasing over the years, with a significant rise in the number of publications related to machine learning-based congestion control techniques. The study identifies the most influential authors, institutions, and countries in this field. The analysis also identifies the most frequently cited papers, which provide valuable insights into the key concepts and developments in this field. This study provides a comprehensive overview of the trends in computer networking congestion control research and highlights the most promising research directions for future work. The outcome of the review highlights issues that are beneficial to reforming policy and informing network practitioners.

Keywords: computer networking · congestion control · bibliometric analysis · research trends · influential authors

1 Introduction

Computer networking is a rapidly growing field, driven by the increasing demand for high-speed data transmission and the growth of the Internet [1]. As more and more people rely on the Internet for various purposes, including work, education, entertainment, and communication, the efficient and reliable transmission of data has become critical. There is a belief that one of the key challenges in computer networking is congestion control,

T. Guarda et al. (Eds.): ARTIIS 2023, CCIS 1935, pp. 483–497, 2024.
https://doi.org/10.1007/978-3-031-48858-0_38

which refers to the mechanisms and techniques used to prevent network congestion and ensure that data is transmitted efficiently [2].

Congestion occurs when the number of packets transmitted over a network exceeds its capacity, resulting in delays, dropped packets, and degraded performance [3]. Congestion can have a significant impact on the performance of the network, including increased latency, decreased throughput, and reduced reliability. To address this problem, researchers and practitioners in computer networking have developed various congestion control mechanisms and techniques that aim to mitigate congestion and ensure efficient data transmission.

Over the past two decades, congestion control research in computer networking has grown significantly, driven by the increasing complexity of computer networks and the growing demand for high-speed data transmission. Researchers have explored various aspects of congestion control, including the design and evaluation of congestion control algorithms, the analysis and modeling of network traffic, and the development of new techniques for managing congestion [4].

Despite the significant progress made in congestion control research, there are still many gaps and challenges that need to be addressed [5]. For example, congestion control for wireless networks, which have unique characteristics and constraints compared to wired networks, is still an open research problem [6]. The growth of the Internet of Things (IoT), which is expected to connect billions of devices, also presents new challenges for congestion control [7].

In this context, there is a need to identify the current research trends and gaps in congestion control research in computer networking. Such an analysis can help researchers and practitioners to understand the state of the art in congestion control research, identify the most influential authors, institutions, and publications in the field, and identify future research directions and challenges.

To this end, in this study, the researchers conducted a bibliometric analysis of research trends in computer networking congestion control from 2003 to 2022. Bibliometric analysis is a quantitative method used to analyze patterns in scientific publications, including citation patterns, co-authorship networks, and research topics [8]. By analyzing a large dataset of publications, the researchers can identify the most influential authors, institutions, and publications in the field of congestion control, analyze the evolution of research topics and keywords over time, and identify the current gaps and future research directions.

The rest of this paper is organized as follows. Section 2 provides a brief overview of the related work in the area of congestion control research in computer networking. Section 3 describes the methodology used in this study, including the data collection and analysis techniques. Section 4 presents the results and discussion of the analysis, including publications in the field, the evolution of research topics and keywords over time, and the current research gaps and challenges. Finally, Sect. 5 provides concluding remarks and suggestions for future work.

2   Related Work

This section aims to provide an overview of the relevant background information and context for the study, highlighting the key contributions and limitations of previous research. The review of relevant research publications, including articles, conference papers, and other literature in the field, is intended to identify gaps in current knowledge and to establish the research questions for the study. By examining the previous work in the field, the authors aim to provide a basis for their analysis and to contextualise their findings in relation to the broader body of literature.

2.1   Computer Networking Congestion Control

Over the past two decades, researchers and practitioners in computer networking have conducted extensive research on congestion control mechanisms and techniques to ensure efficient data transmission. Several studies have focused on analysing the performance of existing congestion control algorithms, such as Transmission Control Protocol (TCP) and User Datagram Protocol (UDP). Other studies have proposed new congestion control algorithms that aim to address the limitations of existing algorithms, such as the fairness and stability issues of TCP [9].

Furthermore, some studies have focused on the analysis and modeling of network traffic to improve the accuracy of congestion control mechanisms. They have proposed various techniques to capture the characteristics of network traffic, such as packet size distribution, inter-packet arrival time, and packet loss rate [10]. Other studies have proposed new methods for network measurement and monitoring to identify and mitigate congestion in real-time [11].

Moreover, some studies have investigated the impact of congestion control mechanisms on specific applications and protocols, such as multimedia streaming, peer-to-peer (P2P) networks, and wireless networks. They have proposed various techniques to optimise the performance of these applications while ensuring efficient congestion control [12].

However, despite the significant progress made in congestion control research in computer networking, there are still several challenges and gaps that need to be addressed. For instance, congestion control for wireless networks and IoT devices, which have unique characteristics and constraints compared to wired networks, is still an open research problem [13]. Additionally, the effectiveness and scalability of congestion control mechanisms in large-scale networks and cloud computing environments are also areas of active research [14].

2.2   Bibliometric Analysis

Bibliometric analysis is a popular and rigorous method for exploring and analysing large volumes of scientific data [15]. It enables us to unpack the evolutionary nuances of a specific field, while shedding light on the emerging areas in that field [16]. Bibliometric analysis has gained immense popularity in business research in recent years and its popularity can be attributed partly to the advancement, availability, and accessibility of bibliometric software such as Gephi, Leximancer, VOS viewer, and scientific databases such as Scopus and Web of Science [17]. The bibliometric approach incorporates the use of quantitative procedures (i.e., bibliometric analysis) on bibliographic data (e.g., units of publication and citation) [18]. It is a solid and sensible approach of research having applications in many different branches of science, including management. It is largely related to the assessment of research using publishing statistics and the degree to which they are used as measures of the productivity and effect of science [19]. It is reproducible, repeatable, and transparent [20].

An original addition to research is made by bibliometrics. Bibliometrics conducts dataset reviews in a competent way when the dataset is too big to be evaluated manually [21]. Additionally, bibliometrics emerges as the best choice for analysis when the review's scope is vast and the dataset spans a significant amount of time. These are alternative possibilities that this study will not explore at this time. Such methods of using bibliometrics for mapping research specialties introduce a measure of objectivity into the evaluation of scientific literature and hold the potential to increase rigor and mitigate researcher bias in reviews of scientific literature by aggregating the opinions of multiple scholars working in that field [22].

In essence, a bibliometric analysis goes through four steps [23]. The purpose and parameters of the bibliometric research must first be established. The extraction of what is known as bibliographic data comes second. The methods to be employed for the bibliometric analysis must be decided upon thirdly. Finally, the bibliometric analysis must then be performed, and the results critically reported. The bibliometric analysis is divided into two groups, namely Analysis of performance and Science mapping [24] respectively.

As it exposes trends in research performance, research components, and relationship patterns of a research field, bibliometrics was selected for this investigation. It demonstrates the organisation and key ideas of a study area when used in conjunction with social network analysis. Bibliometrics plays a significant role in spotting both existing and new trends in a field of study or journal. It also helps in identifying and predicting on potential future research directions [25].

This paper advances in three stages as it continues. Initially, a more thorough explanation of the paper's methodology is provided, particularly as it relates to the search approach and data analysis. Afterwards, the outcomes of the bibliometric study, including general publication trends, co-author analysis, and co-word analysis, are then provided. Lastly, all of these results are collected and analysed to figure out the best way to move forward in the future with research on computer networking congestion control.

3   Methodology

To conduct a comprehensive bibliometric analysis of research trends in computer networking congestion control, the researchers collected data from two major databases: Web of Science and Scopus. The researchers chose these databases because they are widely used in bibliometric analysis and cover a wide range of scientific disciplines, including computer networking. We searched for publications that contained the keywords "congestion control" in the title or abstract and limited the search period from 2003 to 2022. The bibliometric approach that is adopted uses quantitative techniques on bibliometric data and describes the bibliometric factors of the topic. This information highlights the contribution of various authors and identifies patterns or gaps [26]. The researchers then used the bibliometric analysis tool, bibliometrics, to analyse the data. Bibliometrics is a software tool that enables the visualisation and analysis of bibliometric networks, such as co-authorship networks, citation networks, and co-occurrence networks of keywords.

Using bibliometrics, the researchers first conducted a co-authorship analysis to identify the most influential authors in the field of congestion control. The researchers then conducted an institutional analysis to identify the most influential institutions. The researchers also conducted a co-citation analysis to identify the most influential publications in the field. To identify the current research topics and trends in congestion control, the researchers conducted a co-occurrence analysis of keywords in the publications. The researchers also analysed the evolution of research topics and keywords over time.

Finally, the researchers identified the current gaps and challenges in congestion control research in computer networking. The researchers used the analysis results to identify the areas that require further research and development. In this study, a procedure was devised for selecting the search words, suitable databases, search criteria, data analysis software as well as findings analysis. Table 1 (below in Sect. 3.3) depicts these actions, which are further described in the subsequent paragraphs.

3.1 Determining the Search Terms

The objectives of the current paper are to (i) identify and assess the nature and development of the literature on computer networking congestion control; and (ii) identify the major thematic areas of study on computer networking congestion control and their connections to different academic disciplines. These objectives are described in the introduction. The heterogeneous or multidisciplinary character of computer networking congestion control research is the particular emphasis of this study. In order to narrow and focus results on the relevant subject, "computer networking" and "congestion control" were the only search terms used.

3.2 Selection of Databases

The Scopus and Web of Science databases were selected as the study's data repositories as these are two of the most popular bibliographic databases used by researchers worldwide. According to a study by [27], Scopus and Web of Science are the two most preferred databases among researchers for their scholarly work, with Scopus being used by 46.4% and Web of Science by 37.5% of the respondents. In the study surveyed by [27], 3,065 researchers from 27 countries were asked to determine their preferences for bibliographic databases. The results showed that Scopus and Web of Science were the top two choices for researchers. These among others informed the researchers' decision in choosing both Scopus and the Web of Science databases for this research work.

3.3 Selection Criteria

On September 7, 2022, a topical search using the terms "computer network*" and "congestion control" (title, abstract, author keywords, Keyword Plus; TS = "computer networking congestion control") were carried out on both the Scopus and Web of Science

Table 1. Methodological Scheme for the bibliometric analysis

Steps	Events	Description
STEP 1	Search Terms	Computer, networking, congestion
STEP 2	Selected data	Scopus and the Web of Science
STEP 3	Selection criteria	Document types: articles, review articles, and proceeding papers
STEP 4	Data Extraction	File type: Microsoft excel (Data types include: – author; abstract; title; publishing year; DOI; etc.)
STEP 5	Selected Software	Bibliometrics: Duplicates removal, bibliometric network analysis & mapping, data merging Mendeley: For citations and references
STEP 6	Performance Analysis	Publication and citation trends, contributions by top journals, frequently cited documents, top disciplines
STEP 7	Performance Results	Science Mapping: co-keyword analysis, co-author analysis, co-country analysis

databases. The results covered all articles, review articles, book chapters, and conference papers from 2003 to 2022. This twenty-year period was chosen to have a fair view of what has gone on in history with regards to computer networking congestion control till date. In light of major non-journal contributions that are regularly acknowledged in books on computer networking congestion control, it was decided to expand the results beyond journal publications. English was used as a language refining tool. To put it briefly, the search term and parameters were selected to represent the diversity of research on computer networking congestion control and the innately broad nature of bibliometric analysis. After these criteria were applied in both Scopus and the Web of Science databases, bibliographic data was extracted in bibTeX (.bib) format from the Scopus database whilst Plain text formatted files (.txt) were extracted from the Web of Science database.

3.4 Data Extracted

After the selection process had ended focusing on both Scopus and the Web of Science databases as data repositories, the RStudio integrated development environment (IDE) was used to merge these two files and at the same time remove duplicated files. Table 2 shows the number of documents extracted from each database, the initial total of data extracted, tool used in merging the extracted data from the two data repositories, the number of duplicates removed, the tool used to remove the duplicates, and finally the total number of documents left for analysis.

Due to their differences in formats, they have to be merged into one file and be used for the needed analysis. This is where different types of data are taken out, such as author, abstract, title, publishing year, DOI, etc.

Table 2. Twenty-Year Data Extracted from 2003 to 2022

No	SCOPUS		WEB OF SCIENCE	
1	Year Range	Documents Extracted	Year Range	Documents Extracted
2	2003–2022	1058	2003 - 2022	355
3	2003–2022	After Refinement	2003 - 2022	After Refinement
4		971		251
5	File Type	bibTex	File Type	Plain Text
6	Total Documents = (Scopus Data + Web of Science Data) = 971 + 251 = 1222			
7	Total Duplicates removed using the RStudio IDE = 66 (documents)			
8	Available documents merged into one file after duplicates removal: 1222 − 66 = 1156			

Because bibliometrics is repeatable, replicable, and transparent [28], it behooves that anytime anyone accesses the internet to enquire and pull the said query (queries) of the searched results, the value should be just the same as opposed to records which keep changing, especially if the year has not ended; subsequent publications add up to the existing documents, thus always increasing the documents even within a day, week, or month as you access the internet with the same uniform resource locator (URL) and query. This could be suspicious when the question of integrity comes up as to the exact time data was extracted.

Fig. 1. QR code for Scopus Db

Fig. 2. QR code for the Wos Db

The researchers have thus brought onboard the usage of a system which will ensure the exact value you quoted will be made available even after ages. These are the simple steps that you have to follow: (i) you copy the query into your appendix; (ii) you copy the

URL for the searched database into your appendix; (iii) you snip the page of the database to include the query, the URL, and the total number of documents, which always appears on top of the query as the total number of documents of the searched results; and (iv) you generate a Quick Response (QR) Code and paste into your methodology and into your appendix with item (iii). The two generated QR Codes for this research paper are clearly showed by Fig. 1 and Fig. 2, where Fig. 1 is the QR code with captured data from the Scopus, and Fig. 2 is the QR Code with captured data for the Web of Science databases respectively for this research. With this, the reviewer, reader, or publisher, will always see the captured data, which shows up on top of the query, as the total documents of the searched results. Here, verification could be done by any QR code reader e.g., smart phone to scan the QR code. This will display the Query, URL, and the total document for the given search results. They could then double-check the validity and authenticity of what they read on the internet and quoted in the work. They could also verify it from the appendix section, which is not available in this paper.

3.5 Selected Software

Four software packages were used for this work. Firstly, the RStudio application, which is an Integrated Development Environment (IDE), It is a tool with which the differently formatted files from the Scopus and Web of Science databases are used to merge both and, at the same time, used in removing duplicated files. Secondly, the biblioshiny app, created with the RStudio ide, was used to call the bibliometrix analytics to perform the needed analysis. However, it works only when the internet is available. Thirdly, the Vos Viewer analytical tool, like the bibliometrix analytical tool, is also a free analytical software tool for constructing and visualising bibliometric networks. It was used to get authorship, citation, and keyword data and to do co-citation, and co-word analysis whilst managing data tables and making graphs about publication trends, citation trends, the most cited papers, the most cited authors, and the research fields working on computer networking congestion control. The Vos Viewer can be used without the need for an internet connection. Finally, Microsoft Excel was used in putting some of the graphs together for clarity and to conserve space as well.

3.6 Data Analysis

Two stages of data analysis were completed. The first was a performance analysis that mapped publication growth trends, highlighted the contributions made by academic institutions, and authors, and determined the top journals covering computer networking congestion control. The second part of the investigation concentrated on a scientific map that built bibliometric maps to examine the field's intellectual structure. Here, the co-occurrences of titles, authors, keywords, and sources were specifically studied. A narrative review of keyword clusters was completed to supplement this. At the very least, the titles and abstracts of the top 40 most cited publications having at least one of the top five keyword clusters in each manuscript were examined. With this analysis, it was still possible to make sense of the huge amount of content that bibliometric analysis creates while summarising some of the most important trends and discoveries in a cluster.

4   Results and Discussion

In the present study, a total of 1,156 records, authored by 2,545 professionals and which have attracted 24,081 references from 2003 to 2022 were analyzed. As illustrated in Fig. 3, there had been substantial growth in publications from 2003 to 2006 as well as 2008. For this 20-year period, these have been the best years getting close to 140 in terms of publications with 2013 being the worst year as it dropped to a record low of 19 publications. However, there was also a sharp drop in publications from 2021and it is still on the downward trend. This could be attributed to the Covid-19 pandemic which swept across the entire globe and thus affected almost everything in this world including publications of articles. The highest number of published articles was captured in 2005. Also, the highest citation was recorded in 2003 and it had seen a constant linear decline from 19 down to 1 in 2021. Seventy-three authors single-authored Documents, evaluating 3.13 co-authors per Document. Also, an average of 12.28 citations per Document, indicated an interest in the said topic.

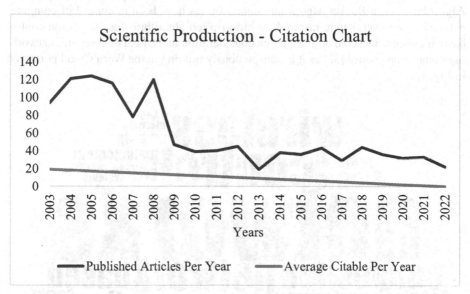

Fig. 3. Computer Networking Congestion Control Articles Published from 2003 to 2022

4.1   Frequently Used Words

The 20 most frequently-used words captured in the Word Cloud are very conspicuously identified, as shown in Fig. 4. The keywords of network Congestion Control stand out uniquely, indicating their high frequency of usage in the computer networking domain. This prominence underscores the importance of addressing network congestion through effective control measures. While the term "control" also garners attention, it is apparent that greater emphasis is required to bring it on par with the significance of "networks," as evidenced by the Word Cloud. Other words like "TCP," "performance," "sensor," "traffic," "wireless," and "algorithm" are also contending for frequency of usage, signalling emerging research areas. [29] argues that Transmission Control Protocol (TCP) continues to be a major stakeholder in congestion control, encompassing various TCP variants such as Vegas, Tahoe, Reno, New Reno, and Cubic. Researchers often employ SWOT analysis to identify strengths and weaknesses, aiming to develop superior mitigatory solutions. The assessment of network performance, measured by data input and output, plays a crucial role in evaluating the efficiency of congestion control mechanisms [30]. With Internet of Things (IOT) emerging, it is reflected as seen by the frequency of the keyword, sensor. Traffic on the other hand replicates the flow of data on the network, which is highly used than sensor, routing, or even protocol in this context. The frequency of the usage of wireless is an indication that wireless networking is much more considered ahead of wired networking for a number of reasons including portability, mobility, convenience, and urbanisation [31]. Algorithm, even though mentioned, could be seen to be having less attention when controlling of computer networking congestion is looked at. Additive Increase Multiplicative Decrease (AIMD) algorithm, Leaky Bucket Algorithm, Token Bucket Algorithm, among others have been in control of computer networks. However, nature-inspired, or bio-inspired algorithms for congestion control have not been considered or given much consideration in the field of computer networking congestion control [32] as it is conspicuously missing in the Word Cloud portrayed in Fig. 4.

Fig. 4. WordCloud for Computer Networking Congestion Control

In graph analytics, Centrality is a very important concept in identifying important nodes in a graph. It is used to measure the importance (or "centrality" as in how "central" a node is in the graph) of various nodes in a graph. Now, each node could be important from an angle depending on how "importance" is defined. Traditionally, impact (Density) has been measured by the number of times a particular article is cited in other comparable publications, or more broadly by the "impact factor" of the journal in which an article appears. While the ability to demonstrate impact can still be an equally important tool in the promotion and tenure process, complementary or "alternative metrics" for measuring disciplinary impact using formal and informal communications are also becoming more common. The thematic keywords have been captured in the four quadrants as in Fig. 5.

The first quadrant (Motor Themes) fully accommodates congestion control for computer networks and Transmission Control Protocol (TCP). It also includes queueing theory, performance evaluation, active queue management, and queueing networks. Factors with high centrality and high impact are trending, matching their frequency of publicity in the Word Cloud.

The second quadrant (Niche Themes) includes Wireless Sensor Networks and Computer Networks publications, but lacks the needed impact in networking domains. The wireless sensor network cluster's position could be closer to making an impact or expanding its impact on livelihoods.

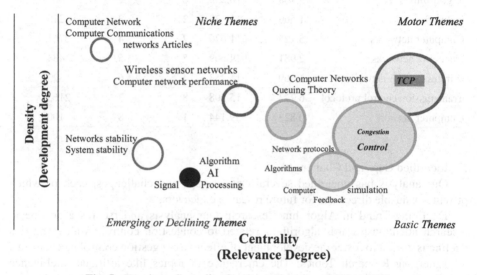

Fig. 5. Density – Centrality Quadrant Chart from 2003 to 2022

The third quadrant (Emerging or Declining Themes) in Fig. 5 highlights network stability and a combination of algorithms, artificial intelligence, and signal processing. The algorithms are seen as less considerate and may be declining in research and publication. However, when clustered with artificial intelligence, both could be emerging, though at different rates.

Finally, the publications in the fourth quadrant (Basic Themes) dialogs about algorithms, computer simulation, and feedback fully. It also partially accommodates both congestion control (communication) for network protocols, computer networks, and a combination of queueing theory, computer network performance evaluation, active queue management, and queueing networks.

These have low centrality (relevance degree) yet having high impact (development degree). Note that cluster 1 (Networks) is about 60% in the Basic Theme (Fourth Quadrant) and 40% in the Motor Theme (First Quadrant). As the already-linked clusters 1 (Networks) and 2 (Algorithms) are also linked to cluster 3 (TCP), there is the possibility of both clusters 1 and 3 getting "pulled" into the Motor Theme Quadrant. That said, it is still vivid that algorithms still have low centrality relevance degree as in Table 3 on a 1 to 8 scale and thus having less research considerations as compared to TCP. Also, the trend highlights network queueing, which also contributes to congestion according to the Density ranking table as in Table 3.

Table 3. Thematic Map with Density (Impact of Development Degree) Ranking

Cluster	Callon Centrality	Callon Density	Rank Centrality	Rank Density	Cluster Frequency
Algorithm	1.743	9.798	3	1	76
Algorithms	3.708	10.253	6	2	602
Networks	1.566	11.370	2	3	215
Computer networks	5.125	11.626	7	4	2761
Queueing networks	2.981	14.009	5	5	484
Wireless sensor networks	1.869	15.253	4	6	323
Transmission control protocol	6.773	15.508	8	7	2163
Computer network	0.823	39.144	1	8	100

Identified Gaps and Challenges

Our analysis has unearthed several critical gaps and challenges, each of which provides valuable directions for future research endeavors.

Declining Trend in Algorithm Research: Our analysis underscores a decline in research attention towards algorithms related to congestion control. Addressing this decline is crucial to foster the development of effective congestion control mechanisms.

Emerging Research Topics: The emergence of topics like artificial intelligence and signal processing in congestion control suggests new research horizons. Investigating these emerging themes could lead to innovative breakthroughs in congestion management.

Balancing Wireless and Wired Networking: While wireless networking offers distinct advantages, its limitations, such as security concerns and potential vulnerabilities, deserve thorough exploration. Achieving a balance between wireless and wired networking is essential to harness their respective strengths.

Nature-Inspired Algorithms: The lack of consideration for nature-inspired algorithms in congestion control indicates an untapped avenue for research. Exploring bio-inspired solutions may yield novel approaches to congestion management.

Collaboration and Co-Authorship Dynamics: The prevalence of multiple authors per document accentuates the collaborative nature of research in this field. Understanding collaboration dynamics and their impact can enhance the efficacy of future collaborative efforts.

Publication Fluctuations Over Time: The observed fluctuations in publication trends warrant a deeper examination of underlying factors. Such analysis is essential to maintain consistent progress and contributions to the field.

IoT Integration in Congestion Control: As the Internet of Things (IoT) gains prominence, adapting congestion control mechanisms for IoT networks becomes paramount. Research should focus on solutions tailored to this emerging paradigm.

5   Conclusions and Way Forward

In conclusion, our analysis not only sheds light on the trends and dynamics of computer networking congestion control research but also identifies critical gaps and challenges.

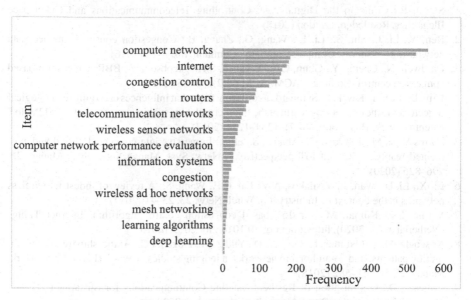

Fig. 6. Topic Trends from 2003 to 2022

Addressing these gaps will not only drive advancements in the field but also pave the way for the development of more robust and adaptable congestion control mechanisms. Future research endeavors should prioritize addressing these challenges to establish a solid foundation for the continuous evolution of networking and congestion control.

The primary objective of this paper is to provide network practitioners with a comprehensive understanding of the current state of computer network congestion control. Through the detailed analysis presented in Fig. 6, this study highlights the key trends and challenges in this area and identifies the essential techniques needed to mitigate congestion effectively with word count frequency. In addition to its primary goal, this research also employs bibliometric analysis to identify various future research directions. These directions include developing more efficient congestion control techniques, exploring the potential of machine learning, investigating the impacts of emerging technologies, addressing security and privacy concerns, and fostering collaboration among researchers. By identifying these areas of research, this study provides valuable insights for researchers to consider when working on future computer network infrastructures.

This paper significantly contributes to computer network congestion control by providing a state-of-the-art analysis and identifying key research directions for the future. By following these directions, network practitioners can work towards more effective congestion control, resulting in faster and more reliable communication. The ongoing evolution of research in this domain will shape the future landscape of computer networking, highlighting the importance of innovation and improvement.

References

1. Smith, R.: Crime in the Digital Age: Controlling Telecommunications and Cyberspace Illegalities. Routledge, London (2018)
2. Ren, Y., Li, J., Shi, S., Li, L., Wang, G., Zhang, B.: Congestion control in named data networking – a survey. Comput. Commun.. Commun. **86**, 1–11 (2016)
3. Cardwell, N., Cheng, Y., Gunn, C.S., Yeganeh, S.H., Jacobson, V.: BBR: congestion-based congestion control. Commun. ACM. ACM **60**(2), 58–66 (2017)
4. Kim, D., Lee, H., Kwak, J.: Standards as a driving force that influences emerging technological trajectories in the converging world of the Internet and things: an investigation of the M2M/IoT patent network. Res. Policy **46**(7), 1234–1254 (2017)
5. Torres Vega, M., Liaskos, C., Abadal, S., et al.: Immersive interconnected virtual and augmented reality: a 5G and IoT perspective. J. Netw. Syst. Manag.Netw. Syst. Manag. **28**, 796–826 (2020)
6. Li, X., Li, D., Wan, J., Vasilakos, A.V., Lai, C.F., Wang, S.: A review of industrial wireless networks in the context of Industry 4.0. Wirel. Netw. **23**, 23–41 (2017)
7. Verma, L.P., Kumar, M.: An IoT based congestion control algorithm. Internet Things (Netherlands) **9** (2020). https://doi.org/10.1016/j.iot.2019.100157
8. Köseoglu, M.A., Okumus, F., Putra, E.D., Yildiz, M., Dogan, I.C.: Authorship trends, collaboration patterns, and co-authorship networks in lodging studies (1990–2016). J. Hosp. Mark. Manag. **27**(5), 561–582 (2018)
9. E-theses, D.: Optimisation of Resilient Satellite Communications for Sustainable Digital Connectivity in Remote Rural Africa. Published online 2020
10. Thomas, S., McGuinness, R., Voelker, G.M., Porter, G.: Dark packets and the end of network scaling. In: Proceedings of the 2018 Symposium on Architectures for Networking and Communications Systems, pp. 1–14 (2018)
11. Liang, F., Hatcher, W.G., Xu, G., Nguyen, J., Liao, W., Yu, W.: Towards online deep learning-based energy forecasting. In: 2019 28th International Conference on Computer Communication and Networks (ICCCN), pp. 1–9 (2019)
12. Ahmad, S., Mir, A.H.: Scalability, consistency, reliability and security in SDN controllers: a survey of diverse SDN controllers. J. Netw. Syst. Manag.Netw. Syst. Manag. **29**, 1–59 (2021)
13. Saleem, Y., Crespi, N., Rehmani, M.H., Copeland, R.: Internet of things-aided smart grid: technologies, architectures, applications, prototypes, and future research directions. IEEE Access **7**, 62962–63003 (2019)
14. Dai, H.N., Wong, R.C.W., Wang, H., Zheng, Z., Vasilakos, A.V.: Big data analytics for large-scale wireless networks: challenges and opportunities. ACM Comput. Surv.Comput. Surv. **52**(5), 1–36 (2019)
15. Park, E.J., Lee, S.: Creative thinking in the architecture design studio: bibliometric analysis and literature review. Buildings **12**(6), 828 (2022)
16. Donthu, N., Kumar, S., Mukherjee, D., Pandey, N., Lim, W.M.: How to conduct a bibliometric analysis: an overview and guidelines. J. Bus. Res. **133**(March), 285–296 (2021). https://doi.org/10.1016/j.jbusres.2021.04.070

17. Horvatinović, T., Matošec, M.: A decade for the books: bibliometric analysis of Economics Letters. Econ. Lett. **216**, 110542 (2022)
18. Zupic, I., Čater, T.: Bibliometric methods in management and organization. Organ. Res. Methods **18**(3), 429–472 (2015)
19. Diem, A., Wolter, S.C.: The use of bibliometrics to measure research performance in education sciences. Res. High. Educ. **54**(1), 86–114 (2013)
20. Zhou, C., Song, W.: Digitalization as a way forward: a bibliometric analysis of 20 years of servitization research. J. Clean. Prod. **300**, 126943 (2021)
21. Vanhala, M., Lu,.C., Peltonen, J., Sundqvist, S., Nummenmaa, J., Järvelin, K.: The usage of large data sets in online consumer behaviour: a bibliometric and computational text-mining–driven analysis of previous research. J. Bus. Res. **106**, 46–59 (2020)
22. Sovacool, B.K., Axsen, J., Sorrell, S.: Promoting novelty, rigor, and style in energy social science: towards codes of practice for appropriate methods and research design. Energy Res. Soc. Sci. **45**, 12–42 (2018)
23. Liu, Y., Avello, M.: Status of the research in fitness apps: a bibliometric analysis. Telemat. Inform. **57**, 101506 (2021)
24. Ellegaard, O., Wallin, J.A.: The bibliometric analysis of scholarly production: how great is the impact? Scientometrics **105**(3), 1809–1831 (2015)
25. Riahi, Y., Saikouk, T., Gunasekaran, A., Badraoui, I.: Artificial intelligence applications in supply chain: a descriptive bibliometric analysis and future research directions. Expert Syst. Appl. **173**, 114702 (2021)
26. Jiang, Y., Ritchie, B.W., Benckendorff, P.: Bibliometric visualisation: an application in tourism crisis and disaster management research. Curr. Issues Tour. **22**(16), 1925–1957 (2019)
27. Jinha, A.E.: The impact of social media on mental health: a systematic review. Article, 258–263 (2010)
28. Walsh, I., Rowe, F.: BIBGT: combining bibliometrics and grounded theory to conduct a literature review. Eur. J. Inf. Syst. 1–22 (2022)
29. Welzl, M.: Network Congestion Control: Managing Internet Traffic. Wiley, Hoboken (2005)
30. Huang, T.K., Lee, C.K., Chen, L.J.: Prophet+: an adaptive prophet-based routing protocol for opportunistic network. In: 2010 24th IEEE International Conference on Advanced Information Networking and Applications, pp. 112–119 (2010)
31. Rashid, B., Rehmani, M.H.: Applications of wireless sensor networks for urban areas: a survey. J. Netw. Comput. Appl.Netw. Comput. Appl. **60**, 192–219 (2016)
32. Nketsiah, R.N., Agbehadji, I.E., Millham, R.C., Freeman, E.: Bio-inspired optimisation algorithm for congestion control in computer networking. **669**, 21–32 (2023). https://doi.org/10.1007/978-3-031-29860-8_3

Use of Anomaly Detection and Object Detection as Basic Support in the Recognition of Outlier Data in Images

Shendry Balmore Rosero Vásquez[(✉)] [iD]

Universidad Estatal Península de Santa Elena, La Libertad avenida principal Km 1.5 vía Santa Elena, La Libertad, Ecuador
`srosero@upse.edu.ec`

Abstract. Despite significant advances in object detection in images, the ability to identify outlier objects in an image remains an unsolved problem. Its challenges arise due to the inherent variability of an outlier object, the limitations of the object detection approach, and the subjective nature of anomalies in different contexts. In addition, traditional object detection approaches focus on identifying previously known objects, which limits their effectiveness in detecting outlier objects. An comparative analysis based on anomaly detection and object detection is then proposed in this preliminary study, techniques that under training would allow learning a "normal" representation of the data, so that they can detect anomalies when reconstructing new data instances. If the reconstruction of a new data differs significantly from the "normal" data, it could indicate the presence of an outlier object.

Keywords: Anomaly · Convolutional auto-encoders · Yolov3 · Object Detection

1 Introduction

Anomaly detection and identification of objects that do not belong to a scene are crucial and complex challenges in the field of computer vision. Despite the significant advances made in object detection in images and videos [1], the ability to detect objects that are unusual or do not fit a given scene remains a largely unsolved problem [2]. This task implies the need for deeper semantic knowledge and contextual understanding in the interpretation of visual scenes. There are several reasons why this task is complex; Anomaly detection faces multiple challenges due to the inherent variability of anomalies, the limitations of object-based approaches, and the subjective nature of anomalies in different contexts. Anomalies can take various forms and do not follow a specific pattern, making it difficult to develop general algorithms capable of detecting all possible anomalies. In addition, traditional object-detection approaches focus on identifying and locating previously known objects, limiting their effectiveness in detecting unusual or mismatched objects.

To address this challenge, a simple but promising approach is proposed for the detection of anomalies and the identification of atypical objects to a given scene, based on a

T. Guarda et al. (Eds.): ARTIIS 2023, CCIS 1935, pp. 498–506, 2024.
https://doi.org/10.1007/978-3-031-48858-0_39

comparative analysis between anomaly detection and object detection using the YOLO3 (You Only Look Once) architecture [3, 4] and the implementation of a convolutional [5] autoencoder. This approach seeks to take advantage of the semantic knowledge acquired through a previous training of a neural network on landscape photographs by using the convolutional autoencoder for image reconstruction and verification of whether a given image fits the training dataset. In this way, it would be possible to identify those images that do not correspond to what would traditionally be expected to be found in the dataset, allowing to detect atypical objects in the scene in specific training circumstances.

In parallel, a second approach based on object detection using YOLO3 is presented, in which an expected set of objects is established [6] for a given scene. This approach seeks to detect any set of objects outside that expected set, which could indicate the presence of anomalous or atypical objects in a photograph or set of photographs.

This research has as its main objective to perform a comparative analysis between these two approaches, evaluating their effectiveness in the detection of anomalies and the identification of objects that do not match the objects that would regularly be expected to be found in the photograph containing the set of objects detected. Although both approaches are rudimentary in their initial formulation, it is hoped that this study will lay the groundwork for future research to develop more advanced and efficient methods to address this complex challenge. The following sections show the theoretical framework on which this research rests, the methodology applied, results and the conclusions that have been preliminarily reached.

2   Theoretical Framework

Autoencoder (Convolutional Auto-encoder or CAE). Convolutional autoencoder is a neural network architecture [7] that is used to learn a compressed representation of input data and then reconstruct it from this representation [8]. It consists of two main components: the encoder, which transforms the input image into a lower-dimensional representation, and the decoder, which reconstructs the original image from this representation. During training, the goal is to minimize the difference between the input image and the reconstructed image. In the context of anomaly detection, a convolutional autoencoder can be used to learn how to reconstruct normal images and then use this trained model to identify images that do not fit well with the expected reconstruction. If an image has a high discrepancy between the original image and the reconstructed image, it could be considered an atypical or anomalous image [9, 10] (Fig. 1).

However, it is important to clarify that the use of a convolutional autoencoder for anomaly detection has some limitations: this approach may have difficulty detecting anomalies that are not present in the training data or that are very different in nature from normal images; Additionally, the detection of anomalies by convolutional autoencoders often requires setting a discrepancy threshold to classify an image as atypical, which can be a challenge in itself, for the moment that analysis escapes the present research.

Under this answer it is useful to describe that computer vision has experienced significant advances thanks to convolutional neural networks (CNN), especially in tasks of classification and detection of objects; However, in many cases the goal is not limited to classification, but also involves understanding and efficiently representing the structure

Fig. 1. Artificial image constructed to generate that subjective uncertainty of identification of an atypical data or object in an image.

and visual content of images. From this point of view, convolutional autoencoders have proven to be powerful tools for feature extraction and image reconstruction in computer vision.

It is also interesting to note that convolutional autoencoders are a variant of traditional autoencoders that take advantage of the ability of convolutional layers to learn spatial representations of images. They consist of an encoder-decoder structure that seeks to compress the information of an image into a lower-dimensional representation and then reconstruct the original image from this compressed representation. The goal of the autoencoder is to minimize the difference between the input image and the reconstructed image, which involves learning meaningful features of the images and capturing information relevant to their reconstruction.

The main advantage of convolutional autoencoders lies in their ability to capture spatial and structural features of images. Convolutional layers allow you to detect local patterns and learn translation-invariant features, which is beneficial for computer vision tasks such as object detection, semantic segmentation, and image generation. In addition, convolutional autoencoders can also be used for image compression and noise removal, as their ability to reconstruct high-quality images allows lost or damaged information to be recovered.

In the field of computer vision, convolutional autoencoders have been applied in various tasks and have proven their effectiveness. For example, in anomaly detection, convolutional autoencoders have been used to learn the representation of normal images and then reconstruct anomalous images, making it possible to identify significant discrepancies between the original images and the reconstructed images as possible anomalies. Also, in image generation, convolutional autoencoders can learn to generate realistic images from a latent representation, which has led to the development of techniques such as generative adversarial networks (GAN) and conditional image generation.

YOLO (You Only Look Once). YOLO is a real-time object detection approach that proposes a unique architecture to perform detection directly in a single execution through the neural network [4]. Object detection is a fundamental subfield in computer vision, whose purpose is to identify and locate objects within an image or video. YOLO is a popular system for object detection. For this particular case, YOLOv3 has been chosen, due to the experience in similar works developed with this version, which has demonstrated high efficiency and speed [11]. Under this premise it can be indicated that YOLO is an object detection algorithm that uses a single neural network to detect objects and their locations in an image in a single pass, hence its name. It can also be indicated that YOLOv3 is the third version of the YOLO algorithm, which introduces notable improvements in the detection of small objects and the use of three different scales for detection, instead of a single one as in previous versions:

YOLO was first proposed by Redmon et al. in 2016 [11]. It was revolutionary because, unlike traditional object detection approaches that first propose candidates and then classify, YOLO takes a complete picture during the testing phase and predicts the locations and categories of objects at once. This makes YOLO much faster than other approaches. YOLOv2, also known as YOLO9000, was introduced in 2017 and allowed the detection of more than 9000 different object classes. In addition, an improvement in detection accuracy was introduced through several changes in architecture. YOLOv3 was introduced in 2018 by the same team. It introduced several improvements over YOLOv2, including detection at three different scales, the introduction of predefined "anchor boxes," and improved detection of small objects [12]. In terms of speed, YOLOv3 can process up to 30 frames per second on a modern GPU, while still maintaining competitive accuracy compared to other object detection algorithms. However, the exact detection rate may vary depending on the dataset and specific test conditions.

The choice of this specific version of YOLO for object detection depended on several factors, including processing speed, accuracy in object detection, the ability to handle different object sizes, and the limitations of available hardware. It can be said that YOLOv3 is a popular choice because it presents a number of improvements over previous versions:

- Multi-scale detection: Unlike previous versions, YOLOv3 makes predictions at three different scales, allowing it to detect objects of different sizes. This is an important advantage in many object detection scenarios, where objects can vary significantly in size.
- Improved small object handling: YOLOv3 introduces predefined "anchor boxes" to improve small object detection. This is useful in situations where small objects are important and must be detected accurately.
- Balance between accuracy and speed: YOLOv3 maintains a balance between accuracy and processing speed. Although there are later versions such as YOLOv4 and YOLOv5 that have introduced additional improvements, YOLOv3 is still a solid choice due to its real-time performance and reasonable accuracy in a wide range of object detection tasks.

3 Methodology

It was necessary to work with a landscape dataset since the objective is to be able to detect atypical objects in a certain scene or photograph, so the landscape dataset of https://www.kaggle.com/datasets/arnaud58/landscape-pictures?resource=download was downloaded.

In general, the dataset was separated into landscape categories, such as mountains, deserts, sea, beaches, islands, etc. Subsequently, the images of each category were resized and normalized.

Specifically, to determine the effectiveness and comparison of the two approaches, we proceeded to work on the following steps:

1. Data preprocessing:
a. A set of "normal" images representing the desired scene was collected. See Fig. 2.
b. Images are resized and normalized.

Fig. 2. Dataset of landscape images for network training, available in www.kaggle.com

Note: no further detail on the dataset is presented to generate the impression of having a subjective idea of what is a "normal" data set.

2. Convolutional Autoencoder Training:
a. A convolutional autoencoder was constructed and trained using the set of normal images.
b. The autoencoder learns to encode and reconstruct normal images.

3. Parallel to this, YOLO training was done for the detection of expected objects:
a. A training dataset was prepared that includes images with expected objects at the scene.
b. The YOLO model was trained using the training dataset to detect the expected objects.

4. Detection of images and atypical objects:
a. A new series of images of the scene was uploaded.
b. The image was entered through the autoencoder to obtain a reconstruction. See Fig. 3. The similarity between the reconstruction of the autoencoder and the image was compared. The image presented on the screen is offered as the result of the image within the set of photographs that does not represent that dataset so it would be considered atypical

c. In parallel using another approach, YOLO was used to detect the objects in the image. See Fig. 4. The image shows the result of applying a list of expected objects to the

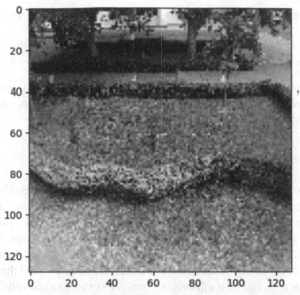

Fig. 3. Result of the application of the algorithm of detection of atypical images by means of the convolutional autoencoder. The image would be considered foreign to the training image set and alien to the assessment dataset.

detection of YOLO in such a way that everything that is not within that list can be considered as atypical

Fig. 4. Result of using YOLO with a list of "expected" items, everything that is not within that list could be considered atypical

d. It was checked if the objects detected by YOLO match the expected objects in the scene.
e. Images and objects that are considered atypical were identified based on the differences and discrepancies found.

For each approach, 10 repetitions of the algorithm were executed with a different set of test images outside the training dataset in the case of autoencoders and in the case of YOLO 10 repetitions were executed with different images.

4   Results and Discussion

Based on the results it was possible to explore that at least for this case the methodology demonstrated a high accuracy in the detection of images (see Table 1) and atypical objects in the landscape test set. A low rate of false positives was observed, indicating that the methodology was able to identify with some accuracy the images and atypical objects present in the photographs that were implemented as objects of study. To understand how this experiment could be highly favorable it is necessary to understand that convolutional autoencoders are a variant of traditional autoencoders that use convolutions instead of fully connected connections, so they are commonly used for dimensionality reduction and for learning features in images [5].

Table 1. Preliminary results of an execution of 10 repetitions of the algorithm used for different cases (images)

Approach	Results obtained considered success	Remarks	% False Positive
Convolutional auto-encoders	*15%*	Considered value of the set of test images in which the success rate was on average 15% for more than 10 images; The lower the number of images to be evaluated, the higher the success rate, consider that if an atypical image was not found, the program did not yield any results	85%
YOLO	*98%*	Considered value of the set of images where some unexpected object was always detected on a 10-pass run	2%

In the context of atypical object detection, CAEs can be trained to learn a "normal" representation of data, so that they can detect anomalies when reconstructing new data instances. If the reconstruction of a new data differs significantly from the "normal" data, it could indicate the presence of an atypical object [13]. Moreover, YOLOv3 is a real-time object detection algorithm that can detect multiple objects in a single image (reference). It is interesting to think of a combination or unification of works of the two approaches; however, there are several considerations that must be taken into account which are detailed in the next section as conclusions. So while the proposal is presented as interesting and could be effective for the detection of atypical objects, it is important to take into account the limitations and associated challenges encountered in this preliminary experimentation.

5 Conclusion

At the end of this preliminary investigation it is necessary to conclude that there are factors that could influence both positive and negative results:

- Quality of CAE reconstruction: The ability of the CAE to detect anomalies will depend on the quality of the reconstruction. If the autoencoder is not able to learn a good representation of "normal" data, it may not be able to detect atypical objects effectively (this was deduced from some experiments performed repeatedly with some images).
- YOLOv3 limitations: YOLOv3 has limitations in detecting small objects and identifying overlapping objects. Whether the atypical objects in the scene are small or overlap with other objects; this aspect must be taken into account when wanting to determine atypical objects in aerial photographs which is where future investigations of this preliminary examination point so YOLOv3 may not be able to detect them correctly.
- Data labeling and YOLOv3 training: YOLOv3 needs to be trained on a labeled dataset that includes the objects expected to be detected. If atypical objects are found that are not in the YOLOv3 training set, they may not be identified correctly.
- Computational complexity: The combination of CAE and YOLOv3 could increase the computational complexity of the task, which could be a problem if a large volume of images needs to be processed in real time.

6 Future Work

The next step is to start working on combining these two approaches together which could offer a robust solution for the detection of atypical objects. On the one hand, CAE could be used to identify regions of the image that differ from "normal," which would provide a kind of pre-filtering. YOLOv3 could then be applied to these regions to identify and categorize any detected objects.

References

1. Xiao, T., Zhang, C., Zha, H.: Learning to detect anomalies in surveillance video. IEEE Sig. Process. Lett. **22**(9), 1477–1481 (2015). https://doi.org/10.1109/LSP.2015.2410031

2. Li, X., Li, W.: Object-oriented anomaly detection in surveillance videos. In: IEEE Conference Publication. IEEE Xplore (2022). https://ieeexplore.ieee.org/document/8461422. Accessed 2 June 2023
3. Koteswararao, M., Karthikeyan, P.R.: Comparative Analysis of YOLOv3–320 and YOLOv3-tiny for optimized real-time object detection system. In: IEEE Conference Publication. IEEE Xplore (2022). https://ieeexplore.ieee.org/document/9853186. Accessed 2 June 2023
4. Lu, Y., Zhang, L., Xie, W.: YOLO-compact: an efficient YOLO network for single category real-time object detection. In: Proceedings of the 32nd China Control and Decision Conference, CCDC 2020, pp. 1931–1936, August 2020. https://doi.org/10.1109/CCDC49329.2020.9164580
5. Zhou, C., Paffenroth, R.C.: Anomaly detection with robust deep autoencoders. In: Proceedings of the ACM SIGKDD International Conference on Knowledge Discovery and Data Mining, vol. Part F129685, pp. 665–674, August 2017. https://doi.org/10.1145/3097983.3098052
6. Redmon, J., Farhadi, A.: YOLOv3: an incremental improvement, April 2018. https://arxiv.org/abs/1804.02767v1. Accessed 02 June 2023
7. Xu, J., Vidal, P.: Deep neural networks an introduction. enlínea, 2018
8. Najari, N., Berlemont, S., Lefebvre, G., Duffner, S., Garcia, C.: Robust variational autoencoders and normalizing flows for unsupervised network anomaly detection. In: Barolli, L., Hussain, F., Enokido, T. (eds.) AINA 2022. LNNS, vol. 450, pp. 281–292. Springer, Cham (2022). https://doi.org/10.1007/978-3-030-99587-4_24
9. Gabryel, M., Lada, D., Kocić, M.: Autoencoder neural network for detecting non-human web traffic. In: Rutkowski, L., Scherer, R., Korytkowski, M., Pedrycz, W., Tadeusiewicz, R., Zurada, J.M. (eds.) ICAISC 2022. LNCS, vol. 13589, pp. 232–242. Springer, Cham (2023). https://doi.org/10.1007/978-3-031-23480-4_19
10. Sevyeri, L.R., Fevens, T.: AD-CGAN: contrastive generative adversarial network for anomaly detection. In: Sclaroff, S., Distante, C., Leo, M., Farinella, G.M., Tombari, F. (eds) ICIAP 2022. LNCS, vol. 13231, pp. 322–334. Springer, Cham (2022). https://doi.org/10.1007/978-3-031-06427-2_27
11. Redmon, J., Divvala, S., Girshick, R., Farhadi, A.: You Only Look Once: Unified, Real-Time Object Detection. http://pjreddie.com/yolo/. Accessed 02 June 2023
12. Koteswararao, M., Karthikeyan, P.R.: Comparative analysis of YOLOv3–320 and YOLOv3-tiny for the optimised real-time object detection system.In: Actas de la 3ª Conferencia Internacional sobre Ingeniería y Gestión Inteligente, ICIEM 2022, pp. 495–500 (2022). https://doi.org/10.1109/ICIEM54221.2022.9853186
13. Chen, S., Guo, W.: Auto-encoders in deep learning—a review with new perspectives. Mathematics 11(8). MDPI, 01 de abril de 2023. https://doi.org/10.3390/MATH11081777

A Machine Learning Approach for the Simultaneous Prediction of Dynamic Modulus and Phase Angle of Asphalt Concrete Mixtures

Fabio Rondinella[1]($\boxtimes$) iD, Fabiola Daneluz[1] iD, Bernhard Hofko[2] iD,
and Nicola Baldo[1] iD

[1] Polytechnic Department of Engineering and Architecture (DPIA), University of Udine,
Via del Cotonificio 114, 33100 Udine, Italy
{fabio.rondinella,fabiola.daneluz,nicola.baldo}@uniud.it
[2] TU Wien, Institute of Transportation, Karlsplatz 13/E230-3, 1040 Vienna, Austria
bernhard.hofko@tuwien.ac.at

Abstract. Road pavements represent the backbone of every road network. Asphalt concrete (AC) mixtures are the main technological solution for road pavement construction. Their composition must be optimized to ensure adequate structural and functional performance. One of the most reliable parameters for the characterization of AC mixtures' viscoelastic behavior is called complex modulus. Such a stiffness property is crucial in the evaluation of pavements' mechanical performance. The complex modulus is usually described in terms of dynamic modulus and phase angle and, to be determined, long and expensive experimental campaigns must be carried out. An interesting alternative is represented by machine learning models that could provide fast and reliable predictions if properly trained on meaningful datasets. In this paper, the results of an extensive 4-point bending test laboratory investigation are thoroughly discussed and an up-to-date artificial neural network (ANN) methodology is outlined to simultaneously predict the dynamic modulus and the phase angle of nine different AC mixtures. To summarize the performance achieved by the developed model, six different metrics were evaluated. The empirical Witczak 1-37A equation, a well-established regression model, was used as a reference to compare the performance obtained by the neural modeling in terms of dynamic modulus. Machine learning predictions showed remarkable accuracy, outperforming regression-based ones with respect to all the evaluation metrics used. Both in terms of dynamic modulus and phase angle, Pearson correlation coefficients and coefficients of determination achieved by the ANN model were higher than 0.98, resulting in a powerful and reliable predictive tool.

Keywords: Machine learning · Artificial Neural Network · Asphalt concrete · Dynamic modulus · Phase angle

T. Guarda et al. (Eds.): ARTIIS 2023, CCIS 1935, pp. 507–520, 2024.
https://doi.org/10.1007/978-3-031-48858-0_40

1 Introduction

A sustainable pavement design requires an efficient optimization procedure with respect to the asphalt concrete mixture components, namely aggregate, filler, and bitumen. Such a complex mixture shows a traditional viscoelastic behavior quantified by means of the complex modulus, an important mechanical property defined through its two main components: dynamic modulus and phase angle. The former is denoted by |E*| and returns the stiffness of a mixture, having defined the test temperature and the frequency of loading conditions. The latter is denoted by Φ and is an indicator of the viscous and elastic quantities corresponding to the set test conditions. These parameters are crucial since they are nowadays used to evaluate pavement performance under assigned traffic conditions or to design asphalt pavements according to the main well-established methodologies [1].

The complex modulus can be determined basically by means of the well-known experimental procedures or computationally. The former approach is the most reliable; however, it is still the most time-consuming and expensive. Along with mechanical testing equipment, experienced technicians are required, and new tests must be performed whenever a condition related to the mixture or test conditions is changed. The latter approach usually involves fine tuning and validation steps but provides far better adaptability to changes in testing conditions. Following the computational approach, several empirical or constitutive equations have been developed over the years [2, 3]. One of the most successful predictive equations for predicting the dynamic modulus based on the analyzed mixture features is named Witczak 1-37A viscosity-based model [4].

In recent years, other computational approaches are progressively becoming well accepted among the scientific community and rely on data science and soft-computing techniques such as artificial neural networks. Their popularity stems from their flexibility about the phenomenon to be modeled and the accuracy of the following predictions. Furthermore, soft-computing techniques represent a promising advanced modeling approach to improve the experimental based methodology conventionally used for the mix design of road pavements.

The goal of this study is to use the results of an experimental campaign carried out by means of 4-point bending test (4PBT) to train a neural model for simultaneously predicting both the dynamic modulus and phase angle values of nine investigated mixtures. With respect to |E*|, a direct comparison with the performance achieved by the well-established Witczak 1-37A model was performed using six different goodness-of-fit metrics. The results achieved are very encouraging and could allow |E*| and Φ values to be quickly determined and implemented within well-established procedures for road pavement design, thus enhancing the sustainability of transport infrastructure.

2 Materials and Methods

2.1 Mix Design and Data Collection

The step-by-step methodology flowchart is shown in Fig. 1. It first involved designing, producing, and testing nine different AC mixtures. Diabase aggregate was used for surface layer mixtures, namely AC11 and SMA11, whereas limestone one was chosen for binder and base mixtures, namely AC22 and AC32. European standards for aggregate in asphalt mixtures were followed (EN 13108-x). Several binders, both unmodified and polymer modified, were used to prepare the mixtures, while filler was always powdered limestone. The optimum binder content was established according to Marshall procedures. Table 1 and Fig. 2 provide more details about the nine investigated mixtures, summarizing the name, the aggregate type, the bitumen content, the performance grade (PG), the air voids content, the Marshall stability, and the bulk specific gravity of the investigated mixtures. The viscoelastic behavior of these mixtures was evaluated through an extensive experimental campaign conducted by means of the 4-point bending test (4PBT). Each mixture was tested at six temperatures (seven for two mixtures) and ten loading frequencies. There were at least three specimens tested for each mixture, and the average resulting values in terms of stiffness and phase angle were recorded. In this way, a large dataset (560 observations) was built up allowing subsequent modeling operations to be carried out.

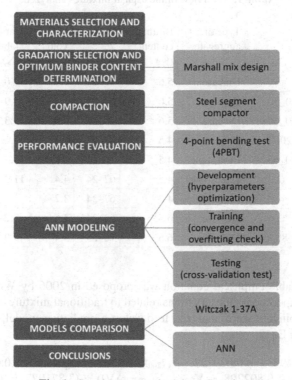

Fig. 1. Step-by-step methodology flowchart.

2.2 Empirical Models

Over the years, the effort of many scientists has been aimed at identifying a reliable correlation between dynamic modulus and the physical/volumetric properties of the corresponding asphalt mixtures. In 1996, Witczak proposed a model based on time-temperature superposition principle (TTSP). Due to shift factors, E* values determined at different temperatures can be shifted both left and right to obtain a single curve referring to a specific reference temperature, known as master curve [5]. To represent the dependence of the dynamic modulus on temperature, this curve is expected to be nonlinear sigmoidal, as given in Eq. 1.

$$\log |E*| = \rho + \alpha / \left(1 + e^{\beta + \gamma \cdot \log(f_{red})}\right) \tag{1}$$

where |E*| stands for the AC mixture dynamic modulus, ρ and $\rho + \alpha$ stand for the logarithms of |E*| minimum value and |E*| maximum value, respectively, β and γ are called shape parameters, and f_{red} stands for the reduced frequency. The representation of the master curves realized for each mixture can be found in Fig. 3.

Table 1. Overview of the asphalt mixtures analyzed.

Mixture name	Type of aggregate	Bitumen content (%)	PG	Air Voids (%)	Marshall Stability (kN)	Bulk specific gravity
AC11_70_100	Diabase	5.6	63–24	3.4	12.6	2.56
AC11_PmB45_80_50	Diabase	5.6	69–27	3.7	13.9	2.56
AC11_PmB45_80_65	Diabase	5.6	76–25	3.4	13.3	2.56
AC22_mB160_220FT	Limestone	4.5	73–22	3.8	11.1	2.62
AC22_PmB45_80_65	Limestone	4.5	76–25	4.1	13.3	2.61
AC22_50_70	Limestone	4.5	67–24	4.4	11.2	2.62
AC32_50_70	Limestone	4.3	67–24	3.2	–	2.64
SMA11_70_100	Diabase	6.5	63–24	3.6	7.2	2.54
SMA11_PmB45_80_65	Diabase	6.5	76–25	3.4	9.9	2.52

Another reliable empirical equation was proposed in 2006 by Witczak et al. [4]. Thousands of experimental observations related to traditional mixtures and/or prepared with modified binders were analyzed to develop a predictive model, called Witczak 1-37A, based on Eq. 2:

$$\log |E*| = -1.249937 + 0.029232 \cdot \rho_{No.200} - 0.001767 \cdot (\rho_{No.200})^2 + 0.02841 \cdot \rho_{No.4} - 0.058097 \cdot AV - 0.802208 \cdot (V_{beff} / (V_{beff} + AV)) + (3.871977 + 0.0021 \cdot \rho_{No.4} + 0.003958 \cdot \rho_{3/8} - 0.000017 \cdot (\rho_{3/8})^2 + 0.005470 \cdot \rho_{3/4}) / (1 + e^{(-0.603313 - 0.313551 \cdot \log(f_l) - 0.393532 \cdot \log(\eta_b))})$$

$$\tag{2}$$

where |E*| stands for the dynamic modulus (10^5 psi), $\rho_{No.200}$, $\rho_{No.4}$, $\rho_{3/8}$, and $\rho_{3/4}$ stand for the aggregate percentage passing No.200, No.4, 3/8-in., and 3/4-in. sieves, respectively, AV stands for the air voids content percentage, V_{beff} stands for the effective binder

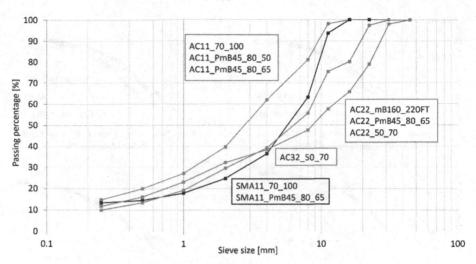

Fig. 2. Particle size distributions of different mixtures.

content percentage, and f_l stands for the loading frequency (Hz). η_b represents the binder viscosity expressed as 10^6 poises and determined as follows:

$$\log_{10}\log_{10}\eta_b = A + VTS \cdot \log_{10}(T_R) \tag{3}$$

where T_R stands for the temperature expressed as Rankine, while A and VTS stand for empirical parameters determined based on PG [4].

Witczak 1-37A empirical model is sufficiently robust and reliable, and it is still used to predict dynamic modulus values in Level 2 and Level 3 asphalt mixture projects, according to M-EPDG [4].

Several performance metrics were evaluated to determine the reliability of the predictive model developed, namely MAE, MAPE, MSE, RMSE, R, and R^2 (Eqs. 4 to 9):

$$MAE = 1/n \cdot \sum_{i=1}^{n} |t_i - p_i| \tag{4}$$

$$MAPE = 1/n \cdot \sum_{i=1}^{n} |(t_i - p_i)/t_i| \cdot 100 \tag{5}$$

$$MSE = 1/n \cdot \sum_{i=1}^{n} (t_i - p_i)^2 \tag{6}$$

$$RMSE = \sqrt{1/n \cdot \sum_{i=1}^{n} (t_i - p_i)^2} \tag{7}$$

$$R = (1/(n-1)) \cdot \sum_{i=1}^{n} ((t_i - \mu_{t_i})/\sigma_{t_i})((p_i - \mu_{p_i})/\sigma_{p_i}) \tag{8}$$

$$R^2 = 1 - (1/n(\sum_{i=1}^{n} (t_i - p_i)^2)/(\sum_{i=1}^{n} (t_i - \mu_{t_i})^2) \tag{9}$$

where t_i and p_i stand for the i-th target and the i-th prediction, respectively, n stands for the number of observations, μ and σ stand for the corresponding average and standard deviation values, respectively.

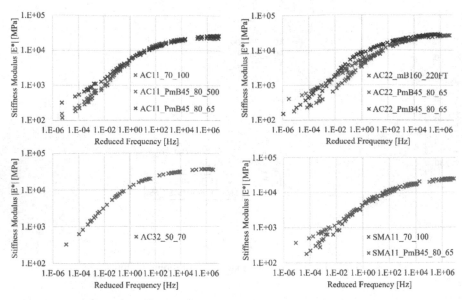

Fig. 3. Master curves of the nine mixtures analyzed at the reference temperature of 15 °C.

2.3 Model Building and Implementation

An artificial neural network (ANN) model is the result of simple units, the artificial neurons, connected through biased and weighted connections and organized in a sequence of layers [6]. The first one is called input layer. It receives a feature vector, and it is composed by a number of neurons equal to the number of features of the feature vector. One or more hidden layers follow the input one. Here computational processes take place. The number of neurons composing the hidden layers determines the computing power of the model. Each neuron activity is here ruled by a particular activation function. Finally, the last one is called output layer, and it returns the outcome of the network.

This research focuses on a shallow neural network, a particular NN composed by three layers, with a single hidden layer. Its architecture is organized as follows: the first twelve rows of the Table 2 composed the feature vector of the input layer; the hidden layer was characterized by a variable number of neurons N (set between 1 and 50), equipped with an activation function selected within a set of the most widely used functions (i.e., positive linear (poslin), exponential linear (ELU), log-sigmoid (logsig), and hyperbolic tangent (tansig)) [7]; finally, two neurons composed the output layer, representing the dynamic modulus |E*| and the phase angle Φ.

On the basis of the same starting input feature vector, the objective of the supervised training process was to identify weights and biases to minimize the errors between the experimental target vector **t** and the predicted neural output vector **p**. The learning rule implemented to update network weights and to compute loss function as iterations proceed is given in Eqs. 10 and 11:

$$\mathbf{W}^{e+1} = \mathbf{W}^{e} - \left[\mathbf{J}^{T}(\mathbf{W}^{e})\mathbf{J}(\mathbf{W}^{e}) + \mu_{e}\mathbf{I}\right]^{-1}\mathbf{J}^{T}(\mathbf{W}^{e})\mathbf{q}(\mathbf{W}^{e}) \qquad (10)$$

Table 2. Summary of variables considered.

Variable	Minimum value	Maximum value	Mean	Standard Deviation
Categorical	–	–	–	–
$\rho_{3/4}$ [%]	0.00	28.01	7.2	9.1
$\rho_{3/8}$ [%]	10.88	47.66	25.9	12.5
$\rho_{No.4}$ [%]	34.35	59.83	50.5	11.2
$\rho_{No.200}$ [%]	6.19	9.56	7.9	1.4
AV [%]	3.2	4.4	3.7	0.4
V_{beff} [%]	11.117	16.160	13.3	1.9
f_1 [Hz]	0.1	40.0	13.0	12.6
T [°C]	−15.40	49.75	14.4	19.9
η_b [10^6 Poise]	0.03	2520654.21	213913.3	520927.3
A	9.458	10.646	10	0.5
VTS	−3.560	−3.116	−3.3	0.2
$|E*|$ [MPa]	97.06	36919.89	10859.5	9607.3
Φ [°]	0.05	63.50	21.8	13.8

$$L(\mathbf{p}(\mathbf{W}^e), \mathbf{t}, \mathbf{W}^e) = \beta||\mathbf{p}(\mathbf{W}^e) - \mathbf{t}||_2^2 + \alpha||\mathbf{W}^e||_2^2 \qquad (11)$$

α and β are called regularization parameters. They are determined according to David MacKay's approach [8], and they are used to reduce the solution complexity by avoiding too high values of connection weights. α/β ratio ranges from 0 to 1. $\mathbf{W}^e$ denotes weight matrix at the generic iteration e, $\mathbf{I}$ denotes the identity matrix, whereas $\mathbf{J}$ stands for the Jacobian matrix of the training loss function $L(\cdot)$, determined with respect to $\mathbf{W}^e$. The scalar μ represents the learning step size taken in the direction towards the minimum loss defined by the gradient $\mathbf{J}^T(\mathbf{W}^e)\mathbf{q}(\mathbf{W}^e)$, with $\mathbf{q}$ representing the error vector ($\mathbf{q}(\mathbf{W}^e) = \mathbf{p}(\mathbf{W}^e) - \mathbf{t}(\mathbf{W}^e)$). As iterations proceed, the learning step size is multiplied by increasing (μ_{inc}) or decreasing (μ_{dec}) factors to achieve fast convergence, by avoiding local minima. The definition of a maximum learning rate μ_{max} was necessary to stop the learning algorithm if this threshold was exceeded.

Model hyperparameters related to the algorithm functioning were set equal to their default values, according to MATLAB®Toolbox [9]. On the other hand, hyperparameters related to network architecture (Table 3) were determined according to a novel procedure called Bayesian optimization (BO) [10]. Once the hyperparameter variation ranges have been established, BO represents a semi-autonomous method to search for the most suited hyperparameter combination. For a detailed description of BO processes, please refer to Snoek et al. [11]. 100 iterations of BO algorithm were run.

Before starting with predictive model training, normalization pre-processing procedures have been carried out (Eq. 12). It means that each feature values have been

Table 3. Hyperparameters determined according to Bayesian optimization procedures.

Hyperparameters	Range of variation
Hidden neurons (N)	$\{1, \ldots, 50\}$
Activation function	$\{poslin, ELU, logsig, tansig\}$

mapped between $[0, +1]$, with 0 and $+1$ representing the lowest and the highest values for each variable, respectively. Such a practice helped to reduce computational time and to improve model efficiency.

$$v_{norm} = (v - v_{min})/(v_{max} - v_{min}) \tag{12}$$

Furthermore, a k-fold cross-validation (with k equal to 5) was implemented. Each of the five subsamples contained randomly selected observations. In this way, $k - 1$ folds were used to train the model whereas the last subsample was used to test it. After k iterations (in which the test fold was always changed), the results were averaged [12]. As a consequence of the iterative resampling, such a procedure allowed the model's predictive performance to be fairly evaluated.

3 Results and Discussion

Pearson correlation matrix [13] was built to determine the correlation strength between every couple of variables (Fig. 4). Pearson correlation coefficients ranged between $[-1, +1]$. An absolute value around one represents a perfect correlation, whereas an absolute value around zero represents no correlation. Plus and minus signs stand for direct and inverse proportionality, respectively. By way of example, it is interesting to notice that a strong negative correlation can be found between dynamic modulus and temperature (R $= -0.90$). On the other hand, a strong positive correlation can be found between phase angle and temperature (R $= +0.88$).

Training outcomes obtained as a result of the 5-fold cross validation coupled with Bayesian optimization returned a minimum value of the average loss function equal to -0.8225. As shown in Fig. 5, it was found for a neural model characterized by an 8-neuron hidden layer, equipped with a logsig activation function (Fig. 5).

Test results are hereafter described. Concerning the dynamic modulus data, a side-by-side comparison between test observations and the ANN-predicted values is shown in Fig. 6. The former are represented by dark blue histograms, whereas the latter are represented by light blue histograms. To identify the 112 test pairs ($|E*|$, Φ), each pair was assigned a test ID, shown on the horizontal axis. It can be noticed how predictions never differed too much from test observations. The same procedure was followed for the phase angle predictions, and the results are shown in Fig. 7. Observed phase angle data are represented by dark blue histograms, whereas ANN-predicted ones are represented by light blue histograms. Once again, the predictions are reasonably reliable and are remarkably close to the test values. This is extremely important from an engineering point of view, as it confirms that the model can simultaneously and accurately predict both the mechanical parameters.

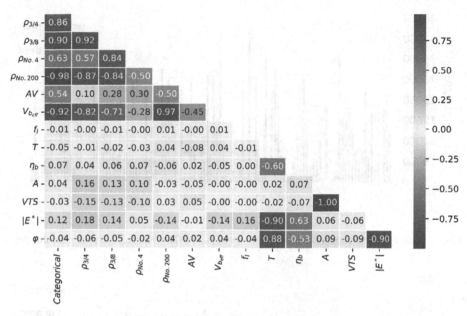

Fig. 4. Summary of Pearson correlations.

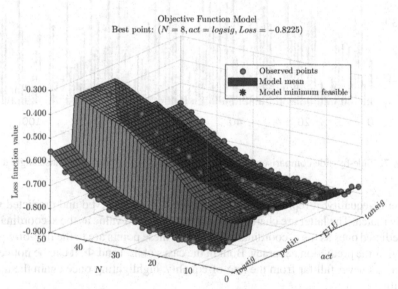

Fig. 5. Observed average loss function values on the 5 folds as a function of hidden neurons and activation functions.

A different representation that provides an even more detailed visualization of the prediction accuracy is provided in Fig. 8 and Fig. 9. In these regression plots, a blue solid line inclined at 45°, and light blue circles can be observed. The former is named

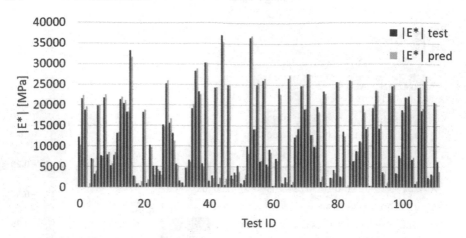

Fig. 6. Side-by-side comparison between observed and ANN-predicted dynamic modulus data.

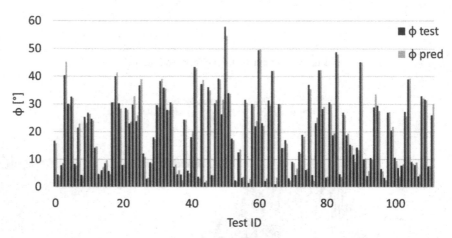

Fig. 7. Side-by-side comparison between observed and ANN-predicted phase angle data.

the line-of-equality: it represents 100% accuracy, where observed and predicted values exactly match. The latter are characterized by the observed value as the x-coordinate and the predicted ones as the y-coordinate. The closer these points are to the line-of-equality, the higher the prediction accuracy. Both in the cases of |E*| and Φ, it can be noticed that predictions never fall far from the line-of-equality, highlighting once again the model's reliability.

Figure 10 shows a comparison between the predictive performance achieved by the empirical model and by the neural model, expressed in terms of error metrics (MAE, RMSE) and coefficient of determination (R^2). Moving from the empirical equation to the neural model, a significant reduction in error metrics can easily be observed, along with a significant increase in the value of R^2. To provide more insight within the predictive performance of the developed models, all the performance metrics evaluated during the testing phase of the two compared models are reported in Table 4. The ANN model

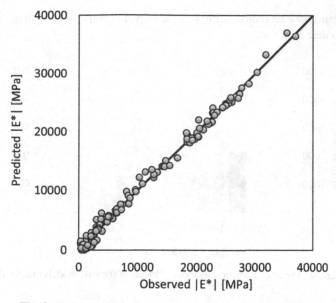

Fig. 8. ANN-model regression plot for dynamic modulus data.

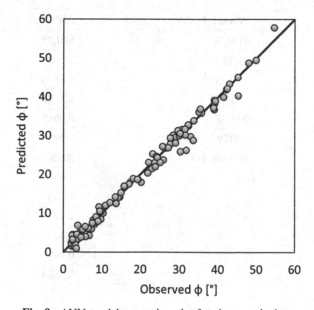

Fig. 9. ANN-model regression plot for phase angle data.

outperformed the empirical model with MAE, MSE, and RMSE values even an order of magnitude lower in terms of dynamic modulus. Both R and R^2 values exceeded 0.99. Furthermore, unlike the Witczak 1-37A model, the neural model allowed the phase angle to be simultaneously predicted, with accuracy levels comparable to those achieved in terms of dynamic modulus.

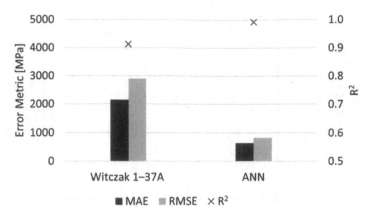

Fig. 10. Predictive performance comparison of the two models analyzed.

Table 4. Comparison between performance achieved by Witczak 1-37A and ANN models.

|E*|	Witczak 1-37A	ANN
MAE	2146.30	640.05
MAPE	41.25	21.60
MSE	$8.43 \cdot 10^6$	$6.88 \cdot 10^5$
RMSE	2904.13	829.21
R	0.9694	0.9965
R^2	0.9129	0.9929
Φ	Witczak 1-37A	ANN
MAE	–	1.05
MAPE	–	10.90
MSE	–	2.17
RMSE	–	1.47
R	–	0.9942
R^2	–	0.9884

4 Conclusions

In the present research, an innovative methodology was developed to predict the mechanical behavior of nine different asphalt concrete mixtures, based on dynamic modulus and phase angle values. Such a methodology relied on the use of an artificial neural network that implemented innovative Bayesian optimization and k-fold cross-validation processes. The experimental campaign carried out by means of the 4-point bending tests resulted in laboratory observations that subsequently allowed the neural model to be trained and tested. Variables used as model inputs are the same as those used by the empirical Witczak 1-37A equation to predict dynamic modulus values. Thus, it was possible to compare the prediction accuracy of both the models. Six different performance metrics defined the performance achieved. ANN showed a significant improvement in prediction accuracy, reducing MAE, MSE, and RMSE by an order of magnitude, and achieving Pearson correlation coefficient and coefficient of determination values both above 0.99. In addition, unlike Witczak 1-37A equation, the neural model also allowed the above mixtures' phase angle values to be simultaneously predicted, adding highly valuable information in terms of mechanical characterization. It is interesting to note that this additional prediction has returned an accuracy comparable to that found for dynamic modulus predictions. Based on these findings, the developed ANN-based methodology represents a reliable alternative to the expensive and time-consuming laboratory procedures for the evaluation of asphalt concretes' complex modulus. It improves the accuracy reached by the well-known empirical equation, allowing the complex modulus to be predicted both in terms of |E*| and Φ at the same time. The current paper contributes to driving the experimental mix design method conventionally used for road pavement construction into a more sustainable and digitally based approach based on machine learning techniques, namely artificial neural networks.

References

1. AASHTO, American Association of State Highway Transportation Officials (AASHTO), Guide for Design of Pavement Structures (1993)
2. Pasetto, M., Baldo, N.: Computational analysis of the creep behaviour of bituminous mixtures. Constr. Build. Mater. **94**, 784–790 (2015)
3. Pasetto, M., Baldo, N.: Creep response of asphalt concretes: visco-elasto-plastic modeling. Int. J. Pavement Res. Technol. **8**(2), 63–71 (2015)
4. Bari, M.J., Witczak, M.W.: Development of a new revised version of the Witczak |E*|: predictive model for hot mix asphalt mixtures. J. Assoc. Asphalt Paving Technol. **75**, 381–423 (2006)
5. Fonseca, O.A., Witczak, M.W.: A prediction methodology for the dynamic modulus of in placed aged asphalt mixtures. J. Assoc. Asphalt Paving Technol. **65**, 532–572 (1996)
6. McCulloch, W.S., Pitts, W.: A logical calculus of ideas immanent in nervous activity. In: Anderson, J.A., Rosenfeld, E. (eds.) Neurocomputing: Foundations of Research 1988, pp. 15–27. MIT Press, Cambridge (1988)
7. Baldo, N., Miani, M., Rondinella, F., Celauro, C.: A machine learning approach to determine airport asphalt concrete layer moduli using heavy weight deflectometer data. Sustainability **13**, 8831 (2021)
8. MacKay, D.J.C.: Bayesian interpolation. Neural Comput.Comput. **4**(3), 415–447 (1992)
9. Beale, M.H., Hagan, M.T., Demuth, H.B.: Neural Network Toolbox. User's Guide. MathWorks: Natick, MA, USA (2010)
10. Baldo, N., Miani, M., Rondinella, F., Manthos, E., Valentin, J.: Road pavement asphalt concretes for thin wearing layers: a machine learning approach towards stiffness modulus and volumetric properties prediction. Periodica Polytechnica: Civil Eng. **66**(4), 1087–1097 (2022)

11. Snoek, J., Larochelle, H., Adams, R.P.: Practical Bayesian optimization of machine learning algorithms. In: Proceedings of the 25th International Conference on Neural Information Processing Systems (NIPS), pp. 2951–2959, Lake Tahoe, NV, USA (2012)
12. Rondinella, F., Daneluz, F., Vacková, P., Valentin, J., Baldo, N.: Volumetric properties and stiffness modulus of asphalt concrete mixtures made with selected quarry fillers: experimental investigation and machine learning prediction. Materials 16(3), 1017 (2023)
13. Pallant, J.: SPSS Survival Manual: A Step by Step Guide to Data Analysis Using IBM SPSS, 7th edn. Routledge, London (2002)

Blockchain and Robotic Process Automation Working Together

Teresa Guarda[1,2]([⊠]) [iD], Samuel Bustos[2] [iD], Manuela Cañizares Espada[1] [iD],
and Daniel Gracia Garallar[1] [iD]

[1] Madrid Open University, Madrid, Spain
tguarda@gmail.com

[2] Universidad Estatal Península de Santa Elena, La Libertad, Ecuador

Abstract. Digital transformation is a change of mindset within the industry, which companies go through with the aim of becoming more modern and keeping up with technological advances. Blockchain and RPA are two disruptive technologies. Being Robotic Process Automation (RPA) itself a driver of digital transformation. RPA is one of the emerging tools which is used for the development of program solutions, creating interactive bots and software which simplify tasks, thus reducing time and operation resources, being. RPA has been changing and revolutionizing the way we work. This technology is capable of imitating human actions, aiming to facilitate the daily life of employees, performing repetitive and high-demand routine tasks, and thus allowing their analytical professional growth. This article presents the relevance of incorporating automation processes in organizations, with the aim to improve the service levels, and minimize operations whose processes are manual in order to use information systems in an agile and secure way, allowing companies to increase productivity, efficiency of the processes, and reinforce their competitive advantage; explaining how to Blockchain and RPA can work together.

Keywords: Blockchain · RPA · Digital Transformation · Security · Competitive Advantage

1 Introduction

Digital transformation refers to the exponential speed and disruptive changes in society, driven by the rapid adoption of technology [1]. This is putting enormous pressure on organizations and, ultimately, many are becoming irrelevant. In this new scenario, two types of organizations can be observed: those that are obtaining incremental gains through digitalization and those that are disruptive in the application of digital tools, which are the ones that are winning.

Digital technologies evolve sharply and exponentially. Currently, we have already experienced the benefits of automating repetitive and routine activities in different workspaces. Even if invisibly, process automation is more than present in our lives: from customer service to the collection, processing, and modeling of corporate data, based on rules. Automation tools are designed to solve problems that affect people [2].

T. Guarda et al. (Eds.): ARTIIS 2023, CCIS 1935, pp. 521–530, 2024.
https://doi.org/10.1007/978-3-031-48858-0_41

In this context of constant evolution, it is worth mentioning that the digital transformation and the new way of working also allowed for the acceleration and development of new and more elaborate business processes, mainly in the digital environment.

The term automation has been used in numerous fields, in this case, it dates from industrial processes, where the term was created due to the need to order and store procedures, optimizing application time [3]. Until the last decade, tools could only learn by following the instructions given by people, which was interpreted as implementing algorithms in a very practical way.

With the increasing competitiveness among organizations in a digital transformation scenario, RPA has attracted more and more corporate attention regarding automation initiatives [4].

RPA is a disruptive technology that allows companies to add value to their processes and operations [5, 6]. With RPA, is possible to automate the execution of business processes, that is, activities within an organization that produced a service or product that are based on Dumas rules (2013) [7], then the execution of tasks such as document data transmission, reading, and writing in databases, filling out forms, and other operational activities can be carried out by software [8, 9].

For this purpose, software robots, commonly called bots, are configured with abilities to learn, simulate and execute an organization's processes [10,11]. In addition, human resources can be directed to less repetitive and more analytical tasks, optimizing service delivery and the quality of processes performed within an organization.

By implementing RPA solutions, an organization increases its workforce [12]. This is possible because RPA offers efficiency and versatility in its applications [12, 13]. However, companies have started adopting Blockchain technology to ensure that automation processes are carried out safely [14].

In this work, we will discuss the relevance of embedding automation processes in organizations, the benefits of RPA and Blockchain technology and how they can work together to increase efficiency and organizational security. We will also examine the competitive advantage that can be gained by integrating RPA and Blockchain technology within organizations.

2 Blockchain

Blockchain is a decentralized ledger technology (DLT) initially designed for Bitcoin electronic financial transactions to be permanently recorded on a Blockchain [15]. The innovations proposed in Nakamoto's (2008) work on bitcoin included the relationship between the concept of Blockchain and a public ledger, which would be a kind of "public book" that can be jointly updated by numerous participants in an open source network, without intermediaries [15, 16].

Blockchain is one of the most innovative and disruptive application technologies today [17]. Blockchain is a technology that works over the Internet, it can be defined as a means of shared public record for point-to-point (chain) transactions safely executed, being an immutable storage system reducing the risk of adulteration [16, 18]. Immutable is defined as resistance to transaction tampering, manifested in the replication of fragments, reversal of unauthorized updates or deletions, regular backups of digital information and cryptographic signature of all transactions, by blocks and uses [18, 19]. In this segment, it stores transactions in a chain of blocks, has characteristics of decentralization, persistence, anonymity, subject to audit [19] and with greater transparency [19].

With Blockchain technology, the chain transfer of value between shares does not depend on an external authority or third parties, and the parties do not need to know each other.

The system that stores Blockchain databases makes it a more secure implementation. Adaptation of databases for use in Blockchain technology is possible. Hence, the data model plays a significant role in Blockchain implementation. Most of the data model systems most suitable for Blockchain implementation are relational, but the key-value oriented data models, and the document oriented ones, or for storing large columns, surpass the previous ones. [18] Blockchain systems follow the principles of databases in terms of permissions, making it possible to define roles and policies [20]. The important thing is that the consistency of the databases is guaranteed.

Blockchain structures rely on digital signatures [20], which allow the authentication of transactions; cryptographic hash functions, which allow the creation of the attached-only ledger structure (algorithm); consensus algorithms, which are used to decide the order of transactions to be processed. Blockchain, by providing users with desirable characteristics of decentralization, autonomy, integrity, immutability, verification, fault tolerance [19], has increased research interest in the subject and meets the needs of organizations. Enabling the action of accumulators, which is a cryptographic function that allows the generation of proofs of inclusion for sets of elements, without revealing any member of the underlying set [21].

Blockchain technology can be used in many sectors, from education, finance, and healthcare, to supply chain management. Among the main benefits of Blockchain we highlight its security and transparency [22,23].

3 Robotic Process Automation

RPA is a software that provides the tools to build an digital robot/bot that automatically simulates repetitive and routine operational tasks, that interacts with applications and information sources, and performs assigned and programmed actions in the same way that humans do [24].

The technology is capable of working 24 h a day, without rest or error, making it an excellent option for repetitive and high-volume tasks.

Although companies today seek process efficiency when implementing this technology, it should also be taken into account that not all tasks can be solved by RPA [25], however, it can be the final answer to tasks that do not require human contact and can be considered stressful.

RPA technology is in charge of ensuring that the solutions are effective, because said software or product for the company will not allow errors to occur as a result of manual processes carried out by humans [26]. In this way, the activities being automated ensure that this tool will be key for an effective mobilization of the flow of information in an adequate and precise manner, thus determining its availability at all times and its efficiency when carrying out the assigned tasks. The objective will be achieved to reduce response times, increase the quality of the information generated and increase customer satisfaction.

It is necessary to take into account what is the risk of this transformation in software or programs, because RPA software interacts directly with business applications and mimics the way in which applications and people use credentials and permissions. This can create conceivable risks when digital workers are involved in processes that require access to privileged credentials, which in turn to sensitive and critical data.

RPA is based on rules, data structuring, including routine tasks [27], RPA in the world of technology brings many benefits of great importance and also consequences for end users without experience regarding the use of these in their business [28,29].

Developing software robots using RPA provides immediate profitability [8], thus increasing the efficiency and production of organizations and industries. RPA offers a solution for any process and can similarly transform and optimize an organization's workflow. Software bots are designed to allow businesses to be scalable and flexible, providing a quick and personalized response to emerging needs [30]. They are easy to develop and integrate seamlessly into any system. They continually report on their progress, are operationally proactive, and help implement the organization's growth and digital transformation strategies.

RPA can be applied in various functions and corporate segments, such as financial services, human resources, logistics, administrative, inventory and purchasing, among other areas.

Process automation brings benefits that go beyond removing the monotonous service from employees. In this sense, some advantages of implementing this technology in the business environment stand out are: increased productivity; scalable; reduces costs; availability; focus on the core business; and talent enabler (Fig. 1) [12, 31, 32].

4 Working Together

Blockchain is a distributed technology that enables secure and transparent transactions, while is a technology that automates repetitive and manual tasks using software robots, in this sense both technologies can work together.

The joint use of Blockchain and RPA pre-results in a robust solution that allows simplify processes, increasing efficiency, and reducing costs [33].

Blockchain and RPA when used together can improve organizational efficiency and security, allowing companies to improve their operational processes, reduce costs and increase transparency.

RPA technology can automate repetitive and high-volume tasks [34], while Blockchain technology can provide a secure and transparent ledger for these transactions [35].

Blockchain technology provides a secure and transparent ledger for transactions, while RPA technology can automate and secure the transfer of data between systems [36].

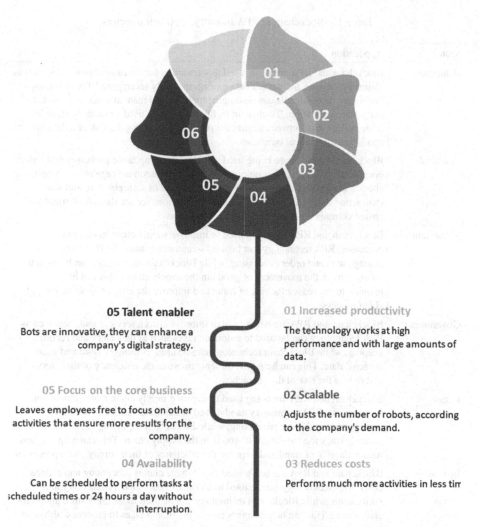

Fig. 1. Advantages of implementing RPA in the business environment.

Blockchain and RPA can be used together to improve organizational efficiency and security across a wide range of industries, including healthcare, finance, manufacturing, government, retail, insurance, energy and transportation [37, 38, 39] (Table 1).

Although these two technologies used together offer many benefits, it must be clear that the constraints and challenges must be considered. In this sense, some of the challenges and restrictions in its integration stand out (Table 2).

Table 1. Blockchain & RPA Industry application sectors.

Sector	Application
Healthcare	Blockchain and RPA are being used to streamline administrative processes such as claims processing and patient data management. By leveraging RPA technology, healthcare professionals can automate repetitive and manual tasks such as data entry and verification. Blockchain technology can be used to securely store and share patient data between healthcare providers, reducing the risk of a data breach and improving patient outcomes
Financial	Blockchain and RPA are being used to automate compliance processes and reduce operational costs. RPA technology can be used to automate regulatory compliance checks, while Blockchain technology can be used to securely store and share transaction data. This can help financial institutions reduce the risk of fraud and ensure compliance with regulatory requirements
Manufacturing	Blockchain and RPA are being used to improve supply chain management processes. RPA technology can be used to automate tasks like inventory management and order processing, while Blockchain technology can be used to securely track the movement of goods in the supply chain. This can help manufacturers reduce the risk of fraud and improve the efficiency of their supply chain processes
Government	Blockchain and RPA are being used to improve citizen services and reduce costs. RPA technology can be used to automate tasks such as data entry and record keeping, while Blockchain technology can be used to securely store and share citizens' data. This can help governments improve the efficiency of their services and reduce the risk of data breaches
Retail	Blockchain and RPA are being used to improve supply chain management and reduce costs. RPA technology can be used to automate tasks like inventory management and order processing, while Blockchain technology can be used to securely track the movement of goods in the supply chain. This can help retailers reduce the risk of fraud and improve the efficiency of their supply chain processes
Insurance	Blockchain and RPA are being used to automate claims processing and reduce costs. RPA technology can be used to automate tasks such as data entry and verification, while Blockchain technology can be used to securely store and share claims data. This can help insurers reduce the time it takes to process claims and improve customer satisfaction
Energy	Blockchain and RPA are being used to improve asset management and reduce costs. RPA technology can be used to automate tasks such as maintenance scheduling and data entry, while Blockchain technology can be used to securely track maintenance history and ownership of energy assets. This can help energy companies reduce downtime and improve asset utilization
Transportation	Blockchain and RPA are being used to improve logistics and reduce costs. RPA technology can be used to automate tasks like order processing and tracking shipments, while Blockchain technology can be used to securely track the movement of goods in the supply chain. This can help transport companies reduce the risk of fraud and improve the efficiency of their logistical processes

Table 2. Main challenges in the integrating Blockchain and RPA

Challenge	Description
Technical Complexity	Blockchain and RPA integration can be technically complex and require a high level of expertise. Organizations may need to invest in specialized software, hardware, and personnel to implement these technologies effectively
Data Privacy	Although Blockchain technology is designed to be secure and transparent, there are still data privacy concerns. Organizations need to ensure that information is only accessible to authorized personnel and that data is encrypted and protected from unauthorized access
Regulatory Compliance	Depending on the industry and jurisdiction, there may be regulatory compliance requirements that need to be met when using Blockchain and RPA. Organizations need to ensure they comply with relevant laws and regulations to avoid legal and financial transfers
Scalability	As organizations increase their use of Blockchain and RPA, they may encounter challenges with scalability. These technologies may require computing power and absorbency and may struggle to handle large volumes of data
Integration with legacy systems	Many organizations have existing legacy systems that may not be compatible with Blockchain and RPA technology. Integrating these technologies with legacy systems can be time consuming and requires a significant investment

5 Conclusions

RPA is a technological application that automates business processes based on rules, structured and repetitive inputs.

Blockchain is a decentralized ledger technology used to record transactions. Transactions are recorded securely and transparently, making data tampering difficult. The blockchain era gives numerous benefits which include elevated safety, transparency and performance.

Blockchain and RPA are two disruptive technology that could work together to enhance organizational efficiency and security. Leveraging the strengths of these two technologies, companies can improve their operational methods, reduce charges and increase transparency. However, cautious planning and implementation are needed to make sure the successful integration of these technologies.

Blockchain and RPA may be used collectively to enhance organizational performance and security throughout a vast variety of industries, along with healthcare, finance, manufacturing, authorities, retail, coverage, electricity, and transportation. Leveraging the strengths of these technologies, businesses can automate repetitive duties, reduce charges, and increase transparency and safety.

References

1. Bottoni, P., Labella, A., Pareschi, R.: A formal model for ledger management systems based on contracts and temporal logic. Blockchain: Res. Appl. **3**(1), 1–15 (2022). https://doi.org/10.1016/j.bcra.2022.100062
2. Capocasale, V., Danilo, G., Perboli, G.: Comparative analysis of permissioned blockchain frameworks for industrial applications. Blockchain: Res. Appl. **3**, 1–13 (2022). https://doi.org/10.1016/j.bcra.2022.100113
3. Chen, Y.L., Bulysheva, L., Kataev, M.Y.: Applications of blockchain in industry 4.0: a review. Inf. Syst. Front. 1–15 (2022). https://doi.org/10.1007/s10796-022-1024
4. Choi, D.R.: Enabling the gab between rpa and process mining: user interface interactions recorder. IEEE Access **10**, 39604–39612 (2022). https://doi.org/10.1109/ACCESS.2022.3165797
5. Cooper, L.A., Holderness, D.K., Jr., Sorensen, T.L., Wood, D.A.: Robotic process automation in public accounting. Account. Horiz. **33**(4), 15–35 (2019). https://doi.org/10.2308/acch-52466
6. Darwish, D.: Blockchain and artificial intelligence for business transformation toward sustainability. In: Namasudra, S., Akkaya, K. (eds.) Blockchain and its Applications in Industry 4.0, pp. 211–255. Springer Nature Singapore, Singapore (2023). https://doi.org/10.1007/978-981-19-8730-4_8
7. Devarajan, Y.: A study of robotic process automation use cases today for tomorrow's business. Int. J. Comput. Tech. **5**(6), 12–18 (2018). http://www.ijctjournal.org/Volume5/Issue6/IJCT-V5I6P3.pdf
8. Dey, S., Das, A.: Robotic process automation: assessment of the technology for transformation of business processes. Int. J. Bus. Process. Integr. Manag. **9**(3), 220–230 (2019). https://doi.org/10.1504/IJBPIM.2019.100927
9. Enríquez, J.G., Jiménez-Ramírez, A., Domínguez-Mayo, F.J., García-García, J.A.: Robotic process automation: a scientific and industrial systematic mapping study. IEEE Access **8**, 39113–39129 (2020). https://doi.org/10.1109/ACCESS.2020.2974934
10. Ganapathy, A.: Robotic process automation: end from entrepreneurial content editing to go live. Acad. Entrepreneurship J. **27**(3), 220–230 (2021). https://doi.org/10.1504/IJBPIM.2019.100927
11. Guarda, T., Augusto, M.F., Haz, L., Díaz-Nafría, J.M.: Blockchain and government transformation. In: Rocha, Á., Ferrás, C., López-López, P.C., Guarda, T. (eds.) ICITS 2021. AISC, vol. 1330, pp. 88–95. Springer, Cham (2021). https://doi.org/10.1007/978-3-030-68285-9_9
12. Guarda, T., Fernandes, C., Augusto, M.F. (eds.): Technology, Business, Innovation, and Entrepreneurship in Industry 4.0. Springer International Publishing, Cham (2023)
13. Guo, H., Yu, X.: A survey on blockchain technology and its security Blockchain. Blockchain: Res. Appl. **3**(2), 1–15 (2022). https://doi.org/10.1016/j.bcra.2022.100067
14. Hacioglu, U.: Handbook of research on strategic fit and design in business ecosystems. IGI Global (2019)
15. Hartley, J.L., Sawaya, W.J.: Tortoise, not the hare: digital transformation of supply chain business processes. Bus. Horiz. **62**(6), 707–715 (2019). https://doi.org/10.1016/j.bushor.2019.07.006
16. Júnior, C.A., Sanseverino, E.R., Gallo, P., Koch, D., Schweiger, H.G., Zanin, H.: Blockchain review for battery supply chain monitoring and battery trading. Renew. Sustain. Energy Rev. **157**, 112078 (2022). https://doi.org/10.1016/j.rser.2022.112078
17. Kalajdjieski, J., Raikwar, M., Arsov, N., Velinov, G., Gligoroski, D.: Databases fit for blockchain technology: a complete overview. Blockchain. Res. Appl. **4**(1), 100116 (2022). https://doi.org/10.1016/j.bcra.2022.100116

18. Kang, T., Lu, J., Yu, T., Long, Y., Liu, G.: Advances in nucleic acid amplification techniques (NAATs): COVID-19 point-of-care diagnostics as an example. Biosens. Bioelectron. **206**, 1–16 (2022). https://doi.org/10.1016/j.bios.2022.114109
19. Kokina, J., Blanchette, S.: Early evidence of digital labor in accounting: innovation with robotic process automation. Int. J. Account. Inf. Syst. **34**, 1–13 (2019). https://doi.org/10.1016/j.accinf.2019.100431
20. Kolberg, D., Zühlke, D.: Lean automation enabled by industry 4.0 technologies. IFAC-PapersOnLine **48**(3), 1870–1875 (2015). https://doi.org/10.1016/j.ifacol.2015.06.359
21. Lacity, M.C., Willcocks, L.P.: A new approach to automating services. MIT Sloan Manag. Rev. **58**(1), 41–49 (2016). http://eprints.lse.ac.uk/68135/
22. Madakam, S., Holmukhe, R.M., Jaiswal, D.K.: The future digital work force: robotic process automation (RPA). ISTEM-J. Inf. Syst. Technol. Manag. **16**(2019). https://doi.org/10.4301/S1807-1775201916001
23. Maheshwari, A.: Digital transformation: Building intelligent enterprises. John Wiley & Sons (2019)
24. Mohamed, S.A., Mahmoud, M.A., Mahdi, M.N., Mostafa, S.A.: Improving efficiency and effectiveness of robotic process automation in human resource management. Sustainability **14**(7), 1–18 (2022). https://doi.org/10.3390/su14073920
25. Mookerjee, J., Rao, O.: A review of the impact of disruptive innovations on markets and business performance of players. Int. J. Grid Distrib. Comput. **14**(1), 605–630 (2021). http://sersc.org/journals/index.php/IJGDC/article/view/35967/19876
26. Nakamoto, S.: Bitcoin: A peer-to-peer electronic cash system. Decentralized Bus. Rev. (21260), 14–19 (2008). https://assets.pubpub.org/d8wct41f/31611263538139.pdf
27. Newland, B., Carlsson-Wall, M.: Blockchain and the Sports Tech Dilemma. En The Routledge Handbook of Digital Sport Management (308–318). Routledge (2023)
28. Păvăloaia, V.D., Necula, S.C.: Artificial intelligence as a disruptive technology—a systematic literature review. Electronics **12**(5), 1102 (2023). https://doi.org/10.3390/electronics1205 1102
29. Radke, A.M., Dang, M.T., Tan, A.: Using robotic process automation (RPA) to enhance item master data maintenance process. LogForum **16**(1), 129–140 (2020). https://doi.org/10.17270/J.LOG.2020.380
30. Rajasekaran, A.S., Azees, M., Al-Turjman, F.: A comprehensive survey on blockchain technology. Sustain. Energy Technol. Assess. **52**, 1–13 (2022). https://doi.org/10.1016/j.seta.2022.102039
31. Riyal, A.K., Sharma, D.K., Gupta, K.D., Srivastava, G.: Blockchain tree powered green communication for efficient and sustainable connected autonomous vehicles. IEEE Trans. Green Commun. Netw. **6**(3), 1428–1437 (2022). https://doi.org/10.1109/TGCN.2022.3166104
32. Saad, W.B., Chen, M.: A vision of 6G wireless systems: applications, trends, technologies, and open research problems. IEEE Netw. **34**(3), 134–142 (2019). https://doi.org/10.1109/MNET.001.1900287
33. Ganeshayya Shidaganti, K.N., Karthik, A., Kantikar, N.A.: Integration of RPA and AI in industry 4.0. In: Bhattacharyya, S., Banerjee, J.S., De, D. (eds.) Confluence of Artificial Intelligence and Robotic Process Automation, pp. 267–288. Springer Nature Singapore, Singapore (2023). https://doi.org/10.1007/978-981-19-8296-5_11
34. Siderska, J.: Robotic Process Automation—a driver of digital transformation? Eng. Manag. Prod. Serv. **12**(2), 21–31 (2020). https://doi.org/10.2478/emj-2020-0009
35. Sobczak, A.: Robotic process automation as a digital transformation tool for increasing organizational resilience in polish enterprises. Sustainability **14**(3), 1–29 (2022). https://doi.org/10.3390/su14031333
36. Suri, V.K.: Functional Automation and Digital Transformation. Dorrance Publishing (2020)

37. Syed, R., et al.: Robotic process automation: contemporary themes and challenges. Comput. Ind. **115**, 1–15 (2020). https://doi.org/10.1016/j.compind.2019.103162
38. Tailor, R.K., Pareek, R., Khang, A.: Robot process automation in blockchain. En The Data-Driven Blockchain Ecosystem (113–125). CRC Press (2020)
39. Tyagi, A.K., Aswathy, S.U., Abraham, A.: Integrating blockchain technology and artificial intelligence: synergies, perspectives, challenges and research directions. J. Inf. Assur. Secur. **15**(5), 178–193 (2020). https://ak-tyagi.com/static/pdf/49.pdf

Data Science Methodologies – A Benchmarking Study

Luciana Machado and Filipe Portela(✉) (iD)

Algoritmi Centre, University of Minho, Guimarães, Portugal
cfp@dsi.uminho.pt

Abstract. There are several Data Science methodologies that entities and organizations have daily contact with however real-time decision support is seen as a decisive factor for success in making a decision. Due to the complexity, quantity, and diversity of data currently existing, a set of Data Science methodologies has emerged that help in the implementation of solutions. This article arises, fundamentally, with the purpose of answering the following question: What is the most complete and comprehensive data science methodology for any Data Science project? In carrying out this article, twenty-four methodologies were found and analyzed in detail. This study was based on a comparative benchmarking of methodologies, consisting of three phases of analysis, a first that evaluates and compares the phases of all the methodologies collected, a second that analyzes, compares and evaluates the cost, usability, maintenance, scalability, precision, speed, flexibility, reliability, explainability, interpretability, cyclicity and the support of OLAP technology by each methodology, and a third phase where the previous evaluations are compiled and the methodologies with the best results are returned. Quotes. After the three analyses, the methodologies that stood out the most were AgileData.io and IBM – Base Methodology for Data Science, however both obtained a quotation of 63.03%, which demonstrates a low percentage compared to the requirements.

Keywords: Data Science · Methodologies · Projects

1 Introduction

Due to the amount of data science methodologies on the market, a study arises, based on the survey of the most varied methodologies, to find the most comprehensive ones in the area of data science. The purpose of this study is to identify the most complete methodology in the data science market through the comparison of phases and variables. A complete and adaptable methodology for any Data Science project provides an organized and efficient structure, allowing a consistent and flexible approach, resulting in greater effectiveness and probability of success in any project.

Benchmarking was used to carry out this study, which consisted of three analysis phases. As such, this article was done through a benchmarking divided into three phases, a first one that compares the methodologies through the phases that compose it, a second

© The Author(s), under exclusive license to Springer Nature Switzerland AG 2024
T. Guarda et al. (Eds.): ARTIIS 2023, CCIS 1935, pp. 531–546, 2024.
https://doi.org/10.1007/978-3-031-48858-0_42

one that compares the methodologies according to the variables cost, usability, maintenance, scalability, accuracy, speed, flexibility, reliability, explainability, interpretability, cyclicity and support of OLAP (Online Analytical Processing) technology, and a third that evaluates the methodology according to the combination of the phases that constitute it and the variables that integrate it.

The phases are characterized by steps, that is, guidelines that guide the methodology. The phases are used as a crucial component in one of the comparison steps, as they convey the ability of the methodology to provide an organized and systematic structure, ensuring consistency, repeatability and reliability in the data analysis processes. The evaluation of the phases allows determining the complete scope of the process of each methodology. The judicious use of the variables cost, usability, maintenance, scalability, accuracy, speed, flexibility, reliability, explainability, interpretability, cyclicity and support of OLAP technology in comparing data science methodologies is justified as a comprehensive and objective analysis, comprehensive because many are the variables chosen, giving relevance to such different themes, and objective because through the analysis of a single variable, very concrete conclusions can be drawn about each methodology. These variables make it possible to assess various aspects relevant to the appropriate choice of a methodology, ranging from economic factors to technical characteristics. By considering these variables, data scientists can make informed decisions that optimize the choice and implementation of data science methodologies. This systematic analysis enhances understanding of strengths and drives the development of more effective and customized solutions.

This article is a scientific article, consisting of: an introduction, to insert the theme and explain the reason for the investigation; the background, which gives an overview of the project; the methods, to explain how the study was carried out; a benchmarking consisting of three phases, this to detail all the investigation and analysis carried out; a discussion/results, to highlight the fruits of the investigation and debate them; the conclusion, serving to close the article.

2 Background

Data science methodologies are systematic approaches that guide data scientists through the entire data analysis process, providing clear steps as a guide. There are already some studies on this subject, however these compared small groups of methodologies. The first study found compares the CRISP-DM, KDD and SEMMA methodologies, all these methodologies with the same cyclic nature. This article [1] compares the three methodologies based on their phases. The results of this are evident in Table 1 and stated in the sentence: "At first glance, it can be concluded that CRISP-DM is more complete than SEMMA. However, looking deeper, we can integrate developing an understanding of the application domain, relevant prior knowledge, and end-user goals into the Sample stage of SEMMA, as data cannot be sampled unless there is a true understanding of all aspects presented".

The second article [2] compares these three methodologies and finally concludes with "most researchers and specialists in data mining follow the KDD process model because it is completer and more accurate. In contrast, CRISP-DM and SEMMA are

Table 1. Phases of the CRISP-DM, KDD and SEMMA methodologies.

CRISP-DM	KDD	SEMMA
Business Understanding	------	------
Data Understanding	Seleção	Sample
------	Pre-Processing	Exploration
Data Preparation	Transformation	Modification
Modeling	Data Mining	Modeling
Evaluation	Interpretation/Evaluation	Evaluation
Application	------	------

primarily enterprise-oriented, especially SEMMA, which is used by the SAS enterprise miner and integrates into its software. However, the study shows that CRISP-DM is more complete compared to SEMMA".

The third article [3] compares the Inomn, Kimball Lifecycle and Data Vault methodologies and ends with the following statement "we conclude that none of the approaches is the best for data warehousing (...) Kimball's approach is preferred for modeling data marts because of the query performance it provides, especially if the requirements are stable and well-defined. While Inmon is recommended if requirements are not defined or are very scalable. Both approaches face many problems, especially if the data sources change, which implies a re-engineering of data storage. To overcome these issues, the Data Vault approach is recommended because it allows for extreme flexibility and scalability." There are effectively more articles that talk about the comparison of methodologies, but these two groups of methodologies are regularly the most named and compared. Although the high number of existing studies, none did a depth analysis of all the most used methodologies regarding their global suitability or performance.

3 Methods

Since the objective of this study is to find the most versatile methodologies that would best adapt to any data science project, it was decided to use benchmarking to determine which ones would be, by comparing all methodologies. Benchmarking acts in this project through three phases, that is, three moments of comparison:

1. analyze and compare the methodologies through the phases that compose them;
2. compares and analyzes the existence of the following variables in the methodology: cost, usability, maintenance, scalability, precision, speed, flexibility, reliability, explainability, interpretability, cyclicity and support of the OLAP technology;
3. where the comparison and analysis of all methodologies is applied in a more general way, compiling the evaluations resulting from the first two moments. The third phase refers more directly to what is intended to be removed from the project, that is, the methodology/s with broader scope.

In terms of the research process, it was done across the scientific libraries, using the following terms "data science methods", "data analytics methodologies", "data mining methodologies", "business intelligence methodologies", "data warehousing methodologies", "big data methodologies", "machine learning methodologies", "data visualization methodologies", "CRISP-DM and the like", "What makes a data science methodology different?", and "best data science methods". The search for terms was carried out in Portuguese and English languages.

The benchmarking model is composed of: Planning, where it was defined which comparison criteria would be interesting and important to analyze in the future and how many analysis phases there would be; Collection Data, it was about gathering all the important information highlighted in the previous step, this resulted in a document that contains a brief summary about each methodology, as well as all its phases described, everything being organized and better prepared to be used in the later stage; Analysis of Data, in which all the information obtained so far was analyzed in order to keep only the relevant data for the study; Data comparison is the next phase, and this is where the calculations are made to highlight the best methodologies, giving rise to the last phase; Choice of Methodology, which is the step that brings together the most prominent methodologies. After that, this process starts again from collection of data to choose of methods, in order to conclude the second phase of benchmarking.

4 Benchmarking

Benchmarking consists of three phases of analysis, comparison, and evaluation of methodologies.

4.1 First Step

The first phase began, through several searches on google, gathering the largest number of methodologies, that is, twenty-four, proceeding with an individual evaluation of each one. In this first phase, a summary of each methodology was carried out individually, containing information that distinguishes it, namely its phases and some interesting variables that could effectively help in the elaboration of this benchmarking. At this time, the methodologies were grouped into three different groups, the first named Analytical Methodologies, containing ten methodologies, namely AgileData.io [4], Big Data Warehouse Methodology [5], Business Dimensional Model and Predictive Methodology [6], Data Lake Methodology [7], Data Science Lifecycle [8], Data Science Process [9], Guided Data Mining [10], IBM Analytics Solution Unified Method [11], IDEA [12], and Knowledge Discovery in Databases [1],

A second called Predictive Methodologies, with eleven methodologies, namely AgileData.io, Agile Data Science [13], Business Dimensional Model and Predictive Methodology, CRISP-DM [1], Data Science Lifecycle, Data Science Process, IBM – Base Methodology for Data Science [14], Lean Data Science [15], OSEMN [16], SEMMA [1] and TDSP [17], and Data Warehouse Methodologies, this being the name of the third group, which has in its constitution seven methodologies that are the Cloud Data Warehouse Methodology, Data Integration Methodology for Analytics, Data Vault

[3], Data Warehouse Automation [18], Dimensional Modeling Lifecycle [19], Inmon [3] and the Kimball Lifecycle [3].

Initially, the intention was to have only the first two groups, however the methodologies of the third group showed limited compatibility with the existing phases in them, which required the creation of a new group, since the methodologies of this group have phases in their constitution similar. The first two groups have four methodologies in common, namely AgileData.io, Business Dimensional Model and Predictive Methodology, Data Science Lifecycle and Data Science Process, this happens because these methodologies contain very precise steps for both exploratory data analysis as for the elaboration of the statistical model, these being the phases that most highlight an analytical or predictive methodology.

Subsequently, a survey was made of all the phases contained in the twenty-four methodologies, reaching a total number of twenty-three phases. These were titled by a general name, since different methodologies often contain identical phases in terms of their tasks but named differently. The constituent phases of the methodologies already with the general names are Business Understanding, Plan, Conceptual Modeling, Dimensional Modeling, Data Requirements, Data Understanding, Design, Storage, Data Mart Creation, Data Preparation, Exploration, Data Loading, Visualization, Decision Making, Modeling, Data Management, Evaluation, Implementation, Training, Monitoring, Feedback, Retrospective and Continuous Improvement.

In the first phase of the benchmarking, three tables were created, Table 2, Table 3 and Table 4, which correspond respectively to the three previously mentioned groups of methodologies aligned with each individual phase.

These Tables 2,3 and 4 contain in the column on the left the methodologies of your group, and in the first line the phases that constitute these methodologies. Between the first column and the line there are numbers, these represent how a given phase is ordered in relation to the methodology that is located in that line, that is, if phase X is found in methodology Y as being the third phase of that methodology, and that phase X corresponds to one of the general phases, even if it does not have the same name, then the number 3 will be positioned in the line of methodology Y and in the column that corresponds to the phase, among those mentioned, with which most relationship has.

Analyzing the Tables 2, 3 and 4, it is possible to understand which phase of each methodology is connected with the general name of the phases, to identify which methodologies contain more or less phases, as well as the phases that are part of the constitution of more or less methodologies. Since 69.57% of the phases are in analytical methodologies, 65.21% in predictive methodologies and 60.87% in data warehouse methodologies.

In Fig. 1, it was found that the methods with more phases are AgileData.io, Business Dimensional Model and Predictive Methodology and IBM – Base Methodology for Data Science with nine phases each, which corresponds to 39.13% against the total number of phases. Then with eight phases (34.78%) there are the methodologies Agile Data Science, Big Data Warehouse Methodology, Data Science Lifecycle and Guided Data Mining. Subsequently, there are the methodologies Data Integration Methodology for Analytics, Data Lake Methodology, Data Science Process, IBM Analytics Solution Unified Method and Lean Data Science with seven phases, that is, 30.43%. With six phases (26.09%) there are the CRISP-DM, Data Warehouse Automation and Kimball

Table 2. Analysis of the phases of analytical methodologies.

	AgileData.io	BDMPM	BDWM	DLM	DSL	DSP	GDM	IBM ASUM	IDEA	KDD	Total (10)	Percentage (%)
Business Understanding	X	X	X		X	X	X	X	X		8	80
Dimensional Modeling		X									1	10
Data understanding	X	X	X	X	X	X	X	X		X	9	90
Design								X			1	10
Storage			X	X							2	20
Data preparation	X	X	X	X	X	X	X	X	X	X	10	100
Exploration	X	X	X	X	X	X	X	X	X	X	10	100
Decision making				X			X		X	X	4	40
Visualization			X	X							2	20
Modeling	X	X			X	X					4	40
Data managements				X							1	10
Evaluation	X	X			X	X	X				5	50
Implementation	X	X	X		X	X	X	X			7	70
Monitoring	X	X	X		X			X			5	50
Feedback							X				1	10
Continuous Improvement	X										1	10
Total (16)	9	9	8	7	8	7	8	7	4	4		
Percentage (%)	56	56	50	43	50	43	50	43	25	25		

Lifecycle methodologies, and the methodologies that have five phases (21.74%) are OSEMN, SEMMA and TDSPM. The remaining methods contain less than five phases, that is, less than 20% of the phases.

In Fig. 2, it can be seen that the phase that appears in the largest number of methodologies, that is, in 70.83%, is Implementation, followed by the Business Understanding, Data Understanding and Data Preparation phases are found in 66,66% of the methodologies, and, next, in twelve methodologies, that is, in 50% are the Exploration and Evaluation phases. All the remaining phases are contained in less than 50% of the methodologies.

4.2 Second Step

After the first phase, where the phases of the twenty-four methodologies were analyzed, the second phase follows, where the methodologies were effectively analyzed and compared, taking into account twelve variables:

- Cost - evaluated considering the cost of implementing and maintaining the methodology, considering all the necessary resources.
- Usability - evaluates the ease of using the methodology, so that professionals without advanced technical knowledge would be perceived.

Table 3. Phase analysis of predictive methodologies.

	AgileData.io	ADS	BDMPM	CRISP-DM	DSL	DSP	IBM - MBDS	LDS	OSEMN	SEMMA	TDSPM	Total (11)	Percentage (%)
Business Understanding	X		X	X	X	X	X	X	X		X	9	81,81
Planning		X					X					2	18,18
Dimensional modelling			X									1	9,09
Data requirements							X					1	9,09
Data understanding	X	X	X	X	X	X	X	X		X	X	10	90,90
Data preparation	X	X	X	X	X	X	X	X	X	X		10	90,90
Exploration	X		X		X	X				X		5	45,45
Visualization									X			1	9,09
Modelling	X	X	X	X	X	X	X	X	X	X	X	11	100
Evaluation	X	X	X	X	X	X	X	X				8	72,72
Implementation	X	X	X	X	X	X	X	X	X		X	10	90,90
Monitoring	X		X		X							3	27,27
Feedback		X					X				X	3	27,27
Retrospective		X										1	9,09
Continuous Improvement	X							X				2	18,18
Total (15)	9	8	9	6	8	7	9	7	5	5	5		
Percentage (%)	60,00	53,33	60,00	40,00	53,33	46,66	60,00	46,66	33,33	33,33	33,33		

Table 4. Phase analysis of Data Warehouse methodologies

	CDWM	DIMA	Data Vault	DWA	DML	INMON	Kimball Lifecycle	Total (7)	Percentage (%)
Business Understanding	X				X		X	3	42,85
Planning	X	X		X	X	X	X	6	85,71
Conceptual Modelling			X		X			2	28,57
Dimensional Modelling		X		X	X		X	4	57,14
Data understanding		X						1	14,28
Design			X					1	14,28
Creating Data Marts						X		1	14,28
Data preparation		X						1	14,28
Exploration				X				1	14,28
Data loading	X	X	X	X	X		X	6	85,71
Evaluation		X		X	X			3	42,85
Implementation	X	X			X		X	4	57,14
Training	X					X		2	28,57
Monitoring	X			X			X	3	42,85
Total (14)	6	7	3	6	7	3	6		
Percentage (%)	42,85	50,00	21,43	42,85	50,00	21,43	42,85		

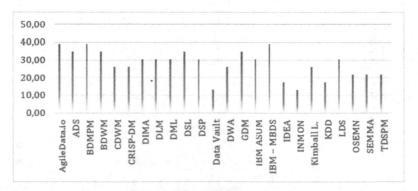

Fig. 1. Step 1: Percentage of methodologies compared to phases.

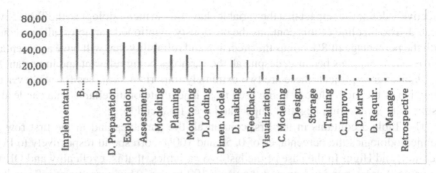

Fig. 2. Step 1: Percentage of phases compared to methodologies.

- The maintenance variable is described as the frequency and intensity with which the data methodology requires maintenance interventions, in order to guarantee its effectiveness, stability and updating.
- Scalability - reflects the ability of the methodology to deal with large volumes of data, in order to be applied in different contexts and situations.
- Precision - allows measuring the accuracy of the results produced by the methodology, that is, how close are the results obtained to the expected or actual results.
- Speed - considers the speed of data processing, which is reflected in the efficiency of the methodology, especially when time is a critical factor.
- Flexibility - measures the ability of the methodology to adapt to different types of data, different problems and scenarios.
- Reliability - measures the ability of the methodology to produce consistent and accurate results in different contexts.
- Explainability - measures the ability of a methodology to explain its results, this variable seeks to maintain transparency.
- Interpretability - translates the ability of a methodology to allow data to be easily interpreted.
- Cyclicity - identifies whether the methodology follows a cycle that allows regression of phase if necessary.
- OLAP - technology that allows you to analyze large volumes of data quickly and interactively, facilitating decision making, and the OLAP variable represents whether or not the methodologies support OLAP technology.

In the follow-up, all methodologies were analyzed, and the Table 5 was created, which records its performance according to the variable to be analyzed. For the analysis process, a systematic approach was taken to allow the evaluation of each of the variables mentioned in relation to each methodology mentioned. With this approach, the objective was to collect, analyze and interpret information in order to be able to identify the impact that the variables have on the methodologies. For each variable, information on its relationship with the methodology in question was sought. To obtain this information, various sources were used, such as articles, reports, books, websites, documents provided by the creators of the methodologies, among other reliable sources. In addition to these sources, all previous knowledge regarding each methodology was considered. In order to effectively define the impact that the variables have on the methodologies, the Table 5 was created. The first line of this contains the previously mentioned variables, all associated with the percentage of 8% minus the precision and reliability that will have a percentage of 10%. This happens because, despite all the variables being relevant and important for any data science project, these are two extremely important variables for whatever the objective of the methodology being used is, as inaccurate or unreliable data can lead to results with a very high negative impact and even financial losses.

The Table 5 contains in the first column all the variables and in the first row all the methodologies the percentages of 0, 50 and 100% correspond respectively to Low, Medium, and High. In the case of the last two variables, that is, cyclicality and OLAP, the value 0 corresponds to no and the value 100 to yes. This percentage reflects how much greater the impact of the variables on the methodologies is, with 100 representing a greater impact and 0 a smaller one, however for some of the variables it is favorable to have a great impact, namely for usability, scalability, accuracy, speed, flexibility, reliability, explainability, interpretability, cyclicality and OLAP, but for others the same does not happen, for example with cost and maintenance, as high cost and high maintenance are negative factors. For this reason and to make everything fairer, the percentages of the cost and maintenance variables will be presented the other way around, that is, the percentage of 100 will correspond to a low cost/maintenance and the percentage 0 to a high cost/maintenance.

Table 5 includes a column named total that represents the sum of the product of the percentages of the variables with the percentage corresponding to the methodologies.

In Table 5 it can be seen that the methodologies that stand out the most in terms of the range of variables are AgileData.io and IBM – Base Methodology for Data Science with 79% of them. AgileData.io stands out as it has high speed, great flexibility, reliability, explainability, interpretability, it is cyclic, it supports OLAP and, in the other variables, it is average, namely in cost, usability, maintenance, scalability and accuracy. IBM – Base Methodology for Data Science is also at the forefront due to its easy use, its high level of scalability, precision, explainability, interpretability, for being a cyclic methodology and for supporting OLAP, for its time, it does not reach a total of 100% since the variables cost, maintenance, speed, flexibility and reliability only act sufficiently in this tool.

Still above 70% are three methodologies, TDSP with 76%, CRISP-DM with 75% and Cloud Data Warehouse Methodology with 71%. The first, that is, the TDSP, stood out for being the methodology that has more than 100% in its composition, with this percentage in the variables usability, scalability, precision, flexibility, reliability, explainability, cyclicality and OLAP, however not ranks first in the total ranking of methodologies, as it has very high implementation and maintenance costs, requires a lot of resources for its maintenance, and its speed and interpretability are considered reasonable. Taking into account the CRISP-DM methodology, it presents very positive values in the usability, precision, explainability, interpretability, cyclicity and OLAP variables, and satisfactory values in the remaining variables, that is, in cost, maintenance, scalability, speed, flexibility and reliability. The last methodology of this group of three, the Cloud Data Warehouse Methodology, presents a total of 71% of the variables since it has a low cost of implementation and maintenance, proves to be easy to use, the accuracy of its

Table 5. Classification of methodologies according to variables

	Costs (8%)	Usability (8%)	Maintenance (8%)	Scalability (8%)	Precision (10%)	Velocity (8%)	Flexibility (8%)	Reliability (10%)	Explainability (8%)	Interpretability (8%)	Cyclicity (8%)	OLAP (8%)	Total (%)
AgileData.io	50	50	50	50	50	100	100	100	100	100	100	100	79
ADS	0	50	50	50	100	50	50	50	100	100	100	0	59
BDMPM	100	100	100	50	100	50	50	100	0	0	100	0	64
BDWM	50	50	50	50	50	50	50	50	0	0	0	0	44
CDWM	100	100	50	50	100	50	50	50	50	50	100	100	71
CRISP-DM	50	100	50	50	100	50	50	50	100	100	100	100	75
DIMA	100	0	100	50	100	50	100	50	100	50	0	100	67
DLM	0	100	50	50	100	50	50	50	100	50	0	0	51
DML	100	100	50	50	50	50	50	50	100	50	0	0	54
DSL	100	50	50	50	50	50	50	50	0	50	0	0	42
DSP	100	50	50	50	100	50	50	50	0	50	0	0	47
Data Vault	0	100	0	100	100	50	100	100	0	50	100	100	68
DWA	0	50	50	50	100	50	50	50	50	50	100	0	51
GDM	0	50	50	50	50	50	50	50	50	50	0	0	38
IBM ASUM	0	50	50	100	50	100	50	50	50	50	100	100	62
IBM – MBDS	50	100	50	100	100	50	50	50	100	100	100	100	79
IDEA	50	100	50	50	50	50	50	50	0	50	0	100	50
INMON	50	100	50	50	50	100	50	50	0	0	100	100	58
Kimball L	50	50	50	50	100	50	50	50	0	0	100	100	50
KDD	100	100	50	50	50	50	50	50	0	50	100	0	59
LDS	100	50	50	50	50	50	50	50	0	50	100	0	50
OSEMN	100	100	50	50	50	50	50	50	50	50	100	0	58
SEMMA	100	100	50	50	50	50	50	50	50	50	100	0	58
TDSPM	0	100	0	100	100	50	100	100	100	50	100	100	76

data is high, is cyclic and supports OLAP technology. This methodology is not completely guaranteed in terms of variables maintenance, scalability, speed and flexibility, reliability, explainability and interpretability, however they are not variables that can be discarded, there are only other methodologies that give more relevance to these variables than the Cloud Data Warehouse Methodology.

All other methodologies are below 70%, and finally, the methodology with the worst rating is Guided Data Mining. This methodology is not cyclical, does not support OLAP technology and has also shown a high cost of implementation and maintenance. This added to the fact that all other variables, ie usability, maintainability, scalability, accuracy, speed, flexibility, reliability, explainability and interpretability, were satisfactory, resulted in 38%.

4.3 Third Step

After evaluating the twenty-four methodologies according to their phases and the variables they support, the third phase has the purpose of joining the classifications obtained in the analysis of the phases and in the analysis of the variables, in order to identify the most complete. Then, it was considered more important that the methodology covers more variables than phases, that is, a methodology with few phases, but that meets all the variables is more effective than the opposite, that is, a methodology with many phases that cannot satisfy all the variables, so to proceed to the final classification of the methodologies, it was understood that the total classification of the phases is equivalent to 40% and the classification of the variables to 60%.

To support the total classification of methodologies, Table 6 was created, which is composed of four columns and four sub columns. The first column consists of all methodologies sorted alphabetically. The second column, named Classification of Phases, represents the classification of methodologies according to the number of phases that compose it. This column is made up of two sub-columns, the first entitled 100%, in which the percentage shown comes from the number of phases that the methodology has, considering the total number of existing phases, which, remember, are twenty-three. In turn, the second sub column, whose name is 40%, identifies the 40% of the methodology's total classification in terms of phases. The third column corresponds to the classification of the variables, this column also contains two sub-columns. The first contains the total percentage of methodologies taking into account the variables, and the second comprises 60% of the value to its left. The fourth and last column represents the total classification and the sum of the 40% that comes from the second sub column of the classification of the phases with the 60% that comes from the second sub column of the classification of the variables.

In Table 6 it can be seen that the best ranked methodologies with 63.05% were AgileData.io and IBM – Base Methodology for Data Science, both had a total percentage of 39.13 in the phase analysis and 79% in the analysis of the variables. Then, in second place, is the CRISP-DM methodology with 55.44%. In third place with a percentage of 54.30 is the TDSP methodology and even after, in fourth place and with 54.05%, is the Business Dimensional Model and Predictive Methodology. With less than 1%, that is, with 53.04%, the Cloud Data Warehouse Methodology appears in fifth place and, shortly after, with 52.37% and in sixth place, the methodology Data Integration Methodology

Table 6. Total classification of methodologies.

Methodologies	Phases	Variables		Total	
	100%	40%	100%	60%	100%
AgileData.io	39,13%	15,65%	79,00%	47,40%	63,05%
ADS	34,78%	13,91%	59,00%	35,40%	49,31%
BDMPM	39,13%	15,65%	64,00%	38,40%	54,05%
BDWM	34,78%	13,91%	44,00%	26,40%	40,31%
CDWM	26,09%	10,44%	71,00%	42,60%	53,04%
CRISP-DM	26,09%	10,44%	75,00%	45,00%	55,44%
DIMA	30,43%	12,17%	67,00%	40,20%	52,37%
DLM	30,43%	12,17%	51,00%	30,60%	42,77%
DML	30,43%	12,17%	54,00%	32,40%	44,57%
DSL	34,78%	13,91%	42,00%	25,20%	39,11%
DSP	30,43%	12,17%	47,00%	28,20%	40,37%
Data Vault	13,04%	5,22%	68,00%	40,80%	46,80%
DWA	26,09%	10,44%	51,00%	30,60%	41,04%
GDM	34,78%	13,91%	38,00%	22,80%	36,71%
IBM ASUM	30,43%	12,17%	62,00%	37,20%	49,37%
IBM – MBDS	39,13%	15,65%	79,00%	47,40%	63,05%
IDEA	17,39%	6,96%	50,00%	30,00%	36,96%
INMON	13,04%	5,22%	58,00%	34,80%	40,02%
Kimball L	26,09%	10,44%	50,00%	30,00%	40,44%
KDD	17,39%	6,96%	59,00%	35,40%	42,36%
LDS	30,43%	12,17%	50,00%	30,00%	42,17%
OSEMN	21,74%	8,70%	58,00%	34,80%	43,50%
SEMMA	21,74%	8,70%	58,00%	34,80%	43,50%
TDSPM	21,74%	8,70%	76,00%	45,60%	54,30%

for Analytics. Subsequently, in seventh, is IBM Analytics Solution Unified Method with 49.37% and even after, in eighth and with 49.31% Agile Data Science. With 46.80% and in ninth place is Data Vault and, already with a beautiful difference, that is, with 44.57%, Dimensional Modeling Lifecycle methodologies are placed in tenth. In eleventh are two methodologies, these being OSEMN and SEMMA, with 43.50%. Subsequently, Data Lake Methodology is in twelfth place with 42.77% and, shortly after, in thirteenth place with 42.36% is Knowledge Discovery in Databases. Still around 42%, specifically, with 42.17% is Lean Data Science in fourteenth place.

The Data Warehouse Automation methodology ranks fifteenth in this ranking with 41.04%. Next, with 40.44% is Kimball Lifecycle in sixteenth and, in seventeenth, with

40.37% is Data Science Process. Soon after, with 40.31%, Big Data Warehouse Methodology is in eighteenth place and, not far away, with 40.02%, maintaining the nineteenth place, is INMON. The remaining three methodologies failed to reach even 40% in their rankings, with Data Science Lifecycle coming in twentieth with 39.11%, IDEA in twenty-first with 36.96% and, finally, Guided Data Mining in twenty second with 36.71%.

5 Discussion

Given the purpose of this study, mentioned in the introduction of this document, which is the identification of the most complete methodology, it was found that the most comprehensive methodologies at the level of the phases were AgileData.io, the Business Dimensional Model and Predictive Methodology and the IBM – Base Methodology for Data Science with nine phases each, which corresponds to 39.13% compared to the total number of phases, and then, with eight phases (34.78%) there are the methodologies Agile Data Science, Big Data Warehouse Methodology, Data Science Lifecycle and Guided Data Mining. On the contrary, that is, with less complete methodologies with regard to the phases, INMON and Data Vault were identified with only 3 steps, which corresponds to 13.04% of the total phases. Regarding the scope of the methodologies regarding the variables cost, usability, maintenance, scalability, precision, speed, flexibility, reliability, explainability, interpretability, cyclicity and support of OLAP technology, it was found that the most evident methodologies were the AgileData.io and the IBM – Base Methodology for Data Science with 79%, TDSP with 76%, CRISP-DM with 75% and Cloud Data Warehouse Methodology with 71%. On the other hand, that is, the ones that were most negatively evidenced were Guided Data Mining with 38%, Data Science Lifecycle with 42%, Big Data Warehouse Methodology with 44%, and Data Science Process with 47%.

That said, the methodologies that obtained the best ratings were AgileData.io and IBM – Base Methodology for Data Science, both with the same classification of 63.05% in terms of phases and variables. These two methodologies showed similar behavior throughout all the analyzes carried out, having always obtained the same evaluations. What effectively distinguishes these two methodologies is the fact that AgileData.o is faster, more flexible and reliable, while IBM – Base Methodology for Data Science is more user friendly, scalable and accurate. The worst ranked were the IDEA methodologies with 36.96% and the Guided Data Mining with 36.71%, both proved to be not very rigorous in terms of their phases and variables.

Analyzing the benchmarking results, the methodologies AgileData.io and IBM – Base Methodology for Data Science, which are the best classified, contain only 63.03% of the final quotation, which indicates that, despite their classification, they still remain below what is expected when talking about a complete methodology. These methodologies proved to be the most demanding and ambitious, having a good composition of phases and an interesting integration of variables. Even so, it is possible to verify in this study that the AgileData.io methodology stands out in relation to IBM – Base Methodology for Data Science, since it can be used both in analytical and predictive projects, while the latter contains in its constitution phases that make it only usable in predictive projects. It should also be noted that the objective would never be for the methodology to obtain a 100% assessment, since a methodology with twenty-three phases in its composition would not be optimized, but a quotation above 75% in its entirety would be expected, with a reasonable number of phases, that is, between 6 and 10, and its variables the highest possible quotation.

6 Conclusion

Although, worldwide, there are some methodologies, in this study it was possible to gather twenty-four. The analysis process was relatively simple, but laborious, due to the peculiarities of each methodology. Throughout the research process many were the methodologies that contained a vast number of support materials, and even more were the ones that there was almost no information about it. Some were inappropriate or nonintuitive, bringing complications with regard to the collection of information, particularly in the second phase.

In the first phase, no conclusion was drawn, since the number of phases that make up the methodology does not add much value to the final result, however this analysis was important in the sense of identifying the most complete methodology and the guidelines that guide it. The second phase was more enriching in terms of adding value and important conclusions, given that it was possible, through this, to identify the methodologies that have the best conditions in their composition, both in terms of implementation and in terms of the results obtained with the same.

Thus, based on this article, it can be concluded that the results obtained are in accordance with the requirements, in the sense that the most complete methodologies were identified, with 63.03%. However, these did not exceed expectations, as none of them was complete enough. Both AgileData.io and IBM – Base Methodology for Data Science can be integrated into data science projects, however, for different reasons, they can at any time fall short of expectations. That said, the future work is to start the idealization of what would be a complete and comprehensive methodology for any data-scientific project, be it able to support different type of projects: predictive, analytical, Data Analytics, Data Mining, Business Intelligence, Data Warehousing, Big Data, Machine Learning or of Data Visualization.

This future study could begin by identifying the essential and sufficient phases for projects of any type of data science. Regarding the variables, the work involves identifying what each methodology is supposed to contain so that it can present good classifications. In addition, and taking into account that this study was based on reading documents, that is, on theoretical research, it would be a future advantage if there was also a practical comparison between the methodologies.

Acknowledgement. This work has been supported by FCT – Fundação para a Ciência e Tecnologia within the R&D Units Project Scope: UIDB/00319/2020.

References

1. Azevedo, A., Santos, M.F.: KDD, semma and CRISP-DM: a parallel overview. IADIS European Conference on Data Mining, pp. 182–185 (2008). http://recipp.ipp.pt/bitstream/10400.22/136/3/KDD-CRISP-SEMMA.pdf
2. Shafique, U., Qaiser, H.: A comparative study of data mining process models (KDD, CRISP-DM and SEMMA). Int. J. Innov. Sci. Res. **12**(1), 217–222 (2014). http://www.ijisr.issr-journals.org/
3. Yessad, L., Labiod, A.: Comparative study of data warehouses modeling approaches: Inmon, Kimball and data vault. In: 2016 International Conference on System Reliability and Science ICSRS 2016 - Proceedings, pp. 95–99 (2017). https://doi.org/10.1109/ICSRS.2016.7815845
4. AgileData.io Limited. AGILEDATA.IO. agiledata.io (2023). https://agiledata.io/
5. Di Tria, F., Lefons, E., Tangorra, F.: A proposal of methodology for designing big data warehouses. Preprints, no. June, p. 2018. https://doi.org/10.20944/preprints201806.0219.v1
6. Paneque, M., del M. Roldán-García, M., García-Nieto, J.: e-LION: data integration semantic model to enhance predictive analytics in e-learning. Expert Syst. Appl. **213**, 118892 (2023). https://doi.org/10.1016/j.eswa.2022.118892
7. Sawadogo, P., Darmont, J.: On data lake architectures and metadata management. J. Intell. Inf. Syst. **56**(1), 97–120 (2021). https://doi.org/10.1007/s10844-020-00608-7
8. Haertel, C., Pohl, M., Staegemann, D., Turowski, K.: Project artifacts for the data science lifecycle: a comprehensive overview. In: Proceedings of - 2022 IEEE International Conference on Big Data (Big Data) 2022, pp. 2645–2654 (2022). https://doi.org/10.1109/BigData55660.2022.10020291
9. geeksforgeeks. Data science process. geeksforgeeks (2023). https://www.geeksforgeeks.org/data-science-process/
10. Campos, L.: A complete guide to data mining and how to use it. HubSpot (2023). https://blog.hubspot.com/website/data-mining
11. IBM. IBM analytics solution unified method. IBM (2015). http://i2t.icesi.edu.co/ASUM-DM_External/index.htm#cognos.external.asum-DM_Teaser/deliveryprocesses/ASUM-DM_8A5C87D5.html
12. Ceri, S., Fraternali, P.: The story of the idea methodology. In: Olivé, A., Pastor, J.A. (eds.) CAiSE 1997. LNCS, vol. 1250, pp. 1–17. Springer, Heidelberg (1997). https://doi.org/10.1007/3-540-63107-0_1
13. Grady, N.W., Payne, J.A., Parker, H.: Agile big data analytics: analyticsops for data science. In: Proceedings of - 2017 IEEE International Conference on Big Data (Big Data) 2017, vol. 2018-Janua, pp. 2331–2339 (2017). https://doi.org/10.1109/BigData.2017.8258187
14. Rollins, J.B.: Metodologia de base para ciência de dados. IBM Anal. Route 100 Somers, NY 10589 (2015). https://www.ibm.com/downloads/cas/B1WQ0GM2
15. Lean. Agile framework for managing data science product and projects. leands.ai (2023). https://leands.ai/
16. Kumari, K., Bhardwaj, M., Sharma, S.: OSEMN approach for real time data analysis. Int. J. Eng. Manag. Res. **10**(02), 107–110 (2020). https://doi.org/10.31033/ijemr.10.2.11
17. Microsoft. What is the Team Data Science Process?. Microsoft (2023). https://learn.microsoft.com/en-us/azure/architecture/data-science-process/overview
18. Astera Software. Automação de data warehouse. Astera.com (2023). https://www.astera.com/pt/knowledge-center/data-warehouse-automation-a-complete-guide/
19. IBM. Dimensional modeling life cycle and work flow. ibm.com (2021). https://www.ibm.com/docs/en/ida/9.1.2?topic=modeling-dimensional-life-cycle-work-flow

Characteristics of Word-of-Mouth (WOM) by the Interaction Between Feedback Willingness and Incentivized WOM Willingness

Takumi Kato[ID] and Toshikuni Sato[✉][ID]

P Meiji University, 1-1, Kanda Surugadai, Chiyoda-Ku, Tokyo 101-8301, Japan
{takumi_kato,tsato}@meiji.ac.jp

Abstract. When designing products/services based on the knowledge obtained by analyzing word-of-mouth (WOM), it is important to remove excessive assertions, both positive and negative. Strong emotions such as affection for a company or a desire for revenge can lead to overestimation. Therefore, it is useful to understand the characteristics of WOM via posting motivation. However, the existing research on WOM contributors is limited to their motives for posting, and there are few examples of examining the influence of motives on the characteristics of WOM. Targeting the Japanese hotel industry, this study clarified those brought about by feedback willingness for companies and incentivized WOM willingness. Hierarchical clustering was applied to the WOM collected in an online survey to classify motivations, and multiple regression analysis was applied. The results revealed that only incentivized WOM willingness increased word count and positive words. In addition, when the intentions of both feedback and incentive posts were high, the total number of characters increased, but the number of positive words decreased. In other words, we speculate that those who want to improve the services through feedback to companies will emphasize the negative aspects. However, even with the positive comments, it is the price that needs attention. WOMs that praise low prices are more common among those with lower loyalty. It is important for practitioners to adopt the method of classifying WOM posting motivations presented herein and to identify consumers who send useful WOMs.

Keywords: Hotel Industry · Word-of-mouth Communications · Motivation

1 Introduction

Comprehending word-of-mouth (WOM) that is helpful for customers and applying such knowledge to the development of products/services is a source of competitiveness for companies [1]. Practitioners are well aware of this, and design products/services based on the knowledge obtained by collecting and analyzing WOMs [2]. At such time, it is important to remove excessive assertions and evaluations, both positive and negative, so as not to be misled by them [3]. For example, consumers with strong negative attitudes toward companies actively post negative WOMs with the aim of taking revenge [4, 5].

© The Author(s), under exclusive license to Springer Nature Switzerland AG 2024
T. Guarda et al. (Eds.): ARTIIS 2023, CCIS 1935, pp. 547–560, 2024.
https://doi.org/10.1007/978-3-031-48858-0_43

It is highly likely that such WOMs do not provide advice aimed at improving products/services, but attack them on all sides regardless of the facts. Conversely, attachment to a company is aimed at supporting that company and promotes positive WOM postings [6, 7]. If practitioners take such strongly biased opinions seriously, there is a risk that they will find it difficult to design appropriate products and services. Hence, it is important to understand the motivations of WOM contributors and their WOM characteristics.

However, existing research often focuses on the impact of WOM on readers rather than authors [8]. Understanding the underlying psychological mechanisms of those who post WOM can help companies empathize with their consumers and use their messages to create value [9, 10]. Existing research on WOM authors focuses primarily on motivation. Evolving from the earliest studies [11], the motivations of positive and negative WOM have recently been recognized as distinct [12]. There are five main positive motivations: product involvement [13, 14], altruism [15, 16], self-enhancement [17, 18], support for companies [6, 7, 19, 20], and financial incentives [21, 22]. Of these, the first three are consumer-to-consumer incentives, and the last two are contributor-business incentives. The focus here is on support for companies and financial incentives in positive WOM.

We clarified the characteristics of WOM brought about by feedback willingness for companies and incentivized WOM willingness. Previous studies have been limited to clarifying the motivations of posters, but the current study extends academic knowledge to the influence of motivations on WOM. In addition, practitioners can know the biases hidden in WOM, making it easier to extract truly meaningful WOM.

2 Related Work and Hypothesis Development

There are mainly five motivations for posting positive WOMs.

Product Involvement: Personal interest in products/services, and the excitement caused by the experience, are basic motivations for consumers to engage in positive WOM [13]. Consumers post their emotions on social media because they enjoy being involved with the product [14].

Altruism: Altruism is the act of doing something for others without expecting anything in return [13]. Altruism serves to promote more positive WOM [15]. People naturally derive satisfaction from helping others overcome difficulties. Helping community members make better purchasing decisions by posting their own experiences on WOM is sufficiently motivating [16].

Self-Enhancement: The desire to advertise one's superiority over others increases the motivation for WOM communication [17]. This is because WOM on positive and successful experiences can serve as a signal of the poster's expertise [18].

Support for Companies: The motivation to support companies with positive WOM has two meanings. One is the motivation to spread positive WOM postings to support companies to which they are attached [6, 7]. The other is providing feedback to improve their products/services [19]. Consumers view social media as a platform for receiving responses from businesses, and there is indeed a dialogue loop between businesses and customers [20]. Therefore, this study formulated the following hypotheses.

H1–1: Feedback willingness for companies has a positive impact on WOM word count.

H1–2: Feedback willingness for companies positively affects WOM positive word count.

Financial Incentives: Financial incentives influence WOM submissions [21]. Satisfaction does not necessarily increase the likelihood of WOM submissions. Satisfied customers are a necessary but not sufficient condition for posting positive WOMs, so incentives are an effective way to encourage satisfied customers to post WOMs [22]. Therefore, the following hypotheses were derived.

H2–1: Incentivized WOM willingness positively influences WOM word count.

H2–2: Incentivized WOM willingness positively affects the number of positive words in WOM.

Furthermore, the two may exhibit synergistic effects. Accordingly, the following hypotheses were derived.

H3–1: The interaction between feedback willingness for companies and incentivized WOM willingness has a positive effect on the number of words in WOM.

H3–2: The interaction between feedback willingness for companies and incentivized WOM willingness positively affects the number of positive words in WOM.

3   Method

3.1   Survey

We conducted an online survey of 3,000 hotel users in Japan from November 10th to 17th, 2022. Among them, 2,892 respondents were used for the analysis after excluding respondents with a small sample size of "junior high school graduates" and "others" in terms of educational background. The following survey items were utilized; (1) gender, (2) age, (3) marital status, (4) presence of children, (5) educational background, (6) household income, (7) use of hotels within a month, (8) purpose of use of the hotel, (9) WOM intention for the hotel (WOM post intention, feedback willingness for companies, incentivized WOM willingness), (10) loyalty indices for the hotel (perceived quality, satisfaction, repurchase intention, recommendation intention), (11) WOM for the hotel. (1)-(6) are basic attributes, and (7)-(8) are hotel usage. (9) corresponds to the study hypotheses, and sample items include: "I love telling others about my experience with this hotel brand," "I would like to provide feedback to companies about my experience with this hotel brand," "Given the financial incentive, I would share my experience with this hotel brand." Options (9) and (10) are rated on a five-point Likert scale (e.g., 1 = Definitely disagree, 5 = Definitely agree). (11) is an open-ended answer. Respondent attributes are presented in Table 1.

3.2   Text Mining for WOM

Natural language processing was used to extract the factors from the WOM for the hotel. As reported in Table 2, five factors and ten words belonging to them were defined

Table 1. Respondent attributes.

Item	Breakdown	Number of Respondents	Ratio
Gender	Male	1,444	49.9%
	Female	1,448	50.1%
Age	20s	446	15.4%
	30s	631	21.8%
	40s	591	20.4%
	50s	630	21.8%
	60s	594	20.5%
Marital status	Unmarried	1,096	37.9%
	Married	1,796	62.1%
Presence of children	No	1,464	50.6%
	Yes	1,428	49.4%
Educational background	High school	450	15.6%
	Junior college	630	21.8%
	University	1,587	54.9%
	Graduate school	225	7.8%
Household income	< 4 m¥	681	23.5%
	4 − 6 m¥	652	22.5%
	6 − 8 m¥	541	18.7%
	8 − 10 m¥	443	15.3%
	10 − 12 m¥	243	8.4%
	12 − 15 m¥	162	5.6%
	15 m¥ ≦	170	5.9%
Purpose of use of the hotel	Business	604	20.9%
	Leisure	2,288	79.1%

based on the frequency of their appearance in the data. The first is a factor related to the direct positive expression. The second to fifth are key factors for the hotel industry (location, price, cleanliness, comfort). A total of ten of the most frequent adjectives related to each factor were set as words (only positive). When any of these registered words were detected in the text, the mention flag (0/1) of the corresponding factor was added. Therefore, if multiple words belonging to the same factor were mentioned multiple times in one text, the flag remained as 1 (i.e., the number of occurrences was counted as 1). As indicated in Table 2, the most frequent factor was F1_Good, which was detected in 757 out of 2,892 responses. Japanese open-source software MeCab was used for morphological analysis and CaboCha was used for parsing.

Table 2. Detection words for each factor.

No	F1_Good	F2_Accessible	F3_Affordable	F4_Clean	F5_Comfortable
1	good	close	affordable	clean	comfortable
2	satisfied	well-located	cheap	beautiful	convenient
3	awesome	accessible	inexpensive	new	helpful
4	fulfilling	downtown	low-price	renovated	quiet
5	wonderful	direct connection	cost performance	fresh	relaxing
6	happy	convenience store	reasonable	spotless	roomy
7	nice	station	privilege	unsullied	cozy
8	fun	parking	free	immaculate	comfy
9	attractive	Disney Resort	discount	pure	safety
10	favorable	Universal Studios	point	brand-new	worry-free
Number of people mentioning each factor	757	153	333	376	276

3.3 Verification

A list of variables used for verification is presented in Table 3. Word_Count indicates the number of words in WOM, and mention dummy (Nos. 16–20 in Table 3) indicates whether each factor is mentioned. Positive_Word_Count is the sum of all mention dummies. As previously mentioned, it is important to remove excessive evaluations that arise from a strong attachment to companies and a desire for revenge. Hence, using the three variables of WOM intention for the hotel (Nos. 8–10), hierarchical clustering was performed to detect people who were biased toward positive and negative. The number of clusters was determined by gap statistics [23].

After excluding clusters with biased evaluations, the hypotheses were verified via multiple regression analysis. In H1–1, H2–1, and H3–1, Model 1 was built with Word_Count (No. 15) as the objective variable, the interaction of Feedback (No. 9), Incentive (No. 10) as the explanatory variable, and the attribute (Nos. 1–7) as the control variables. In H1–2, H2–2, and H3–2, under the same conditions for the explanatory and control variables, Model 2 was built with Positive_Word_Count (No. 21) as the objective variable. Variables were selected stepwise. The analysis environment is statistical analysis software R version 3.6.3.

4 Results

As illustrated in Fig. 1, the number of clusters was set to five considering gap statistics and interpretability. As presented in Fig. 2, the clusters in the dendrogram derived via hierarchical clustering are separated by red lines. The average value of each variable for each cluster is presented in Table 4. In WOM intention for the hotel, Cluster 2 is positive, and Cluster 4 is negative. The reasons for this are evident in the Loyalty Indices, each of which has a prominent attitude toward brands. Cluster 2 (Cluster 4) tends to increase (decrease) the word count and respond positively (negatively) to each factor. Additionally, in Fig. 3, the word count distributions of Clusters 2 and 3 are similar, while in Table 4, the contents of brand loyalty and WOM are significantly different between the two. The results of multiple comparison of Word_Count and Positive_Word_Count are reported in Tables 5 and 6, respectively.

Table 3. Variable list.

No	Variable	Description	Type	Mean	SD
1	Female	Female dummy	0/1	0.501	0.500
2	Age	Age	1:20s, …, 5:60s	3.102	1.366
3	Married	Married dummy	0/1	0.621	0.485
4	Children	Having children dummy	0/1	0.494	0.500
5	Education	Educational background	1: High school, 2: Junior college, 3: University, 4: Graduate school	2.549	0.845
6	Income	Household income	1: < 4 m¥, 2: 4 − 6 m¥, 3: 6 − 8 m¥, 4: 8 − 10 m¥, 5: 10 − 12 m¥, 6: 12 − 15 m¥, 7: 15 m¥ ≦	3.028	1.761
7	Business	Business purpose dummy	0/1	0.209	0.407
8	WOM	Degree of WOM post intention	5-point Likert scale	3.073	1.008

(continued)

Table 3. (*continued*)

No	Variable	Description	Type	Mean	SD
9	Feedback	Degree of feedback willingness for companies	5-point Likert scale	2.981	1.006
10	Incentive	Degree of incentivized WOM willingness	5-point Likert scale	3.314	1.067
11	Perceived_Quality	Degree of perceived quality	5-point Likert scale	3.844	0.846
12	Satisfaction	Degree of satisfaction	5-point Likert scale	3.540	0.971
13	Repurchase	Degree of repurchase intention	5-point Likert scale	3.376	1.031
14	Recommendation	Degree of recommendation	5-point Likert scale	3.536	0.972
15	Word_Count	Word count in WOM	Number (1–437)	33.886	41.864
16	F1_Good	Mention dummy for each factor	0/1	0.262	0.440
17	F2_Accessible		0/1	0.053	0.224
18	F3_Affordable		0/1	0.115	0.319
19	F4_Clean		0/1	0.130	0.336
20	F5_Comfortable		0/1	0.095	0.294
21	Positive_Word_Count	Sum of Nos.16–20	Number (0–5)	0.655	0.841

Data from 2,055 people were used for verification, excluding Cluster 2 with positive bias and Cluster 4 with negative bias. As presented in Table 7, Incentive in Model 1 has a significant positive relationship with Word_Count at the 5% level. Although no significant relationship was found for Feedback, a significant positive effect was confirmed for the interaction between the two. As illustrated in Fig. 4, people with high scores for both feedback willingness for companies and incentivized WOM willingness tend to have higher WOM word counts. Similarly, in Model 2, there is a significant positive relationship with Positive_Word_Count only for Incentive. Contrary to assumptions, the interaction was a significant negative relationship, and people with high scores for both feedback willingness for companies and incentivized WOM willingness tended to have lower WOM positive word counts. Based on the above, H1–1, H1–2, and H3–2 were not supported, and H2–1, H2–2, and H3–1 were supported. Note that H3–2 was rejected because the interaction was a negative effect.

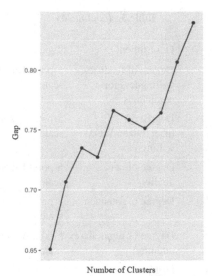

Fig. 1. Gap statistics by cluster.

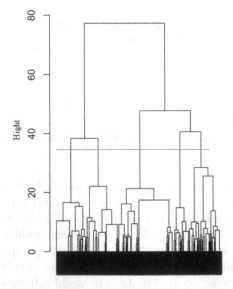

Fig. 2. Dendrogram by hierarchical clustering.

5   Implications and Future Work

5.1   Practical Implications

This study provides three main practical suggestions. First, when using information obtained from WOM for service development, do not be misled by excessive assertions, both positive and negative. If there is a feeling of attachment or revenge toward the

Table 4. Deviation from overall data for each variable.

Category	Variable	Deviation from Total (Each Cluster − Total)				
		1	2	3	4	5
Variables used for cluster analysis	WOM	0.1%	40.9%	−9.0%	−49.7%	−9.7%
	Feedback	7.5%	33.1%	14.0%	−40.7%	−40.7%
	Incentive	−16.9%	29.8%	27.5%	−54.1%	−1.4%
Attribute Variables	Female	−5.7%	2.0%	−4.7%	0.2%	12.2%
	Age	1.4%	−3.2%	1.3%	2.9%	−1.7%
	Married	−2.7%	3.1%	1.8%	4.9%	−2.6%
	Children	−3.1%	1.3%	7.4%	1.6%	−3.6%
	Education	−1.2%	3.5%	−0.5%	0.2%	−1.1%
	Income	−2.3%	6.0%	4.6%	−3.0%	−5.2%
	Business	8.8%	−26.1%	−3.3%	20.2%	−.9%
Loyalty Indices	Perceived_Quality	−2.4%	14.4%	2.7%	−18.7%	−4.2%
	Satisfaction	−3.9%	20.0%	4.7%	−29.1%	−4.3%
	Repurchase	−2.6%	20.7%	6.5%	−28.7%	−9.1%
	Recommendation	−3.8%	20.3%	6.0%	−31.7%	−4.8%
Variables for WOM	Word_Count	−24.2%	28.6%	18.3%	−8.8%	−0.4%
	F1_Good	−9.6%	24.7%	6.0%	−32.8%	1.5%
	F2_Accessible	9.4%	−7.1%	−7.3%	−8.0%	1.8%
	F3_Affordable	−15.7%	−4.0%	27.8%	20.3%	−4.9%
	F4_Clean	−20.5%	22.8%	10.3%	−25.1%	14.6%
	F5_Comfortable	−23.1%	34.2%	2.8%	−21.5%	12.9%
	Positive_Word_Count	−13.3%	18.1%	9.1%	−18.3%	4.7%
Sample Size		968	570	530	267	557

company, there is a concern that it will be overestimated. Practitioners should judge whether WOM is an evaluation born from the heart or a biased evaluation born from strong emotions.

Second, lower prices have a negative impact on loyalty. In hotel services, price is evaluated against other factors. As reported in Table 4, Cluster 2, which has high loyalty, has few mentions of low prices, despite having many positive WOMs. Cluster 4, which has low loyalties, has many references to low prices, even though there are many negative WOMs. In other words, cheapness tends to attract customers with low loyalty without reinforcing loyalty. This is in line with existing literature [24]. Customers who accept high prices with low loyalty are more likely to complain loudly [25].

Third, consumers who are willing to give feedback to companies are an important source of WOM posts, both positive and negative. Feedback intentions can be enhanced

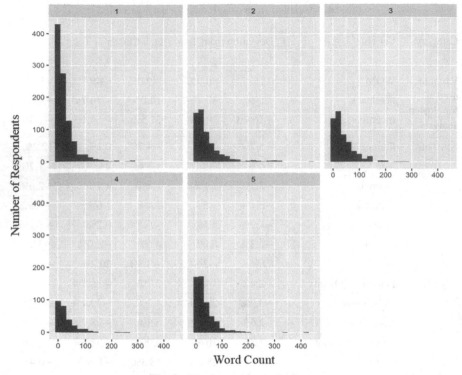

Fig. 3. Word count for each cluster.

Table 5. Results of multiple comparisons by Kruskal-Wallis test for Word_Count.

		Cluster			
		1	2	3	4
Cluster	2	< 0.000***	–	–	–
	3	< 0.000***	1.000	–	–
	4	0.027*	0.008**	0.002**	–
	5	< 0.000***	0.103	0.030*	1.000

Note: *** p < 0.001; ** p < 0.01; * p < 0.05

for companies that want to improve services by sending negative WOM [14, 26]. As a result, the interaction between feedback willingness and incentivized WOM willingness has a negative effect on positive WOM. In Table 3, Clusters 1 and 3 have high feedback intentions, but there is a noticeable tendency to transmit positive and negative WOM. These are thought to be serious responses to service rather than attitudes such as loyalty. Therefore, it is important for practitioners to adopt the method of cluster analysis presented in this study to identify consumers who transmit beneficial WOMs.

Table 6. Results of multiple comparisons by chi-square test for Positive_Word_Count.

		Cluster			
		1	2	3	4
Cluster	2	< 0.000***	–	–	–
	3	0.027*	1.000	–	–
	4	1.000	< 0.000***	0.012*	–
	5	0.053	1.000	1.000	0.018*

Note: *** p < 0.001; ** p < 0.01; * p < 0.05

Table 7. Results of multiple regression analysis including interactions.

Variable	Model 1 (Word_Count)				Model 2 (Positive_Word_Count)			
	Estimate	SE	p-value	VIF	Estimate	SE	p-value	VIF
Intercept	16.016	1.752	0.000 ***	–	0.336	0.067	0.000 ***	–
Female	13.462	1.661	0.000 ***	1.141	0.101	0.036	0.005 **	1.115
Married	3.340	1.602	0.037 *	1.009	−0.053	0.036	0.139	1.011
Business	-6.179	1.994	0.002 **	1.123	0.036	0.021	0.081	1.048
Feedback	1.653	0.916	0.071	1.025	−0.005	0.020	0.814	1.012
Incentive	2.794	0.881	0.002 **	1.011	0.050	0.020	0.011 *	1.025
Word_Count					0.006	0.000	0.000 ***	1.071
Positive_Word_Count	12.495	0.957	0.000 ***	1.023				
Feedback*Incentive	3.264	0.854	0.000 ***	1.012	−0.045	0.019	0.018 *	1.016
R-squared	0.143				0.100			

Note: *** p < 0.001; ** p < 0.01; * p < 0.05

5.2 Limitations and Future Work

This study is limited to word count as a characteristic of WOM given by feedback willingness for companies and incentivized WOM willingness. Others should be extended to other features such as rating distribution [27] and valence [28]. Existing research on WOM contributors is limited to their motives for posting, and there are still few examples of the effects of motives on WOM characteristics, so continued research is needed.

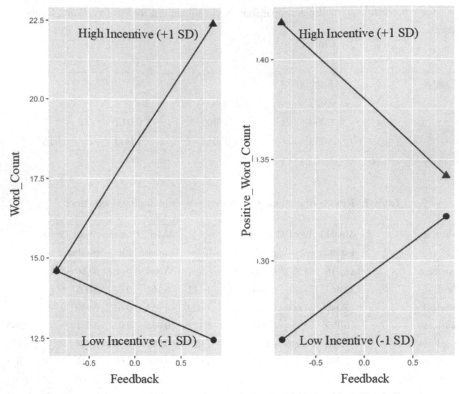

Fig. 4. Simple slope analysis (Left: Word_Count, Right: Positive_Word_Count).

Acknowledgement. The authors gratefully acknowledge the partial supports of JSPS KAKENHI Grant Number 22K13496.

References

1. Filieri, R.: What makes online reviews helpful? A diagnosticity-adoption framework to explain informational and normative influences in e-WOM. J. Bus. Res. **68**(6), 1261–1270 (2015). https://doi.org/10.1016/j.jbusres.2014.11.006
2. Barton, B.: Ratings, reviews & ROI: How leading retailers use customer word of mouth in marketing and merchandising. J. Interact. Advert. **7**(1), 5–50 (2006). https://doi.org/10.1080/15252019.2006.10722125
3. Kumar, V., Aksoy, L., Donkers, B., Venkatesan, R., Wiesel, T., Tillmanns, S.: Undervalued or overvalued customers: capturing total customer engagement value. J. Serv. Res. **13**(3), 297–310 (2010). https://doi.org/10.1177/1094670510375602
4. Sohaib, M., Akram, U., Hui, P., Rasool, H., Razzaq, Z., Kaleem Khan, M.: Electronic word-of-mouth generation and regulatory focus. Asia Pac. J. Mark. Logist. **32**(1), 23–45 (2020). https://doi.org/10.1108/APJML-06-2018-0220
5. Wen-Hai, C., Yuan, C.Y., Liu, M.T., Fang, J.F.: The effects of outward and inward negative emotions on consumers' desire for revenge and negative word of mouth. Online Inf. Rev. **43**(5), 818–841 (2019). https://doi.org/10.1108/OIR-03-2016-0069

6. Wolny, J., Mueller, C.: Analysis of fashion consumers' motives to engage in electronic word-of-mouth communication through social media platforms. J. Mark. Manag. **29**(5–6), 562–583 (2013). https://doi.org/10.1080/0267257X.2013.778324

7. Loureiro, S.M.C., Kaufmann, H.R.: The role of online brand community engagement on positive or negative self-expression word-of-mouth. Cogent Bus. Manag. **5**(1), 1508543 (2018). https://doi.org/10.1080/23311975.2018.1508543

8. Nam, K., Baker, J., Ahmad, N., Goo, J.: Determinants of writing positive and negative electronic word-of-mouth: empirical evidence for two types of expectation confirmation. Decis. Support. Syst. **129**, 113168 (2020). https://doi.org/10.1016/j.dss.2019.113168

9. Chen, Z., Yuan, M.: Psychology of word of mouth marketing. Curr. Opin. Psychol. **31**, 7 (2020). https://doi.org/10.1016/j.copsyc.2019.06.026

10. Fine, M.B., Gironda, J., Petrescu, M.: Prosumer motivations for electronic word-of-mouth communication behaviors. J. Hosp. Tour. Technol. **8**(2), 280–295 (2017). https://doi.org/10.1108/JHTT-09-2016-0048

11. Dichter, E.: How word-of-mouth advertising works. Harv. Bus. Rev. **44**, 147–166 (1966)

12. Fu, J.R., Ju, P.H., Hsu, C.W.: Understanding why consumers engage in electronic word-of-mouth communication: perspectives from theory of planned behavior and justice theory. Electron. Commer. Res. Appl. **14**(6), 616–630 (2015). https://doi.org/10.1016/j.elerap.2015.09.003

13. Sundaram, D.S., Mitra, K., Webster, C.: Word-of-mouth communications: a motivational analysis. ACR North Am. Adv. **25**, 527–531 (1998)

14. Whiting, A., Williams, D.L., Hair, J.: Praise or revenge: why do consumers post about organizations on social media. J. Cetacean Res. Manag. **22**(2), 133–160 (2019). https://doi.org/10.1108/QMR-06-2017-0101

15. Previte, J., Russell-Bennett, R., Mulcahy, R., Hartel, C.: The role of emotional value for reading and giving eWOM in altruistic services. J. Bus. Res. **99**, 157–166 (2019). https://doi.org/10.1016/j.jbusres.2019.02.030

16. Ali, Y.S., Hussin, A.R.C., Dahlan, H.M.: Electronic word of mouth engagement in social commerce platforms: an empirical study. Inf. Dev. **36**(3), 438–456 (2020). https://doi.org/10.1177/0266666919867488

17. Ruvio, A., Bagozzi, R.P., Hult, G.T.M., Spreng, R.: Consumer arrogance and word-of-mouth. J. Acad. Mark. Sci. **48**, 1116–1137 (2020). https://doi.org/10.1007/s11747-020-00725-3

18. Wojnicki, A.C., Godes, D.: Signaling success: word of mouth as self-enhancement. Cust. Needs Solut. **4**(4), 68–82 (2017). https://doi.org/10.1007/s40547-017-0077-8

19. Liu, J.H., North, M., Li, C.: Relationship building through reputation and tribalism on companies' Facebook pages: a uses and gratifications approach. Internet Res. **27**(5), 1149–1169 (2017). https://doi.org/10.1108/IntR-03-2016-0078

20. Rybalko, S., Seltzer, T.: Dialogic communication in 140 characters or less: how fortune 500 companies engage stakeholders using Twitter. Public Relat. Rev. **36**(4), 336–341 (2010). https://doi.org/10.1016/j.pubrev.2010.08.004

21. Ahrens, J., Coyle, J.R., Strahilevitz, M.A.: Electronic word of mouth: the effects of incentives on e-referrals by senders and receivers. Eur. J. Mark. **47**(7), 1034–1051 (2013). https://doi.org/10.1108/03090561311324192

22. Wirtz, J., Chew, P.: The effects of incentives, deal proneness, satisfaction and tie strength on word-of-mouth behaviour. Int. J. Serv. Ind. Manag. **13**(2), 141–162 (2002). https://doi.org/10.1108/09564230210425340

23. Tibshirani, R., Walther, G., Hastie, T.: Estimating the number of clusters in a data set via the gap statistic. J. R. Stat. Soc. Ser. B (Statistical Methodology) **63**(2), 411–423 (2001). https://doi.org/10.1111/1467-9868.00293

24. Nunes, J.C., Drèze, X.: Your loyalty program is betraying you. Harv. Bus. Rev. **84**(4), 124–131 (2006)

25. Kim, M.G., Lee, C.H., Mattila, A.S.: Determinants of customer complaint behavior in a restaurant context: the role of culture, price level, and customer loyalty. J. Hosp. Market. Manag. **23**(8), 885–906 (2014). https://doi.org/10.1080/19368623.2014.896762
26. Verhagen, T., Nauta, A., Feldberg, F.: Negative online word-of-mouth: behavioral indicator or emotional release? Comput. Hum. Behav. **29**(4), 1430–1440 (2013). https://doi.org/10.1016/j.chb.2013.01.043
27. Kato, T.: Rating valence versus rating distribution: perceived helpfulness of word of mouth in e-commerce. SN Bus. Econ. **2**(11), 162 (2022). https://doi.org/10.1007/s43546-022-00338-8
28. Karabas, I., Kareklas, I., Weber, T.J., Muehling, D.D.: The impact of review valence and awareness of deceptive practices on consumers' responses to online product ratings and reviews. J. Mark. Commun. **27**(7), 685–715 (2021). https://doi.org/10.1080/13527266.2020.1759120

Author Index

A

Abdullah, Hanifa II-354
Abid, Muhammad Adil I-297
Agate, Vincenzo I-267
Agbehadji, Israel Edem I-427, I-483
Aguayo, Daniel I-339
Aguiar, Micaela I-88
Aguilar-Vega, Astrid II-58
Alanis, Arnulfo III-210, III-251, III-265
Albuquerque, Robson de Oliveira II-248
Alcalá-Otero, Antony II-370
Almachi, Anthony I. II-205
Almeida, Luis E. II-205
Alturas, Braulio I-65
Alulema, Darwin II-140
Alulema, Verónica II-140
Álvarez-Castro Lamolda, Almudena I-220
Alves, Marcelo III-368
Alves, Toni III-368
Alvin, Jude II-275
Amaro, Isidro R. I-324, III-17
Amigo, Luis I-76
Amouzad Mahdiraji, Saeid I-297
Amri, Samir I-375
Ancajima, Víctor I-352
Andrei, Drozhzhin I-386
Aracelis, Hernandez III-31
Araújo, Sílvia I-88
Arévalo-Huaman, Gianella I-209
Armas-Aguirre, Jimmy I-182
Arseneva, Inna II-87
Atanasov, Stoyan III-73
Augusto, Maria Fernanda II-128
Au-Yong-Oliveira, Manuel II-159
Avalos-Varillas, Kevin II-28
Avilés-Castillo, Fátima II-290
Ayala-Chauvin, Manuel II-290, III-457
Azevedo, Mónica II-3

B

Baldo, Nicola I-507
Balsa, Carlos III-43, III-58

Baltazar, Rosario III-265
Bani, Rkia I-375
Barrera, Diana II-191
Barrera-Barrera, Wendy I-182
Barros, Ana III-368
Bedón, Héctor III-165
Bento, Fernando I-65, I-243
Bezaev, Roman I-400
Biondi, Samuele III-304
Blacio, Manuel Montaño III-417
Bogdanovskaya, Irina II-414
Bolaños-Pasquel, Mónica I-3
Bonilla-Morales, Belen I-14
Bontempi, Franco III-304
Borcoski, Hector I-76
Borissova, Daniela I-457
Borja, Lessly III-391
Bosque, Santiago II-220
Bosta, Athina I-118
Boutiche, Yamina I-364
Brandtner, Patrick I-313
Bravo, Sofia I-230
Briceño, Inesmar C. I-412
Budennyy, Semen I-443
Buele, Jorge II-290
Burga, Daniel I-193
Burga-Durango, Daniel I-182, I-209, II-28,
        II-370
Bustos, Samuel I-521

C

Cajas, Javier III-406
Caldeira, Ana III-502
Calderero, Felipe III-3
Calderón-Díaz, Mailyn I-412
Campos-Vargas, Reinaldo I-339
Camtepe, Seyit II-302
Canessa, Paulo I-339
Carvalho, Denise III-343
Castellanos, German III-406
Castro, R. A. III-180
Castro, Ricardo III-457

T. Guarda et al. (Eds.): ARTIIS 2023, CCIS 1935, pp. 561–565, 2024.
https://doi.org/10.1007/978-3-031-48858-0

Castro, Rodrigo II-72
Castro-Velásquez, Cesar I-182
Chamba, Daniel Jaramillo III-417
Chatzipanagiotou, Niki II-275
Chauca, Luis I-352
Chicchon, Miguel III-165
Churiakova, Tatiana II-45
Cirillo, Teresa III-317
Clunie, Clifton I-255
Coelho, Tiago III-328
Contreras-Pizarro, Carlos H. I-169
Coronado-Hernández, Jairo R. II-102
Coronado-Hernandez, Jairo I-76
Costa, Filipa III-368
Cruz, Patricio J. I-412

D
da Cruz, António Miguel Rosado III-368
da Silva, Maria Braz II-384
da Veiga, Adéle II-354
Da Veiga, Adéle II-426
Daneluz, Fabiola I-507
Dávila, Fabricio I-50
de Padua, Everaldo III-43
De Paola, Alessandra I-267
Delzo-Zurita, Manuel I-193
Denchev, Stoyan III-102
Derawi, Mohammad II-234
Di Loreto, Samantha III-292
Di Paolo, Alessio II-317
Díaz, Mailyn Calderón II-102
Díaz-Nafría, José María III-116, III-151,
     III-165
Diedhiou, Marius Mintu III-237
Dione, Doudou III-237
Diop, Idy III-223, III-237
Durão, Natércia II-3

E
Egor, Loktev I-386
Enriquez-Chusho, Leonardo II-370
Epizitone, Ayogeboh I-427
Espada, Manuela Cañizares I-521
Esposito, Francesco III-317

F
Faye, Demba III-237
Fernandes, António J. G. III-485
Fernandes, José Pedro Teixeira II-159

Fernandes, Margarida III-357
Fernandes, Paula Odete III-471
Fernández, Brayan A. II-205
ferrara, Marta III-292
Ferreira, Flávio III-343
Finocchiaro, Regina III-304
Fonseca, Joao I-243
França, Beatriz III-357
Freeman, Emmanuel I-427, I-483
Fuertes, Walter II-191, II-220

G
Gama, Sílvio III-58
Garallar, Daniel Gracia I-521
García-Cruz, Patricia I-3
Gatica, Gustavo I-76
Giogiou, Natalia II-275
Gomez, Brignith II-264
Gómez, Oscar III-406
Gondim, João José Costa II-248
Gonzales, Guillermo I-50
González-Teodoro, Jorge Rafael I-220
Grados, Billy III-165
Gualli, Anthony III-391
Guarda, Teresa I-521, II-128, III-116
Guennoun, Zouahir I-375
Guerrero, Alexander II-140
Guillén-Guillamón, Ignacio III-433
Guin, Washington Torres III-417
Guise, Catarina III-368
Gupta, Nishu II-234
Gutierrez-Rios, Sandra I-255

H
Hajlaoui, Jalel Eddine II-402
Hermosa-Vega, Gustavo II-58
Herrera, Denisse III-265
Hidrobo, Francisco III-17
Hofko, Bernhard I-507
Holmgren, Johan I-297

I
Ibáñez, Samir F. Umaña II-102
Igor, Lavrov I-386
Infante, Saba I-324, III-17
Ipanaqué-Chero, Robert I-38, I-154
Ipanaqué-Silva, Rolando E. I-154
Iwarere, Samuel A. I-483

J

Jain, Kushi II-149
Janicke, Helge II-302
Jasmonts, Gints I-282
Jiménez, Luis Chuquimarca III-417
Jiménez-Vilcherrez, Judith K. I-38, I-154
Jinez-Tapia, Jose Luis I-26
Jofré, Javiera I-76
Jose, Soto III-31

K

Kato, Takumi I-547
Katynsus, Aleksandr II-87
Kawahara, Miyu II-17
Khatiwada, Pankaj II-234
Khouma, Ousmane III-223
Kolossa, Dorothea II-113
Körei, Attila III-87
Kostadinova, Hristina III-73
Krishnamoorthy, R. II-17
Kritzinger, Elmarie III-444
Kryukovskiy, Alexander I-400

L

Lara-Álvarez, Patricio III-457
Laroze, Nicole Castro II-102
Latchman, Krithica II-354
Lazcano, Vanel III-3
Leiva, Luis I-352
Leon, Alexis III-391
Lima, Camila Lourenço III-471
Lo Re, Giuseppe I-267
Loaiza Chávez, Ramón III-197
Lobo, Carla Azevedo II-3
Lopes, Isabel Maria III-471, III-485
Lorig, Fabian I-297
Lozano, Juan Jose I-133

M

Macas, Mayra II-191, II-220
Machado, Luciana I-531
Macuri, Hiro II-72
Magalhães, Pedro III-357
Magano, José II-159
Maglaras, Leandros II-302
Mansilla, Juan-Pablo I-50, I-230, II-72, II-264
Maraba, Jean II-426

Marković, Nikola II-113
Márquez Lobato, Bogart Yail III-197
Martinho, Domingos I-65, I-243
Mauricio, David I-193
Mbaye, Nalla III-237
Melnichuk, Irina I-400
Mendiguchia, Fernando A. III-433
Mendoza-Correa, Isabel I-169
Mihailescu, Radu-Casian I-297
Millham, Richard C. I-427, I-483
Miñan, Guillermo I-352
Miranda, Rita III-328
Mityagin, Sergey I-400, I-443, II-45, II-87
Monteiro, José I-88
Montelpare, Sergio III-292
Morato, Jorge III-151
Moreno-Achig, Myriam II-58
Morgado, José III-357
Morozov, Aleksandr II-45
Moura, Isabel III-343
Muñoz Zambrano, María E. I-169

N

Naidenov, Naiden I-457
Naranjo, Valery II-191
Nasseri, Mehran I-313
Natykin, Maksim I-443
Ndiaye, Mamadou L. III-223
Nizomutdinov, Boris II-414
Nketsiah, Richard Nana I-427, I-483
Nkuna, Amukelani Lisa III-444
Nolasco, Agata III-317
Nole-Álvarez, Christian I-169
Núñez, L. A. III-180

O

Ocaña, Jesús I-352
Ogura, Sota II-17
Ojo-Gonzalez, Karina I-14
Oliveira, Cristina III-343
Oliveira, João III-368
Oliveira, Jorge III-471
Olmedo-Navarro, Alexis I-76
Opazo, Maria Cecilia I-339
Otero-Espinar, M. Victoria III-58
Ouali, Naima I-364
Ozdamli, Fezile I-143

P

Pantoja, Jenny M.   I-412
Patiño, Efrain   III-251
Pavlova, Anna   II-87
Paz, Daniel   III-165
Pereira, Carla Santos   II-3
Petersson, Jesper   I-297
Peteva, Irena   III-102
Pickman-Montoya, Diego   I-193
Pierantozzi, Mariano   III-292
Pillajo, Hilton B.   II-205
Pinto, Luan   III-43
Placencia-Medina, Maritza D.   I-169
Portela, Filipe   I-531, III-328
Pratas, Antonio   I-65
Puetate-Paredes, Jaime   I-26

Q

Qadous, Munther   I-143
Queirós, Ricardo   III-140
Quintana-Gallardo, Alberto   III-433

R

Ramiro, Carlos Ramiro Peñafiel-Ojeda   I-26
Ramos-Galarza, Carlos   I-3
Rangata, Mapitsi Roseline   I-468
Raza, Ali   II-113
Reina-Cherrez, Marianela   II-58
Ribeiro, Beatriz A.   II-384
Ribeiro, Bernardo   III-343
Ribeiro, Maria I. B.   III-485
Ricciutelli, Alessandro   III-292
Rico-Bautista, Dewar   II-149
Rivas-Carillo, Rafael   II-28
Rivera, Carlos   III-406
Roca-Béjar, Anel J.   I-169
Rodrigues, Filipe   III-357
Rodrigues, J. R.   III-180
Rodrigues, Paula   III-368
Rodrigues, Ricardo   III-328
Rodríguez, Mónica Acuña   II-102
Rogão, Márcia C. R.   III-485
Romahn, Pascal   II-113
Román-Niemes, Stadyn   I-324
Rondinella, Fabio   I-507
Rufino, José   III-43

S

Sá, Miguel   III-368
Saba, Infante   III-31
Saenz, Mayerly   II-140
Salah, Mutaz   I-143
Samaniego, Daniel   II-140
Sánchez Luna, Jonathan   III-251
Sanchez-Cuadrado, Sonia   III-151
Santillan-Valdiviezo, Luis Gonzalo   I-26
Santos, Manuel   III-368
Santos, Vladimir García   III-417
Sarker, Iqbal H.   II-302
Sato, Toshikuni   I-547
Seabra, Cláudia   III-502
Sefara, Tshephisho Joseph   I-468
Sergey, Mityagin   I-386
Shapovalenko, Ekaterina   II-87
Sharma, Swati   II-175
Siddiqi, Shafaq   I-103
Siddiqui, Fahad   I-103
Sidorova, Julia   I-133
Silva, Augusta   III-317, III-357
Silva, Carla Joana   III-368
Silva, Carla   III-317, III-357
Silva, Duarte   I-243
Silva, Mário   III-357
Silva, Pedro   III-357
Silva, Ricardo   III-357, III-368
Silva, Rosa   III-357
Silva-More, César   I-154
Silva-Valencia, Javier   I-169
Šķirmante, Karina   I-282
Sokol, Aleksey   I-400
Sotelo, Javier   III-210
Sousa, João Paulo   III-131
Staab, Marina   I-313
Stalažs, Arturs   I-282
Starikov, Vasilii   II-45
Stavrakis, Modestos   I-118
Sudakova, Vladislava   II-45
Sugiyama, Ko-ichiro   II-17
Sviķe, Silga   I-282
Swaminathan, Jose   II-149
Szilágyi, Szilvia   III-87

T

Tan, Xiao   III-377
Tanaka, Kazuaki   II-17

Tapia-Riera, Guido III-17
Taqi, Agyeman Murad I-143
Tavares, Rogério III-131
Tereso, Marco I-65, I-243
Teti, Antonio III-281
Tipantocta, Fabricio III-406
Tjostheim, Ingvar II-332
Torres, Jesús M. III-131
Totkov, George III-73
Tsvetkova, Elisaveta III-102

U
Uglova, Anna II-414
Ulloa-Jiménez, Ricardo II-102

V
V. Sepulveda, Romina I-339
Valcárcel-Saldaña, María A. I-169
Vallejos-Huaman, Jose I-209
Valle-Oñate, Paulina I-26
Vardasca, Ricardo I-65, I-243
Vargas, Saul II-264
Vargas-Lombardo, Miguel I-14, I-255
Vásconez, Juan Pablo I-412, II-102
Vásquez, Shendry Balmore Rosero I-498
Vaz Serra, Pedro III-502
Velásquez-Fernández, Marcela F. I-38, I-154
Velazquez, Daniel III-265
Velezmoro-León, Ricardo I-38, I-154
Vilaça, Helena III-357

Villao, Datzania II-128
Villarreal-Valerio, Julián I-169
Vinueza-Cajas, Johanna I-324
Virga, Antonio I-267

W
Wolf, Thomas II-113
Wolter-Salas, Sebastian I-339

Y
Yail, Bogart III-210, III-251
Yang, Bian II-234
Yanqui, Anderson III-391
Yiu, Siu Ming III-377
Yoo, Sang Guun II-205
Yordanova, Zornitsa II-344
Yoshinov, Radoslav I-457

Z
Zaimia, Amira II-402
Zakharenko, Nikita I-443
Zambrano, Daliana II-205
Zapata, Diego I-230
Zenkouar, Lahbib I-375
Zhembrovskii, Daniil I-400
Ziediņš, Roberts Ervīns I-282
Zimmermann, Robert I-313
Zinn, Arndt-Hendrik II-113
Zurita, Bryan II-220

Printed in the United States
by Baker & Taylor Publisher Services